Automatic Program Construction Techniques

Automatic Program Construction Techniques

Editors

Alan W. Biermann
Gérard Guiho
Yves Kodratoff

Macmillan Publishing Company
A Division of Macmillan, Inc.
NEW YORK

Collier Macmillan Publishers
LONDON

Macmillan Publishing Company
866 Third Avenue, New York, N.Y. 10022

Collier Macmillan Canada, Inc.

Printed in the United States of America

printing number

1 2 3 4 5 6 7 8 9 10

Library of Congress Cataloging in Publication Data
Main entry under title:

Automatic program construction techniques.

"Outgrowth of a meeting that was held several years ago at the beautiful Centre culturel de Bonas in southern France. The sponsors were the U.S. Army Research and Standardization Group, the French Centre national de la recherche scientifique and the Institut national de recherche en informatique et automatique"—Pref.

Includes bibliographies and index.

1. Automatic programming (Computer science)—Addresses, essays, lectures. I. Biermann, Alan W.,

Library of Congress Cataloging in Publication Data

1939- . II. Guiho, Gérard, 1945- III. Kodratoff, Yves. IV. U.S. Army Research and Standardization Group. V. Centre national de la recherche scientifique (France) VI. Institut national de recherche en informatique et en automatique (France)
QA76.6.A89 1984 001.64′2 83-26817
ISBN 0-02-949070-7

CONTENTS

Preface

SECTION I
INTRODUCTION

1 *An Overview of Automatic Program Construction Techniques* 3
Alan W. Biermann, Gérard Guiho, and Yves Kodratoff

SECTION II
DEDUCTIVE AND TRANSFORMATIONAL METHODS

2 *A Deductive Approach to Program Synthesis* 33
Zohar Manna and Richard Waldinger

3 *LOPS—A System Based on a Strategical Approach to Program Synthesis* 69
W. Bibel and K.M. Hörnig

4 *Combining Program Synthesis with Program Analysis* 91
Ria Follett

5 *Problematic Features of Programming Languages* 109
Zohar Manna and Richard Waldinger

6 *An Interactive Tool for Program Manipulation* 123
Anne Adam, Paul Gloess, and Jean-Pierre Laurent

SECTION III
APPROACHES USING ABSTRACT DATA TYPES

7 *The Design of Efficient Data Representations* 139
John Darlington

8 *Improving Abstract Data Type Specifications by Appropriate Choice of Constructors* 159
Christine Choppy, Pierre Lescanne, and Jean-Luc Rémy

9 *Compiler Construction from High-Level Specifications* 183
M.C. Gaudel, Ph. Deschamp, and M. Mazaud

SECTION IV
OTHER TECHNIQUES FOR SYNTHESIS AND ANALYSIS

10 *The Roles of Knowledge and Deduction in Algorithm Design* 201
David R. Barstow

11 *Invariant Based Programs and Their Correctness* 223
Ralph-Johan Back

12 *Invariance Proof Methods and Analysis Techniques for Parallel Programs* 243
Patrick Cousot and Radhia Cousot

13 *Scheduling Equational Specifications and Non Procedural Programs* 273
A. Pnueli, N.S. Prywes, and R. Zarhi

14 *Constructing Recursive Programs Which Are Memory Efficient* 289
Alberto Pettorossi

SECTION V
PROGRAM SYNTHESIS FROM EXAMPLES

15 *The Synthesis of LISP Programs from Examples: A Survey* 307
Douglas R. Smith

16 *Synthesizing LISP Programs Working on the List Level of Embedding* 325
Yves Kodratoff and Jean-Pierre Jouannaud

17 *Dealing with Search* 375
Alan W. Biermann

18 *Design Directed Synthesis of Lisp Programs* 393
Ted J. Biggerstaff

19 *Theorem Proving by the Study of Example Proof Traces or Theorem Proving by a Correct Theorem Statement* 421
Jacqueline Castaing, Yves Kodratoff and Pierpaolo Degano

20 *Design Issues for Exemplary Programming* 433
D.A. Waterman, W.S. Faught, Philip Klahr, Stanley J. Rosenschein, and Robert Wesson

SECTION VI
LEARNING

21 *Program Synthesis through Concept Learning* 463
Brian Cohen and Claude Sammut

22 *Some Insights into Automatic Programming Using a Pattern Recognition Viewpoint* 483
Ranan B. Banerji

23 *Inductive Inference: Efficient Algorithms* 503
Dana Angluin

24 *Inductive Learning as Rule-Guided Generalization of Symbolic Descriptions: A Theory and Implementation* 517
Ryszard S. Michalski

Appendix: Some Examples of Program Synthesis 553
Alan W. Biermann

Author Index 563

PREFACE

Computer programming has historically been considered an activity reserved for human beings. The sequential lines of code for the machine must be carefully assembled to achieve the desired goals and it has been assumed that humans must be the authors of these commands. However, in recent years, a number of researchers have been examining the possibility that the code might be written automatically, and that the computer users might be required to specify only the goals for the desired program rather than the program itself.

These goals might be given in various forms. They might be composed of a formal specification of the needed input-output behavior, they might be described by an informal interaction with the user, and they could include examples of the desired behavior or other fragmentary information. The result, however, would be that humans could obtain useful work from machines on novel tasks without the necessity of carefully coding a program in the traditional sense. The user would interact with the machine in a convenient dialog, and the machine would program itself to do the required job.

At the core of any such automatic programming system is a mechanism that assembles fragments of information into machine executable code. The mechanism must be able to specify needed data structures, build sequences of commands with the required loops and branches, construct appropriate subroutines, and complete other tasks related to the construction of programs. This book describes the results of several dozen researchers who have been able to build such mechanisms. It contains chapters by most of these individuals, giving their techniques in considerable detail and including examples of their methodologies. The volume should be adequate to give the reader a good view of the field of automatic programming techniques and it points the way toward many new avenues of research. Sections of the book sequentially cover

(a) an overview and introduction to the field,

(b) synthesis methodologies which work from a formal specification of the required input-output behaviors,

(c) techniques based on abstract data structures,

(d) an array of methodologies including knowledge based techniques, and methods arising from the program correctness literature,

(e) synthesis of programs from examples of the desired behavior, and

(f) synthesis methods arising from the literature on learning.

This book emphasizes construction techniques and does not include coverage of any of the large automatic programming systems such as those developed during the 1970's by Robert Balzer at Information Science Institute, Cordell Green at Stanford, George Heidorn at IBM, William Martin at MIT and others. Such large systems need to have a user interface, large databases of programming knowledge, a control system for monitoring dialog and invoking special functions and so forth. This volume examines the central mechanisms related to the synthesis process which will be at the heart of any complete automatic programming system. However, it does not include coverage of such large systems which is a substantial research topic in its own right.

This book is the outgrowth of a meeting that was held several years ago at the beautiful Centre Culturel de Bonas in southern France. The sponsors were the U. S. Army Research and Standardization Group, the French Centre National de la Recherche Scientifique and the Institut National de Recherche en Informatique et Automatique. We are greatly indebted to the Duke University Department of Computer Science which has provided facilities for preparation of the manuscript and we appreciate the encouragement of the Chairman, Merrell Patrick. We would like to especially thank Patricia Land who typed most of the chapters and Steffani Webb, David Mutchler, Bruce Smith, and Elaine Levine who did considerable debugging and formatting in the final stages of the project. The phototypesetting was done by UNICOMP of Los Alamos, New Mexico.

Alan W. Biermann
Gérard Guiho
Yves Kodratoff

SECTION I

INTRODUCTION

CHAPTER 1

An Overview of Automatic Program Construction Techniques

Alan W. Biermann
Duke University
Durham, NC 27706

Gérard Guiho and Yves Kodratoff
Laboratoire de Recherche en Informatique
Université de Paris-Sud
Orsay, France

A. Introduction

The origins of a computer program begin in the mind of a human being and may have many forms. There may be a vision of how the output should look, a few ideas concerning the variety of inputs that will be encountered, some vague thoughts concerning how the computation should be done, some specific examples of desired or disallowed behaviors, and many other kinds of fragmentary information. On the other hand, the target computer program is neither vague nor fragmentary but is a very well defined sequence of instructions that can be loaded into a machine and executed. *Computer programming* is the process of translating those vague inclinations in the mind of a human into machine executable code that will perform the desired action.

The fundamental processes needed for the creation of code have been studied from two viewpoints. The one examines human processes in analyzing and solving problems and tries to generate new methodologies of programming. The other tries to discover what can be totally or partially automated in the process of code creation. We shall consider the second only which is concerned with how to select programming constructs to implement specifications, how to utilize fragmentary information, how to synthesize code from examples of desired behavior, how to utilize domain knowledge and any of many other processes. These methodologies have been called *automatic program construction techniques,* and many of the important results are described in this volume.

The following sections of this chapter introduce these methodologies. We first will examine the process of synthesizing programs from formal specifications. Next abstract data structure methodologies will be described followed by a section on synthesis related issues, program manipulation and correctness. In Section E, techniques for synthesizing programs from examples will be described. The final section will describe recent advances in learning theory and their relationship to automatic programming.

Most of the studies in this introductory chapter will involve a very brief introduction to individual techniques and then an examination of how each approach can be used to create a particular example program. Where possible, the same example has been used so that comparisons can be made. Some of the examples outlined in this chapter are completed in later chapters or the Appendix. All of these sections necessarily leave out much detail but enough is included to give the flavor of each approach and its general characteristics. The later chapters, of course, are designed to give full coverage.

B. Some Logic Based Techniques for Program Synthesis

B.1 Introduction

The first synthesis methods to be studied here will be the formal logic based systems. These methodologies encode information in the "well formed formulas" of logic and utilize deductive procedures in the creation of programs. We will examine in this section the deductive approach of Manna and Waldinger (as is described in Chapter 2), the heuristic but still formal methods of Bibel and Hörnig (Chapter 3), and the goal reduction methodology of Follett (Chapter 4). In each case, we present only an overview of the methodology with all details deferred to the later chapters.

In order to make the discussions concrete and to allow comparisons, the approaches will each be demonstrated on the same example problem which can be defined as follows: a program f is to be created that reads an input list x of integers and returns x with all negative integers removed. For example, if f is given the list (-7 2 9 -3 4), it returns (2 9 4). If f is given NIL, the list of length zero, it returns NIL.

In more formal language, we will write the input specification as P(x) where P is a predicate yielding "true" if x is a list of integers and false, otherwise. The input-output specification will be represented as R(x,z) which is true if and only if x is a list of integers and z is x with all negative integers removed. We will examine in this chapter how seven program synthesis methods approach this problem and create an appropriate program.

B.2 A Deductive Approach

Manna and Waldinger have developed a deductive mechanism which requires that the input-output specifications be given in terms of a theorem to be proven, and a program for realizing the specifications is extracted from a proof of the theorem. For the current problem, the theorem to be proved is

$$\forall a\ \exists z(P(a) \Rightarrow R(a,z))$$

which asserts that for any given input a that satisfies P, an output z is to be found such that R(a,z). The proof of the theorem requires discovering a general method for finding z for each possible a and this method is the desired program.

The Manna-Waldinger approach employs a tabular notation called a *sequent* which has three columns labelled as *assertions, goals,* and *outputs.* A sequent will be typically written as

assertions	*goals*	*outputs*
$A_1(a,x)$		
$A_2(a,x)$		
.		
.		
.		
$A_n(a,x)$		
	$G_1\ (a,x)$	$t_1\ (a,x)$
	$G_2\ (a,x)$	$t_2\ (a,x)$
	.	.
	.	.
	.	.
	$G_m\ (a,x)$	$t_m\ (a,x)$

which has the meaning

$$\begin{aligned}
&\text{if } \forall x\ A_1(a,x) \text{ and} \\
&\quad \forall x\ A_2(a,x) \text{ and} \\
&\quad \cdots\cdots \\
&\quad \forall x\ A_n(a,x) \text{ then} \\
&\qquad \exists x\ G_1(a,x) \text{ or} \\
&\qquad \exists x\ G_2(a,x) \text{ or} \\
&\qquad \cdots\cdots \\
&\qquad \exists x\ G_m(a,x)\ .
\end{aligned}$$

If $x = e$ is the particular value of x such that some $G_i(a,e)$ is true, then the corresponding output $t_i(a,e)$ may be thought of as the program to compute the specified output. All of this can be illustrated by continuing the example. The theorem to be proven for this particular synthesis can be written directly in sequent form.

assertions	*goals*	*outputs*
$P(a)$		
	$R(a,z)$	z

Thus if $P(a)$ is true, we seek z such that $R(a,z)$ and that z is the desired output.

The deductive approach provides techniques for adding assertions and goals with their appropriate output entries to the initial sequent. The aim is to deduce a goal of "true" with a corresponding output entry in terms of primitive machine instructions. We give one method for making additions to the sequent here.

One technique for adding lines to the sequent is called *GG-resolution.* Suppose there are two goals G_1 and G_2 in the sequent with subsentences P_1 and P_2, respectively, that can be unified. That is we assume there is a substitution θ such that P_1 and P_2 are identical: $P_1\theta = P_2\theta$.

goal	*output*
G_1	t_1
G_2	t_2

Then a new goal with its associated output can be created.

goal	*output*
$G_1\theta[P_1\theta \leftarrow \text{true}]$	
$\wedge$	
$G_2\theta[P_2\theta \leftarrow \text{false}]$	if $P_1\theta$ then $t_1\theta$ else $t_2\theta$

This output is correct if the new goal is true for the following reason. If the new goal is true, each conjunct must be true. Thus $P_1\theta = \text{true}$ and $G_1\theta\ [P_1\theta \leftarrow \text{true}]$ is true imply $t_1\theta$ will be the correct output. This is by definition of t_1. If $P_1\theta = \text{false}$, it is not known what $G_1\theta[P_1\theta]$ may evaluate to. However, $G_1\theta[P_2\theta = P_1\theta \leftarrow \text{false}]$ is true by the above argument meaning $t_2\theta$ is the correct output. So the output should be:

if $P_1\theta$ then $t_1\theta$ else $t_2\theta$

To illustrate GG-resolution, we consider the following goals where t is some program.

goal	*output*
(a=NIL)	NIL
not (a=NIL)	t

Let $P_1 = P_2 = (a = \text{NIL})$ and θ is the null substitution. Then the result of a GG-resolution is

goal	*output*
true and not (false)	if(a=NIL) then NIL else t

which reduces to

goal	*output*
true	if a=NIL then NIL else t

The aim of the Manna-Waldinger deductive technique is to deduce a goal of "true" (or an assertion of "false") with a corresponding output entry in terms of primitive machine instructions. After a series of steps similar to the GG-resolution described above, the method generates the following goal and program as described in the Appendix. (Note: A brief introduction to LISP notation appears in the Appendix to this chapter for readers unfamiliar with this language.)

goal	*output*
true	f(a) = if a = NIL then NIL else if neg(car(a))then f(cdr(a)) else cons(car(a),f(cdr(a)))

Once a complete synthesis has been made using the Manna-Waldinger technique, one can make some comments on its characteristics. First one should notice how naturally program control structures emanate from the deduction. For example, GG-resolution, which is a form of the ordinary resolution of the theorem proving literature (Robinson [1965]), generates an if-then-else form. The resulting code is a logical result of the deductive step that is being made. Similarly, recursive looping is introduced through an inductive argument and a resolution step. The well-foundedness of these individual steps and the consequent strength of the complete derivation yields a very satisfying mathematical path from axioms to final program. Once such a synthesis is complete, one has the feeling that the program is completely understood from the most basic logical building blocks.

Furthermore, because of the flexibility of logic, one can have confidence that a wide variety of structures can be handled in aesthetic ways. Thus Manna and Waldinger have pointed out that the method easily handles conjunctive goals where code is to be generated satisfying more than one specification. Furthermore, various kinds of quantification in the specification and also subroutines are dealt with in a straightforward manner as described in Chapter 2.

In the next section, we will examine methods by Bibel and Hörnig that use a nondeductive logic based synthesis method. Their method also emphasizes the use of heuristics to guide the search through the immense solution space.

B.3 A Heuristic System

The Bibel-Hörnig system LOPS, as presented in Chapter 3, attempts to reduce the demands for precision and completeness on the user and to apply a direct and efficient strategy for creation of a program. The methods are heuristic with claims at each point that most of the common cases are covered by the system.

For the example problem, this system would execute a simple dialog with the user of the following form

```
INITIALIZE PROBLEM
f
INPUT VARIABLE
x
INPUT CONDITION
list(x)
OUTPUT CONDITION
if x=NIL then f(x)=NIL
otherwise f(x)=y where
   ∀u [member(u,y) <=> (member(u,x)∧not(neg(u)))]
```

Here list(x) is true if and only if x is a list and member(u,y) is true if and only if u is on list y.

We would expect the system to begin by generating code to handle the trivial case and then seek a recursive solution to the general case. Following this strategy would yield the code

f(x) = if x=NIL then NIL else g(x)

where g(x) is a program yet to be created.

Bibel and Hörnig argue that there are relatively few practical recursion schemes and that a program synthesizer need only try those few. Their method would pose the problem, find g(x) such that

$$g(x) = y \text{ where } x \neq NIL \wedge list(y) \wedge \forall u[member(u,y) <=> (member(u,x) \wedge nonneg(u))] .$$

The strategy dictates that an element of the input is to be "guessed" and then used in computing the output. This "guessed" element can then be removed from the input and a recursive call can be made on the function. The most easily accessed member of input x is its first element car(x), and the method infers that two cases must be handled, the case where car(x) is not in the output and the one where it is. In the first case, it builds the recursive call f(cdr(x)) and in the second it constructs cons(car(x),f(cdr(x))). Finally, it finds a test, as explained in the Appendix, to distinguish between the two and generates

$$g(x) = \text{if } neg(car(x)) \text{ then } f(cdr(x)) \text{ else } cons(car(x), f(cdr(x)))$$

B.4 A Goal Reduction Method

Follett has designed a goal reduction method that creates programs by working backward from the goal specification (Chapter 4). Programming statements are selected that achieve the goal and then their preconditions become new goals to be achieved. Other statements are found to achieve those preconditions, and this process repeats until a precondition is reached that is implied directly by the input specification.

The method employs a concept called the *passback pair* which is the mechanism for passing goals back toward the beginning of the program. Each programming statement has a set of associated passback pairs and any of these may be used to pass a goal back to become a precondition of that statement. For example, the assignment z←1 has passback pair (true,p). The function p is an operator which works on any goal G immediately following z←1 to find a precondition Q for z←1. This may be diagrammed as follows:

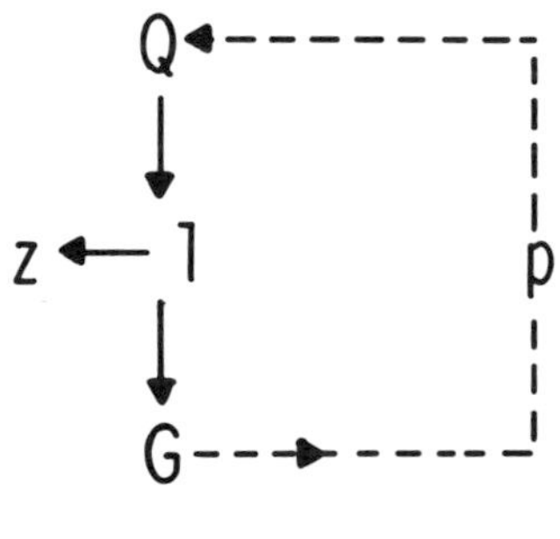

p is designed so that if Q is achieved and z←1 is executed, then G will be achieved. The first argument of the passback pair is a predicate indicating when p is applicable. In this example, p is applicable everywhere (so the first entry is "true") and is the operator that replaces z by 1 in G.

$$p(G) = (G \text{ with } z \text{ replaced by } 1)$$

The use of this passback pair can be illustrated in the synthesis of a simple program. Suppose the input condition $P(x)$ is that x is negative. Suppose the goal condition $R(x,z)$ requires that x be smaller than z.

$$R(x,z) \text{ if and only if } x<z$$

We propose that the goal can be achieved with the statement $z \leftarrow 1$ and use the passback pair to determine the required precondition. But G is $x<z$, so $p(G)$ is $x<1$. Since the input condition $P(x)$ requires x to be negative, the precondition $x<1$ is achieved and the program synthesis is complete. The program is the single statement $z \leftarrow 1$ and it will find for any x such that $P(x)$ a z such that $R(x,z)$.

Another passback pair for $z \leftarrow 1$ is (G does not contain z,I). This states that if the goal following $z \leftarrow 1$ does not mention z, the identity operator may be used to pass the goal back over $z \leftarrow 1$. This means that if the goal is $y=1$ and if $z \leftarrow 1$ is used to try to achieve that goal, the required precondition for $z \leftarrow 1$ is $y=1$. Thus the statement accomplishes nothing toward this goal.

Suppose a program is to be created that yields $z=1$ if x is negative and $z=2$ otherwise. Then a conditional program segment is needed

$$\text{if } A \text{ then } I_1 \text{ else } I_2$$

where A is a predicate and I_1 and I_2 are programs. If I_1 and I_2 have passback pairs (S_1,p_1) and (S_2,p_2), then the conditional statement will have the pair $(S_1 \wedge S_2, \text{ if } A \text{ then } p_1(G) \text{ else } p_2(G))$. To generate the current program, the following substitutions can be made.

Term	*Substitution*	*Passback*
I_1	$z \leftarrow 1$	(true, replace z by 1 in G)
I_2	$z \leftarrow 2$	(true, replace z by 2 in G)
A	$x<0$	

The goal G of the program is

$$(x<0 \wedge z=1) \vee (x>=0 \wedge z=2)$$

and one can check that the passback pair is applicable and yields a precondition of "true" indicating the synthesis is correct.

$$f(x) = \text{ if } x<0 \text{ then } z \leftarrow 1 \text{ else } z \leftarrow 2$$

One can similarly approach the canonical example for this chapter. The goal is

$$(\text{list}(x) \wedge x=\text{NIL} \wedge f(x)=\text{NIL}) \vee$$

$$(\text{list}(x) \wedge \text{not}(x=\text{NIL}) \wedge f(x)=z)$$

where z is list x with negative entries removed. A conditional statement can be proposed to achieve this goal with I_1 = NIL and $I_2 = g(x)$ where $g(x)$ is yet to be created. I_1 will have passback pair (true, $G \wedge f(x)=\text{NIL}$)

and I_2 will have (true,G′) where G′ is G with the requirement removed that f(x)=z where z equals x with negative entries removed. Carrying out the synthesis as in the previous example yields

$$f(x) \;=\; \text{if } x{=}\text{NIL then NIL else } g(x).$$

The synthesis of g(x) requires another invocation of the if-then-else feature and a loop construction using an inductive argument similar to that given by Manna and Waldinger.

B.5 Summary of Logical Based Methods

Section II of this book covers three logic based strategies for program synthesis, as described here, the Manna and Waldinger deductive method that works from formal specifications, the Bibel-Hörnig heuristic method that begins with more informal user inputs, and the Follett goal reduction method. Two additional chapters discuss features of languages that are difficult to represent with formal methodologies, and a programming system for manipulating programs.

C. Approaches Using Abstract Data Types

Ever since the *class* construct of SIMULA (Dahl [1968]), there has been a trend toward the idea of having more and more well defined object types. This can be seen particularly in the design of new languages such as in the concept of *clusters* in CLU (Liskov [1979]) or *packages* in ADA.

However, these types consist only in a specification of the *signature* of the type, i.e. the names of the operations which are visible from outside the type and the types of the objects which are manipulated by these operations. The local part which is added to the type concerns the implementation but, in fact, there is no specification of the *meaning* of the type.

From another point of view, people working on program synthesis have also felt the need for well defined types in order to export strategies from programs built on one type to the same kind of program working on other types of objects (Bidoit *et al.* [1979], Guiho *et al.* [1980]).

Concurrently much research has been done on a more precise specification of the meaning of abstract types. The usual method is to add algebraic axioms to the signature of the type and it is what will be presented informally here (Guttag and Horning [1978], Goguen *et al.* [1978], Gaudel [1978]).

An algebraic specification is given by a set S of sorts, a signature Σ which can be considered a set of operations with an arity on the sorts and a set E of axioms. As an example, let

$$S = \{\text{integer}\}$$

$$\Sigma = \{0, s, +\} \text{ with arities}$$

$$\begin{aligned} &0\text{: } \rightarrow \text{integer} \\ &s\text{: integer } \rightarrow \text{integer} \\ &+\text{: integer, integer } \rightarrow \text{integer} \end{aligned}$$

$$E = \{x+0=x,\ y+s(x)=s(y+x)\}.$$

Many problems arise with this kind of definition. The first one is to discover what has been specified.

We can say that the natural numbers are a suitable model for the previous specification but the integers modulo n are also models and there are many others that are more or less natural. In fact, it is well known that a specification specifies a class of multisorted algebras. Usually we restrict ourselves to algebras that are finitely generated and when this class is reduced to one element (just one model), the type is in some way totally specified and said to be *monomorphic.* When that class is empty or reduced to some kind of trivial type where every sort is composed of only one element, the type is said to be inconsistent.

Many characterizations have been done on types and many difficult problems arise, some of which are still at the research level. The principal ones are as follows.

Errors. How should errors be handled. For instance, in the last type, if one adds the operation d (decrement x by 1) with the axiom d(s(x))=x, one must decide how to define d(0). If we select d(0) = error, then error is a new constant of the sort integer and terms such as s(error) etc. must be defined.

Parameterized types. We can define in the same way the type *stack of integers* or *stack of booleans* with operations in the first case like

$$\text{top: stack-integer} \rightarrow \text{integer}$$

and in the second case like

$$\text{top: stack-boolean} \rightarrow \text{boolean}$$

but it seems more elegant to define the type *stack[data]* with

$$\text{top: stack} \rightarrow \text{data.}$$

This is related to the genericity of package in ADA, for instance. In fact, it is quite easy at the syntactic level as in ADA or CLU but in some cases the semantic conditions are quite complex.

Power of specifications. Can we allow every kind of axiom in the specification? What happens to the decision procedures if we allow conditional axioms like

$$x \neq 0 => s(d(x)) = x$$

or axioms with existential quantifiers as with

$$\exists k \;\; s(k) = 0?$$

Only some strong restrictions on the presentation of axioms make it possible to have effective decision procedures.

Representation of one type by another. When can one say that one type represents correctly another? A natural way is to require that the class of multisorted algebras specified by the representing class is included in the class of the other type. A more effective way is to show that a special homomorphism can be constructed between the two types that will enforce on one the equations of the other. The principal idea of the method of Gaudel *et al.* (Chapter 9) is to consider the computation process as a representation of this homomorphism between the two types which specify the two languages. The chapter shows how this idea can be applied to program construction.

An interesting point when types are described in this way is the fact that one can prove properties of the type using axioms and some kind of deduction or induction principle as in logic. Chapter 7 by Darlington deals with such demonstrations.

Often the presentation of the type is not completely suitable, for instance, for an efficient use of certain operations. Some transformations on the type which attempt to maintain its class of algebra but which allow a more powerful usage can be useful. Chapter 8 by Choppy *et al.* deals with such transformations.

D. Other Techniques for Synthesis and Analysis

Barstow in Chapter 10 has described a knowledge based approach to program synthesis which employs a formal component to guarantee correctness of the generated code. This method assumes a specification of the problem in a language convenient to the user such as English:

> Write a program that inputs a list of integers and outputs the list with all negative entries removed.

The processing of natural language and the subsequent creation of an internal problem representation is beyond the scope of this book. It is dealt with in Balzer [1973], Biermann and Ballard [1980], Green [1977], Green *et al.* [1978], and Martin *et al.* [1974]. We will follow Barstow in this discussion and concentrate on the program synthesis problem.

The Barstow synthesis method follows a producer-consumer paradigm which assumes a process (the producer) that generates pieces of data and a process (the consumer) that uses those pieces to construct an output. This paradigm provides a very natural way of looking at our example problem and we will show briefly how it leads to a solution.

The first step is to divide the processing into the producer and consumer subparts, a straightforward operation in this case. The producer will scan the input list searching for nonnegative values. The consumer will append them to the end of a list as they are found. We, of course, in this short overview do not describe the knowledge rules that lead to this decision but refer the reader to Chapter 10 for details.

The next steps construct sequentially the consumer code and the producer code. Addressing the consumer problem first, the output z is to be initialized. Then objects are to be received from the producer and put on the list. A series of rules built into the system analyze the code requirements and produce the code. For example, in this case the system uses these rules.

> If a consumer builds a set consisting solely of objects received from another process, the set is initially empty.

> If it is known that an object follows every member of an ordered sequence, the object may be added to the sequence by inserting it at the back.

The result is the following template for the consumer.

```
Initialize:
z:=NIL
Action:
v:={received from producer}
insert v at back of z
```

Next we examine the producer which is to move sequentially across the input looking for values to output. The knowledge based rules must be able to extract from the problem description the fact that nonnegative values are sought. The generated producer in this case would be the following:

```
Initialize:
b:=x
Termination test:
Is b NIL?
Each step:
u :=first element of b
remove the first element of b
if u is not negative { send u to consumer }
```

The final step in the synthesis process is the merging of the producer and consumer. Here the system invokes the following rule:

> A transfer program involving a producer and consumer may be refined into a WHILE loop whose condition is the termination test of the producer.

The producer and consumer are thus merged to become a solution to the problem. We use the function consright to append an atom to the right end of a list. As usual, we let x and z stand for the input and output.

```
b:=x
z:=NIL
while b is not NIL do
    u:=car(b)
    b:=cdr(b)
    if not(neg(u)) then
       v:=u
       z:=consright(z,v)
```

Of course, this program is not minimal. In fact, all the intermediate variables b, u, and v can be removed. But synthesis rather than efficiency was the aim of this work. The reader might wish to examine Kant [1979] for a treatment of efficiency concerns.

The knowledge based approach to programming is attractive because it attempts to simulate in some ways the only good programmers known to exist, humans. Standard methodologies for coding, programming tricks, and other programming knowledge can be built into the system rules to gain a human-like approach to program generation. Of course, the rules are manipulating mathematically precise objects, namely, lines of programming code so a deductive component is needed. This is, in fact, a central point in the Barstow contribution.

In Chapter 11, Back gives a methodology for program generation based upon the concept of the *invariant,* a formal specification of the program state at a particular point in the code. This work grows out of the literature on program correctness (Dahl *et al.* [1972], Floyd [1967], Gerhart [1972], Hoare [1969]) and is logic based. A programming language is described for implementation of invariant based programming and examples are given to illustrate the method.

A second chapter coming from the correctness literature is Chapter 12 by Cousot and Cousot. This work introduces a unified approach to the study of various program proof and analysis methods and is based upon state transition systems as models of programs. The approach is used to study the methods of Floyd [1967], Owicki *et al.* [1976], and Lamport [1977] and is offered as a technique for creating and analyzing new proof methods.

Another approach to automatic programming allows the user to make declarative statements relating objects or variables in a problem domain, and an automatic system "executes" the statements to find a solution instantiation for certain output variables. The well known PROLOG language is an example of such a system, and the equational specification language of Chapter 13 by Pnueli, Prywes, and Zarhi is another. This system accepts an equational specification which relates numerical data in arrays but which includes no direct indication concerning the method or order of the calculation to be done. The task of the automatic system is to extract from the equations the operations necessary to do a computation and to program or "schedule" them for execution.

Chapter 14 by Pettorossi studies an issue in the synthesis of recursive programs, the optimum use of memory. The strategy involves a technique for automatically keeping track of which locations contain useful information and releasing those cells which do not.

E. Program Synthesis from Examples

E.1 Introduction

A complaint often made against the synthesis methods described above is that they require too much precision and care from the user. That is, it may be in many cases easier to write a program in a traditional programming language than it would be to write its formal input-output specifications. We address in this section a vastly different type of construction problem, program synthesis from examples. Thus in the canonical example problem of this chapter, instead of constructing the program from input-output specifications, the synthesis will be done knowing only that the desired program must yield z = (2 9 4) if given input x = (−7 2 9 −3 4). The synthesis methods will attempt to produce a program that has this behavior and that will function "similarly" on other examples. If the user observes that the automatically created program has shortcomings either by examining the code or by running examples, then the system can be given additional examples on which to base the synthesis. A surprising experimental fact that has come out of this research is that the desired program, if it is small, often can be very quickly converged upon using only this weak source of information.

Synthesis in this section begins with the example input-output pair: (-7 2 9 -3 4) yields (2 9 4). In fact, we can express this pair with the relationship

```
f(x) = cons(car(cdr(x)),
        cons(car(cdr(cdr(x))),
         cons(car(cdr(cdr(cdr(cdr(x))))),
           NIL)))
```

This is a cons structure which also contains selectors (the car and cdr operations) which "travel inside" the data in order to pick up the desired parts. For instance, the car(cdr(x)) operation selects the 2 from the input list and makes it available for constructing the output. This structure also contains the NIL constructor and the atom predicate will be available to check if some data has reduced to NIL. Finally, this structure contains objects belonging to an *external type* which itself has properties. For instance, one can build lists of integers and the external type will be very rich or lists of variables without any special property. Most of the LISP synthesis methods generate programs to manipulate structure without reference to any external type. Our example will, however, reference integers and the type related fact concerning whether or not they are negative.

The following sections briefly introduce three methods for synthesis from examples.

E.3 Synthesis Through Merge of Primitive Functions

While the above method requires a sequence of input-output pairs for the discovery of recursion relations, one might wish for a method that does the complete synthesis from the single example originally given. The starting point will be the example output z written in terms of the input x.

```
z=cons(car(cdr(x)),
   cons(car(cdr(cdr(x))),
    cons(car(cdr(cdr(cdr(cdr(x))))),
     NIL)))
```

One can create the desired program by first breaking this expression into a set of *primitive forms* and then performing a merge operation on these primitives. As described in Chapter 17, the primitive forms to be used will be

$$
\begin{aligned}
f_i(x) &= \text{NIL} \\
f_i(x) &= x \\
f_i(x) &= f_j(\text{car}(x)) \\
f_i(x) &= f_j(\text{cdr}(x)) \\
f_i(x) &= \text{cons}(f_j(x), f_k(x))
\end{aligned}
$$

and the above expression becomes

$$
\begin{aligned}
z &= f_1(x) \\
f_1(x) &= \text{cons}(f_2(x), f_5(x)) \\
f_2(x) &= f_3(\text{cdr}(x)) \\
f_3(x) &= f_4(\text{car}(x)) \\
f_4(x) &= x \\
f_5(x) &= \text{cons}(f_6(x), f_{10}(x)) \\
f_6(x) &= f_7(\text{cdr}(x)) \\
f_7(x) &= f_8(\text{cdr}(x)) \\
f_8(x) &= f_9(\text{car}(x)) \\
f_9(x) &= x \\
f_{10}(x) &= \text{cons}(f_{11}(x), f_{17}(x)) \\
f_{11}(x) &= f_{12}(\text{cdr}(x)) \\
f_{12}(x) &= f_{13}(\text{cdr}(x)) \\
f_{13}(x) &= f_{14}(\text{cdr}(x)) \\
f_{14}(x) &= f_{15}(\text{cdr}(x)) \\
f_{15}(x) &= f_{16}(\text{carx}) \\
f_{16}(x) &= x \\
f_{17}(x) &= \text{NIL}
\end{aligned}
$$

The construction procedure then produces the target program by performing merge operations on the above seventeen functions. The primary tool used is the conditional of LISP:

$$\begin{aligned}\text{cond}((&p_{i1}, f_{i1}),\\ &(p_{i2}, f_{i2}),\\ &\quad\vdots\\ &(p_{in}, f_{in}))\end{aligned}$$

This function evaluates predicates $p_{i1}, p_{i2}, p_{i3}, \ldots, p_{in}$ sequentially until one is found that is true. If p_{ij} is true, then function f_{ij} is computed and its value returned. In this application, p_{in} will always be T (true) to guarantee that the conditional will always yield a value. The functions f_{ij} will simply be the primitive functions defined above. The predicates p_{ij} must be created by a predicate constructor from primitives.

We will assume for this example that predicates may be assembled from the primitives atom and neg operating on any combination of car's and cdr's of x. The predicate constructor will be given sets of S-expressions and will have the task of finding a predicate that can distinguish between them. For example, if it is given the sets {3} and {(3 4 5)}, it will generate atom(x). In other words, atom(x) yields T for all members of one set and F for all members of the others. If it is given {(-3)} and {(3 4) (6)}, it will find neg(car(x)). Such a constructor is easy to build since its only task is to enumerate the class of allowed predicates until a satisfactory one is found.

Proceeding with the synthesis, the above seventeen functions are modified as described in the Appendix and then every possible merger is attempted. An example merger would be to identify f_9 and f_{16} as the same function. This is a reasonable merger since both functions have the same value. A less obvious merger would be to identify f_1 and f_2 to be a new function g. Since the forms of f_1 and f_2 are different, a conditional is needed. We could write g as either

$$\begin{aligned} g(x) = \text{cond}((&p_1, \text{cons}(f_2(x), f_5(x))),\\ &(p_2, f_3(\text{cdr}(x))))\end{aligned}$$

or

$$\begin{aligned} g(x) = \text{cond}((&p_1, f_3(\text{cdr}(x))),\\ &(p_2, \text{cons}(f_2(x), f_5(x))))\end{aligned}$$

If p_1 and p_2 can be found so that either form can be used to successfully compute the original example, then the merge of f_1 and f_2 is successful. If no such p_1 and p_2 can be found, the merge is not successful, and f_1 and f_2 are proven to be disjoint.

In fact, this merge process can be carried out and it will generate the following code as shown in the Appendix.

$$\begin{aligned} f_1(x) &= \text{cond}((\text{atom}(x)\ ,\ x)\\ &\qquad (\text{neg}(\text{car}(x)),\ f_1(\text{cdr}(x)))\\ &\qquad (T,\ \text{cons}(f_3(x),\ f_5(x))))\\ f_3(x) &= f_1(\text{car}(x))\\ f_5(x) &= f_1(\text{cdr}(x))\end{aligned}$$

This is, in fact, the desired program.

There are a number of interesting points about this synthesis method. First it requires little from the user in terms of precision, knowledge of any formal language, or understanding of the synthesis method. One or two randomly chosen examples are sufficient for the synthesis of most simple programs. Secondly, the method can be defined to be completely algorithmic and so can be programmed to be as reliable as any compiler. In Chapter 17, we describe a version of this system that will generate any program in the class of "regular" LISP programs. The construction of the trace and the modification of its form described here is a simple computation as explained in Chapter 17. The merger computation and the predicate generation are also simple algorithmic procedures but they are expensive. Unfortunately, the merger process is exponentially costly in the length of the target program so that only short programs can be generated.

The program construction methods described next grew out of experiences gained with this function merger technique. It attempts to maintain the simplicity and reliability of the current method and to simultaneously increase the speed of the construction.

E.4 A Production Rule Technique

The function merging technique converges on programs with great reliability. If there exists a merger of the primitive functions that yields a satisfactory program, it can be found by the method. However, the cost of trying all possible mergers can be expensive even if sophisticated pruning methods are employed. A discouraging fact about this search is that, if one examines it carefully, one gains the impression that the method searches every conceivable conglomeration of primitives including a vast array of no conceivable value. The intuition resulting from this work was that perhaps the primitive functions are building blocks too small for efficient program synthesis. A study was then initiated as described in Chapter 17 to find appropriate larger building blocks.

Eventually, a production rule mechanism was created with each rule able to generate all the code for a programming construction. For example, the canonical problem being examined in this chapter is generated by just three production rules, one to create the loop, one to insert the conditional check, and one to append atoms to the output list. Thus the target program is at depth three in a search tree of very limited branching factor and can be generated with remarkable speed. Whereas programs of this complexity would be generated by the function merging method after about a minute of search on a typical machine, they would be generated in less than one second using production rules. The only drawback to the production rule method is that it is not as flexible as the previous method and thus does not generate as broad a class of programs.

An example production rule is as follows:

$$[P^0_w\ (X_0\ XL),\ next] =>$$

$$P^0_w\ (X_0,\ XL)\ = cons(car(X_0),\ next)$$

In order to use the rule, the following variables must be instantiated.

w identifier for the instantiation

XL an unparenthesized list of arguments for program being generated

next an S-expression to which the current result is to be appended.

The rule has two parts, the nonterminal symbol $[P^0_{w,}(X_0\ XL),\ next]$ and the generated string $P^0_w\ (X_0,XL)\ = cons(car(X_0),\ next)$. The nonterminal symbol $[P^0_{w,}(X_0\ XL),\ next]$ can be interpreted to say that program P^0_w is to be defined with arguments $(X_0\ XL)$ and that the result of its computation is to be appended onto "next". The arrow => means "generates" so this rule can be understood to say that the nonterminal symbol $[P^0_w, (X_0\ XL), next]$ with w, XL, and next properly instantiated will generate the code given. Thus if $[P^0_{23}, (X_0\ X_4\ X_6), NIL]$ ever appears during code generation, then the following code will be created:

$$P^0_{23}(X_0,X_4,X_6) = \text{cons}(\text{car}(X_0),\text{NIL})$$

where w=23, XL=$X_4\ X_6$, and next=NIL. Thus a function P^0_{23} has been defined with parameters X_0,X_4,X_6, and the value is computed as shown.

Another production rule of interest is the following which generates looping code.

$[P^i_w, (X_i\ XL), next] =>$

$P^i_w\ (X_i, XL) =$

cond((P^i entry check), next)

(T, $P^k_{w1}\ (X_i,X_i, XL)$))

$[P^k_{w1}, (X_k\ X_i\ XL), P^i_w(cd^mr(X_i), XL)]$

Here the nonterminal $[P^i_w, (X_i\ XL), next]$ generates two things, some LISP code and another nonterminal, $[P^k_{w1},$ ..., ...]. Again, a number of variables need to be instantiated in order to use this rule, i,w,XL,next, (P^i entry check), P^k_{w1}, and m. The functioning of this rule can probably best be understood by examining its action in a complete synthesis.

As an example, suppose a program is needed to generate from input (A B C D) the output (A C). Then the system would first compare the input with output and, using the method described in Chapter 17, determine that the required behavior can be achieved with one scan of the input. It would then select the only rule needed for that scan, the looping rule shown above, and set the variables at appropriate values. Specifically, only one rule is needed, i=1, the needed entry check for the loop is (atom(X_i) or atom(cdr(X_i))), the called routine P^k should be P^0 to append atoms to the output, and the decrement m across the input list should be two. So the looping rule now reads

$[P^1_w, (X_1\ XL), next] =>$
  $P^1_w\ (X_1, XL) =$
    cond((atom(X_1) or atom(cdr(X_1))), next)
     (T, $P^0_{w1}\ (X_1,X_1, XL)$))
    $[P^0_{w1}, (X_0\ X_1\ XL), P^1_w\ (cd^2r(X_1), XL)]$

The production rule method then creates the program by expanding the nonterminal $[P^1, (X_1), NIL]$. Thus to do this expansion with the above rule we set w = (string of length zero),

XL = (string of length zero),

next = NIL.

The rule yields

(a) $P^1(X_1) =$

$\text{cond}((\text{atom}(X_1) \text{ or } \text{atom}(\text{cdr}(X_1))),\text{NIL})$

$(T, P_1^0(X_1,X_1)))$

$[P_1^0, (X_0\ X_1), P^1(\text{cddr}(X_1))]$

The new nonterminal can be expanded using the first rule given above if

w = 1

XL – X_1

next = $P^1(\text{cddr}(X_1))$

to yield

(b) $P_1^0(X_0, X_1) = \text{cons}(\text{car}(X_0), P^1(\text{cddr}(X_1)))$

The combination of (a) and (b) yields the target program.

We show in the Appendix how three rules generate a solution for the canonical example of this chapter:

$P^2(X_2) = \text{cond}((\text{atom}(X_2), \text{NIL})$

$(T, P_1^1(X_2,X_2)))$

$P_1^1(X_1,X_2) = \text{cond}((\text{not}(\text{neg}(\text{car}(X_1))),P_{11}^0(X_1,X_1,X_2))$

$(T, P^2(\text{cdr}(X_2))))$

$P_{11}^0(X_0,X_1,X_2) = \text{cons}(\text{car}(X_0),P^2(\text{cdr}(X_2)))$

F. Learning

F.1 Introduction

The above sections have concentrated on the generation of programs written in traditional languages such as LISP. However, learning theorists have been developing synthesis methods for other structures such as logical formulas, and these structures are close enough to being executable programs to be of interest to us.

The model for the learning theorist is similar to the synthesis-from-examples paradigm of the previous section. Samples of some kind of behavior such as input-output pairs are given and a generalization from them is to be made. However, a learning system may construct a logical formula, grammar, or other entity to represent the generalization. The function of the learning system is to build a representation of the relationship between the input and the output so that if it is given one, it can find the other.

For example, suppose it is desired to train a system such that if its input x is a list of integers, its output z is that list with the negative ones removed. Then we might begin the training process with the input-output pair

$$x=NIL, z=NIL.$$

From this, the learning system constructs the observation

$$x=NIL \wedge z=NIL$$

and then attempts to find a generalization of this assertion. Following the strategy of Cohen and Sammut in Chapter 21, the system would note that

$$x=z \wedge x=NIL$$

is equivalent and a generalization of this formula is that

$$x=z.$$

This assertion thus becomes its first guess at the relationship between x and z.

This is clearly not the desired relationship, so another sample of the target behavior can be given.

$$x=(-1), z=NIL$$

From the new sample the system would assemble the fact

x.head.sign="-" ∧

x.head.mag=1 ∧

x.tail=NIL ∧
z=NIL

using the notation of Chapter 21. Following the same generalization strategy, the formula becomes

x.head.sign="-" ∧
x.head.mag=1 ∧
x.tail=z

This relationship still does not represent the target behavior, but one can begin to see signs of movement in the correct direction. Thus, one can imagine that, after several more learning steps, this expression could be transformed into the equivalent of "if x.head.sign="-" then the output of the current computational iteration should be x.tail."

This complete concept learning task is described in Chapter 21 and the resulting learned concept, "delete", is the following.

```
   delete =
   [ x,z: x=NIL ∧ x=z
∨   [∃ P,Q: x.head.sign="-"
     ∧ x.head.mag=P
     ∧ x.tail=Q
     ∧ x.cardinal(P)
     ∧ delete(Q,z)]


∨   [∃ P,Q: x.head.sign="+"
     ∧ x.tail=P
     ∧ z.tail=Q
     ∧ z.head=x.head
     ∧ delete(P,Q)] ]
```

The meaning is that either

(1) x and z are both NIL,
(2) the head of x is negative and z is obtained by applying delete to the tail of x, or
(3) the head of x is positive (or zero), x and z will have the same head, and the tail of z is obtained by applying delete to the tail of x.

Cohen and Sammut argue this concept is executable like a program and they explain why. For example, if x = (–7 2 9 –3 4), their system will find z = (2 9 4) to satisfy this concept. That is, this concept is like a PROLOG program, a set of logical assertions which are executable. For another example of this kind of work, see Shapiro [1981].

F.2 Generalization and Particularization

It is important to notice that learning is closely related to problems of generalization and particularization. Our aim here is not simply to review the field (and we have no claim toward completeness) but to stress the necessity for a good generalization algorithm. Some important work on this problem has been done by F. Hayes-Roth [1978], under the name of *interference matching* and by S.A. Vere [1981] under the name of *constrained n-to-1 generalization.*

We will discuss here a mechanism which seems to be quite equivalent to theirs and which is nothing but a generalization (see for instance Arsac and Kodratoff [1982] and Costa [1982] for a short description of a generalization algorithm) into an equational theory which takes into account the properties of the logical connectives of the descriptions usually introduced in Artificial Intelligence.

We shall not describe this algorithm here but it must be noticed that it can be efficient only if there is a semantics to drive it.

Let us consider the set of the trees where the node of a tree is a function, its leaves are variables or constants, the number of the sons of a node is the arity of the function. The constants are considered as functions of arity 0. Such a tree is usually called a *term.* The reader knows that comparing two terms t_1 and t_2 is made by means of a unification technique which detects whether or not there exists at least one substitution s such that $st_1 = st_2$. This means that substituting some terms to some variables of t_1 and some other terms to some variables of t_2 will lead to the same tree. Recall that a substitution is a set of pairs of the form $(x_i \backslash t_i)$, where x_i is a variable and t_i a term, which indicates that x_i is to be replaced by t_i.

Example 1.

Let x,y,u,v, be variables. Let t_1 = cons(cons(car(x),NIL),cdr(y)) and t_2 = cons(v,cdr(cons(car(w),NIL))). Then the substitution

$$s = (v \backslash \text{cons(car(x),NIL)},\ \ y \backslash \text{cons(car(w),NIL)})$$

is such that

$$st_1 = st_2 = \text{cons(cons(car(x),NIL),cdr(cons(car(w),NIL)))}$$

In learning, we are concerned with a restriction of unification to the case where there is an s such that $st_1 = st_2$. Given two terms t_1 and t_2, we will say t_1 is *more general* than t_2 when there is a substitution s such that $st_1 = t_2$. Intuitively, this means that the tree t_1 is "shorter" than the tree t_2 since some variables of t_1 have to be replaced by terms to make t_1 equal to t_2.

Example 2.

Let t_1 = cons(cons(car(x),NIL),cdr(y)) and t_2 = cons(v,cdr(y)).
Then s = (v \ cons(car(x)),NIL)) is such that $st_2 = t_1$ and thus t_2 is more general than t_1.

Example 3.

Let t_1 = cons(x,y) and t_2 = cons(v,w). One can unify with the substitution x \ v, y \ w but x,y,v, and w are free variables so there is no change. Therefore, neither t_1 nor t_2 is more general than the other.

Example 4.

Consider example 1. One has st_1 and st_2 and neither t_1 or t_2 is more general than the other.

Example 5.

Let t_1 = cons(x,NIL) and t_2 = cons(x,v). Since NIL is a function of arity 0, it cannot be the left side of a substitution. But the substitution s = (v \ NIL) yields $st_2 = t_1$, so t_2 is more general than t_1. This is the well known rule of "turning constants into variables."

Example 6.

Let t_1 = cons(x,x) and t_2 = cons(x,y). If we attempt to match t_1 to t_2, we obtain x \ x, x \ y which is disallowed since x cannot be given two different names. On the contrary, we can match t_2 to t_1 with s = (x \ x, y \ x) so that $st_2 = t_1$ and t_2 is more general than t_1. This is known by numerous names and expresses the fact that replacing two occurrences of a variable by different variables is a generalization.

Next, we shall be concerned with substitutions into formulas which contain the logical connectives $\wedge$ and $\vee$ considered as 2-ary functions. It happens that their properties make generalization difficult.

Example 7.

Let $t_1 = x$ and $t_2 = x \wedge y$. Then there exists a substitution $s_1 = (x \backslash x \wedge y)$ such that $st_1 = t_2$. Therefore t_1 is more general than t_2. But $t_1 = x = t'_1 = x \wedge \text{True}$. Then there is a substitution $s_2 = (y \backslash \text{True})$ such that $t'_1 = st_2$. Therefore t_2 is more general than $t'_1 = t_1$.

We see here that the substitution rule fails. In fact, it works only when applied to terms within logical formulas and not to predicates which x and y are in this example. A formula with logical connectives such as

$\wedge$ and $\vee$ must connect comparable things so that we can measure the generality of the expression. This is illustrated in the following.

Example 8.

Let $t_1 = EQ(x,1) \wedge EQ(y,2)$. We claim that $t_2 = LOWER(x,y)$ is a generalization of t_1 because there is a substitution s such that $st_2 = t_1$. Of course, this does not appear immediately and one must use some intuition to prove it. Thus one can show that t_1 is equivalent to $t'_1 = EQ(x,1) \wedge EQ(y,2) \wedge LOWER(x,2) \wedge LOWER(1,y)$. Also t_2 can be shown to be equivalent to $t'_2 = EQ(x,x_1) \wedge EQ(y,y_1) \wedge LOWER(x,y_1) \wedge LOWER(x_1,y)$. Then there exists an s such that $st'_2 = t'_1$ and therefore $t'_2 = t_2$ is more general than $t'_1 = t_1$.

F.3 Other Learning Studies

In Chapter 22, Banerji describes a language developed from a pattern recognition viewpoint which has some resemblances to the Cohen-Sammut concept language. He then gives methods for inducing structural descriptions from instances and these descriptions can function as programs for recognition. He very convincingly shows that the same processes are involved in structural pattern recognition as are in program synthesis methods and thus shows how insights in one field lead to results in the other.

Angluin has given in Chapter 23 a survey of theoretical results on inductive inference from examples. In fact, a beautiful theory has developed over the past two decades which gives definitions of learnability, classes of learnable behavior, complexity results, and limits on learnability. This chapter effectively covers most of the important results. Her paper gives particular attention to the question of the cost of doing an induction, an issue not addressed elsewhere in this book.

Finally, Michalski describes in Chapter 24 an object description language developed over a period of many years and methods for inferring descriptions for sets of objects. His methodology is grounded on a strong theoretical foundation and emphasizes the development of programs efficient enough to tackle real world problems. He is interested in automated induction for complex data analysis and computer aided decision making.

G. Conclusion

This chapter has introduced a variety of program synthesis techniques by examining how each approaches the example problem. A summary of the seven methods appears below in Table I. These are, of course, only representative of the complete field of automatic programming and the reader is invited to read the remaining chapters.

Method	Knowledge	Synthesis	Program
Deductive theorem proving (Chapter 2)	Input: P(a), R(a,z) Internal: Three axioms giving properties of P,R. (see Appendix)	Tree search to depth 10. Search method unspecified.	Two nested conditionals with a recursive loop.
Logic with heuristic search (Chapter 3)	Input: Logical specification of I-O characteristics.	Heuristic search.	Two nested conditionals with a recursive loop.
Knowledge based production rules (Chapter 10)	Input: Coded version of English sentence. Internal: Many production rules.	Heuristic search.	Iterative loop with a conditional.
Induction on recursion relations (Chapters 15,16)	Input: 6 examples	Construction of recursion relations. Instantiation of schemas.	Two nested conditionals with a recursive loop.
Merge of primitive functions. (Chapter 17)	Input: 1 example	Uniform search of all merges of 17 primitives with pruning.	Two nested conditionals with a recursive loop.
Syntactic production rules (Chapter 17)	Input: 1 example	Selection and expansion of three production rules.	Two nested conditionals with a recursive loop.
Learning of I-O relation. (Chapter 21)	Input: 3 examples plus the answers to 8 yes-no queries	Construction and generalization of logical relations.	Logic formula for I-0 relation with recursion.

Table I. Summary of seven synthesis methods and their solution to the example problem

Appendix

LISP and Some Notation

Many of the synthesis techniques will use notation and concepts from LISP, and thus a few of the important conventions will be given here. The primary data structure in LISP is the *S-expression* which can be defined to be any string of symbols generated by

<S-expression> → <atom> | (<S-expression>. <S-expression>)

where <atom> may be either an identifier, integer, or NIL. NIL is a special reserved symbol, a LISP constant. Any S-expression defined by the rule

<S-expression> → <atom>

will be called an *atom*. Some example S-expressions are NIL, (3.NIL), and ((A . B) . C).

Three basic LISP functions are car, cdr, and cons which are defined as

$$\text{car}(x) = \begin{cases} s_1 & \text{if } x = (s_1 \,.\, s_2) \\ \text{undefined} & \text{if } x \text{ is an atom} \end{cases}$$

$$\text{cdr}(x) = \begin{cases} s_2 & \text{if } x = (s_1 \,.\, s_2) \\ \text{undefined} & \text{if } x \text{ is an atom} \end{cases}$$

$$\text{cons}(s_1,s_2) = (s_1 \,.\, s_2)$$

where s_1 and s_2 are S-expressions. Conventional LISP notation includes a function f and its arguments $X_1,X_2,\ldots,X_n$ on a list as follows (f X_1 X_2, . . . , X_n) and sometimes the names will be capitalized. Thus one would write (CAR X), (CDR X), and (CONS X Y) instead of car(x), cdr (x), and cons(x,y), respectively. A list is represented by an S-expression as follows:

$$(x_1\ x_2\ x_3 \text{ --- } x_n) \text{ is represented}$$
$$\text{as } (x_1.\ (x_2.\ (x_3 \text{ --- } (x_n.\ \text{NIL}))) \text{ --- })$$

Both list and S-expression notations will be used in this book.

Several predicates will be used as follows (where T and NIL represent, respectively, true and false).

$$\text{atom}(x) = \begin{cases} \text{T} & \text{if } x \text{ is an atom} \\ \text{NIL} & \text{otherwise} \end{cases}$$

$$\text{neg}(x) = \begin{cases} \text{T} & \text{if } x \text{ is a negative integer} \\ \text{NIL} & \text{otherwise} \end{cases}$$

$$\text{not}(x) = \begin{cases} T & \text{if x is NIL} \\ \text{NIL} & \text{if x is T} \\ \text{undefined} & \text{otherwise} \end{cases}$$

If x = ((A . B) . C), then some example evaluations are

$$\begin{aligned} \text{car}(x) &= (A\ .\ B) \\ \text{cdr}(x) &= C \\ \text{cons}(x,x) &= (((A\ .\ B)\ .\ C)\ .\ ((A\ .\ B)\ .\ C)) \\ \text{atom}(x) &= \text{NIL} \\ \text{not}(\text{atom}(x)) &= T \end{aligned}$$

References

Arsac and Kodratoff [1982]
J. Arsac and Y. Kodratoff, "Some techniques of recursion removal from recursive functions," ACM Trans on Prog. Lang. and Syst. 4 (1982) 295-322.

Balzer [1973]
R.M. Balzer, "A global view of automatic programming," Proc. of the Third Joint Conference on Artificial Intelligence (August 1973), pp. 494-499.

Bidoit *et al.* [1979]
M. Bidoit, C. Gresse, G. Guiho, "A system which synthesizes array manipulating programs from specifications," Proceedings 6th IJCAI, Tokyo.

Biermann and Ballard [1980]
A.W. Biermann and B.W. Ballard, "Towards natural language programming," *American Journal of Computational Linguistics,* Vol. 6, No. 2 (Apr. 1980).

Costa [1982]
E. Costa, "Dérécursivation automatique en utilisant des systèmes de réécriture de termes," Thése de 3ème cycle, Paris (1981). Published (in French) by L.R.I. Bât. 490, F 91405 ORSAY CEDEX Publication interne n° 118, juin 1982.

Dahl *et al.* [1972]
O.J. Dahl, E.W. Dijkstra, and C.A.R. Hoare, *Structured Programming,* Academic Press (1972).

Floyd [1967]
R.W. Floyd, "Assigning meanings to programs," Proc. of the Symposium on Applied Mathematics, Vol. 19 (1967), pp. 19-32.

Gaudel [1978]
M.C. Gaudel, "Specifications incompletes mais suffisantes de la representation des types abstraits," Rapport Laboria No. 320, INRIA.

Gerhart [1972]
S.L. Gerhart, "Verification of APL programs," Ph.D. Thesis, Dept. of Computer Science, Carnegie-Mellon University, Pittsburgh, PA (1972).

Goguen *et al.* [1978]
J. Goguen, J. Thatcher, and E. Wagner, "An initial algebra approach to the specification, correctness, and implementation of abstract data types," *Current Trends in Programming Methodology,* Vol. 4, R.T. Yeh, Ed., Prentic Hall (1978).

Green [1977]
C.C. Green, "A summary of the PSI program synthesis system," Proc. of the Fifth International Conf. on Artificial Intelligence, Vol. I (Aug. 1977), pp. 380-381.

Green *et al.* [1978]
C.C. Green, R.J. Waldinger, D.R. Barstow, R. Elschlager, D.B. Lenat, B.P. McCune, D.E. Shaw, and L.I. Steinberg, "Progress report on program understanding systems," Memo AIM-240, Stanford Artificial Intelligence Laboratory, Stanford, CA. (1978).

Guiho and Gresse [1980]
G. Guiho and C. Gresse, "Program synthesis from incomplete specifications," *Proceeding 5th Conference on Automated Deduction,* Les Arcs.

Guttag and Horning [1978]
J. Guttag and J. Horning, "The algebraic specifications of abstract data types," *Acta Informatica,* Vol. 10 (1978).

Hayes-Roth and McDermott [1978]
F. Hayes-Roth and J. McDermott, "An interference matching technique for inducing abstractions," Com. ACM, 21 (1978), 401-411.

Hoare [1969]
C.A.R. Hoare, "An axiomatic basis for computer programming," *Comm. of the ACM,* Vol. 19 (1969), pp. 576-583.

Kant [1979]
E. Kant, "Efficiency considerations in program synthesis: A knowledge-based approach," Ph.D. Thesis, Computer Science Dept., Stanford University (1979).

Kodratoff [1979]
Y. Kodratoff" "A class of functions synthesized from a finite number of examples and a LISP program scheme", *International Journal of Computer and Information Science,* Vol. 8, No. 6 (1979), pp. 489-521.

Lamport [1977]
L. Lamport, "Proving the correctness of multiprocess programs," *IEEE Trans. on Software Eng.,* Vol. SE3 (Mar. 1977), pp. 125-143.

Liskov *et al.,* [1979]
B. Liskov *et al.,* "CLU reference manual," MIT/LLS/TR-225.

Martin *et al.* [1974]
W.A. Martin, M.J. Ginzberg, R. Krumland, B. Mark, M. Morgenstern, B. Niamir, and A. Sunguroff, Internal Memos, Automatic Programming Group, MIT, Cambridge (1974).

Owicki and Gries [1976]
J. Owicki and D. Gries, "An axiomatic proof technique for parallel programs," *Acta Informatica,* Vol. 6 (1976), pp. 319-340.

Robinson [1965]
J. Robinson, "A machine oriented logic based on the resolution principle," *Journal of the ACM,* Vol. 12 (1965), pp. 23-41.

Shapiro [1981]
E.Y. Shapiro, "Inductive inference of theories from facts," Report 192, Dept. of Computer Science, Yale University (Feb. 1981).

Smith [1977]
D.R. Smith, "A class of synthesizable LISP programs," A.M. Thesis, Dept. of Computer Science, Duke University (1977).

Summers [1977]
P.D. Summers, "A methodology for LISP program construction from examples," *Journal of the ACM,* Vol. 24 (1977).

Vere [1981]
S.A. Vere, "Constrained N-to-1 generalizations," Unpublished draft Feb. 1981, 23 pp.

SECTION II

DEDUCTIVE AND TRANSFORMATIONAL METHODS

CHAPTER 2

A Deductive Approach to Program Synthesis*

Zohar Manna
Stanford University and Weizmann Institute

Richard Waldinger
SRI International

This research was supported in part by the National Science Foundation under Grants MCS 76–83655 and MCS 78–02591, in part by the Office of Naval Research under Contracts N00014–76–C–0687 and N00014–75–C–0816, in part by the Defense Advanced Research Projects Agency of the Department of Defense under Contract MDA903–76–C–0206, and in part by the United States-Israel Binational Science Foundation.

Authors' addresses: Z. Manna, Department of Computer Science, Stanford University, Stanford, CA. 94305; R. Waldinger, Artificial Intelligence Center, SRI International, 333 Ravenswood Ave., Menlo Park, CA 94025.

Abstract

Program synthesis is the systematic derivation of a program from a given specification. A deductive approach to program synthesis is presented for the construction of recursive programs. This approach regards program synthesis as a theorem-proving task and relies on a theorem-proving method that combines the features of transformation rules, unification, and mathematical induction within a single framework.

A. Motivation

The early work in program synthesis relied strongly on mechanical theorem-proving techniques. The work of Green [1969] and Waldinger and Lee [1969], for example, depended on resolution-based theorem proving; however, the difficulty of representing the principle of mathematical induction in a resolution framework hampered these systems in the formation of programs with iterative or recursive loops. More recently, program synthesis and theorem proving have tended to go their separate ways. Newer theorem-proving systems are able to perform proofs by mathematical induction (e.g., Boyer and Moore [1975]) but are useless for program synthesis because they have sacrificed the ability to prove theorems involving existential quantifiers. Recent work in program synthesis (e.g., Burstall and Darlington [1977] and Manna and Waldinger [1979]), on the other hand, has abandoned the theorem-proving approach and has relied instead on the direct application of transformation or rewriting rules to the program's specification; in choosing this path, these systems have renounced the use of such theorem-proving techniques as unification or induction.

In this paper we describe a framework for program synthesis that again relies on a theorem-proving approach. This approach combines techniques of unification, mathematical induction, and transformation rules within a single deductive system. We outline the logical structure of this system without considering the strategic aspects of how deductions are directed. Although no implementation exists, the approach is machine oriented and ultimately intended for implementation in automatic synthesis systems.

In the next section we give examples of specifications accepted by the system. In the succeeding sections we explain the relation between theorem proving and our approach to program synthesis.

B. Specification

The specification of a program allows us to express the purpose of the desired program, without indicating an algorithm by which that purpose is to be achieved. Specifications may contain high-level constructs that are not computable, but are close to our way of thinking. Typically, specifications involve such constructs as the quantifiers *for all* ... and *for some* ..., the set constructor {x: ...}, and the descriptor *find z such that* ....

For example, to specify a program to compute the integer square root of a nonnegative integer n, we would write

$$\begin{aligned} \mathrm{sqrt}(n) \Leftarrow\!\!= \text{ find } z \text{ such that} \\ \mathrm{integer}(z) \text{ and } z^2 \leqslant n < (z+1)^2 \\ \text{where } \mathrm{integer}(n) \text{ and } 0 \leqslant n. \end{aligned}$$

Here, the *input condition*

$$\mathrm{integer}(n) \text{ and } 0 \leqslant n$$

expresses the class of legal inputs to which the program is expected to apply. The *output condition*

$$\text{integer}(z) \text{ and } z^2 \leqslant n < (z+1)^2$$

describes the relation the output z is intended to satisfy.

To describe a program to sort a list *l*, we might write

```
sort(l)  <==  find z such that
                  ordered(z) and perm(l,z)
   where islist(l).
```

Here, ordered(z) expresses that the elements of the output list z should be in nondecreasing order; perm(*l*,z) expresses that z should be a permutation of the input *l*; and islist(*l*) expresses that *l* can be assumed to be a list.

To describe a program to find the last element of a nonempty list *l*, we might write

```
last(l)  <==  find z such that
                  for some y, l = y<>[z]
   where islist(l) and l≠[].
```

Here, "u<>v" denotes the result of appending the two lists u and v; [u] denotes the list whose sole element is u; and [] denotes the empty list. (Thus, [A B C]<>[D] yields [A B C D]; therefore, by the above specification, last([A B C D]) = D.)

In general, we are considering the synthesis of programs whose specifications have the form

```
f(a)  <==  find z such that R(a,z)
   where P(a).
```

Here, a denotes the input of the desired program and z denotes its output; the input condition P(a) and the output condition R(a,z) may themselves contain quantifiers and set constructors (but not the *find* descriptor).

The above specification describes an applicative program, one which yields an output but produces no side effects. To derive a program from such a specification, we attempt to prove a theorem of the form

```
for all a,
if P(a)
then for some z, R(a,z).
```

The proof of this theorem must be constructive, in the sense that it must tell us how to find an output z satisfying the desired output condition. From such a proof, a program to compute z can be extracted.

The above notation can be extended to describe several related programs at once. For example, to specify the programs div(i,j) and rem(i,j) for finding the integer quotient and remainder, respectively, of dividing a nonnegative integer i by a positive integer j, we write

```
(div(i,j),rem(i,j))  <==  find(y,z) such that integer(y) and
                              integer(z) and i=y·j+z and 0 ⩽ z and z < j
   where integer(i) and integer(j) and 0 ⩽ i and 0 < j.
```

C. Basic Structure

The basic structure employed in our approach is the *sequent,* which consists of two lists of sentences, the *assertions* $A_1,A_2,...,A_m$, and the *goals* $G_1,G_2,...,G_n$. With each assertion or goal there may be associated an entry called the *output expression.* This output entry has no bearing on the proof itself, but records the program segment that has been constructed at each stage of the derivation (cf. the "answer literal" in Green [1969]). We denote a sequent by a table with three columns: assertions, goals, and outputs. Each row in the sequent has the form

assertions	goals	outputs
$A_i(a,x)$		$t_i(a,x)$

or

	$G_j(a,x)$	$t_j(a,x)$

The meaning of a sequent is that if all instances of each of the assertions are true, then some instances of at least one of the goals is true; more precisely, the sequent has the same meaning as its *associated sentence*

$$
\begin{aligned}
&\text{if for all } x,\ A_1(a,x) \text{ and} \\
&\quad \text{for all } x,\ A_2(a,x) \text{ and} \\
&\quad \vdots \\
&\quad \text{for all } x,\ A_m(a,x) \\
&\text{then for some } x,\ G_1(a,x) \text{ or} \\
&\qquad \text{for some } x,\ G_2(a,x) \text{ or} \\
&\qquad \vdots \\
&\qquad \text{for some } x,\ G_n(a,x)
\end{aligned}
$$

where a denotes all the constants of the sequent and x denotes all the free variables. (In general, we denote constants or tuples of constants by "a,b,c,...,n" and variables or tuples of variables by "u,v,w,...,z".) If some instance of a goal is true (or some instance of an assertion is false), the corresponding instance of its output expression satisfies the given specification. In other words, if some instance $G_j(a,e)$ is true (or some instance $A_i(a,e)$ is false), then the corresponding instance $t_j(a,e)$ (or $t_i(a,e)$) is an acceptable output.

Note that (1) an assertion or goal is not required to have an output entry; (2) an assertion and a goal never occupy the same row of the sequent; (3) the variables in each row are "dummies" that we can systematically rename without changing the meaning of the sequent.

The distinction between assertions and goals is artificial and does not increase the logical power of the deductive system. In fact, if we delete a goal from a sequent and add its negation as a new assertion, we obtain an equivalent sequent; similarly, we can delete an assertion from a sequent and add its negation as a new goal without changing the meaning of the sequent. This property is known as *duality.* Nevertheless, the distinction between assertions and goals makes our deductions easier to understand.

If initially we are given the specification

$$f(a) \Longleftarrow \text{find } z \text{ such that } R(a,z) \text{ where } P(a),$$

we construct the initial sequent

assertions	goals	outputs f(a)
P(a)		
	R(a,z)	z

In other words, we assume that the input condition P(a) is true, and we want to prove that for some z, the goal R(a,z) is true; if so, z represents the desired output of the program f(a). The output z is a variable, for which we can make substitutions; the input a is a constant. If we prefer, we may remove quantifiers in P(a) and R(a,z) by the usual skolemization procedure (see, e.g., Nilsson 1979]).

The input condition P(a) is not the only assertion in the sequent; typically, simple, basic axioms, such as u=u, are represented as assertions that are tacitly present in all sequents. Many properties of the subject domain, however, are represented by other means, as we shall see.

The deductive system we describe operates by causing new assertions and goals, and corresponding new output expressions, to be added to the sequent without changing its meaning. The process terminates if the goal *true* (or the assertion *false*) is produced, whose corresponding output expression consists entirely of primitives from the target programming language; this expression is the desired program. In other words, if we develop a row of form

	true	t

or

false		t

where t is a primitive expression, the desired program is of form

$$f(a) \Longleftarrow t.$$

Note that this deductive procedure never requires us to establish new sequents or (except for strategic purposes) to delete an existing assertion or goal. In this sense, the approach more resembles resolution than "natural deduction."

Suppose we are required to construct two related programs f(a) and g(a); i.e., we are given the specification

$$(f(a),g(a)) \Longleftarrow \text{find}(y,z) \text{ such that } R(a,y,z) \text{ where } P(a).$$

Then we construct an initial sequent with two output columns

assertions	goals	outputs f(a)	outputs g(a)
P(a)			
	R(a,y,z)	y	z

If we subsequently succeed in developing a terminal row, say of form

	true	s	t

where both s and t are primitive expressions, then the desired programs are

f(a) <== s

and

g(a) <== t.

In the remainder of this paper we outline the deductive rules of our system and their application to program synthesis.

D. Splitting Rules

The splitting rules allow us to decompose an assertion or goal into its logical components. For example, if our sequent contains an assertion of form (F and G), we can introduce the two assertions F and G into the sequent without changing its meaning. We will call this the *andsplit rule* and express it in the following notation:

assertions	goals	outputs
F and G		t
F		t
G		t

This means that if rows matching those above the double line are present in the sequent, then the corresponding rows below the double line may be added.

Similarly, we have the *orsplit rule*

assertions	goals	outputs
	F or G	t
	F	t
	G	t

and the *ifsplit rule*

assertions	goals	outputs
	if F then G	t
F		t
	G	t

There is no *orsplit rule* or *ifsplit rule* for assertions and no *andsplit rule* for goals. Note that the output entries for the consequents of the splitting rules are exactly the same as the entries for their antecedents.

Although initially only the goal has an output entry, the *ifsplit rule* can introduce an assertion with an output entry. Such assertions are rare in practice, but can arise by the action of such rules.

E. Transformation Rules

Transformation rules allow one assertion or goal to be derived from another. Typically, transformations are expressed as conditional rewriting rules.

$$r ==> s \quad \text{if } P$$

meaning that in any assertion, goal, or output expression, a subexpression of form r can be replaced by the corresponding expression of form s, provided that the condition P holds. We never write such a rule unless r and s are equal terms or equivalent sentences, whenever condition P holds. For example, the transformation rule

$$u \in v \quad ==> \quad u = head(v) \text{ or } u \in tail(v) \quad \text{if islist}(v) \text{ and } v \neq []$$

expresses that an element belongs to a nonempty list if it equals the head of the list or belongs to its tail. (Here, head(v) denotes the first element of the list v, and tail(v) denotes the list of all but the first element.) The rule

$$u|0 ==> \text{true} \quad \text{if integer}(u) \text{ and } u \neq 0$$

expresses that every nonzero integer divides zero.

If a rule has the vacuous condition *true,* we write it with no condition; for example, the logical rule

$$Q \text{ and true} ==> Q$$

may be applied to any subexpression that matches its left-hand side.

A transformation rule

$$r ==> s \quad \text{if } P$$

is not permitted to replace an expression of form s by the corresponding expression of form r when the condition P holds, even though these two expressions have the same values. For that purpose, we would require a second rule

$$s ==> r \quad \text{if } P.$$

For example, we might include the rule

$$x + 0 ==> x \quad \text{if number}(x)$$

but not the rule

$$x ==> x + 0 \quad \text{if number}(x).$$

Assertions and goals are affected differently by transformation rules. Suppose

$$r ==> s \quad \text{if } P$$

is a transformation rule and F is an assertion containing a subexpression r′ which is not within the scope of any quantifier. Suppose also that there exists a *unifier* for r and r′, i.e., a substitution θ such that $r\theta$ and $r'\theta$ are identical. Here, $r\theta$ denotes the result of applying the substitution θ to the expression r. We can assume that θ is a "most general" unifier (in the sense of Robinson [1965]) of r and r′. We rename the variables of F, if necessary, to ensure that it has no variables in common with the transformation rule. By the rule, we can conclude that if $P\theta$ holds, then $r\theta$ and $s\theta$ are equal terms or equivalent sentences. Therefore, we can add the assertion

$$\text{if } P\theta \text{ then } F\theta[r\theta \leftarrow s\theta]$$

to our sequent. Here, the notation $F\theta[r\theta \leftarrow s\theta]$ indicates that every occurrence of $r\theta$ in $F\theta$ is to be replaced by $s\theta$.

For example, suppose we have the assertion

$$a \in l \text{ and } a \neq 0$$

and we apply the transformation rule

$$u \in v \quad ==> \quad u = head(v) \text{ or } u \in tail(v) \quad \text{if islist}(v) \text{ and } v \neq [\,],$$

taking r′ to be $a \in l$ and θ to be the substitution $[u \leftarrow a;\ v \leftarrow l]$; then we obtain the new assertion

if islist(l) and $l \neq$ []
then (a = head(l) or a $\in$ tail(l)) and a $\neq$ 0.

Note that a and l are constants, while u and v are variables, and indeed, the substitution was made for the variables of the rule but not for the constants of the assertion.

In general, if the given assertion F has an associated output entry t, the new output entry is formed by applying the substitution θ to t. For, suppose some instance of the new assertion "if Pθ then Fθ[r$\theta \leftarrow$ sθ]" is false; then the corresponding instance of Pθ is true, and the corresponding instance of Fθ[r$\theta \leftarrow$ sθ] is false. Then, by the transformation rule, the instances of rθ and sθ are equal; hence the corresponding instance of Fθ is false. We know that if any instance of F is false, the corresponding instance of t satisfies the given specification. Hence, because some instance of Fθ is false, the corresponding instance of tθ is the desired output.

In our deduction rule notation, we write

assertions	goals	outputs
F		t
if Pθ then Fθ[r$\theta \leftarrow$ sθ]		tθ

The corresponding dual deduction rule for goals is

assertions	goals	outputs
	F	t
	Pθ and Fθ[r$\theta \leftarrow$ sθ]	tθ

For example, suppose we have the goal

	a|z and b|z	z+1

and we apply the transformation rule

u | 0 ==> true if integer(u) and u $\neq$ 0,

taking r′ to be a|z and θ to be the substitution [z $\leftarrow$ 0; u $\leftarrow$ a]. Then we obtain the goal

	(integer(a) and a$\neq$0) and (true and b|0)	0+1

which can be further transformed to

	integer (a) and a$\neq$0 and b|0	1

Note that applying the transformation rule caused a substitution to be made for the occurrences of the variable z in the goal and the output entry.

Transformation rules can also be applied to output entries in an analogous manner.

Transformation rules need not be simple rewriting rules; they may represent arbitrary procedures. For example, r could be an equation $f(x) = a$, s could be its solution $x = e$, and P could be the condition under which that solution applies. Another example: the skolemization procedure for removing quantifiers can be represented as a transformation rule. In fact, decision methods for particular subtheories may also be represented as transformation rules (see, e.g., Bledsoe [1977] or Nelson and Oppen [1978]).

Transformation rules play the role of the "antecedent theorems" and "consequent theorems" of PLANNER (Hewitt [1971]). For example, a consequent theorem that we might write as

to prove $f(u) = f(v)$
prove $u = v$

can be represented by the transformation rule

$$f(u) = f(v) \;==>\; \text{true} \quad \text{if } u = v.$$

This rule will have the desired effect of reducing the goal $f(a) = f(b)$ to the simpler subgoal $a = b$, and (like the consequent theorem) will not have the pernicious side effect of deriving from the simple assertion $a = b$ the more complex assertion $f(a) = f(b)$. The axiomatic representation of the same fact would have both results. (Incidentally, the transformation rule has the beneficial effect, not shared by the consequent theorem, of deriving from the complex assertion $not(f(a) = f(b))$ the simpler assertion $not(a = b)$.)

F. Resolution

The original resolution principle (Robinson [1965]) required that sentences be put into conjunctive normal form. As a result, the set of clauses sometimes exploded to an unmanageable size and the proofs lost their intuitive content. The version of resolution we employ does not require the sentences to be in conjunctive normal form.

Assume our sequent contains two assertions F and G, containing subsentences P_1 and P_2, respectively, that are not within the scope of any quantifier. For the time being, let us ignore the output expressions corresponding to these assertions. Suppose there exists a unifier for P_1 and P_2, i.e., a substitution θ such that $P_1\theta$ and $P_2\theta$ are identical. We can take θ to be the most general unifier. The *AA-resolution rule* allows us to deduce the new assertion

$$F\theta[P_1\theta \leftarrow \text{true}] \text{ or } G\theta[P_2\theta \leftarrow \text{false}]$$

and add it to the sequent. Recall that the notation $F\theta[P_1\theta \leftarrow \text{true}]$ indicates that every instance of the subsentence $P_1\theta$ in $F\theta$ is to be replaced by *true*. (Of course, we may need to do the usual renaming to ensure that F and G have no variables in common.) We will call θ the *unifying substitution* and $P_1\theta$ $(= P_2\theta)$ the *eliminated subexpression;* the deduced assertion is called the *resolvent.* Note that the rule is symmetric, so the roles of F and G may be reversed.

For example, suppose our sequent contains the assertions

$$\text{if } (P(x) \text{ and } Q(b)) \text{ then } R(x)$$

and

$$P(a) \text{ and } Q(y).$$

The two subsentences "P(x) and Q(b)" and "P(a) and Q(y)" can be unified by the substitution

$$\theta = [x \leftarrow a;\ y \leftarrow b].$$

Therefore, the AA-resolution rule allows us to eliminate the subexpression "P(a) and Q(b)" and derive the conclusion

$$(\text{if true then } R(a)) \text{ or false},$$

which reduces to

$$R(a)$$

by application of the appropriate transformation rules.

The conventional resolution rule may be regarded as a special case of the above AA-resolution rule. The conventional rule allows us to derive from the two assertions

$$(\text{not } P_1) \text{ or } Q$$

and

$$P_2 \text{ or } R$$

the new assertion

$$Q\theta \text{ or } R\theta,$$

where θ is a most general unifier of P_1 and P_2. From the same two assertions we can use our AA-resolution rule to derive

$$((\text{not } P_1 \text{ or } Q)\theta)[P_1\theta \leftarrow \text{true}] \text{ or } ((P_2 \text{ or } R)\theta)[P_2\theta \leftarrow \text{false}]$$

.i.e.

$$((\text{not true}) \text{ or } Q\theta) \text{ or } (\text{false or } R\theta),$$

which reduces to the same conclusion

$$Q\theta \text{ or } R\theta$$

as the original resolution rule.

The justification for the AA-resolution rule is straightforward: Because F holds, if $P_1\theta$ is true, then $F\theta[P_1\theta \leftarrow \text{true}]$ holds; on the other hand, because G holds, if $P_1\theta (= P_2\theta)$ is false, $G\theta[P_2\theta \leftarrow \text{false}]$ holds. In either case, the disjunction

$$F\theta[P_1\theta \leftarrow \text{true}] \text{ or } G\theta[P_2\theta \leftarrow \text{false}]$$

holds.

A "nonclausal" resolution rule similar to ours has been developed by Murray [1978]. Other such rules have been proposed by Wilkins [1973] and Nilsson [1979].

G. The Resolution Rules

We have defined the AA-resolution rule to derive conclusions from assertions. The *AA-resolution rule*

assertions	goals
F G	
$F\theta[P_1\theta \leftarrow \text{true}]$ or $G\theta[P_2\theta \leftarrow \text{false}]$	

where $P_1\theta = P_2\theta$, and θ is most general.

By duality, we can regard goals as negated assertions; consequently, the following three rules are corollaries of the AA-resolution rule.

The *GG-resolution rule*

assertions	goals
	F G
	$F\theta[P_1\theta \leftarrow \text{true}]$ and $G\theta[P_2\theta \leftarrow \text{false}]$

The *GA-resolution rule*

assertions	goals
G	F
	$F\theta[P_1\theta \leftarrow \text{true}]$ and not $(G\theta[P_2\theta \leftarrow \text{false}])$

The *AG-resolution rule*

assertions	goals
F	G
	not $(F\theta[P_1\theta \leftarrow \text{true}])$ and $G\theta[P_2\theta \leftarrow \text{false}]$

where P_1,P_2, and θ satisfy the same condition as for the AA-resolution rule.

Up to now, we have ignored the output expressions of the assertions and goals. However, if at least one of the sentences to which a resolution rule is applied has a corresponding output expression, the resolvent will also have an output expression. If only one of the sentences has an output expression, say t, then the resolvent will have the output expression $t\theta$. On the other hand, if the two sentences F and G have output expressions t_1 and t_2, respectively, the resolvent will have the output expression

$$\text{if } P_1\theta \text{ then } t_1\theta \text{ else } t_2\theta.$$

(Of course, if $t_1\theta$ and $t_2\theta$ are identical, no conditional expression need be formed; the output expression is simply $t_1\theta$.)

The justification for constructing this conditional as an output expression is as follows. We consider only the GG case: Suppose that the goal

$$F\theta[P_1\theta \leftarrow \text{true}] \text{ and } G\theta[P_2\theta \leftarrow \text{false}]$$

has been obtained by GG-resolution from two goals F and G. We would like to show that if the goal is true, the conditional output expression satisfies the desired specification. We assume that the resolvent is true; therefore both $F\theta[P_1\theta \leftarrow \text{true}]$ and $G\theta[P_2\theta \leftarrow \text{false}]$ are true. In the case that $P_1\theta$ is true, we have that $F\theta$ is also true. Consequently, the corresponding instance $t_1\theta$ of the output expression t_1 satisfies the specification of the desired program. In the other case, in which $P_1\theta$ is false, $P_2\theta$ is false, and the same reasoning allows us to conclude that $t_2\theta$ satisfies the specification of the desired program. In either case we can conclude that the conditional

$$\text{if } P_1\theta \text{ then } t_1\theta \text{ else } t_2\theta$$

satisfies the desired specification. By duality, the same output expression can be derived for the AA-resolution, GA-resolution, and AG-resolution.

For example, let $u \cdot v$ denote the operation of inserting u before the first element of the list v, and suppose we have the goal

assertions	goals	outputs f(a,b)
	head(z) = a and tail(z) = b	z

and we have the assertion

head(u·v) = u		

with no output expression; then by GA-resolution, applying the substitution

$$\theta = [u \leftarrow a;\ z \leftarrow a \cdot v]$$

and eliminating the subsentence

$$\text{head}(a \cdot v) = a,$$

we obtain the new goal

	(true and tail(a·v) = b) and (not false)	a·v

which can be reduced to

	tail(a·v) = b	a·v

by application of the appropriate transformation rules. Note that we have applied the substitution [u ← a; z ← a·v] to the original output expression z, obtaining the new output expression a·v. Therefore, if we can find v such that tail(a·v) = b, the corresponding instance of a·v will satisfy the desired specification.

Another example: Suppose we have derived the two goals

assertions	goals	outputs max(*l*)
	max(tail(*l*)) ⩾ head(*l*) and tail(*l*) ≠ []	max(tail(*l*))
	not(max(tail(*l*)) ⩾ head(*l*)) and tail(*l*) ≠ []	head(*l*)

Then by GG-resolution, eliminating the subsentence max(tail(*l*)) ⩾ head(*l*), we can derive the new goal

	(true and tail(*l*) ≠ []) and (not false) and tail(*l*) ≠ [])	if max(tail(*l*)) ⩾ head(*l*) then max(tail(*l*)) else head(*l*)

which can be reduced to

	tail(*l*) ≠ []	if max(tail(*l*)) ⩾ head(*l*) then max(tail(*l*)) else head(*l*)

H. The Polarity Strategy

Not all applications of the resolution rules will produce valuable conclusions. For example, suppose we are given the goal

assertions	goals	outputs
	P(c,x) and Q(x,a)	

and the assertion

if P(y,d) then Q(b,y)		

Then if we apply GA-resolution, eliminating Q(b,a) we can obtain the resolvent

(P(c,b) and true) and not(if P(a,d) then false),

which reduces to the goal

	P(c,b) and P(a,d)	

However, we can also apply GA-resolution and eliminate P(c,d), yielding the resolvent

(true and Q(d,a)) and not(if false then Q(b,c)),

which reduces to the trivial goal

	false	

Finally, we can also apply AG-resolution to the same assertion and goal in two different ways, eliminating P(c,d) and eliminating Q(b,a); both of these applications lead to the same trivial goal *false*.

A *polarity strategy* adapted from Murray [1978] restricts the resolution rules to prevent many such fruitless applications. We first assign a *polarity* (either positive or negative) to every subsentence of a given sequent as follows:

(1) each goal is positive;
(2) each assertion is negative;
(3) if a subsentence S has form "not α", then its component α has polarity opposite to S;
(4) if a subsentence S has form "α and β," "α or β," "for all x,α," or "for some x,β," then its components α and β have the same polarity as S;
(5) if a subsentence S has form "if α then β," then β has the same polarity as S, but α has the opposite polarity.

For example, the above goal and assertion are annotated with the polarity of each subsentence, as follows:

assertions	goals	outputs
(if P(y,d)$^{+}$ then Q(b,y)$^{-}$)$^{-}$	(P(c,x)$^{+}$ and Q(x,a)$^{+}$)$^{+}$	

The four resolution rules we have presented replace certain subsentences by *true*, and others by *false*. The polarity strategy, then, permits a subsentence to be replaced by *true* only if it has at least one positive occurrence, and by *false* only if it has at least one negative occurrence. For example, we are permitted to apply GA-resolution to the above goal and assertion, eliminating Q(b,a) because Q(x,a), which is replaced by *true*, occurs positively in the goal, and Q(b,y), which is replaced by *false*, occurs negatively in the assertion. On the other hand, we are not permitted to apply GA-resolution to eliminate P(c,d), because P(y,d), which is replaced by *false*, only occurs positively in the assertion. Similarly, we are not permitted to apply AG-resolution between this assertion and goal, whether we eliminate P(c,d) or Q(b,a). Indeed, the only application of resolution permitted by the polarity strategy is the one that led to a nontrivial conclusion.

The deductive system we have presented so far, including the splitting rules, the resolution rules, and an appropriate set of logical transformation rules, has been proved by Murray to constitute a complete system for first-order logic, in the sense that a derivation exists for every valid sentence. (Actually, only the resolution rules and some of the logical transformation rules are strictly necessary.) The above polarity strategy does not interfere with the completeness of the system.

I. Mathematical Induction and the Formation of Recursive Calls

Mathematical induction is of special importance for deductive systems intended for program synthesis because it is only by the application of some form of the induction principle that recursive calls or iterative loops are introduced into the program being constructed. The induction rule we employ is a version of the principle of mathematical induction over a well-founded set, known in the computer science literature as "structural induction."

We may describe this principle as follows: In attempting to prove that a sentence of form F(a) holds for an arbitrary element a of some well-founded set, we may assume inductively that the sentence holds for all u that are strictly less than a in the well-founded ordering $<_w$. Thus, in trying to prove F(a), the well-founded induction principle allows us to assume the induction hypothesis

$$\text{for all u, if } u <_w a \text{ then } F(u).$$

In the case that the well-founded set is the nonnegative integers under the usual $<$ ordering, well-founded induction reduces to the familiar complete induction principle: To prove that F(n) holds for an arbitrary nonnegative integer n, we may assume inductively that the sentence F(u) holds for all nonnegative integers u such that $u<n$.

In our inference system, the principle of well-founded induction is represented as a deduction rule (rather than, say, an axiom schema). We present only a special case of this rule here.

Suppose we are constructing a program whose specification is of form

$$f(a) \Leftarrow\!= \text{find z such that } R(a,z) \text{ where } P(a).$$

Our initial sequent is thus

assertions	goals	outputs f(a)
P(a)		
	R(a,z)	z

Then we can always add to our sequent a new assertion, the induction hypothesis

if u $<_w$ a then if P(u) then R(u,f(u))		

Here, f denotes the program we are trying to construct. The well-founded set and the particular well-founded $<_w$ to be employed in the proof have not yet been determined. If the induction hypothesis is used more than once in the proof, always refer to the same well-founded ordering $<_w$.

Let us paraphrase: We are attempting to construct a program f such that for an arbitrary input a satisfying the input condition P(a), the output f(a) will satisfy the output condition R(a,f(a)). By the well-founded induction principle, we can assume inductively that for every u less than a (in some well-founded ordering) such that the input condition P(u) holds, the output f(u) will satisfy the same output condition R(u,f(u)). By employing the induction hypothesis in the proof, recursive calls to f can be introduced into the output expression for f(a).

As we shall see in a later section, we can introduce an induction hypothesis corresponding to any subset of the assertions or goals in our sequent, not just the initial assertion and goal; most of these induction hypotheses are not relevant to the final proof, and the proliferation of new assertions obstructs our efforts to find a proof. Therefore, we employ the following *recurrence strategy* for determining when to introduce an induction hypothesis.

Let us restrict our attention to the case where the induction hypothesis is formed from the initial sequent. Suppose that at some point in the derivation a goal is developed of the form

	R(s,z')	t(z')

where s is an arbitrary term. In other words, the new goal is a precise instance of the initial goal R(a,z) obtained by replacing a by s. This recurrence motivates us to add the induction hypothesis

if u $<_w$ a then if P(u) then R(u,f(u))		

The rationale for introducing the induction hypothesis at this point is that now we can perform GA-resolution between the newly developed goal R(s,z') and the induction hypothesis. The resulting goal is then

	true and not if s $<_w$ a then if P(s) then false	t(f(s))

This simplifies (by the application of logical transformation rules) to

	s $<_w$ a and P(s)	t(f(s))

Note that a recursive call f(s) has been introduced into the output expression for f(a). By proving the expression $s <_w a$, we ensure that this recursive call will terminate; by proving the expression P(s), we guarantee that the argument s of the recursive call will satisfy the input condition of the program f.

The particular well-founded ordering $<_w$ to be employed by the proof has not yet been determined. We assume the existence of transformation rules of form

$$u <_{w_1} v \implies \text{true} \quad \text{if } Q(u,v)$$

capable of choosing or combining well-founded orderings applicable to the particular theories under consideration (e.g., numbers, lists, and sets).

Let us look at an example. Suppose we are constructing two programs div(i,j) and rem(i,j) to compute the quotient and remainder, respectively, of dividing a nonnegative integer i by a positive integer j; the specification may be expressed as

$$\begin{aligned}(\text{div}(i,j),\text{rem}(i,j)) \Longleftarrow\ & \text{find } (y,z) \text{ such that} \\ & i = y \,.\, j + z \text{ and } 0 \leqslant z \text{ and } z < j \\ \text{where } 0 \leqslant i \text{ and } 0 < j.&\end{aligned}$$

(Note that, for simplicity, we have omitted type requirements such as integer(i).) Our initial sequent is then

assertions	goals	outputs div(i,j)	outputs rem(i,j)
$0 \leqslant i$ and $0 < j$	$i = y \cdot j + z$ and $0 \leqslant z$ and $z < j$	y	z

Here, the inputs i and j are constants, for which we can make no substitution; y and the output z are variables.

Assume that during the course of the derivation we develop the goal

	$i - j = y_1 \cdot j + z$ and $0 \leqslant z$ and $z < j$	$y_1 + 1$	z

This goal is a precise instance of the initial goal

$$i = y \cdot j + z \text{ and } 0 \leqslant z \text{ and } z < j$$

obtained by replacing i by $i - j$. Therefore, we add as a new assertion the induction hypothesis.

if $(u_1,u_2) <_w (i,j)$ then if $0 \leqslant u_1$ and $0 < u_2$ then $u_1 = \text{div}(u_1,u_2) \cdot u_2 + \text{rem}(u_1,u_2)$ and $0 \leqslant \text{rem}(u_1,u_2)$ and $\text{rem}(u_1,u_2) < u_2$			

Here, $<_w$ is an arbitrary well-founded ordering, defined on pairs because the desired program f has a pair of inputs.

We can now apply GA-resolution between the goal

	$i-j = y_1 \cdot j + z$ and $0 \leqslant z$ and $z < j$	$y_1 + 1$	z

and the induction hypothesis; the unifying substitution θ is

$$[u_1 \leftarrow i-j;\ u_2 \leftarrow j;\ y_1 \leftarrow div(i-j,j);\ z \leftarrow rem(i-j,j)].$$

The new goal is

	true and not (if $(i-j,j) <_w (i,j)$ then if $0 \leqslant i-j$ and $0 < j$ then false)	$div(i-j,j)+1$	$rem(i\text{-}j,j)$

which reduces to

	$(i-j,j) <_w (i,j)$ and $0 \leqslant i-j$ and $0 < j$	$div(i-j,j)+1$	$rem(i-j,j)$

Note that the recursive calls $div(i-j,j)$ and $rem(i-j,j)$ have been introduced into the output entry.

The particular well-founded ordering $<_w$ to be employed in the proof has not yet been determined. It can be chosen to be the $<$ ordering on the first component of the pairs, by application of the transformation rule

$$(u_1,u_2) <_{N1} (v_1,v_2) \Rightarrow \text{true} \quad \text{if } u_1 < v_1 \text{ and } 0 \leqslant u_1 \text{ and } 0 \leqslant v_1.$$

A new goal

	$i-j < i$ and $0 \leqslant i-j$ and $i \leqslant 0$ and true and $0 \leqslant i-j$ and $0 < j$	$div(i-j,j)+1$	$rem(i-j,j)$

is produced; this goal ultimately reduces to

	$j \leqslant i$	$div(i-j,j)+1$	$rem(i-j,j)$

In other words, in the case that $j \leqslant i$, the outputs $div(i-j,j) + 1$ and $rem(i-j,j)$ satisfy the desired program's specification. In the next section, we give the full derivation of these programs.

In our presentation of the induction rule, several limitations were imposed for simplicity but are not actually essential:

(1) In the example we considered, the only skolem functions in the initial sequent are the constants corresponding to the program's inputs, and the only variables are those corresponding to the program's outputs; the sequent was of form

assertions	goals	outputs $f(a)$
$P(a)$	$R(a,z)$	z

In forming the induction hypothesis, the skolem constant a is replaced by a variable u and the variable z is replaced by the term f(u); the induction hypothesis was of form

if $u <_w a$ then if $P(u)$ then $R(u,f(u))$		

However, if there are other skolem functions in the initial sequent, they too must be replaced by variables in the induction hypothesis; if there are other variables in the initial sequent, they must be replaced by new skolem functions. For example, suppose the initial sequent is of form

f(a) <== find z such that
for all x_1,
for some x_2,
$R(a, z, x_1, x_2)$
where P(a).

Then the initial sequent is of form

assertions	goals	outputs $f(a)$
$P(a)$	$R(a,z,g_1(z),x_2)$	z

where $g_1(z)$ is the skolem function corresponding to x_1. The induction hypothesis is then of form

if $u <_w a$ then if $P(u)$ then $R(u,f(u),v,g_2(u,v))$		

Here, the skolem function $g_1(z)$ has been replaced by the variable v, and the variable x_2 has been replaced by a new skolem function $g_2(u,v)$.

(2) One limitation to the recurrence strategy was that the induction hypothesis was introduced only when an entire goal is an instance of the initial goal. In fact, the strategy can be extended so that the hypothesis is introduced when some subsentence of a goal is an instance of some subsentence of the initial goal, because the resolution rule can then be applied between the goal and the induction hypothesis. This extension is straightforward.

(3) A final observation: The induction hypothesis was always formed directly from the initial sequent; thus, the theorem itself was proved by induction. In later sections we extend the rule so that induction can be applied to lemmas that are stronger or more general than the theorem itself. This extension also accounts for the formation of auxiliary procedures in the program being constructed.

Some early efforts toward incorporating mathematical induction in a resolution framework were made by Darlington [1968]. His system treated the induction principle as a second-order axiom schema rather than as a deduction rule; it had a limited ability to perform second-order unifications.

J. A Complete Example: Finding the Quotient of Two Integers

In this section, we present a complete example that exploits most of the features of the deductive synthesis approach. Our task is to construct programs div(i,j) and rem(i,j) for finding the integer quotient of dividing a nonnegative integer i by a positive integer j. Portions of this synthesis have been used to illustrate the induction principle in the previous section.

Our specification is expressed as

$$\begin{aligned}(\mathrm{div}(i,j), \mathrm{rem}(i,j)) \Longleftarrow\ & \text{find } (y,z) \text{ such that} \\ & i = y \cdot j + z \text{ and } 0 \leqslant z \text{ and } z < j \\ \text{where } 0 \leqslant i \text{ and } 0 < j.\end{aligned}$$

(For simplicity, we again omit type conditions, such as integer(i), from this discussion.) Our initial sequent is therefore

assertions	goals	outputs div(i,j)	outputs rem(i,j)
1. $0 \leqslant i$ and $0 < j$			
	2. $i = y \cdot j + z$ and $0 \leqslant z$ and $z < j$	y	z

(Note that we are enumerating the assertions and goals.)

In presenting the derivation we sometimes apply simple logical and algebraic transformation rules without mentioning them explicitly. We assume that our background knowledge includes the two assertions

3. $u = u$			
4. $u \leqslant v$ or $v < u$			

Applying the *andsplit rule* to assertion 1 yields the new assertions

5. $0 \leqslant i$			
6. $0 < j$			

Assume we have the following transformation rules that define integer multiplication:

$$0 \cdot v \implies 0$$

$$(u + 1) \cdot v \implies u \cdot v + v.$$

Applying the first of these rules to the subexpression $y \cdot j$ in goal 2 yields

	7. $i = 0 + z$ and $0 \leqslant z$ and $z < j$	0	z

The unifying substitution in deriving goal 7 is

$$\theta = [y \leftarrow 0;\ v \leftarrow j];$$

applying this substitution to the output entry y produced the new output 0.

Applying the numerical transformation rule

$$0 + v \implies v$$

yields

	8. $i = z$ and $0 \leqslant z$ and $z < j$	0	z

The GA-resolution rule can now be applied between goal 8 and the equality assertion 3, $u = u$. The unifying substitution is

$$\theta = [u \leftarrow i;\ z \leftarrow i]$$

and the eliminated subexpression is $i = i$; we obtain

	9. $0 \leqslant i$ and $i < j$	0	i

By applying GA-resolution again, against assertion 5, $0 \leqslant i$, we obtain

	10. $i < j$	0	i

In other words, we have found that in the case that $i < j$, the output 0 will satisfy the specification for the quotient program and the output i will satisfy the specification for the remainder program.

Let us return our attention to the initial goal 2,

$$i = y \cdot j + z \text{ and } 0 \leqslant z \text{ and } z < j.$$

Recall that we have a second transformation rule

$$(u + 1)\cdot v \implies u\cdot v + v$$

for the multiplication function. Applying this rule to goal 2 yields

	11. $i = y_1\cdot j + j + z$ and $0 \leq z$ and $z < j$	$y_1 + 1$	z

where y_1 is a new variable. Here, the unifying substitution is

$$\theta = [y \leftarrow y_1{+}1;\ u \leftarrow y_1;\ v \leftarrow j];$$

applying this substitution to the output entry y produced the new output $y_1{+}1$ in the div program.

The transformation rule

$$u = v + w \implies u - v = w$$

applied to goal 11 yields

	12. $i - j = y_1\cdot j + z$ and $0 \leq z$ and $z < j$	$y_1 + 1$	z

Goal 12 is a precise instance of the initial goal 2,

$$i = y\cdot j + z \text{ and } 0 \leq z \text{ and } z < j,$$

obtained by replacing the input i by $i - j$. (Again, the replacement of the dummy variable y by y_1 is not significant.) Therefore, the following induction hypothesis is formed:

13. if $(u_1,u_2) <_w (i,j)$ then if $0 \leq u_1$ and $0 < u_2$ then $u_1 = div(u_1,u_2)\cdot u_2 + rem(u_1,u_2)$ and $0 \leq rem(u_1,u_2)$ and $rem(u_1,u_2) < u_2$			

Here, $<_w$ is an arbitrary well-founded ordering.

By applying GA-resolution between goal 12 and the induction hypothesis, we obtain the goal

	14. true and not (if $(i-j,j) <_w (i,j)$ then if $0 \leqslant i-j$ and $0 < j$ then false)	$div(i-j,j) + 1$	$rem(i-j,j)$

Here, the unifying substitution is

$$\theta = [u_1 \leftarrow i-j;\ u_2 \leftarrow j; y_1 \leftarrow div(i-j,j);\ z \leftarrow rem(i-j,j)]$$

and the eliminated subexpression is

$$i-j = div(i\text{-}j,j) \cdot j + rem(i\text{-}j,j) \text{ and } 0 \leqslant rem(i-j,j) \text{ and } rem(i-j, j) < j.$$

Note that the substitution to the variable y_1 has caused the output entry $y_1 + 1$ to be changed to $div(i-j,j) + 1$ and the output entry z to be replaced by $rem(i-j,j)$. The use of the induction hypothesis has introduced the recursive calls $div(i-j,j)$ and $rem(i-j,j)$ into the output.

Goal 14 reduces to

	15. $(i-j,j) <_w (i,j)$ and $0 \leqslant i-j$ and $0 < j$	$div(i-j,j) + 1$	$rem(i-j,j)$

The particular ordering $<_w$ has not yet been determined; however, it is chosen to be the $<$ ordering on the first component of the pairs, by application of the transformation rule

$$(u_1,u_2) <_{N1} (v_1,v_2) \implies \text{true} \quad \text{if } u_1 < v_1 \text{ and } 0 \leqslant u_1 \text{ and } 0 \leqslant v_1.$$

A new goal is produced:

	16. $i-j < i$ and $0 \leqslant i-j$ and $0 \leqslant i$ and $0 \leqslant i-j$ and $0 < j$	$div(i-j,j) + 1$	$rem(i-j,j)$

Note that the conditions of the transformation rule caused new conjuncts to be added to the goal.

By application of algebraic and logical transformation rules, and GA-resolution with the assertion 5, $0 \leqslant i$, and assertion 6, $0 < j$, goal 16 is reduced to

	17. $j \leqslant i$	$div(i-j,j) + 1$	$rem(i-j,j)$

In other words, we have learned that in the case that $j \leqslant i$, the outputs $div(i-j,j) + 1$ and $rem(i-j,j)$ satisfy the specification of the div program. On the other hand, in deriving goal 10 we learned that in the case that $i < j$, 0 and i are satisfactory outputs. Assuming we have the assertion 4

$$u \leqslant v \text{ or } v < u,$$

we can obtain the goal

	18. not (i<j)	div(i−j,j) + 1	rem(i−j,j)

by GA-resolution.

The final goal

	19. true	if i < j then 0 else div(i−j,j) + 1	if i < j then i else rem(i-j,j)

can then be obtained by GG-resolution between goals 10 and 18. The conditional expressions have been formed because both goals have a corresponding output entry. Because we have developed the goal *true* and a corresponding primitive output entry, the derivation is complete. The final programs

```
div(i,j)  <==  if i < j
               then 0
               else div(i−j,j) + 1
```

and

```
rem(i,j)  <==  if i < j
               then i
               else rem(i−j,j)
```

are obtained directly from the final output entries.

K. The Formation of Auxiliary Procedures

We have remarked that mathematical induction need not be restricted to apply only to the initial assertion and goal but may legitimately be applied to any subset of the assertions and goals in the sequent. In fact, when induction is applied in this more general setting, *auxiliary procedures* may be introduced into the program being constructed. For example, in constructing a program *sort* to order a list, we might introduce an auxiliary procedure *merge* to insert a number in its place in an ordered list of numbers. In this section we develop the extended form of the induction principle that accounts for the formation of auxiliary procedures. We begin with a description of the recurrence strategy that applies in this extended induction.

Assume that we are in the process of constructing a program f(a) whose specification is of form

```
f(a)  <==  find z such that R(a,z)
           where P(a).
```

Then our initial sequent is of form

assertions	goals	outputs f(a)
P(a)	R(a,z)	z

Let goal A be any goal obtained during the derivation of f(a), and assume that goal A is of form

A:

	R′(a,z′)	t′(z′)

Suppose that by applying deduction rules successively to goal A and to the assertions $P'_1(a), P'_2(a), \ldots, P'_k(a)$ of the sequent, we obtain a goal B of form

B:

	R′(s,z″)	t″(z″)

where s is an arbitrary term. (For simplicity, we assume that no goals are required other than those derived from goal A, and that none of the k required assertions have associated output entries.)

In summation, we have developed a new goal (goal B) that is a precise instance of the earlier goal (goal A), obtained by replacing the input a by the term s. This recurrence motivates us to define an auxiliary procedure fnew(a) whose output condition is goal A; we then hope to achieve goal B by a recursive call to the new procedure.

Let us be more precise. The specification for fnew(a′) is

fnew(a′) <== find z′ such that R′(a′, z′)
where P′(a′).

Here, the input condition P′(a′) is ($P'_1(a')$ and $P'_2(a')$ and ... and $P'_k(a')$). If we succeed in constructing a program that meets this specification, we can employ it as an auxiliary procedure of the main program f(a).

Consequently, at this point we add a new output column for fnew(a′) to the sequent, and we introduce the new rows

A′:

assertions	goals	outputs f(a)	fnew(a′)
P′(a′)			
	R′(a′,z′)	t′(fnew(a))	z′

Note that in these rows we have replaced the input constant a by a new constant a′. This step is logically necessary; adding the induction hypothesis without renaming the constant can lead to false results. The second row (goal A′) indicates that if we succeed in constructing fnew(a′) to satisfy the above specification, then f(a) may be computed by a call t′(fnew(a)) to the new procedure.

By introducing the procedure fnew(a′) we are able to call it recursively. In other words, we are now able to form an induction hypothesis from the assertion P′(a′) and the goal R′(a′,z′), namely,

if u′ $<_{w'}$ a′ then if P′(u′) then R′(u′,fnew(u′))			

If this assertion is employed during a proof, a recursive call to fnew can be introduced into the output column for fnew(a′). The well-founded ordering $<_{w'}$ corresponding to fnew(a′) may be distinct from the ordering $<_w$ corresponding to f(a).

Note that we do not begin a new sequent for the derivation of the auxiliary procedure fnew; the synthesis of the main program f(a) and the auxiliary procedure fnew(a′) are both conducted by applying derivation rules to the same sequent. Those rows with output entries for fnew(a′) always have the expression t′(fnew(a)) as the output entry for f(a).

Suppose we ultimately succeed in obtaining the goal *true* with primitive output entries t and t′:

assertions	goals	outputs	
		f(a)	fnew(a′)
	true	t	t′

Then the final program is

$$f(a) <== t$$

and

$$fnew(a') <== t'.$$

Note that although the portion of the derivation leading from goal A to goal B serves to motivate the formation of the auxiliary procedure, it may actually have no part in the derivation of the final program; its role has been taken over by the derivation of goal B′ from goal A′.

It is possible to introduce many auxiliary procedures for the same main program, each adding a new output column to the sequent. An auxiliary procedure may have its own set of auxiliary procedures. An auxiliary procedure may call the main program or any of the other procedures; in other words, the system of procedures can be "mutually recursive."

If we fail to complete the derivation of an auxiliary procedure fnew(a′), we may still succeed in finding some other way of completing the derivation of f(a) without using fnew, by applying deduction rules to rows that have no output entry for fnew(a′).

To illustrate the formation of auxiliary procedures, we consider the synthesis of a program cart(s,t) to compute the cartesian product of two (finite) sets s and t, i.e., the set of all pairs whose first component belongs to s and whose second component belongs to t. The specification for this program is

$$\text{cart}(s,t) <== \text{find } z \text{ such that}$$
$$z = \{(a,b): a \in s \text{ and } b \in t\}.$$

The initial sequent is then

	assertions	goals	outputs cart(s,t)
		z= {(a,b): a ∈ s and b ∈ t}	z

(Note that this specification has no input condition, except for the type condition isset(s) and isset(t), which we omit for simplicity.)

We denote the empty set by {}. If u is a nonempty set, then choice(u) denotes some particular element of u, and rest(u) denotes the set of all other elements. We assume that the transformation rules concerning finite sets include:

u ∈ v ==> false   if v = {}

u ∈ v ==> u = choice(v) or u ∈ rest(v)   if v ≠ {}

{u:false} ==> {}

{u: P or Q} ==> {u:P} ∪ {u:Q}

rest(u) $<_{s_1}$ u ==> true   if u ≠ {}

{u: u = v} ==> {v}   (where u does not occur in v)

We will not reproduce the complete derivation, but only those portions that concern the formation of auxiliary procedures.

By application of deduction rules to the initial sequent, we obtain the goal

A:

	z′ = {(a,b): a = choice(s) and b ∈ t}	if s = {} then {} else z′ ∪ cart(rest(s),t)

By applying several deduction rules to this goal alone, we obtain the new goal

B:

	z″ = {(a,b): a = choice(s) and b ∈ rest(t)}	if t = {}
		then {}
		else if s = {}
		    then {}
		    else (choice(s), choice(t)) ∪
		        cart(rest(s),t) ∪ z″

This goal is a precise instance of the earlier goal; consequently, our recurrence strategy motivates us to form an auxiliary procedure cartnew(s,t) having the earlier goal as its output specification, i.e.,

$$\text{cartnew}(s',t') \Leftarrow\!\!= \{(a,b): a = \text{choice}(s') \text{ and } b \in t'\}.$$

We therefore introduce an additional output column corresponding to the new procedure, and we add to the sequent the row

A′:

assertions	goals	outputs cart(s,t)	 cartnew(s′,t′)
	z′ = {(a,b): a = choice(s′) and b ∈ t′}	if s = {} then {} else cartnew(s,t) ∪ cart(rest(s),t)	z′

The induction hypothesis corresponding to this goal is then

if $(u',v') <_{w'} (s',t')$ then cartnew(u′,v′) = {(a,b): a = choice(u′) and b ∈ v′}			

By applying deduction rules to the new goal, we obtain the goal

B′:

	z″ = {(a,b): a = choice(s′) and b ∈ rest(t′)}	if s = {} then {} else cartnew(s,t) ∪ cart(rest(s),t)	if t′ = {} then {} else (choice(s′), choice(t′)) ∪ z″

Applying GA-resolution between this goal and the induction hypothesis, and simplifying by transformation rules, we obtain the goal

	$(s',\text{rest}(t')) <_{w'} (s',t')$	if s = {} then {} else cartnew(s,t) ∪ cart(rest(s),t)	if t′ = {} then {} else (choice(s′), choice(t′)) ∪ cartnew(s′,rest(t′))

Note that a recursive call has now appeared in the output entry for the auxiliary procedure cartnew. By further transformation, the well-founded ordering $<_{w'}$ is chosen to be $<_{s_2}$, defined by

$$(u_1,u_2) <_{s_2} (v_1,v_2) \quad \text{if } u_2 \text{ is a proper subset of } v_2.$$

The final program obtained from this derivation is

```
cart(s,t) <== if s = {}
              then {}
              else cartnew(s,t) ∪
                 cart(rest(s),t)

cartnew(s′,t′) <== if t′ = {}
              then {}
              else (choice(s′),choice(t′)) ∪
                 cartnew(s′,rest(t′)).
```

There are a few extensions to the method for forming auxiliary procedures that we will not describe in detail:

(1) We have been led to introduce an auxiliary procedure when an entire goal was found to be an instance of a previous goal. As we remarked in the section on mathematical induction, we can actually introduce an auxiliary procedure when some subsentence of a goal is an instance of some subsentence of a previous goal.

(2) Special treatment is required if the assertions and goal incorporated into the induction hypothesis contain more than one occurrence of the same skolem function. We do not describe the formation of such an induction hypothesis here.

(3) To complete the derivation of the auxiliary procedure, we may be forced to weaken or strengthen its specification by adding input or output conditions incrementally. We do not present here the extension of the procedure-formation principle that permits this flexibility.

L. Generalization

In performing a proof by mathematical induction, it is often necessary to generalize the theorem to be proved, so as to have the advantage of a stronger induction hypothesis in proving the inductive step. Paradoxically, the more general statement may be easier to prove. If the proof is part of the synthesis of a program, generalizing the theorem can result in the construction of a more general procedure, so that recursive calls to the procedure will be able to achieve the desired subgoals. The recurrence strategy we have outlined earlier provides a strong clue as to how the theorem is to be generalized.

We have formed an auxiliary procedure when a goal is found to be a precise instance of a previous goal. However, in some derivations it is found that the new goal is not a precise instance of the earlier goal, but that both are instances of some more general expression. This situation suggests introducing a new auxiliary procedure whose output condition is the more general expression, in the hope that both goals may be achieved by calls to this procedure.

Let us be more precise. Suppose we are in the midst of a derivation and that we have already developed a goal A, of form

A:

assertions	goals	outputs f(a)
	$R'(a,s_1,z_1)$	$t_1(z_1)$

where s_1 is an arbitrary term. Assume that by applying deduction rules only to goal A and some assertions $P'_1(a)$, $P'_2(a)$,..., $P'_k(a)$, we obtain a goal B, of form

B:

	$R'(a,s_2,z_2)$	$t_2\ (z_2)$

where s_2 is a term that does not match s_1. Thus, the new goal (goal B) is not a precise instance of the earlier goal (goal A). Hence, if an induction hypothesis is formed for goal A itself, the resolution rule cannot be applied between goal B and the induction hypothesis.

However, both goals A and B may be regarded as instances of the more general expression $R'(a,b',z')$, where b' is a new constant: goal A is obtained by replacing b' by s_1, and goal B is obtained by replacing b' by s_2. This suggests that we attempt to establish a more general expression (goal A′) hoping that the proof of goal A' will contain a subgoal (goal B′) corresponding to the original goal B, so that the induction hypothesis resulting from goal A′ will be strong enough to establish goal B′.

The new goal A′ constitutes the output condition for an auxiliary procedure, whose specification is

$$\begin{array}{l} fnew(a',b') \Longleftarrow \text{find } z' \text{ such that } R'(a',b',z') \\ \quad \text{where } P'(a'). \end{array}$$

(Here, $P'(a')$ is the conjunction $P'_1(a')$ and $P'_2(a')$ $\cdots$ and $P'_k(a')$.) Consequently, we introduce a new output column to the sequent, and we add the new assertion

assertions	goals	outputs f(a)	outputs fnew(a′,b′)
$P'(a')$			

and the new goal

A′:

	$R'(a',b',z')$	$t_1\ (fnew(a,s_1))$	z'

(Note again that it is logically necessary to replace the input condition a by a new constant a′.) Corresponding to this assertion and goal we have the induction hypothesis

if $(u',v') <_{w'} (a',b')$ then if $P'(u')$ then $R(u',v',fnew(u',v'))$			

There is no guarantee that we will be able to develop from goal A′ a new goal B′ such that the resolution rule can be applied between goal B′ and the induction hypothesis. Nor can we be sure that we will conclude the derivation of fnew successfully. If we fail to derive fnew, we may still complete the derivation of f in some other way.

We illustrate the generalization process with an example that also serves to show how program-synthesis techniques can be applied as well to *program transformation* (see, e.g., Burstall and Darlington [1977]). In this application we are given a clear and concise program, which may be inefficient; we attempt to derive an equivalent program that is more efficient, even though it may be neither clear nor concise.

We are given the program

$$\begin{aligned} \text{reverse}(l) \;\; <== \;\; & \text{if } l = [] \\ & \text{then } [] \\ & \text{else reverse}(\text{tail}(l)) <> [\text{head}(l)] \end{aligned}$$

for reversing the order of the elements of a list l. Here, head(l) is the first element of a nonempty list l and tail(l) is the list of all but the first element of l. Recall that u<>v is the result of appending two lists u and v, [] denotes the empty list, and [w] is the list whose sole element is w. As usual, we omit type conditions, such as islist(l), from our discussion.

This reverse program is inefficient, for it requires many recursive calls to reverse and to the append procedure <>. We attempt to transform it to a more efficient version. The specification for the transformed program rev(l) is

$$\text{rev}(l) \;\; <== \;\; \text{find } z_1 \text{ such that } z_1 = \text{reverse}(l).$$

The initial sequent is thus

A:

assertions	goals	outputs rev(l)
	z_1 = reverse (l)	z_1

The given reverse program is not considered to be a primitive. However, we admit the transformation rules

$$\text{reverse(u)} ==> [] \quad \text{if u} = []$$

and

$$\text{reverse(u)} ==> \text{reverse(tail(u))} <> [\text{head(u)}] \quad \text{if u} \neq [];$$

obtained directly from the reverse program.

We assume that the transformation rules we have concerning lists include

$$\begin{aligned} &\text{head(u}\cdot\text{v)} ==> \text{u} \\ &\text{tail(u}\cdot\text{v)} ==> \text{v} \\ &[\text{u}] ==> \text{u}\cdot[] \\ &(\text{u}\cdot\text{v} = []) ==> \text{false} \end{aligned}$$

(where u·v is the result of inserting u before the first element of the list v; it is the Lisp cons function)

$$u <> v ==> v \quad \text{if } u = []$$
$$u <> v ==> u \quad \text{if } v = []$$
$$u <> v ==> \text{head}(u) \cdot (\text{tail}(u) <> v) \quad \text{if } u \neq []$$
$$(u <> v) <> w ==> u <> (v <> w)$$
$$\text{tail}(l) <_L l ==> \text{true} \quad \text{if } l \neq []$$

Applying transformation rules to the initial goal, we obtain a subgoal

B:

	$z_2 = \text{reverse}(\text{tail}(l)) <> [\text{head}(l)]$	if $l = []$ then [] else z_2

This goal is not a precise instance of goal A. However, both goals may be regarded as instances of the more general expression

$$z' = \text{reverse}(l') <> m'.$$

Goal A is obtained by replacing l' by tail(l) and m$'$ by [] (because $u<>[] = u$), and goal B is obtained by replacing l' by tail(l) and m$'$ by [head(l)]. This suggests that we attempt to construct an auxiliary procedure having the more general expression as an output condition; the specification for this procedure is

$$\text{revnew}(l',m') <== \text{find } z' \text{ such that } z' = \text{reverse}(l') <> m'.$$

Consequently, we introduce a new output column to the sequent, and we add the new goal

A$'$:

assertions	goals	outputs	
		rev(l)	revnew(l',m$'$)
	$z' = \text{reverse}(l') <> m'$	revnew(l,[])	z'

The induction hypothesis corresponding to this goal is then

if $(u',v') <_{w'} (l',m')$ then $\text{revnew}(u',v') = \text{reverse}(u') <> v'$		

By applying deduction rules to the goal A′, we eventually obtain

B′:

assertions	goals	outputs rev(l)	outputs revnew(l',m′)
	z″ = reverse(tail(l')) <> (head(l') · m′)	revnew(l,[])	if l' = [] then m′ else z″

We succeed in applying the resolution rule between this goal and the induction hypothesis.

Ultimately, we obtain the final program

rev(l) <== revnew(l,[])
revnew(l',m′) <== if l' = []
then m′
else revnew(tail(l'),head(l')·m′).

This program turns out to be more efficient than the given program reverse(l); it is essentially iterative and employs the insertion operation · instead of the imperative append operation <>. In general, however, we have no guarantee that the program produced by this approach will be more efficient than the given program. A possible remedy is to include efficiency criteria explicitly in the specification of the program. For example, we might require that the rev program should run in time linear to the length of l. In proving the theorem obtained from such a specification, we would be ensuring that the program constructed would operate within the specified limitations. Of course, the difficulty of the theorem-proving task would be compounded by such measures.

Some generalizations are quite straightforward to discover. For example, if goal A is of form R′(a,0,z_1) and goal B is of form R′(a,1,z_2), this immediately suggests that we employ the general expression R′(a,b′,z′). Other generalizations may require more ingenuity to discover. In the reverse example, for instance, it is not immediately obvious that z_1 = reverse(l) and z_2 = reverse(tail(l)) <> [head(l)] should both be regarded as instances of the more general expression z′ = reverse(l') <> m′.

Our strategy for determining how to generalize an induction hypothesis is distinct from that of Boyer and Moore [1975]. Their system predicts how to generalize a goal before developing any subgoals. In our approach, recurrences between a goal and its subgoals suggest how the goal is to be generalized.

M. Comparison With the Pure Transformation-Rule Approach

Recent work (e.g., Manna and Waldinger [1979], as well as Burstall and Darlington [1977]) does not regard program synthesis as a theorem-proving task, but instead adopts the basic approach of applying transformation rules directly to the given specification. What advantage do we obtain by shifting to a theorem-proving approach, when that approach has already been attempted and abandoned?

The structure we outline here is considerably simpler than, say, our implemented synthesis system DEDALUS, but retains the full power of that system. DEDALUS required special mechanisms for the formation of conditional expressions and recursive calls, and for the satisfaction of "conjunctive goals" (of form "find z such that R_1(z) and R_2(z)"). It could not treat specifications involving quantifiers. It relied on a backtracking control structure, which required it to explore one goal completely before attention could be passed to another goal. In the present system, these constructs are handled as a natural outgrowth of the theorem-proving process. In addition, the foundation is laid for the application of more sophisticated search strategies, in which attention is passed back and forth freely between several competing assertions and goals. The present framework can take advantage of parallel hardware.

Furthermore, the task of program synthesis always involves a theorem-proving component, which is needed, say, to prove the termination of the program being constructed, or to establish the input condition for recursive calls. (The Burstall-Darlington system is interactive and relies on the user to prove these theorems; DEDALUS incorporates a separate theorem prover.) If we retain the artificial distinction between program synthesis and theorem proving, each component must duplicate the efforts of the other. The mechanism for forming recursive calls will be separate from the induction principle; the facility for handling specifications of the form

$$\text{find } z \text{ such that } R_1(z) \text{ and } R_2(z)$$

will be distinct from the facility for proving theorems of form

$$\text{for some } z,\ R_1(z) \text{ and } R_2(z);$$

and so forth. By adopting a theorem-proving approach, we can unify these two components.

Theorem proving was abandoned as an approach to program synthesis when the development of sufficiently powerful automatic theorem provers appeared to flounder. However, theorem provers have been exhibiting a steady increase in their effectiveness, and program synthesis is one of the most natural applications of these systems.

N. Acknowledgments

We would like to thank John Darlington, Chris Goad, Jim King, Neil Murray, Nils Nilsson, and Earl Sacerdoti for valuable discussions and comments.

References

Bledsoe [1977]
W.W. Bledsoe, "Non-resolution theorem proving," *Artif. Intel. J.* 9(1977), pp. 1–35.

Boyer and Moore [1975]
R.S. Boyer and J.S. Moore, "Proving theorems about LISP functions," *J.ACM* 22, 1(Jan. 1975), pp. 129–144.

Burstall and Darlington [1977]
R.M. Burstall and J. Darlington, "A transformation system for developing recursive programs," *J.ACM* 24, 1(Jan. 1977), pp. 44–67.

Darlington [1968]
J.L. Darlington, "Automatic theorem proving with equality substitutions and mathematical induction," *Machine Intell.* 3(Edinburgh, Scotland) (1968), pp. 113–127.

Green [1969]
C.C. Green, "Application of theorem proving to problem solving," in *Proc. Int. Joint Conf. on Artificial Intelligence* (Washington, D.C., May 1969), pp. 219–239.

Hewitt [1971]
C. Hewitt, "Description and theoretical analysis (using schemata) of PLANNER: A language for proving theorems and manipulating models in a robot," Ph.D. Diss., M.I.T., Cambridge, Mass., 1971.

Manna and Waldinger [1979]
Z. Manna and R. Waldinger, "Synthesis: dreams => programs," *IEEE Trans. Softw. Eng.*, SE−5, 4(July 1979), pp. 294−328.

Murray [1978]
N. Murray, "A proof procedure for non-clausal first-order logic," Tech. Rep. Syracuse Univ., Syracuse, N.Y., 1978.

Nelson and Oppen [1978]
G. Nelson and D.C. Oppen, "A simplifier based on efficient decision algorithms," in *Proc. 5th ACM Symp. Principles of Programming Languages* (Tucson, Ariz., Jan. 1978), pp. 141−150.

Nilsson [1979]
N.J. Nilsson, "A production system for automatic deduction," *Machine Intell.* 9, Ellis Horwood, Chichester, England, 1979.

Nilsson [1971]
N.J. Nilsson, *Problem-solving Methods in Artificial Intelligence,* McGraw-Hill, New York, 1971, pp. 165−168.

Robinson [1965]
J.A. Robinson, "A machine-oriented logic based on the resolution principle," *J.ACM* 12, 1(Jan. 1965), pp. 23−41.

Waldinger and Lee [1969]
R.J. Waldinger and R.C.T. Lee, "PROW: A step toward automatic program writing," in *Proc. Int. Joint Conf. on Artificial Intelligence* (Washington, D.C., May 1969), pp. 241−252.

Wilkins [1973]
D. Wilkins, "QUEST—A non-clausal theorem proving system," M.Sc. Th., Univ. of Essex, England, 1973.

CHAPTER 3

LOPS — A System Based On A Strategical Approach To Program Synthesis*

W. Bibel and K.M. Hörnig
Technische Universität München

Abstract

This paper describes LOPS, an interactive system for LOgical Program Synthesis, which is currently being implemented. Given the logical input-output specification of a problem, LOPS attempts to construct an algorithmic solution by following several strategies which result in logical transformations, the correctness of which is established by a theorem prover. One of its further components is an example generator. Its use seems to be a novelty in this field.

* This work has been supported by the Deutsche Forschungsgemeinschaft (DFG).

A. Introduction

As with the previous chapter, our approach to the automation of program construction is based on the view that (human or mechanical) programming is a deductive process which starts with a more or less detailed purely descriptive specification of the given problem in some representation language and after some search guided by several basic strategies eventually ends up with the deduction of a suitable program solving the problem. We also adopt the view that predicate logic (in a wider sense) so far still is the most suitable representation language for studying this process, because of its conciseness, naturalness, flexibility, extendibility, and in particular because of the well-understood deductive mechanisms for it.

The crucial issue in such a deductive approach is the development of strategies which both are generally applicable and are effectively cutting down the otherwise tremendous search space. Strategies of that kind have been presented in Bibel [1980] and successfully applied by hand to a variety of programming problems of a rather different nature. It has been argued that these strategies are suitable for implementation. We discuss in this chapter a number of steps towards such an implementation which have been worked out during the last several years. Our system is called LOPS which stands for LOgical Program Synthesis. It is written in UT-LISP, implemented on a CYBER 175, and currently comprises implementational work of about two man-years.

In this introduction we will outline the structure of LOPS, leaving further details to the subsequent sections. Its top-level conceptual structure is illustrated by figure 1. Note that the flow of control is not shown, since the arrows rather illustrate the flow of relevant information during the synthesis process.

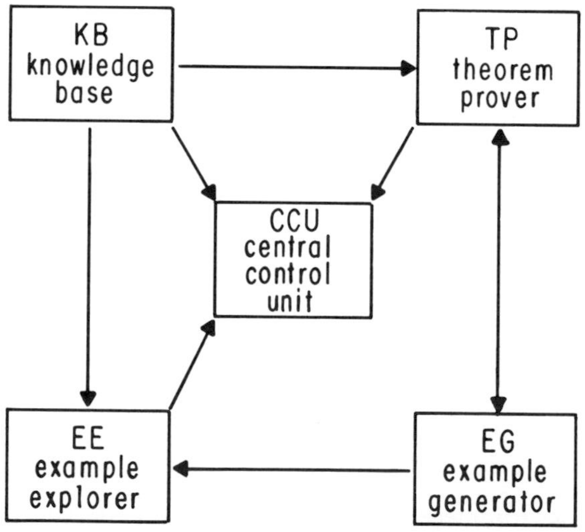

Figure 1. The top-level conceptual structure of LOPS

The heart of the system is the central control unit CCU, which is shown in more detail in figure 2.

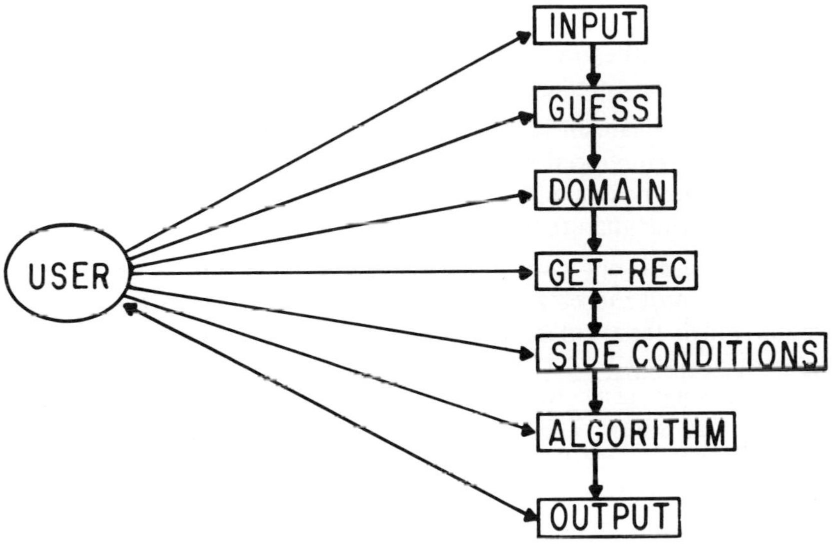

Figure 2. The structure of CCU in LOPS

There, the arrows show the flow of information and of control. Readers who are familiar with Bibel [1980] will notice that each module in the CCU corresponds to a strategy in the theoretical framework. Details on each of these modules may be found in section B.

The CCU on its own would be rather useless. In order to work it needs the communication with several satellite systems: the knowledge base KB, the theorem prover TP, the example generator EG, the example explorer EE, and the user. More on the realization of these satellites will be given in section C. At this point, we confine ourselves with describing some situations where they are actually used.

Scientific questions are usually posed assuming that the addressee has a certain amount of background knowledge, such as basic notation, basic definitions and basic theorems. Similarly we want the system to deal with problem specifications which contain a certain amount of standard knowledge. Whenever the system has to deal with input from the user, it first checks whether it can get any information from KB that will enable it to interpret this input. If this is not possible, then the system has to ask the user to be more explicit. Every good human programmer keeps special programs or programming techniques for future applications. Similarly we want LOPS to store programs it has synthesized in order to use them as subroutines in more complex situations. The place where such information is stored again is KB.

Theorem proving provides a key mechanism in obtaining algorithms from specifications. Readers who are not aware of this fact, hopefully will be convinced by the chapters in this book. Therefore, a theorem prover TP is needed in the system. If a theorem occurs quite often in synthesis processes, then, of course, it might be more appropriate to include it in KB, rather than reproving it each time it is needed.

Often, the theorems to be proved are not given immediately. Instead they have to be set up during the search for a program. For example, in order to obtain an algorithm it may be necessary to find a restatement of a given clause in the specification which then can be evaluated, in the sense that it uses no terms or subproblems which have no computational meaning for the system. Finding such a restatement is a challenging task. Human programmers usually solve such tasks by drawing or imagining a picture of the situation, which apparently is a crucial step towards a solution. This is exactly what the satellites EG and EE are meant to do. EG generates examples (we often call them models following logical terminology) from descriptions (logically playing the role of axioms). EE is supposed to infer statements from such examples. These statements then play the role of conjectures (or theorems) to be proved by TP.

Having mentioned the potential role of each component, we will now explain the function of the arrows in figure 1, which reflect the interactions between these components. KB and TP interact as follows. Any reasonably efficient theorem prover needs background knowledge to guide the search for a proof. Conversely, once a theorem has been proved it is a candidate for KB, since it may be needed in other situations as well. Disproving theorems means to produce counterexamples (see Bledsoe *et al.* [1979]). On the other hand, the construction of complicated models needs theorem proving. This will become clear in section C. These two facts account for the interaction of TP and EG. Clearly, EE depends on EG. In addition to that, background knowledge from KB certainly plays a role in EE. Finally, KB, TP, and EE give their information to CCU. If the system cannot succeed in spite of all efforts, it will try to get help from the user. The extent to which such interaction seems to be desirable depends very much on the taste and expectations of the designer of a program synthesis system. At present, the user is indispensable, but it seems not unrealistic that his role might become more and more marginal at the cost of extending the capabilities of KB, TP, EG, and EE.

This concludes our global view of the structure of LOPS. We are now going to describe the respective parts in more detail.

B. Description of CCU

In this section, we are describing the components of the central control unit, CCU, in LOPS, as introduced in figure 2 from the previous section. For that purpose, their functions are illustrated by use of the following well-known partition problem Bibel [1980] as an example. Given a set S, an element a of S and an ordering relation $<$ on S, we are looking for an algorithm which produces the subset $S_1 \subset S$ of all elements of S smaller than a w.r.t. $<$. Notice that the problem given in the introduction of this book is in fact a special case thereof.

B.1. INPUT

As we said in the introduction, the background for LOPS is predicate logic, that is, the system will manipulate formulas of first order predicate calculus. In the final version of LOPS, however, the user will not have to be deeply familiar with predicate logic; rather he might then communicate with the system in some artificial natural language (see section 4 in Bibel [1982a]).

In logic most problems can be stated in the following canonical way:

$$\forall(\text{input}-\text{variables})\ \exists\ (\text{output}-\text{variables})$$
$$[\text{input-condition} \dashrightarrow \text{output-condition}]$$

In this format our example could be written as follows where we assume all members of S are different.

$$
\begin{aligned}
(1)\quad & \forall\, S, a, <\ \exists\, S_1 \\
& [a \in S \land\ <\ \text{is an ordering on } S \\
& \text{----}> \\
& \quad S_1 \subset S \setminus \{a\} \ \land\ \forall x (x \in S \setminus \{a\} \setminus S_1 \text{ --> } a<x) \\
& \quad \land\ \forall x (x \in S_1 \text{ --> } x<a)
\end{aligned}
$$

Here we have used a semi-formal language for predicate calculus, allowing more natural phrases like "$<$ is an ordering on S" rather than ORD $(<,S)$. We use --> to signify implication and \ to indicate set subtraction. Numerous further liberalizations are possible and a future input-dialogue could proceed as follows (or even more comfortably). Words in capital letters indicate messages of the system.

INITIALIZE PROBLEM:
PART
INPUT-VARIABLES:
S,a,before
OUTPUT-VARIABLES
S1
INPUT-CONDITION:
before ordering on S
INPUT-CONDITION:
a element of S
INPUT-CONDITION:
nil
OUTPUT-CONDITION:
S1 subset of S minus a
OUTPUT-CONDITION:
x element of S minus S1 and x≠a implies a before x
OUTPUT-CONDITION:
x element of S1 implies x before a
OUTPUT-CONDITION:
nil

The system would understand expressions like "element of" or "subset of". If, for example, "ordering on" was not known to the system it would request more information by asking repeatedly GIVE AXIOM FOR "ORDERING ON": The user then would have to specify rules like

- before is binary
- before is transitive
- before is antisymmetric, etc.

In the current state of affairs the problem specification may in fact be presented to LOPS in the way of such a dialogue except that a more formal language still has to be used. The task of designing a suitable user-language has been deferred to the future. As an aside, it should be noted that there are several different (but equivalent from a logical point of view) ways to describe problems and that the efficiency of LOPS may well depend on this description. This effect, however, is certainly well-known to every human programmer as well.

Let us assume that our problem is stored internally in the form of (1) (with $<$ replaced by a binary predicate before) and that the following axioms are known to the system:

(A_1) $\forall x,y(x \text{ before } y \dashrightarrow \sim (y \text{ before } x)$
(A_2) $\forall x,y(x \neq y \dashrightarrow (x \text{ before } y \vee y \text{ before } x))$
(A_3) $\forall x,y,z((x \text{ before } y \wedge y \text{ before } z) \dashrightarrow x \text{ before } z)$

where x,y,z range over the domain of discourse.

"before is an ordering on S" then means "$(A_1)\wedge(A_2)\wedge(A_3)$", with S as the domain of discourse.

B.2. GUESS, DOMAIN, and GET-DNF

In Bibel [1980] the reader finds the introduction and motivation of a number of strategies which will now be applied to the given problem in a certain sequence. In the present problem, the first ones to be applied are GUESS, DOMAIN, and GET-DNF.

GUESS and DOMAIN have to be considered simultaneously. They formalize the idea that the desired output can be obtained by guessing a suitable element which, if we are lucky, is the desired output or an element of it. Otherwise, the information that the guess is faulty may be helpful for obtaining a recursive solution as described in the next section. GUESS decides what should be guessed and DOMAIN restricts the choice for our guess, since obviously it would not be helpful to look for an output in domains which are irrelevant for the problem. For the present problem this intuitive idea is realized by a transformation of it into the following logically equivalent form:

$$
\begin{array}{l}
(2)\ \forall S, a, \text{before}, u \ \exists S_1 \\
\quad u \in S \setminus \{a\} \\
\quad \text{-->} [a \in S \wedge \text{before is an ordering on } S \\
\qquad \text{-->} \\
\qquad S_1 \subset S \setminus \{a\} \\
\qquad \wedge\ \forall x (x \in S \setminus \{a\} \setminus S_1 \text{ --> } a \text{ before } x) \\
\qquad \wedge\ \forall x (x \in S_1 \text{ --> } x \text{ before } a) \\
\qquad \wedge\ (u \in S_1 \dot{\vee} u \notin S_1)]
\end{array}
$$

where $\dot{\vee}$ is the exclusive disjunction, i.e. A $\dot{\vee}$ B holds if and only if exactly one of A or B holds. LOPS obtains this form as follows. The component GUESS analyzes the syntactical structure of the output-condition with respect to the membership relation. Since S_1 occurs on the right hand side of an $\subset$, GUESS conjectures that S_1 is a set. This leads to the alternative $(u \in S_1 \dot{\vee} u \notin S_1)$, capturing the distinction between the cases "lucky" and "not-lucky", where u denotes the guessed element.

In order to realize its task mentioned before, DOMAIN breaks up the output-condition into a set of literals (clauses in more complicated cases). From these it selects a subset (specifying the restricted domain) according to certain criteria. Some of these criteria are of a purely syntactical nature. For instance, the output-variable should occur in a literal of the subset only if it ranges over individuals, since then, if we replace it by our guess we obtain a meaningful formula. This would not be the case, if it would range over sets, since then the output is constructed pointwise, and we could not reasonably replace the output, representing a set, by one of its elements. There are also semantical criteria. A guess should neither prevent its success nor its failure. This seems reasonable, since it is useless to make guesses which are always bound to be wrong. On the other hand, it would be equivalent to the algorithm we wish to produce to make correct guesses every time. In our example this amounts to the demand that both

$$
\begin{array}{ll}
u \in S \setminus \{a\} \wedge u \in S_1 & \text{and} \\
u \in S \setminus \{a\} \wedge u \notin S_1 & \text{are satisfiable for some } u, S.
\end{array}
$$

Checking this means to construct models, and we can see here for the first time the need for a model-generating component. A last very important criterion comes from a look ahead to the situation where we want to transform our logical representation into executable code. Eventually we will need to have an algorithm which is able to make the guess according to the condition chosen by DOMAIN. Hence, we must either know that there is such an algorithm (e.g. in KB) or seek to construct it. If this is impossible we cannot use such a literal as a DOMAIN-condition. If there are literals satisfying all our criteria, then the component has completed its effort, if not, the system turns to the user and asks for help. In our example, the formula $u \in S \setminus \{a\}$ satisfies all requirements and is therefore chosen. An algorithm CHOOSE-SIDIFF (SIDIFF stands for the difference of a set and a singleton), which chooses elements from $S \setminus \{a\}$ if this set is non-empty, is provided by KB (see section B.5).

To apply GET-DNF (get disjunctive normal form) means simply to break up the problem into two mutually excluding cases:

formula (2) restricted to the case $u \in S_1$, and
formula (2) restricted to the case $u \notin S_1$.

B.3. GET-REC

According to Bibel [1980] the next strategy to be applied to our example is GET-REC. This strategy has the task of finding a recursion scheme which fits the description of the problem obtained by GUESS and DOMAIN and which makes an algorithmic solution possible. This is achieved by a matching procedure assisted by a theorem-prover (see section C.1), as will be discussed now. In Bibel [1980] it has been argued that there are only a few practically useful recursion schemata. In the final version of LOPS these schemata will be available for the matching process in a hierarchically structured data-base. The fact that $u \in S$ holds (by the choice $u \in S \setminus \{a\}$ performed by DOMAIN) gives a high priority to such a recursion scheme which, when applied to the present situation, reduces the problem from S to $S \setminus \{u\}$ (see formula (4) below). So, LOPS attempts to replace equivalently S by $S \setminus \{u\}$. As for DOMAIN above, the input- and output-conditions are simply regarded as a set of literals. Each of these literals A determines a new literal A^u, obtained by replacing every occurrence of S by $S \setminus \{u\}$, e.g. $a \in S$ would be replaced by $a \in S \setminus \{u\}$. The equivalence of A and A^u now has to be checked under the side conditions $u \in S \setminus \{a\}$, and $u \in S_1$ or $u \notin S_1$, respectively, according to formula (2).

The following three different reactions can be distinguished:

1. Under the given side conditions, A and A^u are equivalent. For instance, it is true that

$$S_1 \subset S \setminus \{a\} \quad \text{<--->} \quad S_1 \subset S \setminus \{u\} \setminus \{a\}$$

holds under the side condition $u \in S \setminus \{a\}$ and $u \notin S_1$. In this case, A may be replaced by A^u without changing the truth value of the formula.

2. There is a formula B such that A^u is similar to a (not necessarily proper) subformula C of B (in the sense that C can be obtained from A^u by a substitution of terms by terms), and A and B are equivalent under the given side conditions. For instance, under the side conditions $u \in S \setminus \{a\}$ and $u \notin S_1$, we have the following equivalence.

$$\forall y (y \in S \setminus \{a\} \setminus S_1 \text{ --> a before y}) \quad \text{<--->}$$

$$\forall y (y \in S \setminus \{u\} \setminus \{a\} \setminus S_1 \text{ --> a before y}) \wedge \text{(a before u)}$$

In this case the system determines by a matching process that $B \equiv A^u \wedge$ (a before u), which will be used later in the search for the recursion equation.

3. If there is no obvious way to obtain one of the first two cases, then A remains unchanged. An example of such an A is "before is an ordering on S".

Acting as described above the system obtains from (2), splitted by GET-DNF, a new equivalent problem-specification. This equivalence is the following formula (3), where we omit obvious quantifiers:

(3) $u \in S \setminus \{a\}$ --> ($a \in S \wedge$ before is an ordering on S
-->
$S_1 \subset S \setminus \{a\}$
$\wedge \forall x(x \in S \setminus \{a\} \setminus S_1$ --> a before x)
$\wedge \forall x(x \in S_1$ --> x before a)
$\wedge (u \in S_1 \dot{\vee} u \notin S_1))$
<---->
$u \in S \setminus \{a\}$ --> ($a \in S \setminus \{u\} \wedge$ before is an ordering on S
-->
$S_1 \setminus \{u\} \subset S \setminus \{u\} \setminus \{a\}$
$\wedge \forall x(x \in S \setminus \{u\} \setminus \{a\} \setminus S_1$ --> a before x)
$\wedge \forall x(x \in S_1 \setminus \{u\}$ --> x before a) $\wedge$
(u before a)
$\wedge u \in S_1)$
$\dot{\vee}$
($a \in S \setminus \{u\} \wedge$ before is an ordering on S
-->
$S_1 \subset S \setminus \{u\} \setminus \{a\}$
$\wedge \forall x(x \in S \setminus \{u\} \setminus \{a\} \setminus S_1$ -> a before x)
$\wedge$ (a before u)
$\wedge \forall x(x \in S_1$ -> x before a)
$\wedge u \notin S_1)$

To see that this equivalence actually holds, assume the antecedent $u \in S \setminus \{a\}$ and, distinguishing the two cases $u \in S_1$ and $u \notin S_1$, prove the equivalence of corresponding clauses, e.g.

$a \in S$ <---> $a \in S \setminus \{u\}$ (this only needs the assumption $u \in S \setminus \{a\}$)

or

$S_1 \subset S \setminus \{a\}$ <---> $S_1 \setminus \{u\} \subset S \setminus \{u\} \setminus \{a\}$ in the case $u \in S_1$

and

$S_1 \subset S \setminus \{u\}$ <---> $S_1 \subset S \setminus \{u\} \setminus \{a\}$ in the case $u \notin S_1$.

From this by another matching process, which simply compares this new form of specification with the original one, and possibly some simple transformation rules from propositional calculus LOPS obtains the recursion equation:

$$
\begin{array}{c}
(4)\ \mathrm{PART}(S,a,\mathrm{before}) = \mathrm{PART}(S \setminus \{u\},a,\mathrm{before}) \cup \{u\} \wedge (u \text{ before } a) \wedge u \in S_1 \\
\dot{\vee} \\
\mathrm{PART}(S,a,\mathrm{before}) = \mathrm{PART}(S \setminus \{u\},a,\mathrm{before}) \wedge (a \text{ before } u) \wedge u \notin S_1
\end{array}
$$

This is an instance of the recursion scheme we had in mind at the beginning of this section.

The transformation from (3) to (4) is done in two steps. First, LOPS determines a scheme from which all equivalences contained in (3) can be obtained by substitution and possibly addition of formulas. Such a scheme is given by:

$$
\begin{array}{l}
u \in X \setminus \{a\} \rightarrow (a \in Y \wedge \text{before is an ordering on } X) \\
\qquad \rightarrow \\
\qquad Z \subset Y \setminus \{a\} \\
\qquad \wedge\ \forall x(x \in Y \setminus \{a\} \setminus W \rightarrow a \text{ before } x) \\
\qquad \wedge\ \forall x(x \in Z \rightarrow x \text{ before } a)\ \ )
\end{array}
$$

The substitution ((X S) (Y S) (Z S_1) (W S_1)) gives the left hand side of (3), except for the distinction of cases ($u \in S_1 \dot{\vee} u \notin S_1$), ((X S) (Y S \ {u}) (Z S_1 \ {u}) (W S_1)) gives the first alternative ($u \in S_1$), of the right hand side and ((X S) (Y S \ {u}) (Z S_1) (W S_1)) gives the second alternative ($u \notin S_1$), F1 except for the clauses (u before a) and (a before u). In other words, there is a scheme F(X,Y,Z,W) with

$$
\begin{array}{l}
F(S,S,S_1,S_1) \wedge (u \in S_1 \dot{\vee} u \notin S_1) \\
\longleftrightarrow \\
\quad F(S,S \setminus \{u\},S_1 \setminus \{u\},S_1) \wedge (u \text{ before } a) \wedge u \in S_1 \\
\dot{\vee} \\
\quad F(S,S \setminus \{u\},S_1,S_1) \wedge (a \text{ before } u) \wedge u \notin S_1
\end{array}
$$

In the second step LOPS notes that the first and fourth arguments of all F-expressions are equal and thus not relevant for the recursion. LOPS considers the third component as the result of a computation (it corresponds to the output variable) and uses the side conditions $u \in S_1$ and $u \notin S_1$ to get (4). Thus, PART is defined by

$$\mathrm{PART}\ (Y,a,\mathrm{before}) = Z \longleftrightarrow F(S,Y,Z,S_1).$$

This discussion has not yet revealed how the formula B above is obtained; also, in order to obtain an algorithm we must eliminate the clauses $u \in S_1$ and $u \notin S_1$. The latter is done by the following component of LOPS.

B.4. SIDE CONDITIONS

If we confront a suitable theorem prover with the proposition

$$
\begin{aligned}
&\forall y(y \in S \setminus \{a\} \setminus S_1 \dashrightarrow a \text{ before } y)\\
&\texttt{<--->}\\
&\forall y(y \in S \setminus \{u\} \setminus \{a\} \setminus S_1 \dashrightarrow a \text{ before } y)
\end{aligned}
$$

it will react with the counterexample y=u (cf. Bledsoe and Ballantine [1979]), saying that u is a counterexample if and only if u before a holds. Therefore LOPS reacts by adding the negation of this condition, that is a before u to A^u. The theorem prover has to establish the validity of the new equivalence. In general, this technique may be too simple to be successful. To deal with a more complicated situation we use the example generator EG. This will now be illustrated with the substitution of $u \in S_1$ and $u \notin S_1$ by computationally evaluable formulas. Since S_1 is to be determined, any literal containing S_1 is computationally infeasible, and thus has to be substituted. Consider the first case $u \notin S_1$. Only an example can help in this case. Therefore we look for a model (S, before, S_1), say, with $S = \{0,1,2,3\}$, and the following axioms:

$(A_1) - (A_3)$ as before in B.1

(A_4) $\forall x(x \in S_1 \dashrightarrow x \text{ before } 2)$

Among others, the component EG generates the following example

$S = \{0,1,2,3\}$

before $= \{(1\ 2)\ (1\ 3)\ (1\ 0)\ (2\ 3)\ (2\ 0)\ (3\ 0)\}$

$S_1 = \{1\}$

which can be illustrated by

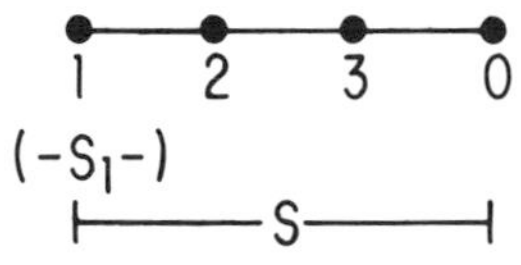

During the construction EG remembers why certain elements do not satisfy certain relations. Therefore looking at a typical example of an element $u \notin S_1$ (e.g. 3), we find that the reason is the failure of (A_4), i.e. not (3 before 2). Therefore, the component EG has to suggest $u \notin S_1$ <---> (u before a). The theorem-prover would then check that this is in fact true and a simplifying procedure would use (A_2) to obtain

$u \notin S_1$ <---> $a=u \vee$ a before u, and since $u \in S \setminus \{a\}$:
$u \notin S_1$ <---> a before u.

At this point two objections to this description of the use of the model program EG in cooperation with EE might arise. Namely it is difficult to see in our very simple example why such a complicated approach is in fact necessary since $u \notin S_1$ <---> a before u expressed hardly more than the definition of S_1. The reason for this is, that we wanted to present the basic ideas behind our approach to program syntheses and not simply ad hoc solutions that apply only to specific problems. The reader, who wants to appreciate the necessity of our general approach, is encouraged to try the maximal spanning tree algorithm (Bibel [1980]). There, one is confronted with a clause $e \in E_o \dot{\vee} e \notin E_o$, where E_o is the desired output. It turns out that $e \notin E_o$ is equivalent to the property of being an edge in a closed circuit of the graph. To us it seems promising to find this and similar equivalences by use of the model program, and in fact we are not aware of any better solution.

Thus SIDE CONDITIONS, the component in LOPS responsible for what has been described in this section, leads to

$$
\begin{aligned}
(5)\quad & \mathrm{PART(S,a,before)} = \mathrm{PART}(s \setminus \{u\},\mathrm{a,before}) \cup \{u\} \\
& \quad \wedge \text{ u before a} \\
& \dot{\vee} \\
& \mathrm{PART(S,a,before)} = \mathrm{PART}(S \setminus \{u\},\mathrm{a,before}) \\
& \quad \wedge \text{ a before u}
\end{aligned}
$$

It remains to transform this into an algorithmic solution, that is to choose suitable data structures and to find a control structure. This will be discussed in the following section.

B.5. ALGORITHM

It is a straightforward task to transform (5) into a PROLOG procedure (Colmerauer *et al.* [1981]). This way LOPS could have finished its task of constructing an algorithm for the partition-problem. However, to obtain more efficient algorithms it is necessary to select suitable data-structures and to eliminate recursion. This particular part has lower priority in our project and will be taken into closer consideration at some time in the future. We note, however, that there are well-explored methods to do this which have been used in other projects like SETL (Dewar [1978]) and PSI (Green [1977]). Eigemeier et al. [1980] describe methods to generate data-types, a project which may be regarded as complementing our efforts in this respect.

In the current version of LOPS there is only a rudimentary version of ALGORITHM which, for instance, translates (5) into the executable LISP-program, shown in figure 3.

```
(DEF
 (PART (S A)
     (PROG (U*)
          (COND ((NOT (MEMBER A S)) (RETURN NIL)))
          (SETQ U* (CHOOSE-SIDIFF (LIST S) (LIST A)))
          (COND (U*
               (COND ((LESSP A U*)
                    (RETURN (PART (REMOVE1 S U*) A)))
                   (T
                    (RETURN (CONS U* (PART (REMOVE1 S U*) A))))
                                        ))
              (T (RETURN NIL))))))

(DEF
 (CHOOSE-SIDIFF (ARGS+ ARGS-)
           (DO
            ((Y (CAR ARGS+) (REMOVE1 Y Z)) (Z NIL)
                      (CHOICE NIL))
            ((OR (NULL Y) CHOICE) CHOICE)
            (SETQ Z (RAND Y))
            (SETQ CHOICE (TEST - SIDIFF Z (CDR ARGS+) ARGS-)))))

(DEF
 (TEST-SIDIFF (CH ARGS+ ARGS-)
          (COND ((TEST-INTERSECTION CH ARGS+)
               (DO ((FLAG T) (Y ARGS- (CDR Y)))
                  ((OR (NULL Y) (NULL FLAG))
                   (COND (FLAG CH)
                        (T NIL)))
                  (SETQ FLAG (NOT (EQUAL CH (CAR Y)))))))))

(DEF
 (RAND (LIST) (NTH LIST) (ADD1 (REMAINDER (TEMPUS) (LENGTH LIST))))))

(DEF
 (TEST-INTERSECTION (CH ARGS)
               (DO ((FLAG T) (Y ARGS (CDR Y)))
                  ((OR (NULL Y) (NULL FLAG))
                   (COND (FLAG CH)
                        (T NIL)))
                  (SETQ FLAG (MEMBER CH (CAR Y))))))
```

Figure 3. The LISP code generated by LOPS for the partition problem

We do not claim that this is the most efficient algorithm to solve the partition-problem. Clearly, a choice of better data-structures, elimination of recursion and other modifications will lead to considerable improvements. But as we said, such techniques might be adapted from other projects, hence they are presently not in the focus of our interest.

C. Description of TP, EG, EE, and KB

In this section, we have a closer look to the satellite components in LOPS, in particular to the example generator.

C.1. THE THEOREM PROVER TP

For the type of theorems which have to be proved within LOPS for the problems in mind, there exist running proof systems powerful enough to establish the required proofs. However, the first author has developed a new proof method, called the *connection method,* which provably is more efficient than traditional methods such as the various resolution methods. A full treatment of this approach is contained in Bibel [1982b], based on a number of earlier publications while an overview may be found in Bibel [1981]. It is therefore quite natural that we are building our own theorem prover. A first test version has just been made available; but it will require some more time until TP may be connected with the rest of LOPS. Until this happens, the validity of theorems has to be confirmed by the user. Since the development of TP may be regarded as a remarkable project in its own right, any further details on this implementation have to be taken from other publications (e.g. see Bibel et al. [1983]).

C.2. THE EXAMPLE GENERATOR EG

We have made experiments with two different approaches to the construction of models which we call the *heuristic* and the *systematic* approach. We shall describe both methods using as an example the task of finding a model of the sentences

$$B1: \forall x\ (Px \vee Qx) \qquad B2: \forall x \sim (Px \wedge Qx)$$

Clearly, a model of B_1, B_2 must be a structure $\underline{M}:=(S,P,Q)$ where S is the domain and $P \subset S$ and $Q \subset S$ determine the subsets of elements x in S for which Px and Qx, respectively, are true. In both approaches we first fix a small number N, let $S:=\{0,1,\ldots,N\}$, and attempt to find suitable relations P and Q. This particular choice of S is, of course, not essential. Instead of numbers we may use other symbols, e.g. LISP-atoms. As an example, let $N=2$, so that $S=\{0,1,2\}$. $\underline{M}$ is called a model of say B_1 if $\underline{M}$ satisfies B_1, in symbols $\underline{M} \models B_1$. The relation $\models$ is defined by the following induction on the structure of sentences. Let G_1 and G_2 be sentences containing at most the predicate symbols P and Q and constants from S.

a) Let $n \in S$.

$\underline{M} \models Pn \ :\longleftrightarrow n \in P$
$\underline{M} \models Qn \ :\longleftrightarrow n \in Q$

b) $\underline{M} \models \sim G_1 : \longleftrightarrow \sim \underline{M} \models G_1$

c) $\underline{M} \models G_1 \wedge G_2 : \longleftrightarrow \underline{M} \models G_1$ and $\underline{M} \models G_2$

d) $\underline{M} \models G_1 \vee G_2 : \longleftrightarrow \underline{M} \models G_1$ or $\underline{M} \models G_2$

e) $\underline{M} \models \exists x G_1[x] : \longleftrightarrow$ there is some $n \in S$ s.t. $\underline{M} \models G_1[n/x]$

f) $\underline{M} \models \forall x G_1[x] : \longleftrightarrow$ for all $n \in S$: $\underline{M} \models G_1[n/x]$.

Here, $G_1[n/x]$ is the result of replacing every occurrence of x in G_1 by n.

This induction yields for B_1,

$\underline{M} \models \forall x (Px \vee Qx)$
$\Longleftrightarrow$ for all $n \in S : M \models Pn \vee Qn$
$\Longleftrightarrow$ for all $n \in S : M \models Pn$ or $M \models Qn$
$\Longleftrightarrow$ for all $n \in S : n \in P$ or $n \in Q$

Similarly

$\underline{M} \models \forall x \sim (Px \wedge Qx)$
$\Longleftrightarrow$ for all $n \in S$: $\sim (n \in P$ and $n \in Q)$
$\Longleftrightarrow$ for all $n \in S$: $n \notin P$ or $n \notin Q$

C.2.1. *The Heuristic Approach*

The algorithm constructs a sequence $\underline{M}_j$ of structures. $\underline{M}_0$ is (S,S,S). If $M_j := (S, P_j, Q_j)$ is defined, then the algorithm checks whether M_j is a model of B_1 and B_2. If this is the case, we are done. Otherwise, we remove elements from P_j, Q_j or both, thus getting $\underline{M}_{j+1}$. The difficulty consists in choosing the right elements to remove. Here we apply several heuristically motivated strategies. Since they may lead us astray, we must allow for backtracking. A first strategy is to attempt to satisfy the axioms A_i in a certain order which reduces the probability of omitting elements whose presence is postulated by an axiom which occurs later in this ordering. This ordering is produced using syntactical information given by the axioms.

As an example, consider the axioms:

B_3 : PO ∧ P1
B_4: ∀xPx-- >Qx
B_5: ∃ x∼Qx

It is rather obvious, that the most direct way to satisfy these axioms is to do it in the sequence B_3,B_4,B_5 which in a way reflects increasing complexity. Syntactically this sequence is found by counting the number of positive and negative occurrences of predicates in the axioms. We get

B_3: (P positive) (P positive)
B_4: (P negative) (Q positive)
B_5: (Q negative)

If we apply the heuristic rule: "List axioms, where the relation R occurs positive before those, where the relation R occurs negative!", then we obtain exactly the sequence B_3,B_4,B_5. The general rules to obtain such a sequence are slightly more complicated, since the structure of positive and negative occurrences is usually not as simple as here. A second strategy is to remove as few elements as possible and to check whether axioms which were valid in $\underline{M}_j$ are still valid in $\underline{M}_{j+1}$. There are more strategies, for which we have no space to go into details.

We only have a further look at our example. Apparently it holds that $\underline{M}_o| = B_1$ and $\underline{M}_o| \neq B_2$ ($\underline{M}_o$ was defined at the beginning of C.2.1). If we choose $P_1 := P_o \setminus \{0\}$ and $Q_1 := Q_o$, we get $\underline{M}_1| = B_1$ and $\underline{M}_1| \neq B_2$. Another such step gives $\underline{M}_2 := (S, \{2\}, S)$. If we define $P_3 := P_2 \setminus \{2\}$, B_1 does no longer hold in M_3. Therefore we better try to reduce Q_2=S. This leads us, for instance, to $\underline{M}_3 := (S, \{2\}, \{0,1\})$. It is easily seen that $\underline{M}_3| = B_1 \wedge B_2$.

It may also occur in the present version that the program can find no model even though such models exist, that is, the procedure is not complete in this sense. Therefore, we have made another, more systematic attempt to construct models.

C.2.2. *The Systematic Approach*

From Bibel [1981] or Bibel [1982b], we know that formulas of propositional calculus can be represented very lucidly by *matrices.* Since S is finite, we can consider existential quantifiers as finite disjunctions and universal quantifiers as finite conjunctions. Thus we can transform the axioms B_1 and B_2 from C.2.1 into formulas of propositional logic. A *negative* (in the terminology of Bibel [1982b]) *representation* K of B_1 and B_2 is given by:

PO	P1	P2	∼PO	∼P1	∼P2
QO	Q1	Q2	∼QO	∼Q1	∼Q2

It represents the propositional formula

(PO∨QO) ∧ (P1∨Q1) ∧ (P2∨Q2)

∧ (∼PO∨∼QO) ∧ (∼P1∨∼Q1) ∧ (∼P2∨∼Q2)

which in turn is equivalent to $B_1 \wedge B_2$. Now, it is not hard to see, that a non-complementary *path* (see Bibel [1982b]) through K determines models of B_1 and B_2. Such paths are obtained by selecting one literal from each column (i.e. clause). As an example consider the path $\{Q0,Q1,P2,\sim P0,\sim P1,\sim Q2\}$. In fact, it can be shown that all models of cardinality 3 can be obtained (up to isomorphism) this way. Now, the proof-procedure given by the first author in Bibel [1981] after an easy modification produces non-complementary paths, if applied to matrices of axioms which possess a model of the cardinality in question. These facts justify the label "systematic". A program which embodies these ideas has been written and is currently undergoing tests. For more details see Hörnig [1981].

C.2.3. *Intended Improvements*

It seems plausible that theorem proving methods dealing with full first order logic with unification can be modified to obtain algorithms for model construction. Some theoretical investigations in this area are currently carried out by the authors.

Both methods which we have introduced in C.2.1 and C.2.2 work efficiently only for models of small cardinality and of few axioms. Since the applications in LOPS ask for the construction of models of e.g. some 100 axioms, the need of extensions becomes obvious. We plan to develop a technique which uses the observation that usually the set of axioms can be split up into smaller groups, each group of axioms describing a separate concept (e.g. graph, tree, matrix in mathematics or chair, table, wall in a model world). For most of these concepts a human being has paradigms

(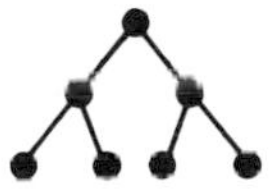 for a tree,  for a table)

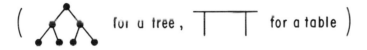

which we call model prototypes. To the system, model prototypes could be made available in three ways, by a data-base installed in the system, by the user, or by a construction using the methods in C.2.1 or C.2.2. What is needed is a procedure which can join several model prototypes into one model. Theorem proving will certainly play an important role in this context. Such a procedure should be feasible, since human beings work in such a way when constructing models, but nothing has been done yet to formalize these ideas.

C.3. THE EXAMPLE EXPLORER EE

This component is still more of an idea. A first approach to an implementation might be a system which "knows" a couple of structural properties of worlds such as:

- transitivity of relations
- uniqueness in arguments
- aboveness in physical spaces
- behindness in physical spaces, etc.

The system then checks which of these properties hold in the model and suggests combinations of them as general facts. The generality has to be checked by TP.

C.4. THE KNOWLEDGE BASE

One might view KB as a global notion for all knowledge which is built into the system. Thus, for example, one might consider the knowledge that all problem specifications are of the form $\forall i \exists o$ IC(i)-- >OC(i,o) as a part of KB. This point of view, however, would blur the difference between CCU and KB. Therefore we regard KB as a collection of various data-bases, each of which is searched by the CCU on different occasions. Such data-bases are

- standard predicates and functions such as
  LESS EQU TIMES PLUS
- standard formal operations such as
  CAR CDR CONCAT
- standard algorithms such as
  CHOOSE-SIDIFF TEST-INTERSECTION RAND
  (see B.5)

  etc.

There are interesting questions concerning the use and updating of these data-structures. They will not be discussed here.

D. Current Performance and Future Extensions

As mentioned above already, LOPS comprises now work of about two man-years, which is not very much in view of the ambitious goal. Therefore emphasis has been laid on providing small, but instructive versions of those parts of the system which to us seem crucial in the whole process. During the implementation we were careful to provide enough power to deal with various interesting problem-specifications, such as the maximum-problem, the partition-problem, the minimum-cost spanning tree problem, the graph-circuit-problem, the pattern-matching problem, etc. (see Bibel [1980]). The component INPUT can handle all these specifications. The components GUESS, DOMAIN and GET-REC need some help from the user to do this. For instance, the component TP is currently simulated by the user. The component EE exists only in a very rudimentary version. Therefore, the component SIDE CONDITIONS is only able to deal with the maximum- and partition-problems. The extensions needed to cover the other problems mentioned above are, however, well-defined and will be made in the near future. We have two versions of EG as described in C.2.1. and C.2.2. At present, LOPS consists of around 15000 lines of code.

The next steps to be taken towards an improvement of the current performance of LOPS come out naturally from our discussion and the above description of the current state.

1. Integration of the component TP.
2. Improvement of the component EG along the lines of C.2.3.
3. Improvement of CCU by
   - addition of strategies to handle more than one output-variable (cf. section 3 and 4 in Bibel [1980])
   - accounting for more recursion schemata
   - improving the user interface.
4. Enlargement of KB (possibly with some learning capabilities)
5. Design and implementation of EE.

E. Relation to Other Work

A related approach to automated program synthesis has been proposed by Guiho-Gresse [1980]. The reader familiar with both Guiho and Gresse [1980] and Bibel [1980] will note at least two major differences between these two methods.

Firstly, Guiho-Gresse transform an abstract program obtained from a canonical statement of the problem step by step into another "evaluable" program, whereas we, as remarked above, transform logical formulas and look for a suitable control structure afterwards. Secondly, the problems they can handle have to fit into one of two schemata which enable them to simplify the strategy DOMAIN and to use recursion schemata like that in (4). These recursion schemata can be found using e.g. the methods of Jouannaud and Kodratoff [1979] and Wegbreit [1976].

This approach is elegant and is perhaps easier to realize on the machine. Nevertheless, we believe that it is worthwhile to proceed differently, essentially for the following two reasons. No matter whether programs or logical formulas are transformed, in either case the correctness of each step has to be proved. This is done using an appropriate logical system. Such a system is naturally given in our case: predicate calculus itself. To handle programs one is forced to use stronger systems like modal logic, since the control structure inherent in programs in addition to their logic causes additional complication. Therefore, instead of several transformations of programs which require such strong and more complicated logical means for their justification, we only have transformations of logical expressions which can be handled by current theorem-provers and one last, usually very simple step, where the control structure, already inherent implicitly in the resulting expression has to be made explicit for the machine. We also believe that one should gain more experience before one finally specifies the strategy DOMAIN. There may be examples where more flexible choices of the domain-specification than the ones in Guiho *et al.* [1980] lead to better algorithms. As far as we can see at present, the approach of Guiho-Gresse could not be easily extended to handle also such examples.

In comparison to other work on program synthesis we restrict ourselves to pointing out the characteristic features of our approach which is deductive like that taken in Manna and Waldinger, Chapter 2, but additionally has a strong strategic feature. Though the various data-bases of LOPS are expected to grow with the system as a whole, the emphasis lies on the conciseness of the strategic approach rather than on hundreds of rules like in PSI (Green [1977]). LOPS actually incorporates also the "programming from examples"—approach (see Biermann [1976]) via its example generator which explores static structures, however, not programs with time-varying, that is, more complicated models, and thus hopefully will prove more successful.

F. Conclusion

We have presented LOPS, an interactive system to construct programs by logical transformations. LOPS consists of a control unit, a knowledge base, a theorem prover, an example generator and an example explorer. After a two man-years implementational investment some of these components are still in a rudimentary state.

The structure of LOPS is patterned after procedures which are believed to be central to human programming efforts. We hope that with the experience of experimenting with LOPS, this system can be improved to such an extent as to strengthen the view that this approach, especially the strategies described in Bibel [1980] is powerful enough to allow the synthesis of algorithms for many practical problems.

G. Acknowledgements

We thank Alan Biermann for a number of detailed comments which provided substantial support for a considerably improved version of this paper.

References

Aho *et al.* [1975]
A. Aho, J. Hopcroft and J. Ullmann, *The Design and Analysis of Computer Algorithms,* Addison Wesley, 1975.

Bibel [1980]
W. Bibel, "Syntax-directed, semantics-supported program synthesis," *Artificial Intelligence,* Vol. 14, No. 3, pp. 243–261.

Bibel [1981]
W. Bibel, "Matings in matrices," *Proceedings German Workshop on Artif. Intelligence 1981,* Bad Honnef, J. Siekmann (ed.), Informatik Fachberichte No. 47, Springer 1981, pp. 171–187.

Bibel [1982a]
W. Bibel, "Logical program synthesis," *Proc. Intern. Conference on Fifth Generation Computer Systems,* Tokyo 1981, T. Moto-oka (ed.), North-Holland P.C. 1982, pp. 227–236.

Bibel [1982b]
W. Bibel, "Automated theorem proving," Vieweg, 1982.

Bibel et al. [1983]
W. Bibel, E. Eder and B. Fronhofer, "Towards an advanced implementation of the connection method," Proc. IJCAI–83, Karlsruhe (1983).

Biermann [1976]
A.W. Biermann, "Approaches to automatic programming," *Advances in Computers,* Vol. 15 (1976), pp. 1–63.

Bledsoe and Ballantine [1979]
W.W. Bledsoe and A.M. Ballantine, "On automatic generation of counterexamples," ATP–44A, Univ. of Texas at Austin (1979).

Colmerauer *et al.* [1981]
A. Colmerauer, H. Kanoui and M. Van Caneghem, "Last steps towards an ultimate PROLOG," *Proc. 7th IJCAI,* Vancouver (1981), p. 947 f.

Dewar [1978]
R. Dewar, "The SETL programming language," Courant Inst., New York University (1978).

Eigemeier *et al.* [1980]
H. Eigemeier, Ch. Knabe, P. Raulefs and K. Tramer, "Automatic implementation of algebraic specifications of abstract data types," Proc. AISB–80, Amsterdam (1980).

Green [1977]
C. Green, "A summary of the PSI program synthesis system," *Proc. IJCAI–77* (1977), pp. 380–381.

Guiho and Gresse [1980]
G. Guiho and C. Gresse, "Program synthesis from incomplete specifications," *Proc. 5th Conf. on Automated Deduction, Lecture Notes in Computer Science,* Vol. 87, Springer, 1980.

Hörnig [1981]
K.M. Hörnig, "Generating small models of first order axioms," *Proc. German Workshop on Artif. Intelligence 1981,* Bad Honnef, J. Siekmann (ed.), Informatik Fachberichte No. 47, Springer 1981, pp. 248–255.

Jouannaud and Kodratoff [1979]
J.P. Jouannaud and Y. Kodratoff, "Characterization of a class of functions synthesized from examples by a Summers-like method using a B.M.W. matching technique," *Proc. IJCAI–79* (1979), pp. 440–447.

Kowalski [1979]
R. Kowalski, "Algorithm = logic + control," *Communications of the ACM,* Vol. 22 (1979), pp. 424–436.

Manna and Waldinger [1979]
Z. Manna and R. Waldinger, "A deductive approach to program synthesis," *Proc. IJCAI–79* (1979), pp. 542–551.

Wegbreit [1976]
B. Wegbreit, "Goal directed program transformations," *IEEE Transactions on Software Engineering,* Vol. 2 (1976).

CHAPTER 4

Combining Program Synthesis With Program Analysis

Ria Follett
Scientia Pty. Ltd. Computer Consultants
Anzac House
26–36 College Street
Sidney, N.S.W. 2010
Australia

Abstract

When synthesizing programs which may have side effects, these side effects must be discovered and taken into account. Program analysis is used to describe the effect of any program segment in sufficient detail to allow the required goal to be achieved and verified. Combining program analysis and program synthesis is especially important when synthesizing recursive programs which may contain arbitrary side effects. The method is illustrated by synthesizing two different sorting algorithms—insertion sort and quick sort.

A. Introduction

A major problem in the synthesis of programs is how to take proper account of the side effects of parts of the program. A side effect is an action which is unplanned. For example, you may open a window to let in some air, and in flies a bee. The bee flying in is a side effect of opening the window. Side effects may be harmful but not necessarily so. Side effects can be used constructively in the synthesis of programs, rather than being purely a destructive element.

Before the side effects of a program segment can be used in program synthesis, these side effects must be discovered and described. Together with a system that synthesizes programs, there must be a method of analyzing any new program segment to obtain its description, which includes all possible side effects. To handle any practical problem methods of analyzing branches, loops and subroutines must be developed. The analysis of the program will result in a detailed program description. The program description should contain sufficient detail to allow the correctness of programs to be proved, while keeping the effort involved in program analysis to a minimum.

A method of program description has been developed which minimizes the amount of analysis required to obtain automatically a description which is adequate for the required verification. The program segment descriptions are then used to synthesize larger programs.

An automatic program synthesis system, PROSYN, has been designed to illustrate these methods. PROSYN allows the synthesis of recursive subroutines, as well as the synthesis of hierarchies of programs. The system has automatically synthesized and analyzed a variety of programs including SORT2, MAX, SUM of an array, solving two simultaneous equations, REMAINDER from dividing two numbers, moving elements up and down arrays, sorting arrays, adding, multiplying and transposing matrices, inverting matrices, finding eigenvectors of matrices, finding the zeros of a function, and solving a set of linear simultaneous equations.

In the following sections the method of describing a program shall be presented, together with methods of program analysis and synthesis. Various sorting algorithms will be used as examples of the variety of programs that may result from using these techniques. Detailed descriptions of two sorting algorithms, insertion sort and quicksort, shall be used to illustrate the process.

B. Defining Side Effects

The actions of programs are usually described by invariants or predicate transformers (see Manna [1974]). Invariants are relations that are unaltered by the program at some point. Predicate transformers show how relations are transformed when passed back through the program. Usually a mixture of the two is used due to difficulty in finding predicate transformers for complicated programs. This is formalized into the concept of a *passback pair,* which allows a wide range of detail to be given in program description.

A passback pair is an ordered pair (S,f) of a predicate S, and a function f, on an arbitrary relation R. It is a description of the effects of a particular program segment p. The second element, f is the function which calculates the precondition of R. For example, consider the assignment statement v:=a. The relation R will be true after executing the assignment statement if f(R) is true before executing the assignment statement. The function f, in this case, may be "substitute a for v in R". The first element, S, is a predicate defining the domain of relations on which f is defined. If S(R) is true, then f can modify R, thus giving the precondition of R. If S(R) is false then the precondition of R may not be calculated using f. The domain of relations on which the function f given above for assignment statements is valid is all relations. Thus a passback pair for v:=a is (TRUE, substitute "a" for "v" in R).

There is a range of passback pairs valid for any program segment. The passback pair (FALSE,I) is valid for all program segments, where I is the identity function, meaning that no relation will be passed back over this segment to produce a valid precondition. Other passback pairs may be obtained for the segment, which allows some relations to be passed back over the segment.

For example, an alternative passback pair for v:=a is

("v" is not contained in R, I)

where I is the identity function. This means that only relations R, where R does not depend on the variable 'v', may be passed back. These relations will be passed back unaffected by the assignment statement.

The variety of passback pairs available for any given program segment means that the depth to which the segment must be analyzed may be varied depending on the depth of description required. For example, no analysis is needed to describe a program segment by the passback pair

(FALSE, I)

As no relations can be passed back over the segment using this passback pair, it is not very useful in either program verification or program synthesis. A variety of more expressive passback pairs of the form

(S,I)

where I is once again the identity function, is often achievable. In these cases, S defines a domain of invariants. Exact descriptions may be unobtainable, and are of the form

(TRUE,f)

where f defines the predicate transformer of all relations. Any combination of invariants and predicate transformers may be used to describe a program segment. If the passback pair is

(S,f)

then invariants are relations R, which lie in the domain defined by S, and for which R <= f(R).

The process of obtaining a more precise passback pair is called *refining* the passback pair. Refining the passback pair implies widening the domain, with a corresponding modification to f.

For example, consider the following program, SORT2, that sorts two numbers

```
IF x ≤ y THEN nil
        ELSE BEGIN temp := x ;
                   x := y ;
                   y := temp
     END
```

A simple passback pair for the above segment is

(x, y and temp not contained in R, I)

where I is the identity function. Using this passback pair, only relations not dependent on the values of x, y or temp may be passed back over the segment, and these may be passed back unaffected.

This passback pair may be refined by passing the relation back separately over both branches. The relation R may be passed back over the ELSE branch resulting in the precondition R''',

where

R''' is obtained by replacing temp by x in R''
and R'' is obtained by replacing x by y in R'
and R' is obtained by replacing y by temp in R.

The relation R may be passed back over the THEN branch unchanged. Thus a refined passback pair for the SORT2 segment is

$$(R''' \equiv R, I)$$

This passback pair means that, whenever x and y may be interchanged in R without affecting R, and R does not contain temp, the R may be passed back unaffected by SORT2. The passback pair may be further refined to

$$(\text{TRUE}, R''' \wedge R).$$

This means that, if both R and R''' are true before SORT2, then R will be true after SORT2.

The passback pair may be still further refined to

$$(\text{TRUE, IF } x \leqslant y \text{ THEN R ELSE } R''')$$

Each passback pair is more complicated than the previous passback pair. The passback pair need only be refined to the level required for program verification or program synthesis.

A passback pair also shows when a primitive, if inserted, will interfere with a *protected relation* R. Protected relations, or protected goals, are widely used in program-synthesis systems, for example in Sussman [1975], Tate [1975] and Waldinger [1977]. After goals are achieved, they are protected, and no further program steps may be added that alter or "undo" the protected goal. A program step, with a passback pair of (S,f), is likely to alter a protected relation R, unless S(R) and R => f(R). For example v := a may be inserted where the y = b is protected, as v is not contained in the relation, but v:=a may not be inserted where v = b is protected. Further refinements may decide that the relation is not affected after all. For example if v=a is protected, then the program segment v:=a may not be inserted if the segment is described by

(v is contained in R, I).

However, if v:=a is described by

(TRUE, substitute a for v in R)

Then f(v=a) is a=a which is true. Thus S(R) and R => f(R) and so the segment may be inserted after all.

C. Program Synthesis

The analysis/synthesis approach has been illustrated by implementing an automatic programming system in LISP, called PROSYN. PROSYN consists of

a) domain specification rules
b) the synthesizer
c) the pattern matching link between the domain and the synthesizer.

An important aim in the development of PROSYN was to show the power of the approach in a wide variety of domains. Hence the synthesizer was designed to be domain independent, and we rely on complementary information supplied for any desired domain, rather than replying on a fixed domain. Domains implemented include BLOCKS, INTEGERS, ARRAYS with REALS, and LISTS. The more primitive domains such as BLOCKS did not need the complete power of the synthesis system.

The domain information consists of

1) the grammar of relations allowed. This grammar determines the format of the input required by the synthesizer. PROSYN assumes a prefix format, whereas in this paper relations are expressed in the more normal infix format. An example used in the grammar is

(VAR 1) = (EXP 1)

where (VAR 1) is a free variable defined in the grammar by VAR, and (EXP 1) is a free expression as defined by EXP. EXP may include in its definition, that EXP is:

(EXP 1) + (EXP 2)
or (VAR 1)
or any atomic value

2) The primitives supplied. The assignment statement was usually the only primitive used. The assignment statement may be described as:

primitive : (VAR 1) := (EXP 1)
achieves goal : (VAR 1) = (EXP 1)
requires precondition : (VAR 1) not in (EXP 1)
passback pairs : ((VAR 1) IN R, I)
or (TRUE,SUBSTITUTE(EXP 1) FOR (VAR 1) IN R)

Note that both S and f are expressed as an executable program.

The following example uses the program segment SWAP which may be built up from assignment statements.

3) The domain dependent logic. The pattern matcher accesses this logic when attempting to show that two expressions match. For example in the REAL domain expl < exp2 is equivalent to exp2 > expl.

4) Any initial assumptions, such as initial values of variables, positions of blocks, etc.

Functions are synthesized by considering goals in turn. After a program to satisfy some of the goals has been created, remaining goals are synthesized by taking into account the side effects of the program already written and the goals that are protected. Strategies (corresponding to programming knowledge) are used to guide the construction. Backtracking occurs when all strategies fail. The strategies, or methods of tackling problems, used include inserting primitives and achieving their preconditions, passing back goals, splitting the goal into cases, and induction. Strategies other than induction lead to straight line or branch programs. The synthesis of recursive programs is far more difficult. In this case the incomplete program must be analyzed so that recursive function calls, which are to be inserted, do not interfere with the goals already achieved.

Recursive functions are achieved in stages by applying induction. Induction is applied whenever the goal consists of a relation defined in the domain to operate on a SET of values, for example the relations FORALL and EXISTS. The induction process may be described as follows

a) if the set cannot be proven to be non-empty, the goal is split into the case of an empty set, and non-empty set.

b) the non-empty set is then split using one of the possible splits indicated in the domain and the new goals attempted.

c) when a future goal is an instance of the original goal, then

d) termination is considered. If termination is assured then

e) the program written so far is analyzed for its passback pair.

f) the recursive function call is inserted if its passback pair does not interfere with any relations protected where it is to be inserted.

g) when completed the function is again analyzed. If only recursive function calls are inserted in the function program, the passback pair as calculated in f) is valid. If other primitives are added, then the passback pair must be re-evaluated, and all recursive function calls checked for consistency with the protected relations. If the program consists of only recursive function calls, the function cannot be synthesized by this method. An alternative split must be used.

h) the program can now be used as a completed subroutine.

The above process can be illustrated by the program that inserts an element in an array. This program was synthesized as part of the synthesis of the insertion sorting algorithm which is described later. The aim of INSERT is to achieve

$$\text{FORALL}\{i = p + 1, n\}\ x(i\text{-}1) \leqslant x(i)$$

assuming that the precondition

$$\text{FORALL}\{i = p + 1, n\text{-}1\}\ x(i\text{-}1) \leqslant x(i)$$

has already been achieved.

The synthesis of INSERT will be described under the points a) to h) given above.

a) The set is empty if $n \leqslant p$. As it cannot be determined whether or not $n \leqslant p$, the goal is split into the two cases. This results in the following program segment:

```
IF n ≤ p THEN NIL
      ELSE ....
```

b) The goal is split into the subgoals

$$x(n\text{-}1) \leqslant x(n)$$
$$\text{and FORALL}\{i = p + 1, n\text{-}1\}\ x(i\text{-}1) \leqslant x(i)$$

These goals are attempted in turn.

i) achieve $x(n\text{-}1) \leqslant x(n)$

The validity of this goal cannot be determined, so it is used as the basis of a branch. If the goal is not already true, swapping will make it true. As no goals are as yet protected, the elements can be swapped, and the following program segment is inserted after the ELSE .... in a):

```
IF x(n-1) ≤ x(n) THEN NIL
  ELSE SWAP (n, n-1)
```

This achieves the goal $x(n\text{-}1) \leqslant x(n)$ which is then protected.

ii) achieve FORALL$\{i = p + 1, n\text{-}1\}\ x(i\text{-}1) \leqslant x(i)$. The validity of this goal cannot be determined, as the SWAP interferes with the assumed precondition (which is, in fact, identical to this goal). The goal is then attempted separately in each branch:

• After the THEN, the only program is the null program, and thus the goal is true given the original precondition.

• After the ELSE, the original precondition is affected by the ELSE. However:

c) The new goal is an instance of the original goal, so induction can be applied.

d) As the set on which the new goal is defined, FORALL$\{i = p + 1, n\text{-}1\}$ is a proper subset of the original goal (FORALL$\{i = p + 1, n\}$), termination is assured, so

e) the program written so far is analyzed for its passback pair. The following passback pair can be derived (see Follett [1980 a,b]) for INSERT (p , n-1)

$$(\text{TRUE, FORALL}\{i = p, n\text{-}1\}\ \text{FORALL}\{j = p, n\text{-}1\}\text{interchange}$$
$$x(i) \text{ with } x(j) \text{ in R}).$$

INSERT(p , n-1) can be inserted after the SWAP if it does not interfere with the protected goal $x(n\text{-}1) \leqslant x(n)$. Denote the above passback pair as (TRUE,f). Then the effect on the protected goal is $f(x(n\text{-}1) \leqslant x(n)\ )$ gives FORALL$\{j = p , n\text{-}1\}\ x(j) \leqslant x(n)$. However, closer analysis shows that the relations already true at this point imply the altered goal (see above reference) and so:

f) INSERT(p , n-1) can be inserted, giving the completed program

```
INSERT(p , n) <-- IF n ≤ p THEN NIL
                  ELSE IF x(n-1) ≤ x(n) THEN NIL
                  ELSE BEGIN
                    SWAP(n , n-1)
                    INSERT(p , n-1)
                   END
```

g) As only a recursive function call has been inserted, the function does not need to be reanalyzed.

h) The program can now be used in the SORT program.

D. The Synthesis of Sorting Algorithms

There is a large variety of sorting algorithms available. Many of these can be synthesized by PROSYN. Only 'inplace' sorts will be considered here. This very specific area has the advantage that the problem is easily expressed, and yet any 'inplace' sorting solution has important side effects. It is used here to demonstrate how the method of dealing with side effects results in vastly different sorting algorithms. The variety of sorting algorithms obtained are also discussed by Darlington [1977] and Green and Barstow [1978].

The goal for sorting an array x, between elements p and n may be given as

$$\begin{aligned} &\text{FORALL}\{i = p + 1 , n\}\ x(i\text{-}1) \leqslant x(i) \\ \wedge\ &\text{FORALL}\{i = p ,n\}\ \text{EXISTS}\{j = p, n\}\ x(i) = s(j) \\ \wedge\ &\text{FORALL}\{i = p ,n\}\ \text{EXISTS}\{j = p ,n\}\ s(i) = x(j) \end{aligned}$$

where s(i) is the initial value of x(i). Note that the last two conjuncts ensure that the resultant array is a permutation of the original array. The first conjunct ensures that the resultant array is sorted.

The last two conjuncts are true initially, and so may be protected over the range of the whole program. They need not be specifically achieved.

The goal that still needs to be achieved is

$$\text{FORALL}\{i = p + 1 ,n\}\ x(i\text{-}1) \leqslant x(i)$$

As the goal is expressed as a FORALL, induction is used. The set on which i operates, being (p + 1 , n) can be divided into the subsets

$$(p + 1 ,m) \text{ and } (m + 1 ,n)$$

The first decision is to determine the value of m. If m is $n-1$, various selection, insertion and bubble sorts result. If m is another predetermined number (such as $(n-p)/2$), then a merge sort results. If the choice of m is left until later, partition sorts (such as a quick sort) result.

Secondly the order in which the goals are attempted must be determined. The order affects the resulting algorithm, but not the correctness, as future goals take into account the program already synthesized and the goals that were achieved or used. For sorting algorithms the order in which the goals are attempted are relatively unimportant. Similar programs are obtained, except that attempting the singleton goal $(x(n\text{-}1) \leqslant x(n))$ first, tends to lead to bubble sorts.

Figure 1 shows how the major sorting algorithms are obtained. These are discussed in detail in Follett [1980 b]. The synthesis method is discussed by illustrating how insertion sort and quicksort are synthesized.

D.1 Exchange Insertion Sort

The exchange insertion sort is one of the many algorithms that result when the induction set is split into the single case m=n and the remainder. Let the subroutine to be synthesized be called SORT(p ,n) which sorts the elements of the array x between the indices p and n. The goal for SORT(p ,n) is thus:

$$\text{FORALL}\{i = p + 1, n\}\ x(i\text{-}1) \leqslant x(i)$$

The goal can be split only if p<n. As this cannot be determined at this stage, a branch is inserted in the program (see B point a). The goal is then split as

$$\text{FORALL}\{i = p + 1, n\text{-}1\}\ x(i\text{-}1) \leqslant x(i) \wedge x(n\text{-}1) \leqslant x(n)$$

These goals are attempted in turn.

Consider first the subgoal

$$\text{FORALL}\{i = p + 1, n\text{-}1\}\ x(i\text{-}1) \leqslant x(i)$$

This can be solved by a recursive call to SORT(p ,n-1), and, as this does not interfere with any protected relation (no relation is as yet protected), the recursive call is inserted. This gives the program

```
SORT(p ,n) <-- IF n ⩽ p THEN NIL
    ELSE 0 BEGIN
          50 SORT(p ,n−1)
          100 END
```

with the goal

$$\text{FORALL}\{i = p + 1, n\text{-}1\}\ x(i\text{-}1) \leqslant x(i)$$

protected between lines 50 and 100.

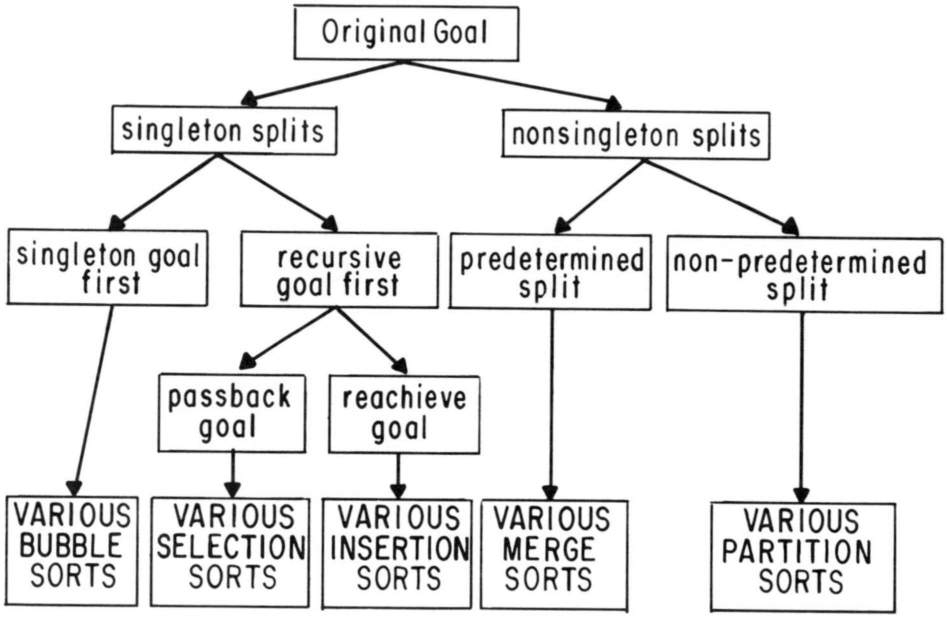

Figure 1
Various Sorting Algorithms

The remaining goal x(n-1) $\leqslant$ x(n) is to be achieved at 100. This can be achieved using SORT2(n-1 ,n), the subroutine that sorts x(n-1) and x(n). Before this can be inserted, any interactions between SORT2 and the goal already achieved must be considered. A passback pair for SORT2(n ,n-1) was developed in section B, as

$$(\text{TRUE}, R''' \wedge R)$$

where R is the relation to be passed back and R''' is the relation with x(n) and x(n-1) interchanged. The effect of SORT2(n, n-1) on the protected goal is considered. The protected goal, G,

$$\text{FORALL}\{i = p + 1 , n\text{-}1\}\ x(i\text{-}1) \leqslant x(i)$$

can be passed back over SORT2(n , n-1) giving f(G) as FORALL{i = p + 1 ,n-1} x(i-1) $\leqslant$ x(i) AND x(n-2) $\leqslant$ x(n). As G $\not\Rightarrow$f(G), the protected goal will be altered if SORT2 is inserted between 50 and 100.

There are two ways of solving this problem:

i) The goal x(n-1) $\leqslant$ x(n) can be passed back over the recursive function call, SORT(p ,n-1) at line 50. This approach leads to various selection sort routines (see Follett [1980 b]), or

ii) The overall goal can be reachieved at 100, given the subgoal already achieved at 50. This approach leads to insertion sorts, and will be described now.

A new subroutine is synthesized, and will be, for the sake of clarity, described as INSERT. The aim of the subroutine is to achieve

$$\text{FORALL}\{i = p + 1 ,n\}\ x(i\text{-}1) \leqslant x(i)$$

assuming, as a precondition

$$\text{FORALL}\{i = p + 1 , n\text{-}1\}\ x(i\text{-}1) \leqslant x(i)$$

The synthesis of this routine was given in section B.

This completes the original program, giving the result

```
SORT(p ,n) <-- IF n ≤ p THEN NIL
               ELSE BEGIN
                  SORT(p ,n-1)
                  INSERT(p ,n)
                END

INSERT(p ,n) <-- IF n ≤ p THEN NIL
                 ELSE IF x(n-1) ≤ x(n) THEN NIL
                 ELSE BEGIN
                    SWAP(n , n-1)
                    INSERT(p , n-1)
                    END
```

D.2 Quicksort

This algorithm is generated when the goal for SORT(p ,n), being

$$\text{FORALL}\{i = p + 1 ,n\}\ x(i\text{-}1) \leqslant x(i)$$

is split into the two conjuncts

$$\text{FORALL}\{i = p + 1 ,m\}\ x(i\text{-}1) \leqslant x(i) \wedge \text{FORALL}\{i = m + 1 ,n\}\ x(i\text{-}1) \leqslant x(i)$$

with m an undefined number, whenever $n > p + 1$.

These goals are attempted in turn. (In this case the choice of order happens to lead to similar programs). The first goal matches the original program goal, with n replaced by m. As it can be determined that $m < n$, by restricting the range of m, the recursive function call can be inserted. This leads to the program

```
SORT(p ,n) <-- IF n ≤ p + 1 THEN NIL
                ELSE 0 BEGIN
                     50 SORT(p ,m)
                     100 END
```

with the goal FORALL{i = p + 1 ,m} x(i-1) $\leqslant$ x(i) protected over 50 to 100.

The goal FORALL{i = m + 1 ,n} x(i-1) $\leqslant$ x(i) is still to be achieved at 100. This goal also matches the original program goal call with $p = m + 1$. The passback pair of SORT(m + 1 ,n) must be determined to test if it interferes with the protected goal.

So far, the only program step is a recursive call to itself. Thus, the passback pair can only be estimated at this stage. The validity will be checked when the synthesis is complete. Assuming that the only primitive available is SWAP(i ,j) which interchanges x(i) and x(j), the passback pair for SORT(p ,n) can be estimated as (Follett [1980 b])

(TRUE,FORALL{i = p ,n}FORALL{j = p ,n}G with x(i) and x(j) interchanged)

The insertion of the recursive function call, SORT(m + 1, n) can be shown to interfere with the protected goal in a manner similar to that described for SORT2 in section C.1.

There are again several ways of solving this problem

i) The overall goal may be reachieved at this point. This leads to a variety of inefficient merge sorts.

ii) The remaining goal may be further split into

$$x(m) \leqslant x(m+1)\ \text{AND}\ \text{FORALL}\{i = m + 2 ,n\}\ x(i\text{-}1) \leqslant x(i).$$

The second subgoal may be achieved with a recursive function call without altering the protected goal. The first subgoal may be achieved using the method described in i) leading to merge sorts, or passed back over the two recursive functions calls, leading to partition sorts, similar to that described in iii)

iii) The remaining goal may be passed back over SORT(p ,m), leading to partition sorts. This option will be investigated below.

The remaining goal,

$$\text{FORALL}\{i = m + 1, n\}\ x(i\text{-}1) \leqslant x(i)$$

is passed back over SORT(p ,m), using the above passback pair, giving the goal to be achieved before the SORT(p ,m) as

$$\text{FORALL}\{i = p, m\}\text{FORALL}\{k = m + 1, n\}\ x(i) \leqslant x(k)$$
$$\wedge\ \text{FORALL}\{k = m + 2, n\}\ x(k\text{-}1) \leqslant x(k)$$

The first conjunction generates a new subroutine, called here PART(p ,n). This subroutine determines the value for m, as m is as yet undetermined. As m will be altered, the SORT routine must be altered to include m as a parameter, effectively making m a local variable. The synthesis of PART(p ,n) is given separately in the next section. The SORT function will be completed here assuming PART, but in fact PROSYN will recursively solve the subgoal PART first. The effect of PART is to swap the values of x(i), and to alter the value of m, but as the values of x(i) and m are not protected at step 25, the subroutine is inserted, leading to the program:

```
SORT(p ,n ,m) <-- IF n ≤ p + 1 THEN NIL
             ELSE  0  BEGIN
                  25  PART(p ,n)
                  50  SORT(p , m , 0)
                  100 END
```

with protected goals:

G1: FORALL{i = p + 1 ,m} x(i-1) $\leqslant$ x(i) from step 50 to 100
G2: FORALL{i = p ,m} FORALL{k = m + 1 ,n} x(i) $\leqslant$ x(k) from 25 to 50
G3: FORALL{i = m + 1 ,n} x(i-1) $\leqslant$ x(i) from 50 to 100

with the goal FORALL{i = m + 2 ,n} x(i-1) $\leqslant$ x(i) still to be achieved at 50.

The goal can be achieved by inserting the recursive function call SORT(m + 1 ,n , 0) at 30. However the side effects must be considered. The goal (given above as G2) is altered by SORT(m + 1 , n , 0) using the passback pair for SORT given earlier, to

FORALL{i = m + 1 ,n} FORALL{j = m + 1 ,n} G2 with x(i),x(j) interchanged.

The altered goal is identical to the original goal. Thus the recursive function call SORT(m + 1 ,n ,0) can be inserted at 30, giving the completed sorting program:

```
SORT(p ,n ,m) <-- IF n ≤ p + 1 THEN NIL
                  ELSE  0 BEGIN
                        25 PART(p ,n)
                        30 SORT(m + 1 ,n ,0)
                        50 SORT(p , m , 0)
                        100 END
```

which, depending on the algorithm given by PART, results in a quicksort.

D.3 PART

This subroutine is synthesized in response to a subgoal in the SORT routine. It is actually synthesized during the synthesis of the SORT routine, but will be described separately to make the synthesis easier to follow.

The goal that needs to be achieved is

$$\text{FORALL}\{i = p ,m\}\ \text{FORALL}\{k = m + 1 ,n\}\ x(i) \leq x(k)$$

where m is an as yet unprotected variable. This means that the value of m may be altered by PART.

The goal can be restated as there exists a y such that

$$\text{FORALL}\{i = p ,m\}\ x(i) \leq y \land \text{FORALL}\{k = m + 1 ,n\}\ y \leq x(k)$$

As m is free, this can be restated as

$$\text{EXISTS}\{m = p - 1 ,n\}\ [\text{FORALL}\{i = p ,m\}\ x(i) \leq y \land \text{FORALL}$$
$$\{k = m + 1 ,n\}\ y \leq x(k)]$$

(Note that m may be p - 1 or n, meaning that either of the FORALL ranges may be null. This allows y to be greater than all the x values, or less than all the x values.)

The EXISTS allows induction on the value of m. Let the induction set considered be split as (p - 1 ,n - 1) and (n ,n). The null condition is first inserted. If p - 1 = n then m exists, and must be n. So the null condition added is

$$\text{IF } p - 1 = n \text{ THEN } m := n.$$

The goal for EXISTS may be split into the sets (p - 1 , n - 1) and (n ,n) giving the goal

$$\begin{aligned}&\text{FORALL}\{i = p\ ,\ n\}\ x(i) \leqslant y\\ \vee\ &\text{EXISTS}\{m = p - 1\ ,\ n - 1\}\ [\text{FORALL}\{i = p\ ,m\}\ x(i) \leqslant y\\ &\qquad \wedge\ \text{FORALL}\{k = m + 1\ ,\ n\}\ y \leqslant x(k)\ ]\end{aligned}$$

The first disjunct is attempted first. As the goal is FORALL induction occurs. The induction set chosen may be (p ,p) and (p + 1 ,n). The first disjunct is split as

$$x(p) \leqslant y \wedge \text{FORALL}\{i = p + 1\ ,n\}\ x(i) \leqslant y$$

The first conjunct is attempted first. The validity cannot be determined, so a branch is synthesized. If the conjunct is true, a recursive call achieves the remainder of the conjunct, giving the partial program

```
PART(p ,n) <-- IF p-1=n THEN m := n
           ELSE IF x(p) ≤ y THEN PART (p + 1 ,n)
                ELSE ...
```

The alternative branch of the worldsplit is the next disjunct. This is the goal

$$\begin{aligned}&\text{EXISTS}\{m = p - 1\ ,n\text{-}1\}\ [\text{FORALL}\{i = p\ ,m\}\ x(i) \leqslant y\\ &\qquad \text{FORALL}\{k = m + 1\ ,n\}\ y \leqslant x(k)]\end{aligned}$$

However the disjunct does not match the original goal for PART as n in the original goal must match both n and n-1 in the current goal. The disjunct can be further split into the sets (p-1 , p-1) and (p ,n-1) giving the goal

$$\begin{aligned}&\text{FORALL}\{k{=}p\ ,n\}\ y \leqslant x(k)\\ \vee\ &\text{EXISTS}\{m{=}p\ ,n\text{-}1\}\ [\text{FORALL}\{i{=}p\ ,m\}\ x(i) \leqslant y\\ &\qquad \text{FORALL}\{k{=}m{+}1\ ,n\}\ y \leqslant x(k)]\end{aligned}$$

The first disjunct is attempted. The goal is split into the sets (p ,n-1) and (n ,n), giving the goals required as

$$y \leqslant x(n) \wedge \text{FORALL}\{k{=}p\ ,n\text{-}1\}\ y \leqslant x(k).$$

The first goal is attempted first. As this cannot be determined, a branch is synthesized, giving the resultant program:

```
PART(p ,n) <-- IF p-1=n THEN m := n
           ELSE IF x(p) ≤ y THEN PART (p + 1 ,n)
              ELSE IF y ≤ x(n) THEN PART (p ,n-1)
                 ELSE ...
```

The remaining goal is

$$\text{EXISTS}\{m=p\ ,n\text{-}1\}\ [\text{FORALL}\{i=p\ ,m\}\ x(i) \leqslant y$$
$$\text{FORALL}\{k=m+1\ ,n\}\ y \leqslant x(k)]$$

This goal may be expressed as

$$\begin{aligned}\text{EXISTS}\{m=p+1\ ,n\text{-}1\}\ [&\text{FORALL}\{i=p+1\ ,m\}\ x(i) \leqslant y\\ &\wedge \text{FORALL}\{k=m+1\ ,n\text{-}1\}\ y \leqslant x(k)\\ &\wedge x(p) \leqslant y\\ &\wedge y \leqslant x(n)]\end{aligned}$$

The goal matches the recursive function call except for the goals $x(p) \leqslant y \wedge y \leqslant x(n)$. These are attempted first. Both of these goals are known to be false from the branch conditions, and neither of these goals can be achieved independently, as x may only be permutated. However, these can be achieved together, still retaining the overall x values, by using SWAP(p ,n).

This is inserted at the end giving

ELSE SWAP(p ,n)

The recursive function call then matches the original function call, giving the completed program.

The only undetermined fact is the choice of y. This requires

a) choosing the value for y (any is sufficient, as otherwise the synthesis would have chosen one)

b) adding this to the parameter list of the procedure PART. Choose y to be x(n).

This gives the completed program as

```
PART(p ,n ,y) <-- IF p-1=n THEN m := n
                  ELSE
                   IF x(p) ≤ y THEN PART (p+1 ,n ,y)
                    ELSE IF y ≤ x(n) THEN PART (p ,n-1 ,y)
                     ELSE BEGIN SWAP (p ,n)
                                PART (p-1 ,n ,y)
                          END
```

The call to PART in SORT now becomes PART(p ,n ,x(n)).

E. Conclusion

The method illustrated here combines program synthesis with program analysis. Methods used in program verification, such as the use of invariants and predicate transformers (Manna [1974]) are utilized in program analysis, and generalized to a form more suitable for combining program analysis with synthesis. The generalization, called the passback pair, allows flexibility in the amount of analysis required without affecting the correctness of the resulting program.

The program synthesis is based on passing back goals, and protecting relations required for verification. These methods are based on those found in Manna and Waldinger [1977 a,b] and Waldinger [1977]. They have been extended for use in generating recursive programs in conjunction with the passback pair. The synthesis is driven by a set of strategies corresponding to programming knowledge. A wide variety of programs have been synthesized by the automatic programming system, PROSYN, based on the above principles, as described in the introduction. The above two examples of sorting algorithms show how the mechanisms work, and their flexibility in the synthesis process.

References

Darlington [1977]
J. Darlington, "A synthesis of several sorting algorithms," DAI Research Report No. 23A, Univ. of Edinburgh, 1977.

Follett [1980a]
R. Follett, "Synthesizing recursive function with side effects," *AI Journal,* Vol. 13, No. 3, May 1980, pp. 175–200.

Follett [1980b]
R. Follett, "Automatic program synthesis," Ph.D. Thesis, Univ. of NSW, Australia.

Green and Barstow [1978]
C. Green and D. Barstow, "On program synthesis knowledge," *AI Journal,* Vol. 10, No. 3, pp. 241–280.

Manna [1974]
Z. Manna, "Mathematical theory of computation," McGraw-Hill Book Co., 1974.

Manna and Waldinger [1977a]
Z. Manna and R. Waldinger, "The automatic synthesis of recursive programs," Proc. of the Symposium on A.I. and Programming Languages, SIGART, August 1977, pp. 29–36.

Manna and Waldinger [1977b]
Z. Manna and R. Waldinger, "Synthesis: dreams => programs," Technical Note 156, SRI International, November 1977.

Sussman [1975]
G. Sussman, "A computer model of skill acquisition," American Elsevier Publishing Co., New York, 1975.

Tate [1975]
A. Tate, "Interacting goals and their use," Fourth Int. Joint Conf. on A.I., 1975, pp. 215–218.

Waldinger [1977]
R. Waldinger, "Achieving several goals simultaneously," *Machine Intelligence 8,* Ed Elcock and Michie, Wiley and Sons, New York, 1977, pp. 94–136.

CHAPTER 5

Problematic Features Of Programming Languages

Zohar Manna
Stanford University and Weizmann Institute

Richard Waldinger
SRI International

Abstract

To construct a program in a given programming language, one must describe the features of that language. Certain "problematic" features, such as data structure manipulation and procedure call mechanisms, have been found to be difficult to describe by conventional techniques. A unified conceptual framework, based on a "situational calculus", has been developed for describing such problematic features. This framework is

This research was supported in part by the National Science Foundation under Grants MCS−78−02591 and MCS−79−09495, in part by the Office of Naval Research under Contracts N00014−75−C−0816 and N00014−76−C−0687, and in part by the Air Force Office of Scientific Research under Contract F30602−78−0099.

The author's addresses: Z. Manna, Department of Computer Science, Stanford University, Stanford, CA 94305; R. Waldinger, Artificial Intelligence Center, SRI International, Menlo Park, CA 94025.

compatible with contemporary theorem-proving techniques, and is suitable for incorporation in automatic program synthesis, transformation, and verification systems.

A fuller description of the material in this chapter appears in Manna and Waldinger [1981].

A. Introduction

The most widely accepted approach to program verification and to the synthesis of programs with side effects has been the one described in Floyd's [1967] paper and formalized by Hoare [1969]. Hoare's formalization requires that each construct of the programming language be described by an axiom or rule, which defines how the construct alters the truth of an arbitrary assertion. Certain features of programming languages have been found to be easier to describe in this way than others:

> Programs with only simple assignment statements and *while* statements can be described adequately.
>
> Programs with arrays are more intractable, but can be treated if the array operations are rewritten in terms of McCarthy's [1962] *assign* and *contents* function.
>
> Operations on other data structures, such as pointers, lists, and records, can be handled only if special restrictions are imposed on the language.
>
> Different varieties of procedure calls have also required programming-language restrictions.
>
> Even the simple assignment statement fails to satisfy the usual Hoare assignment axiom if included in a programming language with other problematic features.
>
> Certain combinations of features have been shown (Clarke [1977]) to be impossible to describe at all by the Floyd-Hoare technique.

It has been argued (e.g., in London et al. [1978]) that features of programming languages whose semantics are difficult to describe by the Floyd-Hoare technique are also difficult for people to understand and use consistently. For this reason, a number of programming languages have been designed with the intention of eliminating or restricting such "problematic" features. Others have objected (e.g., Hoare [1975], Knuth [1974], deMillo et al. [1977]) that the disciplined use of such "unverifiable" programming features can aid the clear and direct representation of a desired algorithm, while their removal may force the programmer into increasingly obscure circumlocutions.

We have recently developed a conceptual framework capable of describing all of these problematic programming features. This framework is suitable to serve as a basis for the implementation of verification systems, as well as synthesis and transformation systems. We do not argue that the problematic features should necessarily be included in programming languages without restriction, but we intend that if a language designer wishes to use some combination of features, that no obstacle should be imposed by verification concerns.

The approach we employ is a "situational calculus", in which we refer explicitly to the states of the computation. In a given state s, the evaluation of an expression e of the programming language produces a new state s;e. The meaning of the expression can then be defined by axioms that relate the characteristics of the new state with those of the original state.

This formalism is quite distinct from that of Hoare, in which no explicit reference is made to states. In this respect, our approach is closer to those adopted by McCarthy [1964] and Burstall [1969] for specifying the semantics of ALGOL-60 subsets, and by Green [1969] for describing robot operations.

To describe the characteristics of the states of a computation, we introduce "situational operators," functions and predicates whose values depend on the state. In defining these operators, we distinguish between the expressions of the programming language, the storage locations of the machine, and the abstract data objects of the program's domain. The precision of this descriptive apparatus enables us to model the effects of programming-language constructs in full detail. We can describe and compare various implementations of the same programming language, or we can ignore the details of implementation if we prefer.

Once we have succeeded in describing the constructs of a programming language, we can use that description in proving that programs in the language satisfy a given specification. The situational operators can be used not only to describe the constructs of the language but also to represent the specifications of a program. Indeed, they are more expressive for this purpose than the conventional input/output assertions, because they enable us to refer in a single sentence to different states of the computation. For example, it is possible to say directly how the *final* value of an identifier relates to its *initial* or *intermediate* values. To show that a program satisfies such a specification, we then prove a corresponding theorem in situational calculus.

The situational-calculus approach can be applied not only to prove that a single program satisfies given properties, but also to prove that an entire class of programs, or a programming language, satisfies given properties. For example, we can state and prove that the "aliasing" phenomenon, in which two identifiers are regarded as different names for the same variable, cannot be created in languages which satisfy certain constraints.

Although the approach has been devised to extend to languages for which the Hoare formalism breaks down, it can also be used to show that the Hoare formalism does actually apply to suitably restricted programming languages. For example, we can show that the Hoare assignment axiom (which fails to apply to most languages used in practice) is true and can be proved as a situational-calculus theorem for languages in which the problematic features have been omitted.

Up to now, we have been discussing the use of a situational-calculus approach for proving properties of given programs and classes of programs. Historically, however, we were led to this approach in developing a method for program synthesis, i.e., the systematic construction of a program to meet given specifications. We have described in Chapter 2 a deductive technique for the synthesis of applicative programs, which yield an output but produce no side effects. We can now construct programs that may produce side effects by applying the same deductive technique within the situational calculus. More precisely, to construct a program to achieve a desired condition, we prove the existence of a state in which the condition is true. The proof is constrained to be "constructive," so that a program to achieve the desired condition can then be extracted from the proof.

The same deductive technique can be applied to the task of transforming a given program, generally to improve its efficiency. Often, the performance of a program can be augmented, at the expense of clarity, by applying transformations that introduce indirect side effects. This transformation process can be conducted within a situational-calculus deductive system, to ensure that the original purpose of the given program is preserved.

The approach of this work is similar in intent and scope to that of denotational semantics, but it relies on a simpler mathematical framework. We do not use functions of higher type, lambda expressions, or fixed points. Situational calculus can be embedded comfortably in a first-order logic to which the well-developed barrage of mechanical theorem proving techniques, such as the unification algorithm, can be applied. In particular, no special difficulty is presented by the existential quantifier, which is outside of the scope of denotational semantics based systems (e.g., Gordon et al. [1979]), but which is valuable for program verification and crucial for program synthesis.

Because of space limitations, it is impossible to present the technical details of our situational-calculus approach here. We must be content with outlining some of the features of programming languages that have caused problems in the past, to indicate sources of the difficulty, and to give some hint of the conceptual framework with which we approach these problems. For a more detailed discussion, see the full version of this paper (Manna and Waldinger [1981]).

We begin with one of the less problematic features—the simple assignment statement.

B. Assignment to Identifiers

By the simple assignment statement we mean one of the form

$$x \leftarrow t,$$

where x is an identifier and t is an expression in the programming language. The Hoare axiom for such an assignment may be expressed as

$$\{P \rightarrow (x \leftarrow t)\}\ x \leftarrow t\ \{P\}$$

indicating that if the assertion $P \rightarrow (x \leftarrow t)$ holds before executing the assignment $x \leftarrow t$, and if the execution terminates, then the assertion P holds afterward. Here, $P \rightarrow (x \leftarrow t)$ is the result of replacing all free occurrences of x in P by t. The rationale for this rule is that the value of x after executing the assignment $x \leftarrow t$ will be the same as the value of t before; therefore, anything that can be said about t before the execution can be said about x afterwards.

However, the above reasoning is faulty, and only applies if certain restrictions are applied to the expression t, the assertion P, and the situation in which the assignment takes place. Let us examine some of these restrictions:

• The expression t must be *static,* in the sense that its evaluation must not itself produce side effects. For example, in the assignment

$$x \leftarrow (x + (y \leftarrow y+1))$$

the evaluation of t, i.e., $x+(y \leftarrow y+1)$, has the side effect of altering the value of the identifier y. Such assignments are legal in the ALGOL dialects and in LISP. If we take the assertion P to be $y=0$, then according to the Hoare axiom, we have

$$\{y = 0\}\ x \leftarrow (x+(y \leftarrow y+1))\ \{y = 0\}.$$

(Note that the assertion $(y=0) \rightarrow (x \leftarrow t)$ reduces to $y=0$ because x does not occur in $y=0$.) However, this sentence is false, because if y is 0 before executing this assignment, then y will be 1, not 0, afterwards.

Similarly, the assignment

$$x \leftarrow f(x),$$

where f is a procedure that has the side effect of increasing the value of the global identifier y by 1, violates the instance of the Hoare axiom

$$\{y = 0\}\ x \leftarrow f(x)\ \{y=0\}.$$

• The assertion P may not refer to the value of an identifier except by mentioning the identifier explicitly. For example, suppose P is the assertion

"there exists an identifier whose value is 2."

Because P contains no occurrences of x at all, the sentence

$$\{P\}\ x \leftarrow 0\ \{P\}$$

is an instance of the Hoare axiom. However, if x is the only identifier whose value is 2 before executing the assignment, then P will become false afterwards.

• Here, the axiom broke down because P referred to the value of x without mentioning x itself.

• In the situation in which the assignment to the identifier x takes place, there must be no way to refer to x indirectly, in terms of other identifiers. For example, suppose x and y are "aliases," i.e., they can be regarded as different names for the same variable. Then changing the value of x will also change the value of y. If P is the condition {y=0}, then the instance of the Hoare axiom

$$\{y=0\} \; x \leftarrow 1 \; \{y=0\}$$

is false, because after executing the assignment, the value of y will be 1, not 0.

In practice, the aliasing phenomenon can arise in languages that admit procedure calls. For example, suppose we have a procedure

$$f(x,y) \Leftarrow x \leftarrow 1$$

whose parameters are passed by a call-by-reference mechanism. In other words, in executing a procedure call f(u,v), where u and v are identifiers, the identifiers x and u become aliases, and the identifiers y and v become aliases. In executing the procedure call f(u,u), all three identifiers x,y, and u become aliases, so altering the value of x will alter the value of y as well. Thus, the assignment statement $x \leftarrow 1$ that occurs in the body of the procedure f(x,y) will violate the instance of the Hoare axiom

$$\{y=0\} \; x \leftarrow 1 \; \{y=0\}.$$

Aliasing can occur in other ways besides the action of the procedure call mechanism. In FORTRAN an alias can be created directly by the action of the "common" or "equivalence" statements.

Other situations, aside from simple aliasing, in which the Hoare axiom is violated occur when the variable x is bound to a substructure of some data structure. Then altering the value of x will indirectly alter the value of the structure.

C. Array Assignments

The direct translation of the Hoare assignment axiom to array assignments is

$$\{P \rightarrow (a[x] \leftarrow t)\} \; a[x] \leftarrow t \; \{P\}.$$

This sentence is false even for straightforward expressions t and assertions P, and for the simplest situations. For example, the sentence

$$\{a[y]=0\} \; a[x] \leftarrow 1 \; \{a[y]=0\}$$

is an instance of the above sentence because a[x] does not occur at all in the assertion a[y]=0; but, of course, the sentence is false if x and y have the same values. The problem is that, while it is exceptional for two identifiers x and y to be aliases, it is commonplace for two array entries a[x] and a[y] to be alternate names for the same entity.

The difficulty has been approached (McCarthy [1962]) by regarding the entire array as a single entity, so that assigning to any of the array's entries produces a new array. More precisely, we regard the entire array a as an ordinary identifier, we treat an array assignment $a[x] \leftarrow t$ as an abbreviation for a simple assignment

$$a \leftarrow \text{assign}(a,x,t),$$

and we treat an array access a[y] as an abbreviation for

$$\text{contents}(a,y).$$

The assign and contents functions are then assumed to satisfy the properties

$$\text{contents}(\text{assign}(a,x,t),y) = t \quad \text{if } x=y$$

and

$$\text{contents}(\text{assign}(a,x,t),y) = \text{contents}(a,y) \quad \text{if } x \neq y.$$

Programs involving arrays can then be treated by the Hoare axiom for simple identifier assignments.

Thus, the previous false sentence

$$\{a[y]=0\} \;\; a[x] \leftarrow t \;\; \{a[y]=0\},$$

expressed in terms of the *contents* and *assign* functions, is

$$\{\text{contents}(a,y)=0\} \;\; a \leftarrow \text{assign}(a,x,t) \;\; \{\text{contents}(a,y)=0\}.$$

This sentence is not an instance of the Hoare assignment axiom, because the assertion contents(a,y)=0 does contain an occurrence of the identifier a. The true instance of the Hoare axiom in this case is

$$\{(\text{contents}(a,y)=0) \rightarrow (a \leftarrow \text{assign}(a,x,t))\}$$

$$a \leftarrow \text{assign}(a,x,t)$$

$$\{\text{contents}(a,y)=0\},$$

i.e.

$$\{\text{contents}(\text{assign}(a,x,t),y)=0\}$$

$$a \leftarrow \text{assign}(a,x,t)$$

$$\{\text{contents}(a,y)=0\}.$$

Although this solution still suffers from the limitations associated with the simple assignment axiom, it resolves the special difficulties arising from the introduction of arrays.

D. Pointer Assignment

To describe the pointer mechanism, let us introduce some terminology. If an identifier is declared in a program, then there is some *location* bound to that identifier; we can regard the location as a cell in the machine memory. If two identifiers are aliases, they are bound to the same locations. A location may contain data, or it may store (the address of) another location; we thus distinguish between *data locations* and *storage locations.* A *pointer* is a storage location which stores (the address of) another storage location. There are many notations for pointers in different programming languages; ours is typical but is not actually identical to any of these.

A pointer is created, for example, by the execution of the simple assignment

$$x \leftarrow \uparrow y,$$

where x and y are both identifiers. Here, the notation ↑ y means the location bound to the identifier y. The result of this assignment is that the location bound to y is stored in the location bound to x. The configuration produced may be represented by the following diagram:

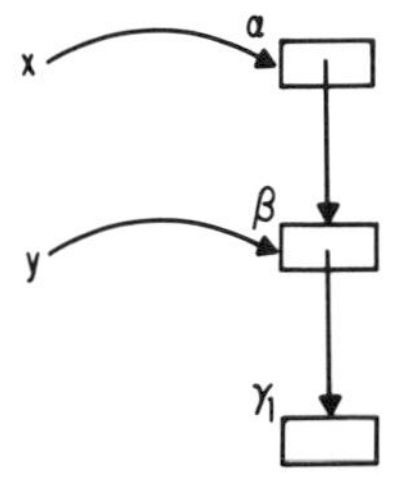

Figure 2.1

Here, α and β are locations bound to x and y, respectively, γ_1 is the location stored in β.

If we subsequently execute a simple assignment statement

$$y \leftarrow t,$$

where t is an expression, we alter the contents of the location β that y is bound to. The location β will then store the location γ_2 yielded by the evaluation of t. The new configuration can be represented by the following diagram:

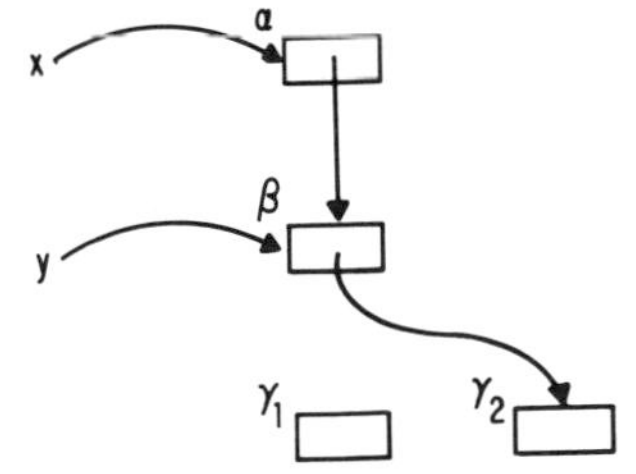

Figure 2.2

We have remarked that such a configuration can easily lead to violations of the Hoare assignment axiom: a simple assignment to y can alter the truth of an assertion about x.

Suppose instead we execute the special *pointer assignment*

$$\downarrow x \leftarrow t.$$

The notation ↓ x means that the location altered by the assignment is not the location α bound to x but rather the location β stored in α. In other words, the effect of the above pointer assignment is precisely the same as that of the simple assignment y ← t, and results in the same configuration depicted above.

A naive extension of the Hoare axiom to pointer assignments is

$$\{P \rightarrow (\downarrow x \leftarrow t)\} \ \downarrow x \leftarrow t \ \{P\}.$$

The sentence

$$\{y=0\} \ \downarrow x \leftarrow 1 \ \{y=0\}$$

is an instance of this axiom, because $\downarrow x$ does not occur in the assertion $y=0$. However, as we have seen, if x "points to" y the assignment $\downarrow x \leftarrow 1$ can set the value of y to 1. In short, the simple adaptation of the Hoare assignment axiom fails to describe the action of the pointer assignment, because the assignment can alter the value of an identifier not mentioned explicitly.

The *assign/contents* technique for arrays has been extended (e.g. see Cartwright et al. [1978]) to pointers by regarding all the identifiers in the program as entries in a single array v, which is indexed not by integers but by identifiers. These array operations can then be treated as simple assignments in terms of the *assign* and *contents* functions, and are correctly described by the Hoare simple assignment axiom and the two McCarthy axioms for *assign* and *contents.*

E. Tree and Record Structure Manipulation

The problems involved with arrays and pointers are compounded in languages with facilities for manipulating more complex structures such as trees and records. Up to now, we have only considered locations that contain data or that store (the address of) a single other location. To treat general data structures, we introduce locations that can store (the address of) arbitrarily many other locations.

For example, in LISP we admit *binary-tree locations,* which can store precisely two locations. If α is a binary-tree location, we will call the two locations stored in α the *left* and *right descendents* of α. Of course, these locations may themselves be binary tree locations. We will refer to the *descendents* of α as a set that includes not only α's left and right descendents, but also their left and right descendents, and so on; we will say that α is one of their *ancestors.*

We will depict a binary-tree location α and its left and right descendents α_L and α_R, by the following diagram:

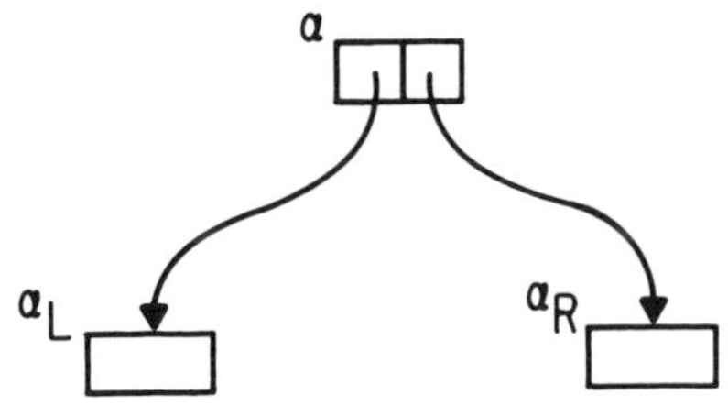

Figure 2.3

We do not exclude the possibility that a binary-tree location is identical to any of its own descendents; such a configuration is called a *circular tree.* For example, the tree below is circular:

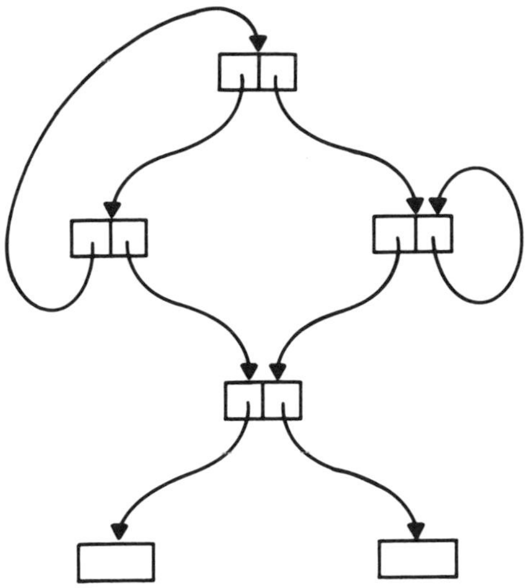

Figure 2.4

LISP provides two functions, which we will call left and right, for accessing the corresponding descendents of a binary-tree location. Suppose t is an expression whose evaluation yields a binary-tree location α; in other words, α represents the value of t. Then the evaluation of left(t) and right(t) yield the left and right descendents of α, respectively.

LISP also provides two operations for altering binary trees: the *replaca* operation, which we denote by

$$\text{left(e)} \leftarrow \text{t},$$

and the *replacd* operation, which we denote by

$$\text{right(e)} \leftarrow \text{t},$$

where e and t are any expressions. If the evaluation of e yields a binary-tree location α, and if the evaluation of t then yields a location β, then the rplaca operation left(e) $\leftarrow$ t will cause β to become the new left descendent of α. The replacd operation behaves analogously.

The problem in describing the rplaca and rplacd operations is precisely the same as for the pointer assignment: a rplaca operation on one binary tree can alter the value of another without mentioning it explicitly. For example, suppose that x and y are identifiers associated with binary-tree locations α and β, respectively, in the following configuration:

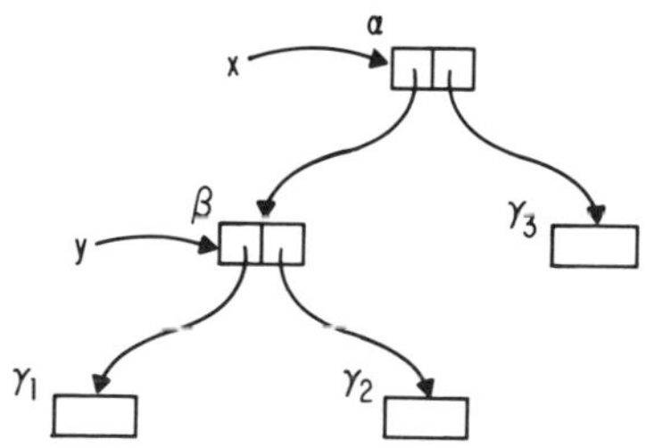

Figure 2.5

If we execute the rplaca operation left(y) ← t, we obtain the configuration

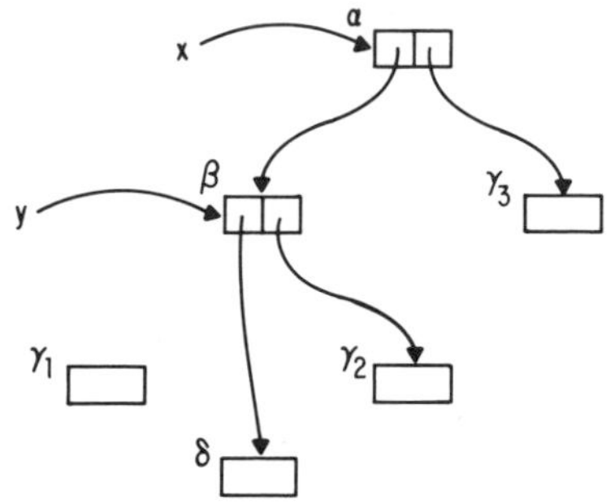

Figure 2.6

where δ is the location yielded by the evaluation of t. Note that the subsequent evaluation of the expression left(left(x)) yields the location δ, not the location γ_1. In other words, the value of x may have been changed by the rplaca operation, even though the operation was applied to y, not to x. Similarly, if α had any other ancestors before the execution of the rplaca, then their values could also have been affected by the operation. It seems that to model the effects of such an assignment completely, we must know all of the ancestors of the altered location.

Many languages admit a more general form of tree structure called a *record,* in which a *record location* can store several other locations. Binary trees can then be regarded as a special type of record. The same problems that arise with trees clearly apply to records as well.

The *assign/contents* formalization of arrays has been extended to apply to tree and record structures by Wegbreit et al. [1972], Cartwright et al. [1978], and Kowaltowski [1979]. Burstall represents the operations that alter tree and record structures by introducing new functions to access the structures. For example, an rplaca operation is said to create a new access function left', which behaves like the left function after the execution of the assignment.

F. Expressiveness of Specifications

Many of the difficulties that prevent us from describing the behavior of individual programming constructs with the Floyd/Hoare approach also obstruct our efforts to express the specifications that describe the desired behavior of entire programs. The only mechanism for forming specifications in that approach is the pair of input and output assertions. We have already encountered one weakness in the expressive power of such assertions: there is no way to refer to an identifier without mentioning it explicitly. For example, we were unable to deal with an assertion such as

"there exists an identifier whose value is 2"

in which we refer to an identifier indirectly.

Such limitations restricted our ability to describe an assignment statement; they also restrict our ability to specify an entire program. For example, suppose we wish to state that a given procedure will behave properly if initially two of its input parameters x and y are not aliases of each other, i.e., they are not bound to the same location.

A natural approach might be to introduce the condition

not(alias(x,y))

as part of the program's input assertions, and to describe the relation alias(x,y) by axioms or rules of inference.

However, this relation cannot be expressed in an assertion because x and y are meant to refer to locations, not values. Thus, the relation will violate even the simple assignment axioms; e.g., the instance of the Hoare axiom

$$\{alias(x,y)\}\ z \leftarrow y\ \{alias(x,z)\}$$

is false: if x and y are aliases, then assigning the value of y to z will not cause x and z to become aliases.

This shortcoming foils a plausible approach to retaining the Hoare formalism by forbidding aliasing to occur in situations where it can lead to trouble. We certainly forbid such occurrences, but we cannot express the condition we want to forbid as a Hoare assertion.

Another awkwardness in the Floyd/Hoare assertion mechanism as a specification device is its inability to refer to more than one state in a single assertion. Thus, it is impossible in an output assertion to refer directly to the initial or intermediate value of an identifier. For example, suppose we want to say that a program reverses the values of two identifiers x and y. The traditional approach is to introduce a "ghost" input assertion

$$\{x=x_0 \text{ and } y=y_0\}$$

at the beginning of the program, so that at the end we can assert that

$$\{x=y_0 \text{ and } y=x_0\}.$$

The purpose of the input assertion is merely to give names to the initial values of x and y. We must be careful, of course, that x_0 and y_0 are new identifiers that do not occur in the program.

The flaw in this solution is apparent if we attempt to use the above program not in isolation but as a segment of a larger program or as the body of a procedure. In this case, we would normally have to prove that the initial assertion

$$\{x=x_0 \text{ and } y=y_0\}$$

is true when control enters the segment; but this is impossible, because x_0 and y_0 are new symbols that cannot occur earlier in the program.

G. Procedures

We have already seen that procedure calls can cause aliasing to occur, which obstructs attempts to axiomatize the assignment statement; we have also seen how global side effects of procedure calls foil the assignment statement axiomatization. Many other problems arise in describing the procedure call mechanism itself. Let us consider only one of these difficulties: expressing how global identifiers of procedures are treated in languages with static binding.

A *global identifier* of a procedure is one that occurs in the procedure's body but that is not one of its parameters. For example, consider the procedure f(x) declared by

$$f(x) <= x \leftarrow x+y.$$

Here, y is a global identifier of f, but x is not.

In a language with *static binding,* such as PASCAL or the ALGOL dialects, the binding of y that would be used in evaluating the procedure is the binding that y had when the procedure was declared. In a language with *dynamic binding,* such as LISP, on the other hand, the binding used would be the one that y had when the procedure was called.

Static binding is difficult to treat by a Hoare rule for a procedure call because it requires that we refer to the binding the global identifier y had in a much earlier state, when the procedure f was first declared. In the meantime, of course, y may have been redeclared.

* * * * *

It is our intention that the situational-calculus approach constitute a single conceptual framework capable of describing all of these problematic programming-language features. This framework is compatible with contemporary theorem-proving techniques, and can be incorporated into systems for the synthesis, verification, and transformation of computer programs.

References

Burstall [1969]
R.M. Burstall, "Formal description of program structure and semantics in first order logic," in *Machine Intelligence* 5, B. Meltzer and D. Michie (eds.), Edinburgh University Press, Edinburgh (1969), pp. 79–98.

Cartwright and Oppen [1978]
R. Cartwright and D. Oppen, "Unrestricted procedure calls in Hoare's logic," *Proc. of the Fifth Annual ACM Symposium on Principles of Programming Languages,* Tucson, AZ (Jan. 1978), pp. 131–140.

Clarke [1977]
E.M. Clarke, Jr., "Programming language constructs for which it is impossible to obtain 'good' Hoare-like axiom systems," *Proc. of the Fourth ACM Symp. on Principles of Programming Languages,* Los Angeles, CA (Jan. 1977), pp. 10–20.

DeMillo *et al.* [1977]
R.A. DeMillo, R.J. Lipton and A.J. Perlis, "Social processes and proofs of theorems and programs," in the *Proc. of the Fourth ACM Symp. on Principles of Programming Languages,* Los Angeles, CA (Jan. 1977), pp. 206–214.

Floyd [1967]
R.W. Floyd, "Assigning meanings to programs," in the *Proc. of the Symp. on Applied Mathematics,* Vol. 19, J.T. Schwartz (ed.), Providence, RI (1967), pp. 19–32.

Gordon *et al.* [1979]
M. Gordon, R. Milner and C. Wadsworth, "Edinburgh LCF," *Lecture Notes in Computer Science,* Springer Verlag, Berlin (1979).

Green [1969]
C. Green, "Application of theorem proving to problem solving," in the *Proc. of the International Joint Conf. on Artificial Intelligence,* Washington, D.C. (May 1969), pp. 219–239.

Hoare [1969]
C.A.R. Hoare, "An axiomatic basis for computer programming," *CACM,* Vol. 12, No. 10 (1969), pp. 576–580.

Hoare [1975]
C.A.R. Hoare, "Recursive data structures," *Intl. Jour. of Computer and Information Sciences,* Vol. 4, No. 2 (June 1975).

Knuth [1974]
D.E. Knuth, "Structured programming with 'go to' statements," *Computing Surveys,* Vol. 6, No. 4 (Dec. 1974), pp. 261–301.

Kowaltowski [1979]
T. Kowaltowski, "Data structures and correctness of programs," *JACM,* Vol. 26, No. 2 (April 1979), pp. 283–301.

London *et al.* [1978]
R.L. London, J.V. Guttag, J.J. Horning, B.W. Lampson, J.G. Mitchell, G.J. Popek, "Proof rules for the programming language Euclid," *Acta Informatica,* Vol. 10, No. 1 (1978), pp. 1–26.

Manna and Waldinger [1980]
Z. Manna and R. Waldinger, "A deductive approach to program synthesis," *ACM Transactions on Programming Languages and Systems,* Vol. 2, No. 1 (Jan. 1980), pp. 90–121.

Manna and Waldinger [1981]
Z. Manna and R. Waldinger, "Problematic features of programming languages: A situational-calculus approach," *Acta Informatica,* Vol. 16 (1981), pp. 371–426.

McCarthy [1962]
J. McCarthy, "Towards a mathematical science of computation," in *Information Processing, Proc. of IFIP Congress,* C.M. Popplewell (ed.), North-Holland, Amsterdam (1962), pp. 21–28.

McCarthy [1964]
J. McCarthy, "A formal description of a subset of ALGOL," Report (AIM–24), Stanford University, Stanford, CA. (Sept. 1964).

Poupon and Wegbreit [1972]
J. Poupon and B. Wegbreit, "Covering functions," Report, Center for Research in Computing Technology, Harvard University, Cambridge, MA. (1972).

CHAPTER 6

An Interactive Tool For Program Manipulation

Anne Adam
Maitre-Assistante at the University of Caen
14032 Caen cedex FRANCE
G.R. 22 of C.N.R.S.

Paul Gloess
International Fellow at Stanford Research Institute
333 Ravenswood Ave., Menlo Park
California 94025, U.S.A.

Jean-Pierre Laurent
Professor at the University of Chambery
B.P. M04 73011 Chambery, FRANCE

Abstract

An interactive system for understanding programs has been designed. This system provides information about control structure and data flow. It also performs powerful semantic transformations that are checked for validity. The system relies on previously implemented algorithms that apply to a graph representation of programs.

A. Introduction

A practical system, LAURA, has been previously implemented by A. Adam and J.P. Laurent [1980] and is used at the University of Caen to debug student programs by comparing them with a program model. LAURA relies on a theoretical work about graphs by A. Adam and J.P. Laurent [1978] and on related algorithms.

We now intend to use these existing algorithms with a different purpose. The system we present in this paper can be used interactively to understand the meaning of a program. Possible applications are debugging, maintenance and improvement of readability.

The system provides information about control structure and data flow. It can also apply powerful transformations to modify the control structure and sometimes extract formulae that express the program's meaning.

Since the system deals with a graph representation of programs which is independent of the source language, it is not concerned with such syntactic transformations as those performed by some program editors or manipulators. It is entirely devoted to powerful semantic transformations. It is also able to check their validity before applying them.

Understanding is a very subjective notion. Hence it is essential to have an interactive system. It is also necessary to have a flexible and well-suited command language, the main features of which are described in this paper.

Special commands allow the user to insert comments, or restore a previous state. They are not described here but the reader should keep their existence in mind to better understand the usefulness of our tool.

B. Example: Discovering the Meaning of a Program

Consider the program that is represented in Fig. 1

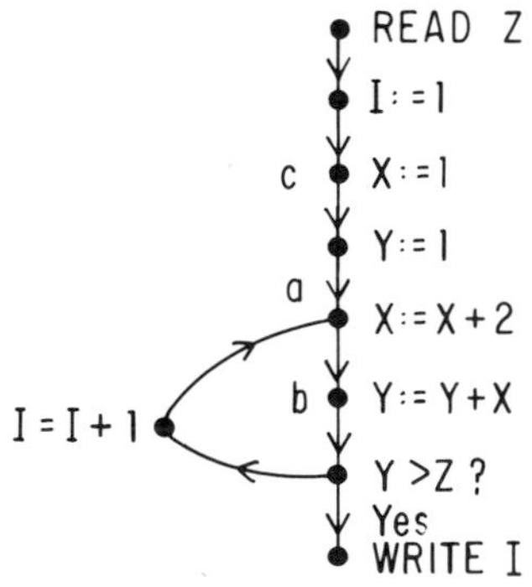

FIGURE 1: The initial program

To understand this program, we may use the following commands:

!RECUR a———→ a becomes X = 1 + 2 * I (1)

!SUBSTX b———→ b becomes Y = Y + 1 + 2 * I (2)

!REMOVE a———→ a is removed (3)

!REMOVE c———→ c is removed (4)

Comments:

command (1): The system solves the recurrence equation X(j) = X(j−1) + 2 with j varying from 1 to I and with X(0) = 1. The result is X(I) = 1 + 2 * I.

command (2): The system finds that the value of X used in b is 1 + 2 * I, and that it may replace X by 1 + 2 * I in Y = Y + X without changing the meaning of the program. It does so.

commands (3) and (4): The system may remove the definitions of X since this variable is no more used.

After execution of these first commands we obtain the graph of Fig. 2

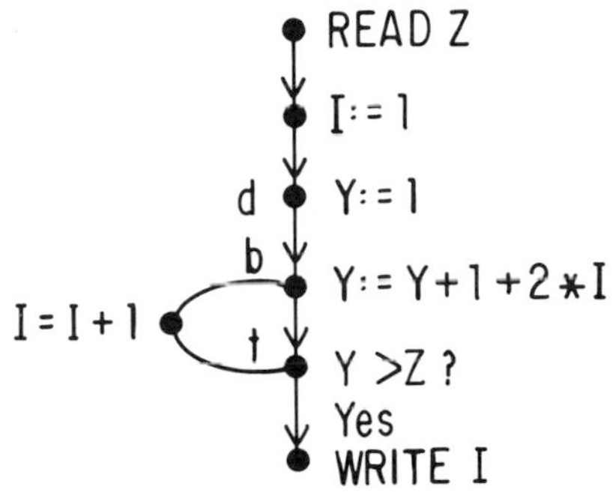

FIGURE 2: After the commands (1), (2), (3) and (4)

It is now possible to ask the system to deal with the variable Y. For that purpose we may use the two commands:

!RECUR b———→ b becomes Y=(1+I)**2 (5)

!SUBST Y d t———→ Illegal substitution of d for Y. Try b. (6)

!SUBST Y b t———→ t becomes (1 + I)**2 > Z (7)

Comments:

command (5): The system solves the recurrence equation Y(j) = Y(j−1) + 1 + 2*(j−1) with j varying from 1 to I and Y(0) = 1. The result is Y(I) = (1 + I)**2.

command (6): The system does not perform the substitution and issues a diagnostic, because the definition d of Y is no longer valid in t since Y as been redefined in b. The system suggests using definition b.

command (7): The system replaces Y in the final test t by its value (1 + I)**2. ("! SUBST Y*t" would have had the same effect).

Then, considering the resulting program in Fig. 3, it is easy to understand that the final value of I is SQRT(Z).

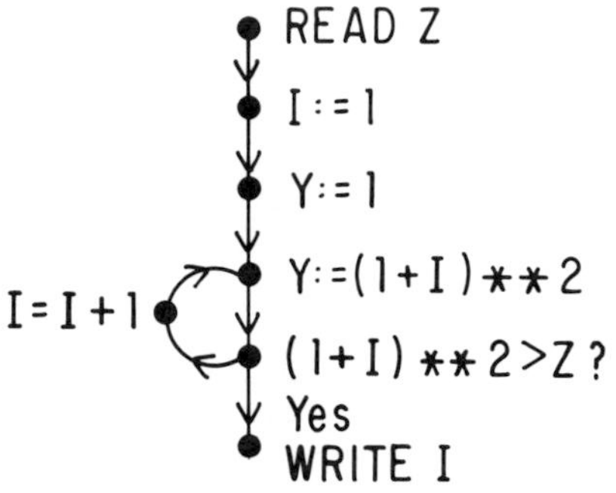

FIGURE 3: The resulting program

It should be emphasized that the meaning of the program, although it was a short one, was not obvious at all from the outset. However, the meaning was easily discovered by issuing a few commands.

In larger programs, other commands, that deal more specifically with the control structure, will be useful to break the complexity.

C. Control Structure Tools

Loops and ovals[1] are subgraphs of great practical interest in a program. Even from the graph representation, they are often difficult to see. Our system is able to find them. It can also modify the structure of loops and move ovals[2].

C.1 Finding and Altering Loops

First, the user can obtain the list of loops containing a node a (see Fig. 4). Loops are numbered for further reference: "(a,n)" will designate the nth loop of the list.

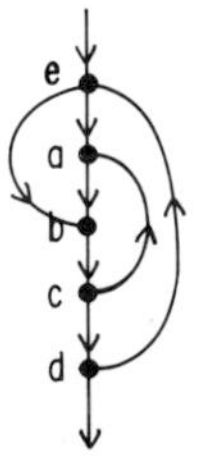

The command ?LOOPS a returns :

1 (a,b,c)
2 (e,a,b,c,d)

FIGURE 4: The ?LOOPS command

1 Intuitively, an oval (a "fuseau" in French) is a piece of program with only one entry point and only one exit point. It is not just a simple succession of assignments. It may have a complex structure since the whole program itself is an oval.

2 Some commands provide information about the program without modifying it: their name starts with "?". The other ones may modify the program: they start with "!".

Note that the system has to look for subgraphs that correspond to the classical programming notion of loops, and not only for simple circuits. According to our system a loop is a union of circuits with same entry and exit nodes (see Fig. 5).

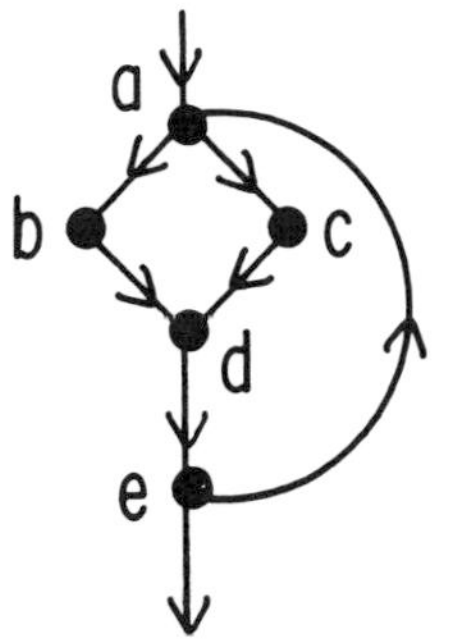

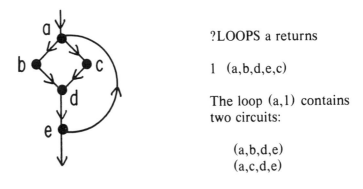

?LOOPS a returns

1 (a,b,d,e,c)

The loop (a,1) contains two circuits:

(a,b,d,e)
(a,c,d,e)

FIGURE 5: A loop is a union of circuits

One can also obtain the entry nodes and the exit nodes of a loop. For example, with the graph of Fig. 4, ?ENTRY (a,1) returns a and b; ?ENTRY (a,2) returns e. ?EXIT (a,1) returns c; ?EXIT (a,2) returns d.

In a programming language with GOTO statements, the loops often have arbitrary structures. For understanding, it is useful to standardize the structure of loops. By splitting some nodes, the system can reduce the number of entry points of a loop. It can also standardize the structure according to the user's preference.

The command !ONE-ENTRY-LOOP (a,n) returns a loop with only one entry node. It is useful for separating intermixed loops. For example the graph of Fig. 4 may be transformed into that of Fig. 6. In this graph, the loop (a,b,c) now has one entry point, which makes the structure more obvious.

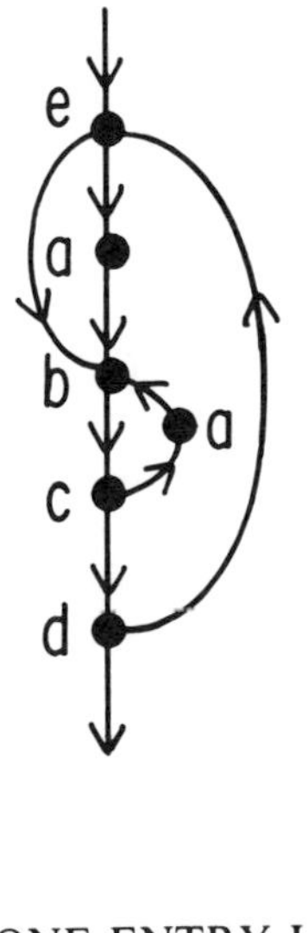

FIGURE 6: The ONE-ENTRY-LOOP command

The command !WHILE-LOOP (a,n) returns a loop in which the entry point is also an exit point. The command !DO-LOOP (a,n) returns a loop in which an exit point is directly connected to the entry point by one arc. After execution of one of these commands, the system can generate a WHILE statement (resp. a DO statement) corresponding to the new loop.

C.2 Finding and Moving Ovals

The user may ask the system if the paths between r and f constitute an oval. If it is the case, the command ?OVAL (r,f) returns the nodes of this oval. Otherwise it returns the empty set.

For example, with the graph of Fig. 4, ?OVAL (e,d) returns {e,a,b,c,d}. ?OVAL (a,c) returns { } since the subgraph defined by {a,b,c} has two entry nodes, a and b.

Ovals are interesting by themselves: they can be studied independently from the rest of the graph. Also, in an oval, one can distinguish internal variables from external variables and build the two sets of external variables that are defined or used in the oval. To deal with the data flow of the whole program, one can consider the oval as a simple node, associated with these two sets.

Another interesting question about ovals is their permutability[3]: there is an appropriate command, ?PERMUT(r_1,f_1) (r_2,f_2), which returns TRUE if ovals (r_1,f_1) and (r_2,f_2) are permutable, FALSE otherwise. The command !PERMUT would effectively perform the permutation whenever possible.

Powerful tools defined in our paper [1978] can check the permutability of any two ovals of the graph. In practice, the PERMUT command will often be applied to a pair such as (a,b) and (b,c) (see Fig. 7).

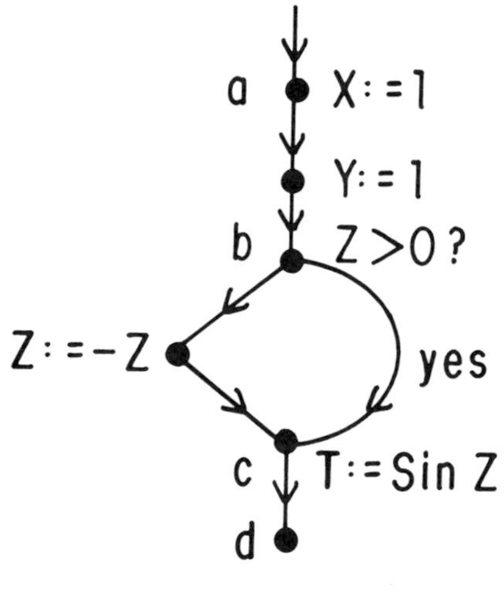

?PERMUT (a,b) (b,c) returns TRUE as it is equivalent to set X and Y to 1 either before dealing with Z and T or after.

FIGURE 7: The ?PERMUT command

Moving ovals is often of great help for understanding. In addition to the permutations, the system can also check and perform transformations that extract an oval from a loop or separate one loop into two loops. The command ?OUT-OF-LOOP (a,n) (r,f) returns TRUE if the oval (r,f) which is inside of the loop (a,n) may be moved before this loop (see Fig. 8). Otherwise, it returns FALSE. The command !OUT-OF-LOOP would effectively perform the movement whenever possible. The command ?DIVIDE-LOOP (a,n) (r,f) returns TRUE if it is possible to separate the loop (a,n) into two loops, one of which has (r,f) for body, the other one computing the rest of (a,n). Otherwise, it returns FALSE. The command !DIVIDE-LOOP would perform this separation whenever possible (see Fig. 9).

---

3 Two ovals are said to be permutable (or interchangeable) if the resulting program would produce the same outputs as the current one.

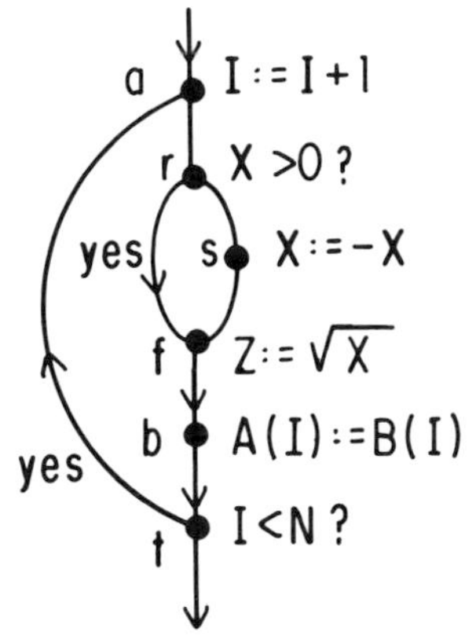

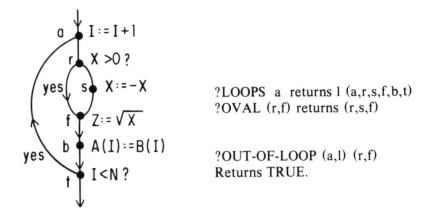

?LOOPS a returns l (a,r,s,f,b,t)
?OVAL (r,f) returns (r,s,f)

?OUT-OF-LOOP (a,l) (r,f)
Returns TRUE.

FIGURE 8: The OUT-OF-LOOP command

Given: !DIVIDE-LOOP (a,l) (r,r) builds:

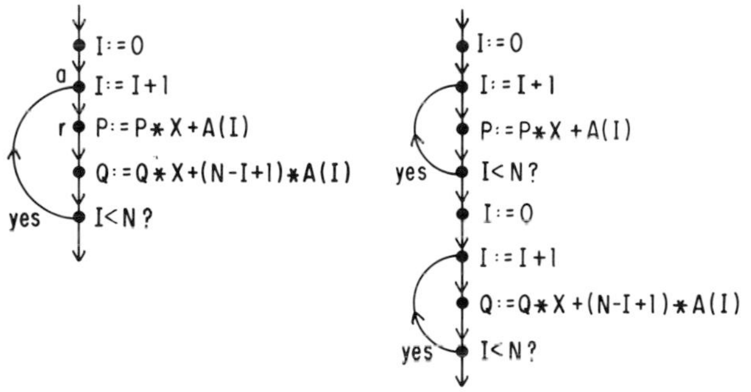

FIGURE 9: The DIVIDE-LOOP command

The two resulting loops may be transformed afterwards into two formulae, using the RECUR command described below.

D. Data Flow

A variable X may be defined at different nodes, for instance by READ X at one node and by X=Y+Z at another one. It is used by nodes such as WRITE X, or Y=X+1. X may eventually be used and redefined in the same node, e.g., X=X+Y.

Studying the various definitions of a variable, as well as the range of each definition, is essential to understanding the meaning(s) of the variable. Graph representation of the control structure is very convenient for dealing with this kind of problem.

D.1 Definition and Range of a Variable

The system can provide information on variable V by execution of the following commands:

?ALL-DEF V: returns the list of all definition nodes of variable V.

?RANGE V a: if a defines V, returns the set of nodes that may use the value of V defined by a. (Note that if this set is empty, a can be deleted using !REMOVE a).

?DEFS V a: returns those definitions of V whose values may be used in a.

An example of utilization of these commands is given in Fig. 10.

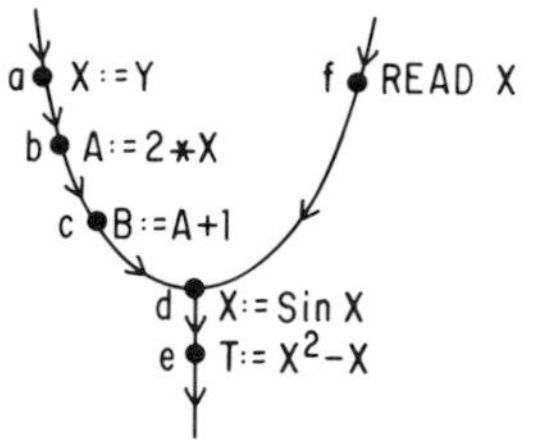

?ALL-DEF X returns (a,f,d)
?RANGE X a returns (b,c,d)
(Note that X does not appear in c,
but A, which depends on X, is used in c)
?DEFS X d returns (a,f)
?DEFS X e returns (d)

(Note that a is not returned, since
X is redefined between a and e)

FIGURE 10: Definition and range of a variable

D.2 Renaming Variables

Let X be a variable and $d_1, \ldots, d_n$ the nodes at which X is defined. By studying the range of each d_i, it is sometimes possible to find out that the same name has been used at different locations of the program for quite different purposes.

An efficient algorithm called "separation" allows renaming of the variable X according to its different meanings, provided that they do not interfere. It is used by the system to execute the command !SEPAR X which, for example, transforms the graph of Fig. 10 into the graph of Fig. 11.

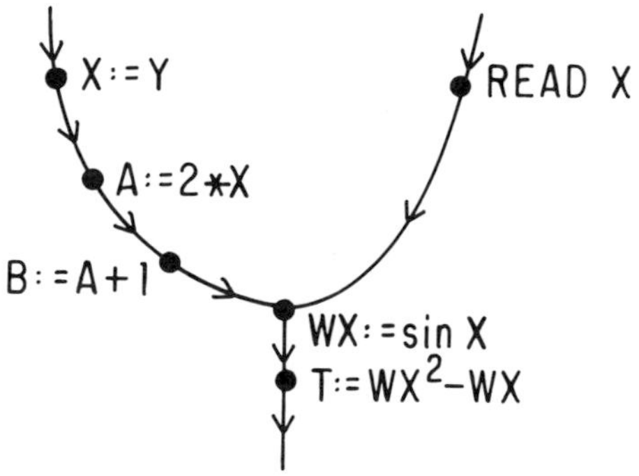

FIGURE 11: Graph 10 after execution of !SEPAR X

The renaming of variables increases the readability of a program and may also help pinpoint a bug.

D.3 Substitutions

Replacing occurrences of a variable by its definition often facilitates understanding. The system can determine whether a substitution is possible or not, and execute the following commands:

!SUBST V d u: substitutes definition d for each occurrence of variable V in node u if possible (for example, in Fig. 11 one can substitute Y to X in b, producing A:=2*Y, but it is not possible to change d into WX:=sin Y).

!SUBST V d *: definition d is substituted for variable V wherever possible. The set of altered nodes is returned.

!SUBST V * u: looks for a definition d such that !SUBST V d u may be performed. If d exists, the substitution is performed.

!SUBST * * u: executes !SUBST V * u for each variable V used in u.

!SUBST * * *: all possible substitutions in the program are performed. The set of altered nodes is returned.

The system may simplify arithmetic expressions, which is often useful after a substitution.

Substitutions may exhibit the meaning of a sequence of computations. This is illustrated by the example of Fig. 12.

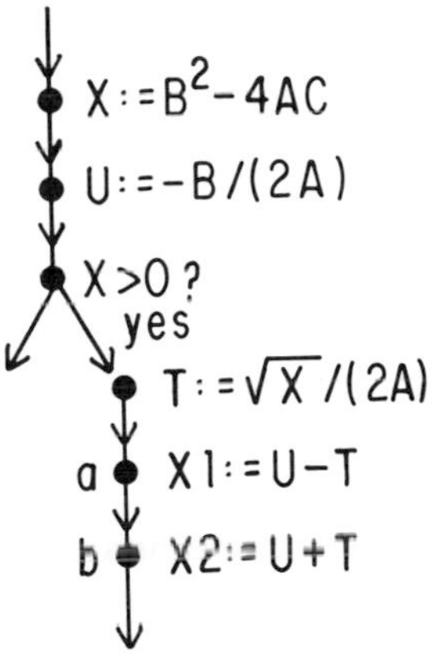

By !SUBST * * a
and !SUBST * * b,
a becomes X1=-B/(2A)-$\sqrt{B**2-4AC/(2A)}$

b becomes X2=-B/(2A)+$\sqrt{B**2-4AC/(2A)}$

which are well-known formulae.

FIGURE 12: The SUBST command

E. Formulae Extraction by Solving Recurrence Equations

As shown by the example above, substitutions of definitions for variables enable the system to extract formulae, thus rendering the program's meaning more obvious.

Another powerful way of extracting formulae is to solve the recurrence equations which appear inside of a loop. (Our introductory example is an illustration of this principle.) This is possible when they are linear and of the first order. Consider the general form given in Fig. 13.

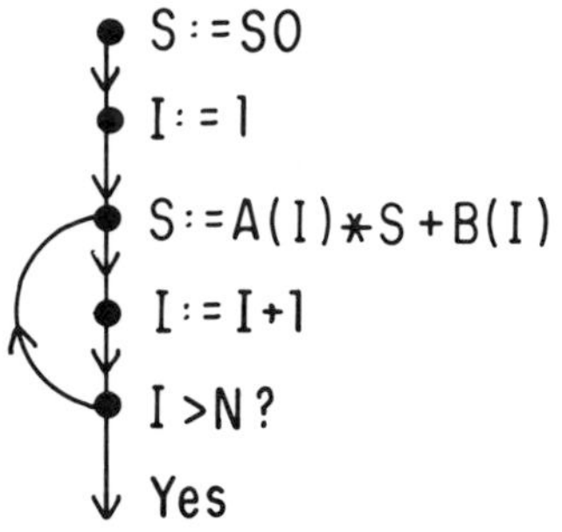

FIGURE 13: The linear recurrence equation of the first order

The resolution of the recurrence equation S(I):=A(I)*S(I−1)+B(I) gives S:=f(N) where:

$$f(N) := SO + \prod_{j=1}^{n} A(j) + \sum_{j=1}^{n-1} (B(j) * \prod_{k=j+1}^{n} A(k)) + B(N)$$

A special command, !RECUR e, looks for the innermost loop containing e, and if there is in e a recurrence equation that is linear and of the first order, solves it. Two cases may then occur:

– if the loop has the general form of Fig. 13, the loop is replaced by the assignment S:=f(N). Two examples of such extractions of formulae are given in Fig. 14.

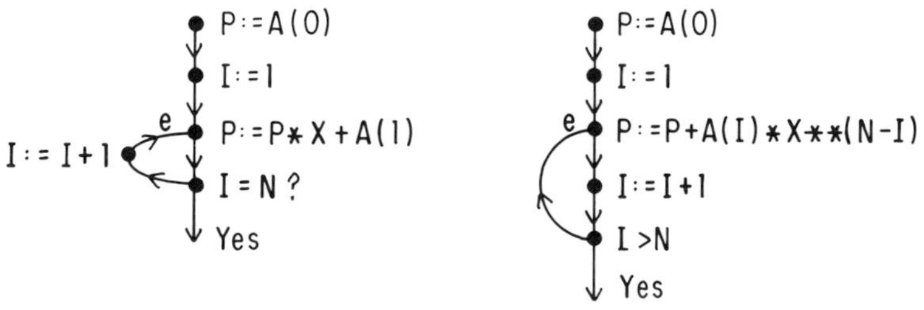

FIGURE 14: Solving recurrent equations

In both cases the command !RECUR a returns:

$$P := \prod_{I=0}^{n} A(I) * X ** (N-I)$$

— if the loop has a more complex form (for instance the exit test is not a comparison between the index and one integer value), the node a is replaced inside of the loop by the assignment S:=f(I). The introductory example demonstrates the powerfulness of this particular transformation.

Conclusion

Text editors that deal with character strings only are widely used to type and modify programs but they cannot help understanding them. More specific systems such as the INTERLISP analyzer MASTERCOPE (e.g. W. Teitelman and Kaplan [1978]) or the program manipulator MENTOR (e.g. V. Donzeau-Gouge et al. [1979]) have some knowledge of the programming language syntax. MENTOR in particular is able to perform complex syntactic transformations, which may be a step towards understanding.

However, a specific system for understanding programs must have some semantic knowledge of the programming language. This is the case for our system which uses graph and data flow transformations that preserve the outputs. It is actually a tool for discovering the meaning of a program.

Interestingly, most of the transformations performed by our system are deoptimizing transformations. This is quite natural since the most optimized programs are generally the most difficult to understand. Understanding and optimization are opposite goals. It is then difficult to compare our system with those which transform programs in order to optimize them, such as the Burstall and Darlington [1978] system.

Our system may be used to debug a program, by checking whether sequences agree with their comments. It may be used to increase readability by adding meaningful comments. In particular, it could also be an efficient tool for maintaining programs: maintenance often requires understanding somebody else's procedures, which is always hard. It also requires modifying specific parts of a program without introducing bugs anywhere else. The ability of our system to locate ovals and to provide information about their external variables may be very helpful for that.

We now intend to realize the system and experiment with it in order to define good strategies for users.

References

Adam and Laurent [1978]
A. Adam and J.P. Laurent, "Decomposition complete d'un graphe en fuseaux. Application au graphe d'un programme," Annexe aux Theses des Auteurs, PARIS VI (November 1978).

Adam and Laurent [1980]
A. Adam and J.P. Laurent, "LAURA: a system to debug programs," *Artificial Intelligence Journal,* Vol. 14 (1980).

Allen and Cocke [1975]
F.E. Allen and J. Cocke, "A program data flow analysis procedure," IBM Research Report RC 5257 (February 1975).

Bidoit *et al.* [1979]
M. Bidoit, C. Gresse and G. Guiho, "A system which synthesizes array-manipulating programs from specifications," *IJCAI 79.*

Boyer *et al.* [1975]
R.S. Boyer, B. Elspas and K. Levitt, "SELECT: a formal system for testing and debugging programs by symbolic execution," International Conf. on Reliable Software, *ACM* (1975), pp. 234–245.

Burstall and Darlington [1978]
R.M. Burstall and J.A. Darlington, "A system which automatically improves programs," Acta Informatica (1978).

Cheatham *et al.* [1979]
T.E. Cheatham, Jr., G.H. Holloway and J.A. Townley, "Symbolic evaluation and the analysis of programs," *IEEE Trans. on Software Engineering,* Vol. SE5 n° (July 1979).

Donzeau-Gouge *et al.* [1979]
V. Donzeau-Gouge, G. Huet, G. Kahn and B. Lang, "Mentor program manipulation system," Technical Report, IRIA Laboria (August 1979).

Gerhart [1975]
S.L. Gerhart, "Knowledge about programs. A model and case study," IEEE Conf. on Reliable Software (1975).

Hecht and Ullman [1975]
M.S. Hecht and J.D. Ullman, "A simple algorithm for global data flow analysis problems," *SIAM J. Computing* 4(December 1975), pp. 519–532.

King [1976]
J.C. King, "Symbolic execution and program testing," *CACM,* Vol. 19 (July 1976), n° 7.

Loveman [1977]
D. Loveman, "Program improvement by source to source transformation," *JACM,* Vol. 24 n° 1(January 1977).

Rosen [1975]
B.K. Rosen, "Data flow analysis for recursive PL/I programs," IBM Res. Report RC 5211 (January 1975).

Rosen [1976]
B.K. Rosen, "Data flow analysis for procedural programs," IBM Res. Report RC 5948 (April 1976).

Osterweil and Fosdick [1976]
L.J. Osterweil and L.D. Fosdick, "DAVE: a validation error detection and documentation system for FORTRAN programs," *Software, Practice and Experience* 6(1976).

Rich *et al.* [1979]
C. Rich, H. Shrobe and R. Waters, "Overview of the programmer's apprentice," IJCAI (1979).

Ruth [1976]
G.R. Ruth, "Intelligent program analysis," *Artificial Intelligence,* Vol. 7 n° 1(1976).

Standish *et al.* [1976]
T.A. Standish, D.C. Harriman, D.F. Kibler and J.M. Neighbors, *The Irvine Program Transformation Catalogue,* Dept. of Information and Computer Sciences, University of CA, Irvine (1976).

Tarjan [1972]
R.E. Tarjan, "Depth-first search and linear graph algorithms," *SIAM Journal Computing* (June 1972), pp. 146–160.

Teitelman and Kaplan [1978]
W. Teitelman and R.M. Kaplan, "INTERLISP Reference Manual, section 20: MASTERCOPE," Technical Report, Xerox Palo Alto Research Center (1978).

Waters [1978]
R.C. Waters, "Automatic analysis of the logical structure of programs," MIT Report TR–492 (December 1978).

Wertz [1978]
H. Wertz, "Un systeme de comprehension, d'amelioration et de correction de programmes incorrects," These de 3[eme] cycle PARIS VI (1978).

SECTION III

APPROACHES USING ABSTRACT DATA TYPES

CHAPTER 7

The Design of Efficient Data Representations

John Darlington
Department of Computing
Imperial College, London

A. Introduction

It is a recognized programming discipline to first approach a task at the appropriate level employing high level data types and then to design appropriate structures that will represent these data types efficiently. For example, priority queues can be efficiently implemented as binomial trees, Vuillemin (1976), or trees as vectors, Floyd (1964). In this chapter we would like to show how consideration of the computations being performed at the higher level can assist in the design of suitable data representations and propose a method whereby an automatic programming system could conceivably invent efficient representations for itself. However we must stress that the ideas presented are very preliminary and we are not intending to incorporate them in any of our experimental program development systems, Darlington [Darlington 1978].

We will use an applicative language, NPL, Burstall [1977], to write our programs and an equational method for defining our data types (Liskov [1975] and Guttag [1977]). The manipulations that we will perform on these programs and data type definitions in order to design efficient representations will be based on the formal system outlined in Burstall and Darlington [1977]. However readers not familiar with that work can regard the manipulations as simple equality replacements.

In section B we outline our method of designing data representations and give a simple example of its application. This method relies on being able to decompose a given function into two or more simpler functions and we describe some techniques for achieving this in section C. In section D we present two examples of representation design, namely the design of the vector of booleans representation for sets of integers and the invention of search trees from consideration of binary search on ordered arrays. Finally, in section E we discuss some possible enhancements to this method.

B. The Origin of Representations

The purpose of a representation is to facilitate some computation. In particular representations are often designed to enable a particular high level operation to be performed efficiently. Thus if we have some high level data type D1 and a high level operation f say mapping D1 to D2

$$D1 \xrightarrow{\ f\ } D2$$

the purpose of a representation for D1 in another domain Dconc may be to facilitate f. It can do this by storing some of the computation of f in a structure in Dconc so that its recomputation can be made more easily. This is equivalent to saying that there is a function rep that encodes some of the computation of f into a data structure in Dconc and a function fconc that takes this encoding and completes the rest of the computation of f, thus

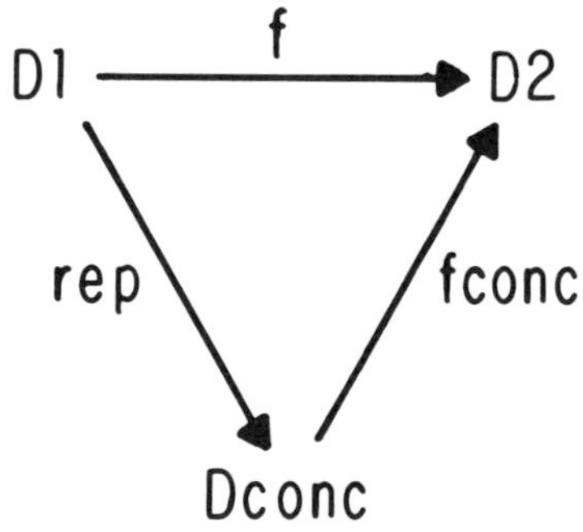

fconc(rep(d1)) = f(d1) for d1 in D1

(In work on the verification or synthesis of implementations, Hoare [1969], Darlington [1979], it is traditional to have the representation function going from the concrete domain Dconc to the abstract D1. This is to keep rep functional as usually many concrete data structures may represent one abstract structure. We have chosen to have rep going the other way purely for manipulative convenience.)

Often D2 will be an abstract domain, often D1 itself. In this case we have the following picture and equation

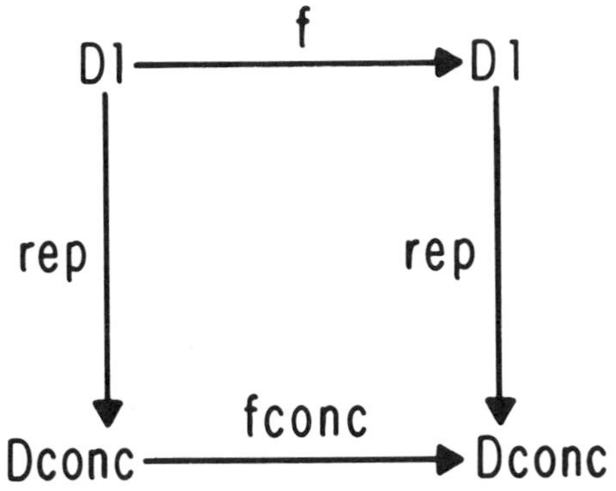

$$fconc(rep(d1)) = rep(f(d1))$$

This is the basis for our method of designing data representations. We choose a higher level operation that we wish to implement efficiently and then attempt to divide its computation into two functions producing a representation function, rep, mapping the higher level data type into a lower level one and a lower level function, fconc, implementing the higher level function in this representation. If we choose our division so that fconc is simple to compute we will have designed an efficient representation for f.

Thus the invention of representations is a simple extension of the techniques used for the synthesis of representation, Darlington [1979]. There we were given two known functions f and rep and required to produce the third fconc. Here we are given just f and need to produce rep and fconc.

Of course having designed a representation on the basis of one high level operation we must check that this still enables any other desired high level operation to be performed. For example, given sets, to compute cardinality all we have to remember is an integer. This would enable us to compute isempty but not membership. Alternatively we may attempt to design a single representation for several abstract functions f1, f2, ... fn. To achieve this we have to split the computations of f1, f2,..., fn into a single common representation function rep and n concrete functions f1conc, f2conc,... fnconc such that

$$ficonc(rep(dl)) = fi(dl) \qquad 1 \leqslant i \leqslant n.$$

B.1 A Simple Example, the Invention of Ordered Lists From Unordered Lists.

To show our technique in action we will first use a very simple example. The reader is warned that two steps used are fairly unmotivated. Happily when we come to more substantial examples things become more mechanical and better motivated.

Our abstract data domain dl will be conventional lists of integers.

type lists

operations

nil: → list

cons: integer x list → list

hd: list → integer

tail: list → list

Axioms

hd(cons(n,l)) = n

tail(cons(n,l)) = l

(We will use the infix :: for cons, e.g. x::l≡cons(x,l))

Assume that we have the operations min and deletemin defined over these lists.

min(x::nil) <= x

min(x1::x2::l) <= x1 if min(x2::l) ⩾x1

min(x2::l) otherwise

deletemin(l) <=delete(min(l),l)

delete(x1,x2::l) <= l if x1 = x2

x2::delete(x1,l) otherwise

Assume that we have decided to stay within lists but we would like to have a representation that enabled us to compute min and deletemin more efficiently. Thus we need to synthesize functions rep, minconc and deleteminconc.

$$\text{rep: lists} \rightarrow \text{lists}$$

$$\text{minconc: lists} \rightarrow \text{integers}$$

$$\text{deleteminconc: lists} \rightarrow \text{lists}$$

such that,

$$\text{minconc}(\text{rep}(l)) = \text{min}(l)$$

and,

$$\text{deleteminconc}(\text{rep}(l)) = \text{rep}(\text{deletemin}(l))$$

Here we take our inventive step mentioned earlier. We are seeking functions for minconc and deleteminconc that are simple to compute. The simplest functions that are of the right type are hd and tail respectively. Let us see what happens if we try these for minconc and deleteminconc. Substituting in our equations we get,

$$\text{hd}(\text{rep}(l)) = \text{min}(l)$$
$$\text{tail}(\text{rep}(l)) = \text{rep}(\text{deletemin}(l))$$

Using the axiom that $l = \text{cons}(\text{hd}(l),\text{tail}(l))$ we can derive,

$$\text{rep}(l) = \text{cons}(\text{min}(l),\ \ \text{rep}(\text{deletemin}(l)))$$

and we can regard this as one equation defining a representation function that orders the list by performing a selection sort. This equation can be used when l has one element or more. To produce a base case we need to consider the case where l has only one element, thus we need rep such that

$$\text{hd}(\text{rep}(x::\text{nil})) = \text{min}(x::\text{nil})$$

and

$$\text{tail}(\text{rep}(x::\text{nil})) = \text{rep}(\text{deletemin}(x::\text{nil}))$$

Thus we have

hd(rep(x::nil)) = x

and

tail(rep(x::nil)) = rep(nil)

To make our recursion terminate we have to evaluate rep(nil). Given min and deletemin alone this is difficult as both min and deletemin are undefined for the empty list but it seems reasonable to take rep(nil) = nil. Thus we have our equations for rep.

```
rep(nil) <= nil
rep(x::nil) <= x::nil
rep(x1::x2::l)  <= min(x1::x2::l) ::rep(deletemin(x1::x2::l))
```

C. The Decomposition of Functions

In Burstall and Darlington [1977] we show how the composition of two recursively defined functions can often be merged to produce a single more efficient recursion. Here we have to reverse this process and decompose a single recursion into two functions.

C.1 Decomposing Functions Using Existing Functions

We will consider first an example where the decomposition is into "pre-existing" functions. Given the append of two lists defined thus

```
append:list x list → list

append(nil,Y) <= Y

append(x::X,Y) <= x::append(X,Y)
```

and,

```
g:list x list x list → list

g(nil,X,Y) <= append(X,Y)

g(x::X,Y,Z) <= x::g(X,Y,Z)
```

can we decompose g into an h and a k such that

$$h,k\text{: list x list} \rightarrow \text{list}$$

$$h(k(X,Y),Z) = g(X,Y,Z) \qquad (A)$$

Looking first at the recursion for the cons case we get

$$\begin{aligned} h(k(x::X,Y),Z) &= g(x::X,Y,Z) \text{ instantiating (A)} \\ &= x::g(X,Y,Z) \text{ unfolding g} \\ &= x::h(k(X,Y),Z) \text{ folding with (A)} \end{aligned}$$

We are attempting to produce a recursion for h. Looking at the right hand side of the last line above we see that it is of the same form as the right hand side of the main equation for append. Thus we are led to the hypothesis that h is similar to append. More precisely we can produce an equation for h

$$h(x::X,Y) = x::h(X,Y)$$

Using this equation to fold the right hand side of our equation we get

$$h(k(x::X,Y),Z) = h(x::k(X,Y),Z)$$

From this we can extract a recursion for k

$$k(x::X,Y) = x::k(X,Y)$$

(We have of course assumed that if $h(X1,Y) = h(X2,Y)$ then $X1=X2$. But this is true for the h we have chosen.)

We have finally to produce base cases for our recursion for h and k. We do this by first considering (A) when X is nil getting

$$\begin{aligned} h(k(nil,Y),Z) &= g(nil,Y,Z) \\ &= append(Y,Z) \qquad \text{(unfolding)} \end{aligned}$$

It seems reasonable to take

$$k(nil,Y) = Y$$

This gives us

$$h(Y,Z) = append(Y,Z)$$

which is stronger than we need. Letting Y be nil gets us

$$\begin{aligned} h(nil,Z) &= append(nil,Z) \\ &= Z \end{aligned}$$

which is enough.

Thus the equations we have developed for h and k are

$$h(nil,Y) = Y \qquad h(x::X,Y) = x::h(X,Y)$$

$$k(nil,Y) = Y \qquad k(x::X,Y) = x::k(X,Y)$$

and h and k are exactly append. This is not always the case as we shall see later even though we may use an already existing equation to base our new equation on the new function when fully defined may be different.

C.2 Decomposing Not Using Existing Equations

In the previous example we used an already existing equation as a guide in our development of new equations. In this section we demonstrate a development of this technique that can be used generally to create totally new functions.

Given

$$g\text{:list of integers} \rightarrow \text{integers}$$

$$g(nil) <= 0$$

$$g(n::X) <= 2n+g(X)$$

can we produce an h and a k such that

$$h(k(X)) = g(X) \qquad \text{(A)}$$

Looking at the main recursion first, we get

$$
\begin{aligned}
h(k(n::X)) &= g(n::X) \\
&= 2n+g(X) \\
&= 2n+h(k(X)) \quad \text{(Folding with (A))} \qquad \text{(B)}
\end{aligned}
$$

Our first step is to decide the intermediate data structure (representation). Information will be written into this structure by k (the representation function) and read out by h (the concrete function corresponding to g). For this example we will choose lists as the intermediate structure. Thus we have

$$k\text{:lists} \rightarrow \text{lists}$$

$$h\text{:lists} \rightarrow \text{integers}$$

Thus we have to rewrite (B) to make this intermediate list explicit. We do this by inserting subexpressions of the right hand side of (B) into a list structure and immediately reading them out again. Thus we rewrite B as,

$$
\begin{aligned}
h(k(n::X)) &= u+h(v) \\
&\quad \text{where } u::v == 2n::k(X)
\end{aligned}
$$

Now we can identify a subexpression on the left hand side with a subexpression on the right hand side getting

$$k(n::X) = 2n::k(X)$$

Returning to (B) we can unfold the left hand side using our new equation getting

$$h(2n::k(X)) = 2n+h(k(X))$$

Generalizing, we get

$$h(u::v) = 2u+h(v)$$

This technique of introducing an intermediary data structure by writing information into it and then immediately reading it out has been called anti-projection by Gerard Terrine in his related work on the invention of data representations, Terrine [1978]. The manipulations performed above are exactly the reverse of the manipulations performed in the more conventional transformation optimizing a composition of two functions to a single recursion. See Burstall and Darlington [1977]. There, projection axioms such as head(cons(u,v)) = u and tail(cons(u,v)) = v are used repeatedly. This connection with well known transformations provides strong heuristic guidance and helps to motivate some of the seemingly unmotivated steps above.

Finally, as always, we have the base cases to establish, thus we have

$$\begin{aligned} h(k(nil)) &= g(nil) \\ &= 0 \end{aligned}$$

We have complete freedom of choice but as k maps lists to lists it seems reasonable to set

$$k(nil) = nil$$

which determines that

$$h(nil) = 0$$

Thus our final equations are

$$\begin{aligned} k(nil) &= nil \\ k(n::X) &= 2n::k(X) \\ h(nil) &= 0 \\ h(n::X) &= n+h(X) \end{aligned}$$

The above manipulations are heavily heuristic in their application. However the equations produced, if they are adequate to define a function, are guaranteed to be correct according to their defining equation. Whether or not they will be useful is a question to be settled by efficiency considerations in the representation context.

D. Examples of Representation Design

D.1 Design of a Representation for Integer Sets

We will consider designing a representation for sets of integers. We are given the data type sets defined thus (following Guttag [1976]).

type sets

operations

empty:set → boolean
nilset: → set
has:set x integer → boolean
add:set x integer → set
remove:set x integer → set

Axioms

empty(nilset) = truc
empty(add(s,i)) = false
has(nilset,i)) = false
has(add(s,i1),i2) = if i1=i2 then true
else has(s,i2)

etc.

We also have the data type vector.

type vector

operations

emptyv: → vector
isemptyv:vector → boolean
assign:vector x integer x item → vector
read:vector x integer → item

Axioms

isemptyv(emptyv) = true
isemptyv(assign(v,in,it)) = false
read(emptyv,in) = error
read(assign(v,in1,it),in2) = if in1 = in2 then it (A)
else read(v,in2).

We will choose has to help us design a representation for sets. We therefore need to synthesize two functions hasconc and rep such that

hasconc(rep(s),i) = has(s,i) (B)

Thus if rep is of type:set → ?, hasconc is of type:? x integer → boolean. Looking first at the case add(s,i1) and expanding has we have

hasconc(rep(add(s,i1)),i2) = has(add(s,i1),i2)
= if i1=i2 then true
else has(s,i2)

Using equation (B) we can rewrite the right hand side getting

= if i1=i2
then true
else hasconc(rep(s),i2)

The computation of the right hand side has now to be split into two, one bit corresponding to hasconc and the other corresponding to rep. Looking at the right hand side above we can see it matches with the right hand side of equation (A) in the vector axioms. Thus we can take this as an equation for hasconc,

hasconc(assign(v,in1,it),in2) = if in1=in2 then it
else hasconc(v,in2)

and use this to fold the previous equation getting

hasconc(rep(add(s,i1)),i2) = hasconc(assign(rep(s),i1,true),i2)

From this we can extract a recursion for rep,

rep(add(s,i1)) = assign(rep(s),i1,true)

Thus rep:set → vector of booleans and hasconc:vector of booleans x integer → boolean and we have designed a representation for our sets of integers as a vector of booleans where the n'th element is true if the integer n is in the set, a traditional 'clever' representation for small sets of integers. Finally, we have to consider the base cases. Looking at the nilset case for equation (B) we get

hasconc(rep(nilset),i) = has(nilset,i)

= falsc

Guided by our recursions for hasconc and rep produced above it seems sensible to parcel this computation up as

rep(nilset) = emptyv
hasconc(emptyv,i) = false

Our final versions are

```
rep(nilset) = emptyv
rep(add(s,i)) = assign(rep(s),i,true)
hasconc(emptyv,i) = false
hasconc(assign(v,i1,it),i2) = if i1=i2
                              then it
                              else hasconc(v,i2)
```

The reader may justifiably complain that this is not quite the traditional representation for small integer sets. Usually the vector length is bounded by the largest integer to be included in the set and the vector contains false for those integers that are not in the set. We can achieve this by reconsidering the base case. We have

hasconc(rep(nilset),i) = false

for all $1 \leqslant i \leqslant n$ where n is the largest integer to be stored. Now if we retain the first equation derived for hasconc as the sole equation for hasconc we see that rep(nilset) must be the vector with false at every position, i.e., assign(...(assign(assign(emptyv,1,false),2,false),...),n,false)

D.2 Search Trees from Binary Search

In this section we will systematically develop the concept of search trees from consideration of a search operation on vectors. Vectors are as defined in C.1 and we define binary trees conventionally.

type tree

operations

niltree : → tree
nulltree : tree → boolean
constree : item x tree x tree → tree
valof : tree → item
lefttree : tree → tree
righttree : tree → tree

axioms

$$\text{nulltree}(\text{niltree}) = \text{true}$$
$$\text{nulltree}(\text{constree}(i,t_1,t_2)) = \text{false}$$
$$\text{valof}(\text{constree}(i,t_1,t_2)) = i$$
$$\text{lefttree}(\text{constree}(i,t_1,t_2)) = t_1$$
$$\text{righttree}(\text{constree}(i,t_1,t_2)) = t_2$$

For this example we assume that the items have some total order, >, defined over them and that our vectors are organized in ascending order. We start our 'invention' of search trees from consideration of an operation that performs a binary search for an item on such an ordered vector.

```
search : vector x item → boolean

search(vec,x) <= bs(vec,1,size(vec),x)

bs : vector x integer x integer x item → boolean

bs(vec,i,j,x) =

    if i > j
    then false
    else if read(vec,mid(i,j)) = x
    then true
    else if read(vec,mid(i,j)) > x
    then bs(vec,i,mid(i,j)-1,x)
    else bs(vec,mid(i,j)+1,j,x)

    mid : integer x integer → integer
    mid(i,j) = if i=j then i
```

$$\text{else} \frac{\lfloor i+j \rfloor}{2}$$

```
   size : vector → integer
   size (emptyv) = 0
   size(assign(v,i,it)) = i if i>size(v)
                          size (v) otherwise
```

where $\lfloor x \rfloor$ is the largest integer less than x.

(At the end of this section the reader may complain that in starting with binary search we already have a lot of the basic idea behind search trees. It would have been possible, though tedious, for us to have started with a search on an unordered vector, then developed ordered vectors and from this developed binary search on ordered vectors.)

We decide to develop a representation for search in trees. We therefore need to synthesize functions rep and treesearch such that

rep : vectors → trees
treesearch : trees x items → boolean
treesearch(rep(vec),x) = search(vec,x)

This equation immediately expands to

treesearch(rep(vec),x) = bs(vec,1,size(vec),x)

Accordingly, we generalize rep to a repl

repl : vector x integer x integer → trees

and let rep(vec) = repl(vec,1,size(vec)).

Thus our defining equation is

treesearch(repl(vec,i,j),x) = bs(vec,i,j,x) (A)

Working on the right hand side, expansion gets us

```
if i>j
then false
else if read(vec,mid(i,j)) = x
then true
else if read(vec,mid(i,j)) > x
then bs(vec,i,mid(i,j)-1,x)
else bs(vec,mid(i,j)+1,j,x)
```

Using equation (A) we can replace the calls to bs in the final two lines getting

```
if i>j
then false
else if read(vec,mid(i,j)) = x
then true
else if read(vec,mid(i,j)) > x
then treesearch(repl(vec,i,mid(i,j)−1),x)
else treesearch(repl(vec,mid(i,j)+1,j),x)
```

Following the strategy outlined earlier we have to make use of an anti-projection to make the intermediate data structure explicit. Here our intermediate data structure or representation is to be trees holding items at their nodes and having similar trees as their left and right subtrees. Looking at the right hand side of the above equation, we see that read(vec,mid(i,j)) is of type item and repl(vec,i,mid(i,j)-1) and repl(vec,mid(i,j)+1,j) are of type tree. Thus using the projections

$$\text{valof}(\text{constree}(n,t_1,t_2)) = n$$

$$\text{lefttree}(\text{constree}(n,t_1,t_2)) = t_1$$

$$\text{righttree}(\text{constree}(n,t_1,t_2)) = t_2$$

backwards, we rewrite the right hand side of the above equation getting

```
= if i>j
  then false
  else if valof(t) = x
  then true
  else if valof(t) > x
  then treesearch (lefttree(t),x)
  else treesearch(righttree(t),x)
  where t = constree(read,(vec,mid(i,j)),
                     repl(vec,i,mid(i,j)-1),
                     repl(vec,mid(i,j)+1,j))
```

For the base case, we see that when i>j we need

```
treesearch(repl(vec,i,j),x) = false
```

Again we have an arbitrary choice. But as repl maps onto trees, it is natural to choose

```
repl(vec,i,j) = niltree if i>j          and

treesearch(niltree,x) = false
```

Having made this choice the right hand side splits cleanly. The 'inner' portion up to the tree is associated with repl and the 'outer' portion with treesearch. Thus we get

```
repl(vec,i,j)

     = if i>j
    then niltree
    else constree(read(vec,mid(i,j)),
              repl(vec,i,mid(i,j)-1),
              repl(vec,mid(i,j)+1,j))

treesearch(t,x)

     = if nulltree(t)
      then false
      else if valof(t) = x
      then true
      else if valof(t) > x
      then treesearch(lefttree(t),x)
      else treesearch(righttree(t),x)
```

Thus our representation function organizes the vector into the traditional search tree, one with all items on the left subtree less than the root and all items on the right subtree greater than the root.

E. Future Developments

Wirsing et al. [1979] stresses the importance of various algebraic models for equational abstract data type specifications. In particular there is a remark, attributed originally to Wand, that as the terminal models contain the least amount of redundancy, they could be the best candidates for efficient representations. We have been thinking along the same lines ourselves and have been considering ways to enrich a data type specification so as to exclude the initial models. This we can do by adding more laws to the specification, making more things equal. Of course if the laws added are derivable from the previous laws then there is no change in the models. We have tried to develop laws that do not change the external behavior of the data type observed through the functions that have as range a type not the type being specified, the TOI in Guttag's terminology. That is, given two terms t1, t2 of type TOI, not equal in the initial model, we try to deduce identities fi(t1) = fi(t2) for all fi with range not the TOI. We can then add the equation t1 = t2 to the specification moving the initial model closer to the terminal without changing the behavior of the type.

Consider for example the simple type SET defined in Wirsing et al. [1979].

```
type SET

  operations

    empty: → set
    incorp: set x integer → set
    iselem: set x integer → boolean

  axioms

    iselem(empty,i) = false
    iselem(incorp(s,i),j) = if i=j
                            then true
                            else iselem(s,j)
```

Here the only external function is iselem. In the initial model of this type incorp(incorp(s,i),j) ≠ incorp(incorp(s,j),i). However, if we consider iselem(incorp(incorp(s,i1),i2),j) we have

```
iselem(incorp(incorp(s,i1),i2)),j)
= if i1 = j
  then true
  else if i2 = j
  then true
  else iselem(s,j)
      (Unfolding twice)

= if i2=j
  then true
  else if i1=j
  then true
  else iselem(s,j)
      (Rearranging the conditional)

= iselem(incorp(incorp(i,i2),i1),j)
      (Folding twice)
```

Thus we can see that adding the law

incorp(incorp(s,i1),i2) = incorp(incorp(s,i2),i1)

will not change the type's external behavior. Similarly, the identity incorp(incorp(s,i),i) = incorp(s,i) can be developed. Having developed this new type it is easy to synthesize a new constructor that keeps everything in the simplest form, e.g., avoiding duplications.

F. Acknowledgements

Many of the ideas presented here were also being developed by Gerard Terrine before his untimely death last year and I greatly benefited from discussions with him and Marie-Claude Gaudel. Thanks also to J. Guttag. The British Science Research Council provided financial support.

References

Burstall [1977]
R.M. Burstall, "Design considerations for a functional programming language," Infotech State of the Art Conference, Copenhagen (1977), pp. 45–57.

Burstall and Darlington [1977]
R.M. Burstall and J. Darlington, "A transformation system for developing recursive programs," *J.ACM,* Vol. 24, No. 1 (1977), pp. 44–67.

Darlington [1978]
J. Darlington, "Program transformation and synthesis: present capabilities," Report 77/43, Department of Computing and Control, Imperial College (1978). To appear in *Artificial Intelligence Journal.*

Darlington [1979]
J. Darlington, "The synthesis of implementations for abstract data types," Report 80, Dept. of Computing and Control, Imperial College (1979).

Floyd [1964]
R.W. Floyd, "Algorithm 245 treesort," *CACM* 7,12 (1964).

Hoare [1972]
C.A.R. Hoare, "Proof of correctness of data representations," *Acta Informatica* 1 (1972), pp. 271–278.

Liskov and Ziller [1975]
B.H. Liskov and S.N. Ziller, "Specification techniques for data abstractions," *IEEE Trans. on Soft. Engineering,* Vol. SE–1, No. 1 (1975), pp. 7–19.

Terrine [1979]
G. Terrine, Personal communication.

Vuillemin [1976]
J. Vuillemin, "A data structure for manipulating priority queues," Internal Report, Department d'Informatique, Universite de Paris Sud, France (1976).

Wirsing *et al.* [1979]
M. Wirsing, P. Depper, W. Partsch, W. Dosch and M. Broy, "Some results on abstract data types," Internal report Project CIP, Technical University, Munich (1979).

CHAPTER 8

Improving Abstract Data Type Specifications By Appropriate Choice Of Constructors

Christine Choppy
Laboratoire de Recherche en Informatique
Université de Paris-Sud

Pierre Lescanne and Jean-Luc Rémy
Centre de Recherche en Informatique de Nancy

Abstract

In this paper, we are concerned with problems involved in transforming abstract data type specifications. The questions are: what are the operations and the conditions involved in transforming a given specification into an equivalent one, what is the gain in this transformation (we define a complexity measure), and finally, is it possible to define systematic strategies for specification transformation. The example we use is a specification built on a cartesian product of two abstract data types (called subtypes), modified by a restriction on a definition domain of a constructor and enriched by some operations.

Introduction

We present here some ideas about how to evaluate and improve an abstract data type specification; we illustrate them with an example inspired from the Bartussek and Parnas [1977] paper.

We adopt the point of view that an abstract data type is a class of algebras on a signature of typed operations (Burstall and Goguen [1977], Guttag and Horning [1978], Goguen *et al.* [1978]). We use equational specifications with preconditions that restrict the operation definition domain (Guttag [1980]).

The construction of abstract data type specification has been studied by various authors (Bauer and Wossner [1979], Darlington [1978], Partsch and Broy [1979], Remy [1980]). An example proposed by Majster [1977] (traversable stacks) and similar to Bartussek and Parnas' has been studied by some authors with an approach close to ours: Thatcher *et al.* [1978] simplify the example and are interested by a very simple model for which they obtain a specification proven thereafter. Veloso and Pequeno [1979] look for the normal forms and work on them as a model.

The example chosen for this paper is built on the cartesian product of two simple data types enriched by additional operations following Burstall and Goguen [1977] terminology. Those operations are difficult to effect and we attempt to transform the specification into another one where calculations are simpler.

In the first part of this paper we describe the techniques we use (and that we either borrowed or developed) in order to build a specification and to allow for systematic transformations:

1) A methodical presentation of the algebraic specification of an abstract data type with preconditions allowing an easy reading of confluence, finite termination and sufficient completeness. (This presentation is tied to Guttag and Horning [1978] and Gaudel [1980]. We differ from these works by orienting each equation into a rewrite rule (Lescanne [1979], Musser [1980], Huet [1980], Rémy [1982])).
2) Proof techniques in rewriting systems proposed by Huet [1980], Burstall and Darlington [1977], (folding, unfolding), Musser [1980] (induction proofs) and Goguen [1980] together with transformation strategies as defined by Feather [1979] (composition of definitions).
3) A measure of the operations complexity defined as the number of rewritings necessary to evaluate them.

We present then the example exhibiting our point:

1) The specifications of a cartesian product of two types is obtained by putting together both specifications and adding commutativity rules between the operations of one and the other.
2) Our example is a cartesian product modified in two ways: a restriction on the objects domain and an enrichment by adding new operations.
3) The complexity evaluation points out the costly operations in the chosen specification.

Finally, we describe the transformation process with some strategies and we give the main steps:

1) Choice of a family of constructors.
2) Choice of the two types in the cartesian product.
3) Transforming the definitions of the operations depending on the two types.

A. Techniques and Concepts Used in the Abstract Data Types Specifications and Their Transformations

A.1 Abstract Data Type Specification and Rewriting System

Using algebraic abstract data types specifications with preconditions, we establish the following presentation:

- *Operations declaration* — The operations are divided into three classes: the *constructors* are the only operation necessary to describe any object of the data type, the *internal operations* are operations with range the type of interest (i.e. the type being specified) which are not constructors, the *external operations* extract values from the abstract data type objects (among those operations are the predicates or operations with range boolean that test properties of the objects).

- *Declaration of the operation profile and restrictions* — In each class, profiles and states (i.e. infixed or postfixed, see further down) are given. Often operations are not defined on their whole domain and restrictions are necessary, they are defined by predicates (predicates are themselves not restricted, therefore using induction, it is possible to define a domain for every term), called *preconditions.*

- *Rewriting rules* — We use rewriting rules to express the operation semantics; both sides play dissymmetrical roles, that is mainly useful to take in account the restrictions. Let $s(x_1,...,x_m) \rightarrow t(y_1,...,y_n)$ be a rule where $V(s) = \{x_1,...,x_m\}$ and $V(t) = (y_1,...,y_n)$ are the variables occurring in s and t. Each rule will be supposed right regular (i.e. $V(t) \subset V(s)$) and left linear (i.e. each variable occurs once in s) ; therefore, t is written $t(x_1,...,x_m)$. Finally, we say that a rule is "sound" if the domain of $s(x_1,...,x_m)$ is included in that of $t(x_1,...,x_m)$.

Furthermore, we use some conventions:

- We replace the notation: u → if p then v else w by a separate cases notation: p => u → v; non p => u → w which is simpler to use in proof techniques.

- We consider specifications where the operations have at most one argument of the type of interest.

- In constructors and internal operations, the argument of the type of interest is denoted in postfixed notation, leaving the other arguments as parameters (Curry and Feys [1958], Backus [1978]). For instance, the term resulting from adding an item x on a stack s (Fig. A.1) is denoted s.Add(x). The advantage of this notation is that it takes into account the chronology of the object construction.

In Fig. A.1. we give two specification examples: the type Stack and the type Pointer (that is a version of type Integer). In the specification of type Stack, we call respectively the operations Take, Front and Isnull, the *destructor,* the *access* and the *test* associated to the operation Add. Numerous specifications present destruction, access and test operations associated with a constructor; in the process of specification transformation, once the family of constructors is chosen, we shall try to associate such operations to them.

It is well known that, in order to perform computations under good conditions, the rewriting system should have the properties of confluence (or Church-Rosser property) and finite termination. The first property insures that every term t is rewritten into at most one irreducible term t' called its normal form. The second property insures that there is no infinite series of rewritings. These two properties insure then that every term has a unique normal form. Usually, the confluence property is proved by using the Knuth and Bendix [1970] algorithm and the Finite termination property is proved by using a well-founded partial ordering on the type expressions (Plaisted [1978], Dershowitz [1979], Kamin *et al.* [1980], Jouannaud *et al.* [1982]).

Fig. A.1. Specifications of the types Stack and Pointer

Type Stack [Item]

Operations with s: Stack, x: Item

Emptystack	: Stack
s.Add(x)	: Stack
s.Take	: Stack def if not Isempty(s)
Front(s)	: Item def if not Isempty(s)
Isempty(s)	: Boolean

Rules for all s : Stack, x: Item

s.Add(x).Take →s

Front(s.Add(x)) →x

Isempty(Emptystack) →True

Isempty(s.Add(x)) →False

Type Pointer

Operations with p: Pointer

Pnull: Pointer

p.Right :Pointer

p.Left : Pointer def if not Isnull(p)

Isnull(p) : Boolean

Rules for all p: Pointer

p.Right.Left →p

Isnull(Pnull) →True

Isnull(p.Right) →False

We require that our specifications are "gracious" in Bidoit [1981]'s terms. Among other things, it means that each internal or external operation admits, with respect to the constructors, either a direct definition or an inductive definition. A direct definition is a rule whose left hand side has the following pattern: $x.f(z_1,...,z_n)$ where x is a variable of the type of interest, $z_1,...,z_n$ are variables of external types. An inductive definition is a family of rules whose left hand sides have the following pattern: $x.c(y_1,...,y_m).f(z_1,...,z_n)$ or $c_o.f(z_1,...,z_n)$ where c_o is a constant constructor and c, a non constant constructor. We need one rule per constructor when the precondition of f is not identically false.

A.2 Proof Techniques in Specification with Preconditions

To transform a specification, we need to compute new relations between the operations. These relations, or theorems, are equations between two terms, in a given context, and can be proved by using specification rules and replacing some terms by other equal terms. This technique, theoretically complete is strongly non-deterministic, each rule being applied either from left to right or from right to left.

In confluent and finite terminating specifications, and especially in gracious ones (cf. A.1.), equality of two terms can always be proved by rewriting them into the same normal form. This technique is classical (Huet 1980]) and we have only to take into account context conditions.

Rewriting in a context — u *rewrites to* v in a context p if there exists a rule p'=>u'→v' and a substitution σ such that

- σu' is a subterm of u
- v is derived from u by replacing σu' by σv', and
- the condition σp' is a rewriting of p

(In the third condition, we use classical rewritings, without preconditions; this is generally sufficient).

Equality proof in a context — Equation u=v is *directly* provable in a context p if there exist some sequences $u_o u_1 \cdots u_n$ and $v_o \cdots v_m$ such that u_o is u, v_o is v, u_n and w_m coincide and each term rewrites to the following in the context p.

Example In Queue Type

$$\text{Frontq(q.Addq(x).Addq(y))} = \text{Frontq(q.Addq(x))} \qquad \text{(true)}$$

The left hand side member rewrites to the right hand side one. We use the substitution σ: q $\rightarrow$ q.Addq(x) and the rule not Isnewq((q) => Frontq(q.Addq(y)) $\rightarrow$ Frontq(q) and σ(not Isnewq(q)) = not Isnewq(q.Addq(x)) $\rightarrow$ not false $\rightarrow$ true.

Induction proof — When an equation is not directly provable, we proceed by induction: let E be an equation u=v (p) to be proven and x a variable of type of interest in E. We can replace the proof of E by the proofs of a family denoted $\frac{\partial E}{\partial C}(x)$ of equations so defined: each equation of $\frac{\partial E}{\partial C}(x)$ is obtained from E by substituting for x a term $x.c(y_1,...,y_n)$ where c is a non-constant constructor of C of the term c_o if c_o is a constant constructor. This notation is due to Bidoit [1981]. Moreover, we can consider x as a constant and use the induction hypothesis to prove the equations of $\frac{\partial X}{\partial C}(x)$.

If an equation has its context reduced to false there is nothing to prove.

Example In Stack type, let the equation

$$\text{s.Take.Add(Front(s))} = \text{s} \qquad \text{(not Isempty(x))}$$

If we replace s by Emptystack, the context is not Isempty(Emptystack) which is reducible to *false*. If we replace s by s.Add(x), the context is reducible to *true* and the left hand side member is s.Add(x).Take.Add(Front(s.Add(x))) which rewrites to the right hand side member s.Add(x).

Application of proof techniques — When we transform a specification, we have to invent the right hand side members of equations. Hopefully, we know the left hand side members since we know a family of constructors and we want some recursive definitions of the other operations. We adopt the following strategy (cf. also Burstall and Darlington [1977] and Feather [1979]).

Direct proof — Beginning with a term u (the left hand side member of an equation)

1) Unfold this term as long as possible, i.e. apply specification rules from left to right. If these rules are conditional, introduce two complementary contexts to deal with successively.
2) Then, fold the resulting term by applying rules from right to left (occasionally, introduce two contexts) and stop when the final term constitutes a recursive definition of u with respect to the new constructors and their associated operations.

Induction proof — Suppose we proved an assertion $E_o : u_o = v_o \ (p_o)$ and there exists a constructor co, a variable x and an assertion E such that $E_o = \frac{\partial E}{\partial co}(x)$. Then we try to prove E by induction.

A.3. Defining and Computing a Complexity Measure for a Specification Rewriting System

The complexity we define has to give a measure of the number of rewritings necessary to transform a ground term (i.e. without variables) into its normal form. This number depends on the rewriting system and the rewriting strategy considered (Vuillemin [1974] ,Huet and Lévy [1979]). Taking in account the specific form of the rules, a call by value strategy, with special consideration for conditionals, is optimal here. Therefore the complexity is totally defined by its value on the terms: $t.o(t_1,...,t_n)$ or $o(t,t_1,...,t_n)$ where t is a normal form of type of interest and $t_1,...,t_n$ constants of external type. We denote by $\hat{o}(t,t_1,...,t_n)$ the number of rewritings needed in computing the normal form of these terms. If t is a term, R a rewriting system, we denote by R(t) the normal form of t in R.

The family of functions $(\hat{o})_{o \in 0}$ verifies a system of equations which can be systematically deduced from R. Instead of formally specifying the process, we propose a sufficiently complete example: let o,o_1,o_2 internal operations, c a constructor, p a predicate and the following rule, recursively defining o on c:

$$p(x,y,z) \; => \; x.c(y).o(z) \; -> \; x.o_1(y).o_2(z)$$

We transform this rule into the following complexity equation:

$$R(p(x,y,z)) \; => \; \hat{o}(x,c(y),z) \; = \; 1 + \hat{p}(x,y,z) + \hat{o}_1(x,y) + \hat{o}_2(R(x.o_1(y)),z)$$

1 holds for the application of the rule itself
$\hat{p}$ holds for test computation
$\hat{o}_1(x,y)$ holds for computing $R(x,o_1(y))$
$\hat{o}_2(R(x.o_1(y)),z)$ holds for computing $R(R(s.o_1(y)).o_2(z))$.

Normal form and valuation — In many examples, the quantity $\hat{o}(x,y_1,...,y_n)$ depends only on numbers of occurrence of constructors in x. We name valuation of a normal form the sequence of these occurrence numbers. For example, let x be a normal form: $c_o.c_1^p(y_1,...,y_p).c_2^q(z_1,...,z_q)$, the valuation of x, denoted $|x|$, is the pair (p,q). In this case we write also $\hat{o}(|x|)$ instead of $\hat{o}(x,y_1, \ldots, y_n)$.

Example — In the type Queue(Item), the normal form of any term q is $R(q) = Newq.Addq^n(x_1, \ldots, x_n)$ and $|R(q)| = n$, n integer, $n \geqslant o$. Here are the rewriting rules we need in this example (the complete specification is classical (cf. Guttag *et al.* [1978])).

Isnewq(Newq) → *true*

Isnewq(q.Addq(x)) → *false*

Isnewq(q) ==> Frontq(q.Addq(x)) → x

not Isnewq(q) ==> Frontq(q.Addq(x)) → Frontq(q)

Immediately, $\hat{\text{Isnewq}}(n) = 1$ for each $n \geqslant o$. By definition $|\text{Newq}| = o$ and $|q.\text{Addq}(x)| = 1 + |q|$. So $\text{Isnewq}(q) = \mathit{true} <==> |q| = o$. We can write

$$|q| = o => \hat{\text{Frontq}}(|q.\text{Addq}(x)|) = 1 + 1 = 2$$

$$|q| > o => \hat{\text{Frontq}}(|q.\text{Addq}(x)|) = 1 + 1 + \hat{\text{Frontq}}(|q|)$$

$$\hat{\text{Frontq}}(1) = 2 \text{ and } \hat{\text{Frontq}}(n+1) = 2 + \hat{\text{Frontq}}(n)$$

Finally $\hat{\text{Frontq}}(n) = 2 \times n$ for all $n \geqslant 1$.

B. Presentation of the Example

B.1. Specification of the Cartesian Product of Two Abstract Data Types

Let T_1 and T_2 be two abstract data types with operation sets O_1 and O_2, and rule sets R_1 and R_2. Their cartesian product is denoted by $T_1(0_1,R_1) \times T_2(0_2,R_2)$ or simpler, $T_1 \times T_2$. Each operation set 0_i is decomposed as $0_i = \text{INIT}_i + 0_i^+$, where INIT_i is the set of "initial" operations (having no argument of the type of interest).

$T_1 \times T_2$ operations are obtained by extending T_1 and T_2 operations in the following way:

- INIT_1 and INIT_2 have a common extension:

$$\text{INIT}_1 \times \text{INIT}_2 = \{(o_1,o_2)/o_2 \in \text{INIT}_1, o_2 \in \text{INIT}_2\}.$$

In our example, INIT_1 and INIT_2 are reduced to one operation; so is $\text{INIT}_2 \times \text{INIT}_2$, it is denoted NULL.

- For each operation $o_1 \in 0_1^+$, its extension $\bar{o}_1$ affects the first component of $T_1 \times T_2$ in the same way as o_1. In the rest of the paper $\bar{o}_1$ will be denoted o_1 (the overlining will be omitted).

$T_1 \times T_2$ rules are composed with extensions R'_1 and R'_2 of the sets of rules R_1 and R_2, each with commutativity rules between:

. T_1 and T_2 constructors

. T_1 external operations and T_2 constructors

. T_2 external operations and T_1 constructors.

Orienting the commutativity axiom between the constructors leads to unique normal forms. An example of cartesian product specification is given in Fig. B.1.

Fig. B.1. Specification of the type Stack x Pointer

Type Stack x Pointer [Item]

Operations with pl: Stack x Pointer, x: Item		**Rules** for all pl: Stack x Pointer, x: Item
NULL	: Stack x Pointer	
pl.Add(x)	: Stack x Pointer	pl.Right.Add(x) → pl.Add(x).Right
pl.Right	: Stack x Pointer	
pl.Take	: Stack x Pointer	pl.Add(x).Take → pl
	def if not Isempty (pl)	pl.Right.Take → pl.Take.Right
pl.Left	: Stack x Pointer	pl.Add(x).Left → pl.Left.Add(x)
		pl.Right.Left → pl
Front(pl)	: Item def if not Isempty(pl)	Front(pl.Add(x)) → x
		Front(pl.Right) → Front(pl)
Isempty(pl)	: Boolean	Isempty(NULL) → True
		Isempty(pl.Add(x) → False
		Isempty(pl.Right) → Isempty(pl)
Isnull(pl)	: Boolean	Isnull(NULL) → True
		Isnull(pl.Add(x)) → Isnull(pl)
		Isnull(pl.Right) → False

B.2. Restriction and Enrichment

To make things clear, let us first give a physical description of the data whose behavior we formalize using an abstract data type called Pointed List (as in Bartussek and Parnas [1977]). Let us take a row of children's blocks covered with a lid. The lid has a window through which one can read (operation Read) the value written on the block under the window, insert (operation Insert) a new block (after having moved to the right the block that was under the window and its eventual neighbors to the right), or remove (operation Delete) the block under the window (the blocks situated to the right are then moved one place to the left). On the lid are two signals indicating whether there is a block to the left (operation Exleft) or to the right (operation Exright) of the current block. The window can be moved one place to the left (operation Left) or one place to the right (operation Right). We lack room to describe in detail the steps leading to this specification (Choppy *et al.* [1980b]). We shall give only an intuitive presentation here. Let us go back to the Stack x Pointer specification (Fig. B.1.): intuitively, the constructor Add allows one to build a row of blocks, while the constructor Right allows one to move the window to the right; the domain of the operation Right has to be restricted in order to avoid generating terms such as $\mathrm{NULL.Right}^n$, n a positive integer. This restriction is expressed through the predicate Exright that is defined on the whole domain (Fig. B.2). In the same way, the definition domain of Left is restricted by means of Exleft. The predicates Isempty and Isnull can be expressed in terms of Exright and Exleft and are therefore removed. The obtained specification is then enriched by the operations Insert, Delete, and Read.

Restricting the domain of Right with Exright causes the rejection of half of the objects generated by the cartesian product. Furthermore, the commutativity rule between the constructors is not symmetrical any more since the left hand side is less defined than the right hand side. What is left is not a cartesian product anymore.

The operations Add, Take, Front are not a formalization for operations on the data; they play an important role in the specification since they are a constructor together with its associated operations, but they are hidden operations (they could not be invoked by a system's user). Enriching the specification with additional operations does not modify the set of the objects.

Fig. B.2. Specification of the type Pointed List

Type Pointed List [Item]

Operations with pl: Pointed List,x: Item		Rules for all pl:Pointed List, x: Item
NULL	: {Pointed List }	
pl.Add(x)*	: {Pointed List }	pl.Right.Add(x) →pl.Add(x).Right
pl.Right	: {Pointed List def if Exright(pl) }	
pl.Take *	: {Pointed List def if Exright(pl) }	pl.Add(x).Take →pl
		pl.Right.Take →pl.Take.Right
pl.Left	: {Pointed List def if Exleft(pl) }	pl.Add(x).Left →pl.Left.Add(x)
		pl.Right.Left →pl
pl.Insert	: {Pointed List }	{non Exright(pl) = >pl.Insert(x) } →pl.Add(x).Right
		Exright(pl) = >pl.Insert(x) →pl.Take.Insert(x).Add(Front(pl))
pl.Delete	: {Pointed List def if Exleft(pl) }	{non Exright(pl) →pl.Delete →pl.Take.Left}
		Exright(pl) = >pl.Delete →pl.Take.Delete.Add(Front(pl))
Front(pl) *	: {Item def if Exright(pl)} {or Exleft(pl) }	Front(pl.Add(x)) →x
		Front(pl.Right) →Front(pl)
Read(pl)	: Item def {if Exleft(pl) }	{non Exright(pl) →Read(pl) →Front(pl)}
		Exright(pl) = >Read(pl) →Read(pl.Take)
Exright(pl)	: Boolean	Exright(NULL) → False
		Exright(pl.Add(x)) → True
		Exright(pl.Right) →Exright(pl.Take)
Exleft(pl)	: Boolean	Exleft(NULL) → False
		Exleft(pl.Add(x)) →Exleft(pl)
		Exleft(pl.Right) → True

* hidden operations

B.3 Complexity Evaluation

Fig. B.3. exhibits definitions of the $\hat{o}$ functions that are the complexity of the Pointed List specification given in Fig. B.2. These functions are computed after principles explained in section A.3. They vary with the valuation of their argument of type of interest (i.e., for all normal form term in the Pointed List type, $R(pl) = NULL.Add^n(x_1, \ldots, x_n)$. $Right^p$, $\hat{o}$ is a function of $|R(pl)| = (n,p)$). When the functions have an argument of type Item, their complexity does not vary with this argument. Details concerning the computation of Insert(n,p) are given in Appendix 1.

C. Transformations

C.1. Transformation of an Abstract Data Type Specification into Another One: Definition and Application

The process of transformation can be compared to the representation process (cf. Gaudel and Terrine [1978]). However, it differs (i) by the implementation: we start from a given specification not knowing a priori the final one, (ii) by the semantics: the final specification is to be equivalent to the initial one, (iii) by

Fig. B.3. Complexity of the rewriting system of the specification of the type Pointed list in Fig. B.2.

$\widehat{\text{NULL}} = 0$

$\widehat{\text{Right}}(n,p) = 0$ $\qquad \widehat{\text{Exleft}}(n,p)$ *if* $p=o$ *then* $n+1$ else 1

$\widehat{\text{Add}}(n,p) = p$ $\qquad \widehat{\text{Exright}}(n,p) = \frac{(p+1)(p+2)}{2}$

$\widehat{\text{Left}}(n,p) = 1$ $\qquad \widehat{\text{Insert}}(n,p) = \frac{(n-p+1)(p+1)(p+2)}{2} + 3(n-p)(p+1) + n + 1$

$\widehat{\text{Take}}(n,p) = p+1$ $\qquad \widehat{\text{Delete}}(n,p) = \frac{(n-p+1)(p+1)(p+2)}{2} + (n-p)(3p+1) + n + 3$

$\widehat{\text{Front}}(n,p) = p+1$ $\qquad \widehat{\text{Read}}(n,p) = (n-p+1)\left(\frac{(p+1)(p+4)}{2} + 1\right)$

the expected goal: reducing the complexity of (nonhidden) operations. At last, in this work, the resulting specification has to be gracious (which implies they have the confluence, finite termination and sufficient completeness properties).

To obtain the new specification, we have, first of all, to find the new constructors, then we compute definition rules for the nonhidden operations (and hidden operations necessary to the specification) in terms of these new constructors.

The input and output specifications have to be equivalent, i.e. their initial algebras have to be isomorphic (Goguen *et al.* [1978]). Without giving formal definitions, it is enough to define an isomorphism between the normal forms generated by the two families of constructors. Classically, we build a new specification by inventing some relations which are theorems in the old specification and, then, we verify that the axioms of the first specification are also theorems for the new one.

In the next paragraph, we see how it is possible to make easier invention and verification in this process.

C.2 Strategy of Transformation for a Specification Built From a Cartesian Product of Abstract Data Types

As shown in section B.2. the example we chose is a cartesian product modified by a restriction on one of its constructors and enriched by some supplementary operations. The specification designed (Fig. B.2.) contains hidden operations which are necessary to the specification but not interesting for the user. So, the specification resulting from the transformation has to contain necessarily all the nonhidden operations of the initial specification.

On the other side, we use the cartesian product structure to change only one constructor at a time (and so, our transformation has two phases) and we try to obtain a specification which is also built from a cartesian product.

1) the first step is the choice of a new constructor and we give some criteria to guide this choice. Recall that one of our goals is reducing the complexity of the specification: we choose, for the first transformation an "expensive" operation, able to form, with another constructor a generating family for the type. In the other side, we seek for a "cartesian product" specification and the new constructor has to commute with the old constructor which is kept. The satisfaction of these conditions leads us to choose, for the second transformation, a constructor which is a composition of operations.

2) As we note in paragraph A.1., we try to associate with the new constructor some operations of destruction, access and test, and test whether these operations verify commutativity rules allowing to identify the components of a cartesian products (cf. para. B.1.).

3) We have finally to complete the specifications by the definition of the operations which are not dealt with yet. It remains now to insure that the resulting specification has confluence, finite termination and sufficient completeness properties (we do not prove that here), to verify that the two specifications are equivalent and to evaluate the complexity in order to estimate the resulting specification.

The equivalence proof is easier because of the special structure of specifications. Let C and C' be the two constructors systems; since only one constructor is modified, we have: $C = C'' \cup \{c\}$ and $C' = C'' \cup \{c'\}$. Let A be the set of the auxiliary operations used in the definitions of c with respect to C' and c' with respect to C. The rules on $C'' \cup \{c,c'\} \cup A$ consist in:

- for the first specification
  - the relation between the constructors of $C'' \cup \{c\}$
  - and the definitions of $\{c'\} \cup A$ with respect to $C'' \cup \{c\}$

- for the second one
  - the relation between the constructors of $C'' \cup \{c'\}$
  - and the definitions of $\{c\} \cup A$ with respect to $C'' \cup \{c'\}$.

Rules of the second specification have been computed in the last step as some theorems of the first one. It remains to verify that the relations in $C'' \cup \{c\}$ and definitions of $\{c'\} \cup A$ are theorems of the second specification. If, in addition, some constructors of the first specification are restricted by preconditions, we have to verify that they have the same preconditions in the transformed specification. For the other operations (which do not belong to $C \cup C' \cup A$) we have computed before, definitions in the new specification which are theorems in the old specification. The fact that the specifications are gracious with respect to C or C' guarantees their equivalence without having to prove that the rules of the old specification are theorems of the new one (Rémy and Veloso [1982]).

C.3 First Transformation of Pointed List Type (Fig. B.2.)

C.3.1. Choice of a new family of constructors

An obvious candidate to be constructor is the operation Insert: it is a type generator since it is the composition of constructors Add and Right for the class of terms for which *not* Exright is verified (cf. Fig. C.3.1.), and its complexity is high (cf. Fig. B.3.).

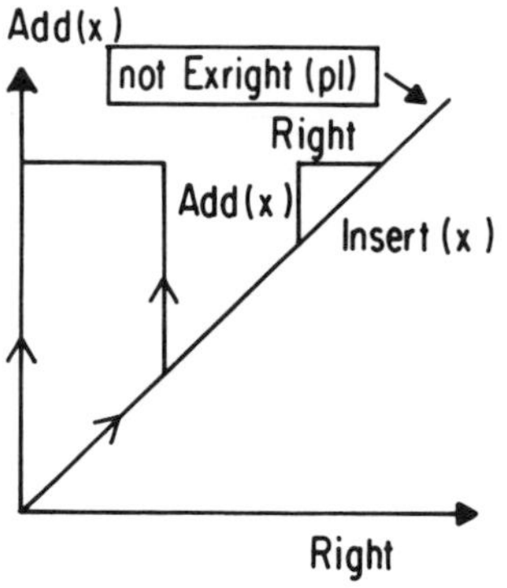

Figure C.3.1.

The constructor to eliminate is Right since the family {Null, Insert, Right} is not generating. So, the new family is {Null,Add,Insert}. It is generating as we can define Right in terms of Add,Insert and the operations associated with Add,Remove and Front (cf. Appendix 2):

Not Exright(pl.Take) => pl.Right → pl.Take.Insert(Front(pl))
Exright(pl.Take) => pl.Right → pl.Take.Right.Add(Front(pl))

Moreover constructors Add and Insert commute with each other:

pl.Add(x).Insert(y) → pl.Insert(y).Add(x).

C.3.2 Identification of the cartesian product components

If we associate with Insert the operations Delete, Read and *not* Exleft, we find the well-known rules of Stack type (cf. Guttag *et al.* [1978]):

pl.Insert(x).Delete → pl
Read(pl.Insert(x)) → x
not Exleft(Null) → True
not Exleft(pl.Insert(x)) → False

Moreover, we find commutativity rules:

. between Insert and Take, not Exright
. between Add and Delete, Read, not Exleft

Only a commutativity rule is missing between Insert and Front.

C.3.3. Definition of not hidden operations

In the two preceding paragraphs, we dealt with almost all the operations. It remains to define Left in terms of Add and Insert. We so obtain a specification (Fig. C.3.3.) which is easily proven to be gracious (cf. para. A.1.).

Fig. C.3.3. Specification of the type Pointed List with constructors {NULL, Add, Insert}

Type Pointed List [Item]

Operations with pl: Pointed List, x: Item		**Rules** for all pl: Pointed list x,y: Item
NULL	: Pointed list	
pl.Add(x)*	: Pointed list	pl.Insert(x).Add(y) →pl.Add(y).Insert(x)
pl.Insert(x)	: Pointed list	
pl.Take*	: Pointed List def if Exright(pl)	pl.Add(x).Take →pl pl.Insert(x).Take →pl.Take.Insert(x)
pl.Delete	: Pointed List def if Exleft(pl)	pl.Add(x).Delete →pl.Delete.Add(x) pl.Insert(x).Delete →pl
pl.Left	: Pointed List def if Exleft(pl)	pl.Add(x).Left →pl.Left.Add(x) non Exright(pl) = >pl.Insert(x).Left →pl.Add(x) Exright(pl) = >pl.Insert(x).Left → →pl.Take.Insert(x).Left.Add(Front(pl))
pl.Right	: Pointed List def if Exright(pl)	non Exright(pl.Take) = >pl.Right → →pl.Take.Insert(Front(pl)) Exright(pl.Take) = >pl.Right → →pl.Take.Right.Add(Front(pl))
Front(pl)*	: Item def if Exleft(pl) or Exright(pl)	Front(pl.Add(x)) →x nonExright(pl) = >Front(pl.Insert(x))) →x Exright(pl) = >Front(pl.Insert(x)) →Front(pl)
Read(pl)	: Item def if Exleft(pl)	Read(pl.Add(x)) →Read(pl) Read(pl.Insert(x)) →x
Exright(pl)	: Boolean	Exright(NULL) → False Exright(pl.Add(x)) → True Exright(pl.Insert(x)) →Exright(pl)
Exleft(pl)	: Boolean	Exleft(NULL) → False Exleft(pl.Add(x)) →Exleft(pl) Exleft(pl.Insert(x)) → True

* hidden operations

C.3.4. Equivalence proof

With the notations of paragraph C.2., we have:

C'' = {Null,Add}
c = Right
c' = Insert
A = {Take, Front, Exright}

We have to verify that commutativity relation between Add and Right and the definition of operations of {c'} ∪ A in the first specification are theorems of the new one.

C.3.5. Evaluation and analysis of the complexity of the rewriting system of the resulting specification

We give in figure C.3.5. the complexity of the rewriting system of the resulting specification. We want to compare this complexity with the one of the original specification (Fig. B.3.). We can adopt several points of view:

a) to compare the complexity by groups of operations

— constructors (the complexity is the same)
— associated destructors (idem)
— boolean operations (or tests) (complexity is slightly lessened for Exright)
— operations with result in the type Item or accesses Read and Front (complexity is globally lessened)
— other operations: Insert and Delete in the first case Right and Left, in the second case (complexity approximately identical)

b) to compare the complexity only for the nonhidden operations. Whatever the point of view adopted, we can note a slight gain. Nevertheless, the second point of view does not satisfy us for the complexity of Right and Left. It leads us to attempt a second transformation.

C.4. Second Transformation of Pointed List Type

C.4.1. Choice of a new family of constructors

For replacing the constructor Add, we choose the operation Insertleft which is the composition of Insert and Left. That may seem to be a total "eureka"; however, we try now to motivate this choice:

— we want to keep Insert as constructor as this is a nonhidden operation and its role of construction gives it a low complexity; so we eliminate Add,
— we seek for a constructor among costly operations (Right and Left); Right is not generating with Insert and Left does not commute with Insert, yet the composition of Insert and Left is convenient. Insertleft can be inductively defined on the constructors Null, Add, Insert by the following rules:

Fig. C.3.5. Complexity of the rewriting system of the specification of the Pointed list in fig. C.3.3.

Normal forms: $\text{NULL.Add}^n(x_1,\dots,x_n).\text{Insert}^p(y_1,\dots,y_p)$

$\widehat{\text{NULL}} = 0$

$\widehat{\text{Add}}(n,p) = p$ $\qquad$ $\widehat{\text{Left}}(n,p) = \dfrac{(2+p)n(n+1)}{2} + 2n(2p+3) + 2(p+1)$

$\widehat{\text{Insert}}(n,p) = 0$ $\qquad$ $\widehat{\text{Right}}(n,p) = \dfrac{(2+p)(n-1)(n-2)}{2} + n(6p+9) - p - 2$

$\widehat{\text{Take}}(n,p) = p+1$ $\qquad$ $\widehat{\text{Exleft}}(n,p) = n + 1$

$\widehat{\text{Delete}}(n,p) = 1$ $\qquad$ $\widehat{\text{Exright}}(n,p) = p + 1$

$\widehat{\text{Read}}(n,p) = 1$ $\qquad$ $\widehat{\text{Front}}(n,p) = n(p+2) + p + 3$

(IGO) Null.Insertleft(y) → Null.Add(y)
(IG1) pl.Insert(x).Insertleft(y) → pl.Insertleft(y).Insert(x)
(IG2) pl.Add(x).Insertleft(y) → pl.Insertleft(y).Add(x)

Then the family {Null, Insert, Insertleft} is generating. Indeed, the eliminated constructor Add is so defined (where $\overline{R}$ denotes the symmetric of rule R):

($\overline{\text{IG0}}$) Null.Add(y) → Null.Insertleft(y)
(COM) pl.Insert(x).Add(y) → pl.Add(y).Insert(x)
($\overline{\text{IG2}}$) pl.Insertleft(x).Add(y) → pl.Add(y).Insertleft(x)

In addition Insert(x) and Insertleft(y) commute (by rule IG1)).

C.4.2. Identification of the cartesian product components

We know that the operations Null, Insert, Delete, Read, not Exleft constitute a stack. For the symmetry of the specification, we add some operations associated with Insertleft: Deleteright and Readright which are respectively compositions with Right of Delete and Read and such that:

pl.Deleteright: Pointed list def if Exright(pl)
pl.Insertleft(x).Deleteright → pl
pl.Insert(x).Deleteright → pl.Deleteright.Insert(x)

Readright(pl): Item def if Exright(pl)
Readright(pl.Insertleft(x)) → x
Readright(pl.Insert(x)) → Readright(pl)

At last, we prove easily that:

not Exright(pl.Insertleft(x)) → False

So, the operations Null, Insertleft, Deleteright, Readright, not Exright constitute a second stack which commute with the first one. We, therefore, have a cartesian product of two stacks.

C.4.3. Definition of the other nonhidden operations

It remains to find the definitions of operations Right and Left in this new system to obtain the specification given in Figure C.4.3.

C.4.4. Equivalence proof

With the notations of C.2., we put

C'' = {Null, Insert}
c = Add
c' = Insertleft
A = ϕ

The proof is here reduced to the commutativity relation of Add and Insert and the definition of Insertleft with respect to Add and Insert.

Fig. C.4.3. Specification of the Pointed list type with constructors (NULL, Insert, Insertleft)

Type Pointed List [Item]

Operation with pl: Pointed list, x: Item

NULL	: Pointed list
pl.Insert(x)	: Pointed list
pl.Insertleft(x)*	: " "
pl.Delete	: " def if Exleft(pl)
pl.Deleteright*	: " def if Exright(pl)
pl.Right	: " def if : Exright(pl)
pl.Left	: " def if Exleft(pl)
Read(pl)	: Item def if Exleft(pl)
Readright(pl)*	: Item def if Exright(pl)
Exleft(pl)	: Boolean
Exright(pl)	: Boolean

Rules for all pl: Pointed list , x,y: Item

pl.Insertleft(x).Insert(y) →
→pl.Insert(y).Insertleft(x)
pl.Insert(x).Delete →pl
pl.Insertleft(x).Delete →pl.Delete.Insertleft(x)
pl.Insert(x).Deleteright →pl.Deleteright.Insert(x)
pl.Insertleft(x).Deleteright →pl
pl.Right →pl.Deleteright.Insert(Readright(pl))
pl.Left →pl.Delete.Insertleft(Read(pl))
Read(pl.Insert(x)) →x
Read(pl.Insertleft(x))→Read(pl)
Readright(pl.Insert(x)) →Readright(pl)
Readright (pl.Insertleft(x))→x
Exleft(NULL) → False
Exleft(pl.Insert(x))→True
Exleft(pl.Insertleft(x))→Exleft(x)
Exright(NULL) → False
Exright(pl.Insert(x))→Exright(pl)
Exright(pl.Insertleft(x))→True

* hidden operations

C.4.5. Evaluation and analysis of the complexity of the final specification

We give in Figure C.4.5. the complexity of the specification resulting from our second transformation. We see that, whatever the point of view adopted (cf. para. C.3.5.), the complexity is strongly lessened for all the operations, hidden or not. It is approximately identical to the complexity of Stack type, i.e. equivalent to the list length. At this point, we can declare ourselves satisfied and stop the transformations.

D. Conclusion

The main ideas in this paper are the following:

a) Changing a type specification boils down to changing its constructors.

b) Using gracious specifications makes easier proofs and, therefore, easier transformations. Bidoit [1981] agrees with this.

Fig. C.4.5. Complexity of the rewriting system of the specification of the type Pointed list in Fig. C.4.3.

Normal forms: NULL.$\mathrm{Insert}^n(x_1, \ldots, x_n)$.$\mathrm{Insertleft}^p(y_1, \ldots, y_p)$	
$\widehat{\mathrm{NULL}} = 0$	
$\widehat{\mathrm{Insert}}(n,p) = p$	$\widehat{\mathrm{Left}}(n,p) = 2(p+1)$
$\widehat{\mathrm{Insertleft}}(n,p) = 0$	$\widehat{\mathrm{Right}}(n,p) = p+1$
$\widehat{\mathrm{Delete}}(n,p) = p+1$	$\widehat{\mathrm{Exleft}}(n,p) = p+1$
$\widehat{\mathrm{Deleteright}}(n,p) = 1$	$\widehat{\mathrm{Exright}}(n,p) = n+1$
$\widehat{\mathrm{Read}}(n,p) = p+1$	$\widehat{\mathrm{Readright}}(n,p) = 1$

c) Considering simple types composition allows us to use particular transformation strategies (Gaudel and Terrine [1978]).

d) Analyzing the operation complexity in a specification and identifying the costly operations is a useful guide in the choice of constructors.

This work should be pursued in the following ways:

a) Apply the strategies presented here to other examples (as was done for the representation of sets by binary trees (Rémy [1980]).

b) Define a complexity measure that distinguishes each type of operation and its cost.

c) Determine computation methods for the complexity functions starting from equations.

d) Deepen the study of heuristics in guiding the choice of new constructors. Extend the field of the operations that can be used. Finally, it could be necessary to test the strategies and techniques in this paper by writing a set of programs or using existing programs such as Darlington's [1979] or Feather's [1979].

E. Acknowledgements

We are grateful to our departed colleague, G. Terrine, for proposing this Bartussek and Parnas example, and for many discussions we had before his untimely death.

We thank M.C. Gaudel, G. Guiho and M. Sintzoff for their encouragements and constructive criticism. At last, we are indebted to our Castor Research Team at the Centre de Recherche en Informatique de Nancy.

Appendix 1

Complexity computation for the Insert operation

Complexity computations are done using the following lemma the proof of which is simple:

Lemma: for all term pl of the Pointed list type such that:

$|R(pl)| = (n,p)$ n,p integers with $0 \leqslant p \leqslant n$:

(1) Exright(R(pl)) = (n≠p and n>0)
(2) Exleft(R(pl)) = (p≠0)
(3) |R(pl.Add(x))| = (n+1, p)
(4) |R(pl.Insert(x))| = (n+1, p+1)

and for all term pl such that |R(pl)| = (n,p) with n>0

(5) |R(pl.Take)| = (n−1, p)

The term pl.Insert(x) is defined for all pl: *Pointed list,* x : *Item.* The definition rules are:

Exright(pl) => pl.Insert(x) → pl.Take.Insert(x).Add(Front(pl))
non Exright => pl.Insert(x) → pl.Add(x).Right

According to the above lemma, the case : Exright(pl) corresponds to the case : n>p, and *non* Exright(pl) corresponds to : n=p. Let us consider both cases separately:

- *Case n > p*

$$\hat{\text{Insert}}(R(pl),R(x)) = 1 + \hat{\text{Exright}}(R(pl)) + \hat{\text{Take}}(R(pl)) + \hat{\text{Insert}}(R(pl.Take),R(x)) + \hat{\text{Add}}(R(pl.Take.Insert(x)),R(Front(pl))) + \hat{\text{Front}}(R(pl))$$

hence :

$$\hat{\text{Insert}}(n,p) = 1 + \hat{\text{Exright}}(n,p) + \hat{\text{Take}}(n,p) + \hat{\text{Insert}}(n-1,p) + \hat{\text{Add}}(n,p+1) + \hat{\text{Front}}(n,p)$$

Using the results concerning complexities of the operations Exright, Take, Add and Front given in Fig. B.3. :

$$\hat{\text{Insert}}(n,p) = 1 + \frac{(p+1)(p+2)}{2} + 3(p+1) + \hat{\text{Insert}}(n-1,p)$$

$$= (n-p)\left[1 + \frac{(p+1)(p+2)}{2} + 3(p+1)\right] + \hat{\text{Insert}}(p,p)$$

- *Case n = p*

$$\hat{\text{Insert}}(R(pl),R(x)) = 1 + \hat{\text{Exright}}(R(pl)) + \hat{\text{Add}}(R(pl),R(x)) + \hat{\text{Right}}(R(pl.Add(x))$$

hence :

$$\hat{\text{Insert}}(p,p) = 1 + \hat{\text{Exright}}(p,p) + \hat{\text{Add}}(p,p) + \text{Right}(p,p+1) = \frac{(p+1)(p+2)}{2} + p + 1$$

Finally :

$$\hat{\text{Insert}}(n,p) = \frac{(n-p+1)(p+1)(p+2)}{2} + 3(n-p)(p+1) + n+1$$

Appendix 2 *Computing the old constructor : Right in terms of the new ones : Add and Insert and their associated operations*

We want either a direct definition (rewriting pl.Right) or an inductive one (rewriting pl.Add(x).Right and pl.Insert(x).Add) using the following results:

(1) pl.Right is defined if Exright(pl)

(2) pl.Right.Add(x) → pl.Add(x).Right

(3) $\begin{cases}\text{Exright(pl.Add(x))} \rightarrow \text{True} \\ \text{Exright(pl.Right)} \rightarrow \text{Exright(pl.Take)}\end{cases}$

(4) $\begin{cases}\text{non Exright(pl)} \Rightarrow \text{pl.Insert(x)} \rightarrow \text{pl.Add(x).Right} \\ \text{Exright(pl)} \Rightarrow \text{pl.Insert(x)} \rightarrow \text{pl.Take.Insert(x).Add(Front(pl))}\end{cases}$

Folding (2) and (4) (and taking preconditions into account) :

(2') Exright(pl) => pl.Add(x).Right → pl.Right.Add(x)

(4') non Exright(pl) => pl.Add(x).Right → pl.Insert(x)

Let us go back to pl.Right and use a theorem similar to the one proved in the section A.2. example :

pl = pl.Take.Add(Front(pl)) (Exright(pl))

The context of this theorem is the same as the definition context for pl.Right :

pl.Right → pl.Take.Add(Front(pl)).Right

Using (2') and (4') :

Exright(pl.Take) => pl.Right → pl.Take.Right.Add(Front(pl))

non Exright(pl.Take) => pl.Right → pl.Take.Insert(Front(pl))

References

Backus [1978]
J. Backus, "Can programming be liberated from Von Neumann style?: A functional style and its algebra of programs" Comm. A.C.M., 21 (1978), pp. 813–841.

Bidoit [1981]
M. Bidoit, "Une méthode de présentation des types abstraits: application", Théses 3éme cycle, Université Paris-Sud (June 1981).

Burstall and Darlington [1977]
R.M. Burstall, J. Darlington, "A transformation system for developing recursive programs" J.A.C.M., 24, (1977), 44–67.

Burstall and Goguen [1977]
R.M. Burstall, J.A. Goguen, "Putting theories together to make specifications" Proc. 5th Int. J. Conf. Artif. Int., (1977), 1045–1058.

Bartussek and Parnas [1977]
W. Bartussek, D. Parnas, "Using traces to write abstract specifications for software modules" University of North California Report TR77, (December, 1977).

Bauer and Wossner [1979]
F.L Bauer, H. Wossner, "Algorithmic language and program development" Prentice Hall International, London, (1979).

Curry and Feys [1958]
H.B. Curry, R. Feys, "Combinatory logic" North Holland, Amsterdam, (1958).

Choppy et al. [1980a]
C. Choppy, P. Lescanne, J.L. Rémy, "Using models to construct and implement abstract data types", Rapport de Recherche du Centre de Recherche en Informatique de Nancy (1980).

Choppy et al. [1980b]
C. Choppy, P. Lescanne, J.L. Rémy, "Improving abstract data types specifications by appropriate choice of constructors," Rapport CRIN (1980).

Darlington [1978]
J. Darlington, "Program Transformation involving unfree date structures. An extended example" Proc. 3rd Int. On Programming (Robinet ed.), Dunod, Paris, (1978), 203–217.

Dershowitz [1979]
N. Dershowitz, "Orderings for term rewriting systems", Proc. 20th Symposium on Foundations of Computer Science (1979), pp. 123–131.

Feather [1979]
M. Feather, "A system for developing programs by transformations" Ph.D. Thesis, Dept. of Artif. Int., Univ. of Edinburgh, (1979).

Gaudel [1980]
M.C. Gaudel, "Génération et preuve de compilateurs basées sur une sémantique formelle des langages de programmation," These de l'Institut National Polytechnique de Nancy, Nancy (1980).

Goguen [1980]
J.A. Goguen, "How to prove algebraic inductive hypotheses without induction", 5th Conf. on Automated Deduction. Les Arcs (1980).

Guttag [1980]
J. Guttag, "Notes on type abstraction", IEEE Trans. on Soft. Engin., 6, (1980), pp. 13–23.

Goguen et al. [1978]
J.A. Goguen, J.W. Thatcher, E.G. Wagner, "An initial algebra approach to the specification of abstract data types", Current Trends in Programming Methodology (R.T. Yeh ed.), Vol. IV Data structuring, Prentice Hall (1978).

Guttag and Horning [1978]
J.V. Guttag and J.J. Horning, "The algebraic specification of abstract data types" Acta Informatica, 10, (1978), pp. 27–52.

Guttag et al. [1978]
J. Guttag, E. Horowitz, D.R. Musser, "The design of data types specifications", Current Trends in Programming Methodology (R.T. Yeh ed.), IV Data Structuring, Prentice Hall, Engl. Cliffs New Jersey, (1978), 60–79.

Guttag et al. [1978]
J. Guttag, E. Horowitz, D.R. Musser, "Abstract data types and software validation," C.A.C.M., 21, 12 (1978), pp. 1048–1064.

Gaudel et al. [1978]
M.C. Gaudel, G. Terrine, "Synthèse de la représentation d'un type abstrait par des types concrets", Actes du Congrès A.F.C.E.T. Théories et Techniques de l'Informatique, Hommes et Techniques, Paris, Tome 1 (1978); pp. 434–445.

Huet [1980]
G. Huet, "Confluent reductions: abstract properties and applications to term rewriting systems", *J.A.C.M.,* 27, 4 (1980), pp. 797–821.

Huet et al. [1979]
G. Huet, J.J. Lévy, "Call by need computations in non-ambiguous linear term rewriting systems," Rapport de recherche Laboria n° 359 (1979).

Jouannaud et al. [1982]
J.P. Jouannaud, P. Lescanne, F. Reinig, "Recursive decomposition ordering", in *Formal Description of Programming Concepts* (Ed. D. Bjorner), North Holland (1982).

Kamin et al. [1980]
S. Kamin, J.J. Lévy, "Attempts for generalizing recursive path orderings", Draft paper (Feb. 1980).

Knuth and Bendix [1970]
D.E. Knuth, P.B. Bendix, "Simple word problems in universal algebras," in *Computational Problems in Abstract Algebra,* (ed. John Leech) Pergamon Press, 1970.

Lescanne [1979]
P. Lescanne, "Etude algébrique et relationelle des types abstraits et de leurs représentations," Thèse de l'Institut National Polytechnique de Lorraine. Centre de Recherche en Informatique de Nancy (1979).

Majster [1979]
M.E. Majster, "Limits of the 'algebraic' specification of abstract data types," SIGPLAN Notices, 12 (1977), pp. 37–42.

Musser [1980]
D. Musser, "On proving inductive properties of abstract data types," 7th ACM Symposium on Principles of Programming Languages (1980).

Partsch and Broy [1979]
H. Partsch and M. Broy, "Examples for change of types and object structures," in *Program Construction* (F.L. Bauer and M. Broy eds.), *Lecture Notes in Computer Science* 69, Springer Verlag, Berlin (1979), pp. 421–463.

Plaisted [1978]
D.A. Plaisted, "A recursively defined ordering for proving termination of term rewriting systems," Dept. of Computer Science Research Report 78–948, University of Illinois, Urbana IL (Sept. 1978)

Rémy [1980]
J.L. Rémy, "Construction, évaluation et amélioration systématiques de structures de données," *R.A.I.R.P Theoretical Computer Science,* 14 (1980), pp. 83–118.

Rémy [1982]
J.L. Rémy, "Etude des systems de réeciture conditionnels et applications aux types abstraits algebraiques", These de l'Institut National Polytechnique de Lorraine, Centre de Recherche en Informatique de Nancy (1982).

Rémy and Veloso [1981]
J.L. Rémy and P.A.S. Veloso, "Comparing data type specifications via their normal forms", *Int. J. of Comp. and Inf. Sciences,* 11,3 (1982), pp. 141–152, see also: "An economical method for comparing data type specifications," SIGPLAN Notices (1981).

Thatcher et al. [1978]
J.W. Thatcher, E.G. Wagner, and J.B. Wright, "Data type specification: Parameterization and the power of specification techniques" Proc. SIGACT Symp. on the Theory of Computing (1978).

Vuillemin [1974]
J. Vuillemin, "Correct and optimal implementations of recursion in a simple programming language" J. Comp. Syst. Sc. 9 (1974), pp. 332–354.

Veloso and Pequeno [1979]
P.A.S. Veloso and T.H.C. Pequeno, "Don't write more than you have to: a methodology for the complete and correct specification of abstract data types with examples," series : Monografias in Ciencia da Computatiao, n° 10/79, Rio de Janeiro, (May 1979).

CHAPTER 9

Compiler Construction From High-Level Specifications

M.C. Gaudel*

Ph. Deschamp

M. Mazaud
INRIA**

"... a general notation for semantic specification would permit the development of a true compiler generator, just as B.N.F. led to the development of parsers generators".

R.D. Tennent, C.A.C.M. 1976.

* Present address: Centre de Recherches de la CGE — MARCOUSSIS Route de Nozay 91460 Marcoussis

** INRIA Domaine de Voluceau 78150 Rocquencourt FRANCE

A. Introduction

For a long time, much attention has been given to the systematic development of compilers. In this area automatic production of parsers from a B.N.F.-like specification of a grammar is now widely known and used, (Boullier [1980]). These tools allow only partial construction of compilers, the syntactic part. The so-called semantic part has to be written most of the time by hand. The discovery of a high level specification method of programming languages which would be well-suited to compiler construction is still an unsolved problem.

In the first part of this paper, we briefly present the current state of the art. In the second part we suggest a formalism for describing the semantics of programming languages which seems to be convenient for compiler specification. As an example, we outline what the semantics of a usual programming language with recursive procedures looks like in this formalism. In the third part, the specification of an implementation of this same language is presented and discussed.

In the last part, the overall structure of the compiler generator PERLUETTE (which accepts such specifications as inputs) is explained and the current state of development and experimentation of the system is given.

B. Current State of the Art

Most of the industrial compilers are developed nowadays using a parser generator and inserting some so-called "semantic routines" or "semantic actions" in the parser. Several more sophisticated methods have been suggested to help the design of the semantic routines. Tools like Knuthian Attributes (W-grammars, Affix-grammars) are useful to specify formally contextual verifications and code generation without worrying about tedious problems such as management of the semantic stacks (Knuth [1968]). These methods definitely make easier compiler design and development. But they are far from providing the ability of implementing programming languages from a high-level semantic definition. Practically speaking, numerous experimental systems have been developed which deal with attributed grammars. As far as the authors know, very few of them are used in industrial contexts. This is probably due to some lack of efficiency and to the inherent complexity of writing an attributed grammar for a real compiler.

The citation given in "exergue" gives a good idea of the author's feeling about compiler generation. Several experiments have been or are currently performed in order to use a formal semantic description of the source language in a compiler generator. Mosses [1975, 1978] and many others use denotational semantics. In Semanol 76 (Anderson *et al.* [1976]) the semantics is described in an operational (or computational) way. At this time, there exist few systems providing an implementation from the semantic definition of a programming language and all of them are used in research projects.

In the author's opinion it is not sufficient to give the source language semantics. To state a complete specification of a compiler, both the source and the target languages (semantics) must be given, as suggested by F.L. Morris [1973]. Then, it becomes possible to produce compilers from any source language into any target language:

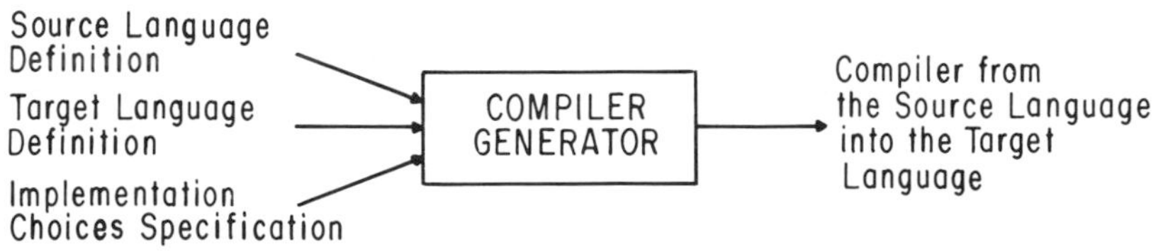

However, to specify and to verify the correctness of the implementation choices is a hard task in the denotational framework (Milne [1977]). We believe it is more realistic to make use of the recent results on the representation of algebraic data types (Guttag and Horning [1978], Guttag *et al.* [1978], Goguen *et al.* [1976]) and the associated proof methods. This is the basic idea of the specification method and the compiler generator we are presenting here.

C. Semantic Description of Programming Languages

Our approach has already been introduced in Gaudel *et al.* [1978]:

— the semantics of the Source Language and of the Target Language are both described with the same formalism;

— the semantic value of a program is a term of an algebraic data type;

— the representation of the semantic values of the source programs in terms of semantic values of target programs is specified and proved as the representation of an abstract data type by another one.

C.1. Algebraic Data Types

First we recall briefly what is an *algebraic data type.* As it is pointed out by the terminology an algebraic data type is a *many-sorted algebra.* The *presentation* of such a type is a triple $<T, F, A>$: T is a set of *names of sorts;* F is a signature, i.e., a set of *names of operations* with the corresponding arities; A is a set of axioms specifying the properties of the operations of F. A classical approach is to consider that the data type corresponding to such a presentation is the *initial algebra* in the category of the F-algebra satisfying the axioms A. A good and complete introduction to these concepts can be found in Guttag *et al.* [1978] and Goguen *et al.* [1976]. An example of a presentation of the *integer* data type is given below.

```
types int;
operations
  (int,int) → int : plus, sub, mult, div;
  . . .
axioms
  plus(x, int'0') = x
  plus(x,plus(y,z)) = plus(plus(x,y),z)
  . . .
```

N.B.: Constants of a data type are enclosed between quotes, preceded by the name of their type. Usually they are considered as nullary operator. In our case we prefer to consider int 'DIGIT-STRING' as a function of *string* into *int.* The axioms on this function are not given here; for a complete presentation see Gaudel [1980a].

C.2. An Example of Semantic Description

As an example of a source language, we consider a typical Pascal-like programming language: SIMPROC. This language allows us to declare and use simple variables, arrays and procedures. Simple and mutual recursivity are possible. Procedure parameters can be called-by-value or called-by-variable. SIMPROC statements are: assignment, procedure call, sequential composition, and conditional composition.

For the sake of simplicity, we assume that all the declared identifiers are different: if necessary, they should be renamed, see Deschamp [1980]. We furthermore consider only correct programs (without so-called compile-time errors). This increases the readability of the semantic functions, since many tests can be omitted.

The complete semantic definition of a language is made up of two parts: in the first one, the presentation of the corresponding abstract data type is given, with some restrictions, i.e. error cases specification; the second part is the definition of the semantic functions, where a meaning is given for each kind of sentence in the language, as a term of the abstract data type.

C.2.1. Semantics of expressions

As an introduction we partially give the abstract data type specification and the semantic functions for arithmetic expressions. Among the sorts, there is the sort *int* given previously but also *variables* [(1)] and *identifiers*.

The semantic function V yields for each expression of SIMPROC a term of the int data type. It is defined by equations such as:

V[E + T] = plus (V[E], V[T])
V[(E)] = V[E]
V[NUMBER] = int 'NUMBER' etc.

where E, T, and NUMBER are some non-terminals of the language. It is important to notice that the functional symbols are not interpreted: we have no more knowledge about "plus" than what is specified in the axioms.

We then describe the properties of identifiers in SIMPROC: every identifier is local to a procedure or to the program (to which the identifier PROG is associated). The identifier types are directly deduced from the data types of SIMPROC:

<u>type</u> *id* = <u>union</u> (*var-id, array-id, proc-id, ref-id*);
<u>operations</u>
(*id*) → *proc-id: scope*,

The *scope* operation gives, for any identifier, the identifier of the procedure to which it is local.

One of the most difficult issues encountered when describing such a language is that a variable identifier, local to a procedure, refers to a different variable for each call of that procedure. In addition, we want to be able to specify which variable is referred to by an identifier non-local to the current procedure. To deal with this problem we introduce the type call of procedure and some operations on it.

<u>type</u> *call*,
<u>operations</u>
( ) → *call* : *currentcall ;*
(call) → *call* : *caller ;*
(call) → *proc-id* : *name ;*

(1): In Algol 68 terminology, one would use the word "name", in denotational semantics the word "location".

An example of the relationship between calls and procedure identifiers is illustrated by the figure below:

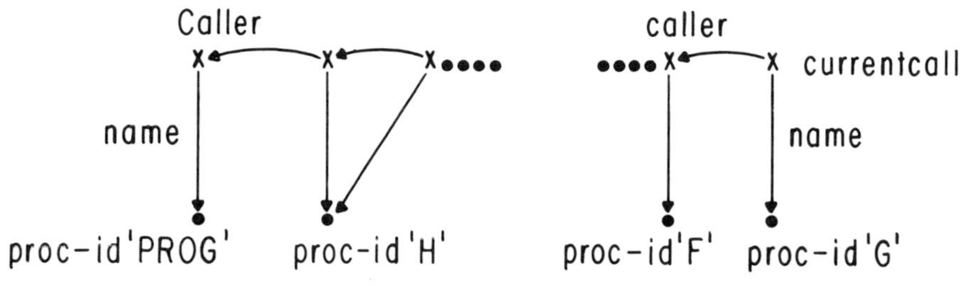

where 'x' stands for a call and '.' stands for a procedure identifier.

An important property we must state is that all the calls in the chain are different. (Some procedure identifiers are possibly the same, as recursive calls are allowed.) We then have the following axioms:

$$(\textit{caller}\,(c1) = \textit{caller}\,(c2)) \supset (c1 = c2)$$
$$\textit{caller}\,(c) \neq \textit{current call}$$

The relationship between identifiers, variables and calls is given by:

<u>type</u> *var* ;

<u>operations</u>
(*var-id, call*) → *var : designates*,
(*var*) → *int : value-of*,

<u>axioms</u>

[1] $(id1 \neq id2) \supset \textit{designates}\,(id1,c1) \neq \textit{designates}\,(id2,c2)$

[2] $(c1 \neq c2) \wedge (\textit{name}(c1) = \textit{name}(c2) = \textit{scope}\,(id)) \supset \textit{designates}\,(id,c1) \neq \textit{designates}\,(id,c2)$

[3] $(\textit{name}(c) \neq \textit{scope}\,(id)) \supset \textit{designates}\,(id,c) = \textit{designates}\,(id,\textit{caller}(c))$

Axiom [1] expresses that two different identifiers designate two different variables. Axiom [2] describes the duplication of local variables for each procedure call. Axiom [3] specifies that, if an identifier is not a local one, it designates the same variable as in the caller, be it local or global to the caller. (Keep in mind that all identifiers are different.)

These axioms are not the most concise ones, but we use them here for reasons of understandability.

To conclude the presentation of this part of the abstract data type, let us give the semantic functions for simple identifiers of SIMPROC: depending on the context where an identifier is used, its meaning can be a term of the *var* data type or of the *int* data type.

L[IDENT] = designates(var-id 'IDENT', currentcall)
V[IDENT] = value-of (L[IDENT])

N.B.: Array elements and called-by-variable parameters are not treated here. See Gaudel *et al.* [1978], Gaudel [1980a], Deschamp [1980].

C.2.2. Semantics of Statements

To describe the semantics of statements, we introduce a new name of type (Gaudel [1980b]):

type *modif*;

The semantic value of a statement is a term of this type. Let S be the corresponding semantic function. Among the operations with *modif* as co-domain, there are:

operations

(var,int)	→ *modif* : *assign;*
(int, int, modif, modif)	→ *modif* : *cond;*
(modif, modif)	→ *modif* : *concat;*

S is defined by the following equations:

$$S[\text{VAR} := \text{E}] = assign\,(L\,[\text{VAR}], \text{V}[\text{E}])$$
$$S[\ \underline{\text{if}}\ \text{E}_1\ \underline{\text{eq}}\ \text{E}_2\ \underline{\text{then}}\ \text{SL}_1\ \underline{\text{else}}\ \text{SL}_2] = cond\,(V[\text{E}_1], V[\text{E}_2], S[\text{SL}_1], S[\text{SL}_2])$$
$$S[\text{S}_1;\text{S}_2] = concat\ \ (S[\text{S}_1],\ S[\text{S}_2])$$

We need some formal definitions of these operations, but before stating them we are going to give an intuitive idea of what a *modif* is. Let us consider, for instance, the modification *assign* (v,i). Its meaning is that the formula "value-of (v) = i" becomes valid. The properties of the *value-of* operation are then changed and, accordingly, the algebraic data type is different. Thus the meaning of a statement is a transformation of the algebraic data type. It is convenient to describe such transformations by using the notion of "formulas of an algebraic data type". We call the set of these formulas a "state".

Definition 1:

Let <T,F,A> be the presentation of the algebraic data type associated with a programming language.

A *state* is a set S of formulas t = t', where t and t' are some *constant* terms of the data type, which satisfies the following properties:

i) $t = t \in S$ for all the terms t of the data type ;
ii) $t = t' \in S ==> t' = t \in S$;
iii) $t = t' \in S$, $t' = t'' \in S ==> t = t'' \in S$;
iv) for all f of F such that the range of f is not modif,
if t and t' belong to the domain of f:
$t = t' \in S ==> f(t) = f(t') \in S$.

Definition 2:

The state *generated by a set of axioms* A is the smallest state which contains all the formulas obtained by substituting, in each axiom a of A, to all the free variables occurring in a, all the constant terms of $<T,F,A>$ of the relevant sort.

These formulas are called 'directly derivable from A'.

Actually, the last definition defines the well-known smallest-congruence relation in $<T,F,A>$. It means that we are considering the initial algebra semantics for the algebraic data types used to characterize a state.

Definition 3:

A state *satisfies a set of axioms* A if it contains all the formulas directly derivable from A.

We have now the elements to describe the semantics of a programming language. Let us call A the set of axioms which defines the operations of the programming language *but* the modifiable ones. This set of axioms is satisfied by all the states of any program of the language. The initial state of a program is the state generated by A.

Given a current state, a modification (an assignment for instance) removes some formulas from the states and adds some new ones. In order to describe these transformations we need, at first, some way to state the semantics of a term of type Modif. Let m be such a term. We note

$$S' = appl(m,S)$$

the resulting state when applying the modification denoted by m to the state S.

The definitions of the operations *concat* and *cond* are:

$$appl(concat(m1, m2), S) = appl(m2, appl(m1, S))$$
$$(i=j) \in S ==> appl(cond(i,j,m1,m2), S) = appl(m1, S)$$
$$(i=j) \notin S ==> appl(cond(i,j,m1,m2), S) = appl(m2, S)$$

To formalize the assignment, one uses a primitive modification *subst* which is called "generalized substitution". Intuitively, subst$(f(\lambda),\mu)$ transforms a state S in such a way that:

- for all x which is equal to λ in S, f(x) is equal to the value of μ in S;
- the other operations, and f(y), where y is not equal to λ in S, are unchanged.
- no contradictions are introduced.

The rather complicated definition of subst given below insures that no inconsistencies are introduced in the resulting state even if there are some occurrences of f in λ or μ.

First, let us consider the following state (where f' does not belong to F and has the same arity as f):

$$\{S + f'(x) = \text{if } eq(x, \lambda) \text{ then } \mu \text{ else } f(x)\}$$

This state is the result of adding a new axiom to S. By definition S + a is the smallest state which contains S and all the formulas which are directly derivable from a (see Definition 2).

Now, the definition of subst can be given:

$$appl(subst(f(\lambda), \mu), S) = \{P \mid P[f'/f] \in \{S + f'(x) = \text{if } eq(x,\lambda) \text{ then } \mu \text{ else } f(x)\}\}.$$

Thus the definition of the *assign* operation above is:

$$assign(v,i) = subst\ (value\text{-}of\ (v),\ i)$$

All the modifications of the Source Language are defined in terms of appl and subst. The same thing is done for the Target Language: it is then possible to prove representations of the modifications.

C.2.3. Semantics of Procedures

One of the interesting points in this approach is that the specification of complex features, as a procedure call, is straightforward. Among the operations of the abstract data type, there are:

<u>operations</u>

(proc-id)	→ *modif : possesses ;*
(proc-id)	→ *var-id : par1 ;*
(proc-id, var-id, modif, proc-id)	→ *modif : proc-decl ;*
(proc-id, int, proc-id)	→ *modif : proc-call ;*

The value possessed by a procedure identifier is a term of type *modif* which is the semantic value of the body of the procedure. There is no problem with recursive declarations since we only consider the term, without interpretation. (We would otherwise have to speak of the least-fixed point theorem and Scott's theory.) The semantics of a procedure call with one called-by value parameter is then:

$$S[\text{call IDENT(E)}] = \text{proc - call (proc - id'IDENT', V[E], name(currentcall))}$$

where proc-call is the concatenation of three modifications:

— a concurrent substitution which describes the change in the calls chain and the assignment of the parameter;
— the body of the procedure;
— the return.

proc-call(p,i,q) =

$$\begin{array}{c} concat^{3}(\,subst(<caller(currentcall'),name(currentcall')), \\ currentcall, value\text{-}of(designates(par1(\mathrm{p}), currentcall'))>, \\ <currentcall, \mathrm{p}, currentcall', i>), \\ possesses(\mathrm{p}), \\ subst(currentcall, caller(currentcall)) \end{array}$$

Note that substitution embodies a very powerful means to specify the creation of a new call and of the new variables associated with it: in every valid formula the occurrences of *currentcall* are replaced by *caller(currentcall),* and from the axioms about *caller* and *designates* one can see that the 'new' *currentcall* is different from all the other calls and that the variables local to the called procedure are different from all the other variables.

D. Specification of an Implementation

D.1. Target Language Definition

As it has been said previously the same formalism is used for the Target Language and the Source Language. As an example of an abstract data type associated with a Target Language, we assume we have:

<u>type</u> *value, address, register, cond-code,...,*
  content = <u>union</u> (*value, address*) ;

<u>operations</u>

(address, value)	→ *address : index ;*
(value, value)	→ *cond-code : compare ;*
( )	→ *cond-code : cc ;*
(address)	→ *content : ca ;*
(register)	→ *content : cr ;*
. . .	
(address, content)	→ *modif : store ;*
. . .	

<u>axioms</u>

index(a, *value* '0') = a ;
index(a, *add*(v1,v2)) = *index*(*index*(a,v1),v2) ;
. . .
store(a,v) = *subst*(*ca*(a), v) ;
. . .

D.2. Representation Specification

The machine resources are managed in a very classical way:

– At run-time the memory is managed as a stack of areas, each of which is related to a current call;

— We assume the existence of an infinite stack of registers. At run-time of the procedure of level i, the first i registers contain the address bases of i areas related to that call and to the current calls of the embedding procedures;
— Each area related to a call includes

- in the first word the address area of the caller,
- in the second word the return label,
- in the two following words, the parameters, and
- the local variables.

— Top pointer designates the top-of-stack register.

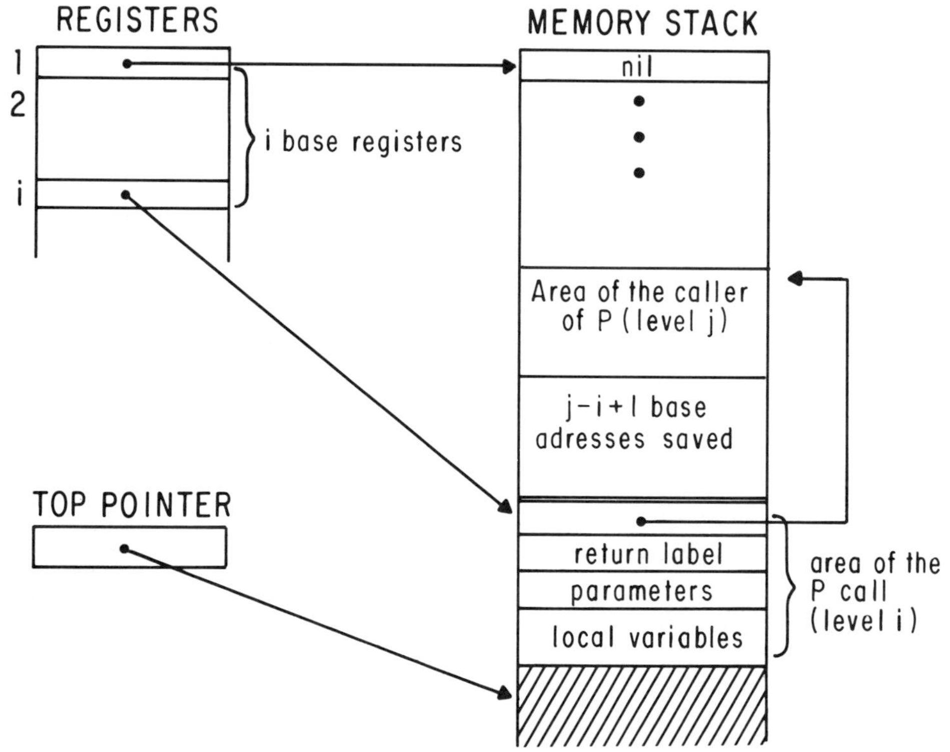

We give here the specification of a very usual representation of variables and assignment: a variable identifier is represented by a constant value which is a displacement from a base register; the content of this register is an address which is the representation of the relevant call; obviously the operation *designates* is represented by indexing.

The formal specification is given below. For each sort of the Source data type, the representing Target sorts are given followed by the representation of the constants (if any). For each source operation, its representation as a composition of the operations of the Target data type is stated.

```
type var-id : value ;
repr var-id 'V' = value 'ALLOC1(V)'
end var-id;
```

[The function ALLOC1 searches in the allocation table for the displacement associated to V; if V is not found the function ALLOC1 returns a displacement depending on its scope. ALLOC1 is an example of a meta function which describes compile-time computations.]

```
type var : address ;
end var ;

type int : value ;
   repr int 'I' = value 'CONVERT(I)'
end int ;

type call : address ;
end call ;
  . . .
repr op designates (var-id v, call c) → var =
   index (cr (register 'NIV(v)', repr v) ;
   [The function NIV returns the procedure level of v.]

repr op value-of (var v) → int =
   ca (repr v) ;

repr op assign (var-id v,int i) → modif =
   store (repr i, repr v) ;

repr op currentcall ( ) → call =
   cr (register 'base') ;
  . . .
```

The specification of the implementation becomes very systematic and formal. It is possible, from this specification, to translate Source terms into Target terms.

But the main advantage is the opportunity to check out that the axioms of the Source data type are kept by the representation and accordingly, to get a proof of the implementation.

E. The System

The PERLUETTE system is a compiler generator. From the definitions of the source and target languages and from the representation specification, a translator working in three steps is built. Only the "syntactic" part of the abstract data types is used. The axioms are necessary only for the proof, not for the translator construction.

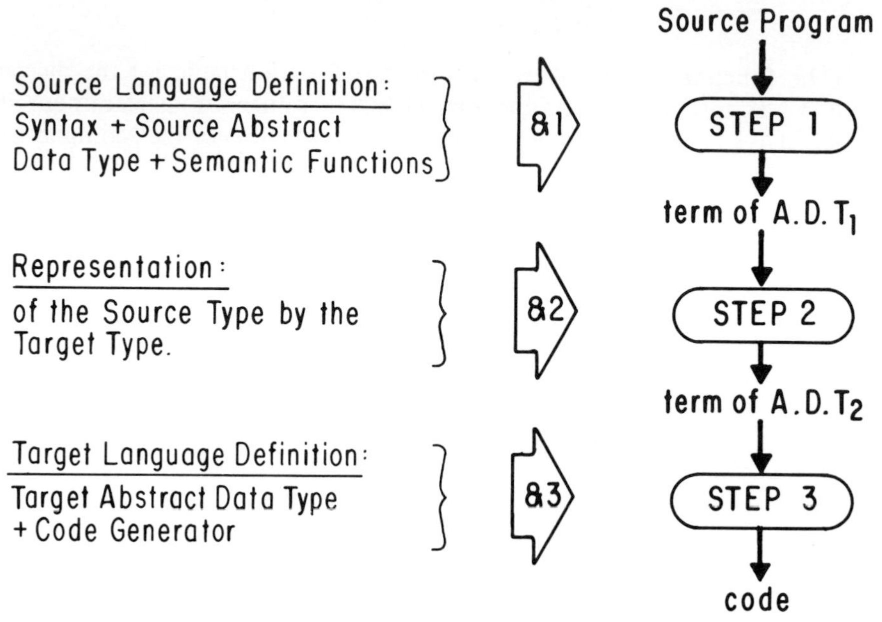

Compiler Specification *PERLUETTE System* *Compiler*

In the source language description the semantic functions are defined by the means of semantic attributes. The type checking is specified in the same way. The module P1 is made of the syntactic constructor and the tabulation part of the DELTA system (Lorho [1975]) with a preprocessor which transforms the functional schemes which occur in attribute definitions into LISP expressions. The STEP1 module is a compound of the parser and the evaluation part of the DELTA system, which have been associated with a LISP system. The result of STEP1 is a LISP form: the Source Term is represented as a tree.

The P2 module builds, from the representation specification, a LISP subsystem which is a list of functions. A lambda (or nlambda) definition is associated to each declaration of type (if there are constants of this type) or operation.

The following definitions are associated respectively to the type *var-id* and to the operations *designates, value-of, currentcall.*

```
(var-id
 (nlambda (v)
     (list 'value (allocl v) v)))
(designates
 (lambda (v a)
     (list 'index
       (list 'cr (list 'register (niv v)))
       v)))
(assign
 (lambda (v i)
     (list 'store (list v i))))
(value-of
 (lambda (v)
     (list 'ca v)))
(currentcall
 (lambda ( )
     (list 'cr 'register 'base)))
```

This subsystem is used to obtain the target term from the source term. STEP 2 evaluates the source term, each of its subterms being considered as a call of a function of the LISP subsystem.

We give now the example of the LISP form generated by STEP 1 for an assignment where the variable j is local to a procedure of level 2, the variable m to a procedure of level 1.

```
(assign(designates(var-id'j') (currentcall))
     (value-of(designates(var-id'm') currentcall)))
```

Let us consider that the displacement associated to j by the meta function ALLOC1 is '3' and the displacement associated with m is 4. Thus the LISP form resulting from STEP 2 is:

```
(store(index(cr(register'2')) value'3')
     (ca(index(cr(register'1'), value'4'))
```

The whole system is currently running on Multics. It is written in PASCAL and largely uses the syntactic constructors SYNTAX and semantic constructor SDELTA. The formal definition of SIMPROC and the specification of the representation presented above have been effectively used as test examples for the available version of the system (P1, STEP 1, P2, STEP 2). The P3 and STEP 3 modules have been tested for the description of the DEC 11 machine language. A code generator for Multics will be described later on.

Meanwhile a Pascal Compiler is described and is used as a realistic test for the PERLUETTE System. By now the implementations are hand-proved but we believe that the proofs can be mechanized: as a first experiment, we have used the DTVS of D. Musser [1977] to prove an implementation of the expressions of a language with flexible arrays, and more recently AFFIRM to prove the representation of booleans as condition-code values.

F. Conclusion

This system is a typical example of an application of theoretical methods to a practical compiler-compiler. The advantages of this formal approach are obvious: the modularity of the compiler specification facilitates the use of the system; the Source and the Target Languages are defined independently and it is feasible to use the corresponding parts of translator (STEP 1 or STEP 3) in several compilers.

Although the system is still an experimental one, it shows the feasibility of automatic compiler construction. This hopeful result is definitely a consequence of the specific class of considered programs and of the large amount of research already performed in the area of programming language semantics.

Appendix

We create a program which inputs a list of integers and returns that list with all nonpositive integers removed.

1) SOURCE LANGUAGE DEFINITION.

1.1) SOURCE DATA TYPE.

```
Type pos_int :
Fin pos_int ;
Type neg_int :
Fin neg_int ;
Type seq :
   op(pos_int, seq) → seq : pos_append ;
   op(pos_int, seq) → seq : neg_append ;
Fin seq ;
axioms
  {There are no axioms because there is no semantics: we are
   specifying a simple syntactic transformation.}
```

1.2) LEXICAL DESCRIPTION.

```
SIMPLE CLASSES
digit = "0123456789" ;
space = " " ;
others = "-" ;
TOKENS
%string = digit {digit} ;
%blancs = space {space} ;
```

1.3) SYNTAX.

```
<prog> = <list> ;
<list> = %string | - %string | %string %blancs <list> | - string %blanc <list> ;
```

1.4) SEMANTIC EQUATIONS.

```
<list> = %string ;
#modele(<list>) : pos_append(pos_int'string', ^)
<list> = -%string ;
#modele(<list>) = neg_append(neg_int'string', ^)
<list> = %string %blancs <list> ;
#modele(<list>) = pos_append(pos_int'string',modele(<list>'))
<list> = - %string %blancs <list> ;
#modele(<list>) = neg_append(neg_int'string',modele(<list>'))
```

2) TARGET LANGUAGE DEFINITION.

2.1) TARGET DATA TYPE.

```
Type pos_int :
Fin pos_int ;
Type pos_seq :
    op( ) → pos_seq: & ;
    op(pos_int, pos_seq) → pos_seq ;
Fin pos_seq ;
```

2.2) CODE GENERATION SPECIFICATION.

```
Code(pos_int'P') = 'P' ;
Code( & ) = ' ' ;
Code(add(p,s)) = Code(p).' '.Code(s) ;
```

3) REPRESENTATION SPECIFICATION.

```
Type pos_int : pos_int ;
        repr pos_int'P' = pos_int'P'
end pos_int
```

```
Type neg_int : pos_int ;   {This is a trick: neg_int must be represented by a target sort. But
                             from the representation of neg_append any representation of a
                             neg_int is going to disappear.}
      repr neg_int'N' = pos_int'N'
end neg_int
Type seq : pos_seq ;
end seq
repr op ^( ) = & ;
repr op pos_append(pos_int p, seq s) = add(repr p, repr s) ;
repr op neg_append(neg_int n, seq s) = repr s ;
```

References

Anderson *et al.* [1976]
E.D. Anderson, F.C. Belz and E.K. Blum, "SEMANOL (73) a metalanguage for programming the semantics of programming languages," *Acta Informatica* 6 (1976), pp. 109–131.

Goguen [1976]
J.A. Goguen, "Abstract data types as initial algebras and the correctness of data representations," *Proceedings of Conference on Computer Graphics and Pattern Recognition and Data Structures* (1976).

Boullier [1980]
P. Boullier, "Generation automatique d'analyseurs syntaxiques avec rattrapage d'erreurs," *Journees Francophones sur la production assistee de Logiciel,* Geneve (1980).

Deschamp [1980]
Ph. Deschamp, "Production de compilateurs a partir d'une description simantique des langages de programmation: le systeme Perluette," These de Docteur-Ingenieur-INPL (Oct. 24, 1980).

Gaudel [1980a]
M.C. Gaudel, "Generation et preuve de compilateurs basees sur une semantique formelle des langages de programmation," These d'Etat, INPL (March 10, 1980).

Gaudel [1980b]
M.C. Gaudel, "On the concepts of state and of states modification in programming languages," *WG 2.2 Meeting,* Lyngby, Danemark (June 1980).

Gaudel *et al.* [1978]
M.C. Gaudel, Ph. Deschamp and M. Mazaud, "Semantics of procedures as an algebraic abstract data type," LABORIA Report n° 334 (1978).

Guttag and Horning [1978]
J.V. Guttag and J.G. Horning, "The algebraic specifications of abstract data types," *Acta Informatica* 10 (1978).

Guttag *et al.* [1978]
J.V. Guttag, E. Horowitz and D.V. Muser, "Abstract data types and software validation," *CACM* 21, n° 12 (1978), pp. 1048–1064.

Knuth [1968]
D.E. Knuth, "Semantics of context free languages," *Mathematical Systems Theory* 2,2(1968).

Lorho [1975]
B. Lorho, "Semantic attributes in the system DELTA," Symposium on Implementation of Algorithmic Languages, Novossibirsk, USSR (1975).

Milne [1977]
R. Milne, "Verifying the correctness of implementations," Advanced Course on Semantics of Programming Languages, Antibes (1977).

Morris [1973]
F.L. Morris, "Advice on structuring compilers and proving them correct," *Proc. of Symp. on Principles of Programming Languages,* Boston (1973).

Mosses [1975]
P.D. Mosses, "Mathematical semantics and compiler generation," Ph.D. Thesis, University of Oxford (1975).

Mosses [1978]
P.D. Mosses, "A compiler-generation system using denotational semantics," Reference Manual, Department of Computer Science, University of Aarhus, Denmark (June 1978).

Musser [1977]
D.R. Musser, "A data type verification system based on rewrite rules," *6th Texas Conf. on Computing Systems,* Austin, Texas (Nov. 1977).

SECTION IV

OTHER TECHNIQUES FOR SYNTHESIS AND ANALYSIS

CHAPTER 10

The Roles Of Knowledge And Deduction In Algorithm Design

David R. Barstow
Schlumberger-Doll Research
P.O. Box 307
Ridgefield, CT 06877

Abstract

In the earliest attempts to apply artificial intelligence techniques to program synthesis, deduction (that is, the use of a general purpose mechanism such as a theorem prover) played a central role. Recent attempts have relied almost exclusively on knowledge about programming in particular domains, with no significant role for

This material is based upon work supported by the National Science Foundation under Grant No. MCS 78−03827. Any opinions, findings, and conclusions or recommendations expressed in this publication are those of the author and do not necessarily reflect the views of the National Science Foundation. The research was done while the author was an Assistant Professor in Computer Science at Yale University. An earlier version of this paper was presented at the Sixth International Joint Conference on Artificial Intelligence, Tokyo, August 1979. Reprinted with permission from Machine Intelligence 10, edited by J.E. Hayes, D.Michie, and Y.H. Pao, 1982 and published by Ellis Horwood Ltd., Chichester.

deduction. Even in such knowledge-based systems, however, there seems to be an important role for deduction in testing the applicability conditions of specific programming rules. This auxiliary role for deduction is especially important in algorithm design, as can be seen in the hypothetical synthesis of a breadth-first enumeration algorithm. The interplay between knowledge and deduction also shows how one can be motivated to consider the central mathematical properties upon which particular algorithms are based, as illustrated in the synthesis of two minimum cost spanning tree algorithms.

A. Introduction

In applying artificial intelligence techniques to the problem of automatic program synthesis, two basic approaches have been tried. In the first approach, deduction (i.e., the use of a general-purpose deductive mechanism such as a theorem prover or problem solver) played a central role. The basic idea was to rephrase the program specification as a theorem to be proved or a problem to be solved. If a proof or solution was found, it could be transformed into a program satisfying the original specification. The Heuristic Compiler [16], the early work of Green [7] and Waldinger and Lee [17], and the recent work of Manna and Waldinger [12,13,14] are all examples of this approach. The second approach, an application of the knowledge engineering paradigm, is based on the assumption that the ability of human programmers to write programs comes more from access to large amounts of knowledge about specific aspects of programming than from the application of a few general deductive principles. For example, the PECOS system [2,3] had a knowledge base of four hundred rules about many aspects of symbolic programming, and could apply these to the task of implementing abstract algorithms.

Although much progress has been made, neither approach has yet "solved" the automatic programming problem, and it is suggested here that neither one alone ever will. There are two problems with the deductive approach. First, for programs of real-world interest, the search space is too large to be explored by a theorem prover. While current systems are capable of synthesizing programs such as "greatest common divisor", no system can yet synthesize any program of significantly greater complexity. And without guiding the theorem prover with some kind of knowledge about how to write programs, it is unlikely that much more progress can be made. Second, since there is a one-to-one correspondence between proofs and programs, if there is a measure by which one program may be preferred to another (e.g., efficiency), then the theorem prover must find, not just any proof, but the "right" proof. That is, the theorem prover needs to know that it is really writing programs and how to relate differences between proofs to differences between programs.

On the other hand, the knowledge-based approach has only been applied to the synthesis of programs from relatively algorithmic specifications. While many rules for algorithm refinement have been developed and tested, very little progress has been made on rules for algorithm design. And, as has been observed elsewhere (e.g., [9]), algorithm design requires a deep understanding of the problem to be solved, an understanding which seems to include the ability to reason (make deductions) about the problem.

In the rest of this paper, a way to combine these two approaches is suggested, as summarized in the following two statements:

> (1) Just as there are specific rules for refining abstract algorithms into concrete implementations, there are also rules for designing algorithms from non-algorithmic specifications.
>
> (2) In testing the applicability conditions of such rules, it is necessary to call on a deductive mechanism to test whether certain properties hold for the program being developed. (See [4] for a similar model of algorithm design, but more closely related to the deduction approach.)

In the next section, these two statements are illustrated with a detailed synthesis of a graph algorithm. In section C, two other algorithm syntheses are used to demonstrate how these roles for knowledge and deduction help identify the mathematical basis for a particular algorithm.

B. Hypothetical Synthesis

The synthesis in this section consists of a sequence of rule applications, with each rule representing some fact that human programmers probably know and that automatic programming systems probably should know. Several of the rules can only be applied if some condition holds for the program under construction. These are the conditions that seem appropriate tasks for a deductive system, and are indicated by the word "PROOF" in the synthesis. The synthesis will be presented in a mixture of English and a hypothetical Algol-like language, in order to focus on the nature of the programming knowledge and the algorithm design process, independent from any formalism used to express them. It should be noted at the outset that this synthesis is beyond the capabilities of any current automatic programming system, and of course, the rules and proofs will have to be formalized before the synthesis could be automated.

B.1 Specification

> Write a program that inputs the root R of a tree with a known successor function CHILDREN(N) and constructs a sequence of all (and only) the nodes of the tree, such that if the distance from R to N1 is less than the distance from R to N2, then N1 precedes N2 in the sequence (where the distance from X to Y, denoted by D(X,Y), is the number of arcs between X and Y; thus, D(R,X) is the depth of X).

This specification is basically a non-algorithmic description of a breadth-first enumeration of the nodes in a tree. One way to deal with this specification would be to recognize that a breadth-first enumeration is the desired program, and to use specific knowledge about breadth-first enumerations (perhaps a template) to produce a program. In this hypothetical synthesis, we will consider the more interesting case in which the basic algorithm must actually be developed.

B.2 Overview

The synthesis process goes through four major stages. First, the task is broken into two parts, a "producer" that generates the nodes in the desired order, and a "consumer" that builds a sequence from the nodes generated by the producer. The second stage involves constructing the consumer, which simplifies into a simple concatenation operation. The third stage, in which the producer is built, is relatively complex but eventually results in a simple queue mechanism in which nodes are produced by taking them from the front and the children of each produced node are added at the back. Finally, the two processes are combined together into a simple WHILE loop.

B.3 The Transfer Paradigm

A common paradigm for many programming problems involves viewing the problem as one of transferring objects from an input set to an output set. For example, selection and insertion sort can both be viewed as instances of the transfer paradigm. One way to implement such a transfer program is to build two processes, with one (a producer) producing the objects in the input set, and the other (a consumer) using the objects to build the output set. If we view the present task this way, the input set consists of the nodes in the tree and the output set is the ordered sequence. Thus, we may apply the following rule to break the task into two subtasks:

> If the task involves using the elements in one set to build another set, try the transfer paradigm, with the producer producing the elements from the first set and the consumer building the second set.

When the transfer paradigm is used, objects are passed from the producer to the consumer in some order, which we may call the transfer order. While the transfer order is often inconsequential, the following rule suggests that a particular order might be useful in this case:

> If a consumer builds an ordered sequence, try constraining the transfer order to satisfy the same ordering.

After applying these two rules, the original task has been broken into two subtasks:

Producer:

> Send the nodes of the tree to the consumer in any order satisfying the following constraint:
>
> if D(R,N1) < D(R,N2), then N1 is produced before N2

Consumer:

> Using the objects received from the producer, build a sequence satisfying the following constraint:
>
> if D(R,N1) < D(R,N2), then N1 precedes N2 in the sequence
>
> The objects are received from the producer in an order satisfying the following constraint:
>
> if D(R,N1) < D(R,N2), then N1 is produced before N2

We may now consider the producer and consumer separately, viewing each as a separate process.

B.4 The Consumer

A process such as the consumer consists of several parts, including an initialization and an action to be performed at each stage. The first rule establishes the initialization part of this consumer:

> If a consumer builds a set consisting solely of objects received from another process, the set is initially empty.

The next rule establishes the action to be performed at each step:

> If a consumer builds a set consisting of all objects received from another process, the action at each step involves adding the object to the set.

Finally, we may apply a special case rule for adding an object to an ordered sequence:

> If it is known that an object follows every member of an ordered sequence, the object may be added to the sequence by inserting it at the back.

Before applying this rule, we must prove its applicability condition: "the object follows every member of the ordered sequence." In this case, the proof is trivial, since the objects are received from the producer in the desired order, and these objects are the only members of the sequence. Having applied the rule, we are now finished with the consumer:

```
Consumer:
   Initialization:
      S := <>
   Action:
      X := {receive from producer}
      insert X at the back of S
```

where "<>" is the empty sequence.

B.5 The Producer

We are now ready to consider the producer, a process that produces the nodes of the tree with a constraint on the order of production. The following rule suggests a way to write the producer:

> If a producer produces all of the nodes of a graph according to some ordering constraint, try using an ordered enumeration of the nodes in the graph, where the action for each step of the enumeration is to produce the enumerated node.

Any such enumeration produces the nodes of the graph, guaranteeing that each node is produced exactly once. In order to do this, the enumerator must know, at each stage, which objects have and have not been enumerated. That is, the state of the enumeration must be saved between "calls" to the producer process. In this case, the objects to be enumerated are all objects which may be reached from the root node by following zero or more arcs. At any point in the process of following these arcs, certain nodes will have been found and others will not. Of those that have been found, some will have had their successors looked at, and others will not. Thus, the enumeration state may be maintained by tagging the nodes (at least conceptually) with one of three labels. This technique for saving the state is summarized in the following rule:

> If a graph is represented as a base set of nodes and a successor function, the state of an enumeration of the nodes may be represented as a mapping of nodes to one of three states: "EXPLORED", "BOUNDARY", and "UNEXPLORED".

(Note that up to this point, no decision has been made about how to implement this mapping. In particular, there is no commitment to explicitly tagging each of the nodes with one of these labels. As will be seen, the final representation of this mapping involves only a single set, consisting of those nodes tagged "BOUNDARY".)

Any enumeration involves several parts, including an initialization, a termination test, a way of selecting the next object to enumerate, and a way of incrementing the state. The following three rules are all based on the technique just selected for saving the enumeration state:

> If the state of an enumeration of the nodes in a graph is represented as a three-state mapping, the state may be initialized by setting the image of all nodes to "UNEXPLORED" and then changing the image of the base nodes to "BOUNDARY".
>
> If the state of an enumeration of the nodes in a graph is represented as a three-state mapping, the termination test involves testing whether any nodes are mapped to "BOUNDARY". If not, the enumeration is over.
>
> If the state of an enumeration of the nodes in a graph is represented as a three-state mapping, the action at each stage consists of selecting some node mapped to "BOUNDARY" (the enumerated node), changing its mapping to "EXPLORED", and changing the mapping of all of its "UNEXPLORED" successors to "BOUNDARY". The "BOUNDARY" node must be selected to satisfy any ordering constraints on the enumeration.

Thus, applying the above rules gives us the following description of the producer (where MARK[X] specifies the image of X under the mapping and MARK-1[Y] specifies the inverse image of Y, that is, the set of all nodes which map to Y under MARK):

```
Producer:
 Initialization:
   for all nodes, X:
     MARK[X] := "UNEXPLORED"
   change MARK[R] from "UNEXPLORED" to "BOUNDARY"
 Termination test:
   is MARK-1["BOUNDARY"] empty?
 Each step:
   X := select any node in MARK-1["BOUNDARY"] such that
        if X1 and X2 are nodes remaining to be selected
          and D(R,X1) <D(R,X2) then X1 is selected before X2
   change MARK[X] from "BOUNDARY" to "EXPLORED"
   for all successors, Y, of X:
        if MARK[Y] = "UNEXPLORED"
          then change MARK[Y] from "UNEXPLORED" to "BOUNDARY"
   {send X to the consumer}
```

Note that the nodes that remain to be enumerated include some tagged "UNEXPLORED" as well as those tagged "BOUNDARY". Thus, the selection operation, and the constraint on it, may be precisely stated as follows:

```
X := select any node in MARK-1["BOUNDARY"] such that
                    D(R,X) ≤D(R,Z) for all Z such that MARK[Z]="BOUNDARY"
                      or MARK[Z] = "UNEXPLORED" and Z is reachable from R
```

If we call the set from which an object is to be selected the "selection set", and the set of which that object must be minimal the "constraint set", the following rule gives us a way to implement the selection operation:

> If a selection operation is subject to an ordering constraint, and every member of the constraint set is dominated by some member of the selection set, the selection operation may be implemented by taking the minimal element of the selection set.

When this rule is applied, we have the following:

X := closest node in MARK-1["BOUNDARY"]

However, before applying the rule we must prove one of its conditions:

PROOF: for all Z such that MARK[Z] = "BOUNDARY"
      or MARK[Z] = "UNEXPLORED" and Z is reachable from R,
   there exists an X such that
      MARK[X] = "BOUNDARY" and $D(R,X) \leqslant D(R,Z)$

If MARK[Z]="BOUNDARY", then Z is such an X. Suppose MARK[Z]="UNEXPLORED" and Z is reachable from R. Since the graph is a tree, there is exactly one path from R to Z, and there must be some node, W, on this path such that MARK[W]="BOUNDARY". This is true since either (i) R is "BOUNDARY" and W can be R; or (ii) the path from R to Z begins with some nonzero number of "EXPLORED" nodes and the next node (which is the desired W) is "BOUNDARY", since all of an "EXPLORED" node's successors are either "EXPLORED" or "BOUNDARY". Since $0 \leqslant D(W,Z)$, $D(R,W) \leqslant D(R,Z)$, and thus W dominates Z. QED

Thus, the action at each stage of the enumeration has been simplified:

```
X := closest node in MARK-1["BOUNDARY"]
change MARK[X] from "BOUNDARY" to "EXPLORED"
for all successors, Y, of X:
  if MARK[Y] = "UNEXPLORED"
    then change MARK[Y] from "UNEXPLORED" to "BOUNDARY"
{send X to the consumer}
```

Part of the body involves a test of whether a node is "UNEXPLORED". The following rule enables this test to be omitted:

> If it is known that the value of a test in a conditional will always be true, the test may be omitted and the conditional refined into the action of the "true" branch.

In order to apply this rule, we must prove one of its conditions:

> PROOF: every successor of X is "UNEXPLORED"
>
> Every successor of X was initially "UNEXPLORED", since every node (except the root, which is not a successor of any node), was initially "UNEXPLORED". The mark of an "UNEXPLORED" node is changed in only one place, when the node is the successor of some other node. Thus, if a successor of X is not "UNEXPLORED", it must be the successor of some node other than X, which is impossible because the graph is a tree. Hence, every successor of X is "UNEXPLORED". QED

With these simplifications to the enumerator, it is clear that only the "BOUNDARY" tag is really being used. Thus, the mapping may be simplified somewhat by getting rid of references to the other two possibilities (i.e., making them implicit instead of explicit). This knowledge is embodied in the following rules:

> If a range element is only used in "set image" and "change image" operations, it may be made implicit.
>
> If the range element of a "set image" operation is implicit, the operation may be omitted.

The result of applying the above rules is as follows:

```
Producer:
 Initialization:
   change MARK[R] from implicit to "BOUNDARY"
 Termination test:
   is MARK-1["BOUNDARY"] empty?
 Each step:
   X := closest node in MARK-1["BOUNDARY"]
   change MARK[X] from "BOUNDARY" to implicit
   for all successors, Y, of X:
     change MARK[Y] from implicit to "BOUNDARY"
   {send X to the consumer}
```

We are finally ready to implement the mapping. When inverse images are frequent operations, the mapping can be inverted, as suggested by the following rule:

> A mapping with domain X and range Y may be represented as a mapping whose domain is Y and whose range consists of subsets of X.

In addition to this data structure representation rule, we need the following rules dealing with operations on such data structures:

> If a mapping is inverted, the inverse image of a range object may be found by retrieving the image of the range object under the inverted mapping.
>
> If a mapping is inverted, a range object may be assigned as the image of a domain object by adding the domain object to the image of the range object under the inverted mapping.
>
> If a mapping is inverted, the image of a domain object may be changed from one range object to another by removing the domain object from the image of the first range object and adding it to the image of the second range object.
>
> If a mapping is inverted, operations on implicit domain objects may be omitted.
>
> If a mapping is inverted, the initial state of the mapping is that all range sets are empty.

Applying these rules gives the following (where MARK' is the inverted mapping):

```
Producer:
  Initialization:
    MARK'["BOUNDARY"] := {}
    add R to MARK'["BOUNDARY"]
  Termination test:
    is MARK'["BOUNDARY"] empty?
  Each step:
    X := closest node in MARK'["BOUNDARY"]
    remove X from MARK'["BOUNDARY"]
    for all successors, Y, of X:
      add Y to MARK'["BOUNDARY"]
    {send X to the consumer}
```

Of course, the inverted mapping must still be represented concretely. Here, the elements of the domain set are known precisely (there is only one) and all references to the mapping involve constants for domain elements, so a record structure is a particularly good technique:

> A mapping whose domain consists of a fixed set may be represented as a record structure with one field for each domain element.

We also need a rule for references to such a data structure:

> If a mapping is represented as a record structure, the image of a constant domain object may be referenced by referencing the corresponding field of the record.

This representation may be simplified further, as suggested by the following rules:

> A record structure with only one field may be represented as the object stored in the field.
>
> If a record structure is represented as the object stored in its single field, the field may be referenced by referencing the record structure itself.

Applying all of the above rules gives us the following (in which the single set is called B):

```
Producer:
  Initialization:
    B := {}
    add R to B
  Termination test:
    is B empty?
  Each step:
    X := closest node in B
    remove X from B
    for all successors, Y, of X:
      add Y to B
    {send X to the consumer}
```

We now have three operations on the B set to consider, and each depends on the representation for that set. Since one of the operations involves taking an extreme element under an ordering relation, it is natural to use an ordered sequence. We thus apply the following rule:

> A set whose elements have an ordering relation may be represented as an ordered sequence.

Having applied this rule, we must consider the operations on B. The "closest" operation may be refined by using the following rule:

> If a set is represented as an ordered sequence, the least element under the ordering may be found by taking the first element of the sequence.

Normally, removing an element from a sequence requires first searching for its position and then deleting that position. In this case, we can avoid the search by applying the following rule:

> If it is known that an element is the first element of a sequence, that element may be removed from the sequence by removing the first element.

Finally, we must consider the two addition operations, one adding R to B and the other adding each successor of X to B. In each case, we may apply the same rule used earlier in writing the consumer:

> If it is known that an object follows every member of an ordered sequence, the object may be added to the sequence by inserting it at the back.

And, in each case, we must prove the applicability condition. The proof when adding R to B is trivial, since B is empty. However, the proof for adding the successors of X to B is somewhat more complicated. Before considering the main proof, we need the following lemma:

LEMMA: for some X in B and for all Z in B,
$D(R,X) \leqslant D(R,Z) \leqslant D(R,X)+1$

> This is clearly true initially, since B = {R}. Suppose it is true at some point. There are only two changes in B that can be made during one step:
>
> (a) X is removed from B
> (b) Y is added to B
>
> (a) After X is removed, either B is empty (in which case adding Y restores the desired property) or there is some new closest node, call it W. We know:
>
> $D(R,X) \leqslant D(R,W)$ and $D(R,W) \leqslant D(R,Z)$ for all Z in B
>
> so substitution (into the inequality that held before X was removed) gives us:
>
> $D(R,W) \leqslant D(R,Z) \leqslant (R,X)+1 \leqslant D(R,W)+1$ for all Z in B

(b) After Y is added to B, since $D(R,Y)=D(R,X)+1$,

$$D(R,W) \leqslant D(R,Z) \leqslant D(R,Y) \leqslant D(R,W)+1 \text{ for all Z in B}$$

Thus, by induction we have:

for some X in B and for all Z in B,
$D(R,X) \leqslant D(R,Z) \leqslant D(R,X)+1$

QED

Note that this lemma holds after each successor of X is added to B. So we are now ready to prove the condition necessary for adding Y at the back of B.

PROOF: Y follows every element of B

The ordering constraint on B is:

if $D(R,X) \leqslant D(R,Z)$ then X precedes Z in B

So what we wish to show is:

if $D(R,X) \leqslant D(R,Z)$ for all Z in B,
and Y is a successor of X,
then $D(R,Z) \leqslant D(R,Y)$ for all Z in B.

The lemma indicates that there is some X in B such that everything else in B is at least as far from the root as X, but not further away than 1 arc. Therefore, this property must hold for the closest node in B. Since $D(R,Y) = D(R,X)+1$, if Y is a successor of X, we know that $D(R,Z) \leqslant D(R,Y)$ for all Z in B. Thus, Y follows every element of B. QED

We have now finished the producer:

```
Producer:
  Initialization:
    B := <>
    insert R at the back of B
  Termination test:
    is B empty?
  Each step:
    X := first element of B
    remove first element of B
    for all successors, Y, of X:
      insert Y at the back of B
    {send X to the consumer}
```

B.6 Recombining the Producer and Consumer

Finally, by applying the following rule, the producer and consumer can be recombined into a single process:

> A transfer program involving a producer and consumer may be refined into a WHILE loop whose condition is the termination test of the producer.

And we have the following algorithm for enumerating the nodes of a tree in breadth-first order:

```
S := <>
B := <>
insert R at the back of B
while B is not empty do
  X := first element of B
  remove first element of B
  for all successors, Y, of X:
    insert Y at the back of B
  insert X at the back of S
```

From this point on, rules about simple symbolic programming (such as those in PECOS) could produce the final implementation. The interesting aspects involve representing the sequences S and B (each is probably best represented as a linked list with a special pointer to the last cell), and the "for all" construct (which depends on the representation of the set returned by CHILDREN(P)).

C. Motivating the Use of Critical Lemmas

As another illustration of this view of the roles of knowledge and deduction in algorithm design, let us look briefly at the problem of finding the minimum cost spanning tree in a weighted undirected graph. The problem may be specified as follows:

> Write a program that inputs a weighted, undirected, connected graph G and constructs a subgraph T such that:
>
> (1) T is a tree;
> (2) T contains every node of G;
> (3) W(T) $\leqslant$min { W(T') | T' is a subgraph of G which is a tree and which contains every node of G}.

(W is the weight function on edges; when applied to a graph it denotes the sum of the weights on the edges.)

There are two standard algorithms for this task, one due to Kruskal [11] and one due to Prim [14]. For each of these, there are a variety of implementations, based on different techniques and representations for the sets and graphs involved. (Cheriton and Tarjan give a detailed discussion of several implementations [5].) Both standard algorithms are based on a single lemma, which may be stated as follows:

> If T is a subgraph of some minimum cost spanning tree of G, T contains all the nodes of G, T' is one of the connected components of T, and x is an edge of minimal weight connecting T' to another connected component of T, then T'+{x} is a subgraph of some minimum cost spanning tree of G.

If one knows this lemma, it is not difficult to come up with either of the standard algorithms. But what if one does not know the lemma? In the rest of this section, we will see that the model of algorithm design discussed in earlier sections leads naturally and directly to the fundamental lemma. In particular, we will consider the minimum cost spanning tree from two different viewpoints, in each case applying a sequence of general programming rules, and in each case arriving at the need to prove the lemma. In the interests of brevity, syntheses will not be pursued at the same level of detail as the breadth-first enumeration algorithm, but only to a sufficient degree to show how one is led to the fundamental lemma in each case. (Note: the rest of this discussion is worded as if the minimum cost spanning tree were unique: this is not crucial to the synthesis process, but simplifies the discussion.)

C.1 Toward Kruskal's Algorithm

The minimum cost spanning tree problem can be viewed as one of selecting a subset of the edges of the original graph. Under such a view, the transfer paradigm (used already for the breadth-first enumeration problem) is appropriate, as suggested by the following rule:

> If the task involves finding a subset of a given set, try the transfer paradigm, with the producer producing the elements from the first set and the consumer testing each for inclusion in the subset.

Of course, this paradigm only succeeds if it is actually possible to test the elements of the set individually as they are produced, which at this point in the synthesis cannot be guaranteed (hence, the word "try" in the rule). If it turns out to be impossible to construct such a test, then a more general paradigm (such as depth-first search allowing back-up by more than one step) or even an entirely different paradigm (such as the tree-growth paradigm of the next section) must be tried.

As with the breadth-first enumeration problem, the transfer order is again important. The following rule suggests that a particular order might be useful in this case:

> If the object being built by the consumer must satisfy a minimality constraint based on some function of the objects being transferred, try constraining the transfer order to be in increasing order of the function.

Again, there is no guarantee that this approach will succeed; this is simply a heuristic suggesting a potentially useful strategy. This heuristic is, in fact, one of the key steps in reaching Kruskal's algorithm, but note that it is far more general than its application to this particular problem. For example, it also plays a role in creating the standard breadth-first algorithm for determining the shortest path from one node in a graph to another. Note also that there are other heuristics that one could apply here. For example, one could try considering the edges in order of decreasing weight, resulting ultimately in an algorithm that gradually removes edges from the original graph until the minimum spanning tree is determined (Kruskal describes this as "Construction A" [11].)

After applying these two rules, the original task has been broken into two subtasks:

```
Producer:
  Send the edges of the graph to the consumer
  in any order satisfying the following constraint:
    if W(E1) < W(E2), then E1 is produced before E2

Consumer:
  Using the objects received from the producer,
  build a subset T of the objects such that:
   (1) T is a tree;
   (2) T contains every node of G:
   (3) W(T) ≤min{W(T') | T' is a subgraph of G which is a tree
                 and which contains every node of G}.
  The objects are received from the producer in an order
  satisfying the following constraint:
   if W(E1) < W(E2), then E1 is produced before E2
```

For this task, the producer is relatively simple, essentially involving only a sort of the edge set of G, either as a pre-process before sending any edges to the consumer, or intermittently during the process of sending. In either case, the algorithm depends on the representation of G and the representation chosen to hold the sorted edge set, but is not particularly complicated. Since it is also not relevant to identifying the critical lemma, the synthesis process for the producer will be skipped in the interest of brevity.

The consumer is a process that produces a subgraph of the original graph, assuming that it receives the edges of G in order of increasing weight. The following rule suggests a way to write the consumer:

> If a consumer builds a subset from the set produced by the producer, try writing a test that determines whether or not an element belongs in the subset, based solely on the subset that has been constructed so far, on the order in which the elements are received, and on the fact that any element already received by the consumer is either not in the desired subset or has been added to the subset already.

In effect, this rule suggests trying to add the elements to the subset one at a time. (A less desirable alternative would be to reconsider the entire set of edges received so far, but this would be somewhat strange in light of the original decision to try the transfer paradigm.) The problem here is to determine a relatively simple test. Before developing the test, we must define the notion of a "preventive" constraint:

> A constraint is preventive if, whenever a set S violates the constraint, there is no superset of S that satisfies it.

Given this definition, the following rule suggests a test to be used in this problem:

> If you know that the following is true (where S is the desired set, S' is the subset constructed so far, x is the element received by the consumer):
> If S' is a subset of S
> and S' + {x} does not violate any preventive constraints on S
> and if y was received before x then y is in S' or not in S
> then S' + {x} is a subset of S.
> then the test for whether a new element may be added to the subset constructed so far may be implemented as a test of whether the new element does not violate any preventive constraints on the subset.

(While this phrasing may seem a bit long for a "rule," its length is due to its precision; a less formal statement would be "Try using only preventive constraints in the test.")

In order to apply the rule, the condition must be tested (here, T is the desired subgraph of G):

> If T' is a subset of T
> and T' + {x} does not violate any preventive constraints on T
> and if y was received before x then y is in T' or not in T
> then T' + {x} is a subset of T.

Which are the preventive constraints? The constraint that T be a tree reduces to two subconstraints: that T be acyclic and that T be connected. Of these, the constraint that T be acyclic is clearly preventive: if a graph is cyclic, no graph containing it can be a tree; the constraint that T be connected is clearly not preventive: any disconnected graph may be extended into a connected graph. The constraint that T contain every node of G is not preventive: any graph that contains a subset of the nodes of G can be extended to contain every node of G. Finally, the minimality constraint is preventive (at least, if all edge weights are positive): if the weight of a graph is greater than some value, then any extension of that graph will also be greater than that value.

The third antecedent in the rule's condition may also be instantiated for this problem: since the edges are being transferred in order of increasing weight, the condition "y was received before x" reduces to "$W(y) < W(x)$". Thus, the condition on the rule becomes:

If T' is a subset of T
  and $T' + \{x\}$ is acyclic
  and $W(T' + \{x\}) \leqslant \min\{W(T') \mid T'$ is a subgraph of G which is a tree
    and which contains every node of G$\}$
  and if $W(y) < W(x)$ then y is in T' or not in T
then $T' + \{x\}$ is a subset of T.

The antecedents of this condition are not independent. In particular:

$W(T' + \{x\}) \leqslant W(T) \leqslant \min\{W(T') \mid T'$ is a subgraph of G which is a tree
  and which contains every node of G$\}$

since T must contain at least one of the edges not yet received by the consumer and since x has the least weight of the edges not yet received. Thus, the condition may be reduced to:

If T' is a subset of T
  and $T' + \{x\}$ is acyclic
  and if $W(y) < W(x)$ then y is in T' or not in T
then $T' + \{x\}$ is a subset of T.

The clause about weights may be rephrased slightly:

if y is in T and not in T' then $W(x) \leqslant W(y)$

that is,

$W(x) \leqslant \min\{W(y) \mid y$ is in T and not in T'$\}$

Since

$$\{ y \mid y \text{ is in } T \text{ and not in } T' \} \text{ is a subset of } \{ y \mid T' + \{y\} \text{ is acyclic} \}$$

the following is sufficient:

$$W(x) \leqslant \min \{ W(y) \mid T' + \{y\} \text{ is acyclic} \}$$

leading to the following condition which, if proved, is sufficient to permit the rule to be applied:

```
If T' is a subset of T
  and T'+ {x} is acyclic
  and W(x) ≤min { W(y) | T'+ {y} is acyclic }
then T'+ {x} is a subset of T.
```

Thus, by applying a sequence of relatively general programming rules, we are led naturally and directly to a (slightly) special case of the fundamental lemma. The rest of the synthesis process is less interesting, and will be omitted. The final algorithm is as follows (assuming that the producer sorts the edges before sending any to the consumer):

```
T := {}
E := edges of G sorted by weight;
while E is non-empty do
   X := first element of E;
   E := rest of  E;
   if T+ {X} is acyclic
      then T := T+ {X}
```

Of course, a considerable amount of work remains to be done. In particular, the test for acyclicity can be very inefficient unless some sophisticated data structures are maintained. Aho, Hopcroft and Ullman describe an efficient implementation of Kruskal's algorithm [1].

C.2 Toward Prim's Algorithm

In the previous section the minimum cost spanning tree was viewed as a problem of finding a particular subset of a known set. The problem can also be viewed in terms more specific to graph theory by applying the following rule:

> If the task involves finding a tree satisfying certain constraints, try starting with a degenerate tree (a single node) and adding edges to the tree until the constraints are satisfied.

As with the transfer paradigm, there is no guarantee that this strategy will succeed. (In particular, it may not be possible to determine an appropriate edge to add at each step.) But it still seems a reasonable strategy to explore.

In applying this strategy, there are two subtasks: determining a technique for selecting the initial node and determining a technique for finding an edge to add at each step. For the first, the following rule may be used:

> If the set of nodes in the desired tree is known, try selecting any node from the set as the initial node.

Of course there are other plausible techniques. (For example, selecting one of the nodes on an edge of minimal weight is another good way to start.) But the unconstrained selection seems as good as any, and is easily implemented (depending on the representation of the nodes of the graph).

The second subtask, determining a technique for finding an edge to add at each step, is more difficult, but the following rule offers a possibility:

> If the tree to be grown must satisfy a minimality constraint, and you know that the following holds.
>
> ```
> if T' is a subtree of T
>   and x extends T'
>   and T'+{x} does not violate any preventive constraints on T
>   and W(x) = min {W(y) | y extends T' }
> then T'+{x} is a subtree of T
> ```
>
> then at each stage select the edge of minimal weight that extends T' and does not violate any preventive constraints.

(This rule is actually just a variant of the minimality heuristic used in developing Kruskal's algorithm.) Before applying the rule, the condition must be proved. As with Kruskal's algorithm, the only preventive constraints are that T'+{x} be acyclic and that the weight of T' be minimal. By similar reasoning, the condition reduces to:

```
if T' is a subtree of T
  and x extends T'
  and W(x) = min { W(y) | y extends T' }
then T'+{x} is a subtree of T
```

Again we are led naturally and directly to a (slightly) special case of the fundamental lemma. In this case, we were led even more directly to the necessary condition than with Kruskal's algorithm, but this is primarily because the rules were specific to graph problems, rather than being oriented more generally toward sets.

The final algorithm is as follows:

```
T := {}
while T does not contain all of the vertices of G do
  X := edge of least weight that connects T to some vertex not in T;
  T := T+{X}
```

Here again, considerable work remains to be done. In this case, the hard part is determining the edge of least weight that extends T. Dijkstra and Kerschenbaum and Van Slyke give implementations of the basic algorithm [6,10].

D. Discussion

The model of algorithm design and program synthesis that emerges from these examples has several parts. First, there is a body of strategic rules, each suggesting a paradigm that may lead to an algorithm for solving the given problem. These strategic rules are relatively specific (more so than condition- or recursion-introduction rules) yet applicable in a variety of situations. Even when applicable, however, there is rarely a guarantee that the paradigm will indeed result in an algorithm: that can only be determined by trying to fill out the pieces. If an algorithm does result, and if the applicability conditions have all been met, then the algorithm will be correct (assuming correctness of the individual rules). Second, there is a larger body of implementation rules which can be used to refine an abstract algorithm into concrete code in some target language. These rules are again relatively specific, but usually independent of any particular target language. Finally, there must also be rules for the chosen target language; while these rules must at some point take over from the implementation rules, this may occur at different levels of abstraction for different languages and problems.

In the process of testing the applicability conditions of any of these rules, deduction plays a very important role. When it is used, it involves properties of the program being developed and properties of the domain. (It is interesting to note that, even if a condition can not be proved, one could apply the rule, resulting in a heuristic program; this would be especially useful if the condition were tested and found to hold on a large number of examples.) Although not illustrated by the hypothetical syntheses, a mechanism for choosing from among applicable rules is also needed. Among the possibilities for such a mechanism are efficiency models of the program being developed (i.e., an evaluation function) and heuristic rules based both on the efficiency of the target program and on the likelihood of a particular strategy succeeding. This latter consideration seems especially important in the initial algorithm design phase.

The rules illustrated here (and the concepts involved in them) are relevant in many more situations than these graph problems. As noted earlier, the transfer paradigm provides a useful model for several sorting algorithms, including selection and insertion sort. In fact, choosing the transfer order seems to be the primary decision involved in differentiating the two types of sorting, and the rule about adding objects to ordered sequences is itself used in deriving an insertion sort. (For a more detailed discussion of this paradigm for sorting, see [8].) As another example, the notion of an enumeration state is critical to any enumeration (in fact, it corresponds to the loop invariant), and the three-state mapping used here is simply a generalization of the standard state-saving schemes used for sequences such as linked lists and arrays.

In fact, many of the rules used in these hypothetical syntheses have already been implemented and tested in the PECOS system. For example, PECOS's knowledge base included the rules about inverted mappings and record structures, and they were used in the implementation of several abstract algorithms, including a reachability algorithm and a simple concept formation algorithm.

E. Conclusions

In order for future automatic programming systems to be truly useful when applied to real-world tasks, they will necessarily have to deal with complex programs at a rather detailed level. It seems to me that this will only be possible if these systems have effective access to large amounts of knowledge about what we today consider to be the task of programming. While some of this knowledge certainly involves general strategies, such as the conditional and recursion introduction rules of deduction-based systems, much of the knowledge also involves rather specific detailed facts about programming in particular domains, such as PECOS's rules about symbolic programming. (This is reminiscent of discussion of the trade-off between generality and power in artificial intelligence systems.) The first attempt to build such programming knowledge into an automatic programming system involved applying the knowledge to algorithmic specifications, in which the programming task was to produce a concrete implementation. The hypothetical syntheses of a breadth-first enumeration algorithm and two minimum-cost spanning tree algorithms demonstrate that specific detailed knowledge about programming can also be of significant value in the algorithm creation process. At the same time, they illustrate an important role to be played by deduction in such knowledge-based automatic programming systems: as a mechanism for answering particular queries about the program under construction, in order to test the applicability conditions of particular rules. Important directions for future research involve adding to the rules that have already been codified and developing deductive techniques for use with such rules.

F. Acknowledgements

Much of this work resulted from discussions during seminars in Knowledge-based Automatic Programming held at Yale in Fall 1977 and Spring 1979. L. Birnbaum helped develop the basis for the section on minimum cost spanning trees. B.G. Buchanan, D. McDermott, A. Perlis, C. Rich, H. Shrobe, L. Snyder, R. Waldinger, and R. Waters provided helpful comments on earlier drafts of the paper.

References

[1] Aho,A.V., Hopcroft,J.E. & Ullman,J.D. (1974). *The Design and Analysis of Computer Algorithms,* Reading, Mass: Addison-Wesley.

[2] Barstow,D.R. (1979). An experiment in knowledge-based automatic programming, *Artificial Intelligence,* **12**, 73–120.

[3] Barstow,D.R. (1979). *Knowledge-based Program Construction,* New-York and Amsterdam: Elsevier North-Holland, 1979.

[4] Bibel,W. (1980). Syntax-directed, semantics-supported program synthesis. *Artificial Intelligence,* **14**, 243–261.

[5] Cheriton,D. & Tarjan,R.E. (1976). Finding minimum spanning trees, *SIAM Journal of Computing,* **5**, 724–742.

[6] Dijkstra,E.W. (1959). A note on two problems in connexion with graphs, *Numerische Mathematik,* **1**, 269–271.

[7] Green,C.C. (1969). The application of theorem proving to question-answering systems. *AIM–96.* Stanford: Stanford University Computer Science Department.

[8] Green,C.C. & Barstow,D.R. (1978). On program systhesis knowledge, *Artificial Intelligence,* **10**, 241–279.

[9] Gries,D. & Misra,J. (1978). A linear sieve algorithm for finding prime numbers, *Communications of the ACM,* **21**, 999–1003.

[10] Kerschenbaum,A. & Van Slyke,R. (1972). Computing minimum spanning trees efficiently, *Proceedings of the 25th Annual Conference of the ACM,* pp. 518–527.

[11] Kruskal,J.B. (1956). On the shortest spanning subtree of a graph and the travelling salesman problem, *Proceedings of the American Mathematical Society,* **7**, 48–50.

[12] Manna,Z. & Waldinger,R. (1975). Knowledge and reasoning in program synthesis, *Artificial Intelligence,* **6**, 175–208.

[13] Manna,Z. & Waldinger,R. (1979). Synthesis: dreams => programs, *IEEE Transactions on Software Engineering,* **4**, 294–328.

[14] Manna,Z. & Waldinger,R. (1978). A deductive approach to program synthesis, Stanford: *AIM–320.* Computer Science Department, Stanford University.

[15] Prim,R.C. (1975). Shortest connection networks and some generalizations, *Bell System Technical Journal,* **36**, 1389–1401.

[16] Simon,H.A. (1963). Experiments with a heuristic compiler, *Journal of the ACM,* **10**, 493–506.

[17] Waldinger,R. & Lee,R.C.T. (1969). A step toward automatic program writing, *International Joint Conference on Artificial Intelligence,* (Washington,D.C.),pp. 241–252.

CHAPTER 11

Invariant Based Programs And Their Correctness

Ralph-Johan Back
Department of Computer Science
University of Helsinki

Editor's Note: The author has included a very complete discussion of our canonical example from Chapter 1. It turns out that through no fault of his own, the specification was understood to be that the output should be a list of all $n > 0$ from the input rather than all $n \geqslant 0$ as was assumed in Chapter 1. Hopefully, this will not cause confusion.

Abstract

The technique of starting from invariants in constructing iterative programs is studied. Invariants are viewed as internal specifications of the program, expressing requirements on the way in which the algorithm should work. The advantages of this view for checking program correctness and for locating possible errors in a program are discussed. A simple language for programs based on invariants is defined. The technique for constructing programs from invariants is described by means of an example. Finally, a system for checking program correctness and locating errors in programs is described.

A. Introduction

One of the main problems in programming is the question whether a given program is correct or not. Correctness is checked by two different techniques, program testing and program verification, neither one of which in itself is sufficient to decide whether a given program is correct or not. The limits of program testing are aptly characterized by Dijkstra's remark that testing only can be used to show the presence of errors, never their absence. This is usually cited as a motivation for program verification. On the other hand, program verification is only useful for showing the absence of errors, i.e. correctness, not their presence. The underlying assumption in program verification is that the program to be proved correct is in fact correct. The methods are not designed to detect program errors.

In practice, one does not know whether a given program is correct or not, and the important thing is to find this out. Moreover, if the program turns out to be incorrect, one wants to know where the errors are. Therefore both testing and verification will usually be needed. In addition, one needs debugging to locate possible errors. Even if testing does reveal that there is an error in the program, it will not provide any information about what kind of error is responsible for the incorrectness or where the error is in the program text. Only when testing results in a run-time error do we get a pointer to a specific location in the program text.

There have been some attempts to strengthen the traditional program verification techniques so that incorrectness of a program could be established (Brand [1978], Katz and Manna [1976]) and conversely to strengthen the testing methods so that correctness could be established (Goodenough and Gerhart [1975]). Debugging, however, is usually left as a more or less informal technique. The situation in checking program correctness should be compared with the elegance by which syntactic correctness is checked by a compiler. The compiler scans the program line for line and either detects one or more syntactic errors, indicating their places in the program text, or does not find any errors, in which case the program is declared syntactically correct. A similar system for checking semantic correctness would, if possible at all, clearly be desirable. We will here consider the possibility of such a system, in some form or another, in the context of simple iterative programs.

To make things more concrete, we will take a simple example program and consider how its correctness is checked. We choose the standard example of this book, i.e., a program which inputs a list of integers and returns that list with all nonpositive integers removed. Thus e.g. input (−7 2 9 −3 4) should produce output (2 9 4).

For simplicity, we assume that we have available a data type for lists, called *list of* T, where T is the type of the list elements (integer in this case). This data type is assumed to have at least the following constants and operations:

null—the empty list
head(L)—the first element in L
tail(L)—L with its first element removed
add(L,x)—L with the element x added as last

The input L and the output M will be lists of integers, declared by

var L,M: list of integer.

The entry and exit conditions are

entry: L = LO,
exit : M is LO with all nonpositive integers removed.

The constant LO denotes the initial value of L. The program will change the value of L, so we cannot refer to L in the exit condition.

We can make the exit condition more precise by introducing some additional notation. If L1 and L2 are lists, we write L1 << L2 to denote the fact that L1 is a sublist of L2, in the sense that L1 can be created from L2 by removing some elements from L2, without disturbing the order of occurrence of the remaining elements. We let e(L) denote the set of elements in the list L. Finally, if P(x) is a property of elements, then we can extend this property to sets of elements A by asserting P(A) if and only if P(x) holds for all x in A. With these conventions, the exit condition can be expressed by

$$\text{exit: } M << LO \text{ and } e(M) > 0 \text{ and } e(LO) - e(M) \leqslant 0$$

This says that M only containsintegers from LO, in their original order of occurrence (M << LO), that all integers in M are positive (e(M) > O) and that all positive integers of LO are included in M (because e(LO) − e(M) ⩽ 0, i.e. all integers in LO and not in M are nonpositive).

The following program is given as a solution to this programming problem:

```
remove: M:= null;
        while L ≠ null do
        begin x:= head(L);
        L:= tail(L);
        if x > 0 then M:= add(M,x)
        end.
```

The question now is whether this program is correct or not, i.e. does it satisfy its specification, given in the form of entry and exit conditions.

We will only consider *partial correctness* of programs here. A program S is partially correct with respect to entry condition P and exit condition Q, denoted P{S}Q, if whenever P holds initially and the execution of S terminates normally, Q will hold upon termination of S. The formula P{S}Q is referred to as a *partial correctness formula*. Thus, partial correctness of the above program is expressed by

$$\text{entry}\{\text{remove}\}\ \text{exit},$$

which says that if initially L = LO holds and the program terminates normally, then upon termination M will be LO with all positive integers removed. (The program is allowed to loop forever or to terminate abnormally.)

We can test this program by executing it for some selected inputs and checking that the outputs satisfy the exit condition. The values LO = (−7 2 9 −3 4) and M = (2 9 4) do e.g. satisfy the exit condition. When confident that the program does not contain any errors, we can try to prove it correct. Partial correctness is usually proved by attaching an assertion to each program loop (referred to as the loop *invariant*), which shows the situation holding prior to each iteration of the loop. A suitable invariant for this program is found by analyzing the behaviour of the program, looking at the situation which holds prior to the test of the loop. An initial part of LO has then been scanned, with its positive integers stored in M and the remaining integers still in L. This situation can be expressed by the invariant:

$$\text{moving: } M{*}L << LO \text{ and } e(M) > 0 \text{ and } e(LO) - e(M{*}L) \leqslant 0.$$

Here M*L denotes the concatenation of the lists M and L. To prove partial correctness, we have to show that this invariant holds initially, when the loop is entered, that it is preserved by each iteration of the loop and that it implies the exit condition, if the loop ever terminates. These conditions are referred to as *verification conditions.*

We can express the verification conditions quite nicely with partial correctness assertions, if we use the *assert-statement,* of the form

assert b

where b is a boolean condition. This statement has no effect if b is true, but if b is false, it forces an abnormal termination of the program.

The verification conditions of the program above are now the following. First, the initialization of the loop:

(1) entry {M:= null} moving.

Next, if the loop terminates, the exit condition must hold:

(2) moving {assert L = null} exit.

(Note that if L $\neq$ null, then an abnormal termination occurs, so the partial correctness assertion is trivially satisfied.) Finally, we have to show that each iteration preserves the loop invariant:

```
moving {assert L ≠ null;
        x:=head(L);
        L:= tail(L);
        if x > 0 then M:= add(M,x) } moving.
```

This last verification condition can in fact be split into two, by treating the cases x $>$ 0 and x $\leqslant$ 0 separately, giving the verification conditions

```
(3a)    moving {assert L ≠ null;
                x:=head(L);
                L:= tail(L);
                assert x > 0;
                M:= add(M,x) }  moving
```

and

```
(3b)    moving {assert L ≠ null;
                x:=head(L);
                L:= tail(L);
                assert x ≤ 0 } moving.
```

Partial correctness is now established by showing that each verification condition holds. This is quite straightforward, by considering the effects of the respective statement sequences. One can also express the verification conditions directly as first-order formulas, thus removing the last traces of program text. The verification conditions (1) and (2) correspond e.g. to the formulas

entry and M = null => moving
moving and L = null => exit.

The last two verification conditions are a little bit more complicated, (3a) corresponds e.g. to the formula

```
moving[x1,L1/x,L] and L1 ≠ null
                  and x = head(L1)
                  and L = tail(L1)
                  and x ≤ 0
                  => moving.
```

The variables x1 and L1 are here used to denote the initial values of x and L. We write moving[x1,L1/x,L] for the formula we get by substituting x1 for each (free) occurrence of x and L1 for each free occurrence of L in the formula moving.

The problem with this verification technique is that it only can provide a positive answer to the question whether the program is correct or not. If all verification conditions are found to be true, then the program is partially correct. If, however, some verification condition is not true, then we know nothing about the correctness of the program. It could still be correct, in which case the loop invariants must have been wrongly chosen, or it could be incorrect, so no choice of invariants could make all verification conditions true. Moreover, even if we could establish incorrectness, by testing or by some other means, we still could not locate the errors in the program. The notion of a specific location of an error is not meaningful when talking about partial correctness; the program is either all right or all wrong.

The situation would, however, be different, if we looked upon the invariants in a slightly different way. Rather than being a tool in verifying partial correctness, we could see them as *internal specifications* of the program, putting certain requirements on the way in which the algorithm is to work. In this case, if some verification condition is found to be false, it means that the algorithm does not satisfy its specifications, i.e. is incorrect, because some internal specification (invariant) or external specification (entry or exit condition) is violated. We could then use a *verification condition generator* to check the correctness of programs. It would compute all the verification conditions of the program (using the given invariants) and feed them to the programmer one by one, asking him (or maybe an automatic theorem prover) to decide whether they are true or false. If all verification conditions were found to be true, then the program would be correct. If some verification condition was found to be false, the program would be rejected as incorrect. Moreover, the places of the errors could also be localized: the parts of the program text from which the false verification conditions were computed.

The price to be paid for this is that the pre- and postconditions of the program together with the loop invariants must now be considered part of the program text. Correctness in the sense above is then turned into an inherent property of the program, which can be decided by a verification condition generator (assuming the availability of an oracle to decide whether an arbitrary verification condition is true or false). We will refer to programs of this kind, in which pre- and postconditions together with all loop invariants are explicitly stated, as *invariant based programs.*

This view of program correctness is acceptable if the invariants really can be understood as *specifications,* to be satisfied by the program code, rather than as *comments,* explaining how the program works. We will try to show below that the first view is defendable, by describing a programming method in which the invariants are designed before the program code is determined, thus serving as specifications for the latter.

The idea of using invariants to prove program correctness is due to Floyd [1967] and Naur [1966]. Hoare [1971] was the first one to use the invariants as guides in constructing programs, combining it with the stepwise refinement technique developed by Dijkstra [1968] and Wirth [1971]. The book by Dijkstra [1976] is an important step further in this direction, with the issue of termination being given special attention. The use of invariants without the restriction to while-programs, which is the approach we will take here, has been described by van Emden [1979] and by Reynolds [1978]. The use of invariants as internal specifications of the program has also been studied by Blikle [1979].

We will in this chapter consider the following questions concerned with invariant based programs:

(1) What is a suitable language for invariant based programs. We will describe a simple language which we think is well-suited to the construction of such programs.
(2) How should invariant based programs be constructed. We will describe, by means of an example, a programming method in which the invariants are designed before the code itself is constructed.
(3) How should the correctness of invariant based programs be checked. We will describe a verification condition generator for the proposed language which works as a compiler, checking for errors in the program text and marking all detected ones, declaring the program to be incorrect or correct depending on whether errors were found or not.

B. A Language for Invariant Based Programs

The use of invariants in program construction is usually combined with the stepwise refinement method, with its emphasis on simple control structures such as compound statements, conditional statements and while-loops *(while-programs).* Invariant based programs are usually expressed as while-programs, with the invariants given as comments in the program text. This is the approach used by Hoare, Dijkstra, Wirth and many others.

With this technique, the program is understood in terms of abstract statements (refinement steps) and their compositions. This approach requires a firm grip of the flow of control in a program. The control flow should therefore be as simple as possible. If, however, the program is understood in terms of its invariants, a simple flow of control becomes less important. Insisting on a restricted set of control structures makes it harder to connect the invariants together by statements. It works if the invariants and the control are designed at the same time, as is usually the case when applying the stepwise refinement technique, but it makes it difficult to design the invariants before the control flow is determined. One is easily forced into changing the original invariants, given as specifications, just to make it easier to connect them by the accepted control structures. Simplicity of control is then bought at the expense of complicating the invariants.

Free use of goto's in programs would give a sufficiently flexible way of connecting the invariants together. Use of goto's would have the additional advantage of providing a natural place where the program invariants could be attached: the program labels. However, a completely free use of goto's and other control structures would, in spite of the invariants, make the program difficult to understand, by hiding the program structure in a maze of jumps and labels.

We would like to have some form of compromise between these two extremes, which would combine the flexibility of goto-programs with the simple structure and safety of while-programs. Our solution is to use a restricted, syntactically sugared form of goto-programs, with the invariants used as carriers of the program structure. We associate invariants with the program labels and allow only certain very simple kinds of transitions between labels. The main design criterion, besides support for using invariants in programs, has been *modularity* of the flow of control: One should be able to understand, construct, change and check the correctness of syntactically separate parts of the program as independently of each other as possible. The program invariants will be used to specify the interfaces between these different parts of the program.

Our proposal should be understood as a suggestion on how invariants could be incorporated into a programming language, along the lines described in the introduction, not as a complete and finished language definition. We only consider flow of control in programs. Important issues, like support for modularity in the form of procedure or data abstractions, are left aside, as are questions concerned with language support for expressing the program invariants.

First, we define *simple statements.* A simple statement S will either be a label identifier, an assignment statement followed by a simple statement or a conditional statement. The syntax of simple statements is defined by

$$S ::= L \mid x := e; S_1 \mid \text{if } b_1 \rightarrow S_1 \,\Box\, \cdots \,\Box\, b_n \rightarrow S_n \text{ fi} \quad (n \geq 1).$$

Here L is a label identifier, x is a variable identifier, e is an expression, $b_1,\ldots,b_n$ are boolean expressions and $S_1,\ldots,S_n$ are simple statements. The syntax of identifiers, expressions and boolean expressions is the conventional one and will not be defined here.

A *compound statement* C is a collection of labelled simple statements. The syntax is

$$C := \text{begin } S_0 \,\Box\, L_1{:}\, S_1 \cdots \Box\, L_n{:}S_n \text{ end} \quad (n \geq 0),$$

where $S_0,\ldots, S_n$ are simple statements and $L_1,\ldots, L_n$ are distinct labels.

A *declaration* D is either a variable declaration or a label declaration. The syntax is

$$D ::= \text{var } x{:}\ T \mid \text{label } L{:}\ Q\,.$$

Here x is a variable identifier, T is a type, L is a label identifier and Q is an invariant. The syntax of invariants and types will not be further defined (first-order formulas can be assumed for invariants, Pascal-types for types).

An *environment* E is a sequence of declarations. The syntax is

$$E ::= D_1;\ldots; D_n,$$

where $D_1,\ldots, D_n$ are declarations.

A *block* B consists of an environment E (the *local* environment) and a compound statement C. The syntax is

$$B ::= E;\ C.$$

Each label in C (labeling a simple statement) must be declared in E.

Finally, an *invariant based program* H consists of an environment E (the *global* environment), an assertion P (the *precondition)* and a block B. The syntax is

$$H ::= E\ \{P\}\ B.$$

All labels and variables used but not declared in B must be declared in the global environment E. No identifier declared in E may be redeclared in B (this restriction could be lifted, with a slight complication in the correctness checking). The *postconditions* of B are given as label declarations in E (we allow more than one exit label for B).

The assignment statement has its usual interpretation and the semicolon is used for compound statements. Note, however, that only a restricted form of compound statements is allowed by the syntax. (The first statement must be an assignment.) The conditional statement is essentially the guarded conditional statement of Dijkstra [1976], i.e. the boolean expressions $b_1,\ldots,b_n$ (the *guards)* are evaluated, one of the guards which evaluate to true is selected, and the corresponding statement is executed. More than one condition may evaluate to true, in which case the choice is nondeterministic. If no condition is true, then an abnormal termination of the program occurs.

A label identifier L in a simple statement stands for the command goto L. It signals a jump to the statement labelled by L in the block, with execution continuing from this statement. If L is a label declared in the global environment, then execution terminates at this label.

The syntax implies that execution of a simple statement always ends in an explicit goto-statement. Simple statements and blocks are thus single entry - multiple exit constructs. They have a tree structure, with labels as leaves and branching points at the conditionals. The essential difference, as compared to while-programs, is that joining of paths which have been split up by a conditional statement is disallowed. More precisely, we do not allow constructs like

$$\text{if } b_1 \text{ -> } S_1 \;\square\; \cdots \;\square\; b_n \text{ -> } S_n \text{ fi; } S.$$

This construct in fact describes n different paths:

$$\text{assert } b_1;\ S_1;\ S,$$
$$\ldots$$
$$\text{assert } b_n;\ S_n;\ S.$$

These paths have different beginnings but the same ending. They can therefore not be designed independently of each other, as each one must fit the common continuation S. This construct would make the design of simple statements more difficult (although the code undoubtedly would be more concise), which is the reason for its rejection.

A block is essentially an ordinary Pascal block, with the symbol '□' standing for ';'. Execution of the block starts with SO and continues according to the usual rules for assignments, conditional statements and goto's. However, because each simple statement ends in an explicit label, the order in which the labeled statements are listed in the block is not significant. This again allows the statements for the different labels to be constructed independently of each other. Nested blocks could be accommodated for quite easily in this language (see e.g. Back [1980]), but we have omitted them for reasons of simplicity.

The programmer states the required behavior of the program with declarations. The declaration var x: T gives the type of the variable x. It states that the variable x should onlv be assigned well-defined values of this type (otherwise a run-time error will occur). The declaration label L:Q gives the invariant at label L. It states that Q may be assumed to hold whenever execution of the block is at label L. The syntax of the language is such that a loop only can be constructed by explicit backward jumps to labels in the block. As all labels must be declared, this makes it illegal to construct a loop without explicitly stating an invariant for it. The label declaration thus serves two different purposes, naming invariants and declaring control points. (It will sometimes be convenient to use a label declaration solely for the first purpose. We do it in the examples, to name the entry conditions of the programs constructed.)

The program E{P}B contains all the information about the intended behavior of the program which is needed to check its correctness. The global environment E declares all global variables and all labels referred to but not declared in B. The precondition P states the condition which may be assumed to hold at entry to the block (the exit conditions are declared as labels in E).

As an example, we show how the example in the introduction is expressed in this language:

```
var L: list of integer;
var M: list of integer;
label entry: L = LO;
label exit: M << LO and e(M) > 0 and e(LO) - e(M) ≤ 0;
{entry}
var x: integer;
label moving: M*L << LO and e(M) > 0 and e(LO) - e(M*L) ≤ 0;
begin M:= null;
    moving
□ moving:
    if L = null ->
         exit
    □ L ≠ null ->
        x:= head(L);
        L:= tail(L);
        if x > 0 ->
              M:= add(M,x);
              moving
        □ x ≤ 0 ->
              moving
        fi
    fi
end.
```

The programming language described here is in content more or less equivalent to the transition diagrams of Reynolds [1978]. A transition diagram is a finite graph, where invariants are associated with the nodes of the graph and assignment or assert statements are associated with the arcs of the graph. The language above provides a linear notation for these transition diagrams and also decreases the number of invariants which need to be explicitly stated.

Another way of describing invariant based programs has been proposed by van Emden [1979]. His suggestion is to express the program directly as a set of verification conditions. Our example program would then be represented as the set of verification conditions {(1), (2), (3a), (3b)} given in the introduction. The language described here is also very close to van Emden's representation, but avoids the repetitions inherent in that approach, as all transitions from an invariant are bundled together to form a single statement. Both Reynolds and van Emden use goto-programs to describe the final executable version of a program. We think that the language proposed here provides a cleaner way of describing the end product, without sacrificing efficiency or losing the information provided by the invariants.

Blikle [1979] has very much the same approach as we, emphasizing the role of invariants as internal specifications of the program, but chooses to extend while-programs to incorporate the invariants and the entry and exit conditions.

The language described above is in form almost identical to the language for tail recursion described by Hehner [1979]. However, Hehner gives a very different interpretation for the labels, taking them to be calls on recursively defined parameterless procedures. This view supports the stepwise refinement technique, but not directly invariant based program construction in the form we want. It is, however, interesting to note that essentially the same language provides a basis for both these, conceptually rather different, methods. (Hehner's tail recursion provides evidence for the fact that stepwise refinement is also useful without insisting on a restricted set of control structures.)

C. Constructing Invariant Based Programs

We will here show, with the help of an example, how invariant based programs can be constructed. Our approach is to start from the entry and exit conditions, then formulate the invariants and finally construct the program code in a way which agrees with the invariants. This approach reverses the usual order of program construction, in which the program code is first designed, after which one tries to find invariants with which the correctness can be shown. The approach outlined here is more or less the same as the methods used by Reynolds [1978] and van Emden [1979].

We will use the following simple lexical analysis problem as our example: Let a line be a sequence of characters (letters and blanks only). A word is a sequence of letters only. The parse of a line is the sequence of words, in order, contained in the line, the words of the line being delimited by blanks or the beginning or end of the line. Our task is to construct a program for obtaining the parse of a line, given the line.

We will use the same data type list of T as in the introduction. Using Pascal notation, let us define the type "string" by

type string = list of char,

where char is the data type of characters. The input will be given in a global variable line, declared as

var line: string

The input may only be manipulated by the operation "read(x)", x a character variable, which has the effect

read(x): x:= head(line); line:= tail(line).

In addition, the boolean function "eol" can be used, defined by

eol = (line = null).

The output will be given in the global variable parse, declared as

var parse: list of string.

The only operations allowed on the output are "reset" and "write(w)", w a string, with the effects

reset: parse:= null,
write(w): parse:= add(parse,w).

The precondition will be that line = line0, where line0 is the given sequence of letters and blanks. (The value of the input variable line will be changed by the program, thus the need for this variable):

entry: only letters and blanks in line0 and line = line0.

The purpose of the program is to compute the parse of line0 and store it in the variable parse. Let parseof(s) denote the parse of a string, i.e. parseof is a function

parseof: string -> list of string.

We will not define this function more precisely here. (The precise definition is given as an exercise.) The program must establish the situation

parse computed: p = parseof(line0).

Thus "parse computed" is the exit label of the program.

We will construct the obvious algorithm for solving this problem, i.e. we are going to scan the input from left to right, accumulating the words met and storing them in the variable parse. During the computation, there will be two basic situations which repeatedly occur: either we are scanning blanks or we are scanning letters. These situations are illustrated by the following picture:

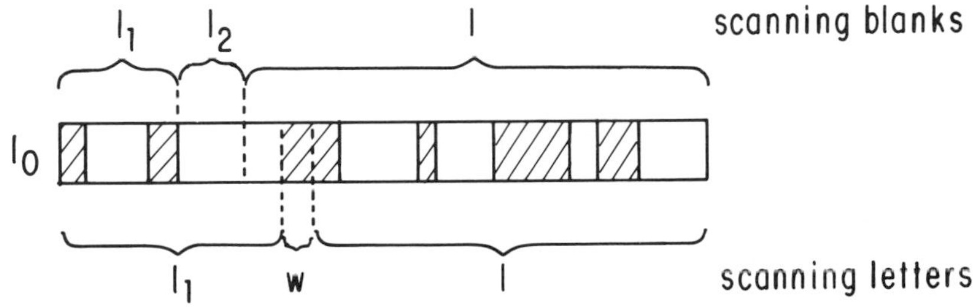

Figure 1. The situations when scanning

The shaded regions in the picture represent strings of letters, while the white regions represent strings of blanks. Consider first the situation in which we are scanning blanks. Part of the input line0 has been scanned, and we can consider line0 as being built up from three consecutive strings, line1, line2 and the current line, i.e.line 0 = line1*line2*line. The words in line1 are already accumulated in the parse, i.e. parse = parseof(line1). The string line2 gives the blanks already scanned, i.e. line2 contains only blanks. Line2 will contain at least one blank, so that we will know that we are scanning blanks, i.e. line2 ≠ null.

These considerations give us the following invariant:

scanning blanks: for some strings line1, line2:
line0 = line1*line2*line
and parse = parseof(line1)
and line2 contains only blanks
and line2 ≠ null.

For the other invariant, when we are scanning words, we need an auxiliary variable w, declared as

var w: string.

The word being scanned will be accumulated into this variable. A similar reasoning as the one above gives us the invariant:

```
scanning letters: for some  string line1:
                      line0 = line1*w*line
                  and parse = parseof(line1)
                  and w contains only letters
                  and w ≠ null
                  and (line1 = null or last(line1) = ' ').
```

(last(line1) is the last character in line1). Here the last conjunct expresses the fact that w must contain all the initial letters of the word being scanned.

The program is constructed by considering the entry condition and each invariant in turn, analyzing what needs to be done to either reach the exit or to reach one of the two invariants (in a way which brings the computation closer to termination). The order in which the invariants are handled does not matter, because of the independence of the labelled statements in the block.

Let us e.g. start by considering how to proceed from the invariant "scanning blanks". Analyzing the situation, we see that there are essentially two different cases, either line = null or line ≠ null. In the first case the task has been completed, i.e. we have established the situation "parse computed". (It follows from the invariant that parse contains all the words of line0.) In the second case, there is at least one character left in line. Let us read this character into the variable c, removing it from line at the same time. We now again have two cases, either c = ' ' or c ≠ ' '. If c = ' ', then we are still scanning blanks. If, however, c ≠ ' ', then we have found the first character of the next word. Initializing w to contain this character will mean that we are scanning letters. In both cases a loop may be created, but at the same time the computation has been brought closer to termination, because the length of the string in variable line has been decreased.

The above analysis is more concisely expressed by the following labelled simple statement:

```
scanning blanks:
      if eol ->
              parse computed
      □ not eol ->
              read(c);
              if c = ' ' ->
                     scanning blanks
              □ c ≠ ' ' ->
                     w:= add(null,c);
                     scanning letters fi fi.
```

This shows the way in which one proceeds from a chosen invariant to other invariants. The initial situation is analyzed and the possible cases are identified. Each case is then handled independently of the others, changing the variable values by assignments and identifying new subcases, which again can be handled independently of the other cases and subcases. The programming language supports this kind of carefully progressing case analysis, by keeping the different cases separate from each other: once a situation has been split into different cases, the way in which one of these cases is handled does not influence the other cases.

The need to check that each loop created does indeed terminate is the main break in the independence of the labelled statements of the block. In this case, the interaction between the statements must be considered. In Back [1980] we show how the language can be extended so that termination also can be handled in a modular fashion. A disadvantage of this language, compared to while-programs, is also evident when termination is considered: identifying the loops of a program is easier in while-programs, because of their explicit looping constructs.

The initial situation, described by the entry condition, and the other invariant are handled in a similar way. The resulting invariant based program is as follows:

```
var line: string;
var parse: list of string;
label entry: only blanks and letters in line0 and line = line0;
label parse computed: parse = parseof(line0);
{entry}
var w: string;
var c: char;
label scanning blanks: .....;
label scanning letters: ....;
begin reset;
      if eol ->
                parse computed
      □ not eol ->
                read(c);
                if c = ' ' ->
                          scanning blanks
                □ c ≠ ' ' ->
                          w:= add(null,c);
                          scanning words  fi fi
□ scanning blanks:
      if eol ->
                parse computed
      □ not eol ->
                read(c);
                if c = ' ' ->
                          scanning blanks
                □ c ≠ ' ' ->
                          w:= add(null,c);
                          scanning letters  fi fi
□ scanning letters:
      if eol ->
                write(w);
                parse computed
      □ not eol ->
                read(c);
                if c = ' ' ->
                          write(w);
                          scanning blanks
                □ c ≠ ' ' ->
                          w:= add(w,c);
                          scanning letters fi fi
end.
```

The transitions of this program are shown in the following graph.

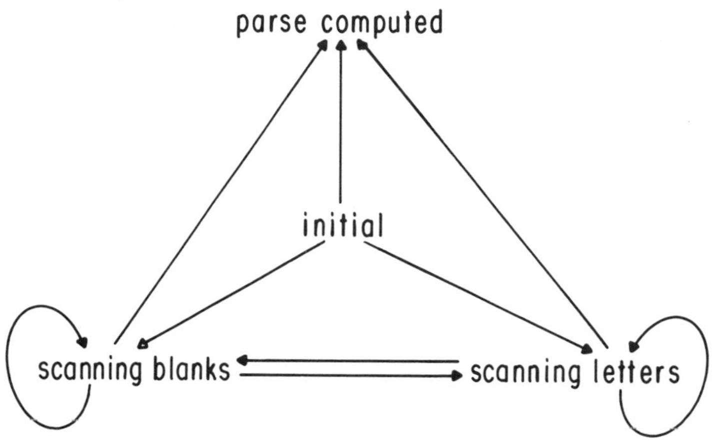

Figure 2. Transitions of the example program

D. Checking Program Correctness

As shown in the introduction, checking program correctness amounts to checking that all verification conditions are satisfied. This is sufficient to establish partial correctness of programs. In addition to this, we will also check that no run-time errors can occur during program execution (that only *clean termination* is possible, Sites [1974]). The proof system will check whether one of the following run-time errors could occur:

(1) A conditional statement for which all guards are false.
(2) An undefined guard in a conditional statement.
(3) An undefined expression in an assignment statement.

One way of checking correctness would be to compute all verification conditions at once and ask the programmer to prove them. This, however, means that the familiar program with which the programmer has been working is turned into something very different, a set of theorems to be proved. Relating this to the original program may be quite difficult and is in any case cumbersome. Moreover, a verification condition is usually computed over a sequence of statements, and will be false if a run-time error could occur when executing this sequence. However, the fact that the verification condition is false does not yet tell us where exactly in this sequence the error is.

We will here describe a correctness checker (verification condition generator), which works directly on the original program code, giving very precise information about the location of the error. The technique is based on symbolic execution (Hantler and King [1976]) and is a forward substitution technique. We prefer this to a backward substitution technique, because it closely follows the method of designing programs by progressing case analysis, described in the previous section. (See Gerhart [1976] for a discussion on forward and backward substitution techniques.)

We assume that the precondition P in a program E{P}B is given in the form

$$R \text{ and } x = t,$$

where R is a first-order formula, x is the list of variables declared in E and t is a list of terms, the number of terms in t being the same as the number of variables in x. No variable declared in E may occur free in R or occur in any term in t. The precondition stands for the formula

$$R \text{ and } x_1 = t_1 \text{and} \cdots \text{ and } x_n = t_n,$$

where n is the length of list x.

The precondition provides for each variable x_i declared in the environment E a value t_i, which is expressed in terms of logical variables (non-program variables whose values remain constant in the block B). The formula R states what we may assume to be true of these variables (they may occur free in R). The use of extra variables allows us to relate the final values of the program variables to their initial values in the postconditions.

The system for checking correctness of invariant based programs is essentially a proof system. The axioms of this system will be all true first order formulas. The proof rules follow the syntax of the language: There will be a proof rule for each program construct of the language.

A proof rule is usually written in the form

$$\frac{K_1,\ldots, K_n}{K}$$

where $K_1,\ldots, K_n$ are the assumptions and K is the conclusion. It says that if $K_1,\ldots, K_n$ are true, then the conclusion K must also be true. We will depart from this standard, writing a proof rule in the form

$$\begin{gathered} H \text{ -> } H_1,\ldots, H_n \\ \text{when } F_1,\ldots, F_m, \end{gathered}$$

$(m,n \geqslant 0)$, where H, $H_1,\ldots, H_n$ are invariant based programs and $F_1,\ldots, F_m$ are first-order formulas. Assuming that H = E{P}B, this stands for the proof rule

$$\frac{\begin{gathered} H_1,\ldots,H_n \\ P{=>}F_1,\ldots, P{=>}F_m \end{gathered}}{H}.$$

This notation is chosen to emphasize the use of the proof rules as a reduction system. The correctness of the program H, with precondition P, can be reduced to the correctness of the programs $H_1,\ldots, H_n$, provided all the formulas $P{=>}F_1,\ldots, P{=>}F_m$ are valid. In proving the correctness of an invariant based program, one starts from the original program and applies these reduction rules as long as possible, each time checking that the conditions for the application of a reduction rule (proof rule) are satisfied. If the reduction terminates with no programs left to reduce, the program is correct, otherwise it is incorrect.

Before going to the proof rules, we introduce some useful notation. First, if L is a label, then E(L) is the invariant associated with L in the environment E. Given a term t (a value expression or a boolean expression), def(t) is an assertion which is true if and only if the expression t has a well-defined value. Finally, for a a list and e a list element, a, e denotes the result of appending e to the end of list *a*.

The proof rules for checking the correctness of invariant based programs are as follows.

1. Variable declaration:

$$\begin{aligned}&E\{R \text{ and } x=t\} \text{ var } y{:}T;B\\ &\text{-->}\ E;\ \text{var } y{:}\ T\{R \text{ and } x,\ y=\ t,\ y'\}B\end{aligned}$$

Here y' is a fresh identifier, not declared in E or B or occurring in R or *t*. Thus the declaration of variable y means that y is initialized to some arbitrary value y'.

2. Label declaration:

$$\begin{aligned}&E\{R \text{ and } x=\ t\} \text{ label } L{:}\ Q;\ B\\ &\text{-->}\ E;\ \text{label } L{:}\ Q\{R \text{ and } x=\ t\}\ B\end{aligned}$$

A label declaration is thus simply moved into the environment, without affecting the precondition in any way.

3. Compound statements:

$$\begin{aligned}&E\{R \text{ and } x=\ t\} \text{ begin } S_0 \,\square\, L_1{:}S_1 \cdots \square\, L_n{:}S_n \text{ end}\\ &\quad\text{-->}\ E\{R \text{ and } x=\ t\}S_0,\\ &\qquad E\{E(L_1)[x'/x] \text{ and } x = x'\}S_1,\\ &\qquad \ldots\\ &\qquad E\{E(L_n)[x'/x] \text{ and } x = x'\}S_n,\end{aligned}$$

where x' is a list of distinct fresh identifiers, not declared in E or occurring free in R or t. Correctness of a compound statement thus reduces to n+1 independent checks: the correctness of the initialization statement SO and of the statements $S_1, \ldots, S_n$.

4. Conditional statements:

$$\begin{aligned}&E\{R \text{ and } x = t\} \text{ if } b_1 \text{ -> } S_1 \,\square \cdots \square\, b_n\text{-> } S_n \text{ fi}\\ &\text{-->}\ E\{R \text{ and } b_1[t/x] \text{ and } x = t\}S_1,\\ &\quad \ldots\\ &\quad E\{R \text{ and } b_n[t/x] \text{ and } x = t\}S_n,\\ &\text{when } \operatorname{def}(b_1), \ldots, \operatorname{def}(b_n),\\ &\qquad (b_1 \text{ or } \cdots \text{ or } b_n).\end{aligned}$$

Thus, correctness of a conditional statement is reduced to the correctness of each alternative (with the guard added to the assumptions), provided that each guard is necessarily well-defined and at least one of the guards is necessarily true.

5. Assignment statement:

$$\begin{aligned}&E\{R \text{ and } x = t\}\ x_i := e;\ S\\ &\text{-->}\ E\{R \text{ and } x = t'\}S\\ &\text{when } \operatorname{def}(e).\end{aligned}$$

Here t' is the list of terms

$$t' = t_1,\ldots,t_{i-1},\ e[t/x],\ t_{i+1},\ldots,t_n.$$

Correctness of an assignment statement construct is thus reduced to the correctness of the statement following the assignment statement, provided that the expression has a well-defined value.

6. Labels:

$$E\{R \text{ and } x = t\}\ L$$
$$\text{-->}$$
$$\text{when } E(L).$$

Reduction thus terminates when a label is reached, provided that the invariant associated with the label is satisfied.

These proof rules allow us to check the correctness of an invariant based program in a way which is similar to the syntax checking done by a recursive descent parser. The environment E corresponds to the symbol table of the parser. R and x function as variables used by the parser to keep relevant information needed to generate the correctness checks (when-conditions). These checks together make up the verification conditions of the program. The difference, as compared to the usual verification condition generators, is that each initial segment of a path in a program generates a verification condition. This allows very precise location of the errors in the program text. An error occurs at the end of an initial segment for which the verification condition produced is true, but the extension of which gives a verification condition which is false.

An alternative way of looking at the proof system, which shows the close relation to the program text, is to look at the precondition {R and x = t} as a marker in the program text. The proof rules show under which conditions this marker can be moved forward in the text. Starting from the initially given invariant based program, with the precondition as the only marker in the text, this marker, and any others which may be created by the proof rules, are moved forward as far as possible in the text. If all markers can be eliminated from the text, then the program is correct. If some marker gets stuck, because some when-condition is false, then the marker shows the place of the error and what is known to be true at that place, while the when-condition shows the nature of the error.

The simple marking scheme we use will give all the information available about the error detected. This would not be the case if joining of paths was allowed, e.g. by the construct

$$\text{if } b_1 \text{ -> } S_1 \,\Box\, \cdots \,\Box\, b_n \text{ -> } S_n \text{ fi;S.}$$

If the marker pointed at the position immediately preceding the statement S, then it would not be clear which one of the cases $b_1,\ldots, b_n$ was responsible for the error (although this information is contained in the verification condition computed). In this case, some indication of the path responsible for the error would have to be added to the error message.

We will illustrate the use of the proof rules with the example program of the introduction. We repeat this program below for ease of reference. We show for selected program points, indicated by numbers in the text, what may be assumed to be true at that point (the marker R and x = t) and what needs to be checked at that point (the when-condition).

```
var L: list of integer;
var M: list of integer;
label entry: L,M = LO,MO;
label exit:  M << LO and e(M) > 0 and e(LO) - e(M) ⩽ 0;
{entry}
var x:  integer;
label moving: M*L << LO and e(M) > O and e(LO)—e(M*L) ⩽ 0;
begin M:= null;
(1) moving
□ moving:
(2) if L = null ->
       (3) exit
     □ L ≠ null ->
          x:= head(L);
       (4) L:= tail(L);
          if x > 0 ->
                  M:= add(M,x);
            (5) moving
          □ x ⩽ 0 ->
                moving
          fi
     fi
end.
```

Let moving' denote the formula moving[L1,M1,x1/L,M,x], i.e. moving' is

$$M1*L1 \ll LO \text{ and } e(M1) > 0 \text{ and } e(LO) - e(M1*L1) \leqslant 0.$$

The assumptions and checks associated with the above program points are then:

(1) Assume: L,M,x = LO,null,xO.
Check: moving.

(2) Assume: moving' and L,M,x = L1,M1,x1.
Check: def(L = null),
def(L ≠ null),
L = null or L ≠ null.

(3) Assume: moving' and L1 = null and L,M,x = L1,M1,x1.
Check: exit.

(4) Assume: moving' and L1 ≠ null and L,M,x = L1,M1,head(L1).
Check: def(tail(L1)).

(5) Assume: moving' ' and L1 ≠ null and head(L1) > 0
and L,M,x = tail(L1), add(M1,head(L1)),head(L1).
Check: moving.

E. Summary

Our main purpose here has been to discuss the use of invariants in programs, when these are understood as internal specifications for the program to be constructed, rather than as comments about the way in which the program works. We have tried to show the advantages of this view for checking program correctness: Not only can we show the correctness of programs, but also incorrectness can be established, and the program errors responsible for the incorrectness can be located.

We have described a simple programming language, intended to support a program construction technique in which the design of invariants precedes the construction of the program code itself. The feasibility of this approach was supported by a simple example of program construction. Finally, we described a simple system for checking program correctness, essentially a verification condition generator, allowing very precise location of program errors in the text.

Acknowledgements

I would like to thank J.W. de Bakker, A. de Bruin, H.B.M. Jonkers, P. Orponen and J.V. Tucker for their critical comments and for the stimulating discussions we had on the topics treated here.

References

Back [1980a]
R.J.R. Back, "Exception handling with multi-exit statements, Programmiersprachen und Programmentwicklung," Darmstadt 1980. Informatik — Fachbereich 25, Springer Verlag.

Back [1980b]
R.J.R. Back, "Checking whether programs are correct or incorrect," Mathematical Center report IW 144/80, Mathematical Center, Amsterdam 1980.

Blikle [1979]
A. Blikle, "Specified programming," in: K.E. Blum, M. Paul and S. Takosu (eds.), *Mathematical Studies of Information Processing,* Lecture Notes in Computer Science 75, Springer Verlag 1979.

Brand [1978]
D. Brand, "Path calculus in program verification," *Journal of the ACM,* Vol. 25, No. 4 (October 1978), pp. 630—651.

Dijkstra [1968]
E.W. Dijkstra, "A constructive approach to the problem of program correctness," BIT 8 (1968), pp. 174—186.

Dijkstra [1976]
E.W. Dijkstra, *A Discipline of Programming,* Prentice-Hall, Englewood Cliffs, NJ., 1976.

van Emden [1979]
M.H. van Emden, "Programming with verification conditions," *IEEE Transactions on Software Engineering,* SE—5, 2(1979).

Floyd [1967]
R.W. Floyd, "Assigning meanings to programs," Proceedings of the AMS Symposium in Applied Mathematics 19 (1967), pp. 19—31.

Gerhart [1976]
S.L. Gerhart, "Proof theory of partial correctness verification systems," *SIAM J. of Computing,* Vol. 5, No. 3 (September 1976), pp. 355−377.

Goodenough and Gerhart [1975]
J.B. Goodenough and S.L. Gerhart, "Towards a theory of test data selection," Proc. Int. Conf. on Reliable Software, Sigplan Notices 10(June 1975), pp. 528−533.

Hehner [1979]
E. Hehner, "Do considered od: a contribution to the programming calculus," Acta Informatics 11 (1979), pp. 287−304.

Hantler and King [1976]
S.L. Hantler and J.C. King, "An introduction to proving the correctness of programs," *Computing Surveys* 8,3(1976), pp. 331−353.

Hoare [1971]
C.A.R. Hoare, "Proof of a program: FIND," *Comm. ACM* 14(January 1971), pp. 39−45.

Katz and Manna [1976]
S.M. Katz and Z. Manna, "Logical analysis of programs," *Comm. ACM* 19 (April 1976), pp. 185−206.

Naur [1966]
P. Naur, "Proof of algorithms by general snapshots," BIT 6(1966), pp. 310−316.

Reynolds [1978]
J.C. Reynolds, "Programming with transition diagrams," in: Gries, D. (ed.), *Programming Methodology,* Springer Verlag, Berlin 1978.

Sites [1974]
R.L. Sites, "Proving that computer programs terminate cleanly," Stanford Report CS−74−418, 1974.

Wirth [1971]
N. Wirth, "Program construction by stepwise refinement," *Comm. of the ACM* 14, 4(1971), pp. 221−227.

CHAPTER 12

Invariance Proof Methods And Analysis Techniques For Parallel Programs

Patrick Cousot
Université de Metz
Faculté des Sciences
Ile du Saulcy
57045 Metz cedex
France

Radhia Cousot
Centre de Recherche en Informatique de Nancy
France

A. Introduction

We propose a unified approach for the study, comparison and systematic construction of program proof and analysis methods. Our presentation will be mostly informal but the underlying formal theory can be found in Cousot and Cousot [1980b, 1979], and Cousot, P. [1981].

We use discrete state transition systems (Keller [1976], Cousot, P. [1979, 1981]) as abstract models of programs so that our approach is independent of any particular programming language. We use parallel programs with shared variables for illustration purposes.

Our approach is also independent of the particular class of program properties which is considered. For simplicity we only consider invariance properties in this paper. Important properties falling under this category are partial correctness, non termination, absence of run-time errors, deadlock freedom, mutual exclusion, etc.

Since programs are finite descriptions of arbitrarily long and sometimes infinite computations, properties of these computations can only be proved using some inductive reasoning. Hence program proof methods rely upon basic induction principles. For a given class of program properties several different induction principles can be considered. For simplicity, only one basic induction principle will be considered in this paper, which underlies Floyd [1967]'s partial correctness proof method. (A number of different although equivalent induction principles for invariance can be found in Cousot and Cousot [1982].)

All proof methods which rely upon the same induction principle intuitively look similar, but can be difficult to compare in the abstract. We offer a unified view for comparing them. It consists in showing that the verification conditions involved in any of these methods can be obtained by decomposition of the global inductive hypothesis used in the induction principle into an equivalent set of local inductive hypotheses. (Such decompositions can be formalized as connections between lattices (see Cousot and Cousot [1979, 1980b]) and in particular obtained by a cover of the set of states of the program where each local inductive hypothesis holds for a given block of the cover (Cousot [1979]). It is possible to find as many proof methods as such different decompositions. We illustrate only three of them which respectively lead to the Floyd [1967], Owicki and Gries [1976], and Lamport [1977, 1980] invariance proof methods. This approach also provides a framework for systematically constructing new sound and complete proof methods based on unexplored induction principles or decompositions. (See for example Cousot, R. [1981], Cousot and Cousot [1980a]).

Static program flow analysis techniques can be used for discovering semantic properties of programs, that is, for discovering properties of the runtime behavior of programs without actually running them. Such analysis methods consist in solving a fixed point system of equations (by elimination or iteration algorithms) associated with the program to be analyzed (Cousot and Cousot [1977]). In the design of such methods the essential part consists in defining correctly the rules for associating the system of equations with the program. We have shown (Cousot and Cousot [1979]) that they can be derived from the verification conditions of a proof method using an approximate decomposition, hence from a basic induction principle. We illustrate this point of view by generalizing Cousot and Cousot [1976] to parallel programs with shared variables. Another example can be found in Cousot and Cousot [1980b] that generalizes Cousot and Halbwachs [1978] to parallel processes communicating by rendezvous.

B. An Abstract Model of Parallel Programs: Non-Deterministic Transition Systems

An essential step in understanding invariance proof methods consists in considering an abstract model of programs so that irrelevant details can be left unspecified. For that purpose we will consider that a program P defines a dynamic discrete transition system that is a quadruple (S,t,b,e) where:

S	is a set of states,
$t \in (S \times S \rightarrow \{tt,ff\})$	is a transition relation,
$b \in (S \rightarrow \{tt,ff\})$	characterizes entry states,
$e \in (S \rightarrow \{tt,ff\})$	characterizes exit states.

The set S of states is a model of the set of possible data that can be contained in the store(s) on which the program operates. We ignore for the moment the particular structure of the states. In practice a state has several memory components (assigning values to program variables, input and output files, ...) and control components (assigning values to program location counters, ...). Program execution always begins with entry states. The total function b from states into truth values {tt,ff} characterizes entry states. This means that b(s) = tt if and only if state s is an entry state and b(s) = ff otherwise. Program execution properly ends when an exit state is reached. Exit states are characterized by e. The transition relation t specifies the effect of executing an elementary program step. More precisely t(s,s') = tt means that starting in state s and executing one program step can put the program in successor state s'. A sequential program is modeled by a deterministic transition relation since a state s can only have one successor state s', if any. A parallel program is modeled by a non-deterministic transition relation since a state s can have no or several successor states s'. This is because the transition relation is usually defined in terms of arbitrarily choosing an active process and executing one step of that process. Some states s may have no successor (that is t(s,s') = ff for all $s' \in S$), in which case they are called blocking states. For example, a sequential program can be in a blocking state after a run-time error or a parallel program can be in a blocking state because all processes which are not terminated are waiting for some event that never happens.

Example B.1: Defining the semantics of a sequential program by means of a deterministic transition system.

We will consider sequential programs with assignment, conditional and iteration commands. Labels will only be used to designate program points. For simplicity, type and variable declarations are left implicit.

For example, the following program computes 2^n for $n \geqslant 0$:

```
L1:
   P:=1;
L2:
   while N > 0 do
L3:
   N:=N-1;P:=2×P;
L4:
   od;
L5:
```

Let Π = {li,...,hi} be the set of integers included between the lowest and greatest machine representable integers li and hi. A state $(l,n,p) \in S$ consists of a memory state, that is a pair $(n,p) \in M$ assigning integer values to program variables N,P and of a control state $l \in C$ which is one of the program points, L1,...,L5. Therefore,

$$C = \{L1,\ldots,L5\}$$
$$M = \Pi^2$$
$$S = C \times M$$

Program execution begins at point L1 and ends at point L5 so that

$$b(l,n,p) = [l = L1] \quad \text{characterizes entry states,}$$
$$e(l,n,p) = [l = L5] \quad \text{characterizes exit states.}$$

We define the transition relation t by the following clauses (where $n \in \Pi$ and $p \in \Pi$):

$$(L1,n,p) \xrightarrow{t} (L2,n,1) \quad \text{iff} \quad 1 \in \Pi$$
$$(L2,n,p) \xrightarrow{t} (L3,n,p) \quad \text{iff} \quad n>0$$
$$(L2,n,p) \xrightarrow{t} (L5,n,p) \quad \text{iff} \quad n \leqslant 0$$
$$(L3,n,p) \xrightarrow{t} (L4,n-1,2\times p) \quad \text{iff} \quad (n-1) \in \Pi \text{ and } (2\times p) \in \Pi$$
$$(L4,n,p) \xrightarrow{t} (L3,n,p) \quad \text{iff} \quad n>0$$
$$(L4,n,p) \xrightarrow{t} (L5,n,p) \quad \text{iff} \quad n \leqslant 0$$

A clause $[s \xrightarrow{t} f(s)$ iff $c(s)]$ means that for all $s \in S$, $t(s,f(s)) = tt$ whenever condition $c(s)$ holds.

Starting with $N=2$ and $P=p$, execution of that program leads to the sequence of states $(L1,2,p) \xrightarrow{t} (L2,2,1) \xrightarrow{t} (L3,2,1) \xrightarrow{t} (L4,1,2) \xrightarrow{t} (L3,1,2) \xrightarrow{t} (L4,0,4) \xrightarrow{t} (L5,0,4)$.□

Example B.2: Defining the semantics of a parallel program by means of a non-deterministic transition system.

We consider parallel programs $[\![P_1 \| \ldots \| P_k]\!]$ which consist of $k>1$ sequential processes $P_1,\ldots,P_k$ executed concurrently. These processes share (implicitly declared) global variables. (If variables need to be local to some process P_i, we will use instead global variables neither used nor modified by the other processes P_j, $j \neq i$.)

It is sometimes necessary that processes have exclusive access to shared global variables. For that purpose we will enclose atomic operations inside square brackets. The execution of such operations is indivisible so that it cannot interfere with the concurrent execution of other processes. For example the program

$$[\![\; [N:=N+1] \;|\; [N:=N+1] \;]\!]$$

will increment N by two, whereas the program

$$[\![\; [T1:=N];[T1:=T1+1];[N:=T1] \;|\; [T2:=N];[T2:=T2+1];[N:=T2] \;]\!]$$

will increment N by one if both processes read the value of N before it is modified by the other process and by two if one process reads the value of N after it has been incremented by the other process.

The following parallel program computes 2^n when $n \geqslant 0$:

```
L0:
  [[
    L11:
        [P1 := 1];
    L12:
        while [N>1] do
    L13:
        [N := N-1; P1 := 2×P1];
    L14:
        od;
    L15:
  |
    L21:
        [P2 := 1];
    L22:
        while [N>1] do
    L23:
          [N := N-1; P2 := 2×P2];
    L24:
        od;
    L25:
  ]];
L1:
  if N = 0 then P := P1×P2 else P := 2×P1×P2 fi;
L2:
```

A state is of the form (c,n,p1,p2,p) where the values n,p1,p2,p of variables N,P1,P2,P belong to Π = {li,...,hi} and the control state c is either L0, L1, L2 or a pair (l1,l2) of labels, one control location for each of the two processes:

$$C = \{L0,L1,L2\} \cup (\{L11,...,L15\} \times \{L21,...,L25\})$$

$M = \Pi^4$

$S = C \times M$

b(c,n,p1,p2,p) = [c = L0]   characterizes entry states

e(c,n,p1,p2,p) = [c = L2]   characterizes exit states

We define the transition relation t by the following clauses (where l1 $\in$ {L11,...,L15}; l2 $\in$ {L21,...,L25}; n,p1,p2,p $\in \Pi$):

(a) $(L0,n,p1,p2,p) \xrightarrow{t} ((L11,L21),n,p1,p2,p)$

(b) $((L11,l2),n,p1,p2,p) \xrightarrow{t} ((L12,l2),n,1,p2,p)$ iff $1 \in \Pi$

(b) $((L12,l2),n,p1,p2,p) \xrightarrow{t} ((L13,l2),n,p1,p2,p)$ iff $n>1$

(b) $((L12,l2),n,p1,p2,p) \xrightarrow{t} ((L15,l2),n,p1,p2,p)$ iff $n \leqslant 1$

(c) (b) $((L13,l2),n,p1,p2,p) \xrightarrow{t} ((L14,l2),n\text{-}1,2\times p1,p2,p)$ iff $(n-1) \in \Pi$ and $(2\times p1) \in \Pi$

(b) $((L14,l2),n,p1,p2,p) \xrightarrow{t} ((L13,l2),n,p1,p2,p)$ iff $n>1$

(b) $((L14,l2),n,p1,p2,p) \xrightarrow{t} ((L15,l2),n,p1,p2,p)$ iff $n \leqslant 1$

... similar clauses for process 2 ...

(d) $((L15,L25),n,p1,p2,p) \xrightarrow{t} (L1,n,p1,p2,p)$

$(L1,n,p1,p2,p) \xrightarrow{t} (L2,n,p1,p2,p1\times p2)$ iff $(n=0)$ and $(p1\times p2) \in \Pi$

$(L1,n,p1,p2,p) \xrightarrow{t} (L2,n,p1,p2,2\times p1\times p2)$ iff $(n\neq 0)$ and $(2\times p1\times p2) \in \Pi$

On program entry, executions of both processes begin simultaneously (a). Then each process progresses at its own speed independently of the other (b). The concurrent execution of commands in different processes is modelled by an interleaved execution which proceeds as a sequence of discrete steps. In each step a command is selected in only one of the processes and is executed to completion before the same or another process may initiate an elementary command and proceed to complete it. Since execution of atomic operations is indivisible it is modelled by a single transition (c). Notice that since P1 and P2 are not shared we could have split [N:=N-1;Pi:=2×Pi] into [N:=N-1];[Ti:=Pi];[Ti:=2×Ti];[Pi:=Ti]. However the update of N must be indivisible. This can be achieved by any hardware or software mutual exclusion mechanism. The concurrent execution of the two processes ends when both have terminated (d).

A possible execution sequence for N=2 could be:

$(L0,2,p1,p2,p) \xrightarrow{t} ((L11,L21),2,p1,p2,p) \xrightarrow{t} ((L12,L21),2,1,p2,p) \xrightarrow{t}$

$((L13,L21),2,1,p2,p) \xrightarrow{t} ((L14,L21),1,2,p2,p) \xrightarrow{t} ((L14,L22),1,2,1,p) \xrightarrow{t}$

$((L15,L22),1,2,1,p) \xrightarrow{t} ((L15,L25),1,2,1,p) \xrightarrow{t} (L1,1,2,1,p) \xrightarrow{t} (L2,1,2,1,4).$

In the above sequence the value of N at L1 was 1. It can also be 0 if both processes simultaneously test that N>1 when N=2. This is the case in the following execution sequence:

$(L0,2,p1,p2,p) \xrightarrow{t} ((L11,L21),2,p1,p2,p) \xrightarrow{t} ((L12,L21),2,1,p2,p) \xrightarrow{t}$

$((L12,L22),2,1,1,p) \xrightarrow{t} ((L13,L22),2,1,1,p) \xrightarrow{t} ((L13,L23),2,1,1,p) \xrightarrow{t}$

$((L14,L23),1,2,1,p) \xrightarrow{t} ((L15,L23),1,2,1,p) \xrightarrow{t} ((L15,L24),0,2,2,p) \xrightarrow{t}$

$((L15,L25),0,2,2,p) \xrightarrow{t} (L1,0,2,2,p) \xrightarrow{t} (L2,0,2,2,4).$

Notice that the undeterminacy about the values of N and P when both processes end can easily be taken into account to yield the correct result. This solution is certainly less costly than the one which would consist in synchronizing the processes in order to avoid possible simultaneous tests of N. Another solution would consist in having one process iterate $\lfloor n/2 \rfloor$ times and the other $\lceil n/2 \rceil$ times. The drawback of this solution is that its efficiency does depend upon the assumption that both processes are executed at about the same speed. On the contrary, the efficiency of the above parallel program does not depend upon the relative speed of execution of the two processes. Another advantage is that it can be easily generalized to an arbitrary number of processes. □

Abstraction from the above examples is left to the reader. In general, the semantics of a programming language can be defined operationally. This consists in defining the transition system associated with each program of the language by induction on the context-free syntax of programs. (See e.g. Cousot, R. [1981]).

C. Invariance Properties of Parallel Programs

Some properties of programs, such as partial correctness, can be proved without reasoning about the set of sequences of states which represent all possible executions of the program starting from any possible entry state. It is sufficient to reason about the set of states which can be reached during execution. This is because the "time" at which a particular state is reached during execution (if ever), is irrelevant for such invariance proverties.

C.1 Definition: Invariance Property

Let t^* be the reflexive transitive closure of t, that is

$$t^*(s,s') = [\exists\, n \geqslant 1,\ s_1,\ldots,s_n \in S^n \mid s{=}s_1 \wedge (\forall i \in \{1,\ldots,n-1\},\ t(s_i,s_{i+1})) \wedge s_n{=}s'].$$

Let $\epsilon \in (S \to \{tt,ff\})$ and $\sigma \in (S \to \{tt,ff\})$ be characterizations of initial and final states.

A relation $\Psi \in (S \times S \to \{tt,ff\})$ is said to be invariant if and only if it is a necessary relation between the initial states and their descendants which are final, that is

$$\forall s,s' \in S,\ [\epsilon(s) \wedge t^*(s,s') \wedge \sigma(s')] \Rightarrow \Psi(s,s').$$

An assertion $\Psi \in (S \to \{tt,ff\})$ is said to be invariant if and only if it characterizes a super-set of the set of final states that can be reached during some execution started with an initial state, that is

$$\forall s,s' \in S,\ [\epsilon(s) \wedge t^*(s,s') \wedge \sigma(s')] \Rightarrow \Psi(s').$$

C.2 Partial Correctness

Proving that a program is partially correct consists in showing that if execution starts at program entry point with initial values $\underline{x}$ of the variables satisfying some precondition $\phi(\underline{x})$ and terminates with final values $\bar{x}$ of the variables then some relation $\theta(\underline{x},\bar{x})$ should hold between the input values $\underline{x}$ and output values $\bar{x}$ of the variables. This is an invariance property which can be stated as

$$\forall \underline{s},\bar{s} \in S,\ [\epsilon(\underline{s}) \wedge t^*(\underline{s},\bar{s}) \wedge \sigma(\bar{s})] \Rightarrow \Psi(\underline{s},\bar{s}).$$

More precisely, if states $s \in S$ are pairs (c,x) consisting of a control state $c \in C$ and a memory state $x \in M$, b characterizes entry states and e characterizes exit states, partial correctness can be stated as

$$\forall\, \underline{c},\bar{c} \in C,\ \underline{x},\bar{x} \in M,\quad [b(\underline{c},\underline{x}) \wedge t^*((\underline{c},\underline{x}),(\bar{c},\bar{x})) \wedge e(\bar{c},\bar{x})] \Rightarrow [\phi(\underline{x}) \Rightarrow \theta(\underline{x},\bar{x})]$$

Notice that the fact that an exit state $(\bar{c},\bar{x})$ can be reached when execution is started with an entry state $(\underline{c},\underline{x})$ is an hypothesis which is assumed to be true for $\Psi((\underline{c},\underline{x}),(\bar{c},\bar{x})) = [\phi(\underline{x}) \Rightarrow \theta(\underline{x},\bar{x})]$ to hold. Therefore termination is not implied. In particular, any non-terminating program is partially correct since $ff \Rightarrow [\phi(\underline{x}) \Rightarrow \theta(\underline{x},\bar{x})]$.

Example C.2.1: Partial correctness of programs B.1 and B.2.

We will prove that programs B.1 and B.2 are partially correct with respect to $\phi(\underline{n},\underline{p}) = [\underline{n} \geqslant 0]$ and $\theta((\underline{n},\underline{p}),(\bar{n},\bar{p})) = [\bar{p} = 2^{\underline{n}}]$. □

C.3 Non termination

A program never terminates if and only if any state which can be reached during execution is not an exit state and has at least one successor state. Non-termination is also an invariance property where ϵ characterizes entry states, σ is identically true and $\psi(\bar{s})$ holds if and only if $\bar{s}$ is neither an exit nor a blocking state.

$$\forall \underline{s},\bar{s} \in S,\ [b(\underline{s}) \wedge t^*(\underline{s},\bar{s})] \Rightarrow [\neg e(\bar{s}) \wedge (\exists\, s \in S \mid t(\bar{s},s))]$$

C.4 Absence of Run-time Errors

Absence of run-time errors is also an invariance property. It means that whenever a state which is not an exit state is reached during execution, a next computation step is possible without causing a run-time error (such as division by zero, arithmetic overflow, subscript out of range, ...).

Example C.4.1: Clean behavior of program B.1.

For each label l of program B.1, let us formulate a necessary and sufficient condition $\gamma_l(n,p)$ which guarantees that execution of the program commands labelled l in memory state (n,p) will not cause a run-time error:

$$\gamma_1(n,p) = [li \leqslant 1 \leqslant hi]$$

$$\gamma_2(n,p) = \gamma_4(n,p) = \gamma_5(n,p) = tt$$

$$\gamma_3(n,p) = [li \leqslant n-1 \leqslant hi \ \wedge\ li \leqslant 2\times p \leqslant hi]$$

For program B.1 the condition that all integers between 0 and $2^{\underline{n}}$ are machine representable is sufficient to avoid run-time errors. This can be stated as

$$[b(\underline{l},\underline{n},\underline{p}) \wedge t^*((\underline{l},\underline{n},\underline{p}),(l,n,p))] \Rightarrow \Psi((\underline{l},\underline{n},\underline{p}),(l,n,p))$$

where

$$\Psi((\underline{l},\underline{n},\underline{p}),(l,n,p)) = [\ [0 \leqslant \underline{n} \wedge li \leqslant 0 \leqslant 2^{\underline{n}} \leqslant hi] \Rightarrow \gamma_l(n,p)]\ .□$$

C.5 Global and Local Invariants

Let P be a program with states $S = C \times M$. A global invariant $\gamma \in (M \rightarrow \{tt,ff\})$ is a predicate on memory states which is always true during execution:

$$\forall\, \underline{s} \in S,\ c \in C,\ x \in M,\ [b(\underline{s}) \wedge t^*(\underline{s},(c,x))] \Rightarrow \gamma(x).$$

A predicate $\delta \in (M \rightarrow \{tt,ff\})$ on memory states which holds whenever control is at program points $l \in L$, where $L \subseteq C$, is called an invariant local to L:

$$\forall\, \underline{s} \in S,\ c \in C,\ x \in M,\ [b(\underline{s}) \wedge t^*(\underline{s},(c,x))] \Rightarrow [(c \in L) \Rightarrow \delta(x)].$$

Example C.5.1: Using program flow analysis algorithms for generating local invariants.

Some program analysis techniques, such as Cousot and Halbwachs [1978], can be used for automatic computation of local invariants of programs. Since the strongest set of local invariants is not computable, only approximate results can be automatically obtained. The invariant $\delta(x)$ associated with program points $l \in L$ is approximate in the sense that it is correct:

$$[b(\underline{s}) \wedge t^*(\underline{s},(l,x))] \Rightarrow \delta(x)$$

but does not provide full information, since we may have

$$[b(\underline{s}) \wedge t^*(\underline{s},(l,x))] \not\Leftarrow \delta(x) \quad \square$$

C.6 Absence of Global Deadlocks

Parallel processes may need to be synchronized for the concurrent access of shared resources. For example a process P_i may be willing to use a common resource, which can only be used by one process at the same time, and which is currently being used by some other process P_j, $j \neq i$. Then P_i has to be blocked temporarily and to wait until this resource is released by process P_j. If several processes are waiting it may be necessary to specify the order in which waiting processes will be allowed to use the common resource.

Because of programming errors, it may happen that all processes are blocked permanently so that there is no way to recover. The absence of such global deadlocks is an invariance property. (It may also happen that some subset of the processes in a program is blocked while the other processes remain permanently active. The absence of such individual starvations or livelock is not an invariance property.)

For illustration purposes, we will use conditional critical regions as the synchronization tool. When a process attempts to execute a command

await [B then C]

it is delayed until the condition B is true. Then the command C is executed as an atomic action, the evaluation of B to true and execution of C being indivisible. Command C cannot contain a nested await command. If two or more processes are waiting for the same condition B, any one may be allowed to proceed when B becomes true while the others continue waiting. When invariance properties are considered the order in which waiting processes are scheduled is often irrelevant.

Let us consider a parallel program $[\![P_1 \| \ldots \| P_k]\!]$. The corresponding states are of the form $((l_1,\ldots,l_k),x)$ where each l_i is a location of process P_i and x the memory state of the shared variables X. Let W_i be the set of waiting locations of process P_i so that P_i contains await commands

Lij:await [B(Lij)(X) then C] , for Lij $\in W_i$.

Let Lie be the exit location of process P_i. We define W as the set of control states $(l_1,\ldots,l_k)$ corresponding to waiting or exit locations, not all of them being exit locations. Formally

$$W = \{(l_1,...,l_k) \mid \forall i \in \{1,...,k\}, l_i \in W_i \cup \{Lie\}\} - \{(L1e,...,Lke)\}.$$

A *blocking state* is a state where not all processes have terminated and all of the processes that have not yet terminated are delayed at an await (because the corresponding condition evaluates to false).

Formally a blocking state is characterized by $\beta \in (S \rightarrow \{tt,ff\})$ such that

$$\beta((l_1,...,l_k),x) = [(l_1,...,l_k) \in W \wedge (\forall i \in [1,k], (l_i \neq Lie) => \neg B(l_i)(x))] .$$

A *sufficient condition ensuring absence of global deadlocks* is that all states that can be reached during execution are not blocking states. This invariance property can be stated as

$$\forall \underline{s},s \in S, [b(\underline{s}) \wedge t^*(\underline{s},s)] => \neg\beta(s)$$

C.7 Mutual Exclusion

Let P be a parallel program $[\![P_1 \| ... \| P_k]\!]$ with states of the form $((l_1,...,l_k),x)$ where each l_i is a label of process P_i and x is the memory state of the shared variables. Two statements labelled L_i and L_j in processes P_i and P_j, i, j $\in \{1,...,k\}$ are mutually exclusive if they cannot be executed at the same time. This invariance property can be formulated as:

$$\forall \underline{s},((l_1,...,l_k),x) \in S, [b(\underline{s}) \wedge t^*(\underline{s},((l_1,...,l_k),x))] => [\neg ((l_i=L_i) \wedge (l_j=L_j))]$$

D. The Basic Sound and Complete Induction Principle for Proving Invariance Properties of Programs

We now begin to introduce our mathematical approach for constructing invariance proof methods. This study is abstract in that by considering a general model of programs (dynamic discrete transition systems) we are not bound to particular programming language features. Also by considering an abstract class of program properties (invariance properties) the study is independent of which particular property in the class is considered. In this paragraph we state the general induction principle underlying almost all methods for proving invariance properties. Next we will explain how particular methods can be derived from this induction principle.

For proving that a program property Ψ is invariant, one usually has to guess a stronger property I which is shown to hold for all descendants of the initial states (a), (b) and to imply Ψ for final states (c). The proof that the inductive invariant I holds for any possible descendant of any initial state is by induction (on the minimal number n of computation steps until execution reaches this descendant of the initial state). The basis (a) consists in proving that the inductive invariant I holds for initial states (that is after n=0 computation step). The induction step (b) consists in proving that if the inductive invariant I holds for some state s' (which is reachable from the initial state by $n \geqslant 0$ computation steps) then I also holds for all possible successors s of that state s' (successors s, which are therefore reachable from the initial states by n+1 computation steps). By induction on n, all descendants of initial states satisfy I. In particular (c), since I implies Ψ for final states, Ψ holds if and when such a final state is reached during execution.

In the following theorem we give a very general formulation of the above invariance proof method using the transition systems framework. In the proof of this theorem we formally rephrase the above soundness (correctness, consistency) argument. We also add a semantic completeness argument (showing that if a property Ψ is invariant, then this can be proved using the general induction principle).

THEOREM D.1

$$[\exists I \in (S \times S \rightarrow \{tt,ff\}) \mid \forall \underline{s},s,\bar{s} \in S,$$

$$\begin{array}{ll} (a) & \epsilon(\underline{s}) \Rightarrow I(\underline{s},\underline{s}) \\ & \wedge \\ (b) & [\exists s' \in S \mid I(\underline{s},s') \wedge t(s',s)] \Rightarrow I(\underline{s},s) \\ & \wedge \\ (c) & [I(\underline{s},\bar{s}) \wedge \sigma(\bar{s})] \Rightarrow \Psi(\underline{s},\bar{s}) \quad] \end{array}$$

$$<==>$$

$$[\forall \underline{s},\bar{s} \in S, [\epsilon(\underline{s}) \wedge t^*(\underline{s},\bar{s}) \wedge \sigma(\bar{s})] \Rightarrow \Psi(\underline{s},\bar{s})]$$

Proof: For the *soundness* proof (= >) we show by recurrence on n that

$$[\forall n \geqslant 1, s_1,...,s_n \in S, [\epsilon(s_1) \wedge (\forall i \in \{1,...,n-1\}, t(s_i,s_{i+1})] \Rightarrow I(s_1,s_n)].$$

Wc usc (a) for the basis n=1 and (b) for the induction step n>1. From this lemma we conclude that $[\epsilon(\underline{s}) \wedge t^*(\underline{s},\bar{s}) \wedge \sigma(\bar{s})] \Rightarrow [I(\underline{s},\bar{s}) \wedge \sigma(\bar{s})]$ which according to (c) implies $\Psi(\underline{s},\bar{s})$.

The *completeness* proof (<=) is also very simple since we can choose $I(\underline{s},s) = [\epsilon(\underline{s}) \wedge t^*(\underline{s},s)]$ so that (a) and (b) follow from the definition of the reflexive transitive closure whereas (c) follows from the hypothesis $[\epsilon(s) \wedge t^*(\underline{s},\bar{s}) \wedge \sigma(\bar{s})] \Rightarrow \Psi(\underline{s},\bar{s})$. □

The invariance property is sometimes not a relation between initial and final states but an assertion on final states. In this case we can use the following induction principle, the soundness and correctness proofs of which are easily derived from the above theorem. (A version of this induction principle was originally proposed by Keller [1976]):

Corollary D.2

$$[\exists i \in (S \rightarrow \{tt,ff\}) \mid \forall \underline{s},s,\bar{s} \in S,$$

$$\begin{array}{ll} (a) & \epsilon(\underline{s}) \Rightarrow i(\underline{s}) \\ & \wedge \\ (b) & [\exists s' \in S \mid i(s') \wedge t(s',s)] \Rightarrow i(s) \\ & \wedge \\ (c) & [i(\bar{s}) \wedge \sigma(\bar{s})] \Rightarrow \psi(\bar{s}) \quad] \end{array}$$

$$<==>$$

$$[\forall \underline{s},\bar{s} \in S, [\epsilon(\underline{s}) \wedge t^*(\underline{s},\bar{s}) \wedge \sigma(\bar{s})] \Rightarrow \psi(\bar{s})]$$

Proof: The *soundness* proof (= >) consists in defining $I(\underline{s},s) = i(s)$, $\Psi(\underline{s},\bar{s}) = \psi(\bar{s})$ and applying theorem D.1. The *completeness* proof (<=) consists in proving that if $I(\underline{s},s)$ satisfies conditions D.1 (a) – (c) then $i(s) = [\exists \underline{s} \in S \mid \epsilon(\underline{s}) \wedge I(\underline{s},s)]$ satisfies conditions D.2 (a) – (c). □

Example D.3: Proving the partial correctness of a parallel program by direct application of the basic induction principle.

The program

$$[\![L11: [N:=N+1];L12: \mid L21: [N:=N+1];L22:]\!]$$

defines a non-deterministic transition system (S,t,b,e) such that

$S = \{L11,L12\}\times\{L21,L22\}\times\Pi$	states
$b(l1,l2,n) = [l1=L11 \wedge l2=L21]$	entry states
$e(l1,l2,n) = [l1=L12 \wedge l2=L22]$	exit states
$(L11,l2,n) \xrightarrow{t} (L12,l2,n+1)$ iff $(n+1) \in \Pi$	transition relation
$(l1,L21,n) \xrightarrow{t} (l1,L22,n+1)$ iff $(n+1) \in \Pi$	

Let us prove that if execution of that program begins with N=0 and happens to end then N=2. This partial correctness property can be formulated as

$$\forall \underline{s},\bar{s} \in S,\ [\epsilon(\underline{s}) \wedge t^*(\underline{s},\bar{s}) \wedge \sigma(\bar{s})] => \psi(\bar{s})$$

where

$\epsilon(l1,l2,n) = [b(l1,l2,n) \wedge n=0]$	input specification
$\sigma(l1,l2,n) = e(l1,l2,n)$	
$\psi(l1,l2,n) = [n=2]$.	output specification

This can be proved using the following inductive assertion:

$$\begin{aligned} i(l1,l2,n) = [&(l1=L11 \wedge l2=L21 \wedge n=0) \vee (l1=L11 \wedge l2=L22 \wedge n=1) \\ &\vee (l1=L12 \wedge l2=L21 \wedge n=1) \vee (l1=L12 \wedge l2=L22 \wedge n=2)] \end{aligned}$$

which, as can easily be checked by the reader, satisfies conditions D.2 (a) – (c). □

Readers familiar with fixpoint theory can consult Cousot, P. [1981] where it is shown that the *invariants can be defined as fixpoints of predicate transformers.* In Cousot and Cousot [1981], *other equivalent induction principles are derived from the above ones,* and this leads to the construction of new invariance proof methods.

E. Design of a Proof Method by Decomposition of the Global Invariant of an Induction Principle into a Set of Local Invariants

We now informally explain how practical invariance proof methods can be constructively derived from induction principles D.1 and D.2. The essential idea is to provide for a standard decomposition of the global inductive invariant I into a (logically equivalent) set of local invariants $\{Q_l \mid l \in L\}$, each one holding when control is at some points of the program. Then the verification conditions D.1 (a) – (c) or D.2 (a) – (c) can be decomposed into a conjunction of simpler verification conditions, each one corresponding to a basic command of the program and each one involving only some of the local invariants Q_l.

Example E.1: The standard decomposition for sequential programs.

Naur [1966], Floyd [1967] and Hoare [1969]'s partial correctness proof method is applicable to sequential programs. A local inductive invariant on memory states Q_l is associated with each program point l. The verification conditions ensure that when execution reaches some program point k which is immediately followed by program point l, then the assumption that Q_k is true when control is at point k implies that Q_l must be true if and when control reaches program point l.

The verification conditions for proving the partial correctness of program B.1 are (for all $\underline{n}, n, \underline{p}, p, p' \in \Pi$):

(a) $[\underline{n} \geq 0] \Rightarrow Q_1(\underline{n},\underline{n},\underline{p})$

(b) $[Q_1(\underline{n},n,p') \wedge 1 \in \Pi \wedge p=1] \Rightarrow Q_2(\underline{n},n,p)$

$[Q_2(\underline{n},n,p) \wedge n>0] \Rightarrow Q_3(\underline{n},n,p)$

$[Q_2(\underline{n},n,p) \wedge n\leq 0] \Rightarrow Q_5(\underline{n},n,p)$

$[Q_3(\underline{n},n',p') \wedge (n'-1) \in \Pi \wedge n=(n'-1) \wedge (2\times p') \in \Pi \wedge p=2\times p'] \Rightarrow Q_4(\underline{n},n,p)$

$[Q_4(\underline{n},n,p) \wedge n>0] \Rightarrow Q_3(\underline{n},n,p)$

$[Q_4(\underline{n},n,p) \wedge n\leq 0] \Rightarrow Q_5(\underline{n},n,p)$

(c) $Q_5(\underline{n},n,p) \Rightarrow [p = 2^{\underline{n}}]$

Observe that by substitutions we could have eliminated Q_2 and Q_4, keeping only the loop invariant Q_3. This leads to Floyd's method.

The reader can check that the following local invariants satisfy the above verification conditions:

$Q_1(\underline{n},n,p) = [\underline{n} = n \geq 0]$

$Q_2(\underline{n},n,p) = [\underline{n} = n \geq 0 \wedge p=1]$

$Q_3(\underline{n},n,p) = [n>0 \wedge p=2^{\underline{n}-n}]$

$Q_4(\underline{n},n,p) = [n\geq 0 \wedge p=2^{\underline{n}-n}]$

$Q_5(\underline{n},n,p) = [n=0 \wedge p=2^{\underline{n}}]$

In order to understand how this partial correctness proof method can be constructively derived from induction principle D.1, let us define

$$\epsilon(\underline{l},\underline{n},\underline{p}) = [\underline{l}=L1 \wedge \underline{n} \geq 0]$$

$$I((\underline{l},\underline{n},\underline{p}),(l,n,p)) = \bigvee_{k=1}^{5} [l=Lk \wedge Q_k(\underline{n},n,p)]$$

Then verification D.1(a) which was

$$(\epsilon(\underline{l},\underline{n},\underline{p}) => I((\underline{l},\underline{n},\underline{p}),(\underline{l},\underline{n},\underline{p})))$$

can be simplified into condition E.1.(a) as follows:

$$\equiv ([\underline{l}=L1 \wedge \underline{n} \geqslant 0] => \bigvee_{k=1}^{5} [\underline{l}=Lk \wedge Q_k(\underline{n},\underline{n},\underline{p})])$$

$$\equiv ([\underline{n} \geqslant 0] => \bigvee_{k=1}^{5} [L1=Lk \wedge Q_k(\underline{n},\underline{n},\underline{p})])$$

$$\equiv ([\underline{n} \geqslant 0] => Q_1(\underline{n},\underline{n},\underline{p}))$$

The same way, condition D.1.(b):

$$[I(\underline{s},s') \wedge t(s',s)] => I(\underline{s},s)$$

can be written as a conjunction of five conditions for $k=1,...,5$:

$$[I((\underline{l},\underline{n},\underline{p}),(Lk,n',p')) \wedge t((Lk,n',p'),(l,n,p))] \;=>\; I((\underline{l},\underline{n},\underline{p}),(l,n,p))$$

Replacing I and t by their definitions further simplifications lead to the verification conditions E.1.(b). Finally E.1.(c) is equivalent to D.1.(c) where:

$$\sigma(\bar{l},\bar{n},\bar{p}) \;=\; [\bar{l} = L5]$$

$$\Psi((\underline{l},\underline{n},\underline{p}),(\bar{l},\bar{n},\bar{p})) \;=\; [\bar{p} = 2^{\underline{n}}]\;. \quad \square$$

More generally, observe that the basic induction principles D.1 and D.2 have verification conditions of the form:

$$(\alpha) \quad (\exists\, I \in A \mid V(I))$$

Invariance proof methods apply induction principles D1 or D2 indirectly in that one uses other verification conditions of the form

$$(\beta) \quad (\exists\, Q \in A' \mid V'(Q)).$$

Using (β) instead of (α) is sound iff $(\beta) => (\alpha)$, complete iff $(\alpha) => (\beta)$ and equivalent iff $(\alpha) <=> (\beta)$.

In practice we can establish a correspondence between I and Q by means of a pair of functions $\rho \in [A \rightarrow A']$ and $\rho' \in [A' \rightarrow A]$ so that a sufficient soundness condition is

$$\forall\, Q \in A',\; V'(Q) => V(\rho'(Q))$$

and a sufficient completeness condition is

$$\forall\, I \in A,\; V(I) => V'(\rho(I)).$$

Example E.2: The standard decomposition for sequential programs leads to sound and complete proof methods.

Coming back to the partial correctness proof method which we illustrated by example E.1 we had:

$$C = \{L1,...,L5\}$$

$$S = C\times\Pi^2$$

$$A = (S^2 \to \{tt,ff\})$$

$$A' = \prod_{l\in C} (\Pi^3 \to \{tt,ff\})$$

That is $Q \in A'$ was a vector of assertions Q_l, $l \in C$ on $(\underline{n},n,p) \in \Pi^3$. The correspondence between A and A' was defined by $\rho' \in [A' \to A]$ such that:

$$\rho'(Q)((\underline{l},\underline{n},\underline{p}),(l,n,p)) = \bigvee_{k=1}^{5} [l=Lk \wedge Q_k(\underline{n},n,p)]$$

and $\rho \in [A \to A']$ such that:

$$\rho(I) = (Q_1,...,Q_5)$$

where

$$Q_l(\underline{n},n,p) = [\exists\, \underline{l} \in C,\ \underline{n},\underline{p} \in \Pi \mid I((\underline{l},\underline{n},\underline{p}),(l,n,p))].$$

This correspondence formally defines what is usually explained as "$Q_l(\underline{n},n,p)$ relates the initial value $\underline{n}$ of N and the current values n,p of variables N,P when control is at program point l".

Notice that ρ is one-to-one-onto and ρ' is its inverse. Since

$$\forall Q \in A',\ V'(Q) = V(\rho'(Q))$$

the method is sound. Moreover,

$$\forall I \in A,\ V(I) \Rightarrow V(\rho'(\rho(I))) = V'(\rho(I)),$$

so that the method is also complete. □

In Cousot and Cousot [1980] we have shown that A and A' can be chosen as *complete lattices* and the pair (ρ,ρ') as a *Galois connection* between these lattices.

Cousot, P. [1981] proposes a systematic method for constructing the set of local invariants A' and the corresponding pair (ρ,ρ') using a *cover of the set* S *of states* of the transition system (S,t,b,e) defined by the operational semantics of a program. There, each local invariant is defined so as to be isomorphic with the restriction of the global inductive invariant to the states belonging to some block of the cover. For example, the decomposition leading to Floyd's method for proving partial correctness of sequential programs (see examples 6.1, 6.2) has been derived in this way, using a partition of the set of states such that states belonging to a given block of the partition all correspond to the same control point of the program.

However our idea of using connections between the lattices A and A' which induce a connection between the predicate transformers corresponding to the verification conditions V and V' (which goes back to Cousot and Cousot [1976]) is more general in that it is suitable for reasoning about program proof methods (where (A,V) and (A′,V′) have to be equivalent) and also for reasoning about mechanizable hence fundamentally incomplete program analysis methods (Cousot and Cousot [1979]).

F. Two Invariance Proof Methods for Parallel Programs

We now present two methods for proving invariance properties of parallel programs. Both are derived from induction principle D.2 but using different decompositions of the global invariant involved in this induction principle. The first decomposition consists in associating a local invariant about memory and control states with each point of each process of the program. Choosing this decomposition we obtain Owicki and Gries [1976] (up to the use of auxiliary variables for simulating control states) and Lamport [1977] invariance proof methods. The second decomposition of the global program invariant consists in associating a global process invariant on control and memory states with each process of the program. Choosing this decomposition leads to the Lamport [1980] invariance proof method. We have chosen these two decompositions on purpose, in order to study from a unified point of view two classical methods which are intuitively understood as variations on Floyd's basic method of invariants but are difficult to compare because dissimilar formalisms are used for assertion languages and for the presentation of verification conditions.

F.1 Decomposition of the Global Program Invariant Leading to Owicki and Gries [1976]-Lamport [1977] Proof Method

F.1.1 Decomposition

Let us consider a parallel program $[\![P_1 \| \ldots \| P_k]\!]$ with memory states M and control states Ci for each process P_i, i = 1, ...,k. A global invariant $I \in (C1 \times \cdots \times Ck \times M \rightarrow \{tt,ff\})$ can be expressed as a conjunction of local invariants $Q_{il} \in (C1 \times \cdots \times Ci-1 \times Ci+1 \times \cdots \times Ck \times M \rightarrow \{tt,ff\})$ on control states (of processes $P_j, j \neq i$) and memory states. A local invariant Q_{il} is attached to each program point $l \in Ci$ of each process P_i, $i=1,\ldots,k$. More precisely,

$$I(c1,\ldots,ck,x) = \bigwedge_{i=1}^{k} \bigwedge_{l \in C_i} [(c_i = l) => Q_{il}(c_1,\ldots,c_{i-1},c_{i+1},\ldots,c_k, x)]$$

and

$$Q_{il}(c_1,\ldots,c_{i-1},c_{i+1},c_k,x) = I(c_1,\ldots,c_{i-1},l,c_{i+1},\ldots,c_k,x).$$

Example F.1.1.1: The global invariant

$$i(c1,c2,n) = [(c1=1 \wedge c2=3 \wedge n=0) \vee (c1=1 \wedge c2=4 \wedge n=2) \vee (c1=2 \wedge c2=3 \wedge n=1) \vee (c1=2 \wedge c2=4 \wedge n=3)]$$

of the parallel program

$$[\![\ 1{:}[N{:}=N+1];\ 2{:} \,\|\, 3{:}\ [N{:}=N+2];\ 4{:}\ ]\!]$$

can be expressed by the set of local invariants

$$Q_1(c2,n) = [(c2=3 \wedge n=0) \vee (c2=4 \wedge n=2)]$$
$$Q_2(c2,n) = [(c2=3 \wedge n=1) \vee (c2=4 \wedge n=3)]$$
$$Q_3(c1,n) = [(c1=1 \wedge n=0) \vee (c1=2 \wedge n=1)]$$
$$Q_4(c1,n) = [(c1=1 \wedge n=2) \vee (c1=2 \wedge n=3)]$$

Notice that if program point l belongs to process i then Q_l holds when control is at l in process i (wherever control can be in the other processes). Therefore these local invariants can be interspread at appropriate places in the program text, with the interpretation that Q_l is a valid comment at program point l . □

F.1.2 Derivation of the verification conditions

Verification condition D.1(b), which for simplicity we denote $I \wedge t \Rightarrow I$ can be decomposed into a conjunction of verification conditions

$$I(c'_1,\ldots,c'_k,x') \wedge t((c'_1,\ldots,c'_k,x'),(c_1,\ldots,c_{i-1},l,c_{i+1},\ldots,c_k,x)) \Rightarrow Q_{il}(c_1,\ldots,c_{i-1},c_{i+1},\ldots,c_k,x)$$

for each process $i \in \{1, \ldots, k\}$ and program point $l \in C_i$ of that process. Since t is defined as a disjunction of cases, one for each elementary command of the program, the above verification condition can be further decomposed. When the transition corresponds to execution of a command of process i we get verification conditions corresponding to the sequential proof (of process i regarded as an independent sequential program):

$$I(c_1,\ldots,c_{i-1},l',c_{i+1},\ldots,c_k,x') \wedge t((c_1,\ldots,c_{i-1},l',c_{i+1},\ldots,c_k,x'),(c_1,\ldots,c_{i-1},l,c_{i+1},\ldots,c_k,x))$$
$$\Rightarrow Q_{il}(c_1,\ldots,c_{i-1},c_{i+1},\ldots,c_k,x)$$

When the transition corresponds to execution of a command of process $j \neq i$, we get verification conditions of the form:

$$I(c_1,\ldots,c_{j-1},l',c_{j+1},\ldots,c_{i-1},l,c_{i+1},\ldots,c_k,x') \wedge t((c_1,\ldots,l',\ldots,l,\ldots,c_k,x'),(c_1,\ldots,l'',\ldots,l,\ldots,c_k,x))$$
$$\Rightarrow Q_{il}(c_1,\ldots,c_{j-1},l'',c_{j+1},\ldots,c_{i-1},c_{i+1},\ldots,c_k,x)$$

which consists in proving that the local invariants of each process are left invariantly true under parallel execution of the other processes. These verification conditions were termed "interference freeness checks" by Owicki and Gries [1976] and "monotonicity conditions" by Lamport [1977]. However, these authors did not exactly propose the above verification conditions but instead the following simpler (and stronger) ones:

— sequential proof:

$$Q_{il'}(c_1,\ldots,c_{i-1},c_{i+1},\ldots,c_k,x') \wedge t((c_1,\ldots,c_{i-1},l',c_{i+1},\ldots,c_k,x'),(c_1,\ldots,c_{i-1},l,c_{i+1},\ldots,c_k,x))$$
$$\Rightarrow Q_{il}(c_1,\ldots,c_{i-1},c_{i+1},\ldots,c_k,x)$$

— interference freeness checks:

$$Q'_{il}(c_1,\ldots,c_{j-1},l',c_{j+1},\ldots,c_{i-1},c_{i+1},\ldots,c_k,x') \wedge Q'_{jl'}(c_1,\ldots,c_{j-1},c_{j+1},\ldots,c_{i-1},l,c_{i+1},\ldots,c_k,x')$$

$$\wedge\ t((c_1,\ldots,l',\ldots,l,\ldots,c_k,x'),(c_1,\ldots,l'',\ldots,l,\ldots,c_k,x)) \Rightarrow Q'_{il}(c_1,\ldots,c_{j-1},l'',c_{j+1},\ldots,c_{i-1},c_{i+1},\ldots,c_k,x)$$

These verification conditions are obviously sufficient since they imply the above ones (because $I = \bigwedge_i \bigwedge_l Q'_{il}$).

Example F.1.2.1:

The verification conditions corresponding to program F.1.1.1 that is:

$$[\![\ 1{:}\ [N{:}=N+1];\ 2{:}\ \|\ 3{:}\ [N{:}=N+2];\ 4{:}\ ]\!]$$

are

(a) initialization:

$\phi(\underline{n}) \Rightarrow [Q'_1(3,\underline{n}) \wedge Q'_3(1,\underline{n})]$, where ϕ is the input specification

(b) induction step:

— sequential proof of process 1:

$[Q'_1(c2,n') \wedge (n'+1) \in \Pi \wedge n=n'+1] \Rightarrow Q'_2(c2,n)$

— absence of interference of the proof of process 1 with process 2:

$[Q'_1(3,n') \wedge Q'_3(1,n') \wedge (n'+2) \in \Pi \wedge n=n'+2] \Rightarrow Q'_1(4,n)$

$[Q'_2(3,n') \wedge Q'_3(1,n') \wedge (n'+2) \in \Pi \wedge n=n'+2] \Rightarrow Q'_2(4,n)$

— sequential proof of process 2:

$[Q'_3(c1,n') \wedge (n'+2) \in \Pi \wedge n=n'+2] \Rightarrow Q'_4(c1,n)$

— absence of interference of the proof of process 2 with process 1:

$[Q'_3(1,n') \wedge Q'_1(3,n') \wedge (n'+1) \in \Pi \wedge n=n'+1] \Rightarrow Q'_3(2,n)$

$[Q'_4(1,n') \wedge Q'_1(3,n') \wedge (n'+1) \in \Pi \wedge n=n'+1] \Rightarrow Q'_4(2,n)$

(c) finalization:

$[Q'_2(4,\bar{n}) \wedge Q'_4(2,\bar{n})] \Rightarrow \theta(\bar{n})$, where θ is the output specification.□

If we define

$$\rho'(Q) = I \text{ iff } I(c_1,\ldots,c_k,x) = \bigwedge_{i=1}^{k} \bigwedge_{l \in C_i} [(c_i=l) \Rightarrow Q_{il}(c_1,\ldots,c_{i-1},c_{i+1},\ldots,c_k,x)]$$

and

$$\rho(I) = Q \text{ iff } Q_{il}(c_1,\ldots,c_{i-1},c_{i+1},\ldots,c_k,x) = I(c_1,\ldots,c_{i-1},l,c_{i+1},\ldots,c_k,x)$$

we have established a formal correspondence between induction principle D.2 and the Owicki-Lamport invariance proof method. We have informally proved that the verification conditions proposed by Owicki-Lamport are sound (i.e. using the notations of paragraph E, that $V'(Q) \Rightarrow V(\rho'(Q))$. The sufficient completeness condition $(V(I) \Rightarrow V'(\rho(I)))$ can also be checked by the reader. Intuitively, this condition is satisfied because each local invariant Q_{il} can always be made strong enough so as to exactly describe the possible states of the whole program when process i is at point l.

F.1.3 Example

Let us prove that program B.2 is partially correct (according to definition C.2.1). Instead of using induction principle D.2 which underlies the Owicki and Gries' method we use D.1 so as to be able to relate the current value n of variable N to its initial value $\underline{n}$. (Owicki and Gries would instead introduce an auxiliary variable in order to memorize the initial value of N).

Since both processes are symmetric we need only reason about process 1. We will prove that the relation

$$Inv(\underline{n},c2,n,p1,p2) = [(c2=L21 \wedge p1=2^{\underline{n}-n}) \vee (c2\neq L21 \wedge p1\times p2=2^{\underline{n}-n})]$$

is invariant in process 1 after initialization of variable P1. To prove this we will show that the invariant remains true after execution of any command of process 1 and that it is not invalidated by execution of some command of process 2. Since partial correctness follows from the invariant with c2=L25 (process 2 has terminated) and $0 \leqslant n \leqslant 1$, we will also show that the value of N after the parallel command is either 0 or 1. Since the initial value $\underline{n}$ of N is assumed to be positive, the only difficulty is for $\underline{n} > 1$. In this case N is decremented until reaching value 2. On one hand both processes can test that N>1 before it is decremented by the other one, then each process will decrement N and terminate. In this case N would equal 0 on exit of the parallel command. On the other hand, when N=2, one process can test for N>1 and decrement N to 1 before the other process tests for N>1. Then both processes terminate and N=1 on exit of the parallel command. For an invariance proof, the above operational arguments can be rephrased in a "time independent manner", which leads to the following local invariants:

$$Q_{11}(\underline{n},c2,n,p1,p2) = Q_{12}(\underline{n},c2,n,1,p2)$$

$$Q_{12}(\underline{n},c2,n,p1,p2) = [Inv(\underline{n},c2,n,p1,p2) \wedge [(c2\in\{L21,L22\} \wedge n=\underline{n} \wedge n\geqslant 0) \\ \vee (c2=L23 \wedge n>1) \vee (c2=L24 \wedge n\geqslant 1) \vee (c2=L25 \wedge 0\leqslant n\leqslant 1)]]$$

$$Q_{13}(\underline{n},c2,n,p1,p2) = [Inv(\underline{n},c2,n,p1,p2) \wedge [(c2\in\{L21,L22,L23\} \wedge n>1) \\ \vee (c2=L24 \wedge n\geqslant 1) \vee (c2=L25 \wedge n=1)]]$$

$$Q_{14}(\underline{n},c2,n,p1,p2) = [Inv(\underline{n},c2,n,p1,p2) \wedge [(c2 \in \{L21,L22,L23\} \wedge n>0) \vee (c2=L24 \wedge n \geqslant 0) \vee (c2=L25 \wedge 0 \leqslant n \leqslant 1)]]$$

$$Q_{15}(\underline{n},c2,n,p1,p2) = [Inv(\underline{n},c2,n,p2,p1) \wedge [(c2=L23 \wedge n=1) \vee (c2 \neq L23 \wedge 0 \leqslant n \leqslant 1)]$$

$$Q_1(\underline{n},n,p1,p2) = [p1 \times p2 = 2^{\underline{n}-n} \wedge 0 \leqslant n \leqslant 1]$$

$$Q_2(\underline{n},p) = [p=2^{\underline{n}}]$$

It is a simple mathematical exercise to show that these local invariants satisfy the following verification conditions (which are universally quantified over $\underline{n},n,n',p1,p1',p2,p2',p \in \Pi$, $c1 \in \{L11,...,L15\}$):

— Initialization:

$$[\underline{n} \geqslant 0] \Rightarrow [Q_{11}(\underline{n},L21,\underline{n},p1,p2) \wedge Q_{21}(\underline{n},L11,\underline{n},p2,p1)]$$

— Sequential proof (similar to E.1):

$$[Q_{11}(\underline{n},c2,n,p1',p2) \wedge 1 \in \Pi] \Rightarrow Q_{12}(\underline{n},c2,n,1,p2)$$
$$[Q_{12}(\underline{n},c2,n,p1,p2) \wedge n>1] \Rightarrow Q_{13}(\underline{n},c2,n,p1,p2)$$
$$[Q_{12}(\underline{n},c2,n,p1,p2) \wedge n \leqslant 1] \Rightarrow Q_{15}(\underline{n},c2,n,p1,p2)$$
$$[Q_{13}(\underline{n},c2,n',p1',p2) \wedge (n'-1) \in \Pi \wedge (2 \times p1') \in \Pi] \Rightarrow Q_{14}(\underline{n},c2,n'-1,2 \times p1',p2)$$
$$[Q_{14}(\underline{n},c2,n,p1,p2) \wedge n>1] \Rightarrow Q_{13}(\underline{n},c2,n,p1,p2)$$
$$[Q_{14}(\underline{n},c2,n,p1,p2) \wedge n \leqslant 1] \Rightarrow Q_{15}(\underline{n},c2,n,p1,p2)$$

— Interference freeness check (for $k=1,...,5$):

$$[Q_{1k}(\underline{n},L21,n,p1,p2') \wedge Q_{21}(\underline{n},L1k,n,p2',p1) \wedge 1 \in \Pi] \Rightarrow Q_{1k}(\underline{n},L22,n,p1,1)$$
$$[Q_{1k}(\underline{n},L22,n,p1,p2) \wedge Q_{22}(\underline{n},L1k,n,p2,p1) \wedge n>1] \Rightarrow Q_{1k}(\underline{n},L23,n,p1,p2)$$
$$[Q_{1k}(\underline{n},L22,n,p1,p2) \wedge Q_{22}(\underline{n},L1k,n,p2,p1) \wedge n \leqslant 1] \Rightarrow Q_{1k}(\underline{n},L25,n,p1,p2)$$
$$[Q_{1k}(\underline{n},L23,n',p1,p2') \wedge Q_{23}(\underline{n},L1k,n',p2',p1) \wedge (n'-1) \in \Pi \wedge (2 \times p2') \in \Pi] \Rightarrow Q_{1k}(\underline{n},L24,n'-1,p1,2 \times p2')$$
$$[Q_{1k}(\underline{n},L24,n,p1,p2) \wedge Q_{24}(\underline{n},L1k,n,p2,p1) \wedge n>1] \Rightarrow Q_{1k}(\underline{n},L23,n,p1,p2)$$
$$[Q_{1k}(\underline{n},L24,n,p1,p2) \wedge Q_{24}(\underline{n},L1k,n,p2,p1) \wedge n \leqslant 1] \Rightarrow Q_{1k}(\underline{n},L25,n,p1,p2)$$

– Finalization:

$[Q_{15}(\underline{n},L25,n,p1,p2) \wedge Q_{25}(\underline{n},L15,n,p2,p1)] \Rightarrow Q_1'(\underline{n},n,p1,p2)$

$[Q_1(\underline{n},n,p1,p2) \wedge n=0 \wedge (p1 \times p2) \in \Pi] \Rightarrow Q_2'(\underline{n},p1 \times p2)$

$[Q_1(\underline{n},n,p1,p2) \wedge n \neq 0 \wedge (2 \times p1 \times p2) \in \Pi] \Rightarrow Q_2'(\underline{n},2 \times p1 \times p2)$

$Q_2(\underline{n},p) \Rightarrow [p=2^{\underline{n}}]$.

Notice that for the whole program we have got 77 verification conditions. Theoretically the number of sequential verification conditions is linear in the size of the program whereas the number of verification conditions for checking interference freeness grows exponentially with the number and size of processes. The practical method for avoiding this combinatorial explosion is to make informal proofs and to choose the local invariants of each process as independent as possible of the other processes. In that case most of the interference freeness checks become trivial.

F.2 Decomposition of the Global Program Invariant Leading to Lamport [1980] Proof Method

F.2.1 Decomposition

Another way to avoid the proliferation of simple verification conditions is to use a coarser decomposition which consists in associating a global invariant Q_i with each process P_i of program $[\![P_1 \| ... \| P_k]\!]$. Each predicate Q_i may depend upon the values of variables as well as upon program control locations. The correspondence with induction principle D2 is established along the lines of paragraph E by defining global inductive invariant I as the conjunction of the global invariants Q_i for each process P_i:

$$I = \rho'(Q) = \bigwedge_{i=1}^{k} Q_i$$

F.2.2 Derivation of the verification conditions

For the basis D.2(a) we must prove that I is initially true and this verification condition can be decomposed into checks that each $Q_i, i = 1,...,k$ is initially true.

The induction step D.2(b) which consists in proving that I is invariant, that is $I \wedge t \Rightarrow I$, can be decomposed into proofs that $I \wedge t \Rightarrow Q_i$ for $i=1,...,k$. Moreover, the induction hypothesis $I = \bigwedge_{j=1}^{k} Q_j$ can be weakened and one can choose (simpler but sufficient since stronger) conditions $(\bigwedge_{j \in S_i} Q_j) \wedge t \Rightarrow Q_i$ for $S_i \subset \{1,...k\}$ and $S_i \neq \emptyset$. (These verification conditions satisfy the completeness criterion of paragraph E for $\rho(I) = Q$ iff $Q_i = I$ for $i = 1,...k$. This formalizes the intuitive idea that the method is complete since all global invariants Q_i for each process $i=1, ...,k$ can always be chosen as the global program invariant which is used for the completeness proof of induction principle D.2.) A further decomposition of the verification conditions $(\bigwedge_{j \in S_i} Q_j) \wedge t \Rightarrow Q_i$ is possible since t is a disjunction of cases. For each process i, one can distinguish between a sequential proof $(\bigwedge_{j \in S_{il}} Q_j) \wedge t_{il} \Rightarrow Q_i$ (when t corresponds to execution of a basic command labelled 1 of process i) and an interference freeness check $(\bigwedge_{j \in S_{hl}} Q_j) \wedge t_{hl} \Rightarrow Q_i$ (when t corresponds to execution of a basic command labelled 1 of process h $\neq$ i).

F.2.3 Example

Let us give another proof of program B.2, using process invariants. Obviously, the proof is just a reformulation of F.1.3 using a global invariant for each process instead of local invariants attached to program points. Since both processes are symmetric, we use the same process invariant for each of them and reason only on process one.

In order to be able to designate program locations let us introduce:

$$\begin{aligned}
\text{Not-started} &\equiv (c1=L11 \wedge c2=L21)\\
\text{P2-started} &\equiv (c1=L11 \wedge c2\neq L21)\\
\text{P1-started} &\equiv (c1\neq L11 \wedge c2=L21)\\
\text{Started} &\equiv (c1\neq L11 \wedge c2\neq L21)
\end{aligned}$$

The central idea of program B.2 is to maintain invariant the following relation:

$$\begin{aligned}
\text{Inv}(\underline{n},c1,c2,n,p1,p2) = {} & [(\text{Not-started} \wedge n=\underline{n}) \vee (\text{P2-started} \wedge p2=2^{\underline{n}-n})\\
& \vee (\text{P1-started} \wedge p1=2^{\underline{n}-n}) \vee (\text{Started} \wedge p1 \times p2=2^{\underline{n}-n}).
\end{aligned}$$

The other essential observation for the partial correctness proof is that the program can only terminate when $0 \leqslant N \leqslant 1$. To prove this, let us introduce:

$$\begin{aligned}
&\text{Before-test} \equiv [(c1 \in \{L11,L21\} \wedge c2 \in \{L21,L22\}) \vee (c1 = L14 \wedge c2 = L24)]\\
&\text{After-test} \equiv [(c1=L13 \wedge c2 \in \{L21,L22,L23\}) \vee (c1 \in \{L11,L12,L13\} \wedge c2=L23)]\\
&\text{After-test-and-decrement} \equiv [(c1=L14 \wedge c2 \in \{L21,L22,L23\})\\
&\qquad\qquad \vee (c1 \in \{L11,L12,L13\} \wedge c2=L24)]\\
&\text{One-decrement-left} \equiv [(c1=L15 \wedge c2=L23) \vee (c1=L13 \wedge c2=L25)]\\
&\text{No-decrement-left} \equiv [(c1=L15 \wedge c2\neq L23) \vee (c1\neq L23 \wedge c2=L25)]
\end{aligned}$$

For each process, one can choose the following global invariant:

$$\begin{aligned}
Q(\underline{n},c1,c2,n,p1,p2) = {} & [\text{Inv}(\underline{n},c1,c2,n,p1,p2) \wedge [(\text{Before-test} \wedge n \geqslant 0)\\
& \vee (\text{After-test} \wedge n>1) \vee (\text{After-test-and-decrement} \wedge n \geqslant 1)\\
& \vee (\text{One-decrement-left} \wedge n=1) \vee (\text{No-decrement-left} \wedge 0 \leqslant n \leqslant 1)]]
\end{aligned}$$

This global invariant satisfies the following verification conditions:

— Initialization.

$[\underline{n} \geqslant 0] \Rightarrow Q(\underline{n},L11,L21,\underline{n},p1,p2)$

— Sequential proof of process 1:

$[Q(\underline{n},L11,c2,n,p1',p2) \wedge 1 \in \Pi] \Rightarrow Q(\underline{n},L12,c2,n, 1,p2)$

$[Q(\underline{n},L12,c2,n,p1,p2) \wedge n>1] \Rightarrow Q(\underline{n},L13,c2,n,p1,p2)$

$[Q(\underline{n},L12,c2,n,p1,p2) \wedge n \leqslant 1] \Rightarrow Q(\underline{n},L15,c2,n,p1,p2)$

$[Q(\underline{n},L13,c2,n',p1',p2) \wedge (n'-1) \in \Pi \wedge (2 \times p1') \in \Pi] \Rightarrow Q(\underline{n},L14,c2,n'-1,2 \times p1',p2)$

$[Q(\underline{n},L14,c2,n,p1,p2) \wedge n>1] \Rightarrow Q(\underline{n},L13,c2,n,p1,p2)$

$[Q(\underline{n},L14,c2,n,p1,p2) \wedge n \leqslant 1] \Rightarrow Q(\underline{n},L15,c2,n,p1,p2)$

— The proof of absence of interference of execution of process 2 with the global invariant of process 1 exactly amounts to the sequential proof of process 2.

— Finalization:

$Q(\underline{n},L15,L25,n,p1,p2) \Rightarrow Q_1(\underline{n},n,p1,p2)$

When compared with F.1.3 the use of a coarser decomposition leads, for that example, to a natural factorization of similar verification conditions.

F.3 Classification of Program Proof Methods

Program proof methods can be classified according to the class of properties that can be proved. Methods for proving properties in a given class can be classified according to the basic induction principle underlying them. Finally for a given induction principle, proof methods can be compared according to the decomposition of the global inductive hypothesis involved in this induction principle into a set of local inductive hypotheses.

Decompositions can be partially ordered, a decomposition being coarser than another if the former can be further decomposed into the latter.

Example F.3.1 A comparison of two invariance proof methods.

The decomposition of the global program invariant of D2 into the global process invariants of F.2 is coarser than the decomposition into the local invariants of F.1. If we have proved program $[\![P_1 \,|\!.\!.\!|\, P_k]\!]$ using global process invariants $G_1,\ldots,G_k$ we can rephrase the proof using local invariants Q_{il}, $i \in \{1,\ldots,k\}$, $l \in C_i$ which are the decomposition of the G_i, in the sense of paragraph E, that is:

$$Q = \rho(G) \text{ s.t. } Q_{il}(c_1,\ldots,c_{i-1},c_{i+1},\ldots,c_k,x) = G_i(c_1,\ldots,c_{i-1},l,c_{i+1},\ldots,c_k,x).$$

Reciprocally, a proof using global process invariants can be derived from a proof using local invariants using

$$G = \rho'(Q) \text{ s.t. } G_i(c_1,\ldots,c_k,x) = \bigvee_{l \in C_i} [(c_i = l) \wedge Q_{il}'(c_1,\ldots,c_{i-1},c_{i+1},\ldots,c_k,x)]$$

since ρ is bijective and ρ' its inverse the methods are equivalent. □

The above informal idea of comparing proof methods corresponding to a given induction principle according to the decomposition of a global invariant into local invariants can be made formal. The partial ordering on program proof methods is chosen as the ordering on the closure operators $\rho' o \rho$ on the partially ordered set of global invariants (A, =>), induced by the Galois connections (ρ, ρ') corresponding to each of these methods. In this way, a complete lattice of proof methods is obtained, which is part of the lattice of program analysis methods considered in Cousot and Cousot [1979].

G. Flow Analysis of Parallel Programs

Approximate semantic analysis of programs also called program flow analysis (Muchnick and Jones [1981]) is "a tool for discovering properties of the run-time behavior of a program without actually running it. The properties discovered usually apply to all possible sequences of control and data flow and so give global information impossible to obtain by individual runs or by inspection of only a part of the program."

G.1 Design of a Flow Analysis Algorithm

Almost all program flow analysis techniques have been designed for sequential programs. Using the approach of Cousot and Cousot [1979], Cousot, P. [1981], the extension of these techniques to parallel programs is trivial. It consists in choosing an induction principle and a decomposition (α, γ) of the global invariant into a set of machine representable local invariants. Once the corresponding verification conditions have been designed, they are considered as a fixed point system of equations $F(X) \Rightarrow X$ (or $X \Rightarrow F(X)$), the least (or greatest) fixed point D of which leads to the best (i.e. more precise) possible set of local invariants (for the given decomposition (α, γ)) since $F(D) = D$ and if $F(X) \Rightarrow X$ then $D \Rightarrow X$ (or $X \Rightarrow F(X)$ then $X \Rightarrow D$). In order to avoid computability problems, the decomposition is chosen to be approximate, so that the verification conditions F are incomplete. If the approximation is strong enough the least (greatest) fixed point of F can be machine computed as $\vee F^i(\bot)$ (or $\wedge F^i(\top)$) where $\bot$ is $\rho(\text{ff})$ (resp. $\rho(\text{tt})$) and $F^0(X) = X$, $F^{i+1}(X) = F(F^i(X))$. If the convergence is not rapid enough extrapolation techniques are available (Cousot and Cousot [1977]).

G.2 Example of Approximate Decomposition for Parallel Programs

In order to illustrate how our approach to program flow analysis applies equally well to parallel programs than to sequential programs, we will use program B.2 (the reasoning on this program can be extended to a programming language via induction on the syntax of programs).

Assume we want to determine statically for each possible point of control in the program a finite description of the set of data states the program could be in when execution passes through that point. The description D_{jl} attached to point l of process j=1,2 is chosen to be an interval of values for each variable and each point $h \in C_{\tilde{j}}$ of the other process $\tilde{j}$ (where $\tilde{1}=2 \wedge \tilde{2}=1$). Therefore $D_{jl}(\tilde{j}h)$ is a triple $<n, p_j, p_{\tilde{j}}>$ of abstract values of variables N, $P_j, P_{\tilde{j}}$ where each $n, p_j, p_{\tilde{j}}$ is either $\bot$ (bottom, which stands for the predicate ff) or a numerical interval [a,b] such that $li \leqslant a \leqslant b \leqslant hi$ where li and hi are the lowest and greatest machine representable integer. We will use the selectors $<n,p_j,p_{\bar{j}}>[N]=n$, $<n,p_j,p_{\bar{j}}>[P_j]=p_j$ and $<n,p_j,p_{\bar{j}}>[P_{\bar{j}}]=p_{\bar{j}}$. The meaning of a description D can be explained in terms of the local invariants Q considered at paragraph F.1 by the connection $Q=\gamma(D)$ such that:

$$Q_{jl}(\underline{n},c_{\bar{j}},n,p_j,p_{\bar{j}}) = \bigvee_{h\in C_{\bar{j}}} ((c_{\bar{j}}=h) \wedge (\forall v\in\{N,P1,P2\},\ D_{jl}(\bar{j}h)[v]\neq\bot \wedge v\in D_{jl}(\bar{j}h)[v])).$$

For example $D_{14}(23) = <[1,hi-1],[2,hi],[1,hi]>$ means that at point L14 of process 1 it is true that $((1\leqslant n\leqslant hi-1) \wedge (2\leqslant p_1\leqslant hi) \wedge (1\leqslant p_2\leqslant hi))$ when control is at point L23 of process 2. Reciprocally a set of local invariants Q can be approximated by $D=\alpha(Q)$ such that

$$D_{jl}(\bar{j}h) = <\bot,\bot,\bot> \text{ iff } Q_{jl}(\underline{n},L_{\bar{j}h},n,p_j,p_{\bar{j}}) = ff$$

$$= <[\min V(N),\max V(N)],[\min V(P_j),\max V(P_j)],[\min V(P_{\bar{j}}),\max V(P_{\bar{j}})]>$$

where

$$V(N) = \{n\in\Pi \mid (\exists\, \underline{n},p_j,p_{\bar{j}}\in\Pi \mid Q_{jl}(\underline{n},L_{\bar{j}h},n,p_j,p_{\bar{j}})\}$$

and similarly for $V(P_j),V(P_{\bar{j}})$.

Notice that $\alpha(Q)$ is an approximation of Q in that, for example, relationships between variables cannot be expressed.

G.3 Fixed Point System of Approximate Equations Associated with a Parallel Program

The verification conditions of paragraph F.1.3 can be written as a system of inequations $Q\Leftarrow V(Q)$ which was obtained by decomposition of

$$I \Leftarrow \lambda(\underline{s},s)\ .\ [\epsilon(\underline{s}) \vee (\exists s' \mid \underline{I}(\underline{s},s') \wedge t(s',s))]$$

using the connection (ρ,ρ') defined at paragraph F.1.1. A further decomposition leads to a fixed point system of approximate equations $D = F(D)$ using the connection (α,γ) of paragraph G.2 and $F = \alpha o V o \gamma$. Then the meaning of the least fixed point lfp(F) of F is an invariant of the program, that is $\forall \underline{s},s\in S$, $[\epsilon(\underline{s}) \wedge t^*(\underline{s},s)] \Rightarrow \rho' o \alpha(\text{lfp}(F))(s)$.

Before giving the system of equations corresponding to program B.2 let us introduce some notations:

- $<n,p1,p2>[p1:p1'] = <n,p1',p2>$ — substitution

  $<n,p1,p2>[p2:p2'] = <n,p1,p2'>$

- $\bot \wedge x = x \wedge \bot = \bot$ for $x\in\{\bot\}\cup\{[a,b] \mid a\leqslant b\}$ — approximate conjunction

  $[a,b] \wedge [c,d] = [\max(a,c),\min(b,d)]$ iff $\max(a,c)\leqslant\min(b,d)$

  $= \bot$ iff $b<c$ or $d<a$

- $\bot \vee x = x \vee \bot = x$ for $x\in\{\bot\} \cup \{[a,b] \mid a\leqslant b\}$ — approximate disjunction

  $[a,b] \vee [c,d] = [\min(a,c),\max(b,d)]$

- $\bot - 1 = \bot$ — approximate decrement

  $[a,b] - 1 = [a-1, b-1] \wedge [li, hi]$

- $2 \times \bot = \bot$ — approximate shift.

  $2 \times [a,b] = [2 \times a, 2 \times b] \wedge [li, hi]$

In the following presentation of the fixed point system of approximate equations for program B.2, it is assumed that initially we must have $n \geqslant 0$. For each equation we distinguish a term corresponding to the sequential proof and a term corresponding to the interference check:

$$D_0 = \langle [0,hi],[li,hi],[li,hi] \rangle$$

$$D_{11}(21) = D_0$$

$$D_{11}(2k) = inter_{11}(2k) \qquad k = 2,\ldots,5$$

$$D_{12}(2k) = D_{11}(2k)[p1:[1,1]] \vee inter_{12}(2k) \qquad k = 1,\ldots,5$$

$$D_{13}(2k) = (D_{12}(2k) \wedge \langle [2,hi],[li,hi],[li,hi] \rangle) \vee (D_{14}(2k) \wedge \langle [2,hi],[li,hi],[li,hi] \rangle) \vee inter_{13}(2k) \qquad k = 1,\ldots,5$$

$$D_{14}(2k) = \langle D_{13}(2k)(n)-1,\ 2 \times D_{13}(2k)(p1),\ D_{13}(2k)(p2) \rangle \vee inter_{14}(2k)$$

$$D_{15}(2k) = (D_{12}(2k) \wedge \langle [li,1],[li,hi],[li,hi] \rangle) \vee (D_{14}(2k) \wedge \langle [li,1],[li,hi],[li,hi] \rangle) \vee inter_{14}(2k) \qquad k = 1,\ldots,5$$

where

$$inter_{1k}(21) = \langle \bot,\bot,\bot \rangle$$

$$inter_{1k}(22) = (D_{1k}(21) \wedge D_{21}(1k))[p2:[1,1]]$$

$$inter_{1k}(23) = (D_{1k}(22) \wedge D_{22}(1k) \wedge \langle [2,hi],[li,hi],[li,hi] \rangle) \vee (D_{1k}(24) \wedge D_{24}(1k) \wedge \langle [2,hi],[li,hi],[li,hi] \rangle)$$

$$inter_{1k}(24) = \langle (D_{1k}(23)(n) \wedge D_{23}(1k)(n))-1,\ D_{1k}(23)(p1) \wedge D_{23}(1k)(p1),\ 2 \times (D_{1k}(23)(p2) \wedge D_{23}(1k)(p2)) \rangle$$

$$inter_{1k}(25) = (D_{1k}(22) \wedge D_{22}(1k) \wedge \langle [li,1],[li,hi],[li,hi] \rangle) \vee (D_{1k}(24) \wedge D_{24}(1k) \wedge \langle [li,1],[li,hi],[li,hi] \rangle)$$

... similar equations for process 2 ....

$$D_1 = D_{15}(25) \wedge D_{25}(15)$$

G.4 Iterative Resolution of the Equations Using Extrapolation Techniques for Accelerating the Convergence

This system of equations can be solved using any asynchronous iterative strategy (Cousot, P. [1977]). Initially one set $D_{il}(\bar{i}h) = \langle \bot,\bot,\bot \rangle$ for $i = 1,2$, $l \in C_i$, $h \in C_{\bar{i}}$. Then one iterates through the system applying any equation until no changes take place.

The convergence can be accelerated using Cousot and Cousot [1976,1977] extrapolation techniques. This consists in defining a widening operation ∇ such as:

$$\bot \nabla x = x$$

$$[a,b] \nabla [c,d] = [\ \underline{\text{if}}\ c < a\ \underline{\text{then}}\ \text{li}\ \underline{\text{else}}\ a,\ \underline{\text{if}}\ d > b\ \underline{\text{then}}\ \text{hi}\ \underline{\text{else}}\ b]$$

and replacing equations $D_{j3,j} = 1,2$ by

$$D_{j3}(\tilde{jk}) = D_{j3}(\tilde{jk}) \nabla [(D_{j2}(\tilde{jk}) \wedge <[2,hi],[li,hi],[li,hi]>) \vee (D_{j4}(\tilde{jk}) \wedge <[2,hi],[li,hi],[li,hi]>) \vee inter_{j3}(\tilde{jk})]$$

and then solving iteratively. The result we have obtained (for process 1) is:

	k=1			k=2			k=3			k=4			k=5		
	n	pl	p2	n	pl	p2	n	pl	p2	n	pl	p2	n	pl	p2
$D_{11}(2k)$	[0,hi]	[li,hi]	[li,hi]	[0,hi]	[li,hi]	[1,1]	[2,hi]	[li,hi]	[1,hi]	[1,hi-1]	[li,hi]	[2,hi]	[0,1]	[li,hi]	[1,hi]
$D_{12}(2k)$	[0,hi]	[1,1]	[li,hi]	[0,hi]	[1,1]	[1,1]	[2,hi]	[1,1]	[1,hi]	[1,hi-1]	[1,1]	[2,hi]	[0,1]	[1,1]	[1,hi]
$D_{13}(2k)$	[2,hi]	[1,hi]	[li,hi]	[2,hi]	[1,hi]	[1,1]	[2,hi]	[1,hi]	[1,hi]	[1,hi-1]	[1,hi]	[2,hi]	[1,1]	[1,hi]	[1,hi]
$D_{14}(2k)$	[1,hi-1]	[2,hi]	[li,hi]	[1,hi-1]	[2,hi]	[1,1]	[1,hi-1]	[2,hi]	[1,hi]	[0,hi-2]	[2,hi]	[2,hi]	[0,1]	[2,hi]	[1,hi]
$D_{15}(2k)$	[0,1]	[1,hi]	[li,hi]	[0,1]	[1,hi]	[1,1]	[1,1]	[1,hi]	[1,hi]	[0,1]	[1,hi]	[2,hi]	[0,1]	[1,hi]	[1,hi]

Notice that the decomposition is approximate enough to allow a computer implementation of this kind of analyses. However, as shown by the above example, the results of such approximate analyses can be useful since we obtain

$$D_1 = <[0,1],[1,hi],[1,hi]>$$

which proves that $N \in \{0,1\}$ on exit of the parallel command of program B.2, a result which is not trivial to obtain by hand.

References

Cousot P. [1977]
P. Cousot, "Asynchronous iterative methods for solving a fixed point system of monotone equations in a complete lattice," Research Report No. 88, IMAG, University of Grenoble, France (Sept. 1977).

Cousot P. [1978]
P. Cousot, "Méthodes itératives de construction et d'approximation de points fixes d'opérateurs monotones sur un treillis, analyse sémantique des programmes," Thése d'Etat, University of Grenoble, France (March 1978).

Cousot P. [1979]
P. Cousot, "Analysis of the behavior of dynamic discrete systems," Research Report No. 161, IMAG, University of Grenoble, France (Jan. 1979).

Cousot P. [1981]
P. Cousot, "Semantic foundations of program analysis," in *Program Flow Analysis, Theory and Applications,* S.S Muchnick & N.J. Jones (eds.), Prentice-Hall, Inc. (1981), pp. 303−342.

Cousot R. [1981]
R. Cousot, "Proving invariance properties of parallel programs by backward induction," Research Report, CRIN−81−P026, Nancy, France (March 1981), to appear in *Acta Informatica.*

Cousot and Cousot [1976]
P. Cousot and R. Cousot, "Static determination of dynamic properties of programs," *Proc. 2nd Int. Symp. on Programming,* Dunod, Paris, France (April 1976), pp. 106−130.

Cousot and Cousot [1977]
P. Cousot and R. Cousot, "Abstract interpretation: a unified lattice model for static analysis of programs by construction or approximation of fixpoints," *Conf. Rec. of 4th ACM Symp. on Principles of Programming Languages,* Los Angeles, CA. (Jan. 1977), pp. 238−252.

Cousot and Cousot [1979]
P. Cousot and R. Cousot, "Systematic design of program analysis frameworks," *Conf. Rec. of 6th ACM Symp. on Principles of Programming Languages,* San Antonio, TX (Jan. 1979), pp. 269−282.

Cousot and Cousot [1980a]
P. Cousot and R. Cousot, "Semantic analysis of communicating sequential processes," *Automata, Languages and Programming, 7th Colloq. Noordwijkerhout, Lecture Notes in Comp. Science 85,* Springer-Verlag (July 1980), pp. 119−133.

Cousot and Cousot [1980b]
P. Cousot and R. Cousot, "Constructing program invariance proof methods," *Proc. Int. Workshop on Program Construction,* Chateau de Bonas, France, Tome 1 INRIA Ed. (Sept. 1980).

Cousot and Cousot [1982]
P. Cousot and R. Cousot, "Induction principles for proving invariance properties of programs," in *Tools and Notions for Program Construction,* Nice, France, (Dec. 7-18, 1981), Cambridge University Press (1982), pp. 75−119.

Cousot and Halbwachs [1978]
P. Cousot and N. Halbwachs, "Automatic discovery of linear restraints among variables of a program," *Conf. Rec. of 5th ACM Symp. on Principles of Programming Languages,* Tuscon, AZ (Jan. 1978), pp. 84−97.

Floyd [1967]
R.W. Floyd, "Assigning meanings to programs," *Proc. Symp. in Applied Math.,* Vol. 19, AMS, Providence, RI (1967), pp. 19−32.

Hoare [1969]
C.A.R. Hoare, "An axiomatic basis for computer programming," *C.ACM* 12, 10(Oct. 1969), pp. 576–580, 583.

Keller [1976]
R.M. Keller, "Formal verification of parallel programs," *C.ACM* 19, 7(July 1976), pp. 371–384.

Lamport [1977]
L. Lamport, "Proving the correctness of multiprocess programs," *IEEE Trans. on Soft. Eng.,* SE3, 2(March 1977), pp. 125–143.

Lamport [1980]
L. Lamport, "The 'Hoare Logic' of concurrent programs," *Acta Informatica* 14 (1980), pp. 21–37.

Muchnick and Jones [1981]
S.S. Muchnick and N.D. Jones (eds.), *Program Flow Analysis: Theory and Applications,* Prentice-Hall Inc. (1981).

Naur [1966]
P. Naur, "Proof of algorithms by general snapshots," *BIT 6* (1966), pp. 310–316.

Owicki and Gries [1976]
J. Owicki and D. Gries, "An axiomatic proof technique for parallel programs I," *Acta Informatica* 6 (1976), pp. 319–340.

CHAPTER 13

Scheduling Equational Specifications and Non Procedural Programs

A. Pnueli
The Weizmann Institute of Science
Rehovot, Israel

N. S. Prywes
University of Pennsylvania
Philadelphia, PA 19104

R. Zarhi
The Weizmann Institute of Science
Rehovot, Israel

The research reported here was supported by the Information Systems Program Office of Naval Research, Contract No. N00014–76–C–0416.

A. Non Procedural Languages and the MODEL System

A non procedural language is by definition a language in which a computational task is described in a non procedural style. One may adopt different interpretations as to what is procedural or non procedural description style. Closely related concepts are descriptive vs. prescriptive styles of programming, where the descriptive approach corresponds of course to the non procedural way of specifying tasks. Other terms frequently used are applicative vs. imperative, etc.

There is very little need to explain the obvious advantages in the non procedural or descriptive approaches to task specification. A descriptive statement of a task is always of a higher level than a prescriptive program. This entails a final program which is necessarily free of errors, easier to debug and carries its own documentation and verification. All these lead directly and indirectly to better utilization of the human resource in program construction and maintenance. The only argument standing in favor of the imperative-prescriptive-procedural style of programming is that of possible efficiency through tighter control of the hardware resources. With the radically decreasing costs of hardware, the steadily increasing cost of software and the emergence of sophisticated automatic software construction tools such as reported in this conference and elsewhere, the case for the high level descriptive style of programming seems stronger than ever.

The basic question the designer of a very high level (descriptive) language has to face, is how high to go. On one hand, the less procedural details that the user of such a language has to face, the better he could concentrate on *what* is to be done rather than on the *how*. On the other hand, the level of the languages should not be so high that specifications written in it cannot be effectively and unambiguously translated into lower level programs. Representative of the maximalist school in this direction are the efforts for program synthesis from specifications given in the form of a first order logical formula. Another approach is that of program construction from examples or partially specified description. All these attempts face the problem mentioned above, that no algorithm exists for the effective translation of a specification expressed on this level into a working program. For most of these cases there is even a theoretical proof that no such algorithm can exist for the general case. This fact shows the problem of program synthesis to properly belong to the realm of artificial intelligence. At best, the solutions hoped for would be heuristic and achieve some degree of success but would never be complete.

At the other end of the spectrum, we find the projects for the construction of very high level languages such as SETL, LUCID, PROLOG and many others. Characteristic to these efforts is the insistence that programs written in these languages must be effectively executable or translatable with tolerable degree of efficiency. Also, they each single out some features in existing programming languages that they try to elevate to a higher level of description. Thus, both SETL and LISP suggest a uniform data structure that frees the user from the need to perform a detailed design of his data structures. The proponents of each system strongly believe that the set or list respectively, is a most natural way for the user to conceptualize and express his specifications. Other languages, usually referred to as *applicative,* try to attack the sequential nature of programming implied by the imperative languages, in which the user explicitly states in his program the exact order in which statements are to be executed and data elements are to be retrieved or computed.

The MODEL project at the University of Pennsylvania belongs to this latter group of bottom-up introduction of non procedurality. A constant constraint that was upheld since its inception was that it be a compiling system and produce reasonably efficient code. Yet, it tried to eliminate from the user's considerations many features which were considered procedural, in particular those associated with the sequentiality of the execution.

The MODEL language is based on the expression of a specification as a set of equations stating relations between the input and output variables. The equations have to be *explicit* in the sense that each equation is a defining equation for a target variable, appearing on its left hand side in terms of source variables appearing on the right hand side. In the simpler specifications the target variables are always the output variables. More involved specifications include auxiliary variables which appear as targets in some defining equations and as sources in other equations. The basic data structure is the array or its generalization, the subscripted hierarchic structure in the style of PL/I. Typical to the strive towards a high level of description, external variables, i.e. variables residing on external files, are treated and participate in equations in exactly the same way as internal variables. The user need not (and cannot) include statements for the reading and writing of external variables in his specification. Conditions are allowed within equations, and so is the definition of an array variable by a subscripted equation which is interpreted as an individual equation for each element of the array obtained by varying the subscripts over the defined range of the array.

Apart from these two conventions, the user has no way of exerting direct control such as conditional statements or looping. The translations system derives the need for loops from subscripted equations and the data declarations which specify the dimensions of the arrays.

As an example of a MODEL specification, consider the task of computing the smallest power of 2 which is larger than 10000. A possible specification for it might be

```
G IS GROUP (A(*))
A IS FIELD
RESULT IS FIELD

A(I) = IF I = 1 THEN 1 ELSE 2*A(I-1)
j = LEAST(I, A(I)  >  10000)
RESULT = A(j)
```

For a more detailed description of the MODEL language and system we refer the reader to Prywes *et al.* [1979].

B. Dependencies and Array Graphs

In the rest of the chapter we concern ourselves with some of the basic problems inherent in the translation of a language such as MODEL. The main task of a translator for MODEL is that of *scheduling.* A MODEL specification is essentially an unordered specification of a set of computational events. Consider for example the very simple specification:

```
A,B,C  ARE EXTERNAL FIELDS
   C = A + B
```

An obvious event in the execution of this specification is the computation of the value of C from the values of A and B. Less obvious but still necessary events are the reading of the values of A and B off some external medium and then that of writing the value of C onto some other external medium. The execution of these separate events is constrained by the natural precedence requirements that an external variable must be read before its value is used, that all the arguments of an expression must be evaluated before the expression itself can be evaluated. In the simplest cases these precedence or dependency constraints can be expressed by a simple graph:

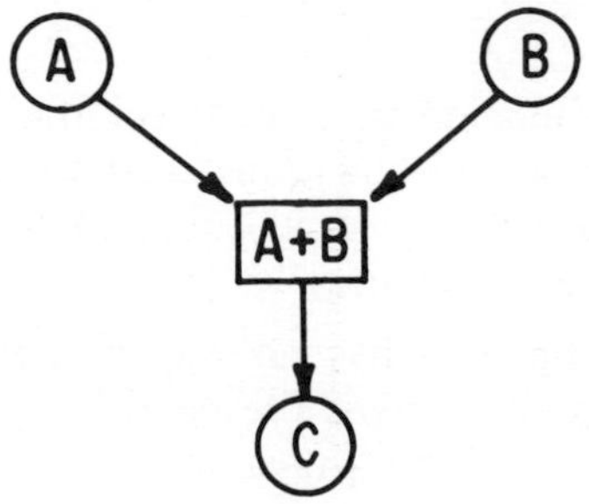

Here the nodes labelled by variable names signify the read and write operations respectively associated with these variables. If we sort this directed graph topologically, i.e. order its nodes in any linear order which conforms with the contraints we obtain a schedule of events in the execution which can immediately be transformed into the simple program:

```
READ B
READ A
C := A+B
WRITE C
```

In the more general case, variables are structured and simple edges do not convey the exact interdependency between the individual elements. Thus considering the specification above for computing the first power of 2 exceeding 10000 we obtain the following dependency graph:

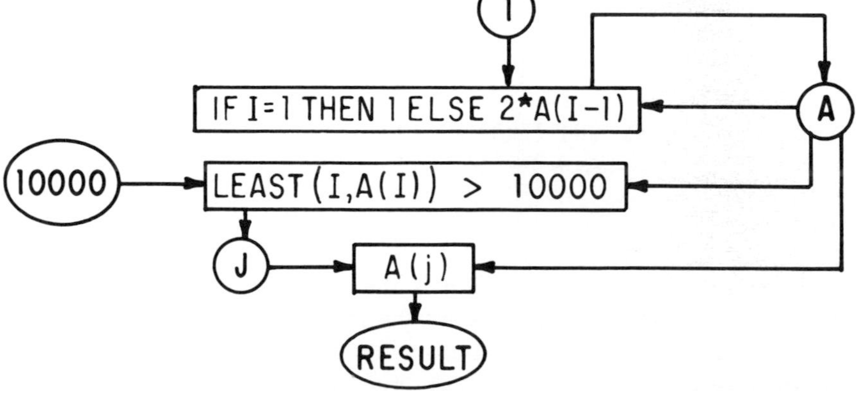

Without deeper analysis of the dependencies, one may conclude from this graph that A depends in general on itself, and therefore this specification cannot be scheduled. This indeed would have been the case if we had slightly changed the expression defining A to read

$$A(I) = \text{IF } I = 1 \text{ THEN } 1 \text{ ELSE } 2*A(I)$$

Consequently we introduce the notion of an *array graph,* in which nodes stand for arrays of individual elements and edges represent dependencies which may be subscripted. The problem of translating a specification reverts therefore to the scheduling of array graphs. Indeed the basic operation of the translator for the MODEL system proceeds in three main phases. In the first phase, the statements of equations and declarations are analyzed and the execution events associated with each statement identified. The main output of the first phase is an array graph representation of the specification. The second phase of the translation consists of the scheduling of the array graph. As will be seen below, this scheduling is tightly coupled with loop identification and construction. The last phase transforms the schedule produced above into a PL/I program, performing essentially a one to one translation of the scheduled events into the respective code for their execution. In this chapter we chose to concentrate on the scheduling algorithm and, in order to simplify the presentation, apply it to a simple set of equations defining rectangular arrays. One should bear in mind, though, that these equations could actually represent arbitrary precedence constraints between arbitrary events in a specification, i.e. are, in fact, an equational representation of an array graph. Thus, the method presented here is actually the basic algorithm used in the MODEL translator for scheduling the array graph representation of the specification.

C. Equational Specifications

In the following sections we address ourselves to the problem of translating an Equational Specification into an equivalent working program.

Typically an equational specification is given by a set of equations of the form:

$$A_1[I_1,\ldots I_{k_1}] = f_1(A_1[E_1^1,..E_{k_1}^1],..\ A_m[E_1^s,..E_{k_m}^s])$$

$$A_m[I_1,..I_{k_m}] = f_m\ (A_1[E_1^p,..E_{k_1}^p],..\ A_m[E_1^t,..E_{k_m}^t])$$

This set of equations defines (recursively) the values of the elements of the possibly infinite arrays $A_1,..A_m$.

The idea is certainly not new. These equations, sometimes representing dependency relations, naturally arise in languages such as Data Flow languages, (Arvind and Gostelow), Lucid (Ashcroft *et al.* [1976]), etc. On the other hand, for anyone familiar with Functional Languages such as LISP, Backus' languages, etc., this is a special case of a mutually recursive set of function definitions when the arguments are restricted to be natural numbers.

There are several reasons for staying within the limitations of recursively defined arrays rather than extending to general functions:

1. The area of applications we have in mind is that of Data Processing usage. In this area, arrays and structures in general play important roles and the direct specification of relations between input structures and output structures seems both natural and adequate.
2. Restricting the arguments of the defined entities to be integers and imposing syntactical restrictions on the expressions that appear as subscripts enable us to perform a much deeper analysis of the situation and hope for a compiling system rather than an interpreting system.

In fact, the subject of this paper is the study of these simplifying assumptions about the language which will enable us to propose a compiling system for its execution.

It is a trivial matter to show that such an array definition language, supplemented with the special function "LEAST" is indeed universal in the sense that every computational task can be programmed in it:

Theorem 0: The Array Definition Language is Universal.

Consider a generic program (actually representing the most general case):

$$\bar{y} = \bar{f}(\bar{x});\ \text{while } p(\bar{y}) \text{ do } \bar{y} := \bar{g}(\bar{y});\ \bar{Z} := \bar{h}(\bar{y})\ .$$

This can be written in our language as:

$$\bar{Y}(I) = \text{if } I = 1 \text{ then } \bar{f}(\bar{x}) \text{ else } \bar{g}(\bar{Y}(I-1))$$

$$j = \text{LEAST}\ (I, \text{not } p(\bar{Y}(I)))$$

$$\bar{Z} = \bar{h}(\bar{Y}(j))$$

In the case that some of the $\bar{y}$ variables are structured, the notation $\bar{Y}(I)$ calls for the addition of one more dimension.

The main question we would like to investigate in this paper is under what conditions can we produce a compiled program for the execution of a given array specification.

Before we formulate this question more precisely, we would like to point out two possible pitfalls that one must beware of, in considering this question.

The first is that obviously, there exists a universal interpreter for this language. The interpreter operation can be described as a continuous search for equations which can be applied to quantities which are either input quantities or already defined array components, and yield a definition for some new array components. Once such an equation is found, the new component is assigned its value, and is flagged as defined. Systematically persisting in this search, the interpreter must either reach a state in which all the output quantities are defined, in which case it can stop, or loop forever. The latter case implies that the specification was inadequate for the definition of all the output variables.

Such an interpreter could indeed be presented as a solution to the general case. But if we insist on having an efficient compiled program, we should rule out the possibility of this trivial solution.

Another complicating factor is that it is easy to devise examples of simple specifications, for which the derivation of the optimal program seems nontrivial.

Consider for example the specification:

Example 1:

$$A(I) = \text{if } I = 25 \text{ then } X \text{ else if } I < 25 \text{ then } A(I+2) + X \text{ else if}$$

$$I \leqslant 50 \text{ then } A(I-1) + A(I-25)$$

The optimal program for it is:

Example 2:

```
A(25):=X;

for I:=23 downto 1 by -2 do A(I):= A(I+2) + X;
    A(26):=A(25) + A(1);

for I:= 24 downto 2 by -2 do A(I) :=A(I+2)+X;

for I:=26 to 50 do A(I):=A(I-1)+A(I-25);
```

As another example consider the following specification for defining A(1..100):

Example 3:

$$A(I) = \text{if } I = 1 \text{ then } 0$$

$$\text{else if even } (I) \text{ then } A(I/2) + 1$$

$$\text{else if } I < 60 \text{ then } A(I+4) + 4$$

$$\text{else } A(I+1) + 2$$

We leave it to the interested reader to a) verify that this specification is adequate for defining a value for each A(I), $1 \leqslant I \leqslant 100$, and b) to derive an efficient loop-while program for the computation of its elements.

It can easily be shown that the general problem of adequacy of the specification, being equivalent to the totality of a number theoretic function given by a recursive definition, is of course undecidable.

In order to avoid the trivial solution of the interpreter on one hand, or getting into undecidable analysis on the other hand, we choose to formulate our problem in schematic terms presenting an abstract model whose solution is more manageable.

D. The Denotational Semantics of Equational Specifications

A specification for the array symbols $A_1, \cdots A_n$ of dimensionalities (arities) $d_1, \ldots d_n$ respectively, is a system of n equations:

$$S\colon A_1(I_1,\ldots I_{d_1}) = \tau_1(I_1,\ldots I_{d_1}, A_1, \cdots A_n)$$

$$\vdots$$

$$A_n(I_1,\ldots I_{d_n}) = \tau_n(I_1, \cdots I_{d_n}, A_1, \cdots A_n)$$

The terms $P_i(I_1,\ldots I_{d_i}, A_1, \cdots A_n)$ are defined recursively as follows:

We use the letters $f_1, \cdots$ to denote functions over array elements values, and $g_1, \cdots$ to denote integer valued functions used as subscripts.

Define first the notion of a subscript.

1. I_k is a subscript. Its appearance in τ_i must satisfy $k \leqslant d_i$. The I_k, $1 \leqslant k \leqslant d_i$ must be disjoint, i.e. if $i \neq j$ then $I_i \neq I_j$.
2. $I_k - c$ for an interpreted integer constant $c > 0$ is a subscript (examples $I_1 - 2$, $I_3 - 7$).
3. If $J_1,\ldots J_m$ are subscripts so is $g_i(J_1,\ldots J_m)$.

We can now define terms:

a) If $J_1,\ldots J_{d_i}$ are subscripts, then $A_i(J_1,\ldots J_{d_i})$ is a term.

b) If $t_1,\ldots t_m$ are terms then so is $f_i(t_1,\ldots t_m)$.

An interpretation for a specification consists of:

a) A domain D over which the array elements will vary.

b) An assignment of concrete D functions to the symbols $\{f_i\}$, i.e., $I[f_i] : (D^+)^m \rightarrow D^+$ where m is the arity of f_i.

c) An assignment of concrete natural number functions to the symbols

$$\{g_i\}, \text{ i.e., } I[g_i]:(Z^+)^m \rightarrow Z^+, \text{ where } m \text{ is the arity of } g_i.$$

We restrict ourselves to the case that $I[f_i]$ and $I[g_i]$ are continuous over their respectively extended domains $(D^+)^m$, $(Z^+)^m$. As usual $D^+ = D \cup \{\perp\}$, $Z^+ = Z \cup \{\perp\}$.

Having an interpreted specification we adopt the least fixpoint semantics to give meaning to the specification. Thus the solution of this set of interpreted equations is taken to be the least fixpoint solution. Each A_i is here specified as a (possibly partial) function $A_i\colon Z^{d_i} \rightarrow D$.

Following are two examples of schematic specifications

$$\begin{aligned} S1\colon\ A_1(I,J) &= f_i\,(A_1(I,J-1),\ A_3(I,J-1)) \\ A_2(I) &= f_2(A_1(I,g)) \\ A_3(I,J) &= f_3(A_1(I,J),\ A_2(I)) \\ S2\colon\ A_1(I,J) &= f_1(A_1(I,J-1),\ A_3(I-1,J)) \\ A_2(I) &= f_2(A_1(I,g)) \\ A_3(I,J) &= f_3(A_1(I,J),\ A_2(I)) \end{aligned}$$

These specifications are identical except for the instance of A_3 in f_1. However, that small difference makes in fact S1 unschedulable while S2 is schedulable.

E. Loop Programs and Their Operational Semantics

Let us consider schematic programs over an alphabet similar to the one used for the specifications. In addition, we add a set of loop variables $k_1, k_2, \cdots$.

A statement has a form similar to an equation:

$$A_i(k^1, \ldots k^{d_i}) := \tau_i(k^1, \ldots k^{d_i}, A_1, \cdots A_n)$$

where some disjoint loop variables have been substituted for the free subscripts $I_1, \cdots I_{d_i}$.

We define the notion of an L-block for L a finite set of loop variables. L specifies the loop variables which are still free in the block.

1. A statement $A_i(k^1 \ldots k^{d_i}) := \tau_i(k^1, \ldots k^{d_i}, A_1, \cdots A_n)$ is a $\{k^1, \ldots k^{d_i}\}$ block.
2. If B_1 is an L_1-block and B_2 is an L_2-block, then $B_1; B_2$ is an $L_1 \cup L_2$ block.
3. If B is an L-block then
   for k do B end;
   is an L-$\{k\}$ block.

A loop program, or simply a program is a 0-block, i.e., a block with no free loop variables.

An interpretation of a loop program consists as before of a domain D, an assignment $\{I[f_i]\}$ and an assignment $\{I[g_i]\}$.

Given an interpreted program <P,I>, we define its N evaluation $E_N(A_1), \cdots E_N(A_n)$, for an integer $N \geqslant 0$ as follows:

1. Replace each "*for* k" clause by "*for* k:=1 *to* N".

2. Execute the program in the conventional way. All the array elements are initialized to $\perp$, and so is interpreted any reference to $A(, \cdots g, \ldots)$ for $I[g] > N$. Since all the concrete functions are total over $(Z^+)^m$, $(D^+)^m$ respectively, each statement yields a value (possibly $\perp$ which is assigned to the corresponding array element.

This computation terminates and yields values over D^+ for $A_i(1 \cdots N, \ldots, 1 \cdots N)$. We extend $E_N(A_i)$ by defining $E_N(A_i)(, \cdots J, \cdots) = \perp$ for any $J > N$.

An immediate consequence of the continuity of the interpretation is that for any $N_1 > N_2$ we have $E_{N_2}(A_1, \cdots A_n) \subset E_{N_1}(A_1, \ldots A_n)$ by which we mean $E_{N_2}(A_i) \subset E_{N_1}(A_i)$ for every $1 \leqslant i \leqslant n$.

Thus $E_N(\overline{A})$ forms a chain for $N = 1, \ldots$ and we define $E^P(A) = (\underset{N}{\text{l.u.b}})(E_N(\overline{A}))$.

Intuitively this definition is equivalent to:

$A_i^P(k_1, \cdots k_{d_i}) = u \in D$ iff for some N the N-execution assigns the value u to $A_i(k_i \cdots k_{d_i})$.

$A_i^P(k_1, \cdots k_{d_i}) = \perp$ iff all N- execution assigns the value $\perp$ to this component.

F. A Problem and Its Solution

Now that we have defined the denotational semantics of a specification and the operational semantics of a loop program we can relate the two:

A program P is said to *realize* the specification S if for every interpretation: $E^P(\bar{A}) = \mu\bar{A} . \tau(\bar{A})$, i.e., the functions (arrays) $A_1, \cdots A_n$ as defined by the limit of N executions are identical to the least fixpoint of the interpreted specification.

Thus a possible realization of the specification S2 is:

```
for k do
  for m do A1(k,m):=f1(A1(k,m-1),A3(k-1,m)) end;
  A2(k):=f2(A1(k,g));
  for m do A3(k,m):=f3(A1(k,m),A2(k)) end
end
```

No similar realizing program can exist for S1.

We can present now our main problem:

Problem: Given a specification, does there exist a program realizing it? If the answer is positive, we would like to also be able to produce such a program.

Because of the high level of abstraction in our problem, our space of candidate programs is actually limited.

We say that a program P is a *schedule* of a specification S, if all the statements in P are substitution instances of the equations in S.

Theorem 1. A specification S is realizable iff it can be realized by a schedule of S.

In the following we present an algorithm which produces a schedule for a given specification iff the specification is realizable.

For the sake of simplicity we will consider here specifications of a somewhat restricted form. A specification is in *normal form* if:

1. All array variables have the same dimension d.
2. A subscript I_k appearing in an expression of the form $I_k - c$ in subscript position j of an array variable must satisfy $j=k$.

The important point in 2 is that the same free index occupies the same position in all the variables in the equation.

Lemma. Every specification can be brought to normal form.

In every specification which does not satisfy condition 1 we can extend the dimensions of every variable to a common maximum d. The extension is performed by adding extra dimensions which are arbitrarily subscripted by free indices not occupying the previous positions.

For the second condition we use an example to show how to handle inconsistent subscripting. Consider the following specification:

$$A(I,J) = F(I,J,A(I-1,J),A(J-1,I))$$

Define a new array B by

$$B(I,J) = A(J,I)$$

Then the following is a consistently subscripted specification which extends the original one:

$$\begin{aligned} A(I,J) &= F(I,J,A(I-1,J),B(I,J-1)) \\ B(I,J) &= F(J,I,B(I,J-1),A(I-1,J)) \end{aligned}$$

This transformation can be applied to the general case to produce a subscript consistent specification.

The algorithm for scheduling a specification in normal form uses a labelled dependency graph which represents the dependencies between elements in the specification. For a given specification S , the dependency graph G_S is defined as follows:

$$G_S = (V_S, E_S, \lambda_S) \text{ where:}$$

V_S — The set of nodes. Each node corresponds to an array variable (or the equation defining it.)

E_S — The set of edges. For each instance of the array A_i in τ_j (the defining expression for A_j), there is an edge leading from node i to node j , implying that elements of A_j depend on elements of A_i, i.e., some elements of A_i have to be computed before the elements of A_j can be computed.

λ_S — For each edge $e = (i,j) \in E_S$, $\bar{\lambda}(e)$ the label for e indicates which elements of A_j depend on which elements of A_i. For an edge $e = (i,j)$ which represents dependency of $A_j(I_1,\ldots,I_d)$ on $A_i(J_1,\ldots,J_d)$ the label $\bar{\lambda}(e) = (\lambda_1(e),\ldots,\lambda_d(e))$ is defined by:

$$\lambda_k(e) = \begin{cases} c & \text{if } J_k = I_k - c \\ -\infty & \text{if } J_k = g(\bar{I}) \end{cases}$$

The following algorithm will attempt to schedule a specification S (in normal form) with the labelled dependency graph G_S:

1. Decompose G_S into maximal strongly connected components $G_1,\ldots,G_p$. Obviously it is sufficient to schedule each component independently and then sequence the resulting schedules. Topologically sort $G_1,\ldots,G_p$. That is, arrange $G_1,\ldots,G_p$ in such an order that if there is an edge connecting a node in G_i to a node in G_j then necessarily $i \leqslant j$. Apply the following steps to each component G_j in order to obtain $P(G_1),\ldots,P(G_p)$ where $P(G_i)$ is the schedule for $G_i, i = 1,\ldots,p$, then $P(G_S)$ — the schedule for S is given by: $P(G_1);\ldots;P(G_p)$.
2. Scheduling a strongly connected component:

   Let G be the component. If G consists of a single node n with no edges then $P(G) = n$.

Otherwise —

Locate a position j such that the index I_j is still free, i.e., has not been bounded by a loop and such that for all edges e in G, $\lambda_j(e) \geqslant 0$. Construct the modified graph G^j obtained from G by deleting all edges e with $\lambda_j(e) > 0$.

3. Construct the program:

$$\begin{array}{l} \text{For } I_j \geqslant 0 \\ \quad P(G^j) \\ \text{END } I_j\ ; \end{array}$$

In order to obtain $P(G^j)$ we apply the scheduling algorithm recursively to G^j.

The algorithm will fail to schedule S iff in some stage step 2 fails to find a free index I_j such that $\lambda_j(e) \geqslant 0$ for every edge e in E_G for some component G. This implies that for *every* index I_j there exists an e such that $\lambda_j(e) = -\infty$ or that $\lambda_j(e) = 0$ for every $e \in E_G$. Since the component G is a nontrivial strongly connected graph it must contain a cycle such that the sum of the labels $\bar{\lambda}(e)$ of its edges is $\leqslant 0$. Consequently every array element $A_i(\bar{u})$ along this cycle depends on another element $A_i(\bar{v})$ with $\bar{u} \leqslant \bar{v}$. Such an element is never computable, and hence the specification is unrealizable. The following example demonstrates the scheduling algorithm.

$$\begin{aligned} A(I,J) &= F(A(I-1,g)\ ,\ B(I-1,J-2)) \\ B(I,J) &= G(B(I,J-1)\ ,\ A(I,J)) \end{aligned}$$

Its dependency graph is given by:

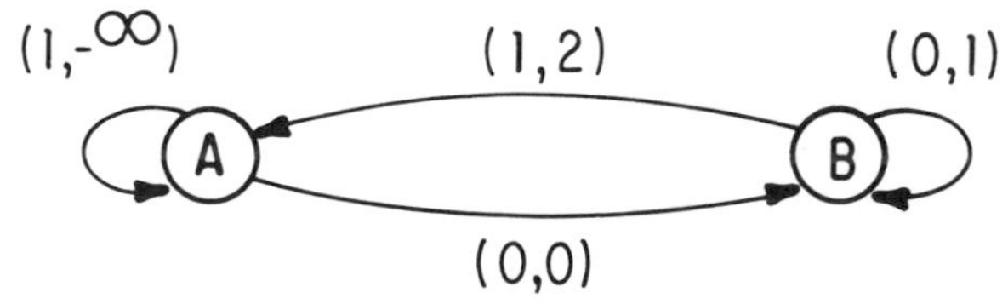

The steps in the construction are:

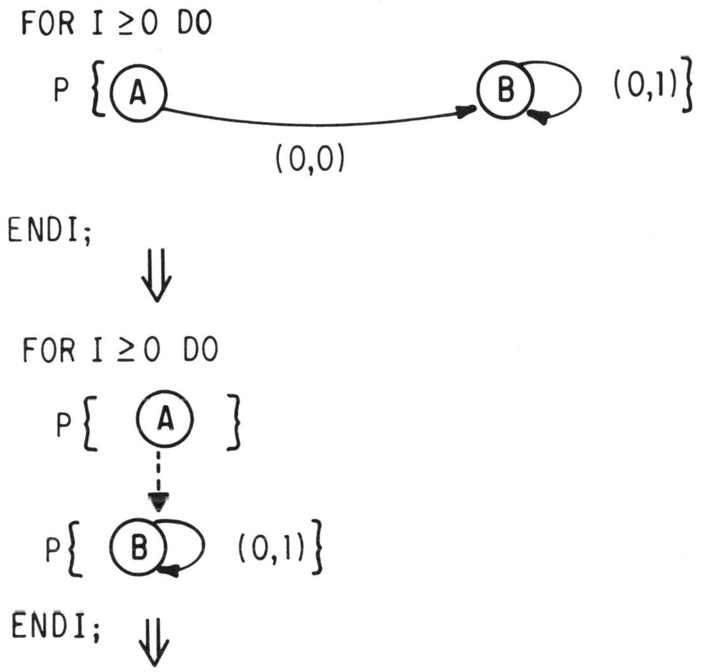


```
FOR I≥0 DO
    FOR J≥0  DO
          A(I,J):  =  F(A(I−1,g), B(I−1, J−2)
    END J
    FOR J≥0 DO
          B(I,J):=G(B(I,J−1),A(I,J))
    END J
END I
```

G. Generalization

A deeper investigation of these problems is reported in Pnueli and Zarhi [1981]. The analysis there considers a significant generalization of the framework and the results presented here. In the more general framework a subscript expression on the right hand side may assume one of the following forms: $I_k - c$, $I_k + c$ for a nonnegative $c \geqslant 0$ and $g_k(\bar{I})$. We may thus have a specification of the following form:

$$\begin{aligned} A(I,J) &= F(B(I+1,J-1)) \\ B(I,J) &= G(B(I,J-1),\ A(I-1,J+2)) \end{aligned}$$

The main algorithm presented there (based on the idea of the algorithm presented here) checks whether a given specification is realizable and produces a program for realizable specifications. The algorithm described in Theorem 1 has to be extended as follows:

Corresponding to each dependency of the form

$$A(\ldots,I_i,\ldots) <\!-\!- F(\ldots B(\ldots,I_i+c,\ldots)\ldots)$$

we construct an edge with the label $-c$ in position i. The labels now may have negative values (not only $-\infty$ as in the case described here). In looking for a free index (step 2) we insist now on identification of subscript position such that the sum of labels (in this position) on every cycle in the dependency graph must be nonnegative. A negative cycle implies a dependency of an array element on another element of the same array with higher subscript. This for example will emerge in the analysis of an equation such as $A(I) = f(A(I+1))$. Naturally with our convention of increasing loops such specification cannot be realized. The more general case where constant subscripts $c \geqslant 0$ are also allowed, and consequently an array may be defined by several equations — is discussed. The problem whether a given specification in this extended form is realizable is proved to be undecidable.

References

Arvind and Gostelow
Arvind and Gostelow, "Dataflow computer architecture: research and goals," Technical Report No. 113, Dept. of ICS, University of California, Irvine.

Ashcroft and Wadge [1976]
E.A. Ashcroft and W. Wadge, "LUCID—a nonprocedural language with iterations," *CACM* 20, No. 7 (1976), pp. 519–526.

Hoffman [1978]
C.M. Hoffman, "Design and correctness of a compiler for a nonprocedural language," *Acta Informatica* 9 (1978), pp. 217–241.

Prywes [1978]
N.S. Prywes, "MODEL II—Automatic program generator user manual," Office of Planning and Research Internal Revenue Service, TIR–77–41 (July 1978), available from CIS Dept., University of Pennsylvania.

Prywes *et al.* [1979]
N.S. Prywes, A. Pnueli and S. Shastry, "Use of a nonprocedural specification language and associated program generator in software development," *ACM TOPLAS,* 1(2) (October 1979), pp. 196–217.

Pnueli and Zarhi [1981]
A. Pnueli and R. Zarhi, "Realizing an equational specification," *ICALP* 81.

Shastry [1978]
S. Shastry, "Verification and correction of a nonprocedural specification in automatic generation of programs," Ph.D. Dissertation, CIS Dept., University of Pa. (May 1978).

Shastry *et al.*
S. Shastry, A. Pnueli and N.S. Prywes, "Basic algorithms used in the MODEL system for design of programs," Moore School Report, CIS Dept., University of Pa.

Wadge [1979]
W. Wadge, "An extensional treatment of dataflow deadlocks," *Proceedings, Semantics of Concurrent Computation,* Evian, France (1979), Springer-Verlag.

CHAPTER 14

Constructing Recursive Programs Which Are Memory Efficient

Alberto Pettorossi
Istituto di Analisi dei Sistemi ed Informatica del C.N.R.,
Via Buonarroti 12, 00185 Roma

Abstract

We present an algorithm for improving memory efficiency of applicative recursive programs. It is based on the method of adding "destructive annotations" to programs as suggested in (Pettorossi, [1978]; Pettorossi, [1979]; Schwarz, [1977]). Memory utilization is improved by the overwriting of cells where intermediate results no longer useful are stored.

The time complexity of the proposed algorithm is also studied.

A. Introduction

Among other methodologies for writing correct and efficient programs, "program transformation" (Burstall and Darlington [1977]; Darlington and Burstall [1976]) has been of great interest over the past years. The basic idea of this approach, in contrast, for example, with the methodology of the stepwise refinements (Dahl *et al.* [1972]; Wirth [1971]), is that the programmer is first asked to be concerned with the program correctness and, only at later stages, with efficiency considerations. The original version of the program, which can be easily proved correct, is transformed (perhaps in several phases) into a program which is still correct, because the strategies used for the transformation preserve correctness, and it is more efficient because the computations evoked by the final program save time and/or space.

Several papers have been published about this methodology concerning: (i) *systems* for transforming programs (Bauer *et al.* [1977]; Burstall and Darlington [1977]; Feather [1978]), (ii) various *strategies* for directing the transformations (Bauer *et al.* [1978]; Chatelin [1977]; Partsch and Pepper [1977]; Pettorossi [1977]), and (iii) some *theories* for proving their correctness (Huet and Lang [1978], Kott [1978]). The list of references is not to be considered exhaustive. For a more extensive bibliography one may refer to Burstall and Feather [1979].

Unfortunately for the program transformation methodology, a general framework in which one can prove that transformations improve efficiency while preserving correctness, is not fully available yet. A first step in this direction was done in Wegbreit [1976]. We have already some partial results and we know that, under given hypotheses, the tupling strategy is a way of reducing time of computation (Burstall and Darlington [1977]) and also the "time × memory product" requirements (Pettorossi [1977]). Other strategies also, as the "generalization strategy" or the "where-abstraction introduction", can improve the running time efficiency.

In this paper we are concerned with the problem of reducing memory requirements in computations evoked by applicative recursive programs, like those studied in (Burstall and Darlington [1977]). In the next section we present the method used and in sections C and D we develop an algorithm which implements it. Possible improvements and directions of further research are outlined in the last two sections.

B. The Method Used

In order to reduce the number of cells necessary for performing computations, we use the so-called "destructive annotation method" as introduced in Pettorossi [1978] and Schwarz [1977]. This method cannot be viewed as a proper program transformation strategy, because indeed the given program maintains its structure unchanged. Nevertheless, using this method, we can transform the behavior of the programs and we can achieve an improvement in memory efficiency; we give, in fact, some information to the interpreter (or the compiler) so that it could rewrite cells where intermediate results no longer useful are stored.

We will show the basic ideas of the "destructive annotation method" through an example. Suppose we are given the following program P1.1 for computing the factorial function:

```
P1.1: fact(n) <= g(1,n)

          g(m,n) <= if n=0 then m else g(mult(m,n),pred(n))
```

A computation history is given in fig. 1. (We did not represent the evaluation of the predicate of the if-then-else construct. The notation pred(n) stands for the predecessor of n.)

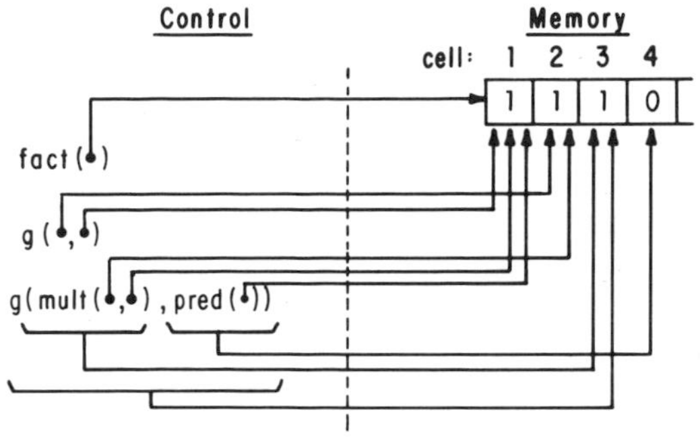

Fig. 1. Computation of fact(1) according to program P1.1

Obviously one could improve the memory utilization by giving to the interpreter the information that it could put the result of mult(m,n) where m was and the result of pred(n) where n was. Doing that, we would have required 2 memory cells instead of 4 (in general 2 cells instead of 2(n+2) when computing fact(n)) (see fig. 2).

As a first step we therefore need to extend the language in which programs are written so that such extra information about the destruction of arguments can be suitably represented. We decided to associate to each *basic function* (i.e. a function which is not explicitly defined in the applicative recursive program, but immediately executable by the interpreter) and each *if-then-else* construct a binary k-tuple. If the i-th component of the k-tuple is 1 the interpreter may reclaim the cell used by the value of the i-th argument of the basic function for storing a new value, which will be computed later on. If it is 0, no reclaim is possible, at least at the moment of the evaluation of that basic function. For example $pred_{<1>}$ (n) means that the result of pred(n), namely, n−1, may be stored in the same cell where n was. We associate with the if-then-else construct a 1-tuple (and not a 3-tuple) denoting the possible destruction of the term of the predicate only (see Pettorossi [1978a]). Therefore we could rewrite program P1.1 as follows:

P1.2: fact(n) <= g(1,n)

$$g(m,n) <= if_{<0>}\ n=0 \text{ then } m \text{ else } g(mult_{<10>}(m,n),\ pred_{<1>}(n))$$

and the computation of fact(1) according to program P1.2 is like the one in fig. 2.

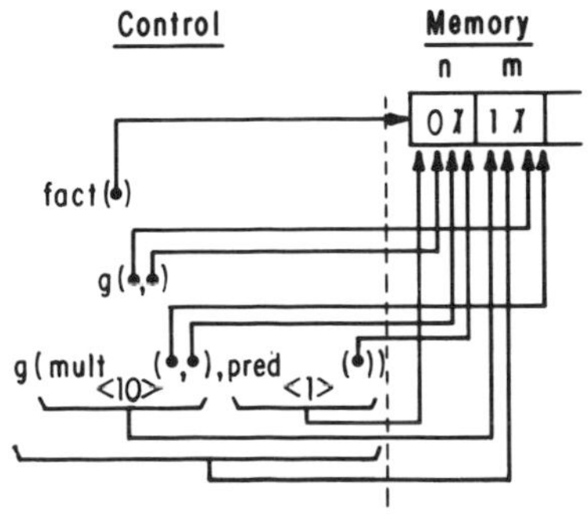

Fig. 2. Computation of fact(1) according to program P1.2.

Only 2 memory cells are used in this case.

Notice that the information we give to the interpreter is a "static" one. In other words, it is not given "at run time", but once and for all before execution and it must be valid for any input value. Since we give "static" information we do not achieve a memory efficiency which is always optimal (as one can see in other examples), but we have the great advantage of being able to "compute" the destructive annotations "off-line". The fact that the given information is "static" is the reason that we associate a 1-tuple to *if-then-else* constructs (and not a 3-tuple, as one could expect of if-then-else being a function with 3 arguments). Since *a priori* we cannot know whether the evaluation of the predicate yields true or false, we should always keep the values of both the left and the right arm of the conditional. So, instead of using the 3-tuple $<x00>$, we use the 1-tuple $<x>$ for $x = 0,1$.

An important feature of the destruction phenomenon needs to be underlined: "destruction is propagating".

In the example we just gave, fact(n) is a not-basic function, therefore it has no destructive annotations; nevertheless it destroys its argument n. It is clear from fig. 2 that the value of n which is 1 is then changed into 0 by $pred_{<1>}(n)$. Since, in general, functions are recursively defined, we have to make sure that the propogation of the destruction is such that correctness is always preserved. In Pettorossi [1978] we studied this problem and we proved some theorems which guarantee, under given hypotheses, the correctness of the destructive annotations.

Notice also that correctness of the annotations depends on the semantics we adopt for the language in which we write our applicative recursive programs. Again it is clear from the given example that, for a correct evaluation of fact(n), it is necessary that $pred_{<1>}(n)$ is performed *after* $mult_{<10>}(m,n)$. Otherwise the value of n which mult will multiply by m cannot be the correct one. The destructive semantics D we consider, is based on the following 3 basic rules:

i) "leftmost innermost" substitution rule for recursively defined functions;
ii) "left to right" evaluation of arguments;
iii) parameters passed by reference if they are variables, by value if they are function applications.

We are going to have two semantics functions: S and D. S is a "standard" semantics and deals with usual programs, i.e. the not annotated ones, and D is a "destructive" semantics which deals with programs which are annotated.

Given a program P, and an algorithm Markprog for synthesizing destructive annotations (or destructive markings, as we call them), the basic facts to be shown are the following ones:

i) the diagram of fig. 3 commutes, and
ii) a suitable implementation of D improves memory utilization w.r.t. a given implementation of S.

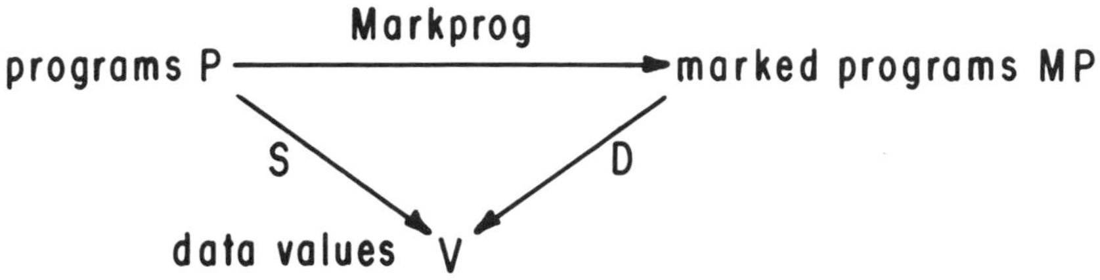

Fig. 3. The commutativity diagram for destructiveness.

In our previous papers (Pettorossi [1978a] and [1978b]) we formally defined the S and D semantics, we proved some theorems and we introduced some heuristics which will validate the Markprog algorithm we are going to present here. Indeed it can be shown that, for our algorithm, under given hypotheses, the diagram of fig. 3 commutes and the memory cells are more efficiently used.

C. Preliminary Definitions and Basic Ideas of the Algorithm

The algorithm has been written in NPL (Burstall [1977]), a language used for the program transformation project at Edinburgh University and its translation into HOPE (Burstall *et al.* [1980]), a language more advanced and more efficiently implemented, is in progress. The complete running version of the algorithm is a bit lengthy (Pettorossi [1979]) and we are going to present here only the main ideas, using a Pascal-like notation. The language L, in which the programs P to be marked with destructive annotations are written, is defined as follows:

X is a set of *variable symbols,* xi ϵ X,
G is a finite set of *basic function symbols,* g ϵ G,
F is a set of *variable function symbols,* f ϵF,
Terms is a set of terms t such that:
t::=x1|x2|...|xn| *if* t0=0 *then* t1 *else* t2|g(t1,...,tk)|f(t1,...,tn)
Programs are functions from F to Terms. Each pair <f,t>, of a program prog such that prog(f) = t, is written as f(x1,...,xn) <=t.

Analogously the language ML, in which the marked-programs MP of fig. 3 are written, has *Marked-terms* which is a set of terms mt defined as follows:

$$\text{mt::=x1}|\text{x2}|\ldots|\text{xn}|\ \text{if}_{\underline{k}}\text{mt0=0 then mt1 else mt2}|\text{g}_{\underline{k}}\text{(mt1,...,mtk)}|\text{f(t1,...,tn)}$$

where $\underline{k}$ is a binary k-tuple. *Marked-programs* are functions from F to Marked-terms. Each pair <f,mt> belonging to a marked-program mprog such that mprog(f)=mt, is written as f(x1,...,xn) $\leqslant$ mt.

The standard semantics S:Terms -> Env -> Programs -> V for terms in L is:

$$S[x_i](r)(prog) = r(x_i)$$

$$S[g(t1,...)](r)(prog) = \beta(g)(S[t1](r)(prog),...)$$

$$S[\text{if } t0{=}0 \text{ then } t1 \text{ else } t2](r)(prog) = COND(S[t0](r)(prog),S[t1](r)(prog), S[t2](r)(prog))$$

$$S[f(t1,...)](r)(prog) = S[prog(f)](<x1,S[t1](r)(prog)>,...)(prog)$$

where Env denotes the environments, i.e., functions from X to V, β:G→ V^n→ V gives the semantics for symbols in G_1 and COND is the semantic conditional.

For a more complete and detailed definition the reader may refer to Pettorossi [1978]. The definition of the destructive semantics D is a bit complicated (Pettorossi [1978]). About D we need only to know that the evaluation of a marked-term like $g_{<b1\ b2>}$(mt1,mt2) proceeds as follows:

> mt1 is evaluated first yielding the value v1, then mt2 is evaluated yielding the value v2, and eventually the value of g(v1,v2) is stored in a new location, with the extra effect that the location where the value of mti was stored, for i = 1, 2, is not certain to contain vi any more, if bi=1.

We will give the algorithm Markprog for synthesizing destructive annotations using the simplifying hypothesis that all *variable values are independent,* i.e. when we destroy the value of one variable we do not affect the value of any other variable. This is indeed a simplifying hypothesis, because when dealing with composite data structures, such as lists or trees, one may have variables denoting subvalues of others (for example y may denote the tail of the list denoted by z). Nevertheless the "independent variables" hypothesis is the first step one has to make as an initial approach to the theory of destructiveness, and it is not too restrictive because it still allows us to deal with data structures like numbers, arrays, etc. and also composite data structures when sharing of values is not present.

In order to be more specific, let us now introduce another example to which we will refer for explaining how the algorithm works. We consider the following program P2.0 for computing 2^{x1}:

P2.0: twoto(x1) <= f(x1,0)
f(x1,x2) <= if minus (x1,x2)=0 then 1 else doubleof(f(x1,succ(x2))).

The algorithm Markprog starts off by producing program P2.1:

P2.1:twoto(x1) <= f(x1,0)
f(x1,x2) $\leqslant$if$_{<\phi>}$minus$_{<\phi\phi>}$(x1,x2)=0 then 1 else doubleof$_{<\phi>}$(f(x1,succ$_{<\phi>}$(x2)))

where all k-tuples are undefined, i.e. made out of ϕ's. Then the algorithm changes each ϕ into either 1 or 0, denoting destruction or preservation of the value of the corresponding argument, according to the fact that destroying that value does or does not keep the diagram of fig. 3 commutative. Since we look for the highest memory efficiency, we have to try to transform all ϕ's into 1's. We may write a first version of the Markprog algorithm as follows:

```
Markprog/1: initialize all k-tuples with ϕ's
             while "there is a ϕ in a k-tuple"
             do "change that ϕ into 1 if commutativity of diagram of
                fig. 3 is preserved, otherwise
             change it into 0"
             od
```

A theorem given in Pettorossi [1978] guarantees the commutativity of diagram of fig. 3 when *correctness* and *consistency,* i.e. two properties defined according to the destructive semantics D, hold. In order to make the checking of the commutativity of the diagram much easier and faster, we would like to have those properties locally testable, i.e. testable looking only at one recursive function definition, like $f(x_1, \ldots, x_n)$ <= mt, at the time. For that purpose we introduce the following notion of *destructive characterization* of recursive functions. Given a marked program mp ϵ F $\rightarrow$ Markedterms, a destructive characterization d is a function from F to 2^X where X = {x1,...,xn}. The informal semantic interpretation of such a function d is such that *if* f ϵ F has arity n and d(f) = $\{x_{i_1},\ldots,x_{i_m}\}$ where x_{i_j}'s are elements of X *then,* after the evaluation of any term of the form f(mt1,...,mtn), the values of the marked terms $mti_1, \ldots, mti_m$ are destroyed.

Example 1. Given d(f) = {x2}, i.e. f destroys its second argument, after the evaluation of f(x1, $succ_{<0>}$(x2))) in program P2.1, the value of succ(x2) is destroyed. □

Now we can informally define the *correctness of a markedterm* mt, *w.r.t. a* given *destructive characterization* d. We say that mt is correct w.r.t. d if, when we evaluate mt according to D and we assume the recursively defined functions occurring in mt to be destructive as specified by d, we get for mt the same value as S[t](r)(prog), i.e. the value which can be obtained using the undestructive semantics.

Example 2. Given d(f) = {x2},mt1 ≡ $if_{<1>}$ $minus_{<00>}$(x1,x2) = 0 then 1 else $doubleof_{<1>}$(f(x1, $succ_{<0>}$(x2))) is correct w.r.t. d, because no useful value is destroyed; but mt2 ≡ $if_{<1>}$$minus_{<10>}$(x1,x2) = 0 then 1 else $doubleof_{<1>}$(f(x1,$succ_{<0>}$(x2))) is *not* correct w.r.t. d, because when we evaluate minus(x1,x2) we destroy x1 which is needed for the evaluation of the right arm of the conditional. Similarly a term like $mult_{<00>}$(f($succ_{<0>}$(x1),x2),x2) is *not* correct w.r.t. d, because after the evaluation of f, x2 has been destroyed, and it will no longer be possible to evaluate correctly the second argument of mult. □

We also say that a marked term mt, such that f(x1,...,xn) <= mt, is *consistent w.r.t. a destructive characterization* d if d(f) ⊆ (d(f) ∪ inspect(mt,d)), where inspect(mt,d) returns the subset of {x1,...,xn} which contains any variable xi which will be destroyed during the evaluation of mt according to D, when the recursively defined functions destroy their arguments according to d.

In other words, we may also say that mt is consistent w.r.t. d if the variable destruction, performed in evaluating mt, is not "greater" than the destruction we assume for the corresponding recursively defined function f.

Example 3. Given d(f) = { },

prog(f)=mt ≡ $if_{<1>}$$minus_{<00>}$(x1,x2)=0 then 1 else $doubleof_{<1>}$(f(x1,$succ_{<1>}$(x2)))

is *not* consistent w.r.t. d, because inspect(mt) = {x2}. Given d(f) = {x1}, prog(f)=mt ≡ $mult_{<00>}$(f($succ_{<1>}$(x1),x2),x2) is consistent w.r.t. d, because inspect(mt) = {x1}. □
Using the result of theorem 2 (Pettorossi [1978]) we can obtain the following version of the algorithm:

Markprog/2:

$\phi \equiv$ {program prog ϵ F $\rightarrow$ Terms}

initialize all k-tuples with ϕ's;
initialize a destructive characterization $\underline{d}$ such that $\forall f \epsilon F\underline{d}(f) = \{\}$;

{every marked term in the marked program, where all ϕ's are considered as 0's, is correct and consistent w.r.t. $\underline{d}$};

while "there is a ϕ in a k-tuple occurring in f(x1,...,xn) <= mt"
do "change that ϕ into 1 if there exists a destructive characterization $\underline{d}$ such that every marked term of the marked program with that ϕ changed into 1 is *correct* and *consistent* w.r.t. $\underline{d}$, otherwise change it into 0"
od

$\psi \equiv$ {diagram of fig. 3 commutes and memory efficiency is maximal}

It is easy to see (Pettorossi [1978]) that the invariant is true after initialization and it remains true for each iteration of the while-loop. In what follows we consider the following two functions as primitive. They are:

correct: Marked terms x destructive characterizations -> bool
and
inspect: Marked terms x destructive characterizations -> set of variables.

They check whether or not correctness and consistency hold. They also depend on the definition of the semantics D and any reasonable definition of D determines a suitable coding of them (and vice versa, according to theorem 2, Pettorossi [1978], any coding defines a D such that the diagram of fig. 3 commutes). We hope that the rules we mentioned at the end of the previous section, and the examples we have given in this section, can convey to the reader the definition of D we have in mind, so that he can anticipate the behavior of the functions *correct* and *inspect* in the examples we are going to give. The interested reader may also find in Pettorossi [1979] the NPL programs for *correct* and *inspect,* which correspond to the semantics D formally given in Pettorossi [1978].

D. Developing the Algorithm

In this section we will develop the algorithm Markprog/2 giving more details on how to execute the body of the while-loop. We are given a marked program mprog:F -> Markedterms and we suppose that a k-tuple with a ϕ is found in a basic function occurring in mti = mprog(fi). Moreover we are given a destructive characterization d such that all marked terms in mprog, considering all ϕ's occurring in them as 0's, are correct and consistent w.r.t. d.

Let us call mti0 and mti1 the marked term mti where the ϕ which has been found is respectively changed into 0 or 1. Considering mti1 and the given d, we can compute corr:=correct(mti1,d) and cons:= issubset(inspect(mti1,d),d(fi)) where issubset(A,B) is true iff $A \subseteq B$. If corr is false then we have to replace mti by mti0 and then look for another ϕ to be replaced. If corr is true, we have to check the value of cons. If cons is true then we replace mti by mti1 and we look for another ϕ to be replaced. Otherwise, if cons is false, we compute the new value for d, namely d'=d[d(fi) $\cup$ inspect(mti1,d)|fi], and then, in order to regain the validity of the invariant, we have to check that all marked terms mtj's of the given marked program, where fi occurs, are correct and consistent w.r.t. the new destructive characterization d'. As usual, f[v|x] denotes a function which is identical to f except that f(x)=v.

Obviously this process of checking correctness and consistency for all mtj's w.r.t. d' can be performed by a "recursive call" of the body of the loop we are describing, which indeed has to check correctness and consistency of mti1 w.r.t. d. This recursive call is a tail-recursive call because what one has to do at the end of a call is either to evoke a new call or to stop the overall process by (i) replacing mti by mti0 or mti1, and (ii) respectively keeping d unchanged or replacing with its last computed value d'. Therefore we can use an inner while-loop to implement this recursion, using the following two extra variables:

i) a set, say "functset", to remember all function symbols fj's for which we have still to check correctness and consistency of the corresponding marked term,

ii) a temporary variable d for storing the initial value of the destructive characterization.

We have the following version Markprog/3 of the algorithm:

Markprog/3:

```
ϕ ≡{program prog ε F -> Terms}

initialize all k-tuples with ϕ's;

initialize a destructive characterization d̲ such that ∀f ε Fd̲(f) = {};


{every marked term in the marked program, where all ϕ's
 are considered as 0's, is correct and consistent w.r.t. d̲}

while "there is a ϕ in a k-tuple occurring in fi(x1,...,xn) <= mti"
do t:=true; functset:={fi}; d:=d̲ ; mprog:=mprog[mti1|fi];

{∀ f ε(F-functset) mprog(f) is correct and consistent w.r.t. d}


    while t and functset ≠ {}
    do f:="choose an element from functset and call it f";
      functset:=functset− {f};
      mt:=mprog(f);
      corr:=correct(mt,d);
      cons:=issubset(inspect(mt,d),d(f));
      d:=d[d(f) ∪ inspect(mt,d)|f];
      if corr then if cons
                   then functset:=functset− {f}
                   else functset:=functset ∪ {fj| f occurs in mprog(fj) }
              else t:=false;

      od
      if t then mprog,d̲:=mprog[mti0|fi],d
          else mprog   :=mprog[mti1|fi]
      od
```

$\psi \equiv$ {diagram of fig. 3 commutes and memory efficiency is maximal}

In Markprog/3:(i) mti0 and mti1 denote the marked term mti where the ϕ which has been found in it is changed into 0 or 1 respectively, (ii) g[v|i] denotes the function g where g(i) = v and all its other values are unchanged. Obviously a correctness proof of Markprog/3 requires the formal specification of the semantics D, of the functions *correct* and *inspect* and of the notion of maximal memory efficiency. It would take too much space here to do so, and we leave to the reader to convince himself of the validity of the algorithm recalling that:

i) if cons = true then d = d[d(f) ∪ inspect(mt,d)|f] by definition,

ii) if no ϕ's occur in mprog and all marked terms in mprog are correct and consistent w.r.t. d then the diagram of fig. 3 commutes by theorem 2, Pettorossi [1978], and no more destruction is possible because all k-tuples have 0's or 1's.

A more detailed analysis is done in Pettorossi [1979].

Example 4. We will analyze the behavior of Markprog/3 for the program P2.0 given in Section C. The initialization phase gives us program P2.1 and the destructive characterization $\underline{d}$ such that $\underline{d}$(twoto) = {} and $\underline{d}$(f) = {}. After the first execution of the body of the main while-loop we get:

P2.2: twoto(x1) <= f(x1,0)
 f(x1,x2) <= $\text{if}_{<1>}\text{minus}_{<\phi\phi>}$(x1,x2) =0 then 1 else $\text{doubleof}_{<\phi>}$ (f(x1,$\text{succ}_{<\phi>}$ (x2)))

and again $\underline{d}$(twoto) = {}, $\underline{d}$(f) = {}. The correctness and the consistency of the terms in P2.2 rely on the fact that no variable value is destroyed. Since x1 and x2 are necessary for the evaluation of the right hand side of the conditional, it is easy to see that during the following two executions of the while-loop body *corr* is false and we get:

P2.3: twoto(x1) <= f(x1,0)
 f(x1,x2) <= $\text{if}_{<1>}\text{minus}_{<00>}$(x1,x2) = 0 then 1 else $\text{doubleof}_{<\phi>}$(f(x1,$\text{succ}_{<\phi>}$ (x2)))

and $\underline{d}$ is still unchanged. Again, changing $\text{doubleof}_{<\phi>}$(...) into $\text{doubleof}_{<1>}$(...) does not create any problem, because the variable values are not destroyed and correctness and consistency are guaranteed. We have therefore:

P2.4: twoto(x1) <= f(x1,0)
 f(x1,x2) <= $\text{if}_{<1>}\text{minus}_{<00>(x1,x2)}$= 0 then 1 else $\text{doubleof}_{<1>}$(f(x1,$\text{succ}_{<\phi>}$(x2)))

and $\underline{d}$(twoto) = {} and $\underline{d}$(f) = {}. When $\text{succ}_{<\phi>}$(x2) is changed into $\text{succ}_{<1>}$(x2), *corr* is true, but *cons* is false because inspect($\text{if}_{<1>}\text{minus}_{<00>}$(x1,x2) = 0 then 1 else $\text{doubleof}_{<1>}$(f(x1,$\text{succ}_{<1>}$(x2))),d) = {x2} while d(f) = {}. Since f occurs in mprog(f), we have again functset = {f}. Now *corr* and *cons* are both true because d has been updated: we have in fact d(twoto) = {} and d(f) = {x2}. Since functset = {}, the outermost while-loop stops and we have the following final program:

P2.5: twoto(x1) <= f(x1,0)

$$f(x1,x2) <= if_{<1>} minus_{<00>}(x1,x2)=0 \text{ then } 1 \text{ else } doubleof_{<1>}(f(x1,succ_{<1>}(x2))).$$

The reader can easily check the improvements on memory utilization one can obtain using program P2.5 instead of program P2.0. In particular *succ* and *doubleof* may overwrite the memory cells where the values of their arguments are stored.

E. Possible Improvements Using Heuristics and Discovering Dependencies

It is possible to speed up the basic algorithm we presented, using some heuristics which *a priori* guarantee the commutativity of the diagram of fig. 3. In particular those heuristics will allow us to start off not from a marked program with completely unspecified k-tuples, but from a program where some decisions on the k-tuples have already been made. The validity of the heuristics depends on the destructive semantics definition D we consider. Since we have not formally defined D here, we cannot prove their validity, but we hope that the informal idea the reader has of our semantic function D, is clear enough to make him accept those heuristics as valid.

Before presenting some of those heuristics, let us give the following definition. An *applicative if-then-else* is an *if-then-else construct with left and right arms which are either an application or an applicative if-then-else.*

Example 5.

i) if x2=0 then g(x2,succ(x1)) else h(x1) is an applicative if-then-else.

ii) if x2=0 then g(x2,succ(x1)) else x2 is *not* an applicative if-then-else because x2 is not an application. □

Heuristic 1. A basic function can be destructive in any argument which is an application or an applicative if-then-else.

Heuristic 2. In $if_{<\phi>}$mt0=0 then mt1 else mt2, ϕ can be 1 if mt0 is an application or an applicative *if-then-else.*

Heuristics 1 and 2 are valid because the value of an argument which is an application or an applicative if-then-else, is used only once. On the contrary, variable values which are passed by pointers can be used several times and by different functions: this is why heuristics 1 and 2 cannot be applied for variables.

Heuristic 3. In $if_{\underline{k}}$mt0=0 then mt1 else mt2, mt0 cannot destroy the variables needed for evaluating mt1 and mt2.

Example 6. Applying heuristics 1,2 and 3 for the program of Example 4 the marking algorithm could have started directly from program P2.4 saving various executions of the outer while-loop body of Markprog/3. □

Some more heuristics are given in Pettorossi [1979].

A second way of improving the Markprog/3 algorithm is to discover dependencies in assigning values to k-tuples, so that, in particular, we change more than one ϕ at the time. Let us show this point through an example.

Example 7. Consider the marked program:

$$f1(x1,x2,x3) <= h_{<\phi\phi\phi>}(x1,f2(x2,p_{<\phi>}(x2),d_{<\phi>}(x2)) , x3)$$

$$f2(x1,x2,x3) <= g_{<\phi\phi>}(x1,f1(x3,r_{<\phi>}(x2), x3))$$

If we choose to change the k-tuple $<\phi\phi\phi>$ of h into $<1\phi\phi>$, since in the body of f2 the function f1 is called with the third argument equal to the first one and variable passing is by reference, destruction of the first argument of f1 implies also destruction of its third argument. Analogously, if we choose to change that same k-tuple into $<\phi\phi 1>$ we destroy the third and the first argument of f1 for the same reason. So we might as well choose to change $<\phi\phi\phi>$ in one step into $<1\phi 1>$ and test correctness and consistency for that k-tuple directly.

There are in general other ways of improving the method and the algorithm we have given, as for example, taking into consideration the semantics of the basic functions occurring in the program. Given a term like g(r(hd(x)),tl(x)) where x is a list, hd and tl are the usual *head* and *tail* functions on lists, we could destroy *in place* the value of hd(x) after having performed the basic operation r because we know that tl(x) would not care about the value of the head of x.

For simplicity reasons we did not analyze this approach here. The reader may have in fact realized that the synthesis of the program annotations as we presented it, is basically done via the analysis of uninterpreted program schemata. We hope to study the problem of destructiveness annotation in interpreted programs in our future research work in this area.

F. Time Complexity of the Algorithm

Now we would like to analyze the time complexity of the Markprog/3 algorithm.

Let us denote by a_{bco} the sum of the arities of the basic functions occurrences plus the number of occurrences of the *if-then-else* constructs, by a_v the sum of the arities of the variable functions and by a_{vo} the sum of the variable functions occurrences.

The structure of the Markprog/3 algorithm is the following:

```
.
.
.
while "there is a ϕ in an equation (call it e) of the program to be marked"
do "check correctness of the equation e";
      "internal while-do loop for checking consistency of the equation e"
od
.
.
.
```

It is easy to see that:

i) the outermost *while-loop* is obviously performed a_{bco} times because the number of ϕ's is initially equal to the sum of the arities of the basic functions occurrences plus the number of occurrences of the *if-then-else* constructs;

ii) the time for checking correctness of the equation is at most of the same order of the time for checking consistency;

iii) since the top of the lattice of destructive characterizations (see Pettorossi [1978a]) is consistent and the longest upward chain in that lattice has length not greater than a_v, the internal *while-do* loop is done at most a_v times;

iv) the worst case for the running time of Markprog/3 is a program with 1 equation only which can be considered as a tree with $a_{bco} + a_{vo}$ nodes, when f(a1,...,an) is represented as:

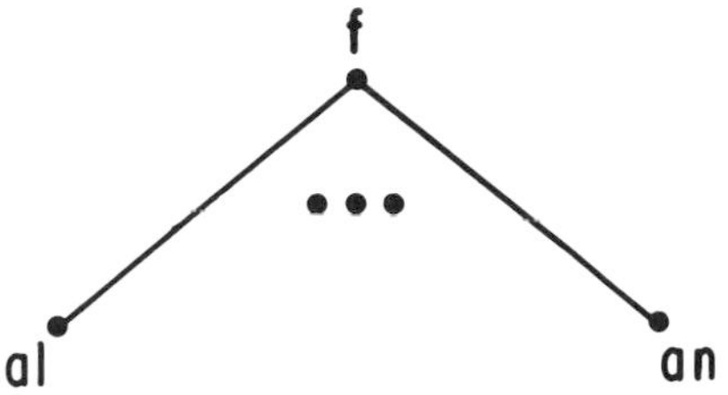

In that case the evaluation of the internal *while-do* loop body takes $(a_{bco} + a_{vo})$ steps, assuming that the evaluation of one node of such a tree takes one step of computation.

From points i) to iv) it follows that the time complexity of Markprog/3 is in the worst case $0((a_{bco} \cdot a_v)(a_{bco} + a_{vo}))$. Therefore the time complexity is quadratic with the sum of the arities of the basic function occurrences. This means that, roughly speaking, it is quadratic with the size of the program to be marked.

G. Conclusions and Acknowledgements

Using the method of adding "destructive annotations" to applicative recursive programs, we constructed an algorithm for improving the memory utilization. The annotations we add, consist in suggesting to the interpreter (or compiler) that it rewrite some memory cells, where intermediate results no longer useful are stored. These suggestions are "static", i.e. given before execution and they must be valid for any input value. Running an annotated program would require less memory and, in particular, we would have the advantage of doing garbage collection less often. We wrote an algorithm which synthesizes those annotations achieving the memory efficient version of a given program, under the basic assumption that variable values are independent, i.e. they do not share any (sub)value. When that assumption is released, the problem of the annotation synthesis is more complicated.

The basic theoretical framework for the algorithm presented here is given in Pettorossi [1978]. Directions of future research include the synthesis of correct annotations when interpretations of basic functions are taken into account.

We would like to thank Professor R.M. Burstall at the Department of Computer Science, University of Edinburgh, for many interesting and stimulating conversations about program transformation and destructiveness. Many thanks to Miss Eleanor Kerse for doing the excellent typing for us.

Related studies concerning the introduction of destructive operators into applicative programs have been recently carried out by A. Mycroft in his Ph.D. Thesis.
(A. Mycroft, "Abstract Interpretations and Optimizing Transformations for Applicative Programs," Ph.D. Thesis, Computer Science Department, Edinburgh University, 1981.)

References

Bauer *et al.* [1978]
F.L. Bauer, M. Broy, H. Partsch, P. Pepper, and H. Wossner, "Systematics of transformation rules," *TUM–INT–BER–77–12–0350, Institut für Informatik, Technische Universität,* München (1978).

Bauer *et al.* [1977]
F.L. Bauer, H. Partsch, P. Pepper and H. Wossner, "Notes on the project CIP: outline of a transformation system," *TUM–INFO–7729,* Institut für Informatik, Technische Universität, München (1977).

Burstall [1977]
R.M. Burstall, "Design considerations for a functional programming language," *Proc. of Infotech State of the Art Conference,* Copenhagen (1977), 45–57.

Burstall and Darlington [1977]
R.M. Burstall and J. Darlington, "A transformation system for developing recursive programs," *JACM,* Vol. 24, No. 1 (1977), 44–67.

Burstall and Feather [1979]
R.M. Burstall and M. Feather, "Program development by transformation: an overview," *Proc. of "Les Fondements de la Programmation"* (eds. M. Amirchahy and D. Neel), Toulouse, 1977. (IRIA-SEFI, France).

Burstall *et al.* [1980]
R.M. Burstall, D.B. MacQueen, and D.T. Sannella, "HOPE: an experimental applicative language," CSR–62–80, Edinburgh University, Computer Science Department (1980).

Chatelin [1977]
P. Chatelin, "Self-redefinition as a program manipulation strategy," *Proc. of Symposium on Artificial Intelligence and Programming Languages,* ACM SIGPLAN Notices and SIGART Newsletter, August 1977, 174–179.

Dahl *et al.* [1972]
O.J. Dahl, E.W. Dijkstra, and C.A.R. Hoare, "Structured programming," Academic Press, London (1972).

Darlington and Burstall [1976]
J. Darlington and R.M. Burstall, "A system which automatically improves programs," *Acta Informatica,* 6 (1976), 41–60.

Feather [1978]
M.S. Feather, "ZAP program transformation system: primer and user manual," *D.A.I. Research Report No. 54,* Dept. of Artificial Intelligence, Univ. of Edinburgh (1978).

Huet and Lang [1978]
G. Huet and B. Lang, "Proving and applying program transformations expressed with second-order patterns," *Acta Informatica,* 11 (1978), 31–55.

Kott [1978]
L. Kott, "About transformation system: a theoretical study," *3ème Colloque International sur la Programmation,* Dunod, Paris (1978), 232–267.

Partsch and Pepper [1977]
H. Partsch and P. Pepper, "Program transformation on different levels of programming," *TUM−INFO−7715,* Institut für Informatik, Technische Universität, München (1977).

Pettorossi [1977]
A. Pettorossi, "Transformation of programs and use of "tupling strategy," *Proc. of Informatica '77 Conference,* Bled, Yugoslavia (1977), 3−103, 1−6.

Pettorossi [1978a]
A. Pettorossi, "Improving memory utilization in transforming programs," *MFCS,* Zakopane, Poland, *Lecture Notes in Computer Science* 64, Springer Verlag (1978), 416−425.

Pettorossi [1978b]
A. Pettorossi, "Destructive marking: a method and some simple heuristics for improving memory utilization in recursive programs," *Informatica '78,* Bled, Yugoslavia (1978).

Pettorossi [1979]
A. Pettorossi, "An algorithm for saving memory in recursive programs using destructive annotations," *Rapp. Istituto di Automatica R.79−19,* Universitá di Roma (1979).

Schwarz [1977]
J. Schwarz, "Using annotations to make recursion equations behave," *D.A.I. Research Report No. 43,* Dept. of Artificial Intel., Univ. of Edinburgh (1977).

Schwarz [1978]
J. Schwarz, "Verifying the safe use of destructive operations in applicative programs," *3ème Colloque International sur la Programmation,* Paris (1978), and *IEEE Trans. Software Eng.* SE−8−1 (1982), 21−33.

Wegbreit [1976]
B. Wegbreit, "Goal-directed program transformation," *IEEE Trans. Software Eng. SE−2* (1976), 69−79.

Wirth [1971]
N. Wirth, "Program development by stepwise refinement," *CACM,* Vol. 14, No. 4 (1971), 221−227.

SECTION V

PROGRAM SYNTHESIS FROM EXAMPLES

CHAPTER 15

The Synthesis of LISP Programs from Examples: A Survey*

Douglas R. Smith
Naval Postgraduate School
Monterey, California

A. Introduction

For some kinds of programs at least, a few well chosen examples of input and output behavior can convey quite clearly to a human what program is intended. The automatic construction of programs from the information contained in a small set of input/output pairs has received much attention recently, especially in the LISP language. The user of such an automatic programming system supplies a sequence of input-output (I/O) pairs $<x_1,y_1>$, $<x_2,y_2>$, ..., $<x_n,y_n>$. The system tries to obtain enough information from the examples to infer the target programs behavior on the full domain of inputs. For example, if a user inputs the sequence <nil,nil>, <(a),(a)>, <(a b),(b a)>, <(a b c),(c b a)> then the system should return a program such as

* The work reported herein was supported by the Foundation Research Program of the Naval Postgraduate School with funds provided by the Chief of Naval Research.

```
(F x) = (G x nil)
(G x z) = (cond ((atom x) z)
    (T (G (cdr x) (cons (car x) z)))).
```

If the system is unable to synthesize a program or needs more examples to verify a hypothesized program then the machine may request more examples. This paper presents an overview of the basic work on program construction from examples and recent approaches to this problem in the domain of the LISP language. It has not been possible to avoid glossing over many details and interesting mechanisms in the synthesis techniques discussed here. Our discussion is a simplified treatment of these techniques aimed at presenting what is essential and novel about them. Further detail may be found by consulting the original papers.

In general the classes of programs which have been studied for synthesis purposes are constructed from the LISP primitives car, cdr, cons, the predicates atom or null, the McCarthy conditional and recursive function procedures. An arbitrary composition of car and cdr functions will be called a *basic* function. e.g., car^cdr is a basic function (usually abbreviated to cadr) where ^ is the composition operator. A *cons-structure* is a function which can be described recursively as follows: i) the special atom nil is a cons-structure, ii) a basic function or a call to a program is a cons-structure, and iii) a function of the form (cons F_1 F_2) is a cons-structure if F_1 and F_2 are cons-structures. For example, (cons (car x) (F (cdr x) z)) is a cons-structure with arguments x and z. The programs to be synthesized usually have the following general form:

```
(F x z) = (cond ((p1 x) (f1 x z))
                ((p2 x) (f2 x z))
                ...
                ((pk x) (fk x z))
                (T (H x (F (b x) (G x z)))))
```

where H and G are themselves programs of this type, $p_1,p_2, ...,p_k$ are predicates, $f_1,f_2, ...,f_k$ are cons-structures, and b is a basic function. For simplicity the arguments are restricted above to x and z; in general more or less will be required. If there is no variable z and no function G then F will be called a *forward-loop program.* If there is no H function then the last line of the above scheme has the form (T (F (b x) (G x z))))), and F is called a *reverse-loop program.*

B. Basic Work

Work on inductive inference properly includes programming by examples because the synthesis of a program generally involves the inference of an extended pattern of program behavior from the patterns discovered in the examples. In the most general setting of computability theory the problem of inductive inference of functions from input/output pairs has been explored in [Gold 1967, Blum & Blum 1975, Barzdin 1977]. The basic result from this work is that a function can be inferred from I/O pairs if it belongs to a class of enumerable functions with a decidable halting problem. Given I/O pairs $\{<x_1, y_1>, <x_2, y_2>, \ldots <x_n, y_n>\}$ our inference mechanism enumerates functions one at a time until one is found which generates y_i given x_i for each $i = 1,2,\ldots n$. If we then extend our examples set and the chosen function does not satisfy some new I/O pair then our mechanism continues its enumeration until a new function is found which does satisfy the examples. Of course such a mechanism is useful only for theoretical purposes since the process of enumerating over a whole class of functions is too expensive for practical use. Nonetheless, this work shows that it is possible to infer large useful classes of programs simply from examples of input/output behavior.

Biermann and his co-workers [Biermann et al. 1975, Biermann and Krishnaswamy 1976] have looked at methods for speeding up this enumerative search process based on the use of a program trace. Given an example input and a desired output, a *semitrace* is a functional expression which correctly computes the example output from the input but which may allow several different orders of evaluation. A *trace* is a semitrace which only has one possible order of evaluation. E.g. a semitrace for a computation of 3! is (times 3 2 1). Because of the associativity of multiplication we obtain two distinct traces from this semitrace: (times 3 (times 2 1)) and (times (times 3 2) 1). Given this kind of information Biermann has shown how to speed up the enumerative process enormously by enumerating over only those programs whose trace on an example input corresponds to some initial subsequence of the given trace. This task is accomplished by partitioning the trace such that each block corresponds to a unique instruction in the desired program. The process of finding such a partition is controlled by a straightforward backtrack search. Pattern matching, generation of predicates and looping control structures are involved in determining whether a given trace instruction belongs to certain block (a process Biermann calls instruction merging). See [Bauer 1979] for recent work on program synthesis from traces.

Despite the great gain which can be realized by using trace information in program synthesis, Biermann's mechanism is again an enumerative method and thus can take large amounts of time in order to synthesize all but the simplest programs. The special attraction of LISP programs is the possibility that a semitrace may be easily constructed from example I/O pairs and furthermore certain restricted classes of LISP programs can be synthesized from the resulting semitraces without the need for enumerative search over the class. Some of the early work on LISP program synthesis [Shaw et al. 1975, Hardy 1975, Siklossy and Sykes 1975] could generate interesting programs but relied on heuristic techniques and provided no characterization of the class of target programs. Summers [Summers 1976, 1978] was the first to put the possibility of LISP program synthesis from examples on a firm theoretical foundation.

All of the methods to be described in this paper derive from Summers' insight that under certain conditions a semitrace of a computation can be constructed from input/output examples in the domain of LISP. Once such a semitrace has been generated a synthesis from traces method can be applied to construct the desired program.

It will be useful to abstract the key elements of a synthesis from traces method in order to facilitate the description and comparison of the LISP synthesis methods. These elements are described below and illustrated by Summers' method.

1. Data Types and Operators

A certain set of data types and operators must be available for use in traces and target programs. Summers used the S-expression data type and the primitive LISP operators cons, car, cdr, atom, nil and occasionally quote. Note that the predicate eq is not used. This means that any predicates constructed in target programs will be concerned with structure rather than semantics of the input S-expression.

2. Control Structures

A set of control structures must be available for constructing target programs. The McCarthy conditional (cond) and recursive function procedures are used in Summers' method.

3. Program Schemas

All of the synthesis methods described here make use of program schemas in order to constrain the way in which the control structures and data operators are used. The basic schema used by Summers' system has the form

$$
\begin{aligned}
F[x] \leftarrow [\ & p_1[x] \rightarrow f_1[x]; \\
& \quad \cdots \\
& p_k[x] \rightarrow f_k[x]; \\
& T \rightarrow A[\ F[b[x]];\ x]\ ]
\end{aligned}
$$

where $f_1,\ldots,f_k$ are cons-structures, and $A[w;x]$ is a cons-structure in which w occurs exactly once. The predicates $p_i[x]$ have the form $atom[b_i[x]]$ where b_i is a basic function.

4. Method of Obtaining a Semitrace

The obvious method for obtaining a semitrace is to ask the user to supply one. As previously mentioned there are other possibilities. In particular there are computational domains in which a semitrace may be obtained from input/output examples. Also one might obtain a semitrace of a computation by simulating an inefficient program in the hope of synthesizing a more efficient version.

In Summers' method the user is required to supply a small set of I/O pairs $<x_1,y_1>,\ldots,<x_k, y_k>$. For each pair $<x_i, y_i>$ a semitrace, called a program fragment, is created based on the following assumptions:

a. the atoms in the input S-expression x_i are unique; i.e., no atoms appear twice in x_i,

b. all atoms in y_i appear also in x_i (except possibly the special atom nil).

Note: x_i and y_i are both lists.

An example I/O pair will be called *self-contained* if the input and output satisfy these properties. The semitrace produced from the pair $<x_i,y_i>$ is a cons-structure formed recursively as follows:

$$ST(x_i,y_i) = \begin{cases} (p\ x) & \text{if } y_i \neq \text{nil and } y_i = p(x) \text{ where p is a basic function} \\ \text{nil} & \text{if } y_i = \text{nil} \\ (\text{cons } ST(x_i, car(y_i))\ ST(x_i, cdr(y_i))) & \text{otherwise} \end{cases}$$

Note that the output of ST is an unEVALed expression. For example ST((a b),(b a)) = (cons (cadr x) (cons (car x) nil)).

5. Detection methods for each control structure

For each control structure allowed in target programs there must be a method for detecting its presence in a trace or semitrace.

If a conditional statement is allowed, as in Summers' method, then we must have a mechanism for determining the number and ordering of cases, the predicates and their corresponding actions in each case. The first step in the synthesis of a recursive LISP program is the creation of a conditional expression which correctly computes all of the examples and has the form

$$F(x) \leftarrow [\ p_1(x) \rightarrow f_1(x); \\ \ldots \\ p_n(x) \rightarrow f_n(x)\ ]$$

where f_i is the semitrace generated by the ith example I/O pair. Summers assumes that the user gives a sequence of examples in which the example inputs form a chain, in the sense that for all inputs x_i and x_j either $x_i \leqslant x_j$ or $x_j \leqslant x_i$ where $u \leqslant v$ iff atom(u) or [car(u) $\leqslant$ car(v) & cdr(u) $\leqslant$ cdr(v)]. For example (a.b) $\leqslant$ (d.e) but the s-expressions u = (a.(b.c)) and v = ((d.e).f) could not both appear as inputs since neither $u \leqslant v$ nor $v \leqslant u$ holds. This assumption provides a natural ordering for the branches of the conditional. The predicates $(p_i\ x_i)$ for $1 \leqslant i \leqslant k$ must have the property that $(p_i\ x_i)$ evaluates to T, but $(p_j\ x_i)$ evaluates to nil for all $1 \leqslant j < i$. Since predicates have the form (atom (b x)) where b is a basic function, a mechanism for generating the predicates must find a basic function b_i such that $(b_i\ x_i)$ is an atom yet $(b_i\ x_{i+1})$ is not an atom (thus $(p_i\ x_{i+1})$ = false). The set of basic functions which so distinguish between example inputs x_i and x_{i+1} can be computed by

$$\text{PRED\_GEN}(x_i,x_{i+1}) = PG(x_i, x_{i+1}, I)$$

(I denotes the identity function)

$$PG(x,y,\theta) = \begin{cases} \phi & \text{if y is an atom} \\ \{\theta\} & \text{if x is an atom and y is not an atom} \\ PG(car(x),car(y),car\hat{}\theta) \cup PG(cdr(x),cdr(y),cdr\hat{}\theta) & \text{otherwise} \end{cases}$$

For example PRED_GEN((A),(A B)) = {cdr}, so a predicate to distinguish between (A) and (A B) is (atom (cdr x)). If Summers' system were given the following set of examples for the function REVERSE

```
{ nil → nil
(A) → (A)
(A B) → (B A)
(A B C) → (C B A) }
```

then by combining the semitraces produced by ST and the predicates generated by PRED_GEN, the following loop-free program is produced:

```
F(x) = (cond ((atom x) nil)
    ((atom (cdr x)) (cons (car x) nil))
    ((atom (cddr x)) (cons (cadr x) (cons (car x) nil)))
((atom (cdddr x)) (cons (caddr x) (cons (cadr x) (cons (car x) nil)))))
```

If recursive function procedures are allowed then mechanisms must be available for detecting recursive patterns in a semitrace, determining the primitive cases for termination, and creating and handling all necessary variables. Summers has shown in his Basic Synthesis Theorem [Summers 1975,1977] the following fundamental result. Suppose that the following recurrence relations hold on a (possibly infinite) set of input-output pairs

$$p_1(x),\ldots,p_k(x),\ p_{k+n}(x) = p_n(b(x)) \text{ for } n \geqslant 1$$

$$f_1[x],\ldots,f_k[x],\ f_{k+n}[x] = C[f_n[b[x]];\ x] \text{ for } n \geqslant 1,$$

where b is a basic function and C is a cons-structure in which $f_n[b[x]]$ occurs exactly once. The function

$$F[x] = \begin{cases} f_j[x] \text{ if } p_j[x] \ \& \ \forall_i\ [1 \leqslant i < j => \neg p_i[x]] \\ \text{undefined otherwise} \end{cases}$$

defined by the recurrence relations can be correctly computed by the following instance of the recursive program schema given above.

```
F[x] ← [ p1[x] → f1[x];
     . . .
   pk[x] → fk[x];
   T → C[ F[b[x]]; x] ]
```

This theorem and its generalizations establish a link between the characterization of a function by a recurrence relation and a recursive program for computing that function. Thus the synthesis of recursive programs reduces to detecting repetitive patterns in the examples and a decision on when enough instances of a pattern have been found to inductively infer that the pattern holds generally. At least two or three instances of a pattern with no counterinstances have been taken as sufficient to allow induction of the pattern. Any decision on this matter though is subject to easily constructed examples which cause the induction of an incorrect pattern.

Recurrence relations are detected between two semitraces f_i and f_{i+k} by finding a basic function b such that $(f_i(b\ x))$ is a substructure of $(f_{i+k}x)$. For example if

$(f_2\ x)$ = (cons (car x) (cons (caddr x) nil))
and
$(f_3\ x)$ = (cons (car x) (cons (caddr x) (cons (caddddr x) nil)))
then
$(f_3\ x)$ = (cons (car x) (f_2 (cdr x))).

One such mechanism makes use of the unification algorithm used in resolution theorem provers. The choice of which semitraces to unify in this way may be done systematically (by trying k = 1,2,...) or by means of heuristics (Kodratoff 1979).

We now can run through a complete example illustrating Summers' synthesis method. Suppose that the user supplies the following examples:

nil → nil
((a b)) → (b)
((a b)(c d)) → (b d)
((a b)(c d)(e f)) → (b d f)

which describes the problem of returning the list of second elements of each sublist of the input list. Applying ST to these examples we obtain the following semitraces

$(f_1\ x)$ = nil
$(f_2\ x)$ = (cons (cadar x) nil)
$(f_3\ x)$ = (cons (cadar x) (cons (cadadr x) nil))
$(f_4\ x)$ = (cons (cadar x) (cons (cadadr x) (cons (cadaddr x) nil)))

Applying the predicate generating algorithm we obtain

$(p_1\ x)$ = (atom x)
$(p_2\ x)$ = (atom (cdr x))
$(p_3\ x)$ = (atom (cddr x))
$(p_4\ x)$ = (atom (cdddr x)).

The following recurrence patterns are obtained

$(f_{i+1}\ x)$ = (cons (cadar x) (f_i (cdr x))) for i=1,2,3 and

$(p_{i+1}\ x)$ = (p_i (cdr x)) for i=1,2,3.

We inductively infer that these patterns hold for all i and using Summers' Basic Synthesis Theorem obtain the following program

```
(F x) = (cond
          ((atom x) nil)
          (T (cons (cadar x) (F (cdr x)))))
```

Note that this program computes a partial function since it assumes that the input is a list of lists where each sublist has length at least two. Thus the program is not defined on inputs (a b) or ((a.b)).

For some example sets, such as the examples given above for REVERSE, the recurrence relation detection mechanisms will not work. A fundamental technique used in Summers' system generalizes the semitraces by replacing some sub-semitrace which occurs in each semitrace by a new variable. It is important to ensure that the value of the new variable will be initialized to the value of the sub-semitrace. The system then checks for recurrence relations amongst the generalized semitraces. Consider the semitraces obtained above for the function REVERSE. If the constant sub-expression nil is replaced by variable z then the semitraces become

```
(g1 x z) = z
(g2 x z) = (cons (car x) z)
(g3 x z) = (cons (cadr x) (cons (car x) z)))
(g4 x z) = (cons (caddr x) (cons (cadr x) ((cons (car x) z)))))
```

and the following recurrence relation is found:

$$(g_{i+1}\ x\ z) = (g_i\ (cdr\ x)\ (cons\ (car\ x)\ z)) \quad \text{for } i=1,2,3.$$

Again we inductively infer that this relation holds for all i, then invoke a form of the Basic Synthesis Theorem to justify the creation of the following reverse-loop program

```
(REVERSE x) = (F x nil)
(F x z) = (cond ((atom x) z)
                (T (F (cdr x) (cons (car x) z)))).
```

C. Recent Approaches to LISP Program Synthesis from Examples.

Biermann [Biermann 1978] has applied the techniques of synthesis from traces to the domain of LISP. The data type, operators, and control structures used in this approach are the same as in Summers' method.

The program schemas, called *semi-regular LISP schemas,* have the form

```
(Fi x) = (cond (p1 f1)
               (p2 f2)
               ...
               (pk fk)
               (T fk+1))
```

where each f_j has one of the following forms: nil, x, (F_j (car x)), (F_j (cdr x)), or (cons (F_g x) (F_h x)). The predicates p_j are required to have the form (atom (b_j x)) where b_j is a basic function and furthermore if (p_{j+1} x) = (atom (b_{j+1} x)) then b_{j+1} = b_j^w where w is a basic function not equal to the identity function. Certain restrictions are placed on the syntax and interpretation of semi-regular LISP schemas to yield a well-behaved subset of instances called *regular LISP programs.* A semitrace is obtained as in Summers' method and from this a trace is constructed in the form of a nonlooping regular program (i.e., no function F_i is called by more than one function f_j). Of course there are no predicates in the trace so each function in the trace has the form

$$(F_i\ x) = f_{k+1}.$$

From the example

$$((a.b).(c.d)) \rightarrow ((d.c).(b.a))$$

the following trace is constructed

$$
\begin{array}{l}
(f_1\ x) = (\text{cons}\ (f_2\ x)\ (f_3\ x)) \\
(f_2\ x) = (f_4\ (\text{cdr}\ x)) \quad (f_3\ x) = (f_5\ (\text{car}\ x)) \\
(f_4\ x) = (\text{cons}\ (f_6\ x)\ (f_7\ x)) \\
(f_5\ x) = (\text{cons}\ (f_8\ x)\ (f_9\ x)) \\
(f_6\ x) = (f_{10}\ (\text{cdr}\ x)) \quad (f_7\ x) = (f_{11}\ (\text{car}\ x)) \\
(f_8\ x) = (f_{12}\ (\text{cdr}\ x)) \quad (f_9\ x) = (f_{13}\ (\text{car}\ x)) \\
(f_{10}\ x) = (f_{11}\ x) = (f_{12}\ x) = (f_{13}\ x) = x.
\end{array}
$$

A regular LISP program can be viewed as a directed graph whose nodes represent functions. Each arc directed from a node representing function f_i is labelled by a branch of the conditional of f_i, i.e., a predicate and a function call. The construction of the graph structure of a regular LISP program from a given trace is performed by a backtrack search. At each point during the search a certain portion of the target graph has been constructed and it accounts for some initial portion of the trace. At this point if all of the trace is accounted for we are done, otherwise there is some function f_i in the trace which invokes a function f_j such that f_i is accounted for but f_j is not. If the target graph has n nodes currently then there are n+1 choices of nodes to identify with f_j (one for each current node plus a new node for f_j if needed). These n+1 alternatives are tried in turn. A choice will fail and be pruned from consideration if for various reasons (for example, knowledge about regular programs or general programming knowledge) the identification of a function with a node is incompatible with other functions identified with the node, or if all of the children of the node fail.

If several arcs emanate from a node g_i then predicates must be synthesized in order to distinguish the different cases. First, for each transition we collect all inputs which cause it to be taken. An extension of algorithm PRED_GEN from Summers' method may be used to build predicates distinguishing the resulting set of inputs.

Consider the trace given in above. Initially we create a new node for f_1 as in Figure 1a. For f_2 we have two possibilities: identify f_2 with g_1, or create a new node g_2 as in Figure 1b. The first alternative fails so we explore further the second. Of the three alternative choices for f_3 shown in Figure 1c only the third does not fail. After merging f_4 and f_5 we have the graph in Figure 1d which accounts for all but f_{10}, f_{11}, f_{12}, and f_{13}. To account for f_{10} a new transition is created from g_1 and predicates must be synthesized to distinguish the two arcs from g_1. From the trace we find that the inputs

$$\{\ ((a.b).(c.d)),\ (c.d)\ \}$$

lead to the function call (cons (g_2 x)(g_3 x)), and the inputs

$$\{\ d\ \}$$

lead to the function call x. The generated predicate which distinguishes these inputs is (atom x). The resulting graph shown in Figure 1e accounts for the entire trace so synthesis halts.

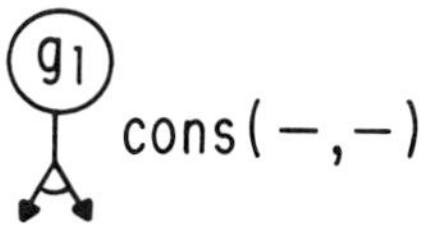

a. A node for f_1

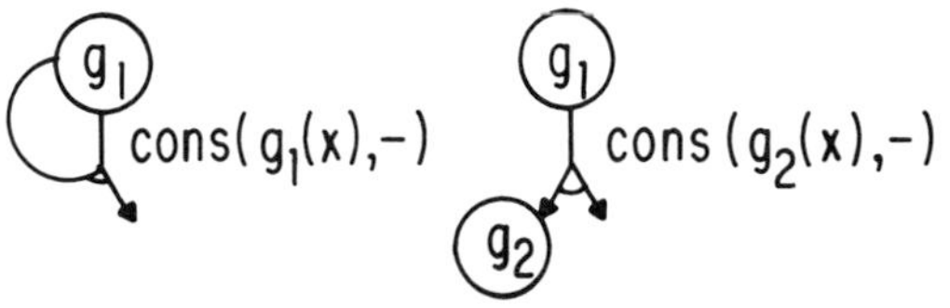

b. Alternatives for f_2.

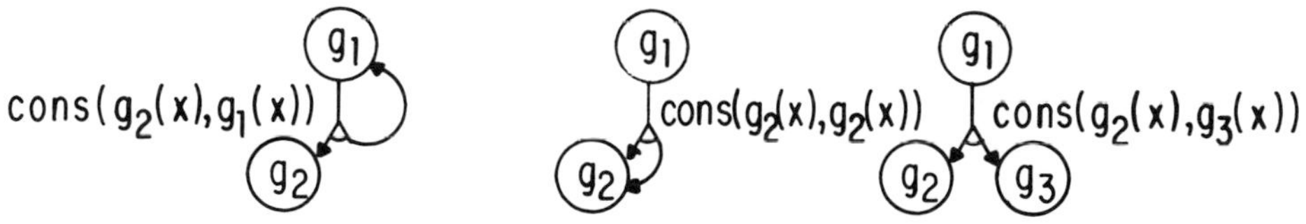

c. alternatives for f_3.

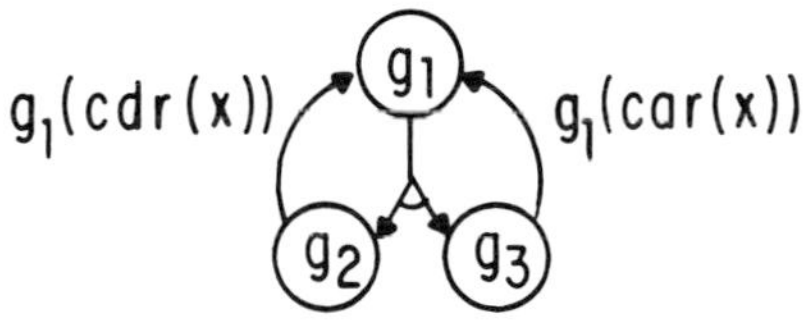

d. After merging f_4 and f_5.

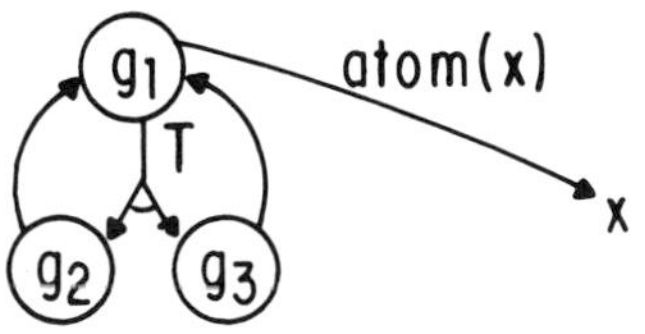

e. Final graph.

Figure 1. Synthesis of a Regular LISP program.

The resulting program is

$$
\begin{aligned}
(g_1\ x) &= (\mathrm{cond}((\mathrm{atom}\ x)\ x)(T\ (\mathrm{cons}\ (g_2\ x)\ (g_3\ x))))\\
(g_2\ x) &= (g_1\ (\mathrm{cdr}\ x))\\
(g_3\ x) &= (g_1\ (\mathrm{car}\ x)).
\end{aligned}
$$

The system is able to generate any regular program from a finite number of examples. Although the system can be sped up by restricting the schema (for example, to programs consisting of a single loop), in general it faces the combinatorial explosion inherent in backtracking mechanisms.

Biermann and Smith [Biermann and Smith 1977, 1979] have studied the synthesis of a class of programs called scanning programs. A scanning program scans its input variables as it generates its output. Synthesis can be based on a single example and the I/O pairs are assumed to be lists of atoms. Data type, operators, and control structures are the same as those used by Summers.

The target program is viewed as a hierarchy of LISP functions and is constructed in a bottom up fashion. A semitrace is constructed for each level of the hierarchy and has the form of a loopless sequence of function calls. Each function call of a semitrace is either nil or consists of a function and an argument. Each level of a semitrace assumes that the output can be computed from the input by appending the results of the sequence of function calls in the semitrace. Since the example input and output are lists,each atom of the output y can be expressed by a function call to a function which has the form (P^O x) = (cons (car x) next) where next is the function call expressing the next atom in the example output.

For example, if the user gives the input/output pair

(a b c d e f) → (a c e f d b)

then the lowest level trace is

(P^O (x) next), (P^O (cddr x) next), (P^O (cd^4r x) next),
(P^O (cd^5r x) next), (P^O (cd^3r x) next), (P^O (cdr x) next), nil.

To obtain the next higher level in the hierarchy the sequence is chopped up into segments such that each segment can be easily generated by either a forward-loop, a reverse-loop, or a straight line function which simply executes a fixed sequence of function calls. The segmenting mechanism works by looking for patterns and extrapolating them as far as they match the sequence of function calls. The above semitrace is segmented as follows

<(P^O (x) next), (P^O (cddr x) next), (P^O (cd^4r x) next)>,
<(P^O (cd^5r x) next), (P^O (cd^3r x) next), (P^O (cdr x) next)>, <nil>.

The first three function calls can be computed by a forward loop, which we call P^1, which in effect computes (a c e) from (a b c d e f), and the next three functions can be computed by a reverse loop which we call P^2. The second lowest level of semitrace is

(P^1 (x) next), (P^2 (cdr x) next), nil.

There is no good way to segment this semitrace so a straightline routine, called P^3, is constructed and we have the highest level semitrace

(P^3 (x) next), nil.

Predicates are generated in a manner similar to Summers' method. The resulting program is

```
(P^3 x) = (P^1 x x)
(P^1 x1 x2) = (cond
                ((atom x1) (P^2 (cdr x2) nil))
                (T (P1^0 x1 x2)))
(P1^0 x1 x2) = (cons (car x1) (P^1 (cddr x1) x2))
(P^2 x z) = (cond
                ((atom (cdr x)) z)
                (T (P^2 (cddr x) (P2^0 x z))))
(P2^0 x z) = (cons (car x) z).
```

Production rule schemas are used to encode both program schemas and the coding knowledge necessary for coordinating the flow of data and control in a hierarchy of functions.

Each function generated by the synthesizer instantiates a rule schema to become a production rule. At the top of the hierarchy is the function F (P^3 in the above example) which when given the example input will produce the example output. The rule for this highest level routine is applied to a start symbol. Each application of a rule adds the code for a routine on the next lowest level of the hierarchy, the correct number and order of variables having been passed down from the coded string, and a sequence of nonterminals, one for each function called by the routine with the correct number and order of variables included to be passed along into the rule for each of these routines. In general it was found necessary to introduce a new variable for each level of nesting of these functions. Rule schemas for forward loops, reverse-loops, straight-line routines, and if-then-else statements were studied.

Kodratoff [Kodratoff 1979] has presented a synthesis technique which is a powerful generalization of Summers' method. The same data type, operators, and control structures are used as in Summers' method. However Kodratoff employs a more powerful schema and technique for detecting looping patterns. Like Summers' method, multiple I/O pairs are required and looping patterns are detected by pattern matching the semitrace of output y_i with a subsemitrace of output y_{i+k} for various values of i and k. In general such a matching divides the semitrace y_{i+k} into three segments $y1_{i+k}$, $y2_{i+k}$, and $y3_{i+k}$, where the middle segment $y2_{i+k}$ matches semitrace y_i. Summers' system stops at this point with the assumption that the initial and the tail segments have no looping structure. Kodratoff's system on the other hand creates two new synthesis problems: one with I/O pairs $<x_i, y1_{i+k}>$ and the other with I/O pairs $<x_i, y3_{i+k}>$. If h is the resulting synthesized program from the former problem, and g is the resulting synthesized program for the latter problem, then these programs can be composed in the following schema:

```
(F x) = (f x,(i x))
(f x z) = (cond ((p1 x) (f1 x z))
            ((p2 x) (f2 x z))
            ...
            ((pk x) (fk x z))
            (T (h x (f (b x) (g x z)))))
```

where b is a basic function, h and g are programs satisfying the schema, and i is an initialization function for variable z.

Notice that this system works in a top-down fashion in contrast to Biermann and Smith's system which works bottom-up. Another point of contrast is the strikingly different ways that the two systems segment the output examples. For example, Biermann and Smith's system would segment the output of the example (A B C D) → (A B C D D C B A) into A B C D and D C B A and conjoin the forward and reverse looping routines which produce these segments. Kodratoff's system, given the examples

(A B C) → (A B C C B A)
(A B C D) → (A B C D D C B A)

would match A B C C B A with the sub-expression B C D D C B of the second output, thus segmenting the second output into A, B C D D C B, and A. Here the function h is (h x z) = (cons (car x) z) and g is (g x z) = (cons (car x) z). The complete synthesized program has the form:

```
(F x) = (f x nil)
(f x z) = (cond ((atom x) z)
          (T (h x (f (cdr x) (g x z)))))
(h x z) = (cons (car x) z)
(g x z) = (cons (car x) z)
```

Another feature of Kodratoff's method is the use of an algorithm he calls BMWk in the matching process of one semitrace against another. As noted above, the introduction of new variables is one of the key problems of program synthesis. In attempting to match A B C C B A against B C D D C B as in the example above it will be noticed that if (cdr x) is substituted for x everywhere in the semitrace for the former expression, we obtain the semitrace of the latter subexpression. The fact that a single substitution suffices is the clue that only one variable is involved. Consider on the other hand, the following example pairs.

(A B) → (B A B B B A)
(A B C) → (C A C B C A C B B)

When we attempt to match B A B B B A against C A C B C A we find two different substitutions. For the first, third and fifth atoms we substitute (cdr x) for x, and for the second, fourth, and sixth atoms we substitute x for x (the identity substitution). Here the two different substitutions are the clue that two variables are involved; the first variable is used to obtain the odd numbered atoms and the second is used to obtain the even numbered atoms. The recurrence relation between these examples then has the form:

$$y_{i+1}(x_1,x_2,z) = y_i(cdr(x_1),x_2,h_i(x_1,x_2,z))$$

where $h_i(x_1, x_2, z)$ computes the right-most segment of y_{i+1}.

Further development of this method is reported in [Kodratoff and Papon 1980, Jouannaud and Kodratoff 1980, Kodratoff and Jouannaud 1983].

Jouannaud and Guiho [Jouannaud and Guiho 1979] have a system called SISP which works on either single or multiple examples. The class of target programs have a somewhat simpler form than those of the above systems since a more powerful class of basic functions is used. Let us call the following functions JG-basic: lcar((A B C D)) = (A) (the list containing the car of its argument), lrac((A B C D)) = (D) (the list containing the last element of the argument list), cdr((A B C D)) = (B C D), and rdc((A B C D)) = (A B C) (the list formed by deleting the last element of the argument list), and any composition of JG-basic functions. In addition to the JG-basic functions SISP uses the predicate null and a multiple-argument version of append.

Given I/O pair <x,y> in which both x and y are lists of atoms SISP segments x such that x = append(px,c,sx) and y = append(py,c,sy) where c is the longest subexpression common to x and y. Since both x and y are lists it is easy to find a JG-basic function f such that f(x) = c. The synthesis task then reduces to two subtasks. SISP finds the shortest subexpressions x_1 and x_2 of x such that $x_1 \rightarrow$ py and $x_2 \rightarrow$ sy are self-contained examples (chosing px, c, or sx if possible), and recursively tries to construct functions satisfying these new examples.

Consider the synthesis of the function REVERSE from example x = (A B C D), y = (D C B A). The largest common subexpression is (A) (in case of a tie in length, a subexpression on either end of y wins out). Thus c = (A), sx = (B C D) and py = (D C B). x = append(nil,(A),(B C D)), y = append((D C B),(A),nil). Since (A) = lcar(x) we have the partial semitrace y = append(py,lcar(x),nil) = append(py,lcar(x)). The smallest subexpression x_1 of x such that $x_1 \rightarrow$ py is self contained is x_1 = (B C D) = cdr(x). Applying the above mechanism recursively to the example $x_1 \rightarrow$ py we end up reducing it to another simpler example, etc. Jouannaud and Guiho diagram the resulting "approximation" structure as follows

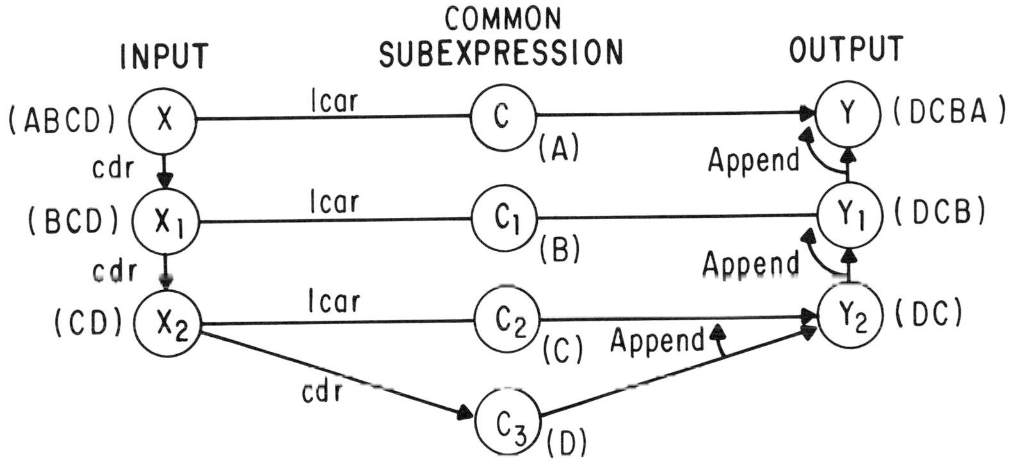

where a transition from Z to Z' that is labeled f means f(Z) = Z', and

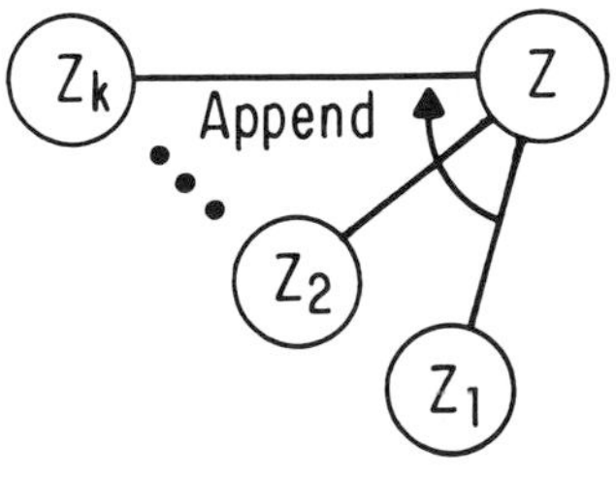

means Z = append(Z_1 Z_2 ... Z_k). Adjacent to each node we have supplied that actual value of the node with respect to the example (A B C D) $\rightarrow$ (D C B A). This structure is similar to the semitrace generated by Summers' method, but its repetitive structure is so clearly brought out that the following recursive program to generate REVERSE is easily created from a single example:

F(x) = (cond
((null x) nil)
(T (append (F (cdr x)) (lcar x))))

If SISP fails to find a satisfactory program based on one example then it can ask for another example whose input has the longest length less than x which is defined on the domain of the program. Examples must be carefully chosen so that the inputs are of decreasing length. Given the examples x → y and x' → y' where b(x) = x' (b is a JG-basic function) SISP segments y into py, c, sx where c now is the largest common segment of y and y'. Synthesis control is based on the following diagram:

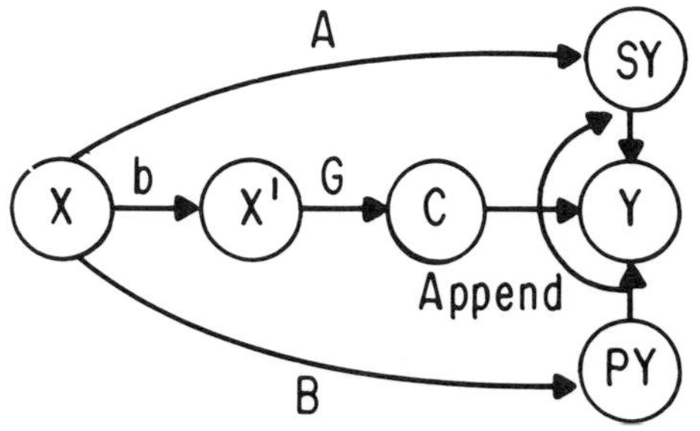

The target program is F and it has the form:

$$F(x) = y = append(py,c,sy) = append(B(x),G(b(x)),A(x))$$

(If c = y' then G is F). The synthesis problem reduces to synthesizing programs for 1) B, using example x → py, 2) G, using example x' → c, and 3) A, using example x → sy. The system can request more examples of F in order to have more examples for each of these subprograms. In theory any number of levels of this process are possible thus enabling SISP to generate arbitrarily deep nestings of recursive loops. The knowledge necessary to map from the repetitive patterns found in the diagrams to program schemas is given by a small set of theorems which are analogous to Summers' Basic Synthesis Theorem.

D. Comparisons and Characterizations of the LISP Synthesis Methods.

Perhaps the most striking point of contrast between the five methods surveyed in this paper lies in their approaches to finding recursion loops. Summers' and Kodratoff's methods detect recurrence patterns by matching the semitraces obtained from different example outputs. In Biermann's Regular LISP system and Biermann and Smith's system recursion is detected by matching or folding a semitrace into itself. In Jouannaud and Guiho's SISP system the control pattern emerges from the match between an example input and its corresponding output.

Table 1 characterizes each of the synthesis techniques discussed above according to several criteria. The first column compares the time complexity of programs which are synthesizeable by each method. The time complexity is closely related to a bound on the number of atoms in the output list since the time complexity bounds the number of cons operations which can be performed. There is an apparent anomaly in Biermann's regular LISP method in that it can generate programs with any finite number of nested loops yet the complexity of such a program is linear in the number of input atoms. This is explained by the structure of S-expressions and the lack of mechanisms in regular LISP programs for copying and reusing the input variable. By way of illustration consider the problem of producing a list of the last elements of each sublist of a given list as in the example

((a b c) (d e) (f g h) (i) (j k l m)) → (c e h i m)

Table 1. Characterization of Several Classes of Synthesizeable Functions

Synthesis Method	Time Complexity of target programs[a]	Depth of nesting of loops	Number of examples required[b]	Closure under function sequencing[c]	Separate resource and control variables	Multiple uses of a resource variable	Nonlinear recursion
Summers (Summers 1977)	O(n)	1	$\geqslant$3k	no	yes	no	no
Regular LISP (Biermann 1976)	O(n)	unbounded	enough to exercise all branches in code	no	no	no	yes
Biermann and Smith (Biermann and Smith 1979)	$O(n^k)$ $k \geqslant O$	unbounded	1	yes	no	no	no
Kodratoff (Kodratoff 1979)	$O(n^k)$ $k \geqslant O$	unbounded	$\geqslant$k(n+2)	no	yes	yes	no
SISP	$O(n^k)$	unbounded	1,several	yes	yes	no	no

a. n is the number of atoms in the input S-expression.

b. n is the depth of nesting and k is the number of conditional branches in the top level routine.

c. A class of LISP functions is closed under function sequcing if whenever F and G are functions in the class then H(x)=append(F(x),G(x)) is a function in the class.

A program to compute this function requires a nested loop which scans down each sublist looking for the last element, yet the program's complexity is clearly linear in the number of input atoms. Columns 6 and 7 compare the uses of program variables. A *resource variable* provides atoms for the output list. A *control variable* is used to control the recursion loops. In many programs constructed by the five methods surveyed the resource variables are also used as control variables. Column six shows which synthesis techniques allow separate resource and control variables. Column seven points out Kodratoff's unique technique of allowing copies of a resource variable to be made then used differently in a program.

An important aspect of any program synthesizer is a characterization of the class of target programs. It is important to know that a system is at least sound but preferably complete also over a class. Characterization of several extensions of the class of programs synthesizable by Summers' method are given in [Smith 1977, Jouannaud and Kodratoff 1979]. Biermann's enumerative methods on input traces are sound and complete over their class of target programs. Guiho and Jouannaud [Guiho and Jouannaud 1977] have shown that SISP can correctly synthesize programs over a well defined class of nonlooping functions.

E. Concluding Remarks

The domain of LISP functions has served as a valuable testbed for the exploration of a number of synthesis mechanisms. Summers' insight that any self-contained input-output pair has a unique semitrace provides one of the fundamental starting points for the synthesis techniques described above. The methods surveyed have explored strikingly different mechanisms for detecting looping patterns in semitraces. Knowledge about how to correctly sequence and nest recursive programs has been gained. Another valuable lesson of this research involves the generation and correct use of auxilliary variables. Despite success in generating ever larger classes of programs the question remains of whether these synthesis techniques can be used in any practical way. It may be that there are some special programming domains in which some of these techniques can be applied. However the real importance of this research probably lies in the abstraction and generalization of the techniques which have been found to be sucessful in the LISP domain and the incorporation of these techniques in synthesis systems of more general scope.

References

Barzdin [1977]
J.M. Barzdin, *"Inductive inference of automata, functions and programs," Amer. Math. Soc. Translations,* Vol. 109(2), 1977, pp. 107−112.

Bauer [1979]
M.A. Bauer, "Programming by examples," *Art. Intell.* 12, 1979, 1−21.

Biermann *et al.* [1975]
A.W. Biermann, R.I. Baum, and F.E. Petry, "Speeding up the synthesis of programs from traces," *IEEE Trans. on Computers,* Vol. C−24(2), 1975, pp. 122−136.

Biermann and Krishnaswamy [1976]
A.W. Biermann and R. Krishnaswamy, "Constructing programs from example computations," *IEEE Trans. on Software Eng.,* Vol. SE−2, Sept. 1976.

Biermann and Smith [1977]
A.W. Biermann and D.R. Smith, "The hierarchical synthesis of LISP scanning programs," in *Information Processing 77,* Ed. B. Gilchrist, IFIP, North-Holland Pub. Co., 1977, pp 41−45.

Biermann [1978]
A.W. Biermann, "The inference of regular LISP programs from examples," *IEEE Trans. on Systems, Man, and Cybernetics,* Vol. SMC−8(8), August 1978, pp 585−600.

Biermann and Smith [1979]
A.W. Biermann and D.R. Smith, "A production rule mechanism for generating LISP code," *IEEE Trans. on Systems, Man, and Cybernetics,* Vol. SMC−9(5), May 1979, pp 260−276.

Blum and Blum [1975]
L. Blum and M. Blum, "Toward a mathematical theory of inductive inference," Inform. Control (28), 1975, pp 125−155.

Gold [1967]
M. Gold, "Language identification in the limit," Inform. Control (5), 1967, pp 447−474.

Green *et al.* [1974]
C.C. Green, "Progress report on program understanding systems," Memo AIM−240,S Stanford Artificial Intelligence Laboratory, Stanford, CA, 1974.

Hardy [1975]
S. Hardy, "Synthesis of LISP functions from examples," Advance Papers 4th Int. Joint Conf. Artificial Intelligence, Tbilisi, Georgia, USSR, Sept. 1975, pp 240−245.

Jouannaud and Guiho [1977]
J.P. Jouannaud and G. Guiho, "Inference of functions with an interactive system," in *Machine Intelligence 9,* Ed. D. Michie, 1979.

Jouannaud and Guiho [1977]
J.P. Jouannaud and G. Guiho, "Program synthesis from examples for a simple class of non-loop functions," Technical Report, Laboratoire de Recherche en Informatique, Universite de Paris-Sud, 91405 ORSAY.

Jouannaud and Kodratoff [1979]
J.P. Jouannaud and Y. Kodratoff, "Characterization of a class of functions synthesized from examples by a Summers-like method using a 'B.M.W.' Matching Technique," Sixth International Joint Conf. on Art. Intell.−Tokyo 1979, pp. 440−447.

Jouannaud and Kodratoff [1980]
J.P. Jouannaud and Y. Kodratoff, "An automatic construction of LISP programs by transformation of functions synthesized from their input-output behavior," *2nd PAIS special issue on induction,* P.S. Michalsky, Ed., 1980.

Kodratoff and Fargues [1978]
Y. Kodratoff and J. Fargues, "A sane algorithm for the synthesis of LISP functions from example problems: The Boyer-Moore Algorithm," Proc. AISB Meeting, Hamburg, Germany, 1978, pp. 169−175.

Kodratoff [1979]
Y. Kodratoff, "A class of functions synthesized from a finite number of examples and a LISP program scheme," *Int. J. of Comp. and Inf. Sci.,* Vol. 8, No. 6, 1979.

Kodratoff and Papon [1980]
Y. Kodratoff and E. Papon, "A system for program synthesis and program optimization," Proc. AISB, Amsterdam, 1980, 1−10.

Kodratoff and Jouannaud [1984]
Y. Kodratoff and J.P. Jouannaud, "Some specifications for the synthesis of LISP programs," to appear in *Automatic Program Construction Techniques,* A.W. Biermann, G. Guiho, Y. Kodratoff (eds.), MacMillan Pub. Co., 1984.

Shaw *et al.* [1975]
D. Shaw, W. Swartout, and C. Green, "Inferring LISP programs from examples," Advance Papers 4th Int. Joint Conf. Artificial Intelligence, Tbilisi, Georgia, USSR, Sept. 1975, pp 260−267.

Siklossy and Sykes [1975]
L. Siklossy and D.A. Sykes, "Automatic program synthesis from example problems," Advance Papers 4th Int. Joint Conf. Artificial Intelligence, Tbilisi, Georgia, USSR, Sept. 1975, pp 268−273.

Smith [1977]
D.R. Smith, "A class of synthesizeable LISP programs," Technical report CS−1977−4, Duke University, Durham, N.C., 1977.

Summers [1975]
P.D. Summers, "Program construction from examples," Ph.D. dissertation, Yale University,

CHAPTER 16

Synthesizing LISP Programs Working On The List Level Of Embedding

Yves Kodratoff *

Jean-Pierre Jouannaud **

Abstract

We describe program transforms that change the semantics of the program to which they are applied. They allow the synthesis of very difficult list programs which mix synthesis from input-output behavior and a program transformation technique.

* Laboratoire de Recherche en Informatique, Université Paris-Sud, Bat. 490, F−91405 ORSAY CEDEX, France.

** Centre de Recherche en Informatique, UER de mathématiques, Université de Nancy 1, 54037 NANCY CEDEX, France.

A. Introduction

Summers' main contribution (Summers [1977]) to the field of LISP program synthesis from input-output examples is in making a clear distinction between the two steps required by the synthesis.

A first step transforms the input-output examples into computation traces. Our contribution to this step is rather formal: we simply noticed that the computation traces are terms (Robinson [1965]) built with the constructors (and their inverses) of an abstract data type. The type used by Summers and us is the type LIST without the constructor of the atoms. The computation traces follow from this assumption: we never use the particular value of an atom but rather compute list structures. The methodology can be applied to any type described by 1— the empty constructor, 2— the predicate checking the result of the empty constructor, 3— the data type constructor, 4— the operators inverse of the constructor, 5— one relation between the constructor and its inverses.

A second step detects recursion among the computation traces. We have improved mainly this aspect of SUMMERS' work and transformed it into a methodology for matching sequences of terms instead of matching terms. It uses successive matchings and generalizations. We shall not describe here the details of our methodology but will give enough examples of how it works to allow a precise description of the semantics of the synthesized programs.

Our main point can be stated as follows. A wild combinatorial explosion can be avoided by synthesizing programs that compute their output atom by atom, i.e. no sequence of atoms may be added "in one piece" to the result.

This chapter will be devoted to the consequences of these semantics and we shall simply point out now that the methodology itself can be also used for the transformation of recursive programs into iterative ones and for the detection of a general enough induction hypothesis for a recurrence proof.

As a consequence of these semantics, our programs can be transformed in three different ways.

The first one, not always possible, transforms some program f defined on any linear ascending domain {x} (described in Jouannaud *et al.* [1979], see here section B) into a program f' defined on flat lists {x'}, in such a way that f(x) = f'(x') for all x and x' such that x' = FLATTEN(x). This means that the new program is defined on flat lists but has the same output as the original one. (The domain is changed; the outputs are conserved.)

The second one transforms any program f' defined on flat lists {x'}, into a program f'', defined on the whole set of the lists {x''}, in such a way that f'' performs on each embedding level of an x' the same operation performed by f' on the top-level of an x''. A good example of this behavior can be seen by considering REVERSE such that (REVERSE(A B C D)) = (D C B A), REVERSE(A (B C) D)) = (D (B C) A) and REVEALL such that (REVEALL (A B C D)) = (D C B A), (REVEALL (A (B C) D)) = (D (C B) A).

The third one, not always interesting, performs directly FLATTEN(f''(x'')) for any x''.

We shall as succinctly as possible describe our methodology for program synthesis (described elsewhere (Kodratoff [1980], Kodratoff et al. [1980])) from input-outputs, mainly in order to be able to show that the three transforms can be applied to the programs we synthesize.

B. The Synthesis From Examples Methodology

More details are given in (Kodratoff [1979], Kodratoff [1980], Kodratoff *et al.* [1978], and Kodratoff *et al.* [1980]).

As we shall see, the input-output sequence $\{x_i,F(x_i)\}$ is transformed into a sequence of predicates and fragments $\{p_i(x),f_i(x)\}$. The predicate $p_i(x)$ is True if x has the same structure as x_i, regardless of the values of their atoms. For instance, (A B) and (E F) have the same structure since they are both lists with only atoms at their top-level (hereafter called flat lists) and they contain two atoms. The fragment $f_i(x)$ describes how the atoms of x_i are used in order to obtain $F(x_i)$. For instance, let x_i = (A B) and $F(x_i)$ = (B A). Then, $f_i(x)$ says that for any flat list containing two atoms, F works by building a flat list containing first the second atom of x (here, the value of this atom is B) and second the first atom of x (here, A).

We shall see also that we restrict our work to sequences such that $p_i(x)$ is easily computable from $p_0(x)$ and a recursion relation $p_{i+1}(x) = p_i(b(x))$ and such that one can find an (often fairly complicated) recursion relation between $f_{i+1}(x)$ and $f_i(x)$.

Let us suppose for the time being that we have found such recursion relations. We shall provc that these relations are equivalent to a program.

When recursion relations are found, we make an induction hypothesis which is (and will stay) the really unprovable part of any work on program synthesis from examples: we suppose that the function we are looking for always fits these recursion relations. An alternate way of saying this is that we synthesize a function which extends to infinity the recursion properties of the first few values given as examples.

When this hypothesis is taken for granted, then it is possible to prove the equivalence between the recursion relations and a recursive program. The first proof, called the "basic synthesis theorem" by Summers [1977] uses the formalism of the fixed point semantics of recursive programs (Manna [1974] and Manna *et al.* [1973]).

In an appendix, we give detailed proofs of extensions to SUMMERS' theorem. We give here an intuitive presentation of these results. As a first approximation, let us state that the following set of recursion relations:

$$p_{i+1}(x) = p_i(b(x)),\ p_0(x) \text{ given,}$$
$$f_i(y) = f'_i(y,\text{constant})$$
$$f'_{i+1}(y,z) = h_i(y,f'_i(a(y),g_i(y,z)))\ ,\ f'_0(y,z) \text{ given,}$$

(h_i and g_i similarly defined by recursion relations) is equivalent to the following recursive function:

$$F(x,y) = F'(x,y,\text{constant})$$
$$F'(x,y,z) = \text{IF } p_0(x) \text{ THEN } f'_0(y,z)$$
$$\text{ELSE } H(x,y,F'(b(x),a(y),G(x,y,z)))$$

where p_0, f'_0,a,b are given in the above recursion relations and where H and G are similarly defined by a recursive scheme of the same type.

The actual scheme is somewhat more complicated by the fact that "constant" may actually be computed by a vector of functions (i.e. we allow a definition by composition), this transforms z into a vector of values and G into a vector of functions. Besides, the variable y is allowed to be a vector of variables and, therefore, the function a to be a vector of functions. Since H and G can be defined similarly to F, one may ask where the process of recursive definition will stop: our scheme includes the fact that this process of recursive definition of embedded function must stop after a finite number of times, by functions defined by the scheme:

$$L(x,y,z) = \text{IF } p_k(x) \text{ THEN } 1_k(y,z)$$
$$\text{ELSE } L(b(x),a(y),z)$$

which embed and are embedded in no other recursively defined function, where $1_k(y,z)$ is given.

Remarks and definition

The above scheme does not forbid cross-recursive calls. We want to forbid them and this will be achieved by defining a *level of recursive embedding* as follows.

A program is of recursive embedding 0 if it appears in no recursive definitions or only once in its own recursive definition. For instance, $F(x), f_{\tau}(xx,\vec{x})$, $\vec{A}(x,x)$ (defined in the appendix) are of recursive embedding 0 in the above scheme.

A program is of recursive embedding n+1 if it appears in the recursive definition of a program of recursive embedding n.

Property of our scheme. The above definition is consistent with our scheme; i.e. a program of recursive embedding level m can call another of recursive embedding level n, only if $m < n$.

Consequence. The programs of recursive embedding level 0 are defined by the original sequence of input-output sequence of examples, their halting condition is thus $p_0(x) = \text{True}$. The programs of recursive embedding 1 are defined by a sequence of examples which starts with the second example, their halting condition is thus $p_1(x) = \text{True}$. For instance, the fragments h_i (see appendix) are defined by $g_{i+1}(\vec{x}) = h_i(\vec{x}, g_i(c_{\vec{i}}(\vec{x})))$, it follows that $g_1(\vec{x}) = h_0(\vec{x}, g_0(c_{\vec{i}}(\vec{x})))$ and $h_0(\vec{x},z)$ is computed when $g_1(\vec{x})$ is computed, i.e. when $p_1(xx) = \text{True}$.

B.1. Notations and Definitions

Let L be the set of LISP lists. A list x of L may be viewed as a cons-tree, each left leaf of which is an atom, each right leaf of which is nil. For instance,

```
x = (A (B) C) =          cons
                        /    \
                       A      cons
                             /    \
                            /      \
                        cons        cons
                       /    \      /    \
                      B     nil   C      nil
```

Definition. A *reduction function* is a finite composition of car and cdr. Let R be the set of reduction functions.

Definition. Let A_i be the i-th occurrence of the atom A in the list x and u be the unique reduction function which verifies $u(x) = A_i$. Then u is said to be the *functional name* of A_i in x.

The cons-tree of a list gives an immediate way to obtain the functional name of each of its atoms: in order to reach an atom, one follows a path into the tree, each left (downward) turn in the path adds a car at the left of the functional name, while each right turn adds a cdr at the left of the functional name (following the path from the father node down to the leaf corresponds to building the functional name from the right to the left).

Example. Consider

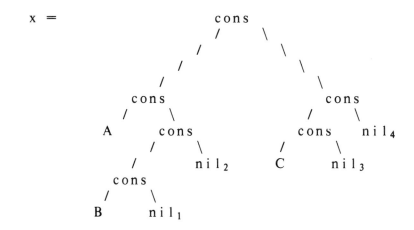

```
x =                      cons
                        /    \
                      /        \
                    /            \
                  /                \
              cons                  cons
             /    \                /    \
            A      cons         cons     nil4
                  /    \       /    \
                /       nil2  C      nil3
            cons
           /    \
          B      nil1
```

then A = car.car(x), B = car.car.cdr.car(x), C = car.car.cdr(x) so that the functional names of A, B, C are respectively car.car, car.car.cdr.car, car.car.cdr, and the functional names of nil_1, nil_2, nil_3, nil_4 are respectively cdr.car.cdr.car, cdr.cdr.car, cdr.car.cdr, cdr.cdr.

Definition. Let u and v belong to R, one says that v is a right factor of u if $u = u_1 . v$. If v is a right factor of u, then uv^{-1} denotes a function of R such that $u = (uv^{-1})\,v$. Let (u modulo v) be the function $u\,v^{-k}$ provided $v^{k'}$ is a right factor of u, iff $0 \leqslant k' \leqslant k$ (i.e. v is not a right factor of $u\,v^{-k}$).

Example:

$$u = \text{car.car.cdr.car.cdr}, \quad v = \text{car.cdr},$$
$$uv^{-1} = \text{car.car.cdr}, \quad (u \text{ modulo } v) = \text{car}.$$

B.2 Linear Ascending Domains

Following Summers [1977], we transform the input-output sequence $\{x_i \rightarrow F(x_i)\}$ into a sequence $\{p_i(x) \rightarrow f_i(x)\}$ of computational traces. A further step of the synthesis requires the existence of recurrence relations between the predicates p_i. We shall therefore characterize the input domains displaying this property.

Definition. Let x_0 and α belong to L, α owning a single *-labelled atom. One denotes $S(\alpha, x_0, *)$ (Knuth *et al.* [1970]) the list obtained by substitution of x_0 to the *-labelled atom of α. The sequence $\{x_0, x_i = S(\alpha, x_{i-1}, *)\}$ is called a ***linear ascending domain:*** $A(x_0, \alpha)$.

A linear ascending domain is totally ordered by the order induced by the substitutions, $x_i < x_j$ for all $i < j$.

Remark. In fact, we change the names of the atoms in order to avoid several occurrences of the same atom in x_i.

Example. Let

```
x0=      cons        and      α =      cons,
        /    \                         /    \
       A      nil                     A      nil.
```

then $A(x_0, \alpha)$ is the set

```
{x0,     cons---------------            cons-------------
        /     \            α           /    \            α
       A       cons-----------        A      cons----------      , ... } =
              /     \      x0               /    \        α
             B       nil--------           B      cons-------
                                                 /    \     x0
                                                C      nil----
```

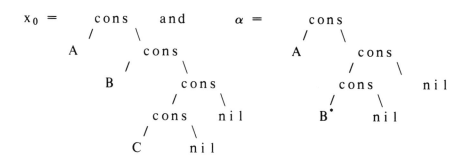

{(A), (A B), (A B C), ...} ,i.e. the set of the flat lists.

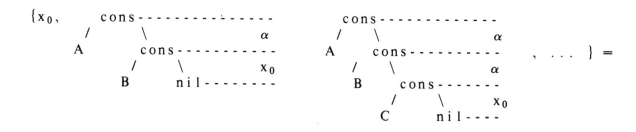

Example. Let

```
x0 =    cons    and      α =     cons
       /    \                   /    \
      A      cons              A      cons
            /    \                   /    \
           B      cons             cons     nil
                 /    \           /    \
               cons    nil       B*     nil
              /    \
             C      nil
```

```
A(x0, α)={x0 ,              cons - - - - - - - - - - ,
                           /    \                   |
                          A      cons               |
                                /    \              α
                            cons      nil           |
                           /    \                   |
                       cons      nil - - - - - - - -
                      /    \                        |
                     B      cons                    |
                           /    \                   |
                          C      cons              x0
                                /    \              |
                            cons      nil           |
                           /    \                   |
                          D      nil  - - - - -

 - - - - - - - - - - - - - - cons                 ,  .  .  .  .  .  }
|                           /    \
|                          A      cons
α                                /    \
|                            cons      nil
|                           /    \
 - - - - - - - - - - - - - cons      nil
|                         /    \
|                        B      cons
α                              /    \
|                          cons      nil
|                         /    \
 - - - - - - - - - - - - cons      nil
|                       /    \
|                      C      cons
|                            /    \
x0                          D      cons
|                                 /    \
|                             cons      nil
|                            /    \
|                           E      nil
 ----------------------------------------------------------------
```

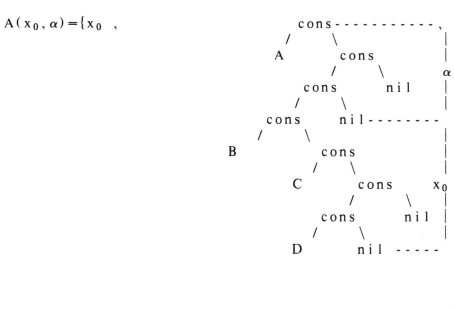

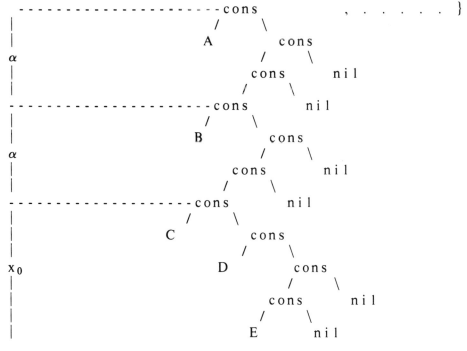

= {(A B (C)), (A ((B C (D)))), (A((B((C D (E)))), ... }.

Definition. An atom of a list is said to be *in the direction* of a reduction function r, iff its functional name u verifies:

$$(u \text{ modulo } r) \text{ is a right factor of } r.$$

From the intuitive point of view, an atom x of a list is in the direction of a reduction function r, iff there exists an integer $k > 0$, such that the path leading to x is a subpath of the path induced by r^k.

Example. Let u = cdr.car.cdr and r = car.cdr. Then (u modulo r) = cdr, and cdr is a right factor of r. An atom the functional name of which is cdr.car.cdr is in the direction of r = car.cdr.

Example. Let u = car.cdr and r = car.car.cdr, (u modulo r) = u and u is a right factor of r. One of the above examples was: x_0 = (A B(C)), α = (A(B•)), the atom of value B• in x_0 is in the direction of the functional name of the labelled atom B• of α since the functional name of B in x_0 is car.cdr and the functional name of B• in α is car.car.cdr.

Property of the linear ascending domains.

Given $A(x_0, \alpha)$, the functional name b of the *-labelled atom in α, the functional name u of the atom of x_0 which is in the direction of b, then the sequence of predicates $\{p_i\} = \{$ atom u . $b^i\}$ is such that $p_i(x_i)$ = True, $p_i(x_j)$ = False if $j > i$, $p_i(x_j)$ = Undefined if $j < i$, where x_i belongs to the linear ascending domain $A(x_0, \alpha)$.

Proof: See (Jouannaud and Kodratoff [1979]).

Consequence. The linear ascending domains are suitable domains for program synthesis from examples.

Let $A(x_0, \alpha)$ be a linear ascending domain and x belongs to $A(x_0, \alpha)$. Then $p_i(x)$ = True if x has the same structure as x_i (regardless of the values of their atoms), $p_i(x)$ = False if x has the structure of $x_j, x_j > x_i$.

Finally, if x has the structure of $x_j, x_j < x_i$, the value of $p_i(x)$ is of no importance since we want to give the form $\{p_i(x) \rightarrow f_i(x)\}$ to the input-output sequence: the p_i are checked in order $p_0, p_1, p_2, \cdots$ and any x has the structure of an $x_i \geqslant x_0$. If $p_0(x)$ = False then x has a structure of an $x_i \geqslant x_1$ and so on.

Besides, this property assures that $p_i(x)$ = atom.u.$b^i(x)$, $p_{i+1}(x)$ = atom.u.$b^{i+1}(x)$, therefore $p_{i+1}(x) = p_i(b(x))$.

Example. The flat lists are defined by

```
x0 =         cons          and        α =         cons.
            /    \                                /    \
           A      nil                            A      nil•
```

The functional name of nil• in α is cdr,b=cdr, and the atom of x_0 in the direction of cdr is nil,u=cdr. The flat lists are characterized by $p_0(x)$ = atom . cdr(x), $p_{i+1}(x) = p_i(\text{cdr}(x))$.

Example. The linear ascending domain construction from x_0 = (A B(C)), α = (A(B•)) is characterized by the functional name of B• in α:b = car.car.cdr, and the functional name of the atom in the direction of b, i.e. B of x_0, is u=car.cdr. It follows that $p_0(x)$ = atom.car.cdr(x),$p_{i+1}(x) = p_i(\text{car.car.cdr}(x))$.

B.3 Construction of the Fragments

We want now to transform each $F(x_i)$ into $f_i(x)$ which is made as follows. The output $F(x_i)$ is taken in its cons-tree form. Each atom, except nil, of this cons-tree is replaced by its functional name in x_i. The process is unambiguous iff there are not several atoms (except nil) bearing the same name in any x_i. Each obtained cons-expression $f_i(x_i)$ is then turned into a partial function $f_i(x)$ by the substitution of x to each x_i of $f(x_i)$. The function $f_i(x)$ is called the i-th *fragment* of F. Notice that f_i is defined for any $x \geqslant x_i$ and $F(x_i) = f_i(x_i)$.

Remark. The fragments could have been constructed in a very different way. For instance, one could try to put into evidence in $F(x_i)$ either x_i or non-atomic parts of x_i. In the case of flat lists cdr(x) or car.cdr(x_i) are such non-atomic parts of x_i. This atomic decomposition in function of the functional names of the atoms of x_i implies that $f_i(x)$ is a cons-tree, the left leaves of which are functional names of atoms of x, the right leaves of which are nil. This remark will be of utmost importance in the following.

Example. Consider the input-output sequence:

$$x_0 = (A) \rightarrow F(x_0) = (A),$$

$$x_1 = (A\ B) \rightarrow F(x_1) = (B\ A),\ x_2 = (A\ B\ C) \rightarrow F(x_2) = (C\ B\ A),$$

$$x_3 = (A\ B\ C\ D) \rightarrow F(x_3) = (D\ C\ B\ A),....$$

The output sequence is put into its cons-tree form:

```
F(x0)  =    cons       ,    F(x1)  =    cons
           /    \                      /    \
          A      nil                  B      cons
                                            /    \
                                           A      nil

F(x2)  =       cons            ,    F(x3)  =  cons         ,  ....
              /    \                          /    \
             C      cons                     D      cons
                   /    \                          /    \
                  B      cons                     C      cons
                        /    \                          /    \
                       A      nil                      B      cons
                                                             /    \
                                                            A      nil
```

From the inputs we know that A in $F(x_0)$ is car(x_0), A and B in $F(x_2)$ are car(x_2) and car.cdr(x_2), A, B and C in $F(x_3)$ are respectively car(x_3), car.cdr(x_3),car.cdr.cdr(x_3),.... The atoms in $F(x_i)$ are replaced by their functional names in x_i:

```
f0(x0) =   cons      ,     f1(x1) =   cons         ,
           /    \                     /      \
        car     nil                car       cons
        x0                         cdr       /      \
                                    x1     car      nil
                                            x1

f2(x2) =         cons          ,
                 /    \
              car      cons
              cdr      /    \
              cdr    car     cons
              x2     cdr     /    \
                     x2   car     nil
                          x2

f3(x3) =       cons
               /    \
            car      cons
            cdr      /    \
            cdr    car      cons
            cdr    cdr      /    \
            x3     cdr    car     cons
                   x3     cdr     /    \
                          x3    car    nil
                                x3
```

Finally, $f_i(x)$ comes from $f_i(x_i)$ simply by replacing x_i by x.

For instance, $f_1(x_1)$ becomes

```
           (        cons             )
           (        /  \             )
f1(x)  =   ( car         cons        )
           ( cdr         /  \        )
           (  x     car        nil   )
           (         x               )
```

The difference between $f_1(x_1)$ and $f_1(x)$ lies in that $f_1(x)$ is defined for all $x \geqslant x_1$ but gives always the same result as $f_1(x_1)$ (if the first two atoms have the same values in x and x_1):

$$f_1((A\ B)) = (B\ A),\ f_1((A\ B\ C)) = (B\ A).$$

Remark. Of the atoms of $F(x_i)$, why is nil not replaced by its functional name in x_i? No real trick is hidden behind this restriction. First, it enables us to treat without ambiguity the cases where several nils appear in the input. Second, even in the unambiguous cases, giving its functional name to nil would add no power to the methodology and would be slightly more complicated.

B.4. The Computation Trace

Embedding the domain predicates and the fragments into IF...THEN...ELSE... functions gives what we call a computation trace. For instance, the above example

$$\{x_i \rightarrow F(x_i)\},\ 0 \leqslant i \leqslant 3,$$

leads to the computation trace:

```
F(x)=IF atom.cdr(x) THEN          cons             ELSE
                                 /     \
                              car       nil
                              x

     IF atom.cdr.cdr(x) THEN         cons          ELSE
                                    /    \
                                 car      cons
                                 cdr     /    \
                                 x     car     nil
                                       x

     IF atom.cdr.cdr.cdr(x) THEN       cons              ELSE
                                      /    \
                                   car      cons
                                   cdr     /    \
                                   cdr   car     cons
                                   x     cdr     /   \
                                         x     car    nil
                                               x

     IF atom.cdr.cdr.cdr.cdr(x) THEN cons              ELSE ⊥
                                    /    \
                                   /      cons
                                  /      /    \
                                 /     car     cons
                               car     cdr    /    \
                               cdr     cdr  car     cons
                               cdr     x    cdr    /    \
                               cdr          x    car     nil
                               x                 x
```

where ⊥ is the undefined value. It follows that the sequence $\{F_n\}$ is an increasing sequence of chains (Manna [1974]).

B.5 Recursion Relations in the Computation Trace

We restricted ourselves to linear ascending domains where a recursion relation links the predicates: this ends the work to be done for the predicates.

On the other hand, a methodology was developed in order to detect recursion relations among the fragments (Kodratoff [1978], Kodratoff [1980], Kodratoff and Papon [1980]). We shall merely give here outlines of this methodology and rapidly exemplify it.

Given a sequence of fragments $f_i(x)$, it is clear that a recursion relation between f_i and f_{i+1} will be found as soon as f_i and f_{i+1} match each other. By definition of the matching (Huet [1976], Robinson [1965]) f_i and f_{i+1} are then identical when some variables of f_i are replaced by terms, this is written: $f_i(x)[x \backslash t_i(x)] = f_{i+1}(x)$ and of course induces the recursion relation: $f_{i+1}(x) = f_i(t_i(x))$. The predicates $p_i(x)$ show this kind of relationship where t_i is a constant b:

$$p_{i+1}(x) = p_i(b(x)).$$

The relationship between fragments is not usually that simple. Our algorithm then uses two different iterations.

First, iterations on the substitutions; as above, one might find x is substituted by a non-constant term $t_i(x)$. The $t_i(x)$ are then looked at as new fragments among which recursion relations are to be detected.

Second, iterations on the generalizations; most often, the matching fails because one variable undergoes different substitutions or because a function (or constant) receives a substitution (we stick to first order matching). One then transforms $f_i(x)$ into a new sequence of generalized fragments $g_i(z_1,...,z_n)$ where $g_i(z_1,...,z_n)$ is the least generalization (Plotkin [1970], Reynolds [1970]) of $f_i(x)$ and $f_{i+1}(x)$. If the matching of g_i and g_{i+1} fails, one iterates on the generalizations, i.e. the sequence g_i is transformed into a new sequence obtained by the least generalization of g_i and g_{i+1}. This process is iterated as long as one does not get a sequence for which the matching of successive terms succeeds.

Example 1. (This example is to be used again in the next section.)

$$x_0 = (A(B)C) \rightarrow F(x_0) = (C\ B\ A),$$

$$x_1 = (A(B(C)D)) \rightarrow F(x_1) = (D\ B\ A\ A),$$

$$x_2 = (A(B(C(D)\ E))) \rightarrow F(x_2) = (E\ B\ A\ A\ B),$$

$$x_3 = (A(B(C(D(E)\ F)))) \rightarrow F(x_3) = (F\ B\ A\ A\ B\ C), \ldots$$

One computes the predicates and fragments as above and finds:

$$P_0(x) = \text{atom.cdr.car.cdr}(x),\ p_{i+1}(x) = p_i(\text{car.cdr}(x)),$$

```
f0(x) =        cons
              /    \
           car       cons
           cdr      /    \
           cdr   car        cons
           x     car       /    \
                 cdr    car       nil
                 x      x
```

```
f1(x) =      cons
            /    \
        car        cons
        cdr       /    \
        cdr    car        cons
        car    car       /    \
        cdr    cdr    car        cons
        x      x      x         /    \
                             car       nil
                             x
```

```
f2(x) =     cons
           /    \
        cdr       cons
        cdr      /    \
        cdr   car        cons
        car   car       /    \
        cdr   cdr    car        cons
        car   x      x         /    \
        cdr                 car        cons
        x                   x         /    \
                                   car       nil
                                   car
                                   cdr
                                   x
```

```
f3(x) =          cons
              /           \
          car               cons
          cdr             /         \
          cdr           car           cons
          car           car           /       \
          cdr           cdr         car        cons
          car           x           x         /       \
          cdr                             car          cons
          car                             x             /     \
          cdr                                    car           cons
          x                                      car            /     \
                                                 cdr         car       nil
                                                 x           car
                                                             cdr
                                                             car
                                                             cdr
                                                             x
```

```
f1 (x) =              cons
                     /         \
                car           cons
                cdr          /         \
                cdr       car           cons
                car       car         /       \
                cdr       cdr       car         cons
                x         x         x         /         \
                                          car           nil
                                          x
```

The matching of f_i and f_{i+1} fails since one gets contradictory substitutions like x\x and x\car.cdr(x). One sees also that the constant nil should undergo a substitution. One therefore transforms the sequence f_i into the sequence of the least generalizations of f_i and f_{i+1}. The least generalization of

```
f0 and f1 is g0(x',x'',z) =      cons
                                  /    \
                                car     cons
                                cdr     /    \
                                cdr   car     cons
                                x'    car     /    \
                                      cdr   car     z
                                      x''   x''
```

```
(with g0(x,x,nil) = f0(x))
```

```
f1 and f2 is g1(x',x'',z) =      cons
                                  /    \
                                car     cons
                                cdr     /    \
                                cdr   car     cons
                                car   car     /    \
                                cdr   cdr   car     cons
                                x'    x''   x''     /    \
                                                  car     z
                                                  x''
```

```
f2 and f3 is g2(x',x'',z) =      cons
                                  /    \
                                car     cons
                                cdr     /    \
                                cdr   car     cons
                                car   car     /    \
                                cdr   cdr   car     cons
                                car   x''   x''     /    \
                                cdr                car    cons
                                x'                 x''    /    \
                                                        car     z
                                                        car
                                                        cdr
                                                        x''
```

. . . . . .

and we can verify that $f_i(x) = g_i(x,x,nil)$ for all i. The matching of g_0 and g_1 succeeds with x'\car.cdr(x'), x''\x'',

```
        ⎛       cons       ⎞
z \     ⎜       /  \       ⎟
        ⎜car          z    ⎟
        ⎝x''               ⎠
```

The matching of g_1 and g_2 succeeds with x'\car.cdr(x'), x''\x'',

```
        ⎛       cons       ⎞
        ⎜       /  \       ⎟
z \     ⎜car          z    ⎟ .
        ⎜car               ⎟
        ⎜cdr               ⎟
        ⎝x''               ⎠
```

The z variable gets a substitution of the form z\h_i(x'',z). Considering h_i(x,z) like new fragments and looking for their recursion relationships leads to h_{i+1}(x,z) = h_i(car.cdr(x),z). We have therefore found recursion relationships between generalized expressions of f_i(x).

```
f_i(x) = g_i(x,x,nil), g_0(x',x'',z) =    cons
                                          /    \
                                         /      \
                                      car        cons
                                      cdr        /    \
                                      cdr   car        cons
                                      x'    cdr        /   \
                                            x''     car      z
                                                    x''

g_i+1(x',x'',z) = g_i(car.cdr(x'), x'',h_i(x'',z)),

h_0(x,z) =       cons,
             /     \
            car      z
            x

h_i+1(x,z) = h_i(car.cdr(x),z).
```

Example 2. The matching of the fragments obtained in section 2.4 fails because the constant nil undergoes a substitution. We accordingly generate the sequence of the least generalizations, which happens to be the same as the initial one except that a variable z is substituted to each nil.

```
g0(x,z) = cons ,                 g1(x,z) = cons ,
          /    \                           /    \
        car     z                        car     cons
                                         cdr     /   \
                                         x     car    z
                                               x

          g2(x,z) = cons , ...
                    /    \
                  car     cons
                  cdr     /   \
                  cdr   car    cons
                  x     cdr    /  \
                        x    car   z
                             x
```

and $f_i(x) = g_i(x,nil)$, where the $f_i(x)$ are those of section 2.3. The matching of g_i and g_{i+1} succeeds with x \ cdr(x) and

```
            cons
z \  (      /  \      )
      car       z
      x
```

for each i, one therefore finds the recursion relations:

```
        fi(x) = gi(x,nil)

                         cons
        g0(x,z) =  (     /  \     )
                     car      z
                     x

      gi+1(x,z) = gi(cdr(x),hi(x,z))

                     cons
   hi(x,z) =  (      /  \      ),  for all i.
                car       z
                x
```

Remark 1. The generalizations of both examples are actually more complicated: they introduce sequences of new variables. In example 1, since 3 variables are introduced at each generalization, we should have written

```
g0(z1, z2, z3)  =  cons
                    /     \
              car          cons
              cdr         /      \
              cdr     car          cons
              z1      car        /       \
                      cdr     car          z3
                      z2      z2
```

```
g1(z4, z5, z6)  =  cons                     , . . .
                    /     \
              car          cons
              cdr         /      \
              cdr     car          cons
              car     car        /       \
              cdr     cdr     car          z6
              z4      z5      z5
```

Since the matching of g_0 and g_1 succeeds, one has: $z_1 \backslash$ car.cdr(z_4), $z_2 \backslash z_5$,

```
          (      cons       )
z3  \     (      /  \       )
          ( car          z6 )
          (  z5             )
```

It is a rule (see remarks 2 and 4) that a variable must be substituted by a term containing this variable. It follows that one must identify z_1 and z_4 to one variable x', identify z_2 and z_5 to one variable x''. We thus write

```
          (      cons       )
z3  \     (      /  \       )
          ( car          z6 )
          (  z5             )
```

as

```
          (      cons       )
z3  \     (      /  \       )
          ( car          z6 )
          ( x''             )
```

where x'' is known, and it follows that one must identify z_3 and z_6 to one variable z. We have shown (Kodratoff [1980]) that this kind of reasoning is always possible when the trees are of polynomial increase. Some extensions to exponential increase are also described in (Papon [1980]).

Remark 2. Our algorithm uses heuristics we have called "lethal successes", since they name matching successes that would not lead to valid recursion relations. We give here an example of this behavior.

Example 3. (Composition)

$x_0 = (A) \rightarrow F(x_0) = (AA)$,

$x_1 = (AB) \rightarrow F(x_1) = (ABAB)$,

$x_2 = (ABC) \rightarrow F(x_2) = (ABCABC)$,...

The domain is the flat lists with

$p_0(x) = \text{atom.cdr}(x)$ and $p_{i+1}(x) = p_i(\text{cdr}(x))$.

The fragments are:

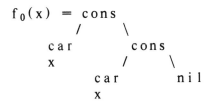

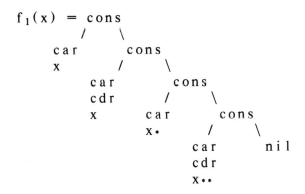

```
f0(x) = cons
          /     \
    car           cons
    x            /     \
             car          nil
             x


f1(x) = cons
          /    \
   car          cons
   x           /     \
        car           cons
        cdr          /     \
        x        car          cons
                 x*          /     \
                         car          nil
                         cdr
                         x**
```

```
f2(x)  =  cons
         /      \
   car           cons
   x            /      \
        car           cons
        cdr          /      \
        x      car           cons
               cdr          /      \
               cdr    car           cons
               x      x            /      \
                              car          nil
                              cdr
                              cdr
                              x
```

The matching of f_1 and f_2 leads to two lethal substitutions. The x* receives cdr.cdr(x) which cannot be a recursion relation, since the fragments cannot recur quicker than the domain (a computation trace could not exist). The x** is such that cdr(x**) \ x which leads to no recursion since cdr has no inverse. The reader can check that these lethal successes occur for other f_i. Since the first lethal success occurs at x, $f_i(x)$ is rewritten as $f_1(x) = h_1(x,g_1(x))$ with

```
              |        cons              |
              |        /  \              |
              | car          cons        |
h1(x,z)   =   |  x           /  \        |
              |        car          z    |
              |        cdr               |
              |        x                 |
```

and

```
              |        cons              |
              |        /  \              |
              | car          cons        |
gi(x)     =   |  x           /  \        |  .
              |        car          nil  |
              |        cdr               |
              |        x                 |
```

In the same way, one could see that $f_2(x)$ must be given the form $f(x) = h_2(x,g_2(x))$, with

```
              |        cons                        |
              |        /  \                        |
              | car          cons                  |
              |  x           /  \                  |
h2(x,z)   =   |        car          cons           |
              |        cdr          /  \           |
              |        x      car          z       |
              |               cdr                  |
              |               cdr                  |
              |               x                    |
```

and

```
                 (        cons                                  )
                 |        /  \                                  |
                 | car          cons                            |
                 |  x           /  \                            |
g2(x)    =       |        car          cons                     |  .
                 |        cdr          /  \                     |
                 |         x     car          nil               |
                 |               cdr                            |
                 |               cdr                            |
                 (                x                             )
```

The fragment $f_0(x)$ is isolated, and the methodology is applied to the sequences $h_i(x,z)$ and $g_i(x)$.

Remark 3. We spoke of *matching* successive fragments. One may also discover recursion relations by matching f_i and a sub-tree of f_{i+1}. This would lead to non-terminal recursive forms, as the following example shows.

Example 4. (matching with a sub-tree).

We come back to the fragments of section 2.4, and shall find other recursion relations than in example 2 of this section.

These fragments are: on the next page

```
                  ------------------
                  |                |
f0(x)  =  cons                     |
          /      \                 |
       car        nil              |
       x                           |
                        -------|---------------
                        |      |              |
          f1(x)  =  cons       |              |
                    /     \    |              |
                 car        cons              |
                 cdr       /      \           |
                 x      car        nil        |
                                              |
                                        -----|-------------------
                                        |    |                  |
                      f2(x)  =  cons         |                  |
                                /      \     |                  |
                             car         cons                   |
                             cdr        /      \                |
                             cdr     car        cons            |
                             x       cdr       /      \         |
                                     x      car        nil      |
                                            x                   |
                                                                |
                                      f3(x)  =  cons            |
                                                /      \        |
                                             car          cons
                                             cdr         /      \
                                             cdr      car         cons
                                             cdr      cdr        /      \
                                             x        cdr     car         cons
                                                      x       cdr        /      \
                                                              x       car        nil
                                                                      x
```

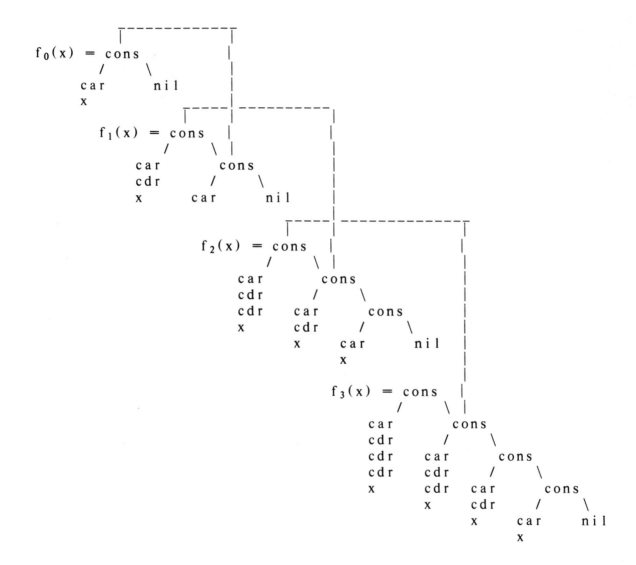

and can be matched as shown by the dotted lines. One then finds:

```
                      cons
                      /  \
f1(x)  =  car                 f0(x) ,
          cdr
          x

                 cons
                 /  \
f2(x)  =  car          f1(x)
          cdr                   ,  . . .
          cdr
          x
```

i.e.,

$$f_{i+1}(x,z) = h_i(x, f_i(x))$$

where

```
                     cons
                     /  \
h0(x,z)  =  car          z,
            cdr
             x

                cons
                /  \
h1(x,z)  =  car      z,  ...
            cdr
            cdr
             x
```

Considering the $h_i(x,z)$ as new fragments, one finds $h_{i+1}(x,z) = h_i(cdr(x),z)$. This ends the recursion relations necessary to describe the recursive behaviour of $f_i(x)$.

Remark 4. We spoke of matching *successive* fragments. Instead of matching f_i and f_{i+1}, one could also attempt a matching of f_i and f_{i+k}. For each $1 \leqslant j \leqslant k$, a different function can in principle be found. In the following, we shall deal with only one function at a time, so this problem will not be studied again.

B.6 More details about the semantics of our scheme

The programs we can synthesize are instantiations of the scheme defined by theorem 2 (see appendix). Two main restrictions express the limit of the class of functions we may synthesize.

B.6.1 The functions are of "polynomial increase".

This means that the number of leaves in the cons-tree $f(x_i)$ increases like a polynomial in the number of leaves in x_i.

Let f be of recursive embedding 0, and h of recursive embedding $n + 1$. By definition, h is called by f either directly (if $n = 0$) or through successive calls to functions f', f'',..., $f^{(n)}$, where $f^{(n)}$ is called by f, $f^{(n-1)}$ called by $f^{(n)}$,...,h called by f'.

In a call by value semantics, the computation of h is ended before the computation of f can be carried on, in a call by name semantics, the value of h is a parameter inside the computation of f. In each case, the number of leaves produced by the computation of h is less than the number of leaves produced by the computation of f, i.e., h increases less rapidly than f.

One must consider now, on the one hand, that our matching process stops until a matching success, i.e., with programs that build a constant number of leaves and have the greatest embedding, on the other hand that a program cannot have embedded calls to himself, i.e., no program can be of exponential increase. Since one must stop with a finite number of recursive embeddings, the lowest increase of our functions is null and the greatest is bounded by the exponential increase: this defines a polynomial increase.

B.6.2. The halting conditions contain reduction functions that compute only atoms.

With respect to the way our programs are built, this property is a mere triviality: each program is obtained as the limit of fragments that, by construction, contain reduction functions computing atoms only. For any x, the computation which takes place is precisely the computation made by the fragment $f_i(x)$ following the predicate $p_i(x) =$ True. This property is not true for any program belonging to the scheme of theorem 2. We shall now make precise how this semantic feature will show up in the scheme. We have given in (Jouannaud and Kodratoff [1979]) a formal description of this condition which was stated as a property of our scheme. We should like to show here, in a somewhat more intuitive way, how the algorithm of section 2.5 shapes the programs we may find.

Example. In example 1 of section 2.5, the recursion relations instantiate the scheme of theorem 2 in order to give the program:

```
F(x)  = G(x,x,nil)

G(x',x'',z)  =  IF atom.cdr.car.cdr(x')  THEN    cons
                                                /    \
                                             car       cons
                                             cdr      /    \
                                             cdr   car      cons
                                             x'    car     /    \
                                                   cdr   car     z
                                                   x''   x''

                                           ELSE
                                       G(car.cdr(x'),x'',H(x'',z))

H(x,z)  =  IF atom.cdr.car.cdr.car.cdr(x)  THEN   cons
                                                 /    \
                                               car     z

                                           ELSE H(car.cdr(x),z)
```

For any x of the domain, car.car.cdr(x) and car(x) are atoms. Since x'' undergoes no substitution, car.car.cdr(x'') and car(x'') are always atoms in the halting condition of G. On the contrary, car.cdr.cdr(x) is an atom only if cdr.car.cdr(x) = True. It follows that x', which undergoes the substitution x' \ car.cdr(x') as long as it does not fulfill this condition is always such that car.cdr.cdr(x') is an atom when the halting condition of G is reached. G is therefore an example of our claim: the halting condition of G contains reduction functions which compute atoms only.

As a counter-example, consider the function G', similar to G where the halting value is

```
           cons
         /      \
car              cons
cdr            /      \
cdr       car          cons
x''       car        /      \
          cdr      car        z
          x'       x'
```

for instance, then G' would not fulfill our condition and we want to show that a function like G' cannot be synthesized from examples by our methodology.

Preliminary remarks. We shall need to consider in greater detail the way a matching may succeed and thoroughly examine the case of the unary functions car and cdr. As before, we shall call $f_n(x)$ the fragments obtained from the examples and $g_n(\vec{x})$ the generalized fragments such that $g_n(\vec{x})$ and $g_{n+1}(\vec{x})$ match.

When the matching between $f_n(x)$ and $f_{n+1}(x)$ is attempted several cases may arise due to the fact that f_n and f_{n+1} are cons-trees made of functional names of atoms: there is a reduction function between the leaves x and the cons which is their nearest father (e.g. in G' above, car.cdr.cdr is between cons and x'').

— a term whose root is cons or a constant is substituted by another term. The generalized expression will thus contain a variable in place of this constant or term. This variable will be said to be *term-typed* and we shall further name it z^i (the upper indices will always characterize variables introduced by a generalization. z at power i will be written $(z)^i$). In other words, each z^i is initiated by a term whose root is cons or a constant. In example 1 of section 2.5, nil is generalized to the term-typed variable z. In the example of section 4, car(x) is generalized to the term-typed variable y.

— a term whose root is a unary function is substituted by an other term. This case is a lethal success and no further generalization takes place. For instance, we do not accept a matching between car.cdr(x) and car.car.car(x). The substitution cdr(x) \ car.car(x) leads to a lethal success.

— an x matches a unary function. In general, this matching is not unique and the generalization will introduce new *x-typed* variables further named x^i. In other words each x^i is initiated by x. In example 1 of section 2.5, we have x' \ car.cdr(x') and x'' \ x'' which are two x-typed variables (where it is understood that the identity is a particular reduction function).

It follows that the generalized fragments are cons-trees, the cons are father of

— another cons

— a reduction function which has an x-typed variable as leaf

— a term-typed variable

— a constant.

The nature of $\vec{c_i}(\vec{x})$ This vector appears in our scheme in the recurrence relations of g_n: $g_{i+1}(\vec{x}) = h_i(\vec{x}, g_i(\vec{c_i}(\vec{x})))$. This vector contains two types of variables, we shall write it as $(c'_{i1}x^1, \ldots, c'_{ip}x^p, c''_{i1}z^1, \ldots, c''_{iq}z^q)$ The c''_i may actually be different for each i but, on the contrary, we shall see that $c'_{ik} = c'_k$ for all i. Recall that b is the constant reduction function such that $p_{i+1}(x) = p_i.b(x)$. The reduction function b may be the r-th power of an irreducible reduction function b', i.e., $b = (b')^r$. For instance, if b = car.cdr.car.cdr then $b = (\text{car.cdr})^2 =$

$(b')^2$. We introduced the following lethal success (see (Kodratoff [1979]) for its reason, it has been here exemplified in example 3 of section 2.5). If c'_{ik} is not equal to $(b')^p$, $0 \leqslant p \leqslant r$, then we have a lethal success. The case $p = 0$ means that c'_{ik} is the identity issued from a substitution $x \setminus x$. If follows that there are at most $r+1$ possible values for c'_{ik} and they cannot be obtained as limits of infinite sequences. To each c'_k we associate an x-typed variable x^k.

Description of $g_0(\overline{x})$

Let u^k_i be the reduction function applied to x^k in $g_i(\overline{x})$. From the above preliminary remarks, one sees that $g_0(\overline{x})$ is a cons-tree the sons of which are

— cons
— a term-typed variable
— $u^k_0 x^k$
— constants

and we know that $u^k_{i+1} = c'_k u^k_i$, where $c'_k = (b')^p$ $0 \leqslant p \leqslant r$, where r is defined by $b = (b')^r$. *These restrictions to the scheme insure that* $u^i_j x^i$ *in the halting values compute atoms only.* By construction of the domain, we know that each x^i is obtained by "adding" the term α to x_{i-1}. We shall write this $x_i = \alpha \dot{+} x_{i-1}$ ($\dot{+}$ is not commutative!). From the input-output examples, we know also that $atom.u_0(x_0) = True$, i.e. u_0 selects an atom out of x_0, $atom.u_1(x_1) = True$, i.e. $u_1 = c'_k.u_0$ selects an atom out of $x_1 = \alpha \dot{+} x_0$, but depending on the relative values of b, u_0, and c'_k this atom may be in x_0 or in α.

Case 1.

If $c'_k = (b')^r = b$, then this atom is always the same atom of x_0 and $u_k(x_k)$ is always an atom.

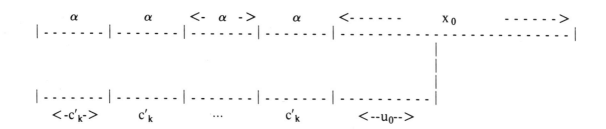

```
      α          α        <-  α  ->      α        <------          x0          ------>
|--------|--------|--------|--------|-------------------------------|
                                                      |
                                                      |
                                                      |
|--------|--------|--------|--------|-------------|
  <-c'k->     c'k       ...      c'k     <--u0-->
```

$c'_k = b.u_0$ always "strikes" x_0 at the same place.

Case 2.

If $c'_k = (b')^p$, $0 \leqslant p \leqslant r$, then after a finite number of steps, say m steps, the atom selected in $\alpha \dot{+} \cdots \dot{+} \alpha \dot{+} x_0$, where $\dot{+}$ appears $m + 1$ times, will be in α.

Let n be the least common multiple of p and r. Let $x_0,\ldots,x_{m+n}$ a sequence for which we have verified that atom $u_i(x_i)$ = True, $0 \leqslant i \leqslant m+n$. The reduction function u_{m+n+1} applied to x_{m+n+1} reaches the same place in α as u_m applied to x_m which is an atom by hypothesis.

It follows that if $u_k(x_k)$ is an atom for the n + m + 1 first examples then $u_k(x_k)$ is an atom for any k. Since each x of the domain has the same structure as some x_k, the proof is completed for this case.

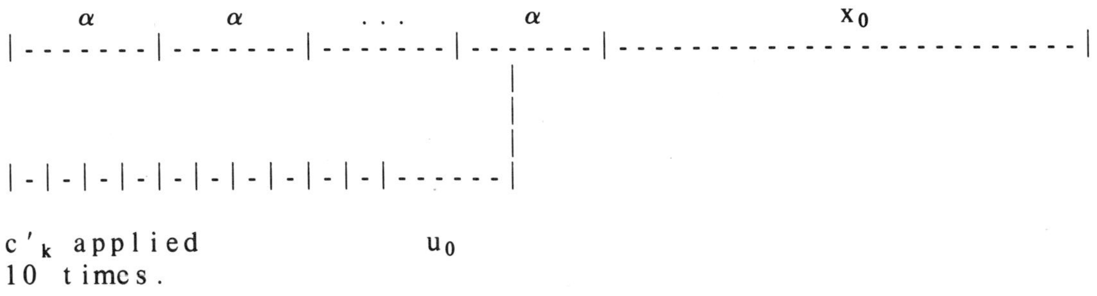

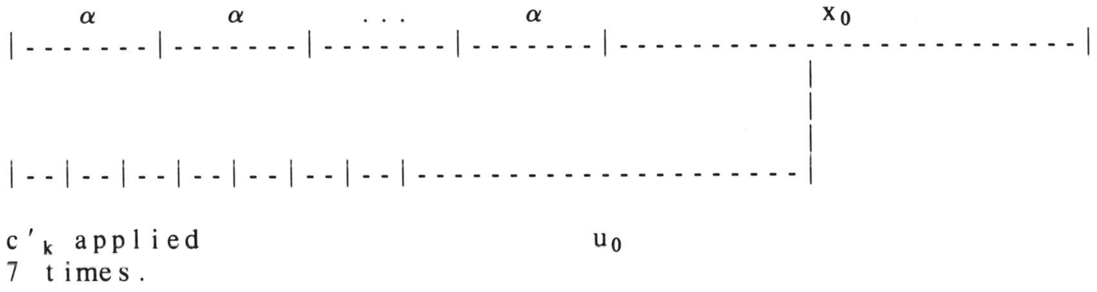

Here, $b=(b')^2$ and $c'_k = b'.u_0$ "strikes" two different places according to whether x_i contains an even or odd number of α's.

Case 3

If $c'_k = (b')^0$ = Identity, the same proof as in case 2 applies, except that it is enough to stop at x_m.

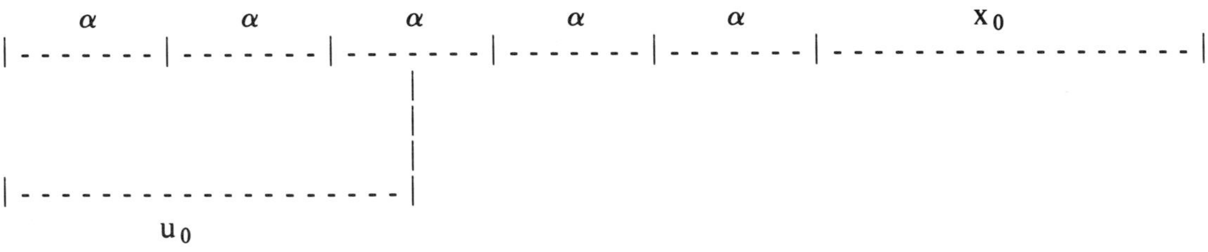

u_0 always "strikes" at the same place in α when at least three α's are added to x_0.

Remark 1. It follows that some recursion relations might appear on the very few first examples that would not be valid for all f_i. One has to verify the recursion relationships up to the $(n + m + 1)$th example in order to insure their validity.

B.6.3

We are now able to characterize the scheme of the functions we synthesize. They formally are instances of the scheme of theorem 2 and their semantics fulfill the restrictions 2.6.1 and 2.6.2.

The last restriction implies that the halting value of the functions of embedding 0 contains only atoms and term-type variables and constants. These term-type variables are in turn computed by functions of embedding 1 which fulfill the same condition. The value $g(\vec{x})$ is thus computed atom by atom, each being put into a frame which expresses the structure of $g(\vec{x})$.

C. The tranformation of f ↔f' where f(x) = f'(x').

This transformation is a simple consequence of the semantics of our scheme. We shall now define a domain adapted (Jouannaud and Kodratoff [1979] and Smith [1978]) to generating couple $[x_0, \alpha]$ because we shall restrict ourselves to this case during section 3.

Definition.

As in section 2.3, b is the functional name of the *-labelled atom in α and u is the functional name of the atom of x_0 which is in the direction of b. The cons-tree x *adapted* to a reduction function r is the smallest cons-tree such that atom.r(x) = True. For instance, let r = car.cdr.car then x has the structure

```
            cons
            /  \
     cons          nil
     /  \
A           cons
            /  \
     B             nil
```

because car.cdr.car(x) = B and any cons-tree which verifies this relation contains x. Let (x_0, α) be a linear ascending domain adapted to b, let x_i be the (i+1)-th representative of this domain and u_j^i, $j \leqslant n$, the functional names of the n non-nil atoms of x_i.

Let us further suppose that b does not contain car only, i.e., we rule out the (left) flat lists: (A), ((A)), (((A))), ... For the sake of simplicity, we shall study only the transformation when $X = \{x\}$ is any linear ascending domain and $X' = \{x'\}$ is the (right) flat lists: (A), (A B), (A B C), ...

Relation between X and X'.

For each x_i belonging to X, let x'_i = FLATTEN(x_i). One can compute directly (x'_0, α') by:

x'_0 = FLATTEN(x_0),

α' = FLATTEN(α) and the * label of α goes to nil in α'.

(there is only one nil since X' is the flat lists).

Because X is adapted, it is trivial that this transformation puts the atoms of any x into a one-to-one correspondence with the atoms of x'. For any f(x) whose halting values compute atoms only, it is therefore evident that f'(x') is obtained by replacing the functional values of these atoms in x by their corresponding values in x'. This is stated more precisely with the following conventions:

Let u_j^i be the functional names of atoms computed in the halting values of f or of functions called by f and u'^i_j the corresponding functional names in X'.

Let p'_0 correspond to p_0. If x_0 contains s non-nil atoms, then $p'_0 = \text{atom.}(\text{cdr})^s$.

Let β correspond to b. If α contains t non-nil atoms then $\beta = (\text{cdr})^t$.

Let γ'_i correspond to recursion relation of the x-typed variables c'_i.

If $b = (b')^r$ one knows that $c'_i = (b')^k$, $0 \leqslant k \leqslant r$, then, if b' contains m cdr, $\gamma'_i = (\text{cdr})^{k*m}$.

We define a transformation $f \rightarrow f'$ by: in the recursive scheme of f, replace $p_i(xx)$ by $p'_i(xx)$, replace u_i^j by u'^j_i, replace b by β, replace c'_i by γ'_i in each level of recursive definition. Then $f\{x\} = f'\{\text{FLATTEN}(x)\}$.

It is quite clear that the number of recursive calls and the names of the atoms can be put in a one-to-one correspondance, and since the halting values in f compute atoms only, f and f' will give the same result.

Example. Consider the sequence of examples:

$$(A) \rightarrow (A),\ (A(B)) \rightarrow ((A)B),\ (A(B(C))) \rightarrow (((A)B)C),\ \ldots$$

in its cons-tree form:

```
x0 =   cons      →      f(xi) =   cons
       /    \                     /    \
      A      nil                 A      nil
```

```
x1 =  cons            →      f(x1) =     cons
      /    \                              /      \
     A      cons                         /        \
           /    \                    cons           cons
        cons     nil                /    \         /    \
       /    \                      A     nil      B     nil
      B      nil
```

```
x1 = cons                  →     f(x2) =        cons
     /    \                                     /      \
    A      cons                                /        \
          /    \                         cons             cons
      cons      nil                     /    \            /    \
      /   \                            /      \          C     nil
     B     cons                    cons        cons
          /    \                  /    \      /    \
      cons      nil              A     nil   B     nil
      /   \
     C     nil
```

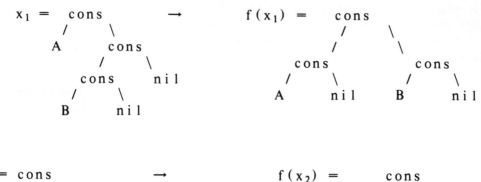

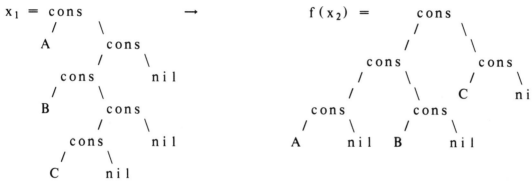

The cons-tree form tells at once that in x_i

$$A = car(x_i),\ B = car.car.cdr(x_i),\ C = car.car.cdr.car.cdr(x_i)$$

and $\{x_i\}$ is generated by

```
                                      cons
             cons                     /  \
(x0 = [     /   \      ] ,  α = [ A        cons            ] ),
       A          nil                      /  \
                                      B*         nil
```

$p_0(x) = atom.cdr(x)$ since nil is in the direction of b,

$p_{i+1}(x) = p_i(car.cdr.(x))$.

One finds the recursion relations between f_i and f_{i+1}:

$$f_i(x) = g_i(x, car(x), nil)$$

$$g_0(x,y,z) = \left[\begin{array}{ccc} & cons & \\ & / \quad \backslash & \\ y & & z \end{array}\right]$$

$$g_{i+1}(x,y,z) = g_i\left(car.cdr(x),\ \left[\begin{array}{ccc} & cons & \\ & / \quad \backslash & \\ y & & z \end{array}\right],\ \left[\begin{array}{ccc} & cons & \\ & / \quad \backslash & \\ \begin{array}{c} car \\ car \\ cdr \\ x \end{array} & & nil \end{array}\right]\right).$$

By an application of theorem 2 these relations are equivalent to the program:

$$F(x) = G(x, car(x), nil)$$

$$G(x,y,z) = \text{IF } atom.cdr(x) \text{ THEN } \left[\begin{array}{ccc} & cons & \\ & / \quad \backslash & \\ y & & z \end{array}\right]$$

$$\text{ELSE } G\left(car.cdr(x),\ \left[\begin{array}{ccc} & cons & \\ & / \quad \backslash & \\ y & & z \end{array}\right],\ H(x)\right)$$

$$H(x) = \left[\begin{array}{ccc} & cons & \\ & / \quad \backslash & \\ \begin{array}{c} car \\ car \\ cdr \\ x \end{array} & & nil \end{array}\right]$$

The domain {FLATTEN} (x) } is given by

$$FLATTEN(x_0) = (A),\ FLATTEN(x_1) = (A\ B),\ FLATTEN(x_2) = (A\ B\ C)$$

and therefore

$$p'_0(x') = atom.cdr(x),\ p'_{i+1}(x') = p'_i(cdr(x))$$

it follows that the halting condition must not be changed but the x-typed variable which recurs like car.cdr(x) must now recur like cdr(x). The halting condition of G contains no reduction function; it is therefore unchanged. The function H is a constant function which stops always at cons(car.car.cdr(x),nil) and since for all x_i, car.car.cdr(x_i) (i.e. B) corresponds to car.cdr(FLATTEN(x_i)), car.car.cdr must be substituted by car.cdr. In the initialization of F, car(x) corresponds to car(x). It follows that F'(x), now defined on the flat lists, computes the same value as F(x) (defined on the above domain).

```
F'(x)   = G'(x,car(x),nil)

G'(x,y,z) = IF atom.cdr(x) THEN   (    cons     )
                                  (    /  \     )
                                  ( y        z  )

            ELSE G(cdr(x),        (    cons     )
                                  (    /  \     )  ,H'(x))
                                  ( y        z  )

H'(x)  =  (      cons          )
          (      /  \          )
          ( car          nil   )
          ( cdr                )
          (  x                 )
```

Remark on the Usefulness of the Transformation

F' is much simpler than F and this transformation may optimize the computation. In the same way, the synthesis of F' is much simpler than the synthesis of F. From a theoretical point of view it shows that all the adapted linear ascending domains are equivalent to some subset of the flat lists.

Remark on the Use of the Transformation

Useful or not, this transformation can be used as a synthesis device. One synthesizes from examples on x, then the specification: "transform the obtained program for x' " allows to obtain f'. The synthesis of f' goes through a synthesis from examples followed by a transformation.

D. All Level Defined Functions

A precise definition of an n-levels recursively defined function asks for a specific description of the lists.

Definitions

— Among the nodes of a binary tree let the *right-most nodes* R be recursively defined by: the root of the tree belongs to R and a node which is a right son of a node of R belongs to R. In

```
(     cons*                          )
(     /  \                           )
( A          cons*                   )
(            /  \                    )
(     cons          \                )
(     /  \           cons*           )
( B          nil     /  \            )
(                 C         nil      )
```

the starred cons are the right-most nodes.

— Let x be a cons-tree. A sub-list of *level* 1 is a left son of a right-most cons. In the above cons-tree, A,(B),C are sublists of level 1.

— Let R_n be the right-most nodes of a sub-list of level n. Then a sub-list of level n+1 is a left son of a cons of R_n.

In

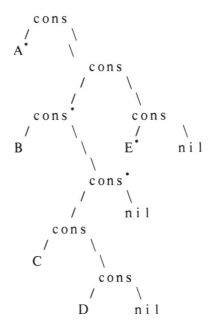

```
              cons
             /    \
           A*      \
                    cons
                   /    \
                  /      \
              cons*       cons
             /    \       /   \
           B       \    E*     nil
                    \
                    cons*
                   /    \
                  /     nil
               cons
              /    \
             C      \
                    cons
                   /    \
                  D      nil
```

the starred sub-lists are of level 1. Its right-most cons are therefore in R_1. The sub-list

```
(     cons                 )
      /  \                 
 C          cons           
            /  \           
      D            nil     )
```

is left son of a cons in R_1, this sub-list is of level 2.

— let F be a function defined on the flat lists only and F' be the all-levels recursively defined function associated to F. We shall first define F' by its semantics.

The computation of F'(x) is carried as follows: all sub-lists of level 0 in x are given a symbolic name s_i^0, i.e. x is re-written as $(s_1^0,\ldots, s_n^0)$ which is a flat list. The first computation of F'(x) is then carried on, it is the computation of $F((s_1^0,\ldots,s_n^0))$. The same operation is recursively applied to each s_i^0 in $F((s_1^0,\ldots,s_n^0))$ as long as s_j^i is not an atom.

Syntactic Definition of F'

We said that F' is derived from F because it works like F on sub-lists of x, this being repeated at each level. Let F be a function which computes F(x) atom by atom, F might not belong to the scheme of theorem 2 but it will anyway have a halting value like the halting values of our scheme: it contains cons the sons of which are cons, a reduction function which computes atoms only: u^i x^i, constants and term-typed variables. These last variables are also computed by functions that compute their result atom by atom.

The construction of F' follows its semantics. F'(x) will have the same overall structure as F except when $u^i x^i$ are computed in F or the functions called by F. Each $u^i x^i$ is replaced by a program which is:

$$\text{If atom}(u^i x^i) \text{ THEN } u^i x^i$$
$$\text{ELSE } F'(u^i x^i).$$

It could be possible to prove formally by induction on the level that the syntactic F'(x) will have the behavior of the F'(x) defined by its semantics. This proof is quite trivial since it is evident that the syntactic F'(x) will compute level by level as far as F computes atom by atom.

Example. We have elsewhere given examples of this transformation in the frame of our scheme (Jouannaud and Kodratoff [1979]). We shall now give an example which does not belong to our scheme.

Let fib(x) be a FIBONACCI-like function defined on flat lists. The length of fib(x) equals the length of fib(cdr(x)) plus the length of fib(cdr(cdr(x))).

```
fib(x)  =  fi(x,nil)
                                              cons
fi(x,z)  =  IF  atom.cdr(x)  THEN             /  \
                                          car      z
                                           x
                                                                   cons
                              ELSE  IF  atom.cdr(x)  THEN          /  \
                                                              car      z
                                                               x
                                                        ELSE
                                      fi(cdr(x),fi(cdr.cdr(x),z))
```

We obtain the function fiball(x), the all-level recursively defined function associated to fib(x), by transforming the car(x) of

```
      cons
      /  \
  car      z
   x
```

into:

```
IF atom.car(x) THEN car(x)
          ELSE  fiball(car(x))
```

One therefore has:

```
fiball(x) = fiall(x,nil)

fiall(x,z) = IF atom.cdr(x) THEN              cons
                                              /    \
                                             /      \
                                            /        z
     ______________________________________/___
     | IF atom.car(x) THEN car(x)              |
     |                ELSE fiball(car(x))      |
     |_________________________________________|

                                ELSE

                 IF atom.cdr.cdr(x) THEN       cons
                                              /    \
                                             /      \
                                            /        z
      _____________________________________/___
      | IF atom.car(x) THEN car(x)             |
      |                ELSE fiball(car(x))     |
      |________________________________________|

                                 ELSE fiall(cdr(x),fiall(cdr.cdr(x),z)).
```

The reader can easily verify that fib((A B)) = (A), fib((A B C)) = (B C),fib((A B C D E)) = (D E D D E),

fiball((A(B C D)(E F G H)(I J K)(L M)) = ((J K)(L)(J K)(L)(J K)(J K)(L))

One sees that

$$x=(A(B\ C\ D)(E\ F\ G\ H)(I\ J\ K)(L\ M))=(s_1^0\ s_2^0\ s_3^0\ s_4^0\ s_5^0)$$

with $s_4^0 = (I\ J\ K)$ and $s_5^0 = (L\ M)$

The semantic definition of fiball implies that fiball computes first

$$fib((s_1^0 s_2^0 s_3^0 s_4^0 s_5^0)) = s_4^0 s_5^0 s_4^0 s_4^0 s_5^0)$$

This operation is recursively applied to this list and since $fib(s_4^0)$=fib((I J K))=(J K) and $fib(s_5^0)$ = (L), one verifies that fiball(x) is the good result.

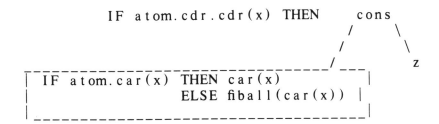

Remark. This transformation solves the following problem. We have said that we are able to synthesize functions whose domain is linear ascending. One could try to synthesize all-level recursively defined functions from examples given on sequences of linear ascending domains from the (right) flat lists: (A),(A B),(A B C),... to the left flat lists: (A),((A)),(((A))), · · · . The methodology we advise is a combination of synthesis from examples and from transformations: give the examples on the flat list and add the specification "to be extended to all-level" which will imply the above transformation of the synthesized function.

Extension up the n-th level

Let F(x) a function defined on the flat list, let F'(x) be the associated all-levels recursively defined function, then we shall call the extension of F(x) up to the n-th level the function $F'_n(x,n)$ where $F'_n(x,n)$ works like F'(x) on the sub-lists of level $m \leqslant n$, and like F(x) on the sub-lists of level $m > n$. $F'_n(x,n)$ has the same overall structure as F'(x) except that each function contains the variable n. In the recursive calls that exist in F(x), n is not transformed. In the recursive calls introduced in F'(x), n becomes $n-1$, and the halting condition atom.$u^i(x^i)$ becomes (n=0) OR (atom.$u^i(x^i)$).

Example. fiball becomes fibaIln:

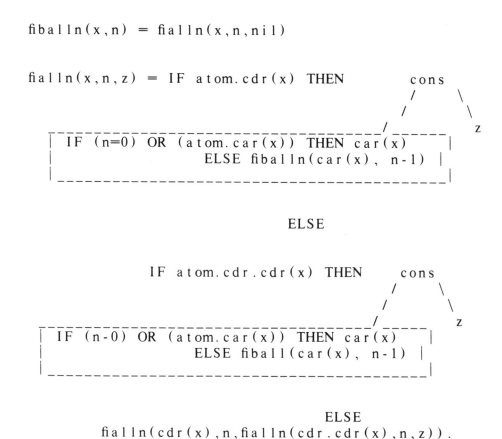

```
fiballn(x,n) = fialln(x,n,nil)

fialln(x,n,z) = IF atom.cdr(x) THEN            cons
                                                /    \
                                               /      \
 ____________________________________________/______    z
| IF (n=0) OR (atom.car(x)) THEN car(x)              |
|                  ELSE fiballn(car(x), n-1)         |
|____________________________________________________|

                              ELSE

                 IF atom.cdr.cdr(x) THEN       cons
                                               /    \
                                              /      \
 ___________________________________________/______    z
| IF (n-0) OR (atom.car(x)) THEN car(x)             |
|                  ELSE fiball(car(x), n-1)         |
|___________________________________________________|

                                ELSE
          fialln(cdr(x),n,fialln(cdr.cdr(x),n,z)).
```

E. The Flattening of All-Level Defined Functions

Let F be a function defined on flat lists. Let F' be the all-level defined function associated to F. We want to transform F' into F'' such that $F''(x) = \text{FLATTEN}(F'(x))$. F' checks the atomic nature of each embedding level of x, F' contains thus explicitly the specification of the embeddings computed in F'(x). One can imagine a first transformation: each time an expression the atomicity of which is not checked is consed in the result, replace cons by appen. The function appen is nearly the classical APPEND, except that it must make the difference between nil and other atoms:

```
appen(x,y)  =  IF(x=nil) THEN y
                         ELSE IF atom(x) THEN cons(x,y)
                              ELSE APPEND(x,y).
```

This transformation has no limitation but will not be further described here since it leads to no new result. On the contrary, we shall study another transformation which applies to a very restricted scheme:

— F'(x) takes always the form F'(x)=FF'(x,nil) with only one accumulator.

— all the halting level in F' and the programs it calls contain only one term-typed variable and have a flat list form: the atoms computed by $u_j^ix^i$ are consed in the term-typed variable. This means that the halting values of F and the programs called by it are:

```
        cons
       /    \
  ui1x1      .
              .
               .
                \
                 cons
                /    \
           uipxp      z
```

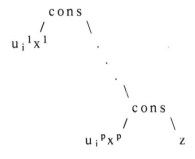

They become in FF':

```
                                   cons
                                  /    \
                                 /      .
IF atom(ui1x1) THEN ui1x1                .
               ELSE FF'(ui1x1)            .
                                           .
                                            \
                                             cons
                                            /    \
                                           /      z
           IF atom(uipxp) THEN uipxp
                          ELSE FF'(uipxp)
```

We now define F'' by the following transformation: F''(x) = FF''(x,nil) and F'' recurs like FF' but its halting values are:

IF $atom(u_i^1x^1)$ THEN $cons(u_i^1x^1, \cdots,$ IF atom $(u_i^px^p)$ THEN $cons(u_i^px^p, z)...)$

ELSE $F''(u_i^px^p, z)...)$

ELSE $F''(u_i^1x^1, \ldots,$ IF $atom(u_i^px^p)$ THEN $cons(u_i^px^p, z)...)$

ELSE $F''(u_i^px^p, z)...)$

Otherwise stated, if $u_i^jx^j$ is an atom then the sub-tree of the halting value in F:

```
(          \                  )
            cons
            /  \
   u_i^j x^j        \
```

is not changed, but if u_i^j is not an atom it becomes

```
(          \                  )
            F''
            /  \
   u_i^j x^j        \
```

When we use this transformation, on the one hand the recursive calls necessary when $u_i^jx^j$ is not an atom are kept as in F' but, on the other hand, the flat list structure of the halting values is also kept because each halting value has a flat list structure. We shall study this transformation on an example issued from $F(x) = x$ synthesized on flat lists. The transformation of section 4 is used in order to obtain an $F'(x) = x$ defined at all-levels, then $F''(x) = FLATTEN(F'(x)) = FLATTEN(x)$. The interest of this transformation lies in the fact that F'' is quite efficient.

E.1 The Synthesis of $F(x) = x$

Recall first that we can synthesize functions that build their result atom by atom. We thus cannot synthesize the identity which builds x in one piece. We shall obtain a function which constructs again x from its atoms, i.e. a COPY function. The input-output sequence is

$$\{x_0 = (A) \rightarrow f(x_0) = A \; ; \; x_1 = (A\ B) \rightarrow f(x_1) = (A\ B\ C) \rightarrow f(x_2) = (A\ B\ C); \cdots \}$$

We deduce from it the following predicates and computation trace sequences:

$p_0(x)$ = (atom(cdr x)) → $f_0(x)$ = (cons(car x)nil);

$p_1(x)$ = (atom(cddr x)) → $f_1(x)$ = (cons(car x)(cons(cadr x)nil));

p_2 (x) = (atom(cdddr x)) -> f_2 (x) = (cons(car x)(cons(cadr x)
(cons(caddr x)nil))); ...

Matching p_i and p_{i+1} leads trivially to the recursion relation $p_{i+1}(x) = p_i(cdr(x))$. Matching f_i and the "tail" of f_{i+1} (as the arrows show) leads to the recursion relation:

$$f_{i+1}(x) = cons(car(x),\ f_i(cdr(x)))$$

which we shall rather write for further transformation purposes:

$$f_{i+1}(x) = h(x,f_i(cdr(x)))$$

where

$$h(x,z) = (cons(car\ x)z).$$

We finally obtain a program whose stopping conditions are given by the first predicate and the first trace and whose recursive body is given by the recursion relations:

```
COPY(x) = IF atom.cdr(x) THEN cons(car(x),nil)
                         ELSE H(x, COPY(cdr(x)))
H(x,z) = cons(car(x),z)
```

The Synthesis of F'(x') = x' (all-levels)

The function copy is defined on flat lists only. We shall apply the transformation of section 4 in order to obtain an all-level recursively defined function. The only appearance, in the halting conditions of COPY and H, of a reduction function is car which is transformed into IF atom.car(x) THEN car(x) ELSE F'(car(x)). One obtains:

```
COPYALL(x) = IF atom.cdr(x) THEN IF atom.car(x) THEN
                                   cons(car(x),nil)
                                       ELSE
                                 cons(COPYALL(car(x)),nil)
                             ELSE HALL(x,COPYALL(cdr(x)))
HALL(x,z) = IF atom.car(x) THEN cons(car(x),z)
                           ELSE cons(COPYALL(car(x)),z)
```

The Synthesis of FLATTEN(F′(x′)) = FLATTEN(x′)

COPY does not present the required form since it is not rewritten as FF(x,nil). We first put it in the required form by writing

```
COPY(x)=COPY(x,nil)
COPY(x,z) = IF atom.cdr(x) THEN cons(car(x),z)
                           ELSE H(x,COPY(cdr(x),z))
```

where H is the same as in the above COPY. The new variable z undergoes no substitution, its value will always be z=nil. One would obtain in the same way a COPYALL(x,z) where z has always the value nil. We apply now the transformation of this section: cons(COPYALL(car(x)),z) which is now present in COPYALL and HALL must become FF"(car(x),z) since we know in this call that car(x) is not atomic. One obtains:

```
MQFLAT(x) = FLATTEN(x)
          = FQQ(x,nil)
FQQ(x,z) = IF atom.cdr(x) THEN IF atom.car(x) THEN cons(car(x),z)[FQQ1]

                                ELSE FQQ(car(x),z)[FQQ3]

                   ELSE HQQ(x,FQQ(cdr(x),z))[FQQ4]


HQQ(x,z) = IF atom.car(x) THEN cons(car(x),z)

                 ELSE  FQQ(car(x),z)
```

We shall characterize the called instance of FQQ by the number which points toward it.

When (MQFLAT)'(A)) is evaluated, only 1 call to FQQ1 is needed. When one adds one atom in the list then (MQFLAT'(A B)) calls FQQ1 then HQQ (thus FQQ4), i.e. each new atom induces 2 new recursive calls. When one adds a nesting level, MQFLAT applied to ((A)) needs a call to FQQ1 and a call to FQQ2, i.e., each nesting level adds only 1 supplementary recursive call. It follows that if x contains n atoms and m pairs of parentheses, 2n+m−2 calls to FQQ and HQQ are needed.

Comparison with MCFLAT

An efficient function FLATTEN is "well-known" and due to McCarthy (Moore [1979]). We give below a version of it, using the predicates NULL and ATOM.

```
MCFLAT = FOO(x,nil)
FOO(x,z) = IF(x=nil) THEN z
                ELSE IF atom(x) THEN cons(x,z)
                       ELSE
                         FOO(car(x),FOO(cdr(x),z))
```

In order to study the complexity of this function we shall count the number of times FOO is called when one evaluates (MCFLAT X) where X is a list containing n atoms and m couples of parentheses. In an intuitive way, consider first the list (A) which leads to 3 calls of FOO (the initial one and then 2 recursive calls). When an atom is added to it, say X becomes (A B), 5 calls to FOO are necessary, i.e. we add 2 new calls to FOO per new atom. The same is true when one considers ((A)), i.e. we add 2 calls by new nesting level. This means that FOs by new nesting level. This means that FOO is called $2n + 2m - 1$ times by MCFLAT the complexity of which is the complexity of MQFLAT + m - 1. It is difficult to say that our program is "better" than McCarthy's since the stopping conditions are not the same and since we use cross-recursion. We therefore do not claim that each LISP system should implement MQFLAT. It is nevertheless surprising that a transformation which is systematic enough to be implemented, i.e. a program that can be automatically synthesized can well challenge the programs due to very skillful programmers.

Remark. As we hinted at in the beginning of this section, it could be possible to define a more general flattening transformation. When the above transformation is not allowed, then replace cons by appen.

F. Conclusion

We presented a methodology for program synthesis which mixes synthesis from examples and program transformation. A first version of the desired program is obtained by its input-output behavior and the definitive version is obtained by a transformation of the first one, this transformation being induced by a specification. It must be noticed that the main task is then to define a set of "suitable" specifications, suitable being understood relatively to the domain and relatively to the problem to be solved. The solution we propose to program synthesis from examples is a kind of unification algorithm which unifies sequences of terms rather than two terms. It is a convenient (and theoretically sound!) way to express the fact that one induces from a set of examples by putting into evidence what is common to all the examples and what are the common differences between different examples. From the theoretical point of view, we are not totally satisfied because we have not yet proved the soundness of our methodology. It may happen that we are able to synthesize different programs from one set of examples. How can we be sure that these programs are equivalent? How many examples are necessary to insure this equivalence? An answer to these questions is equivalent to a LaGrange theorem (stated for polynomials on the reals) for the trees of polynomial increase.

G. Acknowledgements

We thank E. Papon who implemented the BMWk algorithm for the synthesis from input-output behavior and F. Dupuy who implemented the transformations for the three specifications developed in the text.

H. APPENDIX

If we start from n examples, we get a computation trace which contains n embedded IF...THEN...ELSE... statements. (See section B.4.)

Theorem 1 Let

$$F_n(x) = \text{IF } p_0(x) \text{ THEN } f_0(x) \text{ ELSE}$$

$$\text{IF } p_1(x) \text{ THEN } f_1(x) \text{ ELSE } \ldots$$

$$\text{IF } p_n(x) \text{ THEN } f_n(x) \text{ ELSE } \perp$$

$$(\perp \text{ is the undefined value})$$

be a trace where $p_{i+1}(x) = p_i(b(x))$, $f_i(x) = g_i(\vec{a}(x))$, $g_{i+1}(\vec{x}) = h(\vec{x}, g_i(\vec{c}(\vec{x})))$ where p_0,b,h, f_0 and the functions contained in the vectors $\vec{a}$ and $\vec{c}$ are strict and monotonic (Manna *et al.* [1973]). Then, the limit of $F_n(x)$ when n tends towards infinity is strongly equivalent to $F(x)$,$F(x) = f_\tau(x,\vec{a}(x))$ where f_τ is the least fixed point of the functional τ defined by:

$$\tau[G](xx,\vec{x}) = \text{IF } p_0(xx) \text{ THEN } g_0(\vec{x})$$

$$\text{ELSE } h(\vec{x}, xx, G(b(xx), \vec{c}(\vec{x}))).$$

Proof:

First part: equivalence of τ with a generalized trace.

Let $G_n(xx,\vec{x})$ be the trace:

$$G_n(xx,\vec{x}) = \text{IF } p_0(xx) \text{ THEN } g_0(\vec{x}) \text{ ELSE} \ldots$$

$$\text{IF } p_n(xx) \text{ THEN } g_n(\vec{x}) \text{ ELSE } \perp.$$

Let Ω be the everywhere undefined function (i.e. $\Omega(x) = \perp$ for all x). We shall prove that G_{n-1} and $\tau^n[\Omega]$ are identical. We use computational induction (Scott [1970]).

+ *initial step*

$G_0(xx,\vec{x}) =$ IF $p_0(xx)$ THEN $g_0(\vec{x})$ ELSE $\bot=\tau[\Omega](xx,\vec{x})$

since h is supposed to be strict and $h(\vec{x},xx,\Omega(b(xx),c(\vec{x}))) = h(\vec{x},\bot) = \bot$.

+ *induction step*

The induction hypothesis is $\tau^n[\Omega](xx,\vec{x}) = G_{n-1}(xx,\vec{x})$ from which we want to prove that $\tau^{n+1}[\Omega](xx,\vec{x}) = G_n(xx,\vec{x})$.

By definition of τ,

$\tau^{n+1}[\Omega](xx,\vec{x}) = \tau[\tau^n[\Omega]](xx,\vec{x})$

$= \tau[G_{n-1}](xx,\vec{x})$ (by induction hypothesis)

$=$ IF $p_0(xx)$ THEN $g_0(\vec{x})$

ELSE $h(\vec{x},\alpha,G_{n-1}(b(xx),\vec{c}(\vec{x})))$ by definition.

We use the definition of G_{n-1} and the distributivity of h relative to the conditional (Manna *et al.* [1973]):

$\tau_{n+1}[\Omega](xx,\vec{x}) =$ IF $p_0(xx)$ THEN $g_0(\vec{x})$ ELSE

IF $p_0(b(xx))$ THEN $h(\vec{x},xx, g_0(\vec{cx})))$ ELSE

IF $p_{x-1}(b(xx))$ THEN $h(\vec{x},xx, g_{n-1}(\vec{c}(\vec{x})))$ ELSE $\bot$.

Using now the recursion relation we find finally that $\tau^{n-1}[\Omega](xx,\vec{x}) = G_n(xx,\vec{x})$ which was to be proven.

Second part: We have still to prove that $F_n(x) = G_n(x,\vec{a}(x))$. The following instantiation lemma, with $\vec{a}^* = (I,\vec{a})$ where I is the identity, proves our point.

The instantiation lemma:

Let G_n be a trace, i.e. a chain the domain of definition of which increases with n. It has therefore a limit when n tends to infinity; let G be this limit. Let $\vec{a}^*$ be a vector of monotonous functions. Then, the chain $F_n(x) = G_n(\vec{a}^*(x))$ tends toward $G(\vec{a}^*(x))$ when n tends toward infinity.

Proof:

It follows from the continuity of the functional: $\rho[H](x) = H(\vec{a}^*(x))$ and from the chain property of F_n and G_n:

$$\lim F_n(x) = \lim \rho[G_n](x)) = \rho[\lim (G_n)](x)$$

$$= \rho[G](x) = G(\vec{a}^*(x)).$$

This ends theorem 1.

As seen above, the recursion relations that may be found are more complicated than those allowed by theorem 1: we need to generalize them to any level of embedded recursive calls.

Definition. A sequence f_i is defined by embedded recursive calls and will be further named a *recurrent* sequence, if it is defined by:

$$\text{either (1)} \quad f_1(x) = g_i(\vec{a}(x))$$

$$g_{i+1}(\vec{x}) = h(\vec{x},g_i(\vec{c}(\vec{x})))$$

$$\text{or} \quad (2) \quad f_i(x) = g_i(\vec{a_i}(x))$$

$$g_{i+1}(\vec{x}) = h_i(\vec{x},g_i(\vec{c}(\vec{x})))$$

where the sequences $\vec{a_i}$; $h_i,\vec{c_i}$ are themselves recurrent sequences.

A trace is said to be recurrent when $p_{i+1}(x) = p_i(b(x))$ and the sequence of fragments is recurrent.

Examples: In section B.5, example 1 has a recurrent trace where g_i are recurrent of type (2), while h_i are of type (1). Example 4 has f_i of type (1) and h_i of type (2). In example 3, one has $f_i(x) = h_i(x,g_i(x))$ so that the vector $\vec{a_i}$ reduces to the function g_i.

Theorem 2. The limit $F(x)$ of a recurrent trace is given

- in case (1), by theorem 1.

— in case (2), by the following. One has

$F_n(x)$=IF $p_{0(xx)}$ THEN $f_0(x)$ ELSE...

IF $p_n(xx)$ THEN $f_n(x)$ ELSE $\perp$, with the relations:

$$p_{i+1}(x) = p_i(b(x)),\ f_i(x) = g_i(a_{\vec{i}}(x)),$$

$$g_{i+1}(\vec{x}) = h_i(\vec{x}, g_i(c_{\vec{i}}(\vec{x}))).$$

$F(x) = \lim F_n(x) = f_\tau(x,\vec{A}(x,x))$ where f_τ is the least fixed point of the functional

$$\tau[G](xx,\vec{x}) = \text{IF } p_0(xx) \text{ THEN } g_0(\vec{x})$$

$$\text{ELSE } H(xx,\vec{x},G(b(xx),\vec{C}(xx,\vec{x})))$$

where $\vec{A},\vec{C}$, H are the limits of the recurrent traces:

$$A_{\vec{n}}(xx,x) = \text{IF } p_0(xx) \text{ THEN } \vec{a_0}(x) \text{ ELSE...}$$

$$\text{IF } p_n(xx) \text{ THEN } a_{\vec{n}}(x) \text{ ELSE } \perp,$$

$$C_{\overrightarrow{n-1}}(\text{ IF } p_1(xx) \text{ THEN } c_{\vec{0}}(\vec{x}) \text{ELSE ...}$$

$$\text{IF } p_n(xx) \text{ THEN } c_{\overrightarrow{n-1}}(\vec{x}) \text{ ELSE } \perp,$$

$$H_{n-1}(xx,\vec{x},y) = \text{IF } p_1(xx) \text{ THEN } h_0(\vec{x},y) \text{ELSE ...}$$

$$\text{IF } p_{n-1}(xx) \text{ THEN } h_{n-1}(\vec{x},y) \text{ ELSE } \perp .$$

When one starts with n fragments, the functions $\vec{C}$ and H are defined from $n-1$ fragments generated as subproblems of the original problem. This explains why we have chosen to write $g_{i+1}(\vec{x}) = h_i(\vec{x}, g_i(c_{\vec{i}}(\vec{x})))$ which, in turn, implies that c_0 and h_0 must be associated to $p_1(xx) =$ True.

Proof:

It uses a double recurrence, first on n as in theorem 1, second on the recurrent property of the trace F_n. It uses also the fact that H is strict if h_0 is strict, which we suppose to be true.

— if F_n is of type (1) one then comes back to theorem 1

— if F_n is of type (2) then one proves first that $\tau^{n+1}[\Omega] = G_n$, then that $G_n(x,\vec{A}(x,x)) = F_n(x)$.
+ *prove that* $\tau^{n+1}[\Omega] = G_n$

The initial step is identical to the initial step in theorem 1. The induction step: (the induction hypothesis is $\tau^n[\Omega] = G_{n-1}$)

$\tau^{n+1}[\Omega](xx,\vec{x}) = \tau[\tau^n[\Omega]](xx,\vec{x})$

$= \tau[G_{n-1}(xx,\vec{x})](xx,\vec{x})$ (induction hypothesis)

$=$ IF $p_0(xx)$ THEN $g_0(\vec{x})$

ELSE $H(xx,\vec{x}, G_{n-1}(b(xx), \vec{C}(xx,\vec{x})))$
(definition of τ)

$=$ IF $p_0(xx)$ THEN $g_0(\vec{x})$ ELSE

IF $p_0(b(xx))$ THEN $H(xx,\vec{x},g_0(\vec{C}(xx,\vec{x})))$ ELSE ...

IF $p_{n-1}(b(xx))$ THEN $H(xx,\vec{x},g_{n-1}(\vec{C}(xx,\vec{x})))$ ELSE

$H(xx,xvec,\perp)$ (definition of G_{n-1} and distributivity of H relative to the conditional) $=$ IF $p_0(xx)$ THEN $g_0(\vec{x})$ ELSE

IF $p_1(xx)$ THEN $H(xx,\vec{x},g_0(\vec{C}(xx,\vec{x})))$ ELSE ⋯

IF $p_n(xx)$ THEN $H(xx,\vec{x},g_{n-1}(\vec{C}(xx,\vec{x})))$ ELSE $\perp$.
(recursion property of p_i,H is strict).

We must now induce on the recurrent form of F_n. It is quite evident that if $p_i(xx) = $ True then

$$H_n(xx,\vec{x},y) = h_{i-1}(\vec{x},y) \text{ for all } n \geqslant i \text{ and}$$

$$C_{\vec{n}}(xx,\vec{x}) = c_{\overrightarrow{i-1}}(\vec{x}) \text{ for all } n \geqslant i.$$

But our induction hypothesis says that $\vec{C}$ and H are limits of traces H_n and $C_{\vec{n}}$ it follows that if $p_i(xx) = $ True then $H(xx,\vec{x},y) = h_{i-1}(\vec{x},y)$ and $\vec{C}(xx,\vec{x})$ $c_{\overrightarrow{i-1}}(\vec{x})$. We can now write:

$$\tau_{n+1}[\Omega](xx,\vec{x}) = \text{IF } p_0(xx) \text{ THEN } g_0(\vec{x}) \text{ ELSE}$$

$$\text{IF } p_1(xx) \text{ THEN } h_0(\vec{x},g_0(c_{\vec{0}}(\vec{x})))\text{ELSE} \ldots$$

$$\text{IF } p_n(xx) \text{ THEN } h_{n-1}(\vec{x}, g_{n-1}(c_{\overrightarrow{n-1}}(\vec{x})))\text{ELSE} \perp.$$

Using the recursion relations of the g_i, it follows

$$\tau^{n+1}[\Omega](xx,\vec{x}) = G_n(xx,\vec{x})$$

+ Prove that $G_n(x,\vec{A}(x,x)) = F_n(x)$

$\vec{A}$ is the limit of traces $\vec{A_n}(xx,x)$ and $p_i(xx) = $ True implies $\vec{A}(xx_i,x) = a_{\vec{i}}(x)$. It follows that:

$$F_n(x) = \text{IF } p_0(x) \text{ THEN } f_0(x) \text{ ELSE } \ldots$$

$$\text{IF } p_n(x) \text{ THEN } f_n(x) \text{ ELSE } \bot.$$

$$= \text{IF } p_0(x) \text{ THEN } g_0(a_0(x)) \text{ ELSE } \cdots$$

$$\text{IF } p_n(x) \text{ THEN } g_n(a_n(x)) \text{ ELSE } \bot.$$

(since $f_i(x) = g_i(a_i(x))$)

$$= \text{IF } p_0(x) \text{ THEN } g_0(\vec{A}(x,x)) \text{ ELSE } \ldots$$

$$\text{IF } p_n(x) \text{ THEN } g_n(\vec{A}(x,x)) \text{ ELSE } \bot.$$

(since $p_i(x)$ = True implies $\vec{A}(x,x)$ $= a_i(x)$)

$$= G_n(x,\vec{A}(x,x)).$$

The instantiation lemma implies that their limits are equal, which completes the proof.

References

Biermann [1978]
A.W. Biermann, "The inference of regular LISP programs from examples," I.E.E.E. Trans. on Systems, Man and Cybernetics, Vol. SMC−8 (1978), pp. 585−600.

Biermann and Smith [1977]
A.W. Biermann and D.R. Smith, "The hierarchal synthesis of LISP scanning programs," Information Processing 77, B. Gilchrist, ed., North Holland (1977), pp. 41−45.

Hardy [1975]
J. Hardy, "Synthesis of LISP functions from examples," Proc. 4th IJCAI, (1975), pp. 268−273.

Huet [1976]
G. Huet, "Unification dans les th'ories d'ordre 1,2,...,ω," Th'se de doctorat, Universit' Paris 7 (1976).

Green, Waldinger, Barstow, Elschlager, Lenat, McCune, Shaw and Steinberg [1974]
C.C. Green, R.J. Waldinger, D.R. Barstow, Q. Elschlager, D.B. Lenat, B.P. McCune, D.E. Shaw, and L.I. Steinberg, "Progress report on program-understanding systems," Memo AIM−240, Report STAN−CS−74−444, A.I. Lab., Stanford (1974).

Jouannaud and Kodratoff [1979]
J.P. Jouannaud and Y. Kodratoff, "Characterization of a class of functions synthesized from examples by a SUMMERS like method using the BOYER-MOORE-WEGBREIT matching technique," Proc. 6th IJCAI, (1979), pp. 440−447.

Jouannaud and Kodratoff [1980]
J.P. Jouannaud and Y. Kodratoff, "An automatic construction of LISP program by transformation of functions synthesized from their input-output behavior," to appear in 2nd PAIS special issue on induction, P.S. Michalsky, ed., 1980.

Knuth and Bendix [1970]
D.E. Knuth and P.B. Bendix, "Work problems in universal algebras," in Computational Problems in Abstract Algebra, J. Leech, ed., (1970), pp. 263−297.

Kodratoff [1978]
Y. Kodratoff, "Choix d'un programme LISP correspondant ' un exemple," Congr's AFCET-IRIA reconnaissance des formes et traitement des images, Châtenay-Malabry (1978), pp. 212−219.

Kodratoff [1979]
Y. Kodratoff, "A class of functions synthesized from a finite number of examples and a LISP program scheme," Int. J. of Comp. and Inf. Sci. 8, (1979), pp. 489−521.

Kodratoff [1980]
Y. Kodratoff, "Un algorithme pour l'obtention de formes terminales recursives a partir de traces de calcul", Actes des journ'es francophones: production assist'e de logiciel, gen've, (1980), pp. 36−63.

Kodratoff and Fargues [1978]
Y. Kodratoff and J. Fargues, "A sane algorithm for the synthesis of LISP functions from example problems: the BOYER and MOORE algorithm," Proc. AISB meeting Hambourg, (1978), pp. 169−175.

Kodratoff and Jouannaud [1979]
Y. Kodratoff and J.P. Jouannaud, "Construction automatique ' partir d'exemples de fonctions de listes r'cursivement d'finies pour tous les niveaux d'imbrication de listes," Actes 2'mes congr's AFCET-IRIA reconnaissance des formes et intelligence artificielle, Toulouse (1979), pp. 162−171.

Kodratoff and Jouannaud [1980]
Y. Kodratoff and J.P. Jouannaud, "Mechanical construction of a new efficient FLATTEN," The LISP bulletin (1980), Greussay-Laubsch, eds., pp. 36−39.

Kodratoff and Papon [1980]
Y. Kodratoff and E. Papon, "A system for program synthesis and program optimization," Proc. AISB meeting, Amsterdam (1980), pp. 1−10.

Manna [1974]
Z. Manna, Mathematical theory of computation, McGraw-Hill (1974).

Manna, Ness and Vuillemin [1973]
Z. Manna, S. Ness, and J. Vuillemin, "Inductive methods for proving properties of programs," C. ACM 16, (1973), pp. 491−502.

Moore [1979]
J.S. Moore, "A tour through a working theorem prover," 4th Workshop on Artificial Intelligence, Bad Honnef (1979).

Papon [1980]
E. Papon, "Th'se de 3'me cycle, Universit' Paris-Sud (1980).

Plotkin [1970]
G.D. Plotkin, "A note on inductive generalization," Machine Intelligence 5, Meltzer and Michie, eds., (1970), pp. 153–163.

Reynolds [1970]
J.C. Reynolds, "Transformational systems and the algebraic structure of atomic formulas," Machine Intelligence 5, Miltzer and Michie, eds., (1970), pp. 135–151.

Robinson [1965]
J. A. Robinson, "A machine oriented logic based on the resolution principle," J. ACM 12, (1965), pp. 23–41.

Scott [1970]
D. Scott, "Outline of a mathematical theory of computation," 4th Annual Princeton Conf. Inf. Sci. and Syst. (1970), pp. 169–176.

Siklossy and Sykes [1975]
L. Siklossy and D.A. Sykes, "Automatic program synthesis from example problems," Proc. 4th IJCAI (1975), pp. 268–273.

Smith [1978]
J. P. Smith, "A class of synthesizeable LISP programs," Report CS–1977–4, Dept. of Computer Science, Duke University, 1978.

Summers [1977]
P.D. Summers, "A methodology for LISP program construction from examples," J. ACM (1977), 24, pp. 161–175.

CHAPTER 17

Dealing With Search

Alan W. Biermann
Duke University
Durham, NC 27710

A. Introduction

All of the program synthesis methods described in this volume involve search. Unfortunately, this means they are all computationally expensive and that a central issue in program synthesis is the problem of dealing with search. For example, if we study almost any methodology in this book, we see it requires about ten or fifteen steps to generate the example program described in Chapter 1. Furthermore, the number of different rules or transformations applicable at any given point is very large so the target program is at depth ten or more in a very bushy tree. If the target program is to be found via a uniform search of the tree, it will probably be out of range of any realistic automatic procedure simply because of the astronomical number of nodes that must be expanded before adequate depth would be reached.

The usual method for addressing such search problems is to apply "heuristic" methods that abridge the complete search tree by making guesses as to which paths to follow. Using analogies with human thought processes and other arguments, the system designers build strategies into the search program for eliminating vast portions of the tree and moving to search depths that would not otherwise be possible. Examples of this approach are described in many chapters of this book. This approach, however, has severe shortcomings because the tree pruning methods are not well understood and may remove the desired target node as well as many others from consideration. In fact, this problem seems to occur in computer chess programs and the result is that uniform search programs seem to be able to dominate heuristic programs. While heuristic methods seem to be the appropriate method for dealing with large search problems, they do not necessarily have a good record of success.

This chapter will argue for a third alternative which attempts to circumvent at least partially the problem of astronomical search and which avoids the dangers of heuristic methods. The technique is to define classes of programs that are much smaller than the set of all possible programs and to find synthesis methods for the individual classes. Since the classes are smaller, it is possible to move through the search to a much deeper level and to find much more complex programs. However, since the synthesis method can generate any member of the class, it can function as reliably as any traditional language compiler.

Using this approach, program synthesis is done as follows. We assume there is a list of classes of programs for which the synthesis problem is solved. Given a new synthesis problem, one attempts to solve it using one of the known synthesis methods. If one of the synthesis methods is successful, the solution is found efficiently and reliably. If none of the synthesis methods are applicable, less efficient or less reliable methods can be tried.

In this chapter, we describe two classes of LISP programs and their associated synthesis methods. Each synthesis procedure is vastly more efficient than a general synthesis method and is completely reliable. In fact, programs of the complexity of the example of Chapter 1 are well within the reach of these methods. In the following sections, we describe the classes of "regular" and "scanning" LISP programs and their associated construction algorithms.

B. Synthesis From Examples

We will first be interested in constructing programs in the class of "regular" LISP programs from examples of their behavior. As an illustration, if our system is presented with the input-output pair (A B C) yields (A), we want our system to find a program that will compute (A.NIL) whenever given an input (A.(B.(C.NIL))). Furthermore, we would like the generated program to do "all similar" calculations by some measure. If we are dissatisfied with the constructed program, we want to be able to give additional input-output pairs until the desired program is found. We want convergence to the target program with a minimal number of examples because the creation of such inputs may be tedious.

Our synthesis procedure will, in fact, have the following properties:

(1) Convergence to the class of regular LISP programs.
(2) Convergence on the basis of minimal input information.
(3) Robust behavior for a variety of inputs.

By (1) we mean that any member of the class or its equivalent can be synthesized by the method. By (2) we mean that no synthesis method could be created which could synthesize every regular LISP program with fewer examples than our method. By (3) we mean that one can choose examples randomly from the behavior of the target program and be sure convergence will be achieved. No carefully designed training process is necessary.

C. Regular LISP

We will be constructing programs from the following five primitives:

$$
\begin{aligned}
f_i(x) &= \text{NIL} \\
f_i(x) &= x \\
f_i(x) &= f_j(\text{car}(x)) \\
f_i(x) &= f_j(\text{cdr}(x)) \\
f_i(x) &= \text{cons}(f_j(x),\ f_k(x))
\end{aligned}
$$

The synthesis process will proceed by breaking the desired input-output relation into these primitives and constructing a general function by a merge operation. Thus if it is desired to generate a program which computes z = (A.NIL) from x = (A.(B.(C.NIL))), we can write z in terms of x as follows.

$$z = \text{cons}(\text{car}(x),\text{NIL})$$

In general, one can always find the composition of z in terms of x by the following construction.

$$
c(x,z) = \begin{cases} \text{NIL} & \text{if } z \text{ is NIL} \\ z \text{ written in terms of } x & \text{if } z \text{ is some atom of } x \\ \text{cons}(c(x,\text{car}(z)),c(x,\text{cdr}(2))) & \text{otherwise} \end{cases}
$$

After the composition of z in terms of x is found, its breakdown into primitive functions is straightforward. In fact, the example composition breaks down as follows:

$$
\begin{aligned}
f_1(x) &= \text{cons}(f_2(x),\ f_4(x)) \\
f_2(x) &= f_3(\text{car}(x)) \\
f_3(x) &= x \\
f_4(x) &= \text{NIL}
\end{aligned}
$$

It turns out that in many situations, there are several ways to decompose a relation into primitive functions. As designers of the synthesis procedure, we might find all possible decompositions and then do all possible mergers on those decompositions. However, it was found that most decompositions have some undesirable properties and actually only one is needed. We will use only decompositions which are both *direct* and free of *car-NIL* and *cdr-NIL instances.*

Directness requires two things. The first is that car and cdr operations be given precedence in the functional decomposition. That is, whenever there is a choice between selecting the cons operation and either car or cdr, one selects the latter. Suppose x = (A.B) and z = (A.A). Then we can write

$$
\begin{aligned}
f_1(x) &= \mathrm{cons}(f_2(x),\ f_3(x)) \\
f_2(x) &= f_4(\mathrm{car}(x)) \\
f_3(x) &= f_5(\mathrm{car}(x)) \\
f_4(x) &= x \\
f_5(x) &= x
\end{aligned}
$$

However, this violates directness because this same input-output relationship can be expressed with a breakdown that applies car before cons.

$$
\begin{aligned}
f_1(x) &= f_2(\mathrm{car}(x)) \\
f_2(x) &= \mathrm{cons}(f_3(x),\ f_4(x)) \\
f_3(x) &= x \\
f_4(x) &= x
\end{aligned}
$$

Direct calculations are usually more efficient because they avoid the unnecessary repetition of some car and cdr operations.

The second requirement for directness is that the calculations be finite. Thus there can be no infinite series of cons operations in a direct computation.

The other property we want is that the decompositions be free of car-NIL and cdr-NIL instances. Suppose a program f_1 has the form

$$
\begin{aligned}
f_1(x) &= f_2(\mathrm{car}(x)) \\
f_2(x) &= \mathrm{NIL}
\end{aligned}
$$

Then it is clear that the value of $f_1(x)$ is NIL and the computation of car(x) is wasted. This is called a car-NIL instance and is another inefficiency to be avoided.

The desired breakdown of z in terms of x is, in fact, given by the following function t(x,z).

$$
t(x,z) = \begin{cases}
(\overline{N}) \quad \text{if } c(x,z) = \text{NIL} \\
(\overline{I}) \quad \text{if } c(x,z) = x \\
(\overline{A}(t(car(x),z))) \text{ if } car(x) \\
\qquad \text{appears in } c(x,z) \text{ and no} \\
\qquad cdr(x) \text{ or } x \text{ appears as} \\
\qquad \text{an argument of cons or} \\
\qquad x \text{ alone appears in } c(x,z) \\
\\
(\overline{D}(t(car(x),z))) \text{ if } cdr(x) \\
\qquad \text{appears in } c(x,z) \\
\qquad \text{and no } car(x) \text{ or } x \text{ as} \\
\qquad \text{an argument of cons or } x \\
\qquad \text{alone appears in } c(x,z) \\
(\overline{O}(t(x,car(z)),\ t(x,cdr(z)))) \\
\qquad \text{otherwise}
\end{cases}
$$

One can illustrate the trace function t(x,z) on the example of this section.

$$
\begin{aligned}
t(x,z) &= (\overline{A}t(car(x),z)) \\
&= (\overline{A}t(A,(A,NIL))) \\
&= (\overline{A}(\overline{O}t(A,car(z))\ t(A,cdr(z)))) \\
&= (\overline{A}(\overline{O}\ \ (\overline{I})\ \ (\overline{N})))
\end{aligned}
$$

The direct and car-NIL, cdr-NIL free decomposition comes from t(x,z) by interpreting $\overline{N}$,$\overline{I}$,$\overline{A}$,$\overline{D}$, and $\overline{O}$ as applications of, respectively, the NIL, identity, car, cdr, and cons operations. Moving in from the outermost parenthesis, one can construct the decomposition

$$
\begin{aligned}
f_1(x) &= f_2(car(x)) \\
f_2(x) &= cons(f_3(x),\ f_4(x)) \\
f_3(x) &= x \\
f_4(x) &= NIL
\end{aligned}
$$

It is shown in Biermann [1978] that synthesis from the decomposition of t(x,z) is capable of generating any "regular" LISP program.

With these concepts, it is now possible to make some key definitions. Many times the car and cdr functions are composed to a considerable depth so space can be saved with an abbreviated form. Specifically, the middle letters of composed functions can be concatenated between "c" and "r" to represent the composition. Thus cdr(cdr(car(x))) will be written cddar(x). The set of such expressions can be written $c(a+d)^*r\ (x)$ with the understanding that cr(x) is the identity function.

A *chain of predicates* will be defined to be a sequence of predicates $p_1,p_2,...,p_n$ such that

(1) $p_i = \text{atom}(c\ w_i\ r\ (x))$ where w_i is in $(a+d)^*$ for $i = 1,2,...,n-1$, and where w_i is a proper suffix of w_{i+1} for $i = 1,2,...,n-2$, and
(2) $p_n = T$.

Predicates constructed by the system described here will be such chains. An example chain of predicates is

$$\begin{aligned} p_1 &= \text{atom}(\text{car}(x)) \\ p_2 &= \text{atom}(\text{cadar}(x)) \\ p_3 &= \text{atom}(\text{cddadar}(x)) \\ p_4 &= T \end{aligned}$$

A *semiregular* LISP program f will be defined to be a finite nonempty set of *component* programs $f_i, i = 1,2,...,m$, with one of them f_1 being designated as the *initial component.* The value of f operating on x will be $f_1(x)$. A component program f_i of f is of the form

$$\begin{aligned} f_i(x) = \text{cond}((&p_{i1},f_{i1}) \\ (&p_{i2},f_{i2}) \\ &- \\ &- \\ &- \\ (&p_{in},f_{in})) \end{aligned}$$

where $p_{i1},p_{i2},...,p_{in}$ is a chain of predicates with arguments x and each $f_{ij}, j = 1,2,...,n$ is one of the following

(1) the NIL function
(2) the identity function
(3) $f_h(\text{car}(x))$
(4) $f_h(\text{cdr}(x))$
(5) $\text{cons}(f_h(x),f_k(x))$

where f_h and f_k are component programs of f.

A *regular* program is any semiregular program that executes only direct and car-NIL, cdr-NIL free computations. Examples of some regular LISP programs appear in the examples section of this chapter.

D. Synthesis

Once the primitive function decomposition is complete, the synthesis can proceed. The concepts related to the construction will be described here but the actual implementation for an efficient construction will not be described. The full details are given in Biermann [1978].

The method is to assume that the total number MAX of component programs is known and to examine all possible mergers of the functions in the primitive decomposition into MAX functions. Thus in the decomposition of the example program, there are four primitives $f_1,f_2,f_3,$andf_4. If MAX = 1, then all four functions would be merged into one.

$$\begin{aligned} f_1(x) &= f_1(car(x)) \\ f_1(x) &= cons(f_1(x), f_1(x)) \\ f_1(x) &= x \\ f_1(x) &= NIL \end{aligned}$$

Of course this is an unacceptable merge because f_1 is not uniquely defined. However, if a chain of predicates could be found such that

$$\begin{aligned} f_1(x) = cond(&(p_1,f_1(car(x))) \\ &(p_2,cons(f_1(x),f_1(x))) \\ &(p_3, x) \\ &(p_4, NIL)) \end{aligned}$$

then f_1 would become well defined. Unfortunately, one can show that no such chain can be found so that this synthesis attempt fails. Furthermore, no reordering of the clauses within the conditional will yield a form for f_1 that will do the example computation, so MAX is increased and another attempt is made.

At MAX = 2, the four functions can be merged in 16 different ways.

1. $f_1 \rightarrow f_1, f_2 \rightarrow f_1, f_3 \rightarrow f_1, f_4 \rightarrow f_1$
2. $f_1 \rightarrow f_1, f_2 \rightarrow f_1, f_3 \rightarrow f_1, f_4 \rightarrow f_2$

-

-

-

16. $f_1 \rightarrow f_2, f_2 \rightarrow f_2, f_3 \rightarrow f_2, f_4, \rightarrow f_2$

The synthesis procedure tries each possible merger and attempts to build conditionals with predicate chains to make the component programs well defined. In this case, it fails again but at MAX = 3 it finds an acceptable merger:

$$f_1 \rightarrow f_1, f_2 \rightarrow f_1, f_3 \rightarrow f_2, f_4 \rightarrow f_3$$

The program is

$$f_1(x) = \text{cond}((\text{atom}(x), \text{cons}(f_2(x), f_3(x)))$$
$$(T, f_1(\text{car}(x))))$$
$$f_2(x) = x$$
$$f_3(x) = \text{NIL}$$

The basic method is thus to try every possible merger. When a merged function becomes doubly defined, a conditional is constructed and a chain of predicates built to remove the ambiguity. If no such conditional can be built, the merger fails and another is attempted. In practice, one can design the synthesis method so that most unsuccessful mergers are never examined, and the correct one is usually found quite directly. This can be seen by working through the example.

At MAX = 1, we examine the merger of the first two primitives.

$$f_1(x) = f_1(\text{car}(x))$$
$$f_1(x) = \text{cons}(f_1(x), f_2(x))$$

The first definition is to hold if x = (A.(B.(C.NIL))) and the second is to hold if x = A. We can build a chain of predicates that will distinguish between these two sets: $p_1 = \text{atom}(x)$, $p_2 = T$. This yields the definition

$$f_1(x) = \text{cond}((\text{atom}(x), \text{cons}(f_1(x), f_1(x)))$$
$$(T, f_1(\text{car}(x))))$$

However, from the third primitive of the decomposition, we have

$$f_1(x) = x \qquad \text{when } x = A$$

which violates the above tentative definition of f_1. Furthermore no new chain of predicates can be found to allow a satisfactory modification of f_1. So MAX = 1 fails and MAX is incremented.

At MAX = 2, various mergers can be tried but all fail because essentially three different behaviors are required on an input of one atom: $\text{cons}(f_i(x), f_j(x))$, x, and NIL. Limitations on the predicate synthesizer disallow predicates that can distinguish one atom from another. So no chain of predicates can be found to separate them and the search must proceed to MAX = 3.

At MAX = 3, both the primitives $f_3(x) = x$ and $f_4(x) = \text{NIL}$ must be distinguished from each other and from f_1 since they all give different outputs on an atomic input. This yields the final program

$$
\begin{aligned}
f_1(x) &= \text{cond}((\text{atom}(x),\text{cons}(f_2(x),f_3(x))) \\
&\qquad (T,\ f_1(\text{car}(x)))) \\
f_2(x) &= x \\
f_3(x) &= \text{NIL}
\end{aligned}
$$

The complete details of the synthesis algorithm are given in Biermann [1978]. If multiple examples are given, all are converted to primitive form and the merge process functions in the same way. The algorithm is guaranteed to find a regular LISP program that will execute the given examples.

E. Convergence and Optimality

The excellent properties of the synthesis algorithm derive from the fact that it effectively (although not literally) enumerates a complete class of programs. (It actually skips most of the members of the class using information from the trace as shown in the previous section.) We will examine here the properties of enumerative algorithms.

A class of programs will be called *admissible* if it is enumerable and if the halting problem is solvable for each member of the class. Let $C = \{g_i \mid i = 1,2,3,...\}$ be any admissible class of programs. A method for generating a program from a set S of example input-output pairs (x_i,z_i) is to examine sequentially $g_1,g_2,g_3, \cdots$ until g_j is found such that $g_j(x_i) = z_i$ for all (x_i,z_i) in S. This technique has the advantage that it always finds a program which can do the given examples (soundness) and that it can always generate every program (or its equivalent) in the class C (completeness). Such a technique can also be shown to make optimal use of its input information (the input-output pairs) in the sense that no other synthesis technique can be found which will generate every program g_j on the basis of less input-output information than the technique given here.

Before beginning these discussions, it should be noted that the class of regular LISP programs is admissible. They are clearly enumerable and they all halt on every input since, by directness, no infinite cons loops are possible.

We model our synthesis procedure given above with the following:

Algorithm A1:

Input: A finite set S of input-output pairs (x_i,z_i) for the desired program.
Output: A program g_j from class C with the property that $g_j(x_i) = z_i$ for each (x_i,z_i) in S.

(1) $j \leftarrow 1$.
(2) while there is (x_i,z_i) in S such that $g_j(x_i)$ is not z_i, increment j.
(3) return result g_j.

The result obtained if algorithm A1 enumerates class C and has input S will be denoted A1(C,S).

A program synthesis algorithm A will be called *sound* if whenever S represents the behavior of a program in C, the program A(C,S) operating on x_i yields z_i for each (x_i,z_i) in S.

Program g_j will be said to *cover* program g_i if the fact that $g_i(x)$ is defined implies that $g_j(x)$ is defined and that $g_i(x) = g_j(x)$. Algorithm A will be called *complete* over class C if for each g in C there is a set S of pairs (x,z) such that A(C,S) will halt, yielding g_j which covers g.

Algorithm A will be called *stable* if $g = A(C,S)$ and $g(x) = z$ for all (x,z) in S' implies $g = A(C,S \cup S')$. Thus if A chooses a program g on the basis of information S and if additional information S' is compatible with g, A will not make a different choice on the basis of $S \cup S'$.

Theorem 1. If C is admissible, then A1 enumerating class C is sound, complete, and stable.

Proof. The soundness and stability properties follow immediately from the construction of A1. The completeness property requires only a simple proof. Let g be an arbitrarily chosen program from C, and let g_j be the first program in the enumeration of C which covers g. For each i = 1,2,3,...,j−1, choose an (x_i,z_i) such that $g_j(x_i)=z_i$ and $g_i(x_i)$ is undefined or $g_i(x_i)$ does not equal z_i. Such an (x_i,z_i) can be found for each i = 1,2,...,j−1 because the absence of such (x_i,z_i) would imply g_i covers g_j and g for i < j which contradicts the definition of g_j. If A1 operates on finite set $S=\{(x_i,z_i)\,|\,i=1,2,\ldots,j-1\}$, it will halt and return g_j as its answer. This completes the proof.

Suppose A0 is a program synthesis algorithm that is sound, complete, and stable over C. If for every S there is an associated $S' \subset S$ such that A0(C,S') = A1(C,S) and if not all such S with associated S' are such that A1(C,S') = A1(C,S), then A0 will be said to be *more input efficient* than A1.

Theorem 2: If a program synthesis algorithm A0 is sound, complete, and stable over C, then A0 is not more input efficient than A1.

Proof: Assume A0 is more input efficient than A1. Then there must be an S and an $S' \subset S$ such that $A1(C,S)=g_j$, $AO(C,S')=g_j$, and $A1(C,S')=g_i$ for i < j. Then there must be a subset $S'' \subset S'$ such that $AO(C,S'-S'')=g_i$ since A0 is more input efficient than A1, and A0 is complete. But for each (x,z) in S'', $g_i(x)=z$ by the soundness of A1. So by the stability property of A0, $A0(C,(S'-S'') \cup S'')=g_i$. But this contradicts the fact that $A0(C,S')=g_j$ for i < j; so it must not be true that A0 is more input efficient than A1. This completes the proof.

F. Some Examples

The theorems of the previous section cannot be fully appreciated until a synthesis system is constructed and tested. The regular LISP synthesizer was programmed and used to construct a wide variety of programs. If the target program was known to be regular and was no larger than about six transitions in size, the synthesizer generated that program (or an equivalent) immediately and with complete reliability. The absence of any tree pruning methods except those proven to remove only nonsolutions makes such reliable behavior possible. The number of examples required to create the target program was small, usually only one.

Of course, the class of regular LISP programs is very large and the cost of synthesis is exponential on the size of the target program. Programs of four transitions or fewer required several seconds of CPU time for synthesis. Programs with five transitions required most of a minute, and larger programs required a minute or more to construct.

As a first illustration, consider the construction of a program to find the third from last atom in a list. For example, list (A B C D E) yields output C. This implementation required that inputs be given in S-expression form with all atoms distinct and non-NIL. So the actual input was (A.(B.(C.(D.(E.F))))) yields C. The synthesized program after ½ second of CPU time was

```
f1(x) = cond((atom(x),x)
             (atom(cdddr(x)),f1(car(x)))

             (T, f1(cdr(x))))
```

This same program would have been generated if any other list of atoms of length 3 or more had been used.

Suppose the user had submitted the above example with the goal in mind that the target program should find the third element of the list instead of the third from last element. Then the program could be tested on (A B C D) with the result that B would be returned. Clearly this is not compatible with the current goal so both examples could be submitted. The following program was generated from them.

$$\begin{aligned} f_1(x) &= \text{cond}((\text{atom}(x),x) \\ &\qquad (T,\ f_2(\text{cdr}(x)))) \\ f_2(x) &= f_3(\text{cdr}(x)) \\ f_3(x) &= f_1(\text{car}(x)) \end{aligned}$$

The synthesis time was 3 seconds. The same program would have been generated if any two lists of length greater than 2 and of differing length had been used.

A problem of similar complexity to the example of chapter 1 was given to the system. (The actual problem of chapter 1 was not solvable since it required predicates not available to the regular LISP synthesizer.) The target program was to collect the atoms in a list of atoms and lists. The example was (A(B) C (D) (E) F) yields (A C F) and the program was generated in 39 seconds.

$$\begin{aligned} f_1(x) &= \text{cond}((\text{atom}(x),x) \\ &\qquad (\text{atom}(\text{car}(x)),\text{cons}(f_2(x),f_3(x))) \\ &\qquad (T,\ f_1(\text{cdr}(x)))) \\ f_2(x) &= f_1(\text{car}(x)) \\ f_3(x) &= f_1(\text{cdr}(x)) \end{aligned}$$

Again almost any single example would generate the same program provided it is long enough to force that program through all of its transitions.

G. Scanning Programs

While the regular LISP synthesizer was both reliable and robust for a variety of inputs, its shortcoming was its inability to generate programs larger than about six transitions. It was decided that the individual building blocks for regular programs, specifically car, cdr, and cons operations, were smaller than necessary. If the building blocks were complete control structures such as a loop or branch, then a program of size, say six, would be of very substantial size in terms of a real user's needs.

Conceptually, *scanning programs* move sequentially across an input list, once or many times, processing each element as it is encountered. They are the programs generated by production rules of the type described in Chapter 1, Section E. The primary problem in the program synthesis of scanning programs is the selection of which production rules to use and how to set the parameters. Once these decisions have been made, actual code generation is very fast and efficient.

Synthesis uses a hierarchical technique, first accounting for the lowest level behavior and then moving higher until all levels are accounted for. In order to illustrate this process a synthesis of the program that converts list (A B C D) to (A B C D B C D C D D) will be given. This construction requires only the two production rules described in Chapter 1, Section E and begins with a graphical display of the desired behavior. The target output is graphed as a sequential selection of input atoms.

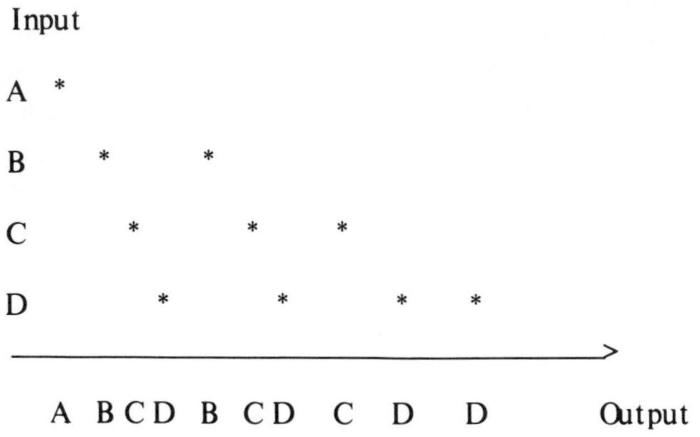

The synthesis proceeds by accounting for the various parts of the figure. First it is noted that the output atoms are simply copied from the input list. The first production rule from Chapter 1 yields this behavior.

$$[P^0_w, (X_0\ XL), \text{next}] ==>$$

$$P^0_w(X_0, XL) = \text{cons}(\text{car}(X_0), \text{next})$$

This accounts for the lowest level behavior, so the synthesis task is now to find a code to call P^0 repeatedly with the correct argument. This is illustrated as follows:

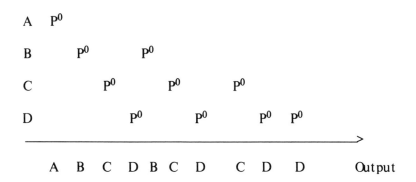

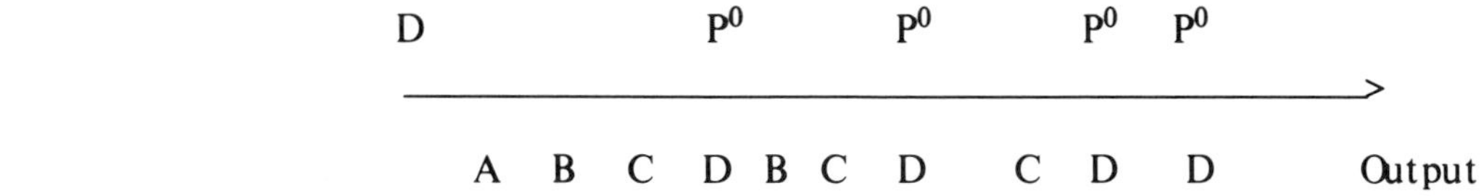

Here P^0 at level A on the graph means call P^0 with $X_0 = (A\ B\ C\ D)$. P^0 at level B means call P^0 with $X_0 = (B\ C\ D)$ and so forth.

Sequential calls of P^0 at regular intervals can be made by looping code as generated by the second production rule from Chapter 1. This rule will generate program P^1 (thus $i=1$) that will scan to the end of the list (thus P^1 entry check is atom(X_1)) decrementing the input list by 1 each time (thus $m=1$). The rule is

$$[P^1_{w},(X_1\ XL),\ next] ==>$$

$$P^1_w(X_1,\ XL) =$$

$$cond((atom\ (X_1),\ next)$$

$$(T, P^0_{w1}\ (X_1, X_1, XL)))$$

$$[P^0_{w1},(X_0\ X_1\ XL),\ P^1_w(cdr(X_1), XL)]$$

This reduces the synthesis problem to the following:

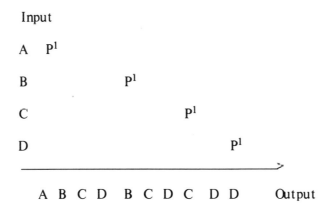

Input

A P^1

B P^1

C P^1

D P^1

A B C D B C D C D D Output

Thus P^1 can account for the descending sequences of P^0's but the descending sequence of P^1's must also be accounted for. But that can be done with another application of the looping production rule schema. In this application, a routine called P^2 will be created by setting $i=2$, the entry check to atom(X_2), $n = 1$, and the subroutine call P^k to P^1. The result is the following rule.

$$[P^2_{w},(X_2\ XL),\ next] ==>$$

$$P^2_w(X_2, XL) =$$

$$cond((atom(X_2),\ next)$$

$$(T,\ P^1_{w1}\ (X_2, X_2, XL)))$$

$$[P^1_{w1},\ (X_1\ X_2\ XL),\ P^2_w(cdr(X_2),\ XL)]$$

Now the problem has been reduced to the one graphical point.

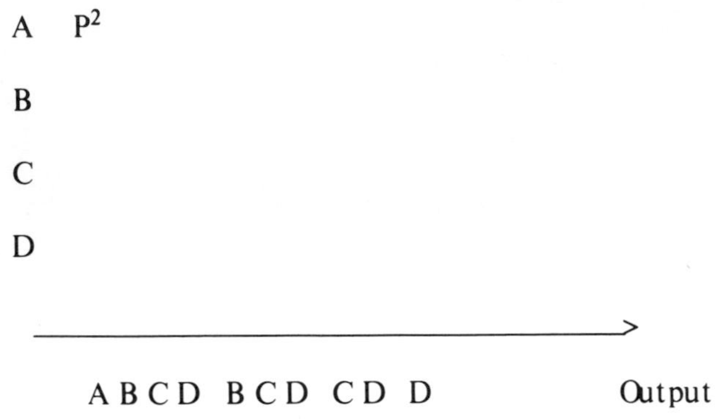

When enough reductions have been made to achieve a one point representation, the program is generated by syntactically expanding the nonterminal for that point, in this case P^2. The nonterminal $[P^2,(X_2), \text{NIL}]$ is expanded. Using the previous rule, we see w and XL must be set to the string of length zero and next = NIL.

$$[P^2,(X_2),\text{NIL}] ==>$$

$$P^2(X_2) = \text{cond}((\text{atom}(X_2), \text{NIL})$$

$$(T, P_1^1(X_2,X_2)))$$

$$[P_1^1,(X_1\ X_2),\ P^2(\text{cdr}(X_2))]$$

This expansion has yielded another nonterminal that can be expanded. The P^1 rule is needed with w=1, $XL=X_2$, and next = $P^2(\text{cdr}\ (X_2))$.

$$[P_1^1,(X_1\ X_2),\ P^2(\text{cdr}(X_2))] ==>$$

$$P_1^1(X_1,X_2) = \text{cond}((\text{atom}(X_1),\ P^2(\text{cdr}(X_2)))$$

$$(T,\ P_{11}^0(X_1,X_1,X_2)))$$

$$[P_{11}^0,(X_0\ X_1\ X_2),\ P_1^1(\text{cdr}(X_1),\ X_2)]$$

This expansion has yielded yet another nonterminal that can be expanded using the above P^0 rule. We set w = 11, XL = X_1,X_2, and next = $P_1^1(\text{cdr}(X_1),\ X_2)$.

$$[P^0_{11}, (X_0\ X_1\ X_2),\ P^1_1(cdr(X_1),\ X_2)] ==>$$

$$P^0_{11}(X_1,X_1,X_2)\ = cons(car(X_0),P^1_1(cdr(X_1),X_2))$$

The final program is the union of the code from the above three expansions.

$$P^2(X_2)\ = cond((atom(X_2),\ NIL)$$

$$(T,\ P^1_1(X_2,X_2)))$$

$$P^1_1(X_1,X_2)\ = cond((atom(X_1),P^2(cdr(X_2)))$$

$$(T,P^0_{11}(X_1,X_1,X_2)))$$

$$P^0_{11}(X_0,X_1,X_2)\ = cons(car(X_0),P^1_1(cdr(X_1),X_2))$$

Reviewing the above synthesis procedure, there is a diagnosis stage in which the problem is hierarchically decomposed and rule schemas are selected and instantiated. Then the actual code is generated by a relatively mechanical syntactic process. In practice, this has been found to be a very fast synthesis procedure and programs with nested loops up to depth six have been diagnosed and constructed in less than a second of CPU time.

It has been shown in Biermann and Smith [1979] that a relatively few rules are necessary (only six) to generate a wide variety of programs. Other kinds of looping behavior, branching structures, and other lowest level routines can be represented in production rule schemas. We will examine one more kind of rule schema here, a rule for generating branching code.

$$[P^i_w, (X_i\ XL),\ next] ==>$$

$$P^i_w(X_i,XL)\ = cond($$

$$((P^i\ condition\ check),\ P^k_{w1}(cdr(X_i),X_i,XL))$$

$$(T,\ next))$$

$$[P^k_{w1}, (X_k\ X_i\ XL),\ next]$$

Instantiated to produce a production rule:

i = rule designation
(P^i condition check)

$P^k_,$ the routine be conditionally executed

Instantiated for each use of the resulting rule:

w, XL, and next as defined above.

This conditional rule can be used in the solution of the problem of Chapter 1. We begin by graphing the problem as above.

```
Input

 -7 |

  2 |   *

  9 |      *

 -3 |

  4 |         *

_________________________________

        2  9  4              Output
```

The lowest level routine P^0 can be used as before.

```
Input

 -7 |

  2 |  P0

  9 |       P0

 -3 |

  4 |            P0

_________________________________

       2   9   4            Output
```

Next, we would like to use a looping schema to make the sequence of calls to P^0. However, the calls are uneven so this tactic will not succeed. Then we can look for something distinguishing the items selected from those not. The predicate generator can quickly discover the selected atoms are not negative and so the branching schema can be used with i = 1,(P^i condition check) = not(neg(car(X_1))), $P^k = P^0$. This yields the rule

$$[P^1_{w'}(X_1\ XL),\ \text{next}] ==>$$

$$P^1_w(X_1,XL) = \text{cond}($$

$$(\text{not}(\text{neg}(\text{car}(X_1)))\ ,\ P^0_{w1}(\text{cdr}(X_1)\ ,\ X_1,XL))$$

$$(T,\ \text{next}))$$

$$[P^0_{w1'}(X_0\ X_1\ XL),\ \text{next}]$$

The graphical representation of the problem can now be modified so that a looping schema can complete the computation.

Input						
-7 |	P^1					
2 |		P^1				
9 |			P^1			
-3 |				P^1		
4 |					P^1	
		2	9		4	Output

The looping schema can then be used to create a P^2 that will call P^1 repeatedly and complete the solution to the problem. The details are given in the Appendix to this book.

H. Conclusion

This chapter began by noting that dealing with search is one of the most difficult issues in automatic programming research. If one attempts to scan a completely general class of programs in the process of program construction, the size of the search becomes unmanageable and even relatively trivial programs will be out of reach. Yet the usual alternative to uniform search may be unsatisfactory: one prunes the search tree using "heuristics" which will hopefully guide the system to an acceptable solution.

The approach advocated here is that automatic programming research be built around the concept of solvable classes of problems. If a given problem is to be addressed and falls into one of the known solvable classes, the automatic synthesis can be achieved by straightforwardly applying the appropriate method. If the size of the target program is known, the cost of doing the construction may be known as well. This approach attempts to make synthesis of moderate sized programs both reliable and efficient.

The regular LISP programs include most of the LISP functions that one might think of which use only the atom predicate and which do not use additional variables. One could broaden the definition but this would result in slower synthesis times. Only by keeping the definition narrow has the synthesis performance described here been possible. One could also seek narrower definitions that would allow larger programs to be generated. The class of scanning programs grew out of such an effort. The scanning programs are able to do most tasks that involve repeated scans of an input list selecting items to be appended to an output. Reasonably satisfactory solutions to the synthesis problem have been found for both classes as has been described here.

I. Acknowledgement

This work was supported by the National Science Foundation under Grants MCS 7904120 and MCS 8113491 and by the Air Force Office of Scientific Research, Air Force Systems Command, USAF, under Grant 81-0221.

References

Biermann [1978]
A.W. Biermann, "The inference of regular LISP programs from examples," *IEEE Transactions on Systems, Man, and Cybernetics,* Vol. SMC–8, No. 8 (1978), pp. 585–600.

Biermann and Smith [1979]
A.W. Biermann and D.R. Smith, "A production rule mechanism for generating LISP code," *IEEE Transactions on Systems, Man, and Cybernetics,* Vol. SMC–9, No. 5 (1979), pp. 260–276.

CHAPTER 18

Design Directed Synthesis Of Lisp Programs

Ted J. Biggerstaff
ITT Programming
Stratford, CT 06497

Abstract

This paper describes the C2, design directed program synthesis system. The C2 synthesis paradigm views program synthesis as the inverse of program evaluation. It uses an abstract design (representing a whole class of specific programs) to direct the simulation of a target program evaluation. It makes a record of the simulated behavior of the target program and induces the target program from that record of behavior.

The specification information used to perform this simulation and synthesis consists of four basic items (specification factors):

- IO Examples,
- IO Spec (similar to IO assertions),
- An abstract design, and
- An abstract definition of the implementation data structures (i.e., LISP lists).

The IO Examples and the IO Spec are supplied by the user. The abstract design and abstract data structure definitions are part of the C2 library. The user need only specify the kind of design and implementation data structures he desires.

A. Introduction

The C2 paradigm (Biggerstaff [1976a, 1976b, 1977]) synthesizes a program by simulating the symbolic execution of the program, and recording the behavior of the program as a symbolic execution trace (state tree). The target program is induced from this record of behavior. For contrasting synthesis paradigms, see Biermann [1976a] and the other chapters of this volume.

The data required to perform such a simulation and construct the state tree is drawn from the four specification sources.

- The IO Examples reveal data structure manipulations which must be performed to generate various forms of the output.
- The IO Spec reveals a class of branching predicate,
- The Abstract Design guides the overall simulation process and provides much of the stereotypical code common to programs of that design, and
- The Abstract Implementation Data Structure definitions provide a class of branching predicate that is needed for loop control and special case constructions.

The C2 design directed paradigm incorporates several important ideas:

- Codification of Generic Design Knowledge
- Program Specification by Factors
- Design Directed Synthesis Procedure

The system codifies generic design knowledge by capturing the essence of an algorithmic method in an abstract design schemata (i.e. algorithm skeleton). This design schemata can be used to synthesize any number of specific programs which use that method. For example, a binary search or a quicksort could both be synthesized from the same "divide-and-conquer" design schemata. The author believes that the codification and reuse of programming knowledge is the key to being able to synthesize large and complex programs. (See also Gerhart [1976], Barstow [1980], Green [1976], Balzer [1976] and Heidorn [1976].)

The system allows target programs to be specified by several separate specification items (called factors) each of which focuses upon a separate aspect of the target program. Program specification by factors provides several desirable consequences. First, it allows the user to focus his attention on one aspect of the program at a time. This leads to clearer, easier to understand specifications, which in turn, should reduce specification errors. Second, there is a direct relationship between specific specification factors and specific classes of constructions within the target program. This aids the user by relating specific target program behaviors to specific specification factors, thus, making it easy for the user to implement changes of mind.

The fundamental idea of design directed program synthesis is that a target program may be efficiently synthesized by use of general plans called design schema. These design schema contribute the control structures which are common to the general algorithmic method of the schema, and the user contributes information necessary to create the specialized constructs required for the specific target program.

This paradigm provides the user with flexibility in controlling the structure of the resulting target program. In the example to be analyzed in this paper, an insertion sort program, the user can insist on a highly efficient algorithm, and get a sort which "replacd-s" the output list and which contains special case constructions for the cases when "replacd" will not work. On the other hand, if the user is not so concerned with efficiency, he will get an algorithm using "append", which requires no special case constructions. Both alternatives are produced from the same design schemata. The first alternative is chosen for the example synthesis shown in this paper.

B. Overview

In this section, we present an example which will be used throughout the paper. We present the specification information required by the C2 system from the user and then overview the role of each specification factor in the synthesis of the example.

B.1 The Example

Before we present the example synthesis of sort, it will clarify the discussion to informally describe the sort we have in mind. Figures 1A and 1B represent two functions synthesized by C2 which together perform an insertion sort.[1] They are annotated to aid the reader. The program named "sort" removes elements from the input list one by one in the order of their occurrence, storing each in the variable X. It then calls the function fp which searches down the output list, OUT, until it finds where X's value should go and (destructively) puts it there. Y and Z are the two pointers used for this search, with the intention that X should be inserted between them.

[1]These functions are expressed in a block structured pseudo-code that will be used throughout the paper.

```
sort(L)    /*L is list to be sorted*/

  {prog OUT,X;  /*Prog variables--
                Output list and current item
                from input list*/
  OUT=NIL;  /*Initialize output*/
   while( not null(L))
        {X=car(L);
        L=cdr(L);
        OUT=fp(X,OUT);} /*fp merges X into OUT*/
   return(OUT);}
```

Figure 1A
Insertion SORT Synthesized by C2[5]

```
fp(X,OUT)    /*Merge item X into the output list OUT,
              generating a new version of OUT*/
  {prog Y,Z; /*Prog variables-Y is the "before insert"
              pointer and Z is the "after insert" pointer*/
  Y=NIL;
  Z=OUT;   /*Initialize Y and Z*/
  if null(Z) V (X ⩽ car(Z))
    then {OUT=cons(X,Z); /*Create new list or put on font*/
        return(OUT);}
    else {do forever;
          {Y=Z; /*Update before and*/
          Z=cdr(Z); /*after pointers*/
          if null(Z) V (X⩽car(Z))
               then {replacd(Y,cons(X,Z));
                     /*Put on end or in middle*/
                     return(OUT);}}}}
```

Figure 1B
Function fp Synthesized by C2

This design leads to several special cases within the function fp. First, if the output list is NIL (i.e., empty), then a list of one element is constructed and assigned to OUT. Second, if X should be the first member of a non-empty output list, then OUT must be reassigned to point to the new, first element, whereas the insertion of X farther down the output list may be effected without reassigning OUT. The C2 optimizer merges these two special cases within fp.

Within fp's loop there are two other special cases. First, X is inserted in the middle of the output list (between X and Z); and second, X is appended to the end of the output list. These two special cases are also merged into one within fp.

Many aspects of the target program structure are under user control. In this case, the user has chosen options which have had the following effects:

- Subfunctions are preferred over in-line code.
- The efficiency option caused the use of "replacd" instead of "append" and this caused the occurrence of the special cases.
- An induction option caused merging of special cases.

B.2. Specification by Factors

In this section, we will introduce the various kinds of specification factors by specifying an insertion sort program. Then we will demonstrate how this specification system is applied to program synthesis.

Table 1 contains the specification information input by the user of the C2 system to specify the example "sort." The most important information supplied by the user is the IO Examples and IO Spec. The remaining information is almost incidental. The user must supply the name of the design routine which will drive the overall synthesis process, "gfp" in this case. In addition, he must supply, for all input and output variables, the role, implementation type and variable name to be used in the synthesis. Finally, he supplies some miscellaneous details such as the program name, order of arguments, etc.

- IO Examples[2]

```
NIL ---> [NIL]
(A) ---> [(A)]
(A B) --> [(A B) (B A)]
(A B C) -> [(A B C) (A C B) (B A C)
            (B C A) (C A B) (C B A)]
```

- IO Spec[3]

```
p(IN,OUT)
   {permute(IN,OUT) ∧
     {null(OUT) ∨
       if  not null(cdr(OUT))
           then{(car(OUT) ≤ cadr(OUT)) ∧
               p(diff(IN,car(OUT)),cdr(OUT))};
            else TRUE;}}
```

- Abstract Design Designation[4]

gfp

- Implementation Data Structure Specification[5]

```
(INPUT LIST IN)
(OUTPUT LIST OUT)
```

where the format is(<ROLE><IMPLTYPE><VBLNAME>)

- Misc(e.g. function name)

OUT=sort(IN)

Table 1
Inputs From User Specifying Sort

In the following sections, we will examine these specification factors in more detail and summarize how they are used in the synthesis process.

---

[2] A,B, etc. are abstract representations of atoms and do not represent the atoms A,B, etc.
[3] "permute" is a predicate which is true when M is a permutation of L, and diff(IN,X) creates a copy of the list IN with the element X removed. If X is not in IN,diff(IN,X) just copies IN.
[4] Name of design routine which will direct the development of the target code.
[5] Both input and output will be LISP style lists.

a. IO Examples

The examples in Table 1 show the input list structure on the left hand side of the arrow and the alternative output list structures which are possible on the right hand side of the arrow. For example, given the input list (A B) of length 2, there are two possible forms for the output: the list (A B) or the list (B A). The IO Examples are, by their nature, strictly limited to information about the structural transformations performed by the target function. They provide no information about what conditions are required for a particular transformation to occur.

How are the IO Examples used in the synthesis paradigm? The IO examples reveal the form of the output list for certain states of the computation. By the nature of the abstract design chosen, C2 knows that successive states of the output list for an arbitrarily long input list (A B C ...) will correspond to a sequence of sort outputs produced by the input lists NIL, (A), (A B), (A B C), etc. Thus, the sequence [NIL, (A), (A B), (C A B)] is one possible sequence of output states for the first three iterations of the "sort" function. By analyzing the difference between states, C2 can determine specific instances of the operations that sort must perform upon the output list. That is, C2 can easily determine that sort must create a list consisting of A, append B to that list, push C onto that list, and so forth.

A number of program synthesis systems based on specification by examples have been developed. Representatives are Biermann [1976b], Hardy [1975] and Summers [1976].

b. The IO Spec

The example IO Spec in Table 1 defines the "predicate function" p, with the parameters IN and OUT, to be the conjunction of two predicate expressions [6]. The first predicate expression, permute(IN,OUT), requires that IN be a permutation of OUT. The second requires, in effect, that for all adjacent items in OUT, the first item is less than or equal to the second item.

How is the IO Spec used in the synthesis paradigm? The IO Spec defines the conditions under which specific IO Example output alternatives would occur. For example, under what conditions would sort('(A B C)) = '(B C A)? The answer is whenever the expression p('(A B C) , '(B C A)) is true; that is, whenever B is less than or equal to C, "(B ⩽ C)", and C is less than or equal to A, "(C⩽A)".

The abstract design will formulate constructs of the form

```
if p(<Input Example>, <Output Possibility>)
    then OUT = <Output Possibility>;
    else . . .;
```

Abstract execution of the predicate expression involving p will produce a simpler (symbolic) predicate expression, such as "(A⩽car(<SpecificListValue>))". A subprocess of inductive generalization, called "variablization", will map this expression into the predicate expression "(X⩽car(Z))" seen in Figure 1B.

The IO Spec mechanism is similar to the specification methods used in deduction based synthesis systems (Manna [1975, 1976]).

[6] The predicate function "p" in Table 1 is the analog of the "output assertion" in more formal approaches. Since the C2 analog of the "input assertion" is not required in this discussion, its introduction will be deferred until later.

c. Abstract Design

The user provides to C2 the name of the desired abstract design. This choice will determine whether the target program produced is an insertion sort, a selection sort or a quicksort, for example. By choosing the "gfp" design, the user has determined that the target routine will be an insertion sort.

A specific design choice will cause a specific design synthesis routine and specific design schema to be chosen from the library. The design synthesis routine implements the specific synthesis procedure and it uses the associated schema. The schema will be the skeleton(s) determining the general structure of the target routine.

The gfp schemata can be described informally as:

> Get the next input element,
> Find where it goes in the output list, and
> Put it there.

An actual design schemata will be exhibited in the synthesis example.

The gfp design schemata produces programs which process their input list(s) members in order of their occurrence. That is, for an input list (A B C ...), the target program would cdr down the input list first processing A, then B, then C, etc. building up to the output list as it went.

The design routine uses the design schema to simulate the behavior of the target routine. It records the behavior of the simulation and induces the target routine from that record of behavior.

d. Abstract Data Structures

Implementation data structures are represented within the system in a form as close to the actual implementation structure as possible. While they are abstracted to some degree, it is in a rather different sense from "abstract data types" of Guttag [1976]. One aspect of the C2 abstraction method has already been seen in the IO Examples. The letters A, B and C in the IO Example list (A B C) represent arbitrary constants which may be atoms or other list structures. Hence, (A B C) represents all three elements lists.

This notation solves directly the problem of how to represent lists of specific lengths, but does not address the problem of representing lists of arbitrary lengths. This is an important problem for the C2 synthesis system because loops are a direct result of the need to process items of arbitrary lengths.

In C2, arbitrarily long lists are represented in two levels of abstraction, the ellipsis and the abstract list constant. They differ only in their level of concreteness and therefore, in their demands upon the deductive mechanisms underlying the evaluator. We will restrict this discussion to the ellipsis, since both are evaluated in much the same way. The rules for evaluating expressions constructed by C2 are given in Table 2. When such expressions include abstract data, such as ellipses, the results of evaluation may contain partially reduced symbolic expressions (i.e., code structures). These codes structures are used as target program building blocks.

- *Abstract Object Constant*

  For A an abstract object constant, eval(A) = A.

- *List of Abstract Object Constants*
  For (A B C) a list of abstract object constants,eval((A B C))=(A B C).

- *Abstract List Constant*
  For L an abstract list, eval(L) returns the expression

```
if null(L)
  then NIL;
  else(car(L) . cdr(L));
```

- *Ellipsis (or Indefinite List)*
  A more concrete form of the abstract list constant is the ellipsis.
  Eval((. . . A B C)) returns the expression

```
if null((... A B C))
  then NIL;
  else(A .( ... B C));
```

  And eval((...)) returns the expression

```
if null((...))
  then NIL;
  else . . .;
```

  where the ". . ." in the "else" clause indicates an open-ended tree branch.

Table 2
Evaluation Rules

- *If-then-else*

For an expression "ex" of the form

```
if Q
   then exp1;
   else exp2;
```

eval(ex) returns

eval(exp1)	if eval(Q)=TRUE,
eval(exp2)	if eval(Q)=FALSE, and
if eval(Q) then eval(exp1)assuming Q; else eval(exp2)assuming not Q	otherwise

- *Distribution of Functions*

For "ex" an expression of the form

```
if ex1
   then exp1;
   else exp2;
```

and for "f" a function, eval(f(ex)) is the expression

```
eval(if ex1
   then f(exp1);
   else f(exp2);)
```

- *Expression Simplification*

Expressions are simplified whenever possible. For example, "(TRUE Λ exp)" simplifies to "exp".

- *Function Invocation*

For f(X,Y,Z) a function defined by the expression "exp",

eval(f(A,B,C))

becomes

eval(σ(exp;(X/A,Y/B,Z/C)))

where the function σ substitutes eval(A) for every occurrence of X in "exp", eval(B) for every occurrence of Y in "exp", etc. σ generalizes in the obvious way for functions with a differing number of parameters.

Table 2 (continued)
Evaluation Rules

An ellipsis is a structure of the form

(... A B C)

and it can be informally thought of as the arbitrarily long conditional expression:

```
if null('( ... A B C))
      then NIL;
      else cons('A
            if null('( ... B C))
                then NIL;
                else cons('B
                     if null('( ... C))
                           then NIL;
                           else . . .
```

This is, in effect, the abstract execution tree of COPY('(... A B C)). This extends the concept of a data structure to include more than just passive data. Arbitrarily long lists now appear more like the execution tree of a single loop. That is, they are indefinitely long and they contain branching predicates. These structures will be woven with the design to form special case branches within the fabric of the target program.

The abstract data structures interact (via abstract evaluation) with the abstract schemata producing new (conditional) branches within the abstract evaluation trace. The predicate expressions, which are to appear in these new conditional branches, migrate out of the abstract data structure definitions, such as the definition of the indefinite LISP list (...A B C). Thus, predicates such as null(M), where M is an abstract list constant, originate in the abstract data structure definitions. They migrate into the record of simulated behavior and are finally generalized into predicate expressions such as null(Z), where "null(Z)" checks for the "special case" in which the first element is to be put onto an empty output list.

C. The Synthesis of Sort

This section will describe an example synthesis.

C.1 An Overview of the C2 Program Synthesis System

One of the fundamental hypotheses of this research is that human programmers are capable of directly and efficiently synthesizing complex algorithms because they make use of stored, abstract knowledge about classes of algorithms (i.e., abstract design knowledge) in conjunction with a variety of target program specific specification information. The fundamental difficulty of developing such a system is discovering a general method for combining all of this disparate information. The C2 paradigm represents one method for accomplishing this.

Recall that there are three steps to the C2 synthesis process. First, the design procedure, which codifies what we have called abstract design knowledge, directs the simulation of the target program applied to abstract data. The details of this simulation are derived from the specification factors of the target program plus built-in knowledge about particular data structures and particular designs. Second, the details of this simulated behavior are recorded as a symbolic execution state tree. Finally, the design procedure completes its work by inducing the target program which would have exhibited such behavior. This is a process of inductive generalization.

The succeeding sections follow the synthesis of an insertion sort program.

C.2. Simulate and Record Target Program Behavior

a. Construct State Tree

The first step of synthesis is the simulation and recording of the target program behavior as a symbolic execution state tree. This state tree represents the unfolded, instantiated form of a gfp sort of function, annotated with state information. This instance of the state tree is developed from two sources of information:

1. The IO examples (see Table 1) which supply information about the values of the output list in various states, and
2. The built-in design schema which supplies the basic control structure framework and code for managing a number of target program variables (e.g., the input list or the current element variable).

The initial state tree for sort is shown in Figure 2. The following comments explain Figure 2.

- The notation for specifying computational states is explained in Figure 3. We will arbitrarily choose OUT as the name of the output list.
- Some states have been omitted from the diagram because, at this point of the development, they only serve to complicate the tree. We will add them as the discussion requires.
- Similarly, a number of value-variable pairs have been omitted from the states at this stage to simplify the state tree.
- Stereotypical code, which is added by the abstract design, is omitted in order to shorten and simplify the example. Typical omissions are the code which manages the "current item variable", X, and the "input list variable", L. The design procedure supplies code of the form

```
X=car(L);
L=cdr(L);
```

  Though the code has been omitted, its effects on the values shown in the states are observable. For example, notice the changes in the values of X and L, from state S0 to state S3.
- (... A B C) is called an ellipsis. It is shorthand notation for a list which may be NIL or may contain the element A cons-ed onto the ellipsis (... B C). Eval((· · · A B C)) returns the expression

```
if null((... A B C))
     then NIL;
     else (A . (... B C))
```

  See the value of L in state S1 and S3 relative to S0, as an example of ellipsis behavior.
- Each of the labelled blocks of code in the figure are created from a subset of the IO examples for sort (see Table 1):

```
Block 1 from NIL -> [NIL],
Block 2 from (A) -> [(A)],
Block 3 from (A B)->[(A B) (B A)]
Block 4 from (A B C)->[ ... (C B A) (B C A) (B A C)]
Block 5 from (A B C)->[(C A B) (A C B) (A B C) ... ]
```

```
{s0:[NIL:OUT,( ... A B C):L,NIL:X]
if null((...A B C))
/*block1*/
    then s1:[NIL:OUT,NIL:L,NIL:X];
/*block2*/
    else{s3:[(A):OUT,(...B C):L,A:X];
       if null((...B C))
         then s4:[(A):OUT,NIL:L,A:X];
/*block3*/
         else{if p((A B),(B A))
            then{s6:[(B A):OUT,(... C):L,B:X];
               if null((... C))
                 then s7:[(B A):OUT,NIL:L,B:X];
/*block4*/
                 else{if p((A B C),(C B A))
                    then {s9:[(C B A):OUT,(...):L,C:X];...}
                    else{s10:[(B A):OUT,(...):L,C:X];
                       if p((A B C),(B C A))
                         then {s11:[(B C A):OUT,(...):L,
                                C:X];...}
                         else {s13:[(B A C):OUT,(...):L,
                                C:X];...}}}}

            else{s15:[(A B):OUT,(... C):L,B:X];
               if null((... C))
                 then s16:[(A B):OUT,(...):L,B:X];
/*block5*/
                 else{if p((A B C), (C A B))
                    then {s18:[(C A B):OUT,(...):L,C:X];...}
                    else{s19:[(A B):OUT,(...):L,C:X];
                       if p((A B C), (A C B))
                         then {s20:[(A C B):OUT,(...):L,
                                C:X];...}
                         else {s22:[(A B C):OUT,(...):L,
                                C:X];...}}}}}}}
```

Figure 2
Formulation of State Tree Using IO Examples

The predicate expressions involving the IO Spec are rationalized as follows. If the current state of the output list (and possible final answer of the function) is (B A), then by the definition of the IO Spec, we know that p((A B),(B A)) must be true. Here, (A B) is the input example associated with output (B A) in the IO Examples. Thus, the statement

```
if p((A B), (B A))
    then {OUT = (B A);
        return(OUT);}
    else ...
```

would be valid code for computing the output value for this specific case.

si:[VAL1:VBL1,VAL2:VBL2,...]

where
- "si" represents state identifier
- "VALi" represents a value for a variable in state "si"
- "VBLi" represents the name of the variable with value "VALi"

Figure 3
State Specification Format

The succeeding sections explain how the gfp design routine processes the state tree to develop the target routine code. The steps of the gfp design procedure are summarized below:

- It will restructure and generalize this state tree into two trees. The first will evolve into a function which gets the elements from the input list and calls a second function. The second function merges the element into the output list.
- It will add code required by the chosen design, e.g. the code that cdr's down the input and extracts the next element to be added to the output list.
- It will reduce predicates, e.g. "p((A B C),(C B A))", to their minimal form, e.g. "(C $\leqslant$ B)".
- It will map specific symbolic values, e.g. "(B C A)", into expressions (involving variables) which would have those specific values at given states of the function's execution. This is called variabilization.
- And finally, it will fold the tree into the control structure of the target routine.

b. Reformulate State Tree

The next step of the target program simulation process is an analysis to determine whether the target routine will contain an embedded loop. This can be determined directly from the IO Examples. For input lists of length n, there are n! output examples for sort. This factorial growth of the output examples indicates an embedded loop. The design procedure will try to restructure the tree into two trees, one associated with the outer loop and one with the inner loop.

The reformulated tree associated with the outer loop is developed by inventing a function which allows the tree's branches to be combined. The design procedure conjectures the existence of a side-effect free function, fp, which will merge the current element with the current state of the output list to create the successor state of the output list. For example, state S6 and S15 can be combined if there exists a function fp which will transform the value of OUT in state S4 into the appropriate value of OUT for either state S6 or S15. The specification of fp's formal parameters is

fp(X,PREFIXL,OUT)

where X is the "current item" being processed by the target function, PREFIXL is the prefix of the original input list containing all items which have been processed so far by the target function, and OUT is the output list being constructed by the target function. PREFIXL is a "virtual variable" introduced by the design procedure which will be "optimized out" of the final code.

Assuming the existence of fp, states S6 and S15 can now be represented as a single state

S6 V S15:[fp(B,(A),(A)):OUT].

Similarly, all states developed for input lists of length three can be represented by the same symbolic value,

[fp(C,(A B),fp(B,(A),(A))):OUT].

Given this, the state tree shown in Figure 2 is reformulated into two state trees; one for the outer loop (in main sort function) and one for the inner loop (the fp function). These are shown in Figures 4 and 6, respectively.

```
{s0:[NIL:OUT];
 if null((...A B C))
   then s1:[NIL:OUT];
   else {s3:[fp(A,NIL,NIL):OUT];
      if null((...B C))
        then s4:[fp(A,NIL,NIL):OUT];
        else{s6 V s15:[fp(B,(A),(A)):OUT];
          if null((... C))
            then s7 V s16:[fp(B,(A),(A)):OUT];
            else{if null((...))
              then s9 V s11 V s13 V s18 V s20 V s22:
                  [fp(C,(A B),fp(B,(A),(A))):OUT];
              else . . . .}}}}
```

Figure 4
Reformulated State Tree Assuming
Existence of fp Function

```
assert p(PREF,OUT);


fp(X,PREF,OUT)
 {prog Y,Z;
 Y = NIL;
 Z = OUT;
 <Develop pattern M' to account for IO examples that map
 append(PREF,cons(X,NIL)) into M'>
 if<there is no such M'>
   then<cannot synthesize>;
   else{while not null(Z)
            {if not p(append(PREF,cons(X,NIL)),M')
               then {Y = Z; Z = cdr(Z);}
               else{OUT = M'; return(OUT);}}
            OUT = M' ;
            return(OUT);}}
```

Figure 5
Find-Put Design Schemata

Since, the synthesis of the main sort loop illustrates only a few aspects of the synthesis procedure, we will not describe the evolution of the state tree of Figure 4 into the target code. Suffice it to say that the state tree of Figure 4 evolves into the target program shown in Figure 1A.

The synthesis of the fp function, however, illustrates many important aspects of the C2 synthesis procedure, and the remainder of this section will follow that synthesis in some detail.

```
assert p(PL,M)
{t0:[M:OUT,undef:Y,undef:Z,W:X,PL:PREF];
Y = NIL;
Z = M;
t1:[M:OUT,NIL:Y,M:Z,W:X,PL:PREF];
if null(M)
  then{t2:[NIL:OUT,NIL:Y,NIL:Z,W:X,NIL:PREF];
      OUT = (W);
      return(OUT);}
  else{t3:[(car(M) . cdr(M)):OUT,NIL:Y,(car(M) . cdr(M)):Z,W:
    X,PL:PREF];
   if p(append(PL,cons(W,NIL)),(W car(M) . cdr(M)))
    then{OUT = (W car(M) . cdr(M))
       return(OUT);}
    else{Y = Z;
       Z = cdr(Z);
       t5:[(car(M) . cdr(M)):OUT,(car(M) . cdr(M)):Y,cdr(M):Z,
            W:X,PL:PREF];
       if null(cdr(M))
         then{t6:[(car(M)):OUT,(car(M)):Y,NIL:Z,W:X,PL:PREF];
            OUT = (car(M) W);
            return(OUT);}
         else{t7:[(car(M)cadr(M) . cddr(M)):OUT,
           (car(M) cadr(M) . cddr(M)):Y,
           (cadr(M) . cddr(M)):Z,W:X,PL:PREF],
         if p(append(PL,cons(W,NIL)),(car(M) W cadr(M)
               cddr(M)))
           then OUT = (car(M) W cadr(M) . cddr(M));
           else . . . . }}}}
```

Figure 6
State Tree Formulated
for Function fp(W,PL,M)

C.3 The Synthesis of the Find-Put Function

a. Simulation of the Find-Put Function

How do we derive the state tree shown in Figure 6? Simulation of the design schemata of Figure 5 will form the skeletal structure of the state tree. Executing explicit code steps in this schemata (e.g. Z=cdr(Z)) using abstracted versions of the IO examples as data will produce symbolic values for the variables in Figure 6 (e.g. Z has the value of "cdr(M)" in state t5). Explicit, stereotypical code from the design schemata is included in the state tree. Now, let us follow the development of Figure 6 step by step.

The first step of simulating the Find-Put function is the re-expression of the IO Examples in a form more suitable for use in an embedded loop. This re-expression involves transforming the IO Examples (see Table 1) so that the (i+1)th state of the output list is expressed in terms of the ith state of the output list. In effect, this parameterizes the IO Examples making PL an arbitrary input list prefix, W an arbitrary element to be inserted, and M an arbitrary state of the output list.

The IO example re-expression is accomplished as follows. Suppose that we are re-expressing the ith IO example set. We will re-express each input list prefix as the symbolic list PL. The re-expression of the associated output possibilities requires a pattern matching process. This pattern matching will treat M and W like variables for the moment, binding M to successive output possibilities of the *previous* IO example set, i.e. the (i−1)th IO example set (and to NULL when (i−1)=0); and binding W to the last element of the input list of the ith IO example set. Thus, for the input list (A B C), M will be successively bound to (A B) and then (B A), while W is bound to C. With these bindings, the output possibilities of the ith IO example set are rewritten as expressions of M and W, which use every element of M and W, and which do not permute the elements of M. For example, for M bound to (A B) and W bound to C:

- (C A B) is re-expressed as (W . M),
- (C B A) does not match this binding of M,
- (A C B) is re-expressed as (car(M) W cadr(M)),
- (B C A) does not match,
- (A B C) is re-expressed as (car(M) cadr(M) W),
- (B A C) does not match.

The resulting re-expressed IO example set is:

PL -->[(W . M),(car(M) W cadr(M)),(car(M) cadr(M) W)]

Binding M to (B A) produces only duplicates of the output possibilities already discovered. Thus, the above set is the complete set of re-expressed output possibilities for input lists of length 3.

We now have a set of IO Examples in which the number of output possibilities grows linearly as the input list length increases. This means that we have parameterized out the effect of the outer loop, and the Find-Put function, fp, will reflect only the process of inserting an element into the output list.

In summary, the IO examples now take the form

(1) PL --->[NIL],
(2) PL --->[(W)],
(3) PL --->[(W . M),(car(M) W)],
(4) PL --->[(W . M),(car(M) W cadr(M)),
(car(M) cadr(M) W)]

where the length of PL is respectively 0, 1, 2, and 3 for the four cases shown above.

These forms of the output will be used for the M' values in the design schemata of Figure 5.

Figure 5 is a simplified version of the Find-Put design schemata which will drive the simulation. The complete Find-Put design schemata includes code for managing a number of variables which are not germane to the sort example, e.g., "first element of input list", "length of the output list", "position of current element in input list", and others. Such unused variables and code are removed from the target routine during optimization. It simplifies the example to simply ignore them from the outset.

The simulation process will unfold the 'while' loop in the design schemata substituting values for PREF, X and M' from the IO Examples above and executing the intervening code to derive values in a given state from those of the preceding state. For example in state t1, of Figure 6, the input prefix variable, PREF; the output variable, OUT; and the "after" pointer, Z, are all bound to symbolic lists. Executing the "while" predicate " not null(Z)", shown in Figure 5, results in the value " not null(M)", and this more specifically determines the values of PREF, OUT and Z in the subsequent states. On the "null(M)" branch (state t2) they are all NIL. On the "notnull(M)" branch (state t3) it is known that the list pointed to by both OUT and Z contains at least one element, car(M), and may possibly contain other elements following the "car(M)" element. This is represented as

(car(M) . cdr(M)).

All values for OUT are derived from the restructured IO examples given above. In line 7 of Figure 6, the form of the output comes from example 2; in lines 10 and 11, from example 4; in line 18 from example 3; and so on. In a later step (see subsection c below), the design procedure will induce the code which would compute values with these forms.

b. Predicate Simplification

The next step of the simulation is the creation of those branching predicates which are expressed in the abstract design as an expression of the IO Spec, p. This step simplifies the predicate expression given in the abstract design to one which is the minimum expression required at that specific point in the target routine.

The predicate simplification process uses a form of symbolic execution (Hantler [1976]) called abstract evaluation (or AE). AE simplifies a predicate expression such as

p(append(PL,cons(W,NIL)),(W car(M) . cdr(M)))

to an expression of the form

$$(W \leqslant car(M))$$

The following discussion steps through this evaluation using the evaluation rules shown in Table 2.

The predicate synthesis process is based on the following axiom expressed in Hoare's notation:

p(PL,M) {if (q) then OUT=g(W,M)} p(append(PL,cons(W,NIL)),g(W,M))

Every expression in this axiom is defined except the predicate expression q. That is, a definition for p is supplied by the user and the specific forms of g (e.g. cons(W,M)) can be derived by differencing the IO Examples (see the following section for details). Given this, we can use abstract evaluation to "solve for q."

The process of "solving for q" consists of two steps:

- Assume p(PL,M) is true, and
- Reduce p(append(PL,cons(W,NIL)),g(W,M)) to q using the abstract evaluation rules given in Table 2.

The following discussion will follow through a specific derivation of q.

Initially, we assert that p(PL,M) is TRUE. From this fact and the definition of p, we derive the additional fact that the symbolic list PL is a permutation of the symbolic list M, i.e., permute(PL,M). These facts will be used in the evaluation of the predicate expression on line 10 of Figure 6:

p(append(PL,cons(W,NIL)),(W car(M) . cdr(M))).

We begin the evaluation of this expression by substituting the arguments in the expression defining p, deriving:

```
{permute(append(PL,cons(W,NIL)),(W car(M) . cdr(M)))
    Λ {null((W car(M) . cdr(M)) V
          if not null(cdr((W car(M) . cdr(M))))
             then {(W ≤ car(M)) Λ p(PL,(car(M) . cdr(M)))};
             else TRUE;}}
```

The truth of the expression involving the predicate "permute" can be deduced as TRUE from permute(PL,M). Next, the evaluator determines that null((W car(M) . cdr(M))) is FALSE. After that, the evaluator begins evaluation of the "if" predicate expression. The cdr of the list (W car(M) . cdr(M)) is the list (car(M) . cdr(M)) which is clearly not null. Next the evaluation begins on the "then" clause. The expression (W ≤car(M)) cannot be further reduced and the value of this expression is just the expression itself. p(PL,(car(M).cdr(M))) is TRUE because the list (car(M) . cdr(M)) is equivalent to M, and p(PL,M) was asserted true at the outset. Thus, the total expression reduces to

```
{TRUE Λ
 {FALSE V
  if TRUE
     then{(W ≤ car(M)) Λ TRUE};
     else TRUE;}}
```

which finally, reduces to

(W ≤car(M)).

Other expressions involving p reduce in a similar fashion, producing the simplified predicates shown in Figure 7.

c. Inductive Generalization and Variablization

Inductive generalization is a process of combining individual instances of code, into the generalized code which would generate such instances by its execution. For example, the expressions (W ≤car(M)) and (W ≤cadr(M)) will generalize to the expression (X ≤car(Z)). Variablization is the subprocess of inductive generalization which maps specific constant values { (e.g. "W", "car(M)" and "cadr(M)") associated with different states of the computation into the variable or expression which would have produced these values in the various states.

The inductive generalization process will fold the open ended execution tree shown in Figure 7 into a graph with a cycle (i.e., a loop). This loop will be the code which searches down the output list to find where the item X should go and puts it there.

The folding process is driven by the structure of the code or expressions to be combined. For example, lines 4 and 5 of Figure 7 are structurally similar to lines 7 and 8. They will combine, if the two lists, "(W)" and "(W car(M) . cdr(M))" can be generated by the same expression. The variablization process will try to create a single expression which will generate the two distinct values for the two distinct states associated with lines 4 and 7.

```
0  fp(X,OUT)
1  {Y = NIL;
2  Z = M;
3  if null(M)
4      then{OUT = (W);           /*Create new list*/
5          return(OUT);}
6      else{if (W ⩽car(M))
7          then{OUT = (W car(M) . cdr(M)); /*Put on front*/
8              return(OUT);}
9          else{Y = Z;
10                 Z = cdr(Z);
11                 if null(cdr(M))
12 /*Put on Tail*/      then{OUT = (car(M) W);
13                           return(OUT);}
14                         else{if(W ⩽cadr(M))

15 /*Put in middle*/          then{OUT = (car(M) W cadr(M) . cddr(M));
16                                 return(OUT);}
17                               else{Y = Z;
18                                 Z = cdr(Z);
19                                 if null(cddr(M))
20 /*Put on tail*/                     then{OUT = (car(M) cadr(M) W);
21                                           return(OUT);}
22                                         else . . . . }}}}}
```

Figure 7
State Tree After Predicate Simplification

There are two steps to the variablization process,

- Differencing two successive output states to produce the instantiated code that would have produced the second state given the first, e.g. the difference of the lists "(car(M))" and "(car(M) W)" is "append((car(m)),cons(W,NIL))."
- Mapping data constants to the variables which would have had those values in the given state, e.g. mapping the data constant variables in "append((car(M)),cons(W,NIL))" will transform the difference expression to either "append(Y,cons(X,NIL))" or "append(Y,cons(X,Z))." The determination of the correct interpretation is made by comparing the interpretation sets from several equivalent states or failing that, by heuristics.

Returning to the problem of folding the pair of lines 4 and 5 into the pair of lines 7 and 8, we find that differencing the output value associated with line 4 and that associated with line 3 produces the following interpretations for the output list value "(W)",

{cons(W,NIL)}.

This is the code which would transform the value of the output list at line 3 (i.e. "NIL") into the value of the ouput list at line 4 (i.e. "(W)"). When the data constants in this expression (i.e. "W" and "NIL" are mapped to variables, the set of variablized interpretations becomes

{cons(X,NIL),cons(X,Z),cons(X,OUT)}.

Interpretations are ordered by heuristic preference.

The same two steps for lines 7 and 6 produce the unvariablized interpretation set

{cons(W,(car(M) . cdr(M))}

and the variablized interpretation set

{cons(X,Z),cons(X,OUT)}

in order of preference. Preference ordering is based on the Find-Put design objective which seeks to interpret modifications of the output list in terms of the "current element", X; the "before pointer", Y; and the "after pointer", Z. Thus, the common, preferred interpretation for the two list instances in lines 4 and 7 is "cons(X,Z)". This interpretation allows lines 3 through 8 to be generalized into

```
if null(Z) V (X ≤car(Z))
    then{OUT = cons(X,Z);
         return(OUT);}
    else ...
```

Note that this choice for an interpretation of the output list value forces the predicate expression instance "(W ≤car(M))" to be variablized to "(X ≤car(Z))".

Similarly, lines 9 through 13 combine with lines 17 through 21. The expressions "(car(M) W)" in line 12, "(car(M) W cadr(M) . cddr(M))" in line 15 and "(car(M) cadr(M) W)" in line 20 all have the common interpretation of "append(OUT,cons(X,Z))", and within the FIND-PUT design context, the synthesizer is allowed to optimize "OUT = append(OUT,cons(X,Z))" to "replacd(Y,cons(X,Z))". The results of these combinations and generalizations are shown in Figure 1B.

Notice that if the design criteria were changed to the minimization of the amount of source code rather than the minimization of computation time (i.e., prefer the use of "append" rather than "replacd"), then "append(OUT,cons(X,Z))" would represent an acceptable interpretation for all four cases—inserting into an empty list, on the front, on the back and in the middle. The resultant form of fp would be a form structurally the same as the original design schemata of Figure 5.

It should be clear that small changes in the design criteria applied during the induction and variablization processes can profoundly effect the resulting target program structure. It is the author's belief that this synthesis paradigm is one of very few in which user can make design choices which can have a significant effect upon the resulting target routine structure.

D. A Second Example

Consider a different problem. Given a list of integers as input, copy the list with all of the non-positive integers removed. For example, given the list (−7 2 9 −3) as input, the function "pcopy," should produce the list (2 9). This problem will introduce several new ideas:

- It will illustrate the role of the input predicate in error proccssing synthesis. An input predicate describes what is known about the input data before the computation starts. As it turns out, this is not really necessary for this example unless the user wants the target program to do error processing (another design option).
- It will reveal that the IO Spec information describing the structural relationships between the input and output lists, is redundant. The job of describing structural relationships is handled by the IO Examples. For example, leaving the clause "permute (IN,OUT)" out of the IO spec definition would make no difference in the sort example discussed earlier.
- It will illustrate another form of optimization allowed by the C2 paradigm.

D.1 The Specification of "pcopy"

The IO Examples for this problem are specified as:

```
NIL   --->[NIL]
(A)   --->[NIL,(A)]
(A B) -->[NIL,(A),(B),(A B)]
```

In this problem, the method requires only three examples in order to synthesize the target program. The pattern that these examples establish is that for each new element of the input list, there are only two alternatives. It is either included in or omitted from the output.

The Input predicate, "i", and the IO Spec, "p", are specified as:

```
i(IN)
  {if null(IN)
     then TRUE;
     else{integer(car(IN)) Λ i(cdr(IN))};}

p(IN,OUT)
  {if null(IN)
     then null(OUT);

     else {(OUT ⊂[1] IN) Λ
          {(car(IN)ϵ[2]OUT) ≡[3](car(IN) ≥0)}Λ   p(cdr(IN),diff(OUT,car(IN))}}
```

The Input predicate asserts that each element of the input list is an integer. Notice that the IO Spec relies on this fact indirectly, only because it uses the arithmetic operator "≥".

[1] ⊂ is a "structural function" which operates upon abstract objects and lists of abstract objects. ⊂ asks the question, "is the abstract list OUT a subset of the abstract list IN." Structural functions ask questions about the abstract objects themselves and not about the values they represent. Hence, structural functions are total functions which always return either TRUE or FALSE. By contrast, the LISP function "subset" might return as its value, an expression containing "eq(A,B)" meaning that the value of subset depends upon the possible equality of the value represented by A and the value represented by B.

[2] ϵ is a structural function which returns TRUE if the "abstract data item," car(IN) is in the "list of abstract objects," OUT, and returns FALSE otherwise.

[3] D.3 "If and only if."

What is the role of the input predicate? In general, the input predicate will influence the abstract evaluation of the IO Spec. However, because the IO Spec is written such that it makes no use of the information from the input predicate, its only role in this example is in the synthesis of the error processing code. The error processing capability can be (optionally) provided through the inclusion of the following code sequence in the loop of the design schemata:

```
if  not i(PREF)
   then <Generate error message and
      return user specified error code >;
   else <Do main line processing >
```

where PREF is the prefix of input elements processed up to this point. The predicate expression i(PREF) will evaluate to the series of branching predicates "integer(A)", "integer(B)", etc. within the state tree and these will generalize to "integer(X)". Since it should be quite clear how such error processing would integrate into the state tree and since these branches would tend to make the example unnecessarily complex, we will omit the error processing from the remainder of the example.

Now consider the IO Spec. It levies two basic constraints upon the input and output lists—that the elements of the output list be a subset of the elements of the input list and that only positive elements are members of the output. Odd as it may seem, the subset requirement is redundant and will contribute nothing to the predicate expression. That information is already implicitly transmitted by the IO Examples.

2. Synthesizing "pcopy"

The state tree for pcopy is shown in Figure 8. This is developed by using the gfp design routine. The synthesis of the branching predicates is the most interesting part of this example. The remaining operations are largely straightforward and are basically, variations of those of the sort example.

```
1    {s0:[NIL:OUT,(... A B):IN,NIL:X];
2    if null((... A B))
3      then s1:[NIL:OUT,NIL:IN,NIL:X];
4      else {s2:[NIL:OUT,(... B),A:X];
5        if p((A),(A))
6          then {s4:[(A):OUT,(... B):IN,A:X];
7            if null((... B))
8              then s5:[(A):OUT,NIL:IN,A:X];
9              else {s6:[(A):OUT,(...):IN,B:X];
10               if p((A B),(A B))
11                 then {s7:[(A B):OUT,(...):IN,B:X];
12                   . . . . }
13                 else {s8:[(A):OUT,(...):IN,B:X];
14                   . . . }
                     }
                 }
15         else {s9:[NIL:OUT,(...):IN,B:X];
16           if p((A B),(B))
17             then {s10:[(B):OUT,(...):IN,B:X];
18               . . . . }
19             else {s11:[NIL:OUT,(...):IN,B:X];
20               . . . . }
                 }
             }
       }
```

Figure 8
State Tree for Example Two

```
pcopy(IN)      /*IN is the list of integers*/
   {prog OUT,X;  /*progr vbls-output list and current element*/
   OUT=NIL;
   while(not null(IN))
        {X = car(IN);
        IN = cdr(IN);
        if(X ⩾0)
            then OUT = cons(X,OUT);}
   return(reverse(OUT));}
```

Figure 9
Copy Positive Integers Function
Synthesized by C2

If the reader takes on faith that the expression p((A),nil) evaluates to "(A < 0)", then we can follow the more interesting evaluation of p((A B),(B)). Substituting values into the definition of p results in

```
{if null((A B))
   then null((B));
   else {((B) ⊂ (A B)) Λ
          {(A ϵ (B)) ≡ (A ⩾ 0)}
           Λ p((B),(B))}}
```

Both null((A B)) and null((B)) evaluate to FALSE, and ((B)) ⊂ (A B)) evaluates to TRUE. (A ϵ (B)) evaluates to FALSE. (A ⩾ 0) evaluates to FALSE because p((A B),(B)) is on a branch on which p((A),NIL) is true, i.e. (A <0) is TRUE. The expression becomes

```
{if FALSE
   then FALSE;
   else {TRUE Λ {FALSE ≡ FALSE} Λ p((B),(B))}}
```

The whole expression reduces to p((B),(B)). Substituting in the definition of p again produces

```
{if null((B))
   then null((B));
   else{((B) ⊂ (B)) Λ
        {(B ϵ (B)) ≡ B ⩾ 0} Λ p(NIL,NIL)}}
```

And this reduces to

```
{if FALSE
   then FALSE;
    else {TRUE Λ {TRUE ≡ (B ⩾ 0)} Λ TRUE}}
```

which reduces to (B ⩾ 0). This will be the predicate in the branch on line 16 of Figure 8.

Induction and variablization operate much like they do in the sort example with OUT being computed by the statement

OUT = append(OUT,cons(X,NIL));

A post-processor, called the optimizer, transforms this statement to

OUT = cons(X,OUT);

and alters "return(OUT)" to

return(reverse(OUT));

The optimizer is a source to source transformation program which analyzes the synthesized program and attempts some simple transformations to optimize the run-time efficiency of the synthesized program. In the case of pcopy, the optimizer recognizes the pattern of the statement which modifies OUT as an inefficient form, and after discovering that this is the only kind of modification to OUT, alters the program as described above.

The optimizer capitalizes upon the design knowledge codified in the C2 synthesis system. For example, the above transformation is designed very specifically for output lists built by the Find-Put design schemata.

The results of the synthesis are shown in Figure 9.

E. Conclusions

There are several conclusions which can be drawn from this research:

- Generic design knowledge can be codified in an easily reuseable form by focusing on a somewhat narrow problem domain (e.g. list combining and restructuring). Importantly, this codification does not compromise the ability to synthesize a wide variety of programs. For example, the "gfp" design can synthesize all set operations, most list searches, most list restructurings such as "flatten", and most operations which remove items from the list.
- Disparate kinds of specification information can be mixed together and used for the synthesis. An added advantage of this is that redundancies within the specification information (e.g. between the IO Examples and the IO Spec), may be exploited to verify the consistency of the specification information.
- The user can influence the target routine structure through the simple use of design options. In many synthesis paradigms, such influence on the target routine could only be accomplished through a large amount of error prone work, such as rewriting a set of axioms.
- In some sense, a specification, factored into pieces is easier to develop and understand than some other kinds of specifications. For example, the IO Examples are a direct and clear expression of the structural manipulations of a target function.

In summary, the design directed paradigm represents one method by which large libraries of generic software designs are possible. The author believes that only through capturing generic software design on a large scale, will it be possible to produce complex real-world target systems in a largely automated manner.

F. Acknowledgements

I would like to acknowledge Professor David Johnson and Dr. Chris Jette for their contributions to this research. Also, I would like to thank the editor for suggestions which significantly changed and improved this paper.

References

Balzer [1977]
R. Balzer, N. Goldman, and D. Wile, "Imprecise program specification," ISI/RR—77—59 (April 1977).

Barstow [1980]
D.R. Barstow, "The role of knowledge and deduction in algorithm creation," International Workshop on Program Construction, Castera-Verduzan, France (Sept. 1980).

Biermann [1976A]
A.W. Biermann, "Approaches to automatic programming," in *Advances in Computers,* Vol. 15, Academic Press, New York (1976).

Biermann [1976B]
A.W. Biermann and R. Krishnaswamy, "Construction programs from example computations," *IEEE Trans. on Software Engineering* 2,3(1976).

Biggerstaff [1976A]
T.J. Biggerstaff, "C2: A super-compiler model of automatic programming," Ph.D. Dissertation, University of Washington, Seattle (Jan. 1976).

Biggerstaff [1976B]
T.J. Biggerstaff and D.L. Johnson, "The C2 super-compiler model of automatic programming," First CSCI/SCEIO Natl. Conf., Univ. of British Columbia, Vancouver (Aug. 1976).

Biggerstaff [1977]
T.J. Biggerstaff and D.L. Johnson, "Design directed program synthesis," CSCI Tech. Rep. 77–02–01, Univ. of Washington (Feb. 1977).

Gerhart [1976]
S.L. Gerhart and L. Yelowitz, "Control structure abstraction of the backtracking programming technique," *IEEE Trans. on Software Eng.* 2,4(Dec. 1976).

Green [1976]
C. Green, "The design of the PSI program synthesis system," 2nd Inter. Conf. on Soft. Eng., Calif. (1976).

Guttag [1976]
J. Guttag, E. Horowitz, and D.R. Musser, "Abstract data types and software validation," Tech. Rep. ISI, Marina del Rey (Aug. 1976).

Hantler [1976]
Sidney L. Hantler and James C. King, "An introduction to proving the correctness of programs," *Computing Surveys,* Vol. 8, No. 3(Sept. 1976).

Hardy [1975]
S. Hardy, "Synthesis of LISP programs from examples," *Proc. of the Fourth Intern. Joint Conf. on Artificial Intelligence* (Sept. 1975).

Heidorn [1976]
G.E. Heidorn, "Automatic programming through natural language dialogue: a survey," *IBM J. of Res. and Develop.* (July 1976).

Manna [1975]
Z. Manna and R. Waldinger, "Knowledge and reasoning in program synthesis," Artificial Intelligence 6,2(Summer 1975).

Manna [1977]
Z. Manna and R. Waldinger, "The logic of computer programming," Stanford AIM–289 (Aug. 1977).

Summers [1976]
P.D. Summers, "A methodology for LISP program construction from examples," *Proc. of the Third ACM Symp. on Principles of Programming Languages,* Atlanta, Ga. (Jan. 1976).

CHAPTER 19

Theorem Proving By The Study Of Example Proof Traces

or

Theorem Proving By A Correct Theorem Statement

Jacqueline Castaing and Yves Kodratoff
Laboratoire de Recherche en Informatique, Bat. 490
Université de Paris-Sud
91405 ORSAY (France)

Pierpaolo Degano
Universita de Pisa
Istituto di Scienze della Informazione
Corso Italia 40, 56100 Pisa, Italy

Abstract

The way a theorem is proven for particular instances of its variables contains information about the way the theorem can be generalized in order to allow its proof by structural induction. We describe a methodology which extracts this information and therefore associates to a given theorem to be proven, the inductive hypothesis suitable for its proof by structural induction.

A. Introduction: The Ideas Underlying Our Methodology

To the best of our knowledge, only one attempt, Degano and Sirovich [1979], has been made in order to use "proof traces" as a tool for theorem proving.

We therefore cannot introduce our work by giving its place in the current flow of the research on theorem proving.

A proof trace has been defined by Degano and Sirovich [1979]. Let us consider a rewriting system like TEL, Levi and Sirovich [1975], for instance. The rewriting system can be used in order to prove a given theorem for particular instances of its variables. During this particular-case-proof, the rewriting rules will be used in some order. The sequence of couples made of the used rules and the expression to which they are applied will be called in the following: *example proof trace* (or simply *proof trace).*

We shall describe our methodology on the example of equivalence between recursively defined functions, proven by structural induction. We suppose that the usual conditions on the domain definition hold (Manna *et al.* [1973]). We do not rule out the case of cross-recursion and terminal recursion so that iterative definitions can be handled. (For the difficulties raised by this problem, see Moore [1975].)

We start from the heuristic remark that some proofs become often surprisingly simple when a more general theorem is proven rather than the original one.

For example suppose that $g_1(x,y,z)$ and $g_2(x,s,t)$ are two recursively defined functions and that we want to prove $g_1(x,1,0)=g_2(x,2,3)$. The induction hypothesis, $g_1(x,1,0)=g_2(x,2,3)$, will be used in order to prove that $g_1(x+1,1,0)=g_2(x+1,2,3)$. Unless we are studying a trivial case, the recursive definition of $g_1$andg_2 bring some transformation on the variables y,z,s,t and the lack of knowledge about the relations between these variables will lead the induction proof to a failure.

We aim at generalizing the theorem to $g_1(x,y,z)$ and $g_2(x,s,t)$ and discover the needed relations between the non-inductive variables y,z and s,t. These relations are found by demanding that $g_1(x,y,z)=g_2(x,s,t)$ can be proven by a use of the recursive proof traces obtained by the rewriting system proving $g_1(0,1,0)=g_2(0,2,3),g_1(1,1,0)=g_2(1,2,3),\ldots$. In other words, we detect relations between y,z,s,t, that allow $g_1(x,y,z)=g_2(x,s,t)$ to be proven with the same proof trace obtained for particular values of the variables. These relations are precisely those needed in order to carry on the induction proof; it is then clear that no real difficulty is left to the theorem prover.

The whole process amounts to a "proof transformation": instead of proving the theorem, we have to prove the relations. It may happen that they are indeed very difficult to prove since they generally have the form of diophantine equations. However, section D shows that the equations to be solved are quite trivial for a wide variety of examples.

In this paper, except for the sake of illustration, we shall limit ourselves to the discovery of the equations between the variables without solving them: we only try to find how some example proof traces make it possible to restate the problem in its most general form. We claim that we have found a problem stater rather than a real problem solver.

B. Description of the Generalization Process

B.1. General Presentation

The process can be divided into five steps.

Step 1. The choice of the induction variables and selection of example proof traces.

One uses the rewriting system in order to choose fertile induction variables (Castaing and Kodratoff [1980]) and prove the theorem for particular values of these variables. We thus obtain the example proof traces.

In practice, if the functions are defined on the natural integers and their stopping condition is $x=0$, one verifies the theorem for $x=0,1,2,3,\ldots$. If the functions are defined on the lists with only atoms at their top level and if their stopping condition is x=NIL, one verifies the theorem for x=NIL, x=(A), x=(B A), x=(C B A), ... (recall that the type list is generally described with a constructor which adds an atom at the left of the list).

We obtain a sequence of example proof traces; let k be the index of this sequence.

Step 2. Cross-fertilization

One has to prove a relation between two functions f and g. Suppose that the k-th trace contains f applied to the values for which the proof has been carried on in trace (k−1). We know that the relation holds for these values (proven in trace k−1), and we apply this relation to obtain a relation depending on g only.

We prove this relation for particular cases and obtain a new sequence of example proof traces to be used in the following.

Step 3. The "wild" generalization

If step 2 has been used, we generalize the relation we have found by putting different variables in place of all the variables (except, of course, the induction ones) and constants.

If step 2 has not been used, we unfold once (Burstall and Darlington [1977], i.e. apply the recursive definition) the functions of the original theorem and generalize the result by putting different variables in place of all the variables (except, of course, the induction ones) and constants.

Let x_i be the set of variables introduced at this step.

Step 4. Relations between the variables

One attempts to prove the generalized relations by following each proof trace. This implies of course some instantiations of the variables which are made as far as any functional symbol remains. One is therefore left with relations between the variables x_i.

Notice that when the cross-fertilization is not used, since the wild generalization is made after one unfolding, one has to start the proof trace after one unfolding has been made.

Each trace provides a new relation and we stop when we obtain a set of k equations between the x_i which can be solved.

We shall suppose here that these equations can be solved. Notice that this step contains the induction hypothesis which gives strength to our methodology: once a system of equations is complete, we induce (with no proof !) that no new information will come from further examples.

Step 5. The desired generalization is obtained. This step calls a theorem prover which will "easily" prove the generalized theorem.

B.2. An Example Without Cross-Fertilization

Let f(x) := IF x=0 THEN 1 ELSE f(x-1)*x,
g(x,y) := IF x=0 THEN y ELSE g(x-1),x*y)

where * is the multiplication supposed to be also defined by a rewriting rule. We want to prove that g(x,1) = f(x).

Remark: The reader may try to prove this by structural induction and find that he needs an infinite sequence of proofs.

Step 1. For x=0 prove that

$g(0,1) = f(0)$ (use the stopping condition of f and g)
$1 = 1$ (use the constructor of the integers)
$0 = 0$ (use the empty constructor of the integers)

The proof trace for x=0 is given by the sequence of doublets $((a_1,b_1),(a_2,b_2),(a_3,b_3))$ where $a_1 := g(0,1) = f(0)$, $a_2 := 1 = 1$, $a_3 := 0 = 0$, b_1 := use the stopping condition f and g, b_2 := use the constructor of the integers, ...

In the following, we shall stop our trace when the definitions of f and g are no longer used since the relations between the variables will appear at this point.

-for x=1
g(1,1) = f(1) unfolding
trace 1: g(0,1*1) = f(0)*1 stopping condition
1*1 = 1*1
...
-for x=2
g(2,1) = f(2) unfolding
trace 2: g(1,2*1) = f(1) * 2 unfolding
g(0,1*(2*1)) = (f(0)*1)*2 stopping condition
1*(2*1) = (1*1)*2
...

Step 3. (step 2 is not used here)

The relation to be proven is g(x,1) = f(x) which gives after one unfolding of both functions: g(x−1,x*1) = f(x-1)*x and a wild generalization of it leads to:

$$g(x,x_2{*}x_3)=f(x){*}x_5$$

Step 4. We follow traces 1 and 2 since the trace for x=0 contains no unfolding.

Trace 1 asks at once for the use of the stopping condition, which can be used only if we instantiate x by 0:

$g(0,x_2{*}x_3)=f(0){*}x_5$ (stopping condition)
$x_2{*}x_3=1{*}x_5$

which proves that $g(0,x_2{*}x_3)=f(0){*}x_5$ provided $x_2{*}x_3=1{*}x_5$.

Trace 2 begins with an unfolding which implies only $x > 0$

$g(x,x_2{*}x_3)=f(x){*}x_5$ (unfolding)
$g(x-1,x{*}(x_2{*}x_3))=(f(x-1){*}x){*}x_5$ (stopping condition)

We must use the stopping condition in order to follow trace 2; this implies: $x-1=0$, or $x=1$. We obtain:

$$1^*(x_2{}^*x_3)=(1^*1)^*x_5,$$

which proves that $g(1,x_2{}^*x_3)=f(1)^*x_5$ provided $1^*(x_2{}^*x_3)=(1^*1)^*x_5$. At this step we suppose that we have a system able to simplify both $x_2{}^*x_3=1^*x_5$ and $1^*(x_2{}^*x_3)=(1^*1)^*x_5$ to $x_2{}^*x_3=x_5$ by computing the function *. No new information about the variables x_2,x_3,x_5 is obtained by the use of trace 2 and we make the induction hypothesis that $x_2{}^*x_3=x_5$ is the relation which will be found within any trace.

Step 5. We replace $x_2{}^*x_3$ by its value x_5 in the relation obtained at step 3. We obtain the new relation $g(x,x_5)=f(x)^*x_5$ which is the generalized theorem we have now to prove.

Remark 1: Suppose that the generalized theorem is proven. The substitution $x_5/1$ proves at once the desired theorem.

Remark 2: For illustration purposes, we shall prove the generalized theorem. The basic case is reduced to $y=y$. Induction hypothesis: $g(x,y) = f(x)^*y$ for all y.

Induction proof: prove that $g(x+1,y) = f(x+1)^*y$ for all y.

Unfolding once g and f gives:

$$g(x+1,y) = g(x,(x+1)^*y) \text{ and } f(x+1)^*y = (f(x)^*(x+1))^*y.$$

We use the associativity of * in order to write: $f(x+1)^*y = f(x)^*((x+1)^*y)$. We thus must prove $g(x,(x+1)^*y) = f(x)^*(x+1)^*y)$ which equals the induction hypothesis with the substitution $(x+1)^*y/y$.

B.3. An Example Using Cross-Fertilization

We use the above example so that the same traces are obtained.

Step 2. We remark (see B.2, step 1) that f(0) appears in the trace for $x=1$. The trace for $x=0$ tells us that $f(0) = g(0,1)$ then the expression $g(0,1^*1) = f(0)^*1$ in the trace for $x=1$ becomes $g(0,1^*1) = g(0,1)^*1$.

We see as well that f(1) appears in the trace for $x=2$, obtaining $g(1,2^*1) = g(1,1)^*2$. In the same way, we would obtain $g(2,3^*1) = g(2,1)^*3$.

These three relations are the new relations we are going to generalize. We therefore study the proof trace of these expressions.

$$\begin{array}{lll}
\text{trace 1: } g(0,1*1) = g(0,1)*1 & & \text{(stopping condition)} \\
\quad 1*1 = 1*1 & & \\
\quad \ldots & & \\
\text{trace 2: } g(1,2*1) = g(1,1)*2 & & \text{(unfolding)} \\
\quad g(0,1*(2*1)) = g(0,1*1)*2 & & \text{(stopping condition)} \\
\quad 1*(2*1) = (1*1)*2 & & \\
\quad \ldots & & \\
\text{trace 3: } g(2,3*1) = g(2,1)*3 & & \text{(unfolding)} \\
\quad g(1,2*(3*1)) = g(1,2*1)*3 & & \text{(unfolding)} \\
\quad g(0,1*(2*(3*1))) = g(0,1*(2*1))*3 & & \text{(stopping condition)} \\
\quad 1*(2*(3*1)) = (1*(2*1))*3 & &
\end{array}$$

Step 3. We generalize the variables and the constants of the relations obtained by cross-fertilization: $g(x,x_2*x_3) = g(x,x_5)*x_6$

Step 4. We follow trace 1 which starts with the stopping condition of g which can be used only if $x = 0$ and obtain

$$x_2*x_3=x_5*x_6$$

We follow trace 2:

$$\begin{array}{ll}
g(x,x_2*x_3) = g(x,x_5)*x_6 & \text{(unfolding)} \\
g(x-1,x*(x_2*x_3)) = g(x-1,x*x_5)*x_6 & \text{(stopping condition)}
\end{array}$$

In order to use the stopping condition we must have $x-1=0$, i.e. $x=1$. This gives:

$$1*(x_2*x_3)=(1*x_5)*x_6$$

We follow trace 3 and obtain:

$$\begin{array}{ll}
g(x,x_2*x_3)=g(x,x_5)*x_6 & \text{(unfolding)} \\
g(x-1,x*(x_2*x_3))=g(x-1,x*x_5)*x_6 & \text{(unfolding)} \\
g(x-2,(x-1)*(x*(x_2*x_3)))=g(x-2,(x-1)*(x*x_5))*x_6 & \text{(stopping condition)}
\end{array}$$

The stopping condition implies $x = 2$ so that we get:

$$1*(2*(x_2*x_3))=(1*(2*x_5))*x_6$$

We are able again to prove that all these expressions are equivalent to $x_2*x_3=x_5*x_6$, so we make the induction hypothesis that this relation is valid for all traces. We find the generalized expression: $g(x,x_5*x_6)=g(x,x_5)*x_6$ obtained by replacing $x_2*x_3=x_5*x_6$ in the relation obtained at step 3.

Remark 1: Assume the validity of this expression. The induction proof of $f(x) = g(x,1)$ can be written as:

Induction hypothesis: $f(x) = g(x,1)$.
Induction proof: prove that $f(x+1) = g(x+1,1)$.

Unfolding once $f(x+1)$, we obtain $f(x+1) = f(x)*(x+1) = g(x,1)*(x+1)$ using the hypothesis.
Unfolding $g(x+1,1)$ gives $g(x,(x+1)*1)$.
We therefore want to prove that $g(x,(x+1)*1) = g(x,1)*(x+1)$ which is an instance of the generalized relation with $x_5/1, x_6/(x+1)$, since $(x+1)*1 = 1*(x+1)$.

Remark 2: Let us prove the generalized expression.

$$g(x,y*z) = g(x,y)*z, \text{ for all y and z.}$$

The basis case is reduced to $y*z = y*z$.

Induction hypothesis: $g(x,y*z) = g(x,y)*z$
Induction proof: prove $g(x+1,y*z) = g(x+1\ ,y)*z$.

We unfold both sides of the equality: we have to prove: $g(x,(x+1)*(y*z)) = g(x,(x+1)*y)*z$.

We use the associativity of * in order to write:

$$(x+1) * (y\ z) = ((x+1) * y) *z.$$

We must prove: $g(x, ((x+1)*y)*z) = g(x, (x+1) * y) * z$ which equals the induction hypothesis with the substitution $y/(x+1)*y$.

C. Discussion

C.1. Cross-fertilization or Not?

The above example seems to imply that cross-fertilization, even when possible, is not needed so that one is tempted to classify it as a useless complication. However, the study of more difficult examples (such as the function described in section D.7), shows that a direct generalization of the theorem to prove is not obtained because the equations have only one solution: the particular values we started from.

Cross-fertilization is the only escape we have found up to now in order to avoid this feature so that if the same phenomenon occurs in cross-fertilization, our methodology becomes useless.

On the other hand, section B.3 nicely shows that the property to be looked for in the proof trace is exactly the property issued from the induction proof. More generally, let us consider two functions f and g, f being recursively defined by $f(x) = a(f(x - 1), h(x))$ and g being defined either by terminal recursion or by recursion. Proving $f(x) = g(x)$ by structural induction is an attempt at proving that $f(x) = g(x)$ implies $f(x+1) = g(x+1)$. If our prover chooses to unfold $f(x+1)$, it obtains

$$a(f(x), h(x+1)) = g(x+1)$$

and the only possibility for using the induction hypothesis is to replace $f(x)$ by $g(x)$, i.e. attempt to prove $a(g(x), h(x+1)) = g(x+1)$. Our cross-fertilization procedure tries to find a generalization of this very expression. When g is also recursively defined, one might cross-fertilize any of g or f and the generalized expression one has to look for depends on the unfolding planned by the prover (Boyer and Moore [1975]).

C.2. What if There is One Functional Symbol?

We have developed the case of proving equalities between two functions. It is however clear that our methodology applies to any proof of this type $P(f_1,...,f_n)$=True where P is a given property.

A particular case can possibly raise difficulties: when P is an equality with a variable or a constant, for instance REVERSE(REVERSE(x)) = x (see section D for proofs of this property for different forms of REVERSE).

This problem can be solved in two different ways.

- The variable or constant is considered as the result of another function. For instance, we define COPY(x) = x (see Kodratoff [1979]) and prove REVERSE(REVERSE(x)) = COPY(x).
- The function is defined as an instance of another function. For example, the iterative REVERSE(X) = REV(x,nil) where REV(x,z) is terminal recursive. At a point in the traces, the value x can be cross-fertilized by a functional expression containing REVERSE or REV.

It may unfortunately happen that the above solutions fail. More theoretical results or heuristic tricks must (and we hope will) be included into our methodology.

D. Examples

The variables are either natural integers or lists with only atoms at their top level. We use the usual definitions for the Predecessor (Pred), the Successor (Suc), the predicates Even, = 0, = 1, integer division by 2(/2), CONS, CAR, CDR, ATOM, nil.

D.0. Basis Functions

We have used the following definitions of PLUS (+), TIMES (*), APPEND.

```
+(x,y):= IF (x=0) THEN y
                  ELSE Suc(+(Pred(x),y).
*(x,y):= IF(x=0) THEN 0
                 ELSE +(*(Pred(x),y),y)
APPEND(x,y):= IF ATOM(CDR(x)) THEN CONS(CAR(x),y)
                         ELSE
                  CONS(CAR(x), APPEND(CDR(x),y)).
```

D.1. Prove: f(x) = FACT(x,0) where f and FACT are:

f(x):= IF(x=0) THEN 1 ELSE f(Pred(x))*x,
FACT(x,y):= IF(x=y) THEN 1 ELSE FACT(x,Suc(y))*Suc(y).

-without cross fertilization:

$f(x)*x_2=FACT(x,x_4)*x_5$WHERE $x_4=0,x_2=x_5$.

Supposing that the equations into the "WHERE" are solved:

$f(x)*x_2=FACT(x,0)*x_2$.

-with cross-fertilization:

$FACT(x,x_2)*x_3=FACT(Pred(x),x_4)*x$WHERE $x_2=x_3,x_4=Pred(x_2)$.

This is equivalent to:

$$FACT(x,x_2)*x_2=FACT(Pred(x),Pred(x_2))*x.$$

Remark: In this case, the sequence of proof traces must be indexed by (x−y) = 0,1,2 ... rather than x = 0,1,2, ... as usual. We have no place here to explain how this can be automatically discovered.

D.2.

```
DIF(x):= IF(x=1) THEN 1
         ELSE IF Even(x) THEN DIF(x/2) ELSE
            +(DIF(Pred(x)/2), DIF(Suc(x)/2)
DIG(x,y,z):= IF(x=1) THEN y
         ELSE IF Even(x)THEN DIG(x/2, +(y,z),z)
                ELSE
            DIG(Suc(x)/2,y,+(y,z))
```

Fails without cross-fertilization.
-IF x is odd, the generalization is:

$$\mathrm{DIG}(\mathrm{Suc}(x)/2,x_2,+(x_3,x_4))=+(\mathrm{DIG}(\mathrm{Pred}(x)/2,x_6,x_7),\mathrm{DIG}(\mathrm{Suc}(x)/2,x_9,x_{10}))$$

$$\begin{aligned}\text{WHERE } &+(x_2,+(x_3,x_4))=+(x_6,+(x_9,x_{10}))\\ &+(x_1,+(x_2,+(x_3,x_4)))=+(+(x_6,x_7),+(x_9+(x_9,x_{10})))\\ &+(+(x_2,+(x_3,x_4)),+(x_3,x_4))=+(+(x_6,+(x_6,x_7)),+(+(x_9,x_{10}),x_{10}))\\ &+(x_2,+(x_2,+(x_3,x_4)))=+(+(+(x_6,x_7),x_7),+(x_9,+(x_9,+(x_9,x_{10}))))\end{aligned}$$

Supposing that the "WHERE" equations are solved, one has:

$$\begin{aligned}&\mathrm{DIG}(\mathrm{Suc}(x)/2,x_2,+(x_3,x_4))=+(\mathrm{DIG}(\mathrm{Pred}(x)/2,x_6,0),\\ &\mathrm{DIG}(\mathrm{Suc}(x)/2,x_2,x_{10})\,\text{WHERE}+(x_3,x_4)=+(x_6,x_{10}).\end{aligned}$$

-If x is even, we find no generalization.

D.3. Prove: FIB(x) = FIBO(x,0) where FIB and FIBO are:

```
FIB(x):= IF ((x=0) OR (x=1)) THEN 1
                  ELSE
            +(FIB(Pred(x)), FIB(Pred(Pred(x)))),
FIBO(x,z):= IF ((x=0) OR (x=1)) THEN Suc(z)
                  ELSE
             FIBO(Pred(x), FIBO(Pred(Pred(x)), z)).
```

Fails without cross-fertilization. Generalization:

$$\begin{aligned}&\mathrm{FIBO}(x,\mathrm{FIBO}(\mathrm{Pred}(x),x_3))=+(\mathrm{FIBO}(x,x_5),\\ &\mathrm{FIBO}(\mathrm{Pred}(x),x_7))\,\text{WHERE } x_3=+(x_5,x_7), \text{ for all } x.\end{aligned}$$

D.4. Prove: REV2(x) = REV1(x) where REV2 and REV1 are:

```
REV2(x):= IF ATOM(CDR(x)) THEN CONS(CAR(x), nil)
                ELSE
          APPEND (REV2(CDR(x)), CONS(CAR(x), nil)),
REV1(x):= FOO(x, nil);
FOO(x,y):= IF ATOM(CDR(x)) THEN CONS(CAR(x),y)
                ELSE FOO (CDR(x), CONS(CAR(x),y))
```

-without cross-fertilization:

$$\text{APPEND}(\text{REV2}(x), x_2) = \text{FOO}(x, x_2) \text{ for all } x \text{ and } x_2$$

(lists with atoms only at their top level).

Remark: We do not use here the associativity of APPEND.
-with cross-fertilization:

$$\text{APPEND}(\text{FOO}(x, x_2), x_3) = \text{FOO}(x, x_5) \text{ WHERE}$$
$$\text{APPEND}(x_2, x_3) = x_5, \text{ for all } x$$

D.5. Prove: REV1(REV1(x)) = x

We use the second solution of section C.2. in order to find:

$$\text{REV1}(\text{FOO}(x, x_2)) = \text{FOO}(x_2, x) \text{ for all } x \text{ and } x_2$$

E. Conclusion

The examples of section D show that a wide variety of problems can be solved by our methodology. We should like to conclude by pointing at its weaknesses.

It may happen that each trace introduces a new relation between the variables so that we have to deal with an infinity of relations.

It may happen that the solution of the obtained equations is more difficult than the proposed problem. Our main point now is to define precisely a class of theorems and functions to which our methodology applies.

In the meanwhile, we are carrying on an implementation of the methodology in order to have more experimental results about its applicability and efficiency.

References

Boyer et al. [1975]
R.S. Boyer and JS. Moore, "Proving theorems about LISP functions," *J.ACM* 22 (1975), pp. 129–144.

Burstall et al. [1977]
R.M. Burstall and J. Darlington, "A transformation system for developing recursive programs," *J.ACM* 24 (1977), pp. 44–67.

Castaing et al. [1980]
J. Castaing and Y. Kodratoff, "Generalisation des theoremes," Actes reunion GROSSEM, Poitiers (1980), LITP editor (1981), pp. 141–167.

Degano et al. [1979]
P.P. Degano, F. Sirovich, "Inducing function properties from computation traces," Proc. IJCAI–79, pp. 208–216.
"Inductive generalization and proofs of function properties," *Comp. Ling. Comp. Lang.* 13 (1979), pp. 101–130.

Kodratoff [1979]
Y. Kodratoff, "A class of functions synthesized from a finite number of examples and a LISP program scheme," *Inter. J. of Comp. and Inform. Sci.* 8 (1979), pp. 489–521.

Manna et al. [1973]
Z. Manna, S. Ness and J. Vuillemin, "Inductive methods for proving properties of programs," *C.ACM* 16 (1973), pp. 491–502.

Levi et al. [1975]
G. Levi and F. Sirovich, "Proving program properties, symbolic evaluation and logical procedural semantics," Lecture notes in Computer Science, 62, Springer, Berlin (1975), pp. 569–574.

Moore [1975]
J.S. Moore, "Introducing iteration into the pure LISP theorem prover," IEEE, SE–1 (1975), pp. 328–338.

CHAPTER 20

Design Issues for Exemplary Programming

D.A. Waterman

W.S. Faught

Philip Klahr

Stanley J. Rosenschein

Robert Wesson

The Rand Corporation
Santa Monica, CA

Abstract

This chapter describes considerations and research questions for the design of an advanced exemplary programming (EP) system. An exemplary programming system typically synthesizes programs from examples of the task to be performed. The EP system "looks over the shoulder" of the user as he performs a task on the computer, and from this example creates a program called an agent to perform the same task or some variant of it. User comments or "advice" are combined with pre-stored knowledge about the task domain to create a general-purpose program for performing tasks illustrated by the example.

The purpose of an EP system is to create small personalized programs capable of acting as interfaces to complex computer systems or as intelligent assistants to aid the user in his work. These programs free users from repeating detailed interactions with applications programs. Yet writing such programs often cannot be justified because of the large number of programs needed, their personalized nature, and their fast-changing specifications. The EP methodology provides a means for exploring quick, easy, and inexpensive methods for creating individualized software of this type.

Our discussion in this chapter centers on design issues related to the next-generation EP system, EP-3, which has not been implemented. Ideas for the EP-3 system design were generated from our experience designing and implementing two earlier EP systems, EP-1 and EP-2.

The most important design issue for EP-3 is the choice of system architecture. We propose a Hearsay-II-type architecture, a pattern-directed system that uses a collection of "experts" called knowledge sources (KSs) to hypothesize and refine procedures for accomplishing some specified task. Furthermore, we propose combining a model-directed top-down approach to program synthesis with a pattern-directed bottom-up approach. The model-directed approach is based on scripts consisting of high-level descriptions of tasks the user might want to perform. This works in conjunction with the pattern-directed approach based on data-directed evocation of rules. Each collection of rules is a KS that fires when it "recognizes" particular information in the trace of the example or in hypotheses generated by other KSs. This modular design permits extensibility: new KSs may be added and modified as needed and new scripts may be acquired by monitoring and analyzing the examples and mapping them into scripts.

A. Introduction

It felt strange to enter my new office for the first time. The highly polished walnut desk was empty, the bookcases in repose, the dictaphone microphone in its cradle. All were silently waiting for me, poised and ready for use by the budding new "data processing manager," as I was to be called.

After depositing my briefcase, I sat down and turned to face the computer terminal stationed where typewriters usually sit. When I turned it on, it beeped and typed the reassuring "*" prompt of an operating system I knew. At last, something familiar! Now, I thought, all I need to do is wade through the new manuals of library programs, transfer my old programs here, and learn the various nuances of this system, and I can begin using it. About that time, someone appeared at the door holding a cup of coffee.

"Hi! I'm your new assistant. They call me E.P.," he said, offering me the coffee. He moved over beside me and sat down next to the terminal. "What would you like to do on the machine today?"

"Glad to meet you, E.P.," I replied. "I'm not very familiar with this particular system, but how about logging in and sending a message via electronic mail to my colleagues back at school letting them know I've arrived and am setting up shop here. Send it to 'Johnston @ ITH-1.' Know my logon here?"

"Sure thing," he replied. "I make it my business to get to know all the computer users around here: who they are, what they use the machine for, and how they do it. Even down to the way they like to name their files. Like, do you use ---.src, ---.txt, or ---.orig for your text files?" As I watched, he had expertly used the shortest logon and message generation commands and was almost finished composing the mail message to Johnston.

"Oh, I usually don't use any extension at all, but I keep all text in a sub-directory called 'TEXT'." He immediately began creating one for me. "Oh, while you're at it, would you retrieve all my Pascal source files from the machine back at school? You might have to make some name changes to get them here."

"Sorry, I don't know how to use your old machine," he confessed, "but if you'll show me a little, I'm pretty quick at getting the hang of it."

I touched the keyboard for the first time and quickly logged into my old machine via the net.

He interrupted, "Let's see. That was logon name, then password, then account number. Right?"

"Uh huh." I continued by listing all my old files with the "PAS:" prefix and using the file-transfer program there to copy them over to my new directory, changing the prefix to an extension ".pas."

When I had done a couple like this, he suggested I let him try to finish it. He did it a little differently, using the local file-transfer program to do it, and I had to correct him once to point out that the files like "PAS:EX-SYS1" and "PAS:EX-BIOSPH" were the executable versions, not source code, and not to transfer them. All in all, though, this guy was going to make using the system fantastically easy!

B. Programming by Example

It would be fantastic, indeed, if we each had an "E.P." assistant to help us at the terminal. How many times we've had to rename a dozen files according to some simple criterion, or had to do some infrequent operation that we didn't quite remember how to do but never had time to construct a macro-program to do for us! With the tremendous increase in useful program libraries and activities available through the terminal, such an assistant seems almost essential, to everyone from the professional who doesn't have the time to learn every detail of a system to the office clerk who needs to do highly repetitive tasks but thinks "DO loops" are some kind of new breakfast cereal.

We are researching the ways and means of creating machine-based versions of "E.P." Through analysis and the actual construction of two preliminary versions, we have arrived at the point where we are ready to tackle the design of a program which itself can learn to mimic example tasks and remember how to perform the routine ones it has seen before—everything that E.P. did above (except, perhaps, bringing the cup of coffee). We call the method exemplary programming, a type of program synthesis based on program specification from examples of the task to be performed (see also Biermann and Krishnaswamy, 1974; Biermann, 1976; Siklossy and Sykes, 1975; Green, 1976). The EP system "looks over the shoulder" of the user as he performs a task on the computer, and from this example creates a program called an agent to perform the same task. User comments or "advice" are combined with pre-stored knowledge about the task domain to create a general-purpose program for performing tasks illustrated by the example.

The basic EP paradigm is illustrated in Figure 1. The user interacts with an application program or operating system to perform a task. The EP program watches and saves the record or "trace" of the interaction as one example of how to perform the task. During the interaction the user may provide the EP program with advice clarifying the example. The trace, advice, and built-in knowledge about the task domain are used by the EP program to construct an agent for performing the task. As the agent attempts to perform the task, it may encounter conditions that did not occur during the example. At this point the user is notified and asked to interact again, providing an example of what to do in this new situation. The EP program monitors the interaction and augments the agent, enabling it to recognize and respond to the new situation when it next occurs. Thus, the agent is developed incrementally based on a number of different examples of task execution.

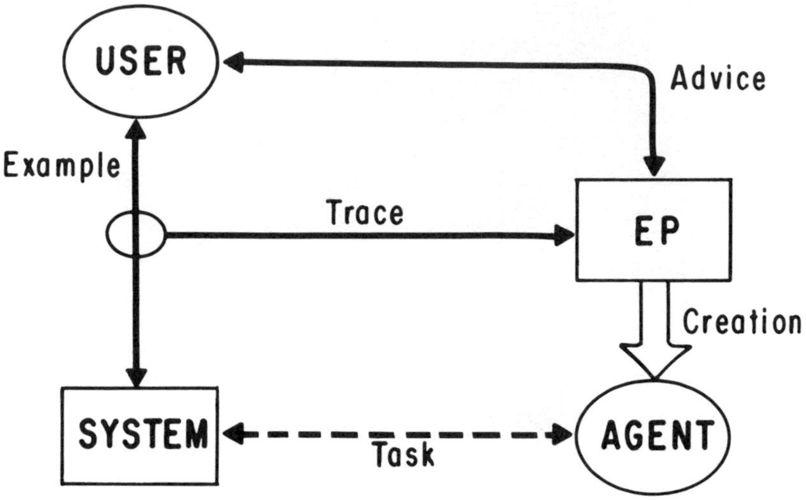

Figure 1. EP Paradigm

The EP approach to program synthesis is based on four important ideas. The most fundamental idea is that of the user agent (Anderson, 1976b; Waterman, 1977a, 1978). This is a program that can act as an interface between the user and the computer systems he wants to access. A user agent is typically a small program residing in a user's terminal or in a portion of a central timesharing system. It may display many of the characteristics of a human assistant, such as the ability to carry on a dialogue with the user or external computer systems or even other agents. The user agent is the target program we are attempting to create through use of the EP system.

Another important idea that pervades the EP system design is that of concurrent processing. By this we mean an organization that permits the user-system interaction to take place concurrently with its analysis by the EP system and the subsequent creation of a user agent. Instead of having the EP system situated between the user and the external system, it sits off to one side (see Figure 1), analyzing the trace as it is being generated. In our current prototype, EP-2, the EP system actually runs on a remote computer linked to the user-system interaction on the user's local computer. Thus the delay in response time seen by the user during agent creation is minimized. Debugging is facilitated by having the EP system execute the agent as the user watches. After debugging is complete, the agent can be compiled into an efficient form that runs directly on the user's local machine.

An important idea that has dominated the EP design philosophy has been learning from examples (Hayes-Roth, 1978). Example-based learning has been studied by researchers in artificial intelligence and cognitive psychology, particularly in the areas of concept formation (Hunt, 1962; Hayes-Roth and Hayes-Roth, 1977; Winston, 1975), serial pattern acquisition (Simon and Kotovsky, 1963; Waterman, 1976), and rule induction from examples (Hayes-Roth, 1976a, 1976b; Vere, 1978; Waterman, 1975). It is our contention that traces of the activity one would like performed in a man-machine environment contain a wealth of information about the task, the user, and the approach suggested by the user for attaining his goals. Specification by example is a natural means of conveying information, one that minimizes the need for training the user in the operation of the program-synthesis technique. When supplemented with advice from the user about his intentions and built-in knowledge about the task domain, the example becomes a powerful tool for program specification.

The final important idea incorporated into both the design of the EP system and the design of the user agents it creates is that of rule-based systems (Waterman and Hayes-Roth, 1978a, 1978b). The rule-directed approach to knowledge acquisition has been the basis for a number of successful research projects in the past few years, including MYCIN (Shortliffe, 1974), a system which contains condition-action rules encoding heuristics for diagnosis and treatment of infectious diseases; TIERESIAS (Davis, 1976), a rule-based approach for transferring expertise from a human to the knowledge base of a high-performance program; and Meta-DENDRAL, a program designed to formulate rules of mass spectrometry which describe the operation of classes of molecular structures (Buchanan, 1974). Other related systems include AM (Lenat, 1976, 1977; Lenat & Harris, 1978), which uses heuristic rules to develop concepts in mathematics, and SLIM and SPROUTER (Hayes-Roth, 1973, 1976a, 1976b; Hayes-Roth & McDermott, 1976, 1978), which infer general condition -> action rules from before-and-after examples of their use. The rule-based system design imposes a high degree of structure on the code, leading to a simple organization that facilitates debugging, verifiability, and incremental modification (Hayes-Roth, Waterman, Lenat, 1978).

The EP paradigm is applicable to tasks that require repetitive, personalized user-system dialogue and can be described by one or more sequences of actions on some external system. Examples of these user-interactive tasks include computer network tasks (e.g., file transfers), operating systems tasks (e.g., file maintenance), data-base retrievals, and edit macros. Development of an advanced EP system will permit us to make inroads into the following problem areas involving effective use of computers: 1) the difficulty of correctly interacting with numerous systems and facilities, each of which requires a unique syntax and protocol; 2) the problem of remembering how to do something that an "expert" previously demonstrated; 3) the frustrating problem of repeating the same sequence of instructions to accomplish a frequently occurring task; and 4) the problem of generalizing specific command sequences to handle a more varied set of problem conditions.

There are, however, certain difficulties associated with the use of example-based programming. First is the basic problem of specifying a complex algorithm from examples of behavior traces. For most interesting classes of algorithms, a single behavior trace will generally be consistent with a large number of alternative algorithms. Since the user of an EP system is trying to build a realization for an algorithm that could be arbitrarily complex, he can never be absolutely sure that the approximation constructed by example is close enough to the desired algorithm to meet his needs. This implies the necessity for an open-ended algorithm-construction paradigm, i.e., the ability to extend the algorithm by example at any time during its construction or application by the user.

Implicit in all the EP work are the following conjectures: 1) there exist interesting classes of algorithms that can be defined by specification of behavior traces, 2) there exist specifiable bases for choosing one algorithm over another as the "intended" one, and 3) programs can be implemented to make this choice and synthesize the algorithms. Reasonable computer scientists may differ as to whether the first two conjectures are plausible. The skeptic might feel that the approach lacks merit because of the idiosyncratic nature of interesting algorithms. However, our previous work with exemplary programming has led us to believe that not only do such classes of algorithms exist, they provide the basis for interesting and practical applications.

Another fundamental problem is how to integrate diverse sources of knowledge in the synthesis of an algorithm. For any particular application domain there will be several unique knowledge sources that can be used to help interpret the behavior trace. For example, in the operating system domain they might include expected input and output strings for each system command, simplified flowcharts of system commands, typical connected sequences of user actions (e.g., telnetting to a remote site and then logging in), and user advice for branches and loops. The problem of integrating knowledge sources necessitates the use of a special mechanisim or representational technique, such as cooperating specialists (see Section D.5).

Another problem is that a strict example-based paradigm tends to present information at a very low level only. High-level information can also be quite useful, e.g., a description of the task, algorithm, etc., in a high-level language that effectively condenses the information in many examples into a few concise statements. In our approach we touch on this idea through the application of "user advice" and pre-defined "scripts" (see Section E.1) that represent high-level abstractions of potential algorithms the user may desire to implement.

Since much knowledge about the task domain is needed to help the system interpret the examples, the task domain must be well defined ahead of time. Thus, unexpected results occurring during the example will be difficult to handle. Even worse, the examples must be error-free, or the EP system must have a way of recognizing errors when they occur. These errors can come from either the user or the system he is accessing.

We feel that the requirement of providing error-free examples is not so great a restriction as to negate the usefulness of the approach.

EP applies only to domains where there is an abundance of low-level feedback at short intervals, i.e., a dialogue that represents or describes the relevant ongoing behavior. Consequently, the exemplary programming approach would not apply to synthesizing a sort function by giving examples of input-output pairs. However, if the algorithm could be demonstrated by actually sorting a list of items, showing all intermediate steps, then this approach might possibly be applicable.

Another problem is that in some interactions involving man-machine dialogue, the man performs crucial activities in his head that are relevant to the task. How to present these activities to the EP system is the question here. For example, a user lists his files and deletes each with the prefix "bin" if he thinks he knows what is in the file. The EP system might be able to infer that files with the prefix "bin" were being deleted but would not be able to deal with the later information.

The ideas we describe for an advanced EP system are clearly speculative, since they have not been implemented and tested. Our inital EP systems have only scratched the surface and do not prove that an advanced EP system such as the one we describe here can be developed. Many researchers have been stymied by the complexities of developing an automatic programming system. In our approach we hope to simplify the problem by limiting the automatic programming system to one that creates programs from examples rather than general specifications. But the task is still complex and difficult. Our approach is based on the deficiencies uncovered in developing previous EP systems. Although these previous systems produced only simple programs, they were both operational and useful. We hope the discussion that follows will shed light on new issues and ideas in the area of program synthesis.

Section C of this Note describes the design and implementation of EP-2, our current EP System. Section D discusses design goals for an advanced version of EP, while Section E describes architectural considerations. The conclusions are presented in Section F.

C. EP-2 System

The current operational EP system, EP-2, is patterned after EP-1 (Waterman, 1977b, 1978), an initial prototype EP system written in RITA (Anderson & Gillogly, 1976a, 1976b; Anderson, et al., 1977). EP-2, however, extends and develops the ideas in that initial prototype.

C.1 Basic Structure

EP-2 operates in three stages: trace acquisition, trace interpretation, and program creation. First, EP-2 watches the user perform a series of operations on the computer and saves the trace of the user-system interaction. Next, EP-2 maps the trace into a model of the interaction that is more general than the trace and is in the form of a graph describing the flow of control during the interaction. Finally, EP-2 transforms the model into a program composed of rules whose conditions represent nodes in the graph and whose actions represent transitions from one node to the next. The program or agent is stored in the user's library under a name supplied by the user. To activate the agent, the user supplies the agent name, usually a natural language command (e.g., "print 2 copies of file foo").

The EP-2 system requires three major information channels: user-system, user-EP, and EP-system. A switch called the front end (FE), situated on the user's local system coordinates and directs the information flow along these channels (see Figure 1). The user-system channel is used by EP-2 to obtain trace information during agent creation, while the user-EP channel permits the exchange of advice and instructions between EP-2 and the user. The EP-system channel is used to send input to the system when executing stored agents.

EP-2 has three basic modes: dormant, create, and execute. When the system is in the dormant mode, the user interacts with it through the front end while EP-2 does nothing. When the system is in the agent-creation mode, the user first gives it the name of the agent, i.e., the agent call. The call may have variable items in it. Values for the variables are subsequently assigned when the user executes the agent. The user then interacts with the system through the FE, and the FE marks and sends all these messages to EP-2 so that they may be incorporated into the trace. The trace is a verbatim description of the interaction, including user advice. EP-2 processes the trace (either incrementally or all at once) to create a model. If the user makes an error and wishes to correct it, he can edit the trace. Whenever the user edits the trace, the current model is deleted and a new model is constructed from the edited (and presumably correct) trace by reprocessing the trace. An interpretable version of the model is then stored as a program (or "agent") in a library under the name provided by the user. (The trace is also stored.) When the user calls an agent, EP-2 goes into execute mode; it locates and reads the model from the library and then interprets it in a manner isomorphic to executing an ordered production system.

The model is a data structure that represents the algorithm the user had in his mind to perform the actions shown in the trace. The model is represented as a graph structure of nodes and arcs. The nodes represent states; the arcs have two components: conditions and actions. Several arcs may originate from each node (state). During execution, EP-2 tests the conditions on all the arcs emanating from a particular node. The arc whose condition is true (there should be at most one) is the branch to be taken. The arc's action is executed and the state of the agent is set to the succeeding node.

C.2 Applications And Examples

We will briefly describe two prototypical applications of EP-2 to illustrate the kinds of agents that have been constructed by example. (The reader is referred to Faught, et al., (1979)) for more detailed discussions and examples.)

The first application is a network access task. An agent is created to retrieve a file from a remote system, print it on a local printer, and delete the extra copy from the local system. The agent call is "print <filename> from <remote system name>." The user demonstrates the protocol using operating system and file transfer commands. A trace of this protocol is shown in Appendix A.

The second application is a data-base retrieval task using the LADDER system (Hendrix, et al., 1978), operating on a naval data-base. This application uses several subagents, all constructed by example. The global agent's call is "<ship type> within <distance> miles." The global agent then calls the subagents in turn. The first subagent logs into a remote system using the ARPANET and starts the LADDER system. The second subagent writes several definitions in the LADDER system's language. The third subagent types a specification to LADDER using the global agent's parameters. The fourth subagent logs out of the LADDER system. Finally, the fifth subagent edits a transcript of the LADDER session and appends the transcript to a log of LADDER sessions. The advantages of the data-base application are that the user does not have to remember a complicated protocol and is freed from a time-consuming, laborious task. See Appendix B for an example of an EP-2 LADDER scenario.

EP-2 is also useful for constructing tutorial agents that demonstrate the use of some applications programs, e.g., a message system, and then allow the user to try it. Subagents can even be created to demonstrate various system commands. This capability of EP can be used to provide a general facility for creating tutorial programs on any user-interactive system.

The current EP-2 system is limited to creating agents with straight-line code and simple loops, which severely restricts the usefulness of the resulting agent. Biermann (1976) developed algorithms for synthesizing flowcharts that could be applied to EP. The main problem is limiting the search space of possible flowcharts. A semantic knowledge base (see Section D) is needed to help limit this space. EP-2 relies primarily on simple syntactic information, e.g., system prompts, and does not contain semantic knowledge of the user-system interaction. What EP-2 needs are knowledge bases containing both domain and programming constructs. For example, a data-base of typical programming constructs, such as "for" loops or sequential file reading, could greatly simplify understanding the branch conditions and data flow in user protocols. Tables of system inputs and outputs could be used to help select candidate global agent variables and track data flows through the agent. Finally, flowcharts of system programs could list the possible system responses at each point and help EP-2 identify potential branches in the agent.

D. Design Goals for EP-3

As a result of our experience with EP-2 we are now able to formulate some basic design goals for the next-generation EP system, EP-3. This section discusses four basic goals to be used to guide the design of the EP-3 system.

The first basic goal is example-generalization, that is, mapping specific examples of user interactions into a general procedure applicable in other situations. The example-generalization ability of EP-2 is somewhat superficial; it does not represent deep learning in the sense of producing analogous behavior in new contexts. The second goal involves the acquisition and application of domain knowledge. In EP-2 little domain knowledge is built-in and no accommodations are made for acquiring new knowledge of this type automatically. The third goal is induction of program structure. This involves recognizing regularities in the trace and mapping them into appropriate program constructs, e.g., loops and branches. Because EP-2 is not able to handle this problem it is severely limited in its scope of application. The final goal is human engineering. Although significant effort is put into making EP-2 helpful and easy to use there is much room for improvement. For each area, we consider several feasible approaches for an advanced exemplary programming system and attempt to reach realistic design goals for EP-3.

D.1 Superficial vs. Deep Learning

The task of the EP system is to observe a user's behavior and acquire the ability to produce analogous behavior on future occasions. The problem arises in defining the intended sense of "analogous."

On the one hand, we would certainly not want to equate "analogous" with "identical"; a system capable of creating only "verbatim" agents would be of little utility. On the other hand, it is unreasonable to define "analogous" as "achieving the user's main goal by whatever means available," since this implies unlimited problem-solving abilities on the part of EP. EP's capabilities should lie somewhere between these two extremes.

In defining EP's ability to analogize, two components can be discerned: (1) how do we define the class of behaviors that EP can recognize, and (2) once recognized, to what extent can these behaviors be operationalized or instantiated in new contexts? The most realistic approach to (1) is to provide EP with an extensible set of schemata and some rules for recognizing instances of a schema or relatively simple combinations of schemata. Since (2) potentially involves the ability to synthesize arbitrary programs, a realistic approach would be to provide EP with a repertoire of specialized techniques guaranteed to operationalize those schematic actions it can recognize.

The EP system can still exhibit a good deal of flexibility in learning even if schemata are provided in advance. For instance, a schema may be only partially specified, with the remaining parts to be extracted from the trace. The complexity of the resulting structures may be considerable and, in a sense, may blur the distinction between "mere" recognition and "true" learning.

D.2. Domain-Specific Knowledge

The EP system will require domain-specific knowledge to be effective in helping users perform useful tasks. For example, to create an agent to help the user log on to a variety of machines, EP must know the appropriate logon sequence for each machine and must recognize that this is the agent the user wants. By observing the user complete a logon sequence on a familiar machine, EP might infer that the user is interested in a "logon" agent.

A more complicated task would be creating an agent capable of executing an analysis program on a text file and printing the result, given the name and directory location of the program and file. If the example trace illustrates this process for program and data residing in the local machine, a basic problem is determining the kind of knowledge EP needs to generalize to the case of arbitrary machines accessed over a network.

EP would have to know how a program's input dataset is defined under different operating systems. EP would have to know what operating system was running on a particular machine. These facts could be learned by having observed the user on other occasions (given that EP can recognize specific operating systems), or they could be built-in knowledge. EP would also have to know how to log on to remote systems and transfer files. Some of this knowledge is obviously general and should be built-in. Nonetheless, many details (e.g., specific logon sequences) could be learned from repeated observations or from user advice.

Consequently, one promising approach is to build into EP numerous descriptions of commonplace activities that require domain knowledge. This should be done in a way that allows EP to fill in details later through observation and advice. Thus EP will learn not only what the user does, but relatively permanent domain knowledge as well.

D.3. Learning Algorithmic Structures

Much of EP's effort will be spent determining the desired internal structure of the agent it is to construct. It will be trying to answer questions like: Are these three user commands that look so similar really instances of a single command being executed repeatedly in a loop, or are the similarities coincidental? Why did the user put the results of a certain operation in a certain file? Which file should be used in general?

To answer questions like these, EP needs more than just domain knowledge. It must know what kinds of things users typically do, and how they do them. This knowledge should be at various levels of abstraction. For instance, EP should be able to interpret a segment of a user-typed string from multiple viewpoints: a string, the name of a file, an argument of a certain operator, and so on. Furthermore, EP should contain heuristics for identifying common control structures using all the syntactic and semantic cues at its disposal.

D.4. Human Engineering

Looking at the intended users of EP and the anticipated characteristic applications, it becomes clear why the success of EP depends crucially on effective human engineering. EP is for use by both novices and experts. It helps them use computers by letting them do things they don't know how to do themselves, and by doing things faster and more conveniently. A poorly designed system that frustrates the user would defeat the purpose of EP.

The design should explicitly take into account the various classes of users EP will serve: ARPANET users, application programmers, editors, novices using special subsystems, etc. Each type of user has different needs, approaches to programming, and levels of understanding. For example, it may be convenient to allow an experienced programmer to give EP advice using standard notions like "variable," "parameter," etc. Yet a non-programmer who just uses the computer to send and receive messages should not have to confront these concepts when using EP.

The general characteristics we seek are reliability, clarity, and ease of use. EP should make it easy to correct errors, make small modifications to existing agents, and retrieve agents by name and by a description of their purpose. The user should be able to give EP advice, where appropriate, in a natural and concise way. These considerations play a role in the design of both the user interface and the agents themselves.

D.5. General Considerations

Since this knowledge is likely to be diverse, incomplete, and often fragmented, it is essential that EP's basic design take these characteristics into consideration. A design well suited to handling information of this type is one based on cooperating specialists. For EP, each specialist would offer a partial characterization of the trace from its own point of view (e.g., file command specialist, common loop recognizer, etc.). Synthesis specialists would integrate these views, thus producing the final agent. An important advantage of this approach is the ability to directly control the allocation of processing resources by intelligent scheduling of specialists. This is especially important for EP, given the large space of alternative interpretations of a trace and the amount of unnecessary, spurious information (e.g., the exact contents of a file being displayed but not used in any other way).

E. Architectural Considerations for EP-3

In this section, we explore the architectural alternatives for the EP-3 system. Drawing from our research discussions and experience, as well as from implementations of related ideas, we delineate the specific EP-3 architectures that satisfy the design goals of Section C and are most likely to achieve high performance using current technology.

Recall that the problem for our new system is to (a) construct a structure that accounts for the sequence of user actions (the trace) in some general sense, (b) both acquire and apply domain-specific knowledge to the problem of recognizing user intentions, (c) learn the algorithmic structure of complex agents, and (d) provide a helpful, friendly interface for both naive and sophisticated users. A good model for what we expect this structure to be can be found in the interaction between an experienced computer terminal user and a novice. "Now, compile the programs, leaving the source code in the SOURCE directory and the object code in the RUN directory," is a typical high-level instruction from the experienced teacher. It specifies a goal-oriented task, omitting such details as the implicit loop when more than one program exists and the syntactic distinctions which must be made between source and object code names in the machine. Like the novice, our EP-3 must be capable of storing the general and specific knowledge about user activities and using that knowledge to understand the trace at various levels of abstraction.

At the foundation of many of the architectures we have considered is the "generate-and-test" problem-solving paradigm. EP-3 will operate by proposing explanations of the trace and correlating them with what is actually present. One possibility is to make EP-3 a model-directed system, proceeding from the more abstract to the specific by initially assuming a particular user activity, deducing the required specifics, and checking them against the trace. Another is to make EP-3 a data-directed system, using specific trace sequences to suggest the more abstract concepts. Or EP-3 could apply both of these approaches, combining the best of both worlds. These approaches are detailed and evaluated below.

A common framework for this discussion may be laid by recalling the Hearsay-II speech-understanding system (Lessor and Erman, 1977). A somewhat modified form of its terminology will be used here, as the following synopsis of its structure and operation suggests: A common data structure, the *blackboard,* is shared among many knowledge source (KS) modules. Each KS, an expert at whatever it does, is responsible for a specific subpart of the problem. The KSs share their information by writing hypotheses on the blackboard. A hypothesis may be an explanation of some part of the data stream, or it may be a prediction that some datum should be present. KSs support and reject the hypotheses posed by other KSs. Whenever a set of mutually supportive hypotheses emerges beyond some threshold level, or the computational resources are exhausted, the program stops with the hypotheses being its solution. This short description of the Hearsay-II architecture should suffice for our purposes. We will, of course, be introducing other concepts and terms and redefining the ones above for our purposes, but their basic meanings remain.

E.1. Model-Directed Inference

Consider first a goal-directed technique—hypothesize first and confirm later. We call this technique "model-directed inference," because the system is assumed to initially possess models of the computer systems to be used, the tasks to be performed, and possibly the user himself. Such a system operates by inferring the meaning of the trace from these models, as well as by using the trace to extend the models.

Turning to the novice user mentioned above for illustration, assume that EP-3 could somehow represent the concepts necessary for temporal sequencing as well as more primitive ones such as compiling, file transfer, and directory. It could thus have models representing expected user activities at various levels of detail and generality encoded in these concepts. The syntax, expected output, and reasons for issuing a compile monitor command would be included in system models, while more specific information such as the fact that this user typically renames the compiler output files according to some convention before storing them away would be part of a user model. Using these concepts, EP-3 could make predictions about what it should see in the trace. The selection of specific components of models to represent hypotheses about segments of user activity could be activated by many clues, from the compile statement in the trace to a user directive stating, "I'm going to do some compiling now." When activated, these components automatically establish a complex context that simplifies EP-3's understanding of the lower-level actions appearing in the trace.

We will call the action sequences that represent a unified higher-level activity scripts because they resemble drama scripts by specifying contexts and temporal sequences of actions yet to be performed (cf. Schank and Abelson, 1977). Our scripts are more general than those of the playwright because they allow choice points and alternative behaviors. A compile script for our imaginary user might look like this:

1 Locate the source code to be compiled, say, <source>

2 Issue the monitor command "Compile <source>"

3 Then do any of the following:

Edit and recompile if errors; or
Test-run the object code; or
Rename the object code; or
Do nothing here

4 Save the object code.

Scripts might exist at various levels of abstraction. The above script, for instance, could be part of a larger "program construction" script while being composed of many lower-level scripts which further specify its own abstractions (e.g., there might be a "locate source code" script for the first action above).

We envision the hypothesizing of user activities to begin at the highest level. Thus, for example, there will be scripts that specify a typical user's daily activites, e.g., logging in, checking and reading mail, deleting old or unused files, editing some files, etc. There will also be scripts for different "types" of users, e.g., system maintainers, editors, application programmers, ARPAnet users, etc. Thus, the EP-3 system would initially have some idea of what a user typically accomplishes in a computer session.

These models of potential user activities will generate expectations about what the user is doing and is going to do. We anticipate that they will not be used in a purely top-down manner, but rather will guide the pattern-matching inherent in both model-directed and pattern-directed inference. Particular items in the trace might suggest that a specific script is being used, and the expectations generated by that script can then be matched against the actual trace data and the script instantiated or rejected in favor of another. Once a particular script has been validated as what the user did, it provides a high-level representation of that behavior and can be reinstantiated as desired to replicate it. When a script includes alternative means of accomplishing a goal, the reinstantiation might perform the task more efficiently than the original user keystrokes, thereby realizing true expertise by helping the user perform his task even better than before.

In summary, we see four main uses for our proposed scripts:

- Recognizers: Scripts recognize that certain activities are being performed by a user.
- Predictors: Scripts predict subsequent commands and activities in the trace. The confirmation of such predictions will improve the credibility of the proposed scripts.
- Evaluators: Scripts can support or refute existing hypotheses about user actions.
- Generators: Scripts can generate agents by being instantiated within a particular computer environment.

Notice that the use of scripts as generators enables an EP-3 agent to be specified at a high, abstract level. Executing an agent would involve the instantiation of the specified scripts relative to the current computer environment. Thus, for example, an agent can be created on one machine and then executed on another machine. The data independence of these high-level scripts is a necessary requirement for transferring agents between system environments.

E.2 Pattern-Directed Inference

At the other end of the spectrum of understanding programs lie those whose activities are almost purely data-directed. Many pattern-directed inference systems are of this character (Waterman and Hayes-Roth, 1978). They possess little control structure; instead, the incoming data stream fires recognition rules that perform actions upon that stream and other internal data.

Applied to the domain of exemplary programming, such a system would proceed in a bottom-up fashion, drawing inferences from what the user did at the lowest level—the primitive trace actions—to determine what higher-level goals he was trying to accomplish. Encoded within a production system framework (Davis & King, 1976), the knowledge sources for EP-3 might be of the following sort:

Rule "Look for a compile call":

IF there is a "Compile <source>" monitor call anywhere
in the trace
THEN generate the hypothesis "Compiling <source> at trace
location x"

Rule "Look for a save call":

IF there is a "Save <program>" monitor call anywhere
in the trace
THEN generate the hypothesis "Saving <program> at trace
location y"

Rule "Look for a compile sequence":

IF there is a hypothesis "Compiling <source> at trace
location x"
& there is a hypothesis "Saving <program> at trace
location y"
& <program> is the object version of <source>
& location x is just before location y
THEN generate the hypothesis "Compile sequence between x
and y"

An EP-3 with perhaps hundreds of these rules would successively generate more and more abstract hypotheses directly from the trace. As with most data-directed behavior, this approach might achieve impressive levels of accomplishment if there are enough constraints and redundancies in the data. Care must be taken however, to avoid pursuit of long search paths obviously at odds with the overall solution being generated.

E.3. Suggested Architecture

The most promising architecture appears to be one that combines the model-directed and pattern-directed approaches (cf. Nii & Feigenbaum, 1978). Working top-down when a script is being checked out and bottom-up to generate the script hypotheses, this architecture would use each approach when appropriate. Control, and therefore search, would proceed opportunistically, much as humans are said to do (Hayes-Roth & Hayes-Roth, 1978). While there would be a knowledge source to provide overall focus when required, for the most part, each knowledge source would be free to operate in a manner most amenable to its particular specialty. Some would, for example, examine the data and propose explanations (pattern-directed), while others would try to instantiate high-level scripts (model-directed).

The architecture proposed below follows this theme. We have tried to be specific whenever possible, making the design choices necessary to achieve opportunistic analysis along the lines of a Hearsay-II type of structure. The executive, for example, is not specified but clearly needs to contain a scheduler to resolve duplicate KS firings. This architecture results from our efforts to produce an EP-3 design that will achieve the highest level of performance possible with current technology.

The data structure chosen is the first instance of a change to the Hearsay-II structure. As others have done (e.g., Englemore and Nii, 1977), we divide the blackboard into several levels. The example we present below concerns the transfer of a set of files from one machine to another machine. An initial specification of blackboard levels and examples relative to transferring files includes:

1) scripts:
top-level knowledge about typical activities users
are likely to do and how they do them, e.g.,

STORE-FILES script:
    copy {fileset} from <from-machine> to <to-machine>

2) abstract procedures:
the steps necessary for accomplishing a script specified
at an abstract level, e.g.,

for STORE-FILES script:
    log on to <from-machine>
    determine set of files to transfer--{fileset}
    execute <file-transfer-program> (<to-machine>)
    log on to <to-machine>
    foreach <file> in {fileset} do
        copy <file> from <from-machine> to <to-machine>

These abstract procedures become concrete when they are instantiated according to a particular computer environment.

3) specific procedures:
instantiations of the above steps in a formalized language. For example, the "foreach" statement above represented as a specific procedure:

```
ENVIRONMENT:
    <FROM-MACHINE>: unix
    <TO-MACHINE>: ecl
    <FILE-TRANSFER-PROGRAM>: ftp
VARS:
   fileset: SET OF unix-FILE;
   from-filename: unix-FILE;
   to-filename: ecl-FILE;

WHILE NOT NULL(fileset) DO
BEGIN
 from-filename  <-  NEXT-ELEMENT(fileset);
    USER-SEND (CONCAT("store",from-filename,to-filename);
    note: to-filename is bound to anything
            fitting type descr.
    IF NOT (SYS-SEND(...,"250...",...,"252...",">"))
    THEN ERROR("bad file transfer" etc.)
    END.
```

4) abstract trace:
a generalization of the actual trace, with specific commands and their parameters replaced by typed variables. For example, the last part of the STORE-FILES script:

```
Sys: Connect...            LOGON
Sys: 300 USC-ECL..           variables:
Sys: >                         to-machine
Usr: USER WATERMAN               TYPE: op-sys
Sys: 330...                      VALUE: ecl
Sys: >                         environment
Usr: PASS ABC          =>        TYPE: program
Sys: 230...                      VALUE: ftp
Sys: >                         user-sent
Usr: ACCT 701                    TYPE: Boolean
Sys: 200...                      VALUE: true
                               password-sent
                                 TYPE: Boolean
                                 VALUE: true
                               acct-sent
                                 TYPE: Boolean
                                 VALUE: True
```

```
Sys: >                    STORE
Usr: store...               variables:
Sys: 200...                   from-filename
Sys: 255...         =>          TYPE:  <from-machine>file
Sys: 250...                     VALUE: code.ep
Sys: 252...                    to-filename
     .                          TYPE:  <to-machine>file
     .                          VALUE: code.ep
     .                         successful-transfer
     .                          TYPE: Boolean
     .                          VALUE: True
```

5) Actual trace
   Obvious, e.g., the left column above.

We will then have the KSs operating between the levels, generating, evaluating, and deleting hypotheses. Some of the KSs might look like:

ENVIRONMENT-SCANNER (level 5 -> level 4)
Task: Scans the actual trace to instantiate the environment variables at the abstract-trace level.
Knowledge: Operating systems, application programs

TRACE-GENERALIZER (level 5 -> level 4)
Task: Scans the actual trace trying to recognize trace segments that it can hypothesize on the abstract trace level.
Knowledge: Operating systems, application programs

HYPOTHESIZE (levels 2, 3, 4 -> 1)
Task: At any time, sufficient information may be present in the lower levels to make a very good guess about what the user is doing. Once a script hypothesis has been made, the system can operate top-down trying to instantiate its holes. In this domain, particularly, it may be possible to accurately guess at the correct script early on.
Knowledge: User goals, script descriptions

SPECIFY-PROCEDURES (levels 2 -> 3)
Task: Instantiate the abstract procedures at level 2 by hypothesizing specific procedures at level 3.
Knowledge: User goals, operating systems, application programs

REALIZE-SCRIPT (level 1 -> levels 2, 3)
Task: Once a script has been hypothesized, generate all hypotheses spawned by it at level 2. A lot of "user-specific" knowledge might be incorporated here, e.g., "User X usually lists his files before doing a transfer" might signify a step at level 2, or "User X usually lists his files using 'ls -l' " might appear at level 3.
Knowledge: Script description, user goals

DATA-VALIDATION (levels 4, 5 -> 3)
Task: By looking at the trace, some information may be found to validate hypotheses at level 3.
Knowledge: Operating systems, application programs, programming constructs

DATA-FLOW (levels 4, 5 -> 3)
Task: By looking at the trace, some information may be hypothesized at level 3.
Knowledge: Operating systems, application programs, programming constructs

ADVICE-TAKER (level 5 -> all other levels)
Task: Advice is used to interpret the trace and make hypotheses at all other levels. Trying to figure out what someone is doing without specific knowledge of his intentions is extremely difficult. Allowing EP-3 to take even the simplest advice may be the avenue to large increases in performance. Information from the user on the trace ("now I'm doing...") can be applied at almost every level to limit the number of alternative hypotheses being considered.
Knowledge: Advice grammar, user goals, operating systems, application programs

STATE-DETERMINER (levels 4, 5 -> levels 1, 2, 3)
Task: Determining the relevance of trace information. The upper levels will need to know whether certain "spurious" trace information affected their hypotheses. For example, if the user does:

```
% dir
 ...system lists his files
% pwd
 ...prints working directory
% ftp ecl
 ...executes file transfer program
```

the KS hypothesizing a "STORE-FILES" script needs to know if "pwd" is important. This KS should know about such things.

Knowledge: User goals, operating systems, application programs

SYMBOLIC-EXECUTOR (level 3 <-> level 4)
Task: When a specific program has been hypothesized enough to symbolically execute it, this KS does so and compares the results to the trace information at level 4.
Knowledge: programming constructs

A novel feature of this particular representation comes as a side-effect of the recognition process. When the entire trace has been "explained" as a particular instance of some script, what falls out is a rather formal program, complete with state and environment variables, loops, etc. The program can then be used to tackle EP-3's "generational" problem—performing the same tasks itself. This model operates similar to the opportunistic planner in that it generates its plan as a data-driven side-effect of the more direct answer to the question, How do we get from START to GOAL (or FINISH)?

Once such a plan (program) has been generated, with suitable KSs available, EP-3 can proceed to apply it to new tasks:

1. Directly, by substituting new values for variables where requested and defaulting to the stored ones when necessary; or
2. Even more intelligently, by using the script information and some evaluation KSs to generate alternate, more efficient ways of accomplishing the same thing.

As noted above, the realization of this scheme requires that EP possess a great deal of domain-specific knowledge—in this example, various ways of doing a file transfer.

F. Conclusions

The EP methodology has the potential for making a significant impact on the computing community because it cuts across task domains, system requirements, and user types. It is most appropriate for repetitive tasks involving extensive man-machine dialogue. The program created by the EP system acts as a repository of information about how to perform the task and as an autonomous agent capable of performing that task. As shown by the discussion of EP-2 applications, the EP paradigm is also useful for tasks composed of many similar subtasks. The user performs a few of the subtasks as the EP system watches and then tells it to do the rest itself. Not only is an agent created to perform the task, the user is relieved of providing the EP system with a repetitious example.

An essential part of the design of an advanced EP system is a pattern interpretation component. We have described a multilevel framework for this component based on the Hearsay-II architecture that combines a model-directed top-down approach to program synthesis with a pattern-directed bottom-up approach.

The model-directed approach, based on scripts, provides a concise way of representing contiguous, context-dependent knowledge. It merges nicely with the learning-by-example paradigm, suggesting more sophisticated future extensions such as automatic script acquisition by example. The mechanism suggested for the advanced EP system contains most of the machinery needed for monitoring, analyzing, reformulating, and storing examples as new scripts. Thus, this approach lends itself to the problem of learning permanent domain knowledge.

The pattern-directed approach, based on data-directed evocation of rules, is a useful way to represent the knowledge sources that map knowledge from one level to another. It facilitates both recognizing behavior in a trace and operationalizing that behavior in new contexts. Maintaining these specialized KS "experts" not only gives us the modularity and clarity needed to promote good human engineering but also allows us as system designers to incorporate as much high-level expertise as is needed in the individual modules. Thus KSs involved in particularly difficult tasks such as recognizing regularities in the trace and mapping them into conventional programming constructs can be easily expanded and augmented until they contain enough expertise to perform as desired.

A fundamental problem related to the use of exemplary programming for program construction is the handling of unexpected or novel tasks that are demonstrated by example. In this situation the model-directed approach may be of little help, since existing scripts will tend not to match the example in a consistent manner. Furthermore, the data-directed approach may lead to false interpretations of the user's intent, since without sufficiently primed knowledge sources, the example could appear ambiguous. To handle this difficult type of situation, the EP approach may have to be used in conjunction with other program synthesis techniques, such as summarizing the task in a high-level language or describing the algorithm used.

Appendix A

Example EP-2 Scenario

The following is a scenario of the current EP system in operation. The user interacts with the UNIX operating system. He wishes to create a program to print a file that he has on a remote system on the local printer. To do this, the program must retrieve the file from the remote system using FTP, print it, and delete it.

In this protocol, the unix prompt is "%." The user-system interaction is at the left margin. The EP-user interaction is indented 20 spaces. User input is shown in italics. Annotation is in braces at the right.

% *ep*
Telnetting · · · logging in · · · starting EP · · ·

{The user starts the EP system.}

The GOTO button is control-P
For help type GOTO and one of the following
(equivalent) commands:
help
HELP
?

%

{EP starts up and displays a standard "help" message. To get EP's attention, the user types a special character, <control-P>.}

[EP]: *create*

{The user tells EP to create an agent.}

Name of agent: *print do.doc from ecl*

{EP responds by asking for the name of the agent.}

Variables in agent call: *do.doc*

{EP then asks the user what variables are in the agent call.}

Making new var: VAR1, with value: do.doc

{EP makes variables for later instantiation.}

Describe agent · · ·
Text: *This agent retrieves the file do.doc*
Text: *from ecl and prints it locally.*
Text:

{The user can give a description of the agent as a form of documentation.}

EP is watching
-EP waiting-

{EP is finished acquiring the initial information about the agent, and now watches the user as he interacts with the system.}

% *ftp ecl*

{The user starts up FTP, and logs onto the remote server.}

Connections established.

300 USC-ECL FTP Server 1.44.11.0 - at WED 12-JUL-78 14:12-PDT
> *user faught*
330 User name accepted. Password, please.
> *pass*
Password:
230 Login completed.
> *retr do.doc*

{The user tells FTP what remote file he wishes to retrieve. EP recognizes the file name as being a variable in the agent call. EP creates a piece of the model to evaluate the variable at run time.}

localfile:

temp.bak

The user selects a temporary filename as the local destination.

255 SOCK 3276867075
250 ASCII retrieve of <FAUGHT>DO.DOC;2 started.
252 Transfer completed.
> *bye*
231 BYE command received.
% *print temp.bak*

{The user prints and deletes the local file.}

% *del temp.bak*
temp.bak

%

[EP]: *end*

{The user tells EP that he is done with the task.}

End agent called: print do.doc from ecl
End agent construction
Agent stored in library
Trace stored in library
-EP dormant-

%

{The agent is now available for use. The user calls it on a different file.}

[EP]: *print pattern from ecl*

Calling: print pattern from ecl

%

{This agent retrieves the file pattern from ecl and prints it locally.}

{The agent starts running by first printing the description of its task.}

% ftp ecl

{The agent types to the system, just as the user did.}

Connections established.

300 USC-ECL FTP Server 1.44.11.0 - at WED 12-JUL-78 14:15-PDT
> user faught
330 User name accepted. Password, please.
> pass
Password:
230 Login completed.
> retr pattern

{The agent tells FTP which remote file is to be retrieved. The file "pattern" is instantiated from the agent call.}

localfile: temp.bak
255 SOCK 3276867075

250 ASCII retrieve of <FAUGHT>PATTERN.;1 started.
252 Transfer completed.
> bye
231 BYE command received.
% print temp.bak

{The agent prints and deletes the local file.}

% del temp.bak
temp.bak

%

Ending agent - print pattern from ecl
-EP dormant-

%

Appendix B

Example EP-2 Ladder Scenario

This is an example of using an existing EP-2 agent to perform a data-base retrieval task within the LADDER data-base system. First, we show the user-system interaction necessary to carry out the retrieval. Note that the user is required only to access EP and give it the agent name.

% *ep*

[EP]: *ships status 200 miles*

POSITION	DATE	PCFUEL	READY	RANK	NAME	SHIP
37-00N,	076-00W 17Jan76,	1200	0	C5	CAPT HALSEY W	AMERICA
37-00N,	076-00W 17Jan76,	1200	100	C1	CAPT BROWN A	SARATOGA
37-00N,	076-00W 17Jan76,	1200	100	C1	CDR SMITH R	STURGEON
37-00N,	076-00W 17Jan76,	1200	100	C1	CDR COHEN X	WHALE
37-00N,	076-00W 17Jan76,	1200	100	C1	CDR HIGH J	TAUTOG
37-00N,	076-00W 17Jan76,	1200	100	C1	CDR DAUGHERTY R	GRAYLING

To illustrate the work the agent must perform, a trace of the agent-system interaction required to effect the retrieval is shown below. This is what the user would have to go through if he did not have access to the agent. User input is in italics.

% *ep*
Telnetting · · · logging in · · · starting EP · · ·
%

The GOTO button is control-P
For help, type GOTO and "help<carriage return>".

%

[EP]: *ships status 200 miles*

-Calling: ships status 200 miles

```
%
                        [This agent uses the LADDER system to print the status of all ships within 200 miles of
                        the default location (currently NORFOLK).  Types of ships recognized by LADDER are:
                        ships  submarines  carriers  cruisers]
%
                        [PHASE 1: Start the LADDER system.]
%
                                  -Calling: ladder
%
                        [This starts the LADDER system at SRI-KL.]
%
                        [Telnet to SRI with a TEE for saving results of this session.]
% tn sri|tee ladder.temp
Open

SRI-KL, TOPS-20 Monitor 101B(116)
System shutdown scheduled for Mon 18-Sep-78 00:01:00,
Up again at Tue 19-Sep-78 04:00:00
There are 43+8 jobs and the load av. is 8.94
@
                        [Login as a LADDER user.]
@login
(user) fhollister
(Password)
(account)
Job 84 on TTY251 14-Sep-78 17:09
Previous login: 13-Sep-78 15:46 from host RAND-UNIX
[There are 3 other jobs in group DA]
@
                        [Logged in; now start LADDER.]
@ladder
     Language Access to Distributed Data with Error Recovery
                                  -- SRI International --
Please type in your name:
                  [User's name (for repeated requests).]
Please type in your name: epdemo
When you are finished, please type DONE.
This will close the Datacomputer files.
Do you want instructions? (type FIRST LETTER of response)
          [Bypass the instructions.]
Do you want instructions? (type FIRST LETTER of response) No
Do you want to use 2 Data Computers?
          [Use only 1 Data Computer.]
Do you want to use 2 Data Computers? No
Do you want to specify a current location (default = Norfolk)?
          [Use the default location (for this user).]
Do you want to specify a current location (default = Norfolk)? No
Do you wish distance/direction calculations to default to GREAT CIRCLE, or RHUMB LINE?  (you can over-
ride by specifying in the query)
          [Use the Great Circle calculation.]
or RHUMB LINE?  (you can override by specifying in the query) Great Circle
```

[Suppress the Data Computer specification.]
1 _ set verbosity to be -1
PARSED!
- 1
2 _
[LADDER is now waiting for English input.]
2 _
-Ending agent: ladder
2 _
[PHASE 2: Define special terms.]
2 _
-Calling: ladstatus
2 _
[This defines opstatus in LADDER.]

2 _ define (what is the opstatus of jfk)
and commanding officer of jfk)

PARSED!

WHAT IS THE CURRENT POSITION FUEL STATUS STATE OF READINESS AND COMMANDING OFFICER OF JFK

PARSED!

For SHIP equal to KENNEDY JF, give the POSITION and DATE and PCFUEL and READY and RANK and NAME.

May LIFER assume that "CURRENT POSITION FUEL STATUS STATE OF READINESS AND COMMANDING OFFICER" may always be used in place of "OPSTATUS"? Yes

<RELN> => OPSTATUS
(OPSTATUS)
3_
["Opstatus" is now defined.]
3_
-Ending agent: ladstatus
3_
[PHASE 3: Type the specific retrieval request.]
3_
[LADDER processes the request by interacting
with the Data Computer
3_what is the opstatus of all ships within 200 miles
FROM NORFOLK
PARSED!

For great circle distance to 37—00N, 76—00W less than or equal to 200, give the POSITION and DATE and PCFUEL and READY and RANK and NAME and SHIP.

Connecting to Datacomputer at CCA:
>> ;0031 780915001150 IONETI: CONNECTED TO SRI-KL-30700010
>> ;J150 780915001151 FCRUN: V='DC-5/01.00.13' J=7 DT='THURSDAY, SEPTEMBER 1978 20:11:51-EDT' S='CCA'
>> ;J200 780915001151 RHRUN: READY FOR REQUEST

*> Set parameters
*<   Exit
*> Set parameters
*< V   Verbosity (-1 to 5): -1......

POSITION	DATE	PCFUEL	READY	RANK	NAME	SHIP
37-00N,	076-00W 17Jan76,	1200	0	C5	CAPT HALSEY W	AMERICA
37-00N,	076-00W 17Jan76,	1200	100	C1	CAPT BROWN A	SARATOGA
37-00N,	076-00W 17Jan76,	1200	100	C1	CDR SMITH R	STURGEON
37-00N,	076-00W 17Jan76,	1200	100	C1	CDR COHEN X	WHALE
37-00N,	076-00W 17Jan76,	1200	100	C1	CDR HIGH J	TAUTOG
37-00N,	076-00W 17Jan76,	1200	100	C1	CDR DAUGHERTY R	GRAYLING

4_

-Calling: beep

4_

[This beeps the user's terminal.]

4_

-Ending agent: beep

4_

-Ending agent: ships status 200 miles
-EP dormant-

4_

[EP]: ladexit

-Calling: ladexit

4_

[Exiting LADDER, back to unix...]

4_

[PHASE 4: Exit from the LADDER system.]

4_done
PARSED!
@k
[Confirm]
System shutdown scheduled for Mon 18-Sep-78 00:01:00,
Up again at Tue 19-Sep-78 04:00:00
Logout Job 84, User FHOLLISTER, Account DA, TTY 251, at 14-Sep-78 17:14:02
Used 0:0:12 in 0:4:56
%

[PHASE 5: Format, print, and save the transcript.]

%

-Calling: ladsave

```
%
                    [This saves the results of each LADDER run
                    by appending them on the file LADDER.RESULTS
                    and printing them on the RCC computer.]
%
                    [Delete cr's and DEL's.]

% tr -d "015177" <ladder.temp> ladder.temp1
%
                    [Use the ED editor to delete unwanted parts
                    of the LADDER protocol.]
% ed ladder.temp1
3211
/^-1/p
-1
1,-d
/._done/p
?
w
?
q
%
                    [Append the results to the archive file.]
% cat ladder.temp>>ladder.results
%
                    [Print a hard copy of today's results.]
% print ladder.temp1
%
                    [Remove the temporary files.]
% del ladder.temp ladder.temp1
ladder.temp
ladder.temp1
                              -Ending agent: ladsave

%
                    [You are now talking to unix.]
%
                              -Ending agent: ladexit
                               -EP dormant-
%
```

References

Anderson, R. H., and J. J. Gillogly, "The Rand Intelligent Terminal Agent (RITA) as a Network Access Aid," *AFIPS Proceedings,* Vol. 45, 1976, pp. 501–509. (a)

Anderson, R. H., and J. J. Gillogly, *Rand Intelligent Terminal Agent (RITA): Design Philosophy,* The Rand Corporation, R–1809–ARPA, 1976. (b)

Anderson, R. H., et al. *RITA Reference Manual,* The Rand Corporation, R–1808-ARPA, 1977.

Biermann, A. W. "Regular LISP Programs and their Automatic Synthesis from Examples," Computer Science Department Report CS–1976–12, Duke University, 1976.

Biermann, A. W., and R. Krishnaswamy, "Constructing Programs from Example Computations," Computer and Information Science Research Center Report CISRC–TR–74–5, Ohio State University, 1974.

Buchanan, J. R., *A Study in Automatic Programming,* Computer Science Report, Carnegie-Mellon University, 1974.

Davis, R., "Applications of Meta Level Knowledge to the Construction, Maintenance and Use of Large Knowledge Bases," Stanford AI Memo AIM–283, Stanford University, 1976.

Davis, R., and J. King, "An Overview of Production Systems," in E. W. Elcock and D. Michie (eds.), *Machine Intelligence,* Wiley, New York, 1976, pp. 300–332.

Englemore, R. S., and H. P. Nii, "A Knowledge-Based System for the Interpretation of Protein X-ray Crystallographic Data," STAN–CS–77–589, Stanford University, 1977.

Erman, L. D., and V. R. Lesser, "A Multi-Level Organization for Problem Solving Using Many Diverse Cooperating Sources of Knowledge," *Proceedings of the Fourth International Joint Conference on Artificial Intelligence,* 1975, pp. 483–490.

Faught, W. S., et al., *A Prototype Exemplary Programming System,* The Rand Coporation, R–2411–ARPA, 1979.

Green, C., "The Design of the PSI Program Synthesis System," *Proceedings of the Second International Conference on Software Engineering,* San Francisco, California, 1976, pp. 4–18.

Hayes-Roth, B., and F. Hayes-Roth, "Concept Learning and the Recognition and Classification of Exemplars," *Journal of Verbal Learning and Verbal Behavior,* Vol. 16, 1977, pp. 321–338.

Hayes-Roth, B., and F. Hayes-Roth, *Cognitive Processes in Planning,* The Rand Corporation, R–2366–ONR, 1978.

Hayes-Roth, F., "A Structural Approach to Pattern Learning and the Acquisition of Classificatory Power," *Proceedings of the First International Joint Conference on Pattern Recognition,* I.E.E.E., New York, 1973.

Hayes-Roth, F., "Patterns of Induction and Associated Knowledge Acquisition Algorithms," in C. H. Chen (ed.), *Pattern Recognition and Artificial Intelligence,* Academic Press, New York, 1976. (a)

Hayes-Roth, F., "Uniform Representations of Structured Patterns and an Algorithm for the Induction of Contingency-Response Rules," *Information and Control,* Vol. 33, 1976, pp. 87–116. (b)

Hayes-Roth, F., "Learning by Example," in A. M. Lesgold et al. (eds.), *Cognitive Psychology and Instruction,* Plenum, New York, 1978.

Hayes-Roth, F., and J. McDermott, "Learning Structured Patterns from Examples," *Proceedings of the Third International Joint Conference on Pattern Recognition,* Coronado, California, 1976.

Hayes-Roth, F., and J. McDermott, "Knowledge Acquisition From Structural Descriptions," *Communications of the ACM,* May 1978.

Hayes-Roth, F., D. A. Waterman, and D. Lenat, "Principles of Pattern-Directed Inference Systems," in D. A. Waterman and F. Hayes-Roth (eds.), *Pattern-Directed Inference Systems,* Academic Press, New York, 1978.

Hendrix, G., et al., "Developing A Natural Language Interface to Complex Data," *ACM Transactions on Database Systems* Vol. 3, No. 2, June 1978, pp. 105–147.

Hunt, E. B., *Concept Formation: An Information Processing Problem,* Wiley, New York, 1962.

Lenat, D., "AM: An Artificial Intelligence Approach to Discovery in Mathematics as Heuristic Search," SAIL AIM–286, Artificial Intelligence Laboratory, Stanford University, 1976.

Lenat, D., "Automated Theory Formation in Mathematics," *Proceedings of the Fifth International Joint Conference on Artificial Intelligence,* 1977, pp. 833–842.

Lenat, D., and G. Harris, "Designing a Rule System that Searches for Scientific Discoveries," in D. A. Waterman and F. Hayes-Roth (eds.), *Pattern-Directed Inference Systems,* Academic Press, New York, 1978.

Lesser, V. R., and L. D. Erman, "A Retrospective View of the Hearsay-II Architecture," *Proceedings of the Fifth International Joint Conference on Artificial Intelligence,* MIT, 1977, pp. 790–800.

Nii, H. P., and E. A. Feigenbaum, "Rule-Based Understanding of Signals," in D. A. Waterman and F. Hayes-Roth (eds.), *Pattern-Directed Inference Systems,* Academic Press, New York, 1978.

Schank, R. C., and R. P. Abelson, *Scripts, Plans, Goals, and Understanding,* Lawrence Erlbaum Associates, New Jersey, 1977.

Shortliffe, E. H., "MYCIN: A Rule-Based Computer Program for Advising Physicians Regarding Antimicrobial Therapy Selection," Memo AIM–251, Artificial Intelligence Laboratory, Stanford University, 1974.

Shortliffe, E. H., *Computer-Based Medical Consultations: MYCIN,* American Elsevier, New York, 1976.

Siklossy, L., and D. A. Sykes, "Automatic Program Synthesis from Example," *Proceedings of the Fourth International Joint Conference on Artificial* Intelligence, 1975, pp. 268–273.

Simon, H. A., and K. Kotovsky, "Human Acquisition of Concepts for Sequential Patterns," *Psychological Review,* Vol. 70, 1963, pp. 534–546.

Vere, S. A., "Inductive Learning of Relational Productions," in D. A. Waterman and F. Hayes-Roth (eds.), *Pattern-Directed Inference Systems,* Academic Press, New York, 1978.

Waterman, D. A., "Adaptive Production Systems," *Proceedings of the Fourth International Joint Conference on Artificial Intelligence,* 1975, pp. 296–303.

Waterman, D. A., "Serial Pattern Acquisition: A Production System Approach," in C. H. Chen (ed.), *Pattern Recognition and Artificial Intelligence,* Academic Press, New York, 1976.

Waterman, D. A., *Rule-Directed Interactive Transaction Agents: An Approach to Knowledge Acquisition,* The Rand Corporation, R–2171–ARPA, 1977. (a)

Waterman, D. A., *A Rule-Based Approach to Knowledge Acquisition for Man-Machine Interface Programs,* The Rand Coporation, P–5895, 1977. (b)

Waterman, D. A., "Exemplary Programming in RITA," in D. A. Waterman and F. Hayes-Roth (eds.), *Pattern-Directed Inference Systems,* Academic Press, New York, 1978.

Waterman, D. A., and F. Hayes-Roth, *Pattern-Directed Inference Systems,* Academic Press, New York, 1978.

Waterman, D. A., and F. Hayes-Roth, "An Overview of Pattern-Directed Inference Systems," in D. A. Waterman and F. Hayes-Roth (eds.), *Pattern-Directed Inference Systems,* Academic Press, New York, 1978. (b)

Winston, P. H., "Learning Structural Descriptions from Examples," in P. H. Winston (ed.), *The Psychology of Computer Vision,* McGraw-Hill, New York, 1975.

SECTION VI

LEARNING

CHAPTER 21

Program Synthesis Through Concept Learning

Brian Cohen and Claude Sammut
School of Electrical Engineering and Computer Science
University of New South Wales,
P.O. Box 1, Kensington, N.S.W., Australia 2033

Abstract

A learning program produces, as its output, a boolean function which describes a concept. The function returns true if and only if the argument is an object which satisfies the logical expression in the body of the function. Concepts may be learned by interacting with a trainer or by providing a set of positive and a set of negative instances. An interpreter has been written which performs the reverse of the learning process. The concept description is regarded as a program which defines the set of objects which satisfy the given conditions. The interpreter takes as its input, a predicate and a partially specified object. It produces, as its output, the completed object. The interpreter is used to aid the learning of complex concepts involving existential quantifiers. This paper presents algorithms for learning concepts and generating objects.

A. Introduction

When a programmer is given an assignment it is usually of the form, "here is a problem which we would like the computer to solve" or "we would like to get this type of information given these data." The first step in good software design or "software engineering" is to analyze the problem and to produce high level specifications. The programmer should determine the class of problem he is dealing with. In doing this he formulates a description of the problem (the specifications) which demonstrates the relationship between the program's input space (the data) and its output space (the results). That is, he forms some concept which specifies what the required program is meant to achieve. This concept may be viewed as the description of the relation between the input and the output of the desired system. The program then, may be seen as the implementation of this relation.

The concept description may be considered a recognition device that classifies input/output pairs. Whereas execution of the program, given relevant input, will produce the appropriate output. Effectively, the program is the generator of the input/output pairs.

Clearly, there is a fine distinction between the concept and the program. Historically, this distinction has seemed significant mainly because the intent of programs was buried deep in the rigid syntax of the language, most of which was not too far removed from the instruction code of the computer. For example, even in a high level language like Pascal, an algorithm to append a list onto the end of another would look like this:

```
type
    list = ^ listcell;
    listcell = record
                  head: integer;
                  tail: list
               end;

    procedure append(x,y:list; var z: list);
    var
      p: list
    begin
      if x = nil then z:= y
      else
        begin
          new(z); p:= z;
          p^.head:= x^.head;
          x:= x^.tail;
          while x <> nil do
          begin
            new(p^.tail); p:= p^.tail;
            p^.head:= x^.head;
            x:= x^.tail
          end;
          p^.tail:= y
        end
    end;
```

[In Pascal this could have been more neatly expressed as a recursive function, however other common languages such as FORTRAN do not allow recursion.]

As more high-level languages have been developed, the trend has been to encode more of 'what' to do rather than 'how' to do it. These languages are closer to English than machine code. Through their use, programs come much nearer to describing the solution to the problem at an understandable level, and not just the details of the implementation. Such is the case with a language like PROLOG (Roussel [1975]), where irrelevant details are largely hidden from the user.

Consider the Prolog version of 'append':

```
append(nil,X,X).
append(cons(A,B), X, cons(A,B1)) :- append(B,X,B1).
```

This states that the result of appending any list, X, to the empty list is X. The result of appending X to a list whose head is A and whose tail is B is the list whose head is also A and whose tail is the result of appending X to B. Thus the Prolog program is a succinct description of the concept of appending lists.

In effect, the difference between the concept and the program lies only in the level of specification and detail given in their description. Conventional languages specify a great amount of detail, whereas high-level languages such as Prolog and other AI systems require much less detail, although some efficiency is lost.

Taking the notion of identity of concept and program a step further we may develop a novel approach to automatic program synthesis. This step involves the incorporation of a computerized concept formation system. Concept learning provides the initial important part of the automatic programming process.

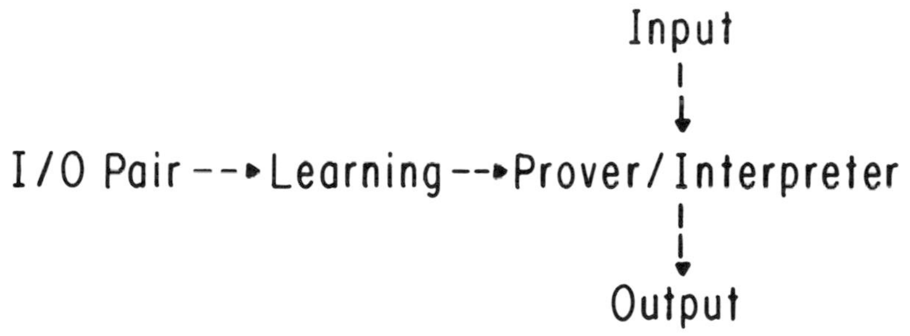

Figure 1. Schematic diagram of system.

Figure 1 summarizes the method. Input/Output pairs are supplied to the learning system. It produces a concept description which recognizes these pairs. Given an input, the interpreter uses the concept description to guide the generation of the corresponding output.

B. Background

The ideas given above form the basis of an automatic programming system which has been implemented at the University of N.S.W. An earlier version of the system was described in Cohen [1978]. This has been considerably enhanced by extending the syntax of the description language to include quantifiers (Sammut and Cohen [1980] and Sammut [1981]). These improvements are enabled by the use of theorem proving techniques.

The project began as an attempt to answer three questions posed by Banerji [1969].

1. How should a concept be described so as to use as small an amount of memory as possible?
2. How should the description of such a concept be stored and processed so that, given an object, we can determine as quickly as possible whether the object is contained in the concept?
3. Given two sets of objects, how should we construct a short description of a concept that contains all elements of the first set and none of the second?

As a result of this attempt a structural concept learning system, CONFUCIUS, was designed and implemented (Cohen [1978]). The description language, CODE, represents as boolean combinations of predicates. These predicates can include relational statements and can refer to other previously or partially learned concepts, thus, providing the language with the ability to grow and include recursive concepts. Restricting the predicates to one free variable obviated the need for instantiation (c.f. Hayes-Roth [1978]) while still providing a reasonable degree of generality, as the variable could be highly structured (this restriction has been lifted in the new system).

A concept can be learned by CONFUCIUS in one of two ways:

1. By interaction with a trainer, or
2. by examining a set of positive instances and a set of negative instances, both provided by the trainer.

CONFUCIUS uses a conservative focusing strategy (Bruner *et al.* [1956]) to generalize positive instances. In the first method the trainer shows a positive instance and then CONFUCIUS asks if the hypothetical concepts it generates are subconcepts of the concept to be learned (the *target* concept).

In the second method the questions are replaced by recognition tests with the set of negative instances.

The structural description language and learning algorithms of CONFUCIUS form the stepping-stones on the way to the new system. What is of interest here is that earlier it was noted that by enforcing recognition of partially specified objects in a concept by filling in the spaces as directed by the concept description, a crude form of program interpretation was being performed.

Initially it seemed that object construction as such, was an interesting extension to the learning system. The syntax of the language has some subtle refinements made to it so that the interpreter could process recursive concepts and the like. However, when the description language was properly extended to include the existential quantifier, it soon became apparent that object construction was an integral part of a learning strategy capable of handling the extended language. It will be shown later that in order to learn concepts involving quantified variables, objects need to be constructed from components of the data so that new pertinent concept statements can be generated.

Moreover, with the ability to generate objects, the concept learning system can show likely objects to the trainer for questioning rather than the more complex concepts they represent. This more closely corresponds to the psychological concept formation procedures (Bruner *et al.* [1956]).

Finally, the occurrence of the existential quantifier in a concept statement implies a search through some domain with associated pattern matching to correctly instantiate the quantified variable. However, by using the construction techniques during the recognition process, this search becomes highly constrained as the target of the search is actually generated.

Thus, it can be seen that the areas of automatic programming and concept formation are interrelated. A concept learning system may provide the basis for a logical form of automatic program synthesis. Such a system is outlined in this paper.

C. The Language

The syntax of the language is quite simple, being a form of predicate calculus. There are two basic types:

1. *objects,* which are the 'constants' of the language, and
2. *concepts,* which are the definitions or statements of the language.

An object is a set of property/value pairs. A property is a symbol. A value can be a symbol or another object (implemented as a name or pointer to that object). Ultimately, values must be symbols. Thus, we can have structured objects. For example, the binary digit 'one' is simply described as:

dl: <value: 1>

Adding some structure, the object of binary number 'one' may be described as:

one: <head: nil; tail: dl>

and the binary number 'two' (10) as:

two: <head: one; tail: dO>

where

dO: <value: O>

With this structure a list, or ordered n-tuple, of objects is an object. For this special case, the property names (first, second, third ...) are omitted for convenience. The descriptions of concepts which classify such an n-tuple may also be considered as descriptions of n-ary relations. Thus, if we have some concept *C* which recognizes all and only all pairs of the form

pair: <X, Y>

where X is less than Y for some ordering relation *R,* then the technique used in describing *C* equally applies to *R*. Such a relation (concept) is described later.

The basic predicates of the language are of the form

x.p = v

where 'p' is a property, 'x' is an object and 'v' is a value. The predicate is true if 'v' is the right hand side of the property/value pair in 'x' whose left hand side is 'p'. Thus, using the above example dl.value = 1 is true.

These predicates are generalized by allowing 'x' and 'v' to evaluate to an object and value respectively (Banerji [1978] gives the formalism for this). Thus, we can have statements of the form

$$\text{one.tail.value} = 1$$

and

$$\text{x.colour} = \text{y.colour}$$

The description of a concept is built up as a boolean combination of these predicates. Thus the concept of binary digit is defined as:

$$\text{digit} = [\text{x: x.value} = 1 \lor \text{x.value} = 0]$$

where 'x' is the object passed to the concept (i.e. its parameter). Another way of looking at this expression is to consider it as the generator of the set of all 'x' such that value of 'x' is 0 or 1.

If *C* is a concept with one parameter, then C(x) is a predicate which is true for an object 'x' which satisfies the predicates in the body of *C* after 'x' is substituted for the formal parameter. If C(x) is true, then 'x' is said to be *recognized* by *C* or that *C classifies 'x'* (Cohen [1974]). Predicates of this form can be included in a concept definition. Thus, the concept of binary number (with no leading zero) may be defined recursively as:

```
number = [x: x.head = nil ∧ x.tail.value = 1
         ∨ number(x.head) ∧ digit(x.tail)
        ]
```

This says, either the number is 'one' or its head is a number and its tail a digit. Now, the description of the relation, given earlier, of 'less' as applied to binary numbers may be defined by the following concept:

```
less = [x,y: number(x) ∧ number(y)
       ∧ (
                x.head = nil ∧ y.head ≠ nil
        ∨ x.head = y.head ∧ x.tail.value = 0
        ∨ less(x.head, y.head)
       )
      ]
```

(The reader may like to verify this for himself.)

The description of complex concepts may require a language with more expressive power than simple expressions joined by "and" or "or" operations. For example, the existential quantifier may be used in the description of the concept of "maximum number in a list":

```
maximum =
[list, max:
  list.tail = nil ∧ max = list.head
  ∨ [ ∃ x: maximum(list.tail, x) ∧
      (
         less(x, list.head) ∧ max = list.head
       ∨ less(list.head, x) ∧ max = x
      )
    ]
]
```

("list" and "max" are the two arguments to "maximum").

However, the introduction of quantifiers raises many problems in the evaluation of an expression. How do we test a statement which claims the existence of an object? It would be impossible to search for such an object since the set of all possible objects may not be specified and may not even be finite. This leads us to ask, is it possible to construct an object which will satisfy the given conditions? Thus, the task of our language is to take as input a predicate and attempt to produce, as output, an instance of the concept. This is the reverse of the learning process.

D. Generation of Objects from Concepts

Consider the case where we wish to treat a concept description as a specification of an object that is to be created. For example, the concept 'append' may be defined as:

```
append = [x, y, z: x = nil ∧ y = z
              ∨ x.head = z.head ∧ append(x.tail, y, z.tail)
         ]
```

Compare this with the Prolog description in section 1.

Suppose x' is the list (1 2) and y' is (3). The third parameter is not instantiated, but the intention is that the program should produce the result

z = (1 2 3)

If we assert that

[∃ z: append(x', y', z)]

then the system is required to *prove* the assertion. Thus the interpretation of the language is very similar to that of PROLOG.

The following may be loosely considered as the main "axioms" used in proving the correctness of a concept/program.

1. X = X is always true.
2. X = Y if X is a variable and X is bound to the value of Y.
3. X = Y if Y is a variable and Y = X.
4. The value of X is X if X is a constant.
5. The value of X is Y if X is a variable and X is bound to Y.
6. The value of X.P is V if the value of X is an object and V is bound to P in that object.
7. X ∧ Y is true if X can be achieved and Y can be achieved.
8. X ∨ Y is true if X can be achieved and is consistent with any other constraints or Y is true. ("Other constraints" may be present if this expression occurs in a concept which is called by another concept).
9. [∃ x: P(x)] if P(x) where x is a variable which will be instantiated during the execution of P(x).
10. P(x', y' ..) is true if P(x, y, ...) is of the form [x, y, ...: <expr>] and the values x', y', ... are bound to the variables x, y, ... respectively and the expression "expr" is true.

The specification given above is similar to that given in Banerji [1978]. The most important difference is that in this system, expressions may contain references to other concepts. And since concepts may be disjunctive, we must consider the possibility of backtracking as discussed above.

Given a method of using a concept as a program, we now consider ways in which new concepts may be introduced to the system, that is, the ways in which new concepts may be learned.

E. Learning

The original model for learning used in CONFUCIUS was the "Conservative Focusing" algorithm described in Bruner *et al.* [1956]. This algorithm was developed by studying the behavior of human subjects in tests of their learning abilities. One experiment consisted of showing the subject a positive instance of a conjunctive concept. He could then modify the appearance of the object and ask if the object was now recognized by the concept. As the name of the algorithm implies, changes to the object are made in conservative steps. If a modified version of the object is still recognized by the concept, then the property of the object that was changed is considered irrelevant. However, if the new object fails to be recognized then the property changed is important.

The learning strategies used in CONFUCIUS went considerably beyond the capabilities of Bruner's methods. However, CONFUCIUS was incapable of learning concepts which require existential quantifiers in their description.

The new system operates in the same environment as CONFUCIUS (i.e. the experimental situation described above). However, the algorithm used to choose which features of the object are to be changed now bears little resemblance to conservative focusing. Before discussing the algorithm we will first define some of the terms used.

Definitions

1. A statement, X, is *implied* by a set of statements $\{Y_i\}$ if and only if any object satisfying all Y_i also satisfies X.
2. A statement X is *directly implied* by $\{Y_i\}$ if and only if it is implied by $\{Y_i\}$ and there does not exist a Y' implied by $\{Y_i\}$ such that X is implied by some set $\{Y'_i\}$ where $Y'_i=Y_i$ for all i except one, say j, where $Y'_j = Y'$.

Refer to the following section for some examples of implication:

(5) is directly implied by (1) and (4).

(7) is implied by (1) and (4) and (6).

3. A concept of C' is a *generalization* of C if and only if every statement in C' is implied by some subset of statements in C.

   The concept, C, defines a set of objects. These objects are said to be recognized by C. If C' is a generalization of C, then C' must define a set of objects which is a *superset* of that defined by C.

4. Conversely, C' is a *restriction* or *particularization* of C if C is a generalization of C'. That is, C' is more specific than C.

5. C' is a *valid generalization* of C if C' is a generalization of C and the target concept is a generalization of C'.

Generalization Rules

During the course of the learning procedure, a trial concept description is maintained. This is the current hypothesis for the correct description. The program either replaces or adds new statements in order to alter the generality of the trial. The following rules indicate how a concept description may be made more general.

1. If there exists a statement of the form

$$X = V$$

and another of the form

$$Y - V$$

then we claim that

$$X = Y$$

may be used to replace the first two statements in the trial. The new concept is more general since the values of X and Y are no longer restricted to the value V but may be any value, provided that they are the same.

2. Concepts are stored in the program's memory in disjunctive normal form. That is, as a disjunction of conjunctions. A conjunction can be viewed as a set of statements. Let the concept C, contain a conjunction consisting of the set $\{s_i\}$. Also let the trial concept be a set of statements which has a subset, $\{s'_j\}$ such that $\{s_i\}$ is equivalent to $\{s'_j\}$ for some substitution of variables, σ. For example,

$$C = [x,y,z: (x = nil \wedge y = z) \vee \quad ...]$$

and the trial contains,

$$... \wedge q = nil \wedge v = w \wedge ...$$

The two sets $\{x = nil, y = z\}$ and $\{q = nil, v = w\}$ are equivalent, for $\sigma = \{x/q, y/v, z/w\}$.

The s'_j may be replaced by a single statement of the form

$$C(x, y, ...)$$

The arguments x, y, ... are obtained from σ. From the example above, the two statements in the trial could be replaced by C(q, v, w).

The new trial is more general if C is a disjunctive concept, since the other disjuncts of C will recognize more objects than the one disjunct which appeared in the trial originally. For example, if C is "append", as defined earlier, then by replacing the matched statements, the trial description admits new objects, q, v, w which were not recognized by the previous trial.

3. A statement of the form

$$C(x,y, ...)$$

may be replaced by

$$[\exists x', y', ... : C(x', y', ...)]$$

where x', y', ... are unique variable names. This new statement is implied by,

$$C(x, y, ...) \land x' = x \land y' = y \land \cdots$$

The Algorithm

The program begins by generating a simple, ungeneralized, description of the training instance. Some statements in the description may directly imply more complex relationships. These implications may be replaced by the more complex statement in order to generalize the concept. As long as the generalization is valid, we continue to replace more specific predicates with those that are more general. However, it is possible for a generalization to "overshoot" and become too general. In this case implied relationships are *added* to the concept (rather than replacing existing predicates) in order to make the concept more specific.

Once the concept has been restricted to the point where it is once again contained in the target concept, generalization can proceed again. Sometimes one line of generalization may be bound to fail and must be abandoned. In general, however, *this algorithm may be regarded as producing successively better approximations of the concept, oscillating between over-generalization and under-generalization until the target is finally reached.*

The basic ideas behind the algorithm can best be illustrated by considering an example. Suppose we wish to learn the concept "maximum of a list" as described earlier.

1. We begin by generating a set of predicates (statements) which describe the training instance in the simplest possible terms. As "maximum" is a recursive concept, the first positive instance the trainer shows the system must teach it what the termination condition is. Let this instance be the pair <(1), 1>. That is, the maximum of the list (1) is the number 1. The initial hypothesis for the concept is:

$$X.head = 1 \land X.tail = nil \land Y = 1$$

where X is the first sub-object in the pair and Y is the second. These are the *primary* statements, which do no more than correspond to the object description.

2. The system now attempts to *generalize* the concept description by making some simple deductions (implications) from the hypothesis. It is possible to deduce that X.head = Y. A new hypothesis is proposed:

$$X.tail = nil \land X.head = Y$$

When two statements are used to deduce a new one, they are temporarily removed from the concept description.

3. Employing the construction techniques of the previous section, the hypothesis is used to generate an object which the system shows to the trainer. For example $<(0), 0>$ is consistent with the constraints above. When asked if this object is recognized by 'maximum' the trainer answers 'yes'. The generalization made is valid.

   * When an object is generated for display to the trainer, the program must ensure that the object does *not* conform to any of the conditions imposed by statements which have been temporarily removed.

4. The program now attempts to generalize further by trying to make other deductions from the new hypothesis. Let us assume at this stage that no further generalizations are possible. This implies that one disjunct of 'maximum' has now been learned.

5. In response to a question asking if the complete concept has now been learned, the trainer answers "no". The system then asks for a new training instance so that it may learn another disjunct.

6. The trainer shows the object $<(2\ 1), 2>$. The primary statements now generated are:

$$\begin{aligned} &\text{X.head} = 2 && (1)\\ \wedge\ &\text{X.tail.head} = 1 && (2)\\ \wedge\ &\text{X.tail.tail} = \text{nil} && (3)\\ \wedge\ &\text{Y} = 2 && (4)\end{aligned}$$

7. The first generalization attempted uses statements (1) and (4). These generate the relational statement (5). The new hypothesis is,

$$\begin{aligned} &\text{X.tail.head} = 1 && (2)\\ \wedge\ &\text{X.tail.tail} = \text{nil} && (3)\\ \wedge\ &\text{X.head} = \text{Y} && (5)\end{aligned}$$

8. This concept will construct the object $<(0, 1), 0>$ to query the trainer. As this object is not recognized by 'maximum', the hypothesis must be too general. Therefore, it should be *restricted* (i.e. made more specific). A concept may be made more specific by adding statements to its description. The problem becomes: which statements should be added? The introduction of the new statement (5) is responsible for the overgeneralization. Thus, too much information was removed when the implicants (1) and (4) were replaced. Additional statements will be chosen to restrict the trial by attempting to form new relationships based on the implicants which have been removed. Thus (1) can be used in combination with (2) to produce:

$$\begin{aligned} &\text{X.tail.head} < \text{X.head} && (6)\\ \wedge\ &\text{X.head} = \text{Y} && (5)\\ \wedge\ &\text{X.tail.tail} = \text{nil} && (3)\end{aligned}$$

   which is a restriction of the earlier hypothesis as statement (6) represents an added constraint on X.head.

9. A new object, $<(1\ 0), 1>$, is constructed. This is recognized by "maximum", that is we have a successful generalization. Statements temporarily removed may now be discarded by the generalization process. (They may still be referred to by the object construction process.)

10. The program continues by attempting to generalize. Statements (5) and (6) may be used to deduce the following:

$$X.tail.tail = nil \tag{3}$$

$$\wedge\ X.tail.head < Y \tag{7}$$

* When the program attempts a generalization, it begins by trying to find simple relationships, such as equality, between sub-objects. If these possibilities are exhausted then more complex relationships are examined such as "<" above.

11. In this case the generalization (7) is too great since the object <(0 0), 1>, which is not recognized by 'maximum' could be constructed. Since the implicants (1) and (2) can not be used to make the trial more specific, statement (7) must be abandoned as a generalization.

12. The program must now try a new approach to restricting the trial.

Suppose that all the built-in relations such as "=" and "<" have been tried without success. The program may now attempt to use a concept that it has learned before to make the description more specific. The problem is, which of the concepts stored in the program's memory are relevant? The method used for discovering potentially useful concept is based on generalization rule 2. The program looks for a concept which contains at least one statement which matches a statement in the trial. In this case remember that the first disjunct of 'maximum' contains "X.tail = nil" which matches statement (3) and "X.head = Y" which matches statement (2) with the substitution {X/X.tail, Y/1}.

As a restricted hypothesis the program may produce this concept:

$$[\exists P, Q:$$

$$maximum(P, Q) \tag{8}$$

$$\wedge\ P = X.tail \tag{9}$$

$$\wedge\ Q = 1 \tag{10}$$

$$\wedge\ X.head = Y \tag{5}$$

$$]$$

* Whenever a reference to a concept is introduced, its arguments are existentially quantified as above. The values of P and Q can be determined from the substitution obtained during the statement matching operation.

* In order to speed up the search for matching statements, the program keeps a directory of concepts and indexes them according to the form of statements contained in them. It is then only necessary to consult this directory to find the must concepts which might be useful.

* In this example, all the statements in one conjunction of the concept stored in memory were matched. However, to learn more complex concepts such as "quick-sort" it must be possible to allow only partial matches to occur. In such cases the values of some of the parameters to the introduced concept must be left free. As a heuristic, the concept with the largest number of matching statements is selected first.

13. This trial is now a valid generalization, since it is able to construct the object <(3, 1), 3>.

14. Continuing to generalize, the program uses (1) and (10) to produce:

$$
\begin{aligned}
&[\exists P, Q: \\
&\text{maximum}(P, Q) && (8)\\
&\wedge\ Q < X.\text{head} && (11)\\
&\wedge\ X.\text{head} = Y && (5)\\
&\wedge\ P = X.\text{tail} && (9)\\
&[
\end{aligned}
$$

This is a valid generalization since any object that it constructs always satisfies the concept that the trainer is trying to teach the system.

15. In fact the program will not be able to generalize any further. That is, the second disjunct of 'maximum',

$$[\exists\ Q: \text{maximum}(X.\text{tail}, Q) \wedge Q < Y \wedge X.\text{head} = Y]$$

has been learned.

* Before being stored the final trial is simplified by eliminating redundant variables. Hence P has disappeared, and "Q < Y" replaces (11).

16. The same process is repeated to learn the final disjunct of 'maximum'.

Note: Throughout this example, "=" and "<" are referred to as built-in predicates. In the present system, "<" is not, in fact, built-in but is a learned concept similar to 'maximum'. The inclusion of statements involving "<" should therefore proceed along similar lines. However, this would complicate the example. For reasons of clarity, it is treated in the same way as "=".

Heuristics Used in Learning

In addition to the algorithm given above, a number of extra features can be added to the program to improve its performance.

During the course of the learning process, the program constructs a number of objects to show the trainer. It is useful to store these objects in two lists, containing those that are recognized by the target concept (positive instances) and those that are not (negative instances). If the new approximation to the target recognizes some negative instances then the introduction of that predicate has made the concept too general. In fact, in this case it is more general than a previous hypothesis known to be too general. Some restrictions may be sought immediately. Thus the program may not need to ask many unnecessary questions of the trainer as it can work out the answers for itself from previously obtained information.

To increase the effectiveness of this method, the program may generate more than one object at any time, only one of which is shown to the trainer. If many objects, which differ substantially, are known then the number of generalizations possible can be restricted to a reasonable size.

The ideas above lead naturally to having the system learn concepts without interacting with the trainer. Instead a list of positive and a list of negative instances are provided. These are dealt with in much the same way as the instances which the program itself generates.

* The first positive instance is used to make the initial hypothesis.

* As above, negative examples are used to test the validity of the hypothesis.

* Positive examples recognized by valid generalizations are pruned from the list as they must be recognized by the same disjunct.

* When there is a choice of generalizations to be made, those that recognize other positive examples should be tried first. This would guide the process into learning a concept with a minimal number of disjuncts to cover the positive instances.

* When no more valid generalizations can be made from the current hypothesis, the hypothesis is added as another disjunct to the concept being learned.

* At this point the next positive instance in the list is used to initiate the learning of a new disjunct.

* The concept is learned when the positive list is exhausted.

Clearly, as has been shown elsewhere (Winston [1970]), the sequence of positive instances provided is critical to the learning. For example, when learning a recursive concept, an instance representing the termination condition must be given first. An alternative to the ordering of instances fixed by the trainer is to have the program choose its own order. The positive and negative lists may be given as unordered sets, and the learning program charged with the responsibility of ordering the examples on some simplicity criteria. Such an ordering may be based on the complexity of the structuring of object—thus, <(0), 0> is "simpler" than <(0 1), 1>.

It was already mentioned that the program chooses concepts for inclusion in the hypothesis on the basis of the forms of the statements it contains. As each disjunct of a concept is learned, its statements are entered into a directory. Such an entry may be:

statement: "X.head = Y"
occurs_in: (append, maximum, ...)

During the learning of 'maximum', the system tried to use "X.head = Y" to deduce some new information. Since this statement matches the above directory entry, it would know that 'append' and 'maximum' and possibly other concepts are worth trying. Since the directory look-up will find more matches with 'maximum' than 'append', 'maximum' is considered more likely to be included in the concept. Therefore, it is tried first. 'Append' would involve the construction of objects before it could be implied.

The entries in the directory of concepts may be ordered according to frequency of access. Thus, statements which occur often can be reached quickly. These statements are also most likely to lead to useful concepts since the frequent occurrence of that statement implies the frequent occurrence of the concepts in which it is contained. (The concepts within an entry may be similarly ordered). If the directory is of limited size, then statements which are rarely referred to may "fall off the bottom" thus resulting in "loss of memory".

F. A Further Example

Let us now turn to the problem of generating a program which, given a list of numbers X (some of the numbers may be negative), produce a list, Y, the same as X except that the negative numbers have been deleted.

As with "maximum" a list will be represented by an object, <head: A; tail: B> where "head" and "tail" are the equivalent of LISP's "car" and "cdr". A number will be represented by an object, <sign: S; mag: M> where S is either "+" or "−" and M is the magnitude of the number, that is an unsigned cardinal number. For this problem, zero will be considered positive. Let us assume that the concepts cardinal(X) (true if X is any unsigned integer) and number(X) (true for any signed number, X) are already known to the system.

The concept "delete" which is to be learned may be described as follows: If X is nil then Y is nil. If the head of X is negative then Y is obtained by deleting the negative numbers from the tail of X. If the head of X is positive then the head of Y is the same as the head of X and the tail of Y is obtained by deleting the negative numbers from the tail of X.

```
delete =
[X, Y:
                  X = nil ∧ X = Y
             ∨
                  [∃P, Q:
                        X.head.sign = "−"
                      ∧ X.head.mag = P
                      ∧ X.tail = Q
                      ∧ cardinal(P)
                      ∧ delete(Q, Y)
                  ]
             ∨
                  [∃P,Q:
                        X.head.sign = "+"
                      ∧ X.tail = P
                      ∧ Y.tail = Q
                      ∧ Y.head = X.head
                      ∧ delete(P, Q)
                  ]
             ]
```

To teach the program the first disjunct, the trainer shows the example <nil, nil>. The initial trial concept is:

$$X = nil \land Y = nil$$

This can be generalized to:

$$X = Y$$

Since this can recognize any pair of objects which are the same, the trial is invalid and must be restricted. This can only be done by reintroducing one of the implicants.

$$X = \text{nil} \wedge X = Y$$

This cannot be generalized any further, so the program accepts this description as the first disjunct.

To learn the second disjunct the trainer shows, <(−1), nil> which results in:

$$\begin{aligned} &X.\text{head.sign} = \text{"}-\text{"} \\ \wedge\ &X.\text{head.mag} = 1 \\ \wedge\ &X.\text{tail} = \text{nil} \\ \wedge\ &Y = \text{nil} \end{aligned}$$

Since X.tail = nil and Y = nil the trial can be generalized to:

$$\begin{aligned} &X.\text{head.sign} = \text{"}-\text{"} \\ \wedge\ &X.\text{head.mag} = 1 \\ \wedge\ &X.\text{tail} = Y \end{aligned}$$

It is possible for this trial to produce the example object <(−1, −1), (−1)>. Therefore it must be made more specific. As in the first disjunct, one of the implicants must be returned to the trial. This results in a description equivalent to the initial trial.

$$\begin{aligned} &X.\text{head.sign} = \text{"}-\text{"} \\ \wedge\ &X.\text{head.mag} = 1 \\ \wedge\ &X.\text{tail} = \text{nil} \\ \wedge\ &X.\text{tail} = Y \end{aligned}$$

The magnitude of the head of X is recognized as a cardinal number by the concept "cardinal" therefore the next generalization is:

$$\begin{aligned} &[\exists P: \\ &\qquad X.\text{head.sign} = \text{"}-\text{"} \\ &\qquad \wedge\ X.\text{head.mag} = P \\ &\qquad \wedge\ X.\text{tail} = \text{nil} \\ &\qquad \wedge\ X.\text{tail} = Y \\ &\qquad \wedge\ \text{cardinal}(P) \\ &] \end{aligned}$$

This generalization is now used to generate an object to show to the trainer. <(−2), nil> is shown. Since this is recognized by the target "delete", the trainer answers "yes" and the program continues to generalize its trial.

Since "X.tail = nil" and "X.tail = Y" match the statements in the first disjunct of "delete" for the substitution {X/X.tail, Y/Y} the following generalization is tested:

```
[∃P, Q:
       X.head.sign = "−"
    ∧  X.head.mag = P
    ∧  X.tail = Q
    ∧  cardinal(P)
    ∧  delete(Q,Y)
]
```

Given this concept, the object generation procedures produce the example <(−2, −1), nil>, which is also valid. Therefore, the program may continue to generalize the trial.

The head of X has a sign and magnitude, therefore it is recognized as a number therefore the statements describing X.head are replaced in the trial:

```
[∃P, Q, R:
       X.head = R
    ∧  X.tail = Q
    ∧  number(R)
    ∧  delete(Q, Y)
]
```

This concept results in the example <(+1, −1), nil> which is incorrect. Thus the last generalization was invalid.

The program is unable to restrict the trial in any way as long as *number(R)* is present. Therefore the trial is abandoned and the program returns to the previous trial. It is also impossible to generalize that any further, so the definition of the second disjunct of "delete" is:

```
[∃P, Q:
       X.head.sign = "−"
    ∧  X.head.mag = P
    ∧  X.tail = Q
    ∧  cardinal(P)
    ∧  delete(Q, Y)
]
```

To teach the final disjunct, the trainer shows the program <(+1), (+1)>. The initial trial is:

```
   X.head.sign = "+"
∧  X.head.mag = 1
∧  X.tail = nil
∧  Y.head.sign = "+"
∧  Y.head.mag = 1
∧  Y.tail = nil
```

The first generalization that can be made is that the signs are equal:

$$
\begin{aligned}
& \text{X.head.mag} = 1 \\
\wedge\ & \text{X.tail} = \text{nil} \\
\wedge\ & \text{Y.head.mag} = 1 \\
\wedge\ & \text{Y.tail} = \text{nil} \\
\wedge\ & \text{X.head.sign} = \text{Y.head.sign}
\end{aligned}
$$

With this definition, the object $<(-1), (-1)>$ may be generated, which is incorrect. The implicants, which have been removed, are now used to look for ways of making the trial more specific. There is no concept stored in the program's memory which has a conjunction to match the statements in the trial. So the program can only reintroduce one of the implicants.

$$
\begin{aligned}
& \text{X.head.sign} = \text{"+"} \\
\wedge\ & \text{X.head.mag} = 1 \\
\wedge\ & \text{X.tail} = \text{nil} \\
\wedge\ & \text{Y.head.mag} = 1 \\
\wedge\ & \text{Y.tail} = \text{nil} \\
\wedge\ & \text{X.head.sign} = \text{Y.head.sign}
\end{aligned}
$$

Of course, this is identical to the original trial, so the program must look for other ways of generalizing the trial. Another equality is possible:

$$
\begin{aligned}
& \text{X.head.sign} = \text{"+"} \\
\wedge\ & \text{X.tail} = \text{nil} \\
\wedge\ & \text{Y.tail} = \text{nil} \\
\wedge\ & \text{X.head.sign} = \text{Y.head.sign} \\
\wedge\ & \text{X.head.mag} = \text{Y.head.mag}
\end{aligned}
$$

Since this may produce the object $<(+2), (+2)>$, the generalization is valid.

Continuing to find equalities, the program attempts to add "X.head = Y.head", replacing the two equalities just introduced. The resulting trial is identical to previous trial, so the program continues to look for more generalizations.

Yet another quality is "X.tail = Y.tail" resulting in the generalization:

$$
\begin{aligned}
& \text{X.head.sign} = \text{"+"} \\
\wedge\ & \text{X.head} = \text{Y.head} \\
\wedge\ & \text{X.tail} = \text{Y.tail}
\end{aligned}
$$

However, this can result in the object $<(+1, -1), (+1, -1)>$ being produced, hence the trial must be made more specific. The implicant "X.tail = nil" must be returned to the trial. However, "X.tail = nil" and "X.tail = Y.tail" match the first disjunct of delete with the substitution {X/X.tail, Y/Y.tail}. Thus a new generalization,

$$
\begin{array}{l}
[\exists P, Q: \\
\quad X.head.sign = "+" \\
\quad \wedge\ X.tail = P \\
\quad \wedge\ Y.tail = Q \\
\quad \wedge\ X.head = Y.head \\
\quad \wedge\ delete(P,Q) \\
]
\end{array}
$$

can produce the object $<(+2, -1), (+2)>$ which is correct. No more generalization can be made, so the complete concept "delete" has been learned.

G. Conclusion

Initially, the intent of the research was to provide a concept learning system—thus CONFUCIUS was (re)born. However, in extending the language it was found necessary to incorporate object construction procedures. In effect, the result is a "computer language", since programs will be written by the learning system and executed without human intervention. Thus, the complete system represents a new approach to automatic program synthesis.

An area where such a system may find application is in the solution of robot-type planning problems. QLISP [Rulifson, 1972] is a language which facilitates the writing of problem solving and theorem proving programs. Although it is a procedural language it also exhibits goal directed behavior in its "GOAL" expression:

(GOAL goal-class goal)

Here the programmer asks the system to attempt some goal. For example, a robot planner might have an expression of the form:

(GOAL $DO (INROOM BOX1 ROOM4))

The system maintains a list, "goal-class", of programs which might help to achieve this goal. One such program is chosen. If it is not successful, the system backtracks and tries another alternative. If no alternative is left, a failure occurs.

This example has, in common with our system, the fact that a program tells it what is to be done, but says very little about how it is to be done. That is left to the interpreter. That is, a statement in the language is regarded as a command to a problem solver.

The ability to construct objects allows our system to solve problems, also. For example, the trainer may teach the robot the concept which describes how its arm is to move a block from one place to another. The object which is produced by an execution of this concept, given the initial state, then describes the state of the system after such a movement. The change in state may be interpreted by machinery, resulting in a real block actually being moved.

With the development of complex structural description languages and learning systems, of the character described here, the distinction between "programming" and "concept learning" becomes less obvious.

References

[Bruner, 1956]
J.S. Bruner, J.J. Goodnow, and G.A. Austin, *A Study of Thinking,* Wiley, New York (1956).

[Banerji, 1969]
R. Banerji, *Theory of Problem Solving: An Approach to Artificial Intelligence,* American Elsevier, New York (1969).

[Banerji, 1978]
R. Banerji, "Using a descriptive language as a programming language," *Fourth International Joint Conference on Pattern Recognition,* 346, 350 (1978).

[Cohen, 1977]
B.L. Cohen, "A powerful and efficient structural pattern recognition system," *Artificial Intelligence,* 9, 223,256 (1977).

[Cohen, 1978]
B.L. Cohen, *A Theory of Structural Concept Formation and Pattern Recognition,* Ph.D. thesis, Dept. of Computer Science, University of N.S.W. (1978)

[Hayes Roth, 1978]
F. Hayes Roth and J. McDermott, "An interference matching technique for inducing abstractions," *Communications of the ACM* (21) 5, 410,411 (1978).

[Michalski, 1980]
R.S. Michalski, "Pattern analysis as rule guided inductive inference," *IEEE Transactions on Pattern Analysis and Machine Intelligence* (2) 4, 349–361 (1980).

[Roussel, 1975]
P. Roussel, "Prolog: Manual de reference et d'utilisation," Groupe d'Intelligence Artificielle, Marseille Luminy.

[Rulifson, 1972]
J.F. Rulifson, J.A. Derksen, and R.L. Waldinger, "QA4: a procedural calculus for intuitive reasoning," S.R.I. Artificial Intelligence Center, Technical Note 73.

[Sammut, 1980]
C. Sammut and B. Cohen, "A language for describing concepts as programs," *Language Design and Programming Methodology,* Springer Verlag Lecture Notes in Computer Science, Vol. 79, Editor: J.M. Tobias.

[Sammut, 1981]
C. Sammut, *Learning Concepts by Performing Experiments,* Ph.D. Thesis, Dept. of Computer Science, University of N.S.W.

[Winston, 1970]
P.H. Winston, *Learning Structural Descriptions from Examples,* Ph.D. Thesis, MIT Artificial Intelligence Laboratory.

CHAPTER 22

Some Insights Into Automatic Programming Using A Pattern Recognition Viewpoint

Ranan B. Banerji
Saint Joseph's University, Philadelphia, USA

Abstract

A formalism has been exhibited which unifies the basic structures of programs as learned from examples and patterns as recognized from instances. This indicates that certain techniques of program construction are available in the pattern-recognition field. Although these techniques would lead to much greater flexibility and strength in pattern recognition, they are seldom used: there has been a marked reluctance to the use of subroutines in the pattern recognition field. It is believed that the formalism exhibited here would remove some of the roadblocks. The limitations of some of the program-learning techniques are also illuminated by the method.

Introduction

This paper is addressed to a wide area of activity, including hopefully the entire field of activity of Program Construction and Automatic Programming and the area of Pattern Recognition involved with what I have previously called (in Banerji [1979]) "Interpreted Logical Descriptions." This area is often also called "Structural Descriptions". I use the former term to avoid confusion with what is known as "Syntactic Descriptions" (Fu and Swain [1969]).

Naturally, if one has to embrace such a wide area, one has to do it at a level of abstraction which may seem useless. For the purposes of transferring techniques from one sub-area of activity to another such abstraction may indeed be useless. However, it is my belief that even at this abstract level there will be enough structure left as to allow us to pinpoint certain problems and insights that permeate the entire area addressed. For some sub-areas, this pinpointing will have to be informal. For others, it will be so close to the technical level as to perhaps allow transfers of technique.

In a very informal way we may say that an Automatic Programming System is a device which has computer programs at the output. We are not terribly concerned here as to the language in which the program is written — as long as one is convinced that a state-of-the-art compiler can be written to convert its sentences to a program for a present-day digital computer.

By the same token, what the pattern-recognition expert wants as the output of a "learning system" is the specification of some device which, given formal objects (e.g., "scenes", "feature vectors") yields a classification signal. There is a wide divergence in the pattern recognition field as to the form this specification takes at the output of the system. In the Interpreted Logical Description area (Cohen [1978], Cohen and Sammut [1978], Banerji [1964] and [1976], Sammut [1981], Banerji [1978], and Chapter 21, this volume) one makes the specification into a statement in symbolic logic: the state-of-the-art dictates statements in some subset of a first order predicate calculus.

What brings Interpreted Logical Descriptions close to Automatic Programming is the fact that a number of workers (Warren [1974], Bibel *et al.* [1978], Kowalski [1979]) have used the descriptive language of predicate calculus to specify programs. Interpreters exist for making this happen. The problems posed by this interpreter have some commonality with the problems of pattern recognition. Moreover, since all "learning" in pattern recognition is done on the basis of examples, the entire technique becomes analogous to learning of programs from input-output.

The major bridge between automatic programming and pattern recognition then, has the learning of programs from input-output pairs at one end and recognizing relations by ordered-pair examples with logical description languages at the other.

So far we have talked about the inputs to the automatic programming system, except in passing immediately above. A wide divergence occurs at this end between different workers in the field of automatic programming. At one end of the spectrum we have workers who feel that the specification can and should be given in natural language. Then there are others, motivated by problems of Robotics, who feel that the specification should be in the form of examples of what inputs are to be transformed into what outputs. There are those who are trying to understand what would be involved if the specification were given interactively (Biermann [1972]): i.e. if instead of acting upon the entire specification initially, the system interrogated the specifier (whether a cooperating human or an impersonal "world of the robot" responding to an experiment with results) during the development of the program.

At the very comfortable opposite end of the spectrum are the workers who feel that the specification needs to be given with the same precision and the same kind of a language as is used by workers in the field of program verification (Manna and Waldinger [1977]) for specifying the output of a program.

In my own work I have straddled the two extremes. On the one hand I have tried to insist that the specification language should have the same precision of syntax and semantics as a formal language like symbolic logic. On the other hand I have felt that the specification itself should be in the form of a set of examples. This latter feeling came from my continued interest in pattern recognition. As a matter of fact, my rather recent interest in automatic programming arose only when I recognized that the pattern recognition language I was using could describe executable functions.

As I have indicated, my preoccupation has been with program development from examples. However, there are some linguistic aspects of the specification language which holds also when the specification of the input is done by a precise language (Warren [1974], Bibel *et al.*) other than that of input-output pairs. When the input specification is by input-output pairs (Biermann and Feldman [1972], Summers [1977], Jouannaud [1977], Guiho and Jouannaud [1978], Treuil *et al.* [1977]) commonality with pattern recognition problems is of course much greater. A remarkable amount of these problems also are of a linguistic nature.

I believe that the discussion of all these common problems would be facilitated if we tried to translate the techniques used by various authors into a single syntactic and semantic framework. In this paper, I shall choose a system used by myself (Banerji [1979]) and (in somewhat modified form) some colleagues (Cohen [1978], Cohen and Sammut [1978], Sammut [1981], and Chapter 21, this volume). In what follows, we shall introduce the syntax of the system and—to the extent possible—its semantics.

A. Syntax and Semantics of a Description Language

Let us assume that a pattern recognition environment has the following basic elements. There is an universe U whose elements we shall call objects. Several functions are pre-defined on this universe. Some of these map objects to names and others map objects to objects. We shall also assume that if A and B are subsets of U then A×B is also a subset of U, i.e. that one has ordered pairs in the universe and so some of the predefined functions could be projection functions. Also, a subset of the universe can on some occasion be a relation between two other subsets of the universe.

The predefined functions naturally define certain subsets of U, i.e. the elements of the partitions induced by these functions. Also, since some of the functions map objects into objects some of these partitions are induced by compositions of functions.

Set theoretical combinations of these pre-defined sets can be used to define new functions and predicates. Very often in pattern recognition literature, the formsof these compositions are compressed by using algebraic techniques, assuming (or recognizing) that often the names of the pre-defined sets are numbers. The algebraic and statistical techniques of pattern recognition are all based on this supposition that the predefined functions map objects to numbers. In our discussion here we shall not make any such assumptions and stick to the standard connectives of logic.

In our presentations, the basic form of the atomic predicates are f(x)=v where f and v may be atomic symbols or may have structures of their own (vide ultra).

The definition of a predicate would attach a name to the description, e.g.

$$x \in \text{digit} \equiv \text{value}(x) = 0 \lor \text{value}(x) = 1 \quad (1)$$

If one allows the use of these defined predicates inside other definitions, one can obtain considerable compression. For instance, if one wants to define pairs of binary digits one could write

$$x \in \text{digpr} \equiv (\text{value}(\text{first}(x)) = 1 \lor \text{value}(\text{first}(x)) = 0)$$

$$\land (\text{value}(\text{second}(x)) = 1 \lor \text{value}(\text{second}(x)) = 0) \qquad (2)$$

However, the chaining of function applications could be reduced and considerable compression obtained if we write

$$x \in \text{digpr} \equiv (\text{first}\ (x) \in \text{digit}) \wedge (\text{second}\ (x) \in \text{digit}) \qquad (3)$$

Another convenient compression we shall often use forms a basis of what is to follow. The pre-defined predicates satisfied by a member of "digit" (i.e. value(x) = 0) can be written

$$x \in (\text{value}, 0) \qquad (4)$$

Expressions like the one to the right of the "∈" sign will be called "objects". As an example of a more complex object, note that a typical member of "digpair" might satisfy

$$\text{value}\ (\text{first}\ (x)) = 0 \wedge \text{value}\ (\text{second}\ (x)) = 1 \qquad (5)$$

This we can compress to

$$\text{first}\ (x) \in (\text{value}, 0) \wedge \text{second}\ (x) = (\text{value}, 1) \qquad (6)$$

and further to

$$x \in (\text{first}, (\text{value}, 0)\ ;\ \text{second}, (\text{value}, 1)) \qquad (7)$$

As we proceed with a formal definition of the syntax, it will be found that the symbol "∈" as used in the discussion above is syntactically correct in equations (1), (2) and (3) above, but is not so in (4), (6) and (7). In the last three cases, the syntax demands that the "∈" sign be replaced by the "=" sign. The "=" sign, as well as the "∈" sign seem to have different interpretations in different syntactic contexts. Only further research can tell whether the ambiguities are an inherent part of the technique or can be removed by careful syntactic redefinition. For the present, we shall have matters as they are and stick to the syntax as was previously defined by us. We shall discuss the semantics, as well as the ambiguous interpretations as we proceed.

A.1. The Formal Syntax of Terms

We start with the following definitions:

1. *Constants* are strings of letters from the early part of the alphabet and digits. *Variables* are strings of letters from the end of the alphabet. A constant is a *term* and a variable is a term.
2. If A and B are terms, then A, B is an *ordered pair* (called "op" for short). A is its *left hand side* (called "lhs") and B is the *right hand side* (called "rhs") of this op. Every op is a *string of ordered pairs* (called "sop"). If A is an op and B is a sop, then A; B is a sop.
3. If A is a sop then (A) is an *object*. An object is a term.
4. If A is a term and B is a term, then A(B) is a term.

The reader will notice that of these four paragraphs, 1 and 4 define terms almost in the usual logical sense and can be interpreted in the same way. The main deviation from standard logic is in 2 and 3 above, which define the objects. It is our belief that the use of this syntactic form gives us an efficient method for proving a class of theorems whose proof using standard methods would be less efficient.

A.2. The Value of Terms: Syntactic Definition

Instead of having proof-procedures, our system has a set of syntactic processes for converting one syntactic structure to another. One of the components of the processor is a routine which, given a term yields another term—its "value". The following definitions of value also describe the processor.

5. The *value* of a constant is itself. The value of a variable is itself. The value of an op A,B is A^1 , B^1 where A^1 and B^1 are the values of A and B respectively when they are defined. The value of the sop A;B is A^1 ; B^1 where A^1 and B^1 are values of A and B when they are defined. In other cases the value of ops and sops are undefined.
6. The value of an object (A) is defined if and only if the value A^1 of A is defined and there are no two ordered pairs in A^1 whose lhs are identical and their rhs are distinct constants (or when one is a constant and the other is an object). In such cases, the value of A is (A^1).
7. The value of a term in the form A(B) is defined only if the values A^1 and B^1 for A and B, respectively, are defined and B^1 is an object. In all such cases, if A^1 is the lhs of an ordered pair of B^1 and the rhs of all such order pairs (i.e. with A^1 as the lhs) are identical, the value of A(B) is this unique rhs. Else the value of A(B) is A^1 (B^1).

The reason for the continuous recursion in the definitions will become clear when we start to give some more realistic examples. Meanwhile, it ought to be pointed out that by the above definition the term

shape ((color, red; shape, square))

has the value "square". This tempts one to think of the object in the parenthesis as an individual. From our discussion above however there is also reason to think of the object as a set, or, as a short-hand for a conjunction of atomic predicates. The need for this will become clearer as we proceed.

A.3. The Formal Semantics of Statements

We shall give some realistic examples after the following formal definitions.

8. If A and B are terms, then (A = B) is an *atom-statement* (called an "atom" for short). F and T are atom statements. An atom is a *conjunction.* If A is a conjunction or an empty string and B is an atom, then A ∧ B is a conjunction. (If A is an empty string, then A ∧ B is written in the form B. Also, if B is a conjunction and A is an empty string, then B can be written as B ∧ A.)

   A conjunction is a *disjunction.* If B is a disjunction and A a conjunction, then A ∨ B is a disjunction. A disjunction is a *statement.* If A is a statement and B is a variable, then (∃B) (A) is a statement. If A is a term and C is a term, then A ∈ C is a statement.
9. If C is a variable, D a constant, and E a statement, then C ∈ D = E is a *description* of D.

   Once again, one is tempted to interpret the symbol ∈ in 9 as the ⊂ symbol. The description

$$x \in \text{redthing} \equiv \text{color}(x) = \text{red}$$

for instance, looks harmlessly like symbolic logic (with "x ∈ redthing" interpreted as having the same meaning as "redthing (x)" with "redthing" as a predicate). However, if "≡" is interpreted normally, then, since our definitions say that the value of "color ((color, red))" is "red", the statement

(color, red) ∈ redthing

is true. But if (color, red) denotes a set, then ∈ should be replaced by ⊂.

The use of defined predicates as in 9 above gives us the ability to express infinite disjunctions without, essentially, leaving the propositional calculus. To see this, let us consider the two following descriptions

$$x \in \text{digit} \equiv x = 0 \vee x = 1$$

$$x \in \text{num} \equiv \text{tail}\ (x) \in \text{digit} \wedge (\text{head}(x) = \text{nil} \vee \text{head}(x) \in \text{num})$$

from which we can deduce (vide ultra)

$$0 \in \text{digit}$$

as well as an infinite class of statements like

$$(\text{head, nil; tail, } 1) \in \text{num}$$

$$(\text{head, (head, nil; tail, } 1); \text{ tail, } 0) \in \text{num}$$

$$(\text{head, (head, (head, nil; tail } 1); \text{ tail, } 0); \text{ tail, } 1) \in \text{num}$$

and so on. Purely as a matter of motivation, and also since these examples will continue to play an important role in our examples, the reader may find it convenient to think of "elements of num" as representing binary strings, the "tail" standing for the least significant digit and the "head" as the remainder of the string— including the empty string, here called "nil". The three objects shown here can then be written as "1", "10" and "101". In what follows, we shall often use this "shorthand" for brevity.

To give meaning to my proposed bridge between program learning and pattern recognition, I would like to point out that i) a binary predicate is really a unary predicate on objects on which projection functions are defined (indeed this is true of n-ary predicates also for all n), and ii) an unary function, defined as a binary predicate, often has enough information in the definition so as to enable the calculation of the output component from the input component. Take, for instance, the successor function on numerals (looked upon as strings of binary digits) as follows

$$x \in \text{succ} \equiv [(\text{tail (first (x))} = 0 \wedge (\text{tail (second (x))} = 1)$$

$$\wedge\ (\text{head (first (x))} = \text{head(second (x)))}]$$

$$\vee\ [(\text{tail (first (x))} = 1) \wedge (\text{tail (second (x))} = 0)$$

$$\wedge\ (\text{head (first (x))} = \text{nil} \wedge (\text{tail (head (second (x)))} = 1)$$

$$\wedge (\text{head (head (second (x)))} = \text{nil})]$$

$$\vee\ [(\text{tail (first (x))} = 1) \wedge (\text{tail (second (x))} = 0) \wedge$$

$$((\text{first, head(first (x)); second, head(second (x)))} \in \text{succ})] \tag{8}$$

We ask the reader to convince himself that "(first, 11; second,100) ∈ succ" is true, interpreting the symbols as belonging to standard logic.

What is more interesting (and gives our system the aspect of a programming language) is that the processor (which can replace the logical processes we asked the reader to simulate above), can also check the statement

$$(\text{first, 11; second, x}) \in \text{succ} \tag{9}$$

to yield the result

$$x = 100 \tag{10}$$

or (removing the "shorthand") to transform

$$(\text{first,(tail, 1;head,(tail, 1;head,nil)); second,x}) \in \text{succ} \tag{11}$$

to

$$x = (\text{tail, 0; head, (tail,0; head, (tail,1; head, nil)))} \tag{12}$$

The processor derives what I have called the "substituted form" of statements. If a statement is true in a standard (or nearly standard) sense and has no free variables, this form is "T". For false statements the form is "F". For statements with free or existentially quantified variables (note once more the alienation from standard logic), the form can be a conjunction of atomic statements of the form "x = A" where A is an object.

A.4. Reduced Form of Statements: Syntactic Definition

In what follows we define this "substituted form", using on the way the definitions of "merged form", "sorted form" and "reduced form". Once more, these definitions are also descriptions of the processors which construct these forms.

A few preliminary comments are in order. First, there is no way that I can see of having the substituted form T for a statement having free variables, since neither negation nor implication belongs in the language. Many theorems, hence,can not be stated in the language.

10. The *reduced form* of $(\exists B)$ (A) is the same as the reduced form of A. This reduced form is said to *construct* B. If the reduced form does not contain B, then B is arbitrary. If the reduced form is F, the construction fails.

11. The reduced form of $A \vee B$ is the same as the reduced form of A unless the reduced form of A is F, in which case it is the reduced form of B.

12. The reduced form of $A \wedge B$ depends heavily on the form of the atom B. These are separately discussed below. In all that follows B is $(C = D)$. C^1 is the value of C and D^1 the value of D. Also, the reduced form of an empty string is defined to be the empty string. The reduced form of A will be denoted by A^1. $(C^1 = D^1)$ will be denoted by B^1.

12a. If C^1 and D^1 are both constants, then the reduced form of $A \wedge B$ is F, unless C^1 and D^1 are identical; in this case, it is A^1. If A is an empty string, then A^1 is T.

12b. If C^1 is a variable and D^1 a constant or object, then the reduced form is $B^1 \wedge A^1$, where A^1 is the reduced form of A. If D^1 is a variable, then it is $B^1 \wedge A^1$. If C^1 and D^1 are identical, then it is A^1, unless A^1 is empty in which case it is T.

12c. If D^1 is a variable and C^1 is not, then the reduced form of $A \wedge B$ is the same as the reduced form of $A \wedge (D^1 = C^1)$.

12d. If C^1 is a variable, constant, or object, and D^1 is of the form E(F), then the reduced form of $A \wedge B$ is the same as the reduced form of $A \wedge (F = (E, C^1))$.

12e. If C^1 and D^1 are of the form E(F), or if they are both objects, then the reduced form of $A \wedge B$ is the same as the reduced form of $A \wedge (G = C^1) \wedge (G = D^1)$, where G is a variable which does not occur in A, C^1, or D^1.

13. A conjunction is said to be in *stable form* if it is the reduced form of all its cyclic permutations.

It is conjectured that the reduced form of all statements will reach a stable form only if it is the conjunction of atoms of the form $C = D$ where C is a variable and D is a constant, object or variable (unless, of course, the reduced form is F or T). We now proceed to obtain the "merged form" of these.

Avoiding for the time some of the (often important) details, one of the major merger processes takes two sentences like "x = (color, red)" and "x = (shape, square)" and yields the sentence "x = (color, red; shape, square)". This process is completely unjustified, of course if "=" stood for identity of objects as strings or if objects were interpreted as individuals. I have found no good way to interpret equality as the identity of constants named by the equated terms. The natural interpretation of objects seems to be as sets. However, interpreting variables as having sets for values would not justify the "merger" process if equality stands for identity of sets. Hence the tentative interpretation for equality as membership suggested above, at least in this context.

All this, of course, is happening because of "merger", whose importance I intend to justify with an example. However, we still need at least one more definition before we can even get started.

14. Let M be a set of descriptions (see Definition 9). A sentence has the *reduced form given M* as we have defined above unless it contains a predicate of the form $A \in B$. In the latter case, the reduced form is F unless the value B' of B is a constant and a description of B' occurs in M. In this case, if $C \in B' \equiv S$ is that description, then in the reduced form $A \in B$ is replaced by the reduced form of S^1, where S^1 is obtained from S by replacing each occurrence of C by A.

Let us now illustrate the stable reduced form of the statement

(first,(tail, 1;head,(tail,0;head,nil)); second,y) ∈ succ (13)

which is slightly simpler, for ease of discussion, than the examples in lines (9) to (12) above.

Replacing the object on the lhs of the ∈ sign in (13) for x on the rhs of ≡ in the definition of succ (eqn 8) we obtain three disjuncts. One immediately negates the first since the first conjunct

tail (first (x)) = 0

becomes, by evaluation, into

1 = 0.

and then by 12a to F.

In a similar manner the second disjunct also is negated since the third conjunct yields

(tail, 0; head, nil) = nil,

and by 11 we are forced to reduce the third disjunct.

To satisfy the third disjunct we note that we have automatically satisfied the first conjunct

tail (first (x)) = 1.

To satisfy the third disjunct one has to satisfy

(first, (tail, 0; head, nil);

second, head (second x)) ∈ succ.

This new object immediately satisfies the first conjunct of the first disjunct of the definition of succ. The other two disjuncts simplify to

nil = head (head (y))

and

tail (head (y)) = 1

while the second conjunct of the original third disjunct already was

tail (y) = 0

The first of the above three atoms reduces by 12d to

$$\text{head}\ (y) = (\text{head, nil})$$

and by a second application, to

$$y = (\text{head}, (\text{head, nil})) \quad (14)$$

The second one reduces similarly to

$$y = (\text{head}, (\text{tail}, 1)) \quad (15)$$

and the third to

$$y = (\text{tail}, 0) \quad (16)$$

A.5. The Merged Form of Statements: Syntactic Description

The next step is the merger. We assume that a linear order "$<$" is imposed on the variables.

15. If $A \wedge (x_1 = t_1) \wedge (x_2 = t_2)$ is in stable form, then its sorted form is the sorted form of $B \wedge (x_2 = t_2)$ if $x_1 < x_2$. Else it is the sorted form of $C \wedge (x_1 = t_1)$. In the above, B is the sorted form of $A \wedge (x_1 = t_1)$ and C is the sorted form of $A \wedge (x_2 = t_2)$.
16. If $A \wedge (x = t_1) \wedge (x = t_2)$ is in sorted form, then its *merged form* is given as follows:

16a. If t_1 and t_2 are both variables, then the merged form is the merged form of the sorted form of $A \wedge (x = t_1) \wedge (t_1 = t_2)$.

16b. If t_2 is a variable, then the merged form is the merged form of the sorted form of $A \wedge (x = t_1) \wedge (t_2 = x)$: similarly, if t_1 is a variable. In both cases, it is assumed that 15a is inapplicable.

16c. If t_1 is a constant and t_2 an object, then the merged form is F.

16e. If t_1 is an object (A_1) and t_2 is an object (A_2) then the merged form is the merged form of the sorted form of the reduced form of $A \wedge B$ where B is constructed as follows:

16e-1. If all the lhs of all the ops in the sop $A_1 ; A_2$ are distinct, then B is $(x = (A_1 ; A_2))$.

16e-2. If there are two ops a, b_1 and a, b_2 with the same lhs then B is of the form $(x = B^1) \wedge (G = b_1) \wedge (G = b_2)$ where G is a variable other than x which does not occur in A, t_1 or t_2 and B^1 is obtained from $(A_1; A_2)$ by deleting a, b_1 and a, b_2 and adding a, G.

In the light of these, let us go back to merging the atoms 14, 15 and 16.

The first two atoms, by 16e-2 yield the conjunction

$$(y = (\text{head}, x)) \wedge (x = (\text{tail}, 1)) \wedge (x = (\text{head}, \text{nil}))$$

of which the last two merge by 16e-1, giving us

$$(y = (\text{head}, x)) \wedge (x = (\text{tail}, 1; \text{head}, \text{nil}))$$

which can merge easily with "y = (tail, 0)" by 16e-1 to yield

$$(y = (\text{head}, x; \text{tail}, 0)) \wedge (x = (\text{tail}, 1; \text{head}, \text{nil}))$$

Now we merely need one more definition to get the substituted form.

17. If a conjunction A is in merged form, then its *substituted form* is itself if none of the terms on the right-hand side of the atoms of A contain any variable which occurs on the left-hand side of any atom of A. Otherwise, if A is of the form $B \wedge (y = t_1) \wedge (x = t_2(y))$ (or an equivalent form under commutativity), then the substituted form of A is the same as the substituted form of $B \wedge (x = t_2(t_1))$.

Applying this rule to the above conjunction we obtain

$$(y = (\text{head}, (\text{tail}, 1; \text{head}, \text{nil}); \text{tail}, 0)) \wedge (x = (\text{tail}, 1; \text{head}, \text{nil}))$$

B. Learning Program From Examples

In what has gone above I have tried to indicate how statements can be interpreted as programs. So far I have not tried (and in this paper, will not) to relate the processes involved with the kind of instantiations that go on during a resolution proof, although close relations obviously exist, and this is a subject of study of some importance to me.

It appears that we have here a description language which can describe relations as well as sets and having the property that the construction of objects from the descriptions is nearly mechanical. As a result, the language can be looked upon as capable of describing programs.

The next question one needs to address is: can one develop the descriptions of programs in this language on the basis of examples of input-output pairs? I shall say that the answer is yes only to the extent that one can develop the description of any set on the basis of examples of its members.

In what follows, we shall describe one method of such "description learning" among a number of alternative ones that are available for learning Interpreted Logical Descriptions. In the process of describing it we shall be exposing difficulties which are exact analogs of difficulties in learning programs. This is done in the hope that as heuristics for surmounting such problems occur in the field of pattern recognition or in the field of program synthesis they can be transferred to the other field.

In what follows, we shall exemplify a learning process by showing how the process learns from examples the following description, equivalent to the description of "succ" in section A.3 (eqn 8)

$$
\begin{aligned}
&x \in \text{succ} \equiv (\text{first}(x) \in \text{num}) \wedge (\text{second}(x) \in \text{num}) \\
&\wedge \{ [(\text{tail}(\text{first}(x)) = 0) \wedge (\text{tail}(\text{second}(x)) = 1) \\
&\wedge (\text{head}(\text{first}(x)) = \text{head}(\text{second}(x)))] \\
&\vee [(\text{tail}(\text{first}(x)) = 1) \wedge (\text{tail}(\text{second}(x)) = 0) \\
&\wedge (\text{head}(\text{first}(x)) = \text{nil}) \wedge (\text{tail}(\text{head}(\text{second}(x))) = 1 \\
&\wedge (\text{head}(\text{head}(\text{second}(x))) = \text{nil})] \\
&\vee [(\text{tail}(\text{first}(x)) = 1) \wedge (\text{tail}(\text{second}(x)) = 0) \wedge \\
&(\exists z)\ (z \in \text{succ}\ \&\ (\text{first}(z) = \text{head}(\text{first}(x))) \\
&\wedge (\text{second}(z) = \text{head}(\text{second}(x))))] \}
\end{aligned}
$$

It will be noticed that the third disjunct of the third conjunct has an existentially quantified statement of which the third conjunct of the third disjunct in section A.3 is an instantiation. A little introspection will show that recognition of an ordered pair as satisfying $x \in$ succ will go almost exactly the same way with the two descriptions.

The other point to notice is that we now have two other conjuncts to the description, namely "first $(x) \in$ num" and "second $(x) \in$ num". The learning process will learn this part of the description in the same way it will learn the rest: indeed, the learning of this part will facilitate the learning of the rest as the following discussion will show.

For purposes of discussion, we shall write members of succ as ordered pairs of strings of binary digits. That is, instead of writing

(first, (tail, 1; head, (tail, 1; head, nil));

second, (tail, 0; head, (tail, 0; head, (tail, 1; head, nil)))).

we shall write (11,100). Also, we shall assume that "num", instead of the description in Section A.3, has the description

$$x \in \text{num} \equiv [(\text{tail}(x) = 0) \vee (\text{tail}(x) = 1)] \wedge [(\text{head}(x) = \text{nil}) \vee (\text{head}(x) \in \text{num})]$$

—which, the reader will notice, is somewhat simpler than the one in Section A.3—in the interest of convenience.

The general strategy we shall assume is the following. We shall concentrate on one positive example and write down all the statements about the examples that can be mechanically deduced from it. We shall work with the following positive instances

(1010, 1011), (10,11), (0,1)

(1, 10)

(11, 100), (01, 10)

and the following negative instances

(1011, 1011), (1010, 1010), (1010, 110),

(1100, 1010), (5,51) (50,5), (0, 10), (11, 101),

(10, 100), (11, 101)

Starting with the first positive example, the following statements can be extracted as true

first (x) ∈ num
second (x) ∈ num
head (first (x)) = 101
head (second (x)) = 101
head (first (x)) = head (second (x))
tail (first (x)) = 0
tail (second (x)) = 1

For simplicity we are leaving out various other deductions, like head (head (first (x)) = 10 etc. These contribute great inefficiencies to the system (we shall discuss these later: workers in the field of program learning will recognize these). However, in this section we are merely illustrating a method, not exalting it in any way.

Continuing with our learning technique, the system now constructs objects which hold all but a few of the above statements true. The first two statements can not be changed without changing the third, fourth and fifth statements, so these latter are changed first. None of these can be changed individually without changing one of the others. Changing the fourth and fifth together yields the third negative example and changing the third and fifth together yields the fourth negative example. Changing the third and fourth together yields no negative examples (some of the positive examples on the first row are produced this way). So the learning program marks the third and fourth statements inessential and the fifth essential. Similarly, changing the sixth and seventh statements yield the first two negative examples. Removing any of the first two statements yield the fifth and sixth negative examples. Hence, these two are essential.

Removing the inessential statements from the above list of statements yields the conjunction induced by the first disjunct of the third conjunct of the description of succ. This description is satisfied by the first row of positive examples. However, the rest of the positive examples do not satisfy the description, so the system picks another positive example to focus on.

The learning of the second disjunct from the second row of positive examples is an identical process and we shall not expand on it here. However, a third kind of deduction becomes essential for the learning of the rest of the description, starting with the first element of the third row as the focus. At this moment the first two disjuncts in the description of succ is already in memory as a partial description.

Using the focus one deduces, in addition to first(x) ∈ num and second(x) ∈ num, also tail (first (x) = 1) and tail (second (x)) = 0 which can be changed to yield the negative examples on the third row. However, a new deduction is suggested by the fact that we can also deduce head (first (x)) ∈ num. This, together with the fact that first (x) ∈ num is an essential part of the description of all succ seen so far, "suggests" (a word which hides many blind alleys and heuristics) that (∃z) (z ∈ succ & first (z) = head (first (x))) is a possible deduction. This yields the following:

$$z = (1, 10)$$

and one "notices" that second (z) = head (second (x)) is true.

Once this deduction is made, a repetition of the previous method of removing and testing conjuncts yields the third disjunct of "succ," completing the description.

In the discussion that follows, we shall try to bring the subject-matter of this section in line with automatic programming.

C. Pattern Recognition and Program Learning

Although program construction from specification is not my particular area of discussion, it will be worthwhile to point out that the atomic operators and predicates used to build the programs and the descriptions play an essential role in determining the difficulty of the construction task, whether we are constructing programs or descriptions. This applies to the program construction task whether the construction be from examples or from specifications. We shall comment in some detail on the former case in what follows. In the latter case I will merely comment that there are certain specifications which are readily convertible to programs and others which take "some doing". Taking an example from Bibel *et al.* [10], the maximum m of a two-elements set {a, b} satisfies the property

$$(a \leqslant b \wedge m = b) \vee (b \leqslant a \wedge \& m = a)$$

which is readily converted into a program. On the other hand, the maximum m of a larger set S, satisfying the property

$$m \in S \,\&\, \wedge\, (\forall m')\, (m' \in S \longrightarrow m' \leqslant m)$$

needs to be converted into a quantifier-free recursive form to match it to the basic predicates and operators of the programming language. If the programming language had quantifications among the basic building blocks, this second statement would be equally easily convertible to a program.

To bring out the importance of the basic predicates in the case of learning by examples (either of programs or of descriptions), let me invoke the description of dig and num in Section A.3.

The two conjuncts of the definition of "num" are

$$\text{tail } (x) \in \text{digit}$$

and

$$\text{head } (x) = \text{nil} \vee \text{head } (x) \in \text{num}.$$

Of these the first succinctly expresses what with a slightly greater effort, could be written

$$\text{value (tail (x))} = 0 \lor \text{value (tail (x))} = 1.$$

This would not only complicate the description but would also lengthen the learning process.

The matter becomes even more critical if we imagine what would happen if the second disjunct of the second conjunct of "num" above was not available to us. We would be forced to learn longer and longer disjunctions.

Some workers (Summers [1977], Jouannaud [1977]) in the area of program learning from examples invoke a special procedure in the learning algorithm for converting such a growth into a recursion. Others (Cohen and Sammut [1978], Treuil *et al.* [1977]) as in my work, build the recursion by matching a part of the developed program to a previously developed program.

But this is taking us somewhat ahead of ourselves. The major point I want to make is that the beginning of any learning task—be it learning descriptions or programs—lies in deducing the truth of certain statements about the examples. An important part of SISP (Guiho [1978]) is the matching of (stating the equality between) substrings of the input and output. In THESYS (Summers [1977]) these predicates come in two parts: the recognition of the position of the input in parts of the Summers hierarchy and the equality of the output with some function of the input. While THESYS restricts these structures to be built out of only CAR, CDR, CONS and ATOM, the Paris school allows itself the liberty of using their LCAR, LRAC, RDC and APPEND. A lot of the strength of their system comes from the use of these stronger building blocks.

However, Jouannaud [1977] in his thesis used another technique (later used by Treuil *et al.* [1977]), somewhat stronger than the technique I have illustrated above in the learning of "num" and "succ". They develop (rather than invoke) subprograms which make the expression of the final program simpler.

It may be worthwhile at this point to indicate the kind of analogy I am drawing between program-learning and description-learning by using the language of section A to describe a LISP program learned by the technique described by Kodratoff [1979]. The example I use appears in his paper in section 4.4.

Some of the examples (x'_i and y'_i) used by him, rewritten as objects would be:

(first, (car, A; cdr, nil); second, (car, A; cdr, nil))

(first, (car, A; cdr, (car, B; cdr, nil));

second, (car, (car, A; cdr, nil); cdr, (car, B; cdr, nil)))

(first, (car, A; cdr, (car, B; cdr, (car, C; cdr, nil)));

second,(car,(car,(car,A; cdr,nil); cdr,(car,B; cdr,nil));

cdr, (car, C; cdr, nil)))

and this sequence would have to satisfy the relation FARG(x) = y or, in the nomenclature of section A:

(first, x;second, y) $\in$ FARG

while FARG, as an unary relation, is defined as follows:

$$\begin{aligned} \alpha \in \text{FARG} \equiv (\exists\beta)\ \{&\text{third}\ (\beta) = \text{second}\ (\alpha) \\ &\wedge \text{first}\ (\beta) = \text{first}\ (\alpha) \\ &\wedge \text{second}\ (\beta) = \text{first}\ (\alpha) \\ &\wedge \beta \in \text{F}\} \end{aligned}$$

paralleling the definition of FARG in his paper.

The use of F as a subroutine for FARG, in any of the learning algorithms suggested by the users of the language of Section A (particularly in Banerji [1979], Cohen and Sammut (Chapter 21)), would presuppose that F (and its subroutine G) were already in the set M of definition 14 of Section A.4; also, of all the deductions possible from the examples, deductions involving F would be the ones tried early. The descriptions of F and G are not simple, as the following transliterations will show

$$\alpha \in F \equiv [\ (\mathrm{cdr}(\mathrm{second}(\alpha)) = \mathrm{nil}) \wedge$$

$$(\mathrm{car}\ (\mathrm{third}(\alpha)) = \mathrm{car}(\mathrm{first}(\alpha))) \wedge$$

$$(\mathrm{cdr}\ (\mathrm{third}(\alpha)) = \mathrm{nil})\ ]$$

$$\vee\ (\exists\beta)\ (\mathrm{third}(\alpha) = \mathrm{fourth}(\beta) \wedge \beta \in G$$

$$\wedge\ \mathrm{first}(\beta) = \mathrm{first}(\alpha)$$

$$\wedge\ \mathrm{second}(\beta) = \mathrm{second}(\alpha)$$

$$\wedge\ (\exists\gamma)\ (\mathrm{third}(\beta) = \mathrm{third}(\gamma)$$

$$\wedge\ \gamma \in F \wedge \mathrm{first}(\gamma) = \mathrm{first}(\alpha)$$

$$\wedge\ (\mathrm{second}(\gamma) = (\mathrm{car}(\mathrm{cdr}(\mathrm{second}(\alpha))))))$$

$$\alpha \in G \equiv \{\ (\mathrm{cdr}(\mathrm{car}(\mathrm{cdr}(\mathrm{second}(\alpha)))) = \mathrm{nil})$$

$$\wedge\ (\mathrm{car}(\mathrm{fourth}(\alpha)) = \mathrm{third}(\alpha))$$

$$\wedge\ (\mathrm{car}(\mathrm{cdr}(\mathrm{fourth}(\alpha)))$$

$$= (\mathrm{car}(\mathrm{car}(\mathrm{cdr}(\mathrm{first}(\alpha))))))$$

$$\wedge\ (\mathrm{cdr}(\mathrm{cdr}(\mathrm{fourth}(\alpha))) = \mathrm{nil})\ \}$$

$$\vee\ (\exists\beta)(\beta \in G \wedge \mathrm{fifth}(\alpha) = \mathrm{fourth}(\beta)$$

$$\wedge\ \mathrm{first}(\beta) = \mathrm{car}(\mathrm{cdr}(\mathrm{first}(\alpha)))$$

$$\wedge\ \mathrm{second}(\beta) = \mathrm{car}(\mathrm{cdr}(\mathrm{second}(\alpha)))$$

$$\wedge\ \mathrm{third}(\beta) = \mathrm{third}(\alpha))$$

In my work the sub-descriptions ("dig" inside "num", "num" inside "num" and "succ", "succ" inside "succ") are extracted from descriptions previously learned. The Paris school develops them "on the run" by restricting the development to a narrow class.

A learning algorithm which was not guided by any preconception of the class of deductions which would be useful, would have to learn exactly these descriptions (and few else, if any semblance of efficiency is to be maintained) by examples, before the description of FARG can be learned. The reason the Kodratoff technique is capable of learning FARG (and can deduce F and G without prior training) lies in the fact that the class of programs is circumscribed to make certain deductions useful and that the learning program is biased towards making just such deductions.

It is not clear to me which method of generating these subprograms is superior. One of these (discussed in sec. B) is open ended in that its flexibility grows with learning—and its efficiency begins to drop at the same time. The Paris school seems to keep a degree of flexibility and efficiency which reaches saturation. On the other hand, the Paris school has always been very careful in circumscribing very carefully the class of functions amenable to their techniques. This sets a laudable example of "engineering specification" which is not available to our system yet.

To summarize, and especially to firm up the "bridge" I have been claiming to build, let us make the following initial statement. In all learning, program or pattern, the main thingsare the examples. In program learning, the examples are input-output pairs or n-tuples. In pattern recognition, they are what I call "objects", i.e. n-tuples of measurement values. At both ends of the bridge, the different members of the example n-tuples have structures of their own—numbers or list structures (mostly) in program construction, and further objects in (at least our version of) pattern recognition.

The major source of efficiency in both activities is the power to recognize that the examples satisfy many statements other than the ones specified at the input. Given the set of ordered pairs (1,1), (2,3), (3,6), (4,10) (5,15) .... the recognizing device can glean right away that $(x=1 \& y=1) \vee (x=2 \& y=3) \cdots$. are viable descriptions (albeit it changes every time a new example comes in). A more sophisticated learner would recognize in addition that if one subtracts 1 from x and x from y, the resulting pair also forms a member of the set. This results in a much more efficient finite program of a recursive nature. The greater strength comes from the program constructors' previous knowledge of another program—that of subtraction. The advantage is offset by the effort spent in deciding what to subtract from what. Interpolation-theory received its impetus from the recognition that the subtraction of the second elements of two examples yield a large class of functions (the polynomials). Present day workers in program learning also use certain restricted deductions. (We do not dare, for instance, say that any synthesizer notices that all examples satisfy $y = x(x+1)/2$ in the above example.) Some limit these restricted deductions to a small class of predicates, others allow the class of predicates to grow as more programs are learned. A recursive class of programsresult, determined by the restriction on the deductions allowed on the examples; this restriction probably has to be made in the interest of efficiency.

In the field of pattern recognition, the only innovations in the seventies have been in the use of stronger logical connectives in the description language and allowing the use of n-ary over unary predicates in the specification of the input. These predicates have always come from a fixed repertoire and no flexible method has been even attempted to the growth of this repertoire. So some of the problems that are being actively addressed by the program construction group have not yet been visualized in pattern recognition.

Standing in the middle of the bridge, I have to admit that one of the banks looks distinctly greener.

Acknowledgment

The preparation of this final manuscript was supported by the National Science Foundation under grant MCS—8110104.

References

Banerji [1979]

R.B. Banerji, "Pattern recognition: structural description languages," *Encyclopedia of computer science and technology,* Vol. 12 (Marcel Dekker, Inc., 1979).

Fu [1969]

K.S. Fu and P. Swain, "On syntactic pattern recognition," Third International Symposium on Computer & Information Science, 1969.

Cohen [1978]

B. Cohen, "A powerful and efficient structural pattern recognition system," Artificial Intelligence 9, 223(1978).

Cohen [1978]
B. Cohen and C.A. Sammut, "Pattern recognition and learning with a structural description language," *Proc. 4th Int. Jt. Conf. on Pattern Recognition* (Kyoto, 1978).

Banerji [1964]
R.B. Banerji, "A language for the description of concepts," General Systems, 9 (1964), p. 135.

Banerji [1976]
R.B. Banerji, "A data structure which can learn simple programs from examples of input-output," *Pattern Recognition and Artificial Intelligence* (C. Chen, Ed.), Academic Press, (N.Y., 1976).

Banerji [1978]
R.B. Banerji, "Using a descriptive language as a programming language," *Proc. of the 4th Int. Joint Conf. on Pattern Recognition* (Kyoto, 1978).

Warren [1974]
D. Warren, "Epilog (400, 400)—A user's guide to the DEC-10 prolog system," Internal Memo, Dept. of Artificial Intelligence, University of Edinburgh (1974).

Manna [1977]
Z. Manna and R. Waldinger, "Studies in automatic programming logic," North-Holland, N.Y. (1977).

Bibel [1978]
W. Bibel, U. Furbach, and J.F. Schreiber, "Strategies for the synthesis of algorithms," in *Programmiersprachen,* Vol. 12, Informatik-Fachberichte, Springer-Verlag, NY, 1978.

Biermann [1972]
A.W. Biermann and J.A. Feldman, "On the synthesis of finite machines from samples of their behavior," *IEEE Trans. on Computers* C-12 (June 1972).

Summers [1977]
P.D. Summers, "A methodology for LISP program construction from examples," *Journal Assoc. Comp. Mach.* 24 (1977).

Jouannaud [1977]
J.P. Jouannaud, "Sur l'Inference et la synthese automatique de fonctions LISP a partir d'examples," Thesis, University of Paris VI (Nov. 1977).

Guiho [1978]
G. Guiho and J.P. Jouannaud, "Program synthesis from examples for a simple class of non-loop functions," Research Report, Laboratoire de Recherche en Informatique, Universite de Paris-Sud (Mar. 1978).

Treuil [1977]
J.P. Treuil, J.P. Jouannaud, and G. Guiho, "LQAS un Systeme-Question-Reponse base sur l'apprentissage et la synthese de programmes a partir d'examples," Institut de Programmation, Universite de Paris-VI (Mar. 1977).

Biermann [1972]
A.W. Biermann, "On the inference of Turing machines from sample computations," *Artificial Intelligence* 3, 181(1972).

Kowalski [1979]
R. Kowalski, "Logic for problem solving," North Holland, NY (1979).

Sammut [1981]
C. Sammut, "Concept learning by experiment," *Proc. of the Int. Joint Conf. on Artificial Intelligence,* Vancouver, B.C. (Aug. 1981), p. 104.

Cohen [1980]
B. Cohen, "Program synthesis through concept learning," this volume.

Kodratoff [1979]
Y. Kodratoff, "A class of functions synthesized from a finite number of examples and a LISP program schema," *Int. Jour. of Comp. and Infor. Sciences,* Vol. 8 (1979), p. 489.

Banerji [1979]
R.B. Banerji, "Artificial intelligence: a theoretical approach," North Holland, NY (1979).

CHAPTER 23

Inductive Inference: Efficient Algorithms*

Dana Angluin
Yale University

Abstract

In this paper we describe some recent results on efficient procedures for identification of formal languages from examples. These results are based on structural information concerning the particular domains considered, and begin to suggest what kinds of structure theory are relevant for inductive inference.

A. Introduction

We begin with two examples. Given the strings of digits

104994, 106446, 108118, 10100001, ...

* This work was supported by the National Science Foundation under grant number MCS 8002447.

one natural sequence of observations is that each string begins with 10, that the remainder of each string is a palindrome of the form xx^r, and that the values of the x's, namely, 49, 64, 81, 100, are squares of consecutive integers. If instead we were presented with the strings

0000, 11, 1100, 1010, 000110, 1001, 0011, ...

we might conjecture that what is common to them is that each one contains an even number of 0's and an even number of 1's. Can we find some fruitful theory to account for inferences of this kind, or is this domain intrinsically beyond analysis? The study of inductive inference is one attempt to find such a theory.

One question that arises immediately is how to define the 'correctness' of inferences of this kind. Since there are in general infinitely many different rules compatible with any finite sample, any guess is subject to being contradicted by the next example. As an illustration, the initial segment 2,4,6,8,10,12,... strongly suggests the even numbers, but if instead it is the sequence of values of Euler's totient function, then the next element is 16. (This example is taken from Sloane's instructive and entertaining book of integer sequences [1973].)

Gold [1967] proposes the concept of 'identification in the limit' to define the correctness of inductive processes. This paper is a study of the problem of how a child is able to learn a grammar for its native language from examples. Gold models this as the acquisition of a formal grammar from examples and obtains a number of fundamental theoretical results, some of which are described in subsequent parts of this paper.

The idea of identification in the limit is the following. There is a fixed domain D of rules, and two players, say N (Nature) and M (Man). N selects a rule from D and begins giving M examples of it in such a way that every possible example of the rule will eventually be given after some finite time. M reads the examples provided by N and occasionally conjectures elements of D. If the sequence of M's guesses is eventually constant (i.e., stops changing after some finite time) and correct (i.e., names the rule that N selected at the start), then we say that M correctly identifies the rule in the limit.

One simple example of a domain of rules that may be correctly identified in the limit by an inference algorithm M is the set of all integer sequences of the form f(1),f(2),f(3),..., where f is a polynomial. When M has the first $m+1$ terms of such a sequence, it interpolates a polynomial of degree m through them and conjectures this polynomial. If N has chosen a polynomial of degree d to start with, then after $d+1$ terms, M's guesses will stabilize on the correct conjecture.

Even in this simple domain, M itself is not able to tell whether the sequence of its guesses has converged yet. For example, the polynomial

$$f(n) = (n-1)(n-2)(n-3)+1$$

is 1 for $n = 1,2,3$ and then jumps to 7. This is analogous to the residual uncertainty we must have about our current scientific theories.

The criterion of identification in the limit (and variations of it) has been widely accepted as a useful definition of correctness for inductive processes. However, since we are distinctly finite beings, the question of measuring the 'goodness' of the answers at finite stages of an inductive process is of vital interest. Complexity theory, with its emphasis on attempting to distinguish problems that are practical to solve from those that are solvable in theory but infeasible in practice, is a natural tool for the more detailed study of inductive inference procedures. Some inductive inference processes and problems are directly amenable to standard notions of complexity theory, while others seem to require new definitions.

The evidence from preliminary studies suggests that an 'efficient' inference procedure must rely on a fairly rich structure theory for the domain in question, and that such a theory in turn illuminates the concept of 'identifiability' in its domain. The remainder of this paper is a description of some of the theoretical work on measures of efficiency for inference methods, and algorithms that are provably efficient with respect to these measures. General surveys of other aspects of abstract and concrete work in inductive inference may be found in Angluin and Smith [1982], Biermann and Feldman [1972], Case and Smith [1983], Fu [1975], Fu and Booth [1975], Gonzalez and Thomason [1978], and Smith [1980]. A general bibliography of abstract and concrete work in inductive inference may be found in Smith [1979].

B. Identification of Formal Languages, Basic Definitions

Identification may be defined for various kinds of objects: languages, functions, sequences, and relations. For simplicity we shall consider only languages—analogous definitions may be given for the other types of objects. The definitions we give below are essentially those of Gold [1967].

An *alphabet* is any finite set of symbols. If A is an alphabet, a *language* over A is any set of finite strings of symbols from A. For example, the set of all strings of 0's and 1's that contain an equal number of 0's and 1's is a language over the alphabet {0,1}.

To specify an inference domain, we must specify a set of languages and also a system of names for these languages. Let C be a set of languages over some alphabet A. A *system of descriptions* for C consists of a recursively enumerable set D of strings over some alphabet B and a function L that maps D onto C. In other words, for each string d in D, L(d) is a language in C, and for each S in C, there exists d in D such that L(d) is S. The requirement that D be recursively enumerable means that there is an effective procedure to enumerate all the legal descriptions d in this system. D is called the set of *descriptions* of C, and L(d) is the *language denoted* by the description d.

Thus, an inference domain is specified by giving a class of languages C and a system of descriptions D and L for C. For example, we could take C to be the class of regular sets over {0,1}, D to be the set of regular expressions over {0,1} and L to be the usual inductively defined language map.

Samples of a language will consist of members, and possibly nonmembers, of the language. More formally, if S is a nonempty language a *positive presentation* of S is any infinite sequence

$$u_1, u_2, u_3, \cdots$$

of strings, such that every u_i is an element of S, and every element of S appears somewhere in the sequence (possibly repeated). If S is any language, a *complete presentation* of S is any infinite sequence

$$(u_1,t_1),(u_2,t_2),(u_3,t_3), \cdots$$

such that for each i, u_i is a string and t_i is 1 if and only if u_i is in S, and for every string u over the alphabet, there is some i such that $u = u_i$. Thus, a positive presentation of a language gives only examples of the language, while a complete presentation gives both members and nonmembers. As an example, if S is the set of all strings of 1's over the alphabet {0,1}, then a positive presentation of S might begin:

1,111,11,11,1,111111,1,...

while a complete presentation might begin:

(1,1),(111,1),(0,0),(101,0),(11111,1),(00,0),(0001,0),(00,0),... .

Another form of presentation of a language S is by *informant*. In this case, the inference machine has access to an oracle for S, which will answer any query of the form "is the string u in S?" with yes or no. In a formal sense an informant for S and a complete presentation of S contain the same information about S, but in practice inference methods for the two types of presentation tend to be rather different. Some authors have considered mixtures of given data and informant presentation.

An *inference machine* is an algorithmic device that from time to time may request inputs and produce outputs. To run such a machine on an infinite sequence of inputs, we start the machine and whenever it requests an input, we give it the next element of the input sequence, and whenever it produces an output, we append the output to the (initially null) output sequence. Thus, we may consider the output of the machine to be the null, finite, or infinite sequence of outputs produced while being run on the input sequence. (A more formal definition may be found in Angluin [1980a].) This definition may easily be modified for the case of informant presentation, but we omit this development.

We now define a notion of convergence for the output of such a machine. A finite nonempty sequence of strings $d_1,d_2,\ldots, d_n$ is said to *converge* to the value d if and only if d_n is equal to d. An infinite sequence of strings $d_1,d_2,d_3, \cdots$. is said to *converge* to the value d if and only if there exists a number N such that d_n is equal to d for all n greater than N.

An inference machine M is defined to *identify the language* S *in the limit from positive data* if and only if for every positive presentation $u_1,u_2,u_3, \cdots$ of S, the sequence of outputs produced by M with this sequence as input converges to some d in D such that L(d) = S. The definition of *identification in the limit from complete data* is the same, with "complete presentation" replacing "positive presentation".

If C is a class of languages with a system of description D and L, C is defined to be *identifiable in the limit from positive data* if and only if there exists an inference machine M that identifies in the limit every S in C from positive data. Identifiability from complete data is defined analogously.

A number of variations of the definition of identification in the limit have been considered, some of which we now sketch. In "finite identification", the inference machine is required to be able to detect when it has converged (Freivald and Wiehagen [1979], Kugel [1977]). "Behavioral correctness" requires only that the language denoted by the guess converge correctly—the descriptions of it may continue to change (Case and Smith [1983], Feldman [1972]). Another approach permits a finite number of "bugs" or "anomalies" in the final guess (Case and Smith [1978,1983], Smith [1979]). Still another idea is to allow a finite "team" of inference machines to work in parallel on one problem (Daley [1981], Smith [1981]). A considerable amount of work has been done studying the classes of languages identifiable with respect to these criteria and others.

C. Enumeration and Search Methods

We now turn to methods for identifying classes of languages in the limit from complete data. One basic method, called the enumeration algorithm, is to enumerate all the descriptions from D in a fixed order, and to guess the earliest one that is compatible with all the data received at a given point. This is formalized below.

A system of descriptions D and L for a class of languages C is called *recursive* if and only if there is an effective procedure to decide membership of a string u in the language L(d) given u and d.

Theorem 1: (Gold [1967]) If D and L is a recursive system of descriptions for the class C, then C is effectively identifiable in the limit from complete data.

Proof: The elements of D are effectively enumerable by definition, so let $d_1,d_2,d_3, \cdots$ be some effective enumeration of them. Let some input sequence

$$(u_1,t_1),(u_2,t_2),(u_3,t_3), \cdots$$

be given. For each n, search for the least k such that u_i is in $L(d_k)$ if and only if $t_i = 1$ for all $i=1,2,\ldots,n$, and output d_k as the nth guess if such is found. It is clear that if the given sequence is a complete presentation of any language L(d) in C, the sequence of outputs produced by this process will converge to the first description of L(d) in the given enumeration of D. []

This theorem shows that the regular sets described by finite automata or regular expressions are effectively identifiable in the limit from complete data. The same is true of the context free or context sensitive languages described by their customary grammars. The simple enumerative inference procedure described in the proof above will be referred to as the *enumeration algorithm*. It is guaranteed to produce as its n th guess the earliest description (if any) compatible with the first n terms of the input sequence.

The enumeration algorithm does not seem very practical. However, if we think of it as a systematic search, certain possibilities suggest themselves. In the enumeration algorithm, each incompatibility between the current hypothesis and the data results in the elimination of one hypothesis from consideration, because of the simple linear ordering of the hypotheses. In concrete domains, it is often possible to organize the class of hypotheses in a more complex way, allowing a whole subclass to be eliminated from further consideration by each incompatibility. Wharton [1977] compares straight enumeration with a more sophisticated search for inferring context free languages. Other search-based methods are described by Biermann [1978,1972,1975,1976], Gaines [1976], Horning [1969], Maryanski and Booth [1977], Mitchell [1979], Shapiro [1981], and Van der Mude and Walker [1978]. Cook *et al.* [1976] describe an inference method based on a hill-climbing search for a local optimum.

D. The Complexity of Minimum Size Inference

Many of the concrete inference methods based on searching have the property that they return the "smallest" description in some fixed ordering that is compatible with the given data. We may ask what the intrinsic computational complexity of this task is, independent of the particular means to accomplish it.

Suppose D and L are a system of descriptions for a class of languages C, and suppose s is a map from D to the positive integers. We think of s(d) as the "size" of the description d. Then the *minimum size inference problem* is the following. Given a pair (S_1,S_0) of disjoint finite sets of strings, find a description d in D such that L(d) contains S_1 and is disjoint from S_0, and s(d) is minimum. Concerning the minimum size inference problem we have the following results.

Theorem 2: (Gold [1978]) The minimum size inference problem is NP-hard for D = deterministic finite automata and s(d) = the number of states in d.

Theorem 3: (Angluin [1978]) The minimum size inference problem is NP-hard for D = regular expressions and s(d) = the length of the expression d.

These results, and refinements of them, suggest that the computational problem of minimum size inference, although natural and rather appealing in its formulation, may prove intractable for classes as simple as the regular sets with natural size functions. Search-based algorithms that solve these problems may be improved in various ways, but are fundamentally up against NP-hard problems.

One approach to NP-hard problems is to analyze heuristic methods for them, in order to establish statistical or approximation guarantees for the methods. There have not as yet been any such studies in the domain of inductive inference. Another open problem in this area is to give a general method for analyzing the complexity of minimum size inference problems—so far, only a few specific problems have been analyzed.

E. Other Objective Functions

Minimum size inference, finding a "smallest" description compatible with given positive and negative data, is not the only objective function that has been considered for the finite stages of inductive inference from given data. Another quantity of interest is how well the guess "fits" the data. These two measures may be considered separately or combined.

One approach to combining these two measures uses Bayes' Theorem. A probability distribution is defined on the space of all descriptions, P(d) representing the "a priori" probability of the description d. For each finite set of strings S and description d, a probability $P(S|d)$ is defined, representing the probability of the event that d generates S. (Stochastic grammars may be used in defining these probabilities.) The objective, given a finite positive sample S, is to find d to maximize P(d|S), which by Bayes' Theorem may be accomplished by maximizing P(d)P(S|d). We may think of P(d) as a kind of inverse of a size function, and P(S|d) as a measure of the "fit" of the description d to the sample S.

Horning [1969] considers this objective function for stochastic context free grammars. He gives a search-based algorithm to maximize P(d|S) and shows that it correctly converges in the limit with probability one under appropriate assumptions. Related studies are those of Solomonoff [1964,1978,1975], Cook *et al.* [1976], and Van der Mude and Walker [1978]. Feldman [1972] gives an abstract treatment of objective functions that combine size and derivational complexity for grammars, and Feldman and Shields [1977] extend this treatment to functions. Other mixed measures have been studied by Maryanski and Booth [1977] and Gaines [1976] for stochastic deterministic regular grammars. Essentially no work has been done studying the computational complexity of optimizing any of these mixed measures.

It is also possible to dispense with "size" entirely and concentrate on "fit" as an objective. One way to do this is as follows. Given a finite set S of strings, find a description d such that L(d) contains S and for any description d' such that L(d') contains S, L(d') is not a proper subset of L(d). That is, L(d) should be minimal in the set containment ordering among all L(d') that contain S. This problem is called the *minimal language inference problem.*

This objective function does not at first seem very promising—for example, in the domain of regular sets, the unique minimal regular set containing the finite sample S is S itself. However, as we shall see in the next two sections, there are nontrivial domains in which this objective leads to correct identification in the limit from positive data, and can be optimized by provably efficient algorithms.

F. Identification From Positive Data

In this section we consider the general question of what classes of languages may be identified in the limit from positive data.

Let C be a fixed class of languages with a system of descriptions D and L. Let L(d) be an element of C. A set T is called a *marker* for L(d) and C if and only if T is a finite subset of L(d) and there is no language L(d') in C that both includes T and is properly included in L(d). If T is a marker for L(d) and C and T is included in some positive input sample, then we may guess d with the assurance that L(d) is not "too big". That is, if the guess of d is wrong, then the input data must eventually contain some string u not in L(d). We have the following theorem characterizing identifiability of classes of recursive languages from positive data.

Theorem 4: (Angluin [1980a]) Suppose that C is a class of languages with a recursive system of descriptions D and L. Suppose also that every language in C is nonempty. Then C is identifiable in the limit from positive data if and only if there is an effective procedure to enumerate a marker for L(d) and C given d, for every description d in D.

As a corollary we have Gold's theorem on positive data.

Theorem 5: (Gold [1967]) Any class of languages containing all the finite languages and at least one infinite language is not effectively identifiable in the limit from positive data.

Proof: There are no markers for the infinite languages in such a class. []

Thus, even the class of regular languages is not effectively identifiable from positive data. Nonetheless, there are some nontrivial classes of languages that may be effectively identified in the limit from positive data, as we shall describe.

G. Three Efficient Algorithms for Inference From Positive Data

In this section we consider three different domains in which identification in the limit is achievable by optimizing the set containment measure at finite stages, and this optimization may be done in polynomial time.

G.1. Free Operator Precedence Grammars

Crespi-Reghizzi [1972] considers the problem of inferring bracketed free operator precedence grammars from positive samples. An operator precedence grammar is defined to be *free* if no two distinct nonterminals have the same left and right terminal sets. A bracketed free operator precedence grammar is obtained from a free operator precedence grammar G as follows. Let '[' and ']' be two terminal symbols not appearing in G. Replace every production $X \rightarrow y$ of G by $X \rightarrow [y]$. Sentences in the new grammar correspond to parse trees in the old grammar with their nonterminal labels removed. The problem is then one of assigning these labels properly, and then "reading off" the productions from the parse trees.

The label assigned to a given node by Crespi-Reghizzi's procedure is the ordered pair consisting of the left and right terminal sets of the subtree rooted at the node. It is clear that this algorithm may be implemented to run in polynomial time as a function of the input sample. Crespi-Reghizzi shows that this algorithm solves the minimal language inference problem in this domain, that is, the answer produced by the algorithm is the smallest free operator precedence language compatible with the sample. He also shows that this procedure correctly identifies in the limit the class of free operator precedence languages.

Some generalizations of this approach to labelling unlabelled or partially labelled parse trees of sentences are explored in Berger and Pair [1978], Crespi-Reghizzi [1971], and Crespi-Reghizzi *et al.* [1978]. Two assumptions appear to contribute to the success of this approach: one is the structural information available in the input, and the other is the existence of local and easily computed determining information for the identity of a nonterminal in a parse tree. When these two assumptions are satisfied, this seems to be a very promising class of methods.

G.2. Pattern Languages

Angluin [1980] considers the problem of inferring a "pattern" common to a finite set of strings. For example, given the strings 1000, 101212, 10336336, it seems reasonable that the pattern "best" describing these is 10xx. This problem is defined formally below.

Let A be some fixed finite alphabet, and X be a countably infinite set of variable symbols disjoint from A. A *pattern* is defined to be a nonempty concatenation of alphabet and variable symbols. If p is a pattern then the *language of* p, denoted L(p), is the set of all strings obtained by substituting a nonempty string of alphabet symbols for each variable of the pattern. As an example, let A be the set of decimal digits and X be the set of variables $\{x,y,z,x_1,y_1,z_2,\ldots\}$. Then 10xx, 3xyy4x5, 33x, and 1001 are patterns. Also, 1000, 101212, 10336336 are elements of L(10xx), while 33, 1001, 1045 are not.

The class of pattern languages appears not to have been studied classically. It is incomparable with the class of context free languages and the class of regular languages. In Angluin [1980] there are basic structural, decidability, and complexity results about the pattern languages and the set of patterns generating a given string.

In this domain, the minimal language inference problem is as follows. Given a finite nonempty set S of nonnull strings over the alphabet A, find a pattern p such that L(p) contains S and for no other pattern q such that L(q) contains S is L(q) properly contained in L(p). (Such a pattern always exists, but may not be unique.) As an example, 10xx is an optimal answer for the sample consisting of the strings 1000, 101212, 10336336.

Angluin [1980] shows the following results concerning inference of the pattern languages. A strategy that solves the minimal language inference problem at finite stages of an inductive inference process leads to correct identification in the limit of the pattern languages from positive data. Also, in the special case of patterns that contain only one variable, there is a polynomial time algorithm to solve the minimal language inference problem. (This algorithm has good incremental behavior, and is easily extended to handle the "reverse" operator, as in the pattern $10xx^r$ of the first example in this paper.) An open problem in this area is to analyze the complexity of the minimal language inference problem for patterns that contain k variables for any fixed k greater than or equal to 2.

G.3. Reversible Regular Sets

Angluin [1983] considers the problem of inferring a certain subclass of the regular sets from positive data. The basic algorithm used is a modification of a heuristic originally proposed by Feldman [1967]. We now describe the algorithm by means of an example.

Consider the set of strings from the second example in this paper:

$$\{0000, 11, 1100, 1010, 000110, 1001, 0011\}.$$

We first construct an incompletely specified tree-like deterministic acceptor that accepts just these strings. The states are all prefixes of the given strings, with a transition on input b from u to ub provided u and ub are both states. The start state is the null string, and the accepting states are the given strings themselves.

We now proceed repeatedly to collapse certain sets of states of this machine to obtain our final machine. First we collapse all the accepting states. Then we collapse any set of states that are all either b-predecessors or b-successors of a single state in the current machine, where b is either 0 or 1. We continue this process until no further collapsing is possible. The result will be a deterministic finite state acceptor with one initial and one final state that accepts a superset of the original sample. In our example this process will result in the acceptor that recognizes all strings that contain an even number of 0's and an even number of 1's.

This technique works well on this particular example. It fails miserably given the sample consisting of the strings 01, 00011, 00111, 000111—in this case the answer found is the language containing all strings over the alphabet {0,1}. In Angluin [1983] there is a characterization of this technique and generalizations of it, which we now summarize.

Consider deterministic finite state acceptors whose transition functions may be partial. (The interpretation is that if a string attempts to use an undefined transition, it is rejected.) Such an acceptor is defined to be *reversible* if and only if it has exactly one accepting state and the operation of interchanging the initial and accepting state, and reversing the direction of each of the transition arrows produces a deterministic acceptor (also possibly with a partial transition function). Alternatively, such an acceptor is reversible if and only if it has just one accepting state and every input symbol induces an injective mapping on the state set of the machine. A regular language is called *reversible* if and only if it is accepted by some reversible automaton.

In Angluin [1983] the collapsing algorithm sketched above is described and shown to run in polynomial time and to find the smallest reversible regular set containing the given sample. Thus it solves the minimal language inference problem in the domain of the reversible regular sets. It is also shown that using this method at the finite stages of an inductive inference process leads to correct identification in the limit of the reversible regular sets from positive data. (There is also a generalization to k-reversibility, in which the reversed acceptor need only be deterministic with lookahead k.)

The reversible automata contain permutation machines with one accepting state as a subclass. This observation suggests the possibility that this technique might be used in conjunction with the theory of algebraic decomposition of automata to produce more powerful but still efficient inference methods for regular sets. In the domain of regular languages, this collapsing technique and the labelling technique of Crespi-Reghizzi appear to complement one another and perhaps may be usefully combined.

H. Other Complexity Measures for Inference Processes

The results above concern the computational complexity of the task of finding an optimum hypothesis from given data according to particular criteria of optimality. Other measures of the efficiency of inference processes have been defined and studied.

Gold [1967] defines the data efficiency for inference machines with complete presentations as input. The *convergence point* of an inference machine M on a given complete presentation $<u_1,t_1>, <u_2,t_2>, \cdots$ is defined to be the least n such that M does not change its guess after reading in the pair $<u_n,t_n>$. If M identifies in the limit all the languages that M' does, and the convergence points of M do not exceed the corresponding ones of M', then M is said to be *as data efficient as* M'. If, in addition, at least one convergence point of M is less than the corresponding convergence point of M', then M is said to be *strictly more data efficient than* M'. Gold shows that no inference method is strictly more data efficient than the enumeration algorithm. Jantke and Beick [1980] further explore this notion of data efficiency.

Another quantity of interest is the number of different hypotheses output by an inference machine before it finally converges. For concreteness, consider the problem of identifying regular sets described by deterministic finite state acceptors from positive and negative data. If we enumerate finite acceptors in order of size, then more than n^n acceptors precede the first one with $n+1$ states. Barzdin [1972] describes a strategy that conjectures only $0(n\log n)$ different acceptors in the course of identifying any acceptor with n states. Related results on this measure and similar ones have been obtained by Barzdin [1974], Barzdin and Freivald [1972], and Jantke [1979].

In general, the algorithms proposed to optimize data efficiency or numbers of hypotheses are not efficient with respect to other measures. One study of a simultaneous polynomial bound on the number of queries and the total running time of an algorithm to identify regular sets from a mixed presentation may be found in Angluin [1981]. However, a comprehensive theory of the efficiency of inference processes that takes into account various relevant measures of efficiency is sorely lacking.

I. Concluding Remarks

It seems intuitively clear that when humans communicate complex procedures to one another (for example, descriptions of algorithms), they do so most successfully by means of a mixture of general description to fix the outlines of the procedure and specific examples to fill in many of the details. Such a form of communication appears to be more robust than either pure description or pure examples. This may be a chance peculiarity of humanity, or it may be a general phenomenon of communication between complex systems. In either case it is of interest to us as designers of systems that communicate with people. Hence it is important for us to try to elucidate the general principles and assumptions underlying the use of examples to infer rules.

How such knowledge might ultimately be systematized and integrated with a component allowing "outline" description or general broad specification is not at all clear. One possibly promising approach, taken by Shapiro [1982,1981], is to explore the synthesis of logic programs (for example, in PROLOG), in which examples and assertions may quite naturally be expressed in the same language.

A very interesting body of work on efficient algorithms to synthesize LISP programs from input/output data, described for example by Jouannaud and Kodratoff [1979], is more fully treated elsewhere in this book.

This paper has described an approach using complexity theory to explore inductive inference procedures in various specific domains, and emphasized the use of structural information to construct efficient identification algorithms. The results in this area, while very preliminary, appear promising.

References

Angluin [1980]
D. Angluin, "Finding patterns common to a set of strings," J. Comp. Sys. Sci. 21:46–62, 1980.

Angluin [1980a]
D. Angluin, "Inductive inference of formal languages from positive data," Inform. Contr. 45:117–135, 1980.

Angluin [1982]
D. Angluin, "Inference of reversible languages," J. ACM 29:741–765, 1982.

Angluin [1981]
D. Angluin, "A note on the number of queries needed to identify regular languages," Inform. Contr. 51:76–87, 1981.

Angluin [1978]
D. Angluin, "On the complexity of minimum inference of regular sets," Inform. Contr. 39–337–350, 1978.

Angluin and Smith [1982]
D. Angluin and C. Smith, "A survey of inductive inference: theory and methods," Yale Univ. Computer Science Dept., Technical Report #250, Oct. 1982. (To appear in Computing Surveys)

Barzdin [1974]
J.M. Barzdin, "On synthesizing programs given by examples," in Lecture Notes in Computer Science, Volume 5, Springer-Verlag, 1974, pp. 53–63.

Barzdin [1972]
J.M. Barzdin, 'Prognostication of automata and functions," in Information Processing 71, North-Holland, Amsterdam, 1972, pp. 81–84.

Barzdin and Freivald [1972]
J.M. Barzdin and R.V. Freivald, "On the prediction of general recursive functions," Sov. Math. Dokl. 13:1224–1228, 1972.

Berger and Pair [1978]
J. Berger and C. Pair, "Inference for regular bilanguages," J. Comp. Sys. Sci. 16:100–122, 1978.

Biermann [1978]
A. W. Biermann, "The inference of regular LISP programs from examples," IEEE Trans. on Systems, Man, and Cybernetics SMC–8:585–600, 1978.

Biermann [1972]
A.W. Biermann, "On the inference of Turing machines from sample computations," Art. Int. 3:181–198, 1972.

Biermann et al. [1975]
A.W. Biermann, R.I. Baum, and F.E. Petry, "Speeding up the synthesis of programs from traces," IEEE Trans. on Computers C–24:122–136, 1975.

Biermann and Feldman [1972]
A.W. Biermann and J.A. Feldman, "A survey of results in grammatical inference," in Frontiers of Pattern Recognition, Academic Press, NY., 1972.

Biermann and Krishnaswamy [1976]
A.W. Biermann and R. Krishnaswamy, "Constructing programs from example computations," IEEE Trans. on Software Engineering, SE−2:141−153, 1976.

Case and Smith [1978]
J. Case and C. Smith, "Anomaly hierarchies of mechanized inductive inference," in Proc. of the Tenth Symposium on Theory of Computing, ACM, 1978, pp. 314−319.

Case and Smith [1983]
J. Case and C. Smith, "Comparison of identification criteria for machine inductive inference," Theor. Comp. Sci. 23:1−28, 1983.

Cook et al. [1976]
C.M. Cook, A. Rosenfeld, and A.R. Aronson, "Grammatical inference by hill-climbing," Information Sciences 10:59−80, 1976.

Crespi-Reghizzi [1971]
S. Crespi-Reghizzi, "Reduction of enumeration in grammar acquisition," in Proc. Second International Joint Conference on Artificial Intelligence, IJCAI, 1971, pp. 546−552.

Crespi-Reghizzi [1972]
S. Crespi-Reghizzi, "An effective model for grammar inference," in Information Processing 71, North Holland Publishing Co., 1972, pp. 524−529.

Crespi-Reghizzi et al. [1978]
S. Crespi-Reghizzi, G. Guida, and D. Mandrioli, "Noncounting context-free languages," J.ACM 25:571−580, 1978.

Daley [1981]
R. Daley, "On the error correcting power of pluralism in inductive inference," Technical Report, Dept. of Computer Science, Univ. of Pittsburgh, 1981.

Feldman [1967]
J.A. Feldman, "First thoughts on grammatical inference," Technical Report, Stanford University Artificial Intelligence Memo #55, 1967.

Feldman [1972]
J.A. Feldman, "Some decidability results in grammatical inference," Inform. Contr. 20:244−262, 1972.

Feldman and Shields [1977]
J.A. Feldman and P. Shields, "Total complexity and the inference of best programs," Math. Sys. Theory 10:181−191, 1977.

Freivald and Wiehagen [1979]
R.V. Freivald and R. Wiehagen, "Inductive inference with additional information," Electronische Informationsverarbeitung und Kybernetik EIK 15:179−185, 1979.

Fu [1975]
K. S. Fu, Syntactic Methods in Pattern Recognition, Academic Press, NY., 1975.

Fu and Booth [1975]
K.S. Fu and T.L. Booth, "Grammatical inference: introduction and survey," parts 1 and 2, IEEE Trans. on Systems, Man, and Cybernetics SMC−5:95−111 and 409−423, 1975.

Gaines [1976]
B.R. Gaines, "Behavior/structure transformations under uncertainty," Int. J. of Man-Machine Studies 8:337−365, 1976.

Gold [1978]
E. M. Gold, "Complexity of automaton identification from given data," Inform. Contr. 37:302−320, 1978.

Gold [1967]
E. M. Gold, "Language identification in the limit," Inform. Contr. 10:447−474, 1967.

Gonzalez and Thomason [1978]
R.C. Gonzalez and M.G. Thomason, Syntactic Pattern Recognition, An Introduction, Addison-Wesley, Reading, MA., 1978.

Horning [1969]
J. J. Horning, A study of grammatical inference, Ph.D. thesis, Stanford University, Computer Science Dept., 1969.

Jantke [1979]
K.P. Jantke, "Natural properties of strategies identifying recursive functions," Elektronische Informationsverarbeitung und Kybernetik EIK 15:487−496, 1979.

Jantke and Beick [1980]
K.P. Jantke and H.R. Beick, "Combining postulates of naturalness in inductive inference," 1980. (preprint, Humboldt Universitat zu Berlin)

Jouannaud and Kodratoff [1979]
J.P. Jouannaud and Y. Kodratoff, "Characterization of a class of functions synthesized by a Summers-like method using a B.M.W. matching technique," in Proc. Sixth International Joint Conference on Artificial Intelligence, IJCAI, 1979, pp. 440−447.

Kugel [1977]
P. Kugel, "Induction, pure and simple," Inform. Contr. 35:276−336, 1977.

Maryanski and Booth [1977]
F. J. Maryanski and T. L. Booth, "Inference of finite-state probabilistic grammars," IEEE Transactions on Computers C−26:521−536, 1977.

Mitchell [1979]
T. M. Mitchell, "An analysis of generalizations as a search problem," in Proc. Sixth International Joint Conference on Artificial Intelligence, IJCAI, 1979, pp. 577−582.

Shapiro [1982]
E. Shapiro, "Algorithmic program diagnosis," in Proc. Ninth Symposium on Principles of Programming Languages, ACM, 1982.

Shapiro [1981]
E. Shapiro, "A general incremental algorithm that infers theories from facts," in Proc. Seventh International Joint Conference on Artificial Intelligence, IJCAI, 1981, pp. 446–451.

Sloane [1973]
N. J. A. Sloane, A Handbook of Integer Sequences, Academic Press, NY., 1973.

Smith [1979]
C. H. Smith, Hierarchies of identification criteria for mechanized inductive inference, Ph.D. thesis, S.U.N.Y., Buffalo, 1979.

Smith [1979a]
C. H. Smith, "An inductive inference bibliography," Technical Report, Purdue University Computer Science Dept., CSD TR 323, 1979.

Smith [1981]
C. H. Smith, "The power of parallelism for automatic program synthesis," in Proc. 22nd Annual Symposium on Foundations of Computer Science, IEEE, 1981, pp. 283–295.

Smith [1980]
D. R. Smith, "A survey of the synthesis of LISP programs from examples," in Proc. Symposium on Program Construction, INRIA, Bonas, France, 1980.

Solomonoff [1978]
R. J. Solomonoff, "Complexity-based induction systems: comparisons and convergence theorems," IEEE Trans. on Information Theory IT–24:422–432, 1978.

Solomonoff [1975]
R. J. Solomonoff, "Inductive inference theory—a unified approach to problems in pattern recognition and artificial intelligence," in Proc. Fourth International Joint Conference on Artificial Intelligence, IJCAI, 1975, pp. 274–280.

Solomonoff [1964]
R. J. Solomonoff, "A formal theory of inductive inference," Inform. Contr. 7:1–22, 224–254, 1964.

Van der Mude and Walker [1978]
A. Van der Mude and A. Walker, "On the inference of stochastic regular grammars," Inform. Contr. 38:310–329, 1978.

Wharton [1977]
R. M. Wharton, "Grammar enumeration and inference," Inform. Contr. 33:253–272, 1977.

CHAPTER 24

Inductive Learning as Rule-Guided Generalization of Symbolic Descriptions: A Theory and Implementation

Ryszard S. Michalski
Department of Computer Science
University of Illinois
Urbana, Illinois 61801

Abstract

The theory presented here treats inductive learning as a process of generalizing symbolic descriptions, under the guidance of *generalization* rules and *background knowledge* rules. This approach unifies various types of inductive learning, such as learning from examples and learning from observation.

Two inductive learning programs are presented: INDUCE 1.1 — for learning structural descriptions from examples, and CLUSTER/PAF — for learning taxonomic descriptions (conceptual clustering). The latter program partitions a given collection of entities (objects, computational processes, observations, etc.) into clusters, such that each cluster is described by a single conjunctive statement and the obtained assembly of clusters satisfies an assumed criterion of preference.

The presented methodology can be useful for an automated determination of complete and correct program specification for computer-aided decision making, for knowledge acquisition in expert systems, and the conceptual analysis of complex data.

A. Introduction

Our understanding of inductive inference processes remains very limited despite considerable progress in recent years. Making progress in this area is particularly difficult, not only because of the intrinsic complexity of these problems, but also because of their open-endedness. This open-endedness implies that when one makes inductive assertions about some piece of reality, there is no natural limit to the level of detail and to the scope of concepts and operators used in the expression of these assertions, or to the richness of their forms. Consequently, in order to achieve non-trivial general solutions, one has to circumscribe carefully the nature and goals of the research. This includes defining the language in which descriptions may be written and the modes of inference which will be used. Careful definitions will avoid the main difficulty of most current research: attacking problems which are too general with techniques which are too limited.

Recently there has been a growing need for practical solutions in the area of computer induction. For example, the development of knowledge-based expert systems requires efficient methods for acquiring and refining knowledge. Currently, the only method of knowledge acquisition is the handcrafting of an expert's knowledge in some formal systems, e.g., in the form of production rules (Shortliffe [1974], Davis [1976]) or as a semantic net (Brachman [1978]). Progress in the theory of induction and the development of efficient inductive programs can provide valuable assistance and an alternative method in this area. For example, inductive programs could be useful for filling in gaps, and testing the consistency and completeness of expert-derived decision rules, for removing redundancies, or for incremental improvement of the rules through the analysis of their performance. They could also provide a means for detecting regularities in data bases and knowledge bases. For appropriately selected problems, the programs could determine the decision rules directly from examples of expert decisions, which would greatly facilitate the transfer of knowledge from experts into machines. Experiments on the acquisition of rules for the diagnosis of soybean diseases (Michalski *et al.* [1980]), have indicated that rule-learning from examples is not only feasible, but in certain aspects is preferable.

Another potential applicaton of computer induction is in various areas of science, e.g., biology, microbiology, and genetics. Here it could assist a scientist in revealing structure or detecting interesting conceptual patterns in collections of observations or results of experiments. The traditional mathematical techniques of regression analysis, numerical taxonomy, factor analysis, and distance-based clustering techniques are not sufficiently adequate for this task. Methods of conceptual data analysis are needed, whose results are not mathematical formulas but conceptual descriptions of data, involving both qualitative and quantitative relationships.

An important sub-area of computer inductive inference is automatic programming (e.g., Shaw *et al.* [1975], Jouannaud *et al.* [1979], Burstall *et al.* [1977], Biermann [1978], Smith [1980], and Pettorossi [1980]). Here, the objective is to synthesize a program from I/O pairs or computational traces, or to improve its computational efficiency by application of correctness-preserving transformation rules. The final result of learning is thus a program, in a given programming language, with its inherent sequential structure, destined for machine rather than human "consumption" (or, in other words, a description in "computer terms" rather than in "human terms"). In this case, the *postulate of human* comprehensibility, mentioned below, is of lesser importance. Quite similar to research on automatic programming is research on grammatical inference (e.g., Biermann and Feldman [1972], Yau and Fu [1978]) where the objective of learning is a formal grammar.

This paper is concerned with computer inductive inference, which could be called a "conceptual" induction. The final result of learning is a symbolic description of a class or classes of entities typically not computational processes in a form of a logical-type expression (e.g., a specification of the program or a classification rule). Such an expression is expected to be relatively "close" to a natural language description of the same class(es) of entities. Specifically, it should satisfy the following *comprehensibility postulate:*

The results of computer inductive learning should be conceptual descriptions of data, similar to the descriptions a human expert might produce observing the same data. They should be comprehensible by humans as single 'chunks' of information, directly interpretable in natural language, and use both quantitative and qualitative information in an integrated fashion.

This postulate implies that a single description should avoid more than one level of bracketing, more than one implication or exception symbol, avoid recursion, avoid including more than 3—4 conditions in a conjunction and more than 2—3 conjunctions in a disjunction, not include more than two quantifiers, etc. (the exact numbers can be disputed, but the principle is clear). This postulate can be used to decide when to assign a name to a specific formula and use that name inside of another formula. This postulate stems from the motivation of this research to provide new methods for knowledge acquisition and techniques for conceptual data analysis. It is also well confirmed by the new role for research in artificial intelligence, as envisaged by Michie [1977], which is to develop techniques for *conceptual interface* and *knowledge refinement.*

In this chapter we will consider two basic types of inductive inference: learning from examples and learning from observation (specifically, the so called "conceptual clustering").

B. Computer Induction as Generalization and Simplification of Symbolic Descriptions

B.1 Inductive Paradigm

The process of induction can be characterized as the search for an economical and correct expression of a function which is only partially known. In other words, its goal is to generate and validate plausible general descriptions (inductive assertions or hypotheses) that explain a given body of data, and are able to predict new data. Between the two aspects of induction—the generation of plausible inductive assertions and their validation—only the first is the subject of our study. We feel that the subject of hypothesis generation, in particular the problems of generalization and simplification of symbolic descriptions by a computer, is a quite unexplored and very important direction of research. The problems of hypothesis confirmation, in the Carnapian (Carnap [1962]) or similar sense, are considered to be beyond the scope of this work. In our approach, inductive assertions are judged by a human expert interacting with the computer, and/or tested by standard statistical techniques. The research is concentrated on the following inductive paradigm:

Given is

(a) a set of *observational assertions (data rules),* which consist of *data descriptions,* $\{C_{ij}\}$, specifying initial knowledge about some entities (objects, situations, processes, etc.), and the *generalization class,* K_i, associated with each C_{ij} (this association is denoted by the symbol ::>):

$$C_{11} ::> K_1,\ C_{12} ::> K_1 \ldots\ldots C_{1t1} ::> K_1$$
$$C_{21} ::> K_2,\ C_{22} ::> K_2 \ldots\ldots C_{2t2} ::> K_2$$

$$C_{m1} ::> K_m,\ C_{m2} ::> K_m \ldots\ldots C_{mtm} ::> K_m$$

Descriptions C_{ij} can be symbolic specifications of conditions satisfied by given situations, production rules, sequences of attribute-value pairs representing observations or results of experiments, etc. The descriptions are assumed to be expressions in a certain logical calculus, e.g., propositional calculus, predicate calculus, or a calculus specially developed for inductive inference, such as variable-valued logic systems VL_1 (Michalski [1973]) or VL_2 (Michalski [1978]).

(b) a set of *background knowledge rules* defining information relevant to the problem under consideration. This includes definitions of value sets of all descriptors* used in the input rules, the properties of descriptors and their interrelationships and any "world knowledge" relevant to the problem. The background knowledge also includes a *preference (or optimality)* criterion, which for any two sets of symbolic descriptions of the same generalization class specifies which one is preferable, or that they are equivalent with regard to this criterion.

The problem is to determine a set of *inductive assertions (hypotheses):*

$$
\begin{array}{llll}
C'_{11} ::> K_1, & C'_{12} ::> K_1, & \cdots & C'_{1r_1} ::> K_1 \\
C'_{21} ::> K_2, & C'_{22} ::> K_2, & \cdots & C'_{2r_2} ::> K_2 \\
\cdot & & & \\
\cdot & & & \\
C'_{m1} ::> K_m, & C'_{m2} ::> K_m, & \cdots & C'_{mr_m} ::> K_m \\
\text{where } r_m \leqslant t_m, & & &
\end{array}
$$

which is the *most preferred* among all sets of rules in the assumed format, that do not contradict the *background knowledge* rules, and are, with regard to the data rules, *consistent* and *complete.*

A set of inductive assertions is *consistent* with regard to data rules, if any situation that satisfies a data rule of some generalization class either satisfies an inductive assertion of the same class, or does not satisfy any inductive assertion. A set of inductive assertions is *complete* with regard to data rules, if any situation that satisfies some data rules also satisfies some inductive assertion.

It is easy to see that if a set of inductive assertions is consistent and complete with regard to the data rules, then it is semantically equivalent to or more general than the set of data rules (i.e., there may exist situations which satisfy an inductive assertion but do not satisfy any data rule).

From a given set of data rules it is usually possible to derive many different sets of hypotheses which are consistent and complete, and which satisfy the background knowledge rules. The role of the preference criterion is to select one (or a few alternatives) which is (are) most desirable in the given application. The *preference criterion* may refer to the simplicity of hypotheses (defined in some way), their generality, the cost of measuring the information needed for their evaluation, their degree of approximation to the given facts, etc. (Michalski [1978]).

B.2 Types of Inductive Learning

We distinguish two major types of inductive learning:

I. Learning from examples

Within this type, three subclasses of problems were given the most attention:

a. concept acquisition, or learning a *characteristic description* of a class of entities,
b. classification learning, or learning *discriminant descriptions* of classes of objects,
c. sequence prediction, or discovery of a rule that generates a given sequence of entities.

---

* Descriptors are variables, relations and functions that are used in symbolic descriptions of objects or situations.

II. Learning from observation

Under this type we distinguish:

a. conceptual clustering, i.e., discovery of conceptual structure underlying a collection of entities,
b. pattern discovery,
c. theory formation.

Most of the research on computer inductive learning has dealt with a special subproblem of type Ia, namely learning a conjunctive concept (description) characterizing a given class of entities. Here the data rules involve only one generalization class (which represents a certain concept), or two generalization classes; the second class being the set of "negative examples" (e.g., Winston [1970], Vere [1975], Hayes-Roth [1976]). Where there is only one generalization class (the so-called *uniclass generalization)* there is no natural limit for generalizing the given set of descriptions. In such case the limit can be imposed by the form of inductive assertion (e.g., that it should be a most specific conjunctive generalization within the given notational framework, as in (Hayes-Roth [1976]) and (Vere [1975]), or by the assumed *degree of generality* (Stepp [1978]). When there are negative examples the concept of *near miss* (Winston [1970]) can be used to effectively determine the limit of generalization.

A general problem of type Ia is to learn a *characteristic description* (e.g., a disjunctive description, grammar, or an algorithm) which characterizes all entities of a given class, and does not characterize any entity which is not in this class.

Problems of type Ib are typical pattern classification problems. Data rules involve many generalization classes; each generalization class represents a single pattern. In this case, the individual descriptions C_{ij} are generalized so long as it leads to their simplification and preserves the condition of consistency (e.g., Michalski [1980]). Obtained inductive assertions are *discriminant descriptions,* which permit one to distinguish one recognition class from all other assumed classes. A discriminant description of a class is a special case of characteristic description, where any object which is not in the class is in one of the *finite* (usually quite limited) number of other classes. Of special interest are discriminant descriptions which have minimal cost (e.g., the minimal computational complexity, or minimal number of descriptors involved).

Problems of type Ic are concerned with discovering a rule governing generation of an ordered sequence of entities. The rule may be deterministic (as in letter sequence prediction considered in Simon and Lea [1973]), or nondeterministic, as in the card game EULESIS (Dietterich [1980]). Data rules involve here only one generalization class, or two generalization classes, where the second class represents "negative examples."

Problems of type II (learning from observation) are concerned with determining a characterization of a collection of entities. In particular, such characterization can be a partition of the collection into clusters representing certain concepts ("conceptual clustering," Michalski [1980], Michalski and Stepp [1983]). In this case, data descriptions in (1) represent individual entities, and they all belong to the same generalization class (i.e., data descriptions consist of a single row in (1)).

Methods of induction can be characterized by the type of language used for expressing initial descriptions C_{ij} and final inductive assertions C'_{ij}. Many authors use a restricted form (usually a quantifier-free) of predicate calculus, or some equivalent notation (e.g., Morgan [1975], Fikes *et al.* [1972], Banerji [1977], Cohen [1977], Hayes-Roth *et al.* [1978], Vere [1975]).

In our earlier work we used a special propositional calculus with multiple-valued variables, called variable-valued logic system VL_1. Later on we have developed an extension of the first order predicate calculus, called VL_{21} (Michalski [1978]). It is a much richer language than VL_1, including several novel operators not present in predicate calculus, (e.g., the *internal conjunction, internal disjunction,* the *exception,* the *selector).* We found these operators very useful for describing and implementing generalization processes; they also directly correspond to linguistic constructions used in human descriptions. VL_{21} also provides a unifying formal framework for adequately handling descriptors of different types (measured on different scales). The handling of descriptors each according to its type in the process of generalization is one of the significant aspects of our approach to induction.

B.3 Relevance of Descriptors in Data Descriptions

A fundamental question underlying any machine induction problem is that of what information the machine is given as input data, and what information the machine is supposed to produce. Two specific questions here are how relevant the variables in the input data must be to the problem, and how the variables in inductive assertions relate to these input variables.

We will distinguish three cases:

1. The input data consist of descriptions of objects in terms of variables which are relevant to the problem, and the machine is supposed to determine a logical or mathematical formula of an assumed form involving the given variables (e.g., a disjunctive normal expression, a regression polynomial, etc.).
2. The input data consist of descriptions of objects as in case 1, but the descriptions may involve a relatively large number of irrelevant variables in addition to relevant variables. The machine is to determine a soluton description involving only relevant variables.
3. This case is like case 2, except that the initial descriptions may not include the relevant variables at all. Among irrelevant variables, they must include, however, also variables whose certain transformations (e.g., represented by mathematical expressions or intermediate logical formulas) are relevant derived variables. The final formula is then formulated in terms of the derived variables.

The above cases represent problem statements which put progressively less demand on the content of the input data (i.e., on the human defining the problem) and more demand on the machine.

The early work on concept formation and the traditional methods of data analysis represent case 1. Most of the recent research deals with case 2. In this case, the method of induction has to include efficient mechanisms for selecting relevant variables (thus, this case represents *selective induction.* The formal logic provides such mechanisms, and this fact is one of the advantages of logic-based solutions. Case 3 represents the subject of what we call *constructive induction.*

Our research on induction using system VL_1 and initial work using VL_{21} has dealt basically with case 2. Later we realized how to approach constructive induction, and formulated the first constructive generalization rules. We have incorporated them in our inductive program INDUCE 1 (Larson *et al.* [1977], Larson [1977]) and in the newer improved version INDUCE-1.1 (Dietterich [1978]).

The need for introducing the concept of constructive induction may not be obvious. The concept has basically a pragmatic value. To explain this, assume first that the output assertions involve derived descriptors, which stand for certain expressions in the same formal language. Suppose that these expressions involve, in turn, descriptors which stand for some other expressions, and so on, until the final expressions involve only initial descriptors. In this case the constructive induction simply means that the inductive assertions are multi-level or recursive descriptions.

But this is not the only interesting case. Derived descriptors in the inductive assertions may be any arbitrary, fixed (i.e., not learned) transformations of the input descriptors, specified by a mathematical formula, a computer program, or, implemented in hardware (e.g., the hardware implementation of fast Fourier transform). Their specification may require a language quite different from the accepted formal descriptive language. To determine these descriptors by learning, in the same fashion as the inductive assertions, may be a formidable task. They can be determined, e.g., through suggestions of possibly useful transformations provided by an expert, or as a result of some generate-and-test search procedure. In our approach, the derived descriptors are determined by *constructive induction rules,* which represent segments of problem-oriented knowledge of experts.

B.4 The Background Knowledge and the Form of Inductive Assertions

The induction process starts with the *problem* specification and ends with a set of alternative *inductive* assertions. The *problem* specification consists of a) *data* rules, and b) *specification of the problem background knowledge* (which includes a *preference criterion).* We will briefly discuss each of these topics.

B.4.1. Form of data rules and inductive assertions

In program INDUCE 1.1, the data descriptions, C_{ij}, and inductive assertions, C'_{ij}, are c-formulas (or VL_{21} *complexes),* defined as logical products of VL_{21} selectors, with zero or more quantifiers in front (the logical product is represented by concatenation). For example, a C'_{ij} can be:

$$\exists\, P1,P2\ [color(P1) = red \vee blue][weight(P1) > weight(P2)]$$
$$[length(P2) = 3..8][ontop(P1,P2)]\&\qquad [shape(P1)\ \&\ shape(P2) = box]$$

(see Appendix 1 for explanation)

Since selectors can include internal disjunction (see Appendix 1) and involve concepts of different levels of generality (as defined by the generalization tree; see next section), the c-formulas are more general concepts than conjunctive statements of predicates.

Other desirable forms of C_{ij} are:

- Assertions with the exception operator

$$(C1 \vee C2 \vee \ldots) \veebar C \qquad (3)$$

where C, C1, C2, ... are c-formulas, and $\veebar$ is the exception operator (see Appendix 1).

The motivation for this form comes from the observation that a description can be simpler in some cases, if it states an overgeneralized rule and specifies the exceptions. Recently Vere [1978] proposed an algorithm for handling such assertions in the framework of conventional conjunctive statements.

- Implicative assertions

$$C(C_1 \rightarrow C_2) \qquad (4)$$

which consist of a context condition C and an implication $C_1 \rightarrow C_2$, which states that properties in C_2 hold only if C_1 is true.

Production rules used in knowledge-based inference systems are a special case of (4), when C is omitted and there is no internal disjunction. Among interesting inductive problems regarding this case are:

1. developing algorithms for exposing contradictions in a set of implicative assertions
2. deriving simpler assertions from a set of assertions
3. generalizing assertions so that they may represent a wider class of specific assertions.

Various aspects of the last problem within a less general framework were studied, e.g., by Hedrick [1974].

- Case assertions

$$([f = R_1] \rightarrow C_1),([f = R_2] \rightarrow C_2),. \cdots \quad (5)$$

where $R_1, R_2 \cdots$ are pairwise disjoint sets.

This form occurs when a description is split into individual cases characterized by different values of a certain descriptor.

B.4.2 Specification of the background knowledge

The background knowledge is defined by the specifying the types of the descriptors and their value sets, the interrelationships between descriptors, rules for generating new descriptors, the preference criterion and any other information relevant to the problem.

- Types of descriptors

The process of generalizing a description depends on the type of descriptors used in the description. The type of a descriptor depends on the structure of the value set of the descriptor. We distinguish among three different structures of a value set:

1. Unordered

   Elements of the domain are considered to be independent entities, no structure is assumed to relate them. A variable or function symbol with this domain is called nominal (e.g., blood-type).

2. Linearly Ordered

   The domain is a linearly (totally) ordered set. A variable or function symbol with this domain is called *linear* (e.g., military rank, temperature, weight). Variables measured on ordinal, interval, ratio and absolute scales are special cases of a linear descriptor.

3. Tree Ordered

   Elements of the domain are ordered into a tree structure, called a *generalization* tree. A predecessor node in the tree represents a concept which is more general than the concepts represented by the dependent nodes (e.g., the predecessor of nodes 'triangle, rectangle, pentagon, etc.,' may be a 'polygon'). A variable or function symbol with such a domain is called *structured.*

Each descriptor (a variable or function symbol) is assigned its type in the specification of the problem. In the case of structured descriptors, the structure of the value set is defined by inference rules (e.g., see eqs. (8), (9), (10)).

- Relationships among descriptors

In addition to assigning a domain to each variable and function symbol, one defines properties of variables and atomic functions characteristic for the given problem. They are represented in the form of inference rules. Here are a few examples of such properties.

1. Restrictions on Variables

Suppose that we want to represent a restriction on the event space saying that if a value of variable x_1 is 0 (e.g. 'a person does not smoke'), then the variable x_3 is 'not applicable' (x_3 — the brand of cigarettes the person smokes). This is represented by a rule:

$$[x_1 = 0] \rightarrow [x_3 = NA]$$

NA = not applicable

2. Relationships Between Atomic Functions

For example, suppose that for any situation in a given problem, the atomic function $f(x_1,x_2)$ is always greater than the atomic function $g(x_1,x_2)$. We represent this:

$$TRUE \rightarrow \forall\ x_1,x_2[f(x_1,x_2) > g(x_1,x_2)]$$

3. Properties of Predicate Functions

For example, suppose that a predicate function 'left' is transitive. We represent this:

$$\forall x_1,x_2,x_3([left(x_1,x_2)][left(x_2,x_3)] \rightarrow [left(x_1,x_3)])$$

Other types of relationships characteristic for the problem environment can be represented similarly.

The rationale behind the inclusion of the *problem background knowledge* reflects our position that the guidance of the process of induction by the knowledge pertinent to the problem is necessary for nontrivial inductive problems.

B.4.3 The preference criterion

The preference criterion defines what is the desired solution to the problem, i.e., what kind of hypotheses are being sought. There are many dimensions, independent and interdependent, on which the hypotheses can be evaluated. The weight given to each dimension depends on the ultimate use of the hypotheses. The dimensions may be, e.g., the number of operators in the set of inductive assertions, the quantity of information required to encode the hypothesis using operators from an a priori defined set (Coulon and Kayser [1978]), the scope of the hypothesis relating the events predicted by the hypothesis to the events actually observed (some form of measure of degree of generalization), the cost of measuring the descriptors in the hypothesis, etc. Therefore, instead of defining a specific criterion, we specify only a general form of the criterion. The form, called a 'lexicograpic functional' consists of an ordered list of criteria measuring hypothesis quality and a list of 'tolerances' for these criteria (Michalski [1973]).

An important and somewhat surprising property of such an approach is that by properly defining the preference criterion, the same computer program can produce either the *characteristic* or *discriminant* descriptions of object classes (by maximizing or minimizing the number of selectors in the inductive assertions, respectively).

C. Generalization Rules

The transformation from data rules (1) to inductive assertions (2) can be viewed (at least conceptually) as an application of certain *generalization* rules.

A *generalization* rule is defined as a rule which transforms one or more symbolic descriptions in the same generalization class into a new description of the same class which is *equivalent* or *more general* than the initial set of descriptions.

A description

$$V ::> K \tag{6}$$

is *equivalent* to a set

$$\{V_i ::> K\},\ i = 1,2, \cdots \tag{7}$$

if any *event* (a description of an object or situation) which satisfies at least one of the V_i, $i = 1,2, \cdots$, satisfies also V, and conversely. If the converse is not required, the rule (6) is said to be *more general than* (7).

The generalization rules are applied to data rules under the condition of preserving consistency and completeness, and achieving optimality according to the preference criterion. A basic property of a generalization transformation is that the resulting rule has UNKNOWN truth-status; being a hypothesis, its truth-status must be tested on new data. Generalization rules do not guarantee that the generated inductive assertions are useful or plausible.

We have formalized several generalization rules, both for *selective* and *constructive induction.* Selective induction differs from constructive induction in that selective does not generate any new descriptors in the generalization process. (The notation $D_1 |< D_2$ specifies that D_2 is more general than D_1).

Selective generalization:

(i) *The extending reference rule*

$$V[L = R_1] ::> \quad K \quad |< \quad V[L = R_2] ::> K$$

where L is an atomic function

$R_2 \supset R_1$, and R_1, R_2 are subsets of the domain,
Dom(L) of descriptor L.
V - a context description (concatenation means conjunction)

This is a generally applicable rule; the type of descriptor L does not matter. For example, the description: 'objects that are blue or red' is more general than 'objects that are red'.

(ii) *The dropping selector* (or *dropping condition)* rule

$$V[L=R] ::> K \ |< \ V ::> K$$

This rule is also generally applicable. It is one of the most commonly used rules for generalizing information. It can be derived from rule (i), by assuming that R_2 in (i) is equal the value set D(L). In this case the selector $[L = R_2]$ always has truth-status TRUE and therefore can be removed.

(iii) The *closing interval* rule

$$\left.\begin{array}{l} V[L = a] ::> K \\ V[L = b] ::> K \end{array}\right| < \quad V[L = a..b] ::> K$$

This rule is applicable only when L is a linear descriptor.

To illustrate rule (iii), consider as objects two states of a machine, and as a generalization class, a characterization of the states as *normal*. The rule says that if two normal states differ only in that the machine has two different temperatures, say, a and b, then the hypothesis is made that all states in which the temperature is in the interval [a,b] are also *normal*.

(iv) The *climbing generalization* tree rule

$$\text{one or more rules} \left\{\begin{array}{l} V[L=a]::>K \\ V[L=b]::>K \\ \quad\vdots \\ V[L=i]::>K \end{array}\right| < \quad [L=s] \rightarrow K$$

where L is a structured descriptor

s - represents the node at the next level of generality than nodes a,b, ... and i, in the tree domain of L (i.e., is the most specific common generalization of nodes a,b, ... i).

The rule is applicable only to selectors involving structured descriptors. This rule has been used, e.g., in (Winston [1970], Hedrick [1974], Lenat [1976]).

Example:

$$\left.\begin{array}{l} V[\text{shape}(p)=\text{triangle}] ::> K \\ V[\text{shape}(p)=\text{pentagon}] ::> K \end{array}\right| < \quad V[\text{shape}(p)=\text{polygon}] ::> K$$

(v) The *extension against* rule

$$\left.\begin{array}{l} V_1[L=R_1] ::> K \\ V_2[L=R_2] ::> \neg K \end{array}\right| < \quad [L \neq R_2] ::> K$$

where $R_1 \cap R_2 = 0$

V_1 and V_2 - arbitrary descriptions.

This rule is generally applicable. It is used to take into consideration 'negative examples', or, in general, to maintain consistency. It is a basic rule for determining discriminant class descriptions.

(vi) The *turning constants into variables* rule

$$\text{one or more rules} \left\{ \begin{array}{l} V[p(a,Y)] ::> K \\ V[p(b,Y)] ::> K \\ \quad \vdots \\ V[p(i,Y)] ::> K \end{array} \right. \left| < \ \exists\, x, V[p(x,Y)] ::> K \right.$$

where Y stands for one or more arguments of atomic function p.

x is a variable whose value set includes a,b,...,i.

It can be proven that this rule is a special case of the extending reference rule (i). This is a rule of general applicability. It is the basic rule used in inductive learning methods employing predicate calculus.

Constructive Generalization Rules:

Constructive generalization rules generate generalized descriptions of events in terms of new descriptors which are functions of the original descriptors. They can be viewed as knowledge-based rules for generating new descriptors. Here are a few examples.

(i) The *counting rule*

$$V[\text{attribute}_1(P_1)=A]\ldots[\text{attribute}_1(P_k)=A][\text{attribute}_1(P_{k+1})\neq A]$$

$$\cdots[\text{attribute}_1(\text{Pqsubr})\neq A] ::> K \,|\!< V[\#\text{P—attribute}_1\text{—A}=k] ::> K$$

where $P_1, P_2, \ldots, P_k, \ldots, P_r$ - are constants denoting, e.g., parts of an object.

$\text{attribute}_1(P_i)$ - stands for an attribute of P_i, e.g., color, size, texture, etc.

$\text{P\#—attribute}_1\text{—A}$ - denotes a new descriptor interpreted as the 'number of P_i's (e.g., parts) with attribute_i of value A.

Example:

$$V[color(P1) = RED][color(P2) = RED][color(P3) = BLUE] \ ::> \ K$$

$$|< [\#P - color - red = 2] \ ::> \ K$$

This is a generalization rule, because a set of objects with any two red parts is a superset of a set of objects with two parts which are red and one part which is blue.

The rule can be extended to a more general form, in which in addition to the arbitrary context formula V there is a predicate CONDITION(P_1,...,P_k), which specifies some conditions imposed on variables P_1,...,P_k.

(viii) The *generating chain properties* rule (a *chain metarule).*

If the arguments of different occurrences of a transitive relation (e.g., relation 'above', 'left of', 'larger than', etc.) form a chain, i.e., are linearly ordered by the relation, the rule generates descriptors relating to specific objects in the chain. For example:

LST-object - the 'least object', i.e., the object at the beginning of the chain (e.g., the bottom object in the case of relation 'above')

MST-object - the object at the end of the chain (e.g., the top object)

position(object) - the position of the object in the chain.

(ix) The *variable association* detection rule.

Suppose that in the data rules, in the context of condition C, an ascending order of values of a linear descriptor x_i corresponds to an ascending (or descending) order of values of another linear descriptor x_j with the same quantified arguments. For example, whenever descriptor weight(P) takes on increasing values, then the descriptor length(P) also takes on the increasing values. In such situations a two-argument predicate descriptor is generated:

$$\uparrow (x_i,x_j) \text{ - if } x_j \text{ grows with } x_i$$

or

$$\downarrow (x_i,x_j) \text{ - if } x_i \text{ decreases with } x_i$$

If the number of different occurrences of x_i and x_j is statistically significant, then the "monotonic" descriptors $\uparrow (x_l,x_j)$ and $\downarrow (x_i,x_j)$ can be generalized to:

$$\uparrow\uparrow (x_i,x_j) = \begin{cases} \text{True, if } r(x_i,x_j) \geqslant \tau \\ \text{False, otherwise} \end{cases}$$

(positive correlation)

$$\downarrow\downarrow (x_i,x_j) = \begin{cases} \text{True, if } r(x_i,x_j) \leqslant -\tau \\ \text{False, otherwise} \end{cases}$$

(negative correlation)

where $r(x_i,x_j)$ denotes the coefficient of statistical correlation, and τ is a certain threshold, $0 < \tau \leqslant 1$.

The concept of generalization rules is very useful for understanding and classifying different methods of induction (Dietterich and Michalski [1979]).

D. Learning From Examples

We will illustrate some aspects of learning from examples by a simple problem involving geometrical constructions. Suppose that two sets of trains, Eastbound and Westbound, are given, as shown in Figure 1. The problem is to determine a concise, logically sufficient description of each set of trains, which distinguishes one set from the other (i.e., a *discriminant* description). Such a description should contain only necessary conditions for distinguishing between the two sets. Using this example we will first briefly describe the learning methodology implemented in computer program INDUCE-1.1 (Larson *et al.* [1977], Larson [1977], Dietterich [1978]) which successfully solved this problem, and then we will discuss some problems for future research.

At the first step, the initial space of descriptors was determined. They were all descriptors which seem to be relevant for the posed discrimination problem.

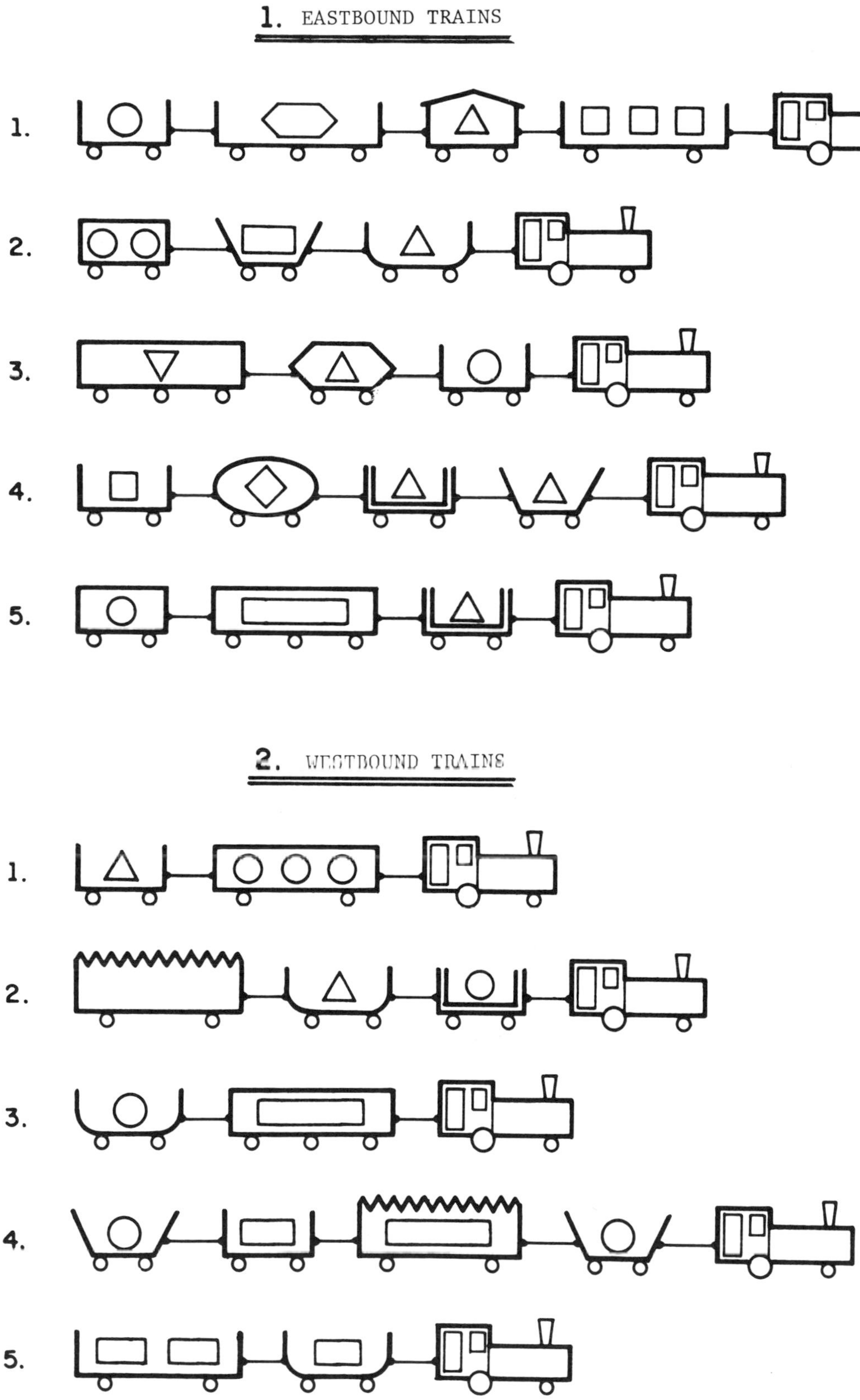

Figure 1. Find a rule distinguishing between these two classes of trains.

Among the eleven descriptors selected in total were:

position(car_i) - the position of car_i, with engine being at position 1
(a linear descriptor)

infront(car_i,car_j) - car_i is in front of car_j
(a nominal descriptor)

length(car_i) - the length of car_i
(a linear descriptor)

car-shape(car_i) - the shape of car_i
(a structured descriptor with 12 nodes in the generalization tree; see eqs. (8) and (9))

contains(car_i,$load_j$) - car_i contains $load_j$
(a nominal descriptor)

load-shape($load_i$) - the shape of $load_i$
(a structured descriptor)
The domain structure is hierarchical:
plane figures may be circles or polygons;
polygons may be hexagons, triangles, rectangles or squares.

nrpts-load(car_i) - the number of parts in the load of car_i
(a linear descriptor)

nr-wheels(car_i) - the number of wheels on car_i
(a linear descriptor)

At the next step, *data rules* were formulated, which characterized trains in terms of the selected descriptors, and specified the train set to which each train belongs. For example, the data rule for the second eastbound train was:

$\exists$ car_1,car_2,car_3,car_4,$load_1$,$load_2$,...
[infront(car_1,car_2)] [infront(car_2,car_3)]...[length(car_1) = long]&
[car–shape(car_1)=engine] [car–shape(car_2)=V–shaped]&
[cont–load(car_2,$load_1$)]&
[load–shape($load_1$)=triangle]...[nrwheels(car_3)=2]..:: >[class=Eastbound]

Background knowledge rules were used to define the structures of structured descriptors (arguments of descriptors are omitted as irrelevant here):

[car – shape=open rctngl V open trapezoid,U – shaped V dbl open rctngl] = >

[car–shape=open top] (8)

[car – shape=ellipse V closed rctngl V jagged top V sloping top] = >

[car–shape=closed top] (9)

[load–shape=hexagon V triangle V rectangle] = >[load–shape=polygon] (10)

and that the relation 'infront' is transitive.

The *criterion of preference* was to minimize the number of rules used in describing each class, and, with secondary priority, to minimize the number of selectors (expressions in brackets) in each rule.

The INDUCE program produced the following inductive assertions*:

Eastbound trains:

$$\exists car_1[length(car_1) = short][car{-}shape(car_1) = closed\ top] :: > [class{=}Eastbound] \tag{11}$$

It can be interpreted:

If a train contains a car which is short and has a closed top then it is an eastbound train.

Alternatively,

$$\exists car_1, car_2, load_1, load_2[infront(car_1, car_2)][contains(car_1, load_1)]\& \\ [contains(car_2, load_2)][load{-}shape(load_1) = triangle]\& \\ [load{-}shape(load_2) = polygon] :: > [class = Eastbound]$$

It can be interpreted:

If a train contains a car whose load is a triangle, and the load of the car behind is a polygon, then the train is eastbound. (12)

Westbound trains:

$$\underline{[nr{-}cars{=}3]} \lor car_1[car - shape(car_1) = jagged{-}top] :: > [class{=}Westbound]$$

Either a train has three cars or there is a car with jagged top. (13)

$$\exists car\underline{[nr{-}cars{-}length{-}long{=}2]}[position(car) = 3][shape(car) = open{-}top \lor jagged{-}top] \\ :: > [class\text{-}Westbound]$$

There are two long cars and the third car has open-top or jagged top.

* It may be a useful exercise for the reader to try at this point to determine his/her own solutions, before reading the computer solutions.

It is interesting to note that the example was constructed with rules (12) and (13) in mind. The rule (11) which was found by the program as an alternative was rather surprising because it seems to be conceptually simpler than rule (12). This observation confirms the thesis of this research that the combinatorial part of an induction process can be successfully handled by a computer program, and, therefore, programs like the above have a potential to serve as a useful aid to induction processes in various practical problems.

The descriptors underlined by the dotted lines ('nr-cars-length-long') are new descriptors, generated as a result of constructive induction. How were they generated? The constructive generalization rules are implemented as modules which scan the data rules and search for certain properties. For example, the *counting rule* of constructive generalization checks for each unary descriptor (e.g., length(car)) how many times a given value of the descriptor repeats in the data rules.

In our example, it was found that the selector [length(car)=long] occurs for two quantified variables in every Westbound train, and therefore a new descriptor called 'nr-cars-length-long' was generated, and a new selector [nr cars-length-long=2] was formed. This selector, after passing a 'relevance test', was included in the set of potentially useful selectors. The relevance test requires that a selector is satisfied by a sufficiently large number of positive examples and a sufficiently small number of negative examples (see the details later). During the generation of alternative assertions, this selector was used as one of the conditions in the assertion (14). The descriptor 'position(car)' was found by the application of the *chain rule.*

Now, how does the whole program work? Various versions of the program were described in (Larson [1977], Michalski [1978], Dietterich [1978]). Appendix 2, provides a description of the top level algorithm. Here we will give a summary of the main ideas, their limitations, and describe some problems for future research.

The work of the program can be viewed essentially as the process of applying generalization rules, inference rules (describing the problem environment) and constructive generalization (generating new descriptors) to the data rules, in order to determine inductive assertions which are consistent and complete. The preference criterion is used to select the most preferable assertions which constitute the solution.

The process of generating inductive assertions is inherently combinatorially explosive, so the major question is how to guide this process in order to detect quickly the most preferable assertions.

As described in Appendix 2, the first part of the program generates (by putting together the 'most relevant' selectors step-by-step) a set of consistent *c-formulas.* A simple relevance test for a selector is to have a large difference between the number of data rules covered by the selector in the given generalization class and the number of rules covered in other generalization classes.

C-formulas are represented as labelled graphs. Testing them for consistency (i.e., for null intersection of descriptions of different generalization classes) or for the *degree of coverage* of the given class is done by determining the subgraph isomorphism. By taking advantage of the labels on nodes and arcs, this operation was greatly simplified. Nevertheless, it consumes much time and space.

In the second part, the program transforms the consistent c-formulas into VL_1 events (i.e., sequences of values of certain many-valued variables (Michalski [1973]), and further generalization is done using AQVAL generalization procedure (Michalski and Larson [1978]). During this process, the *extension against, closing the interval and climbing generalization tree* generalization rules are applied. The VL_1 events are represented as binary string, and most of the operations done during this process are simple logical operations on binary strings. Consequently, this part of the algorithm is very fast and efficient. Thus, the high efficiency of the program is due to the transformation of the data structures representing the rules into more efficient form in the second part of the algorithm (after determining consistent generalizations).

A disadvantage of this algorithm is that the extension of references of selectors (achieved by the application of the *extension against, the closing interval* and *climbing* generalization rules) is done *after* a supposedly relevant set of selectors have been determined. It is possible that a selector from the initial data rules or one generated by constructive generalization rules that did not pass the 'relevance test', could still turn out to be very relevant, if its reference were appropriately generalized. Applying the above generalization rules to each selector represented as a graph structure (i.e., before the AQVAL procedure takes over) is, however, computationally very costly, and we decided against it in the INDUCE program. This problem will be aggravated when the number of constructive generalization rules generating derived descriptors is increased. We plan to seek solutions to this problem by designing a better *descriptor relevance test,* determining more adequate data structures for representing selectors and testing intersections of descriptions, and by applying problem background knowledge.

Another interesting problem is how to provide an inductive program with the ability to discover relevant derived descriptors, which are arithmetic expressions involving the input variables and to integrate them as parts of inductive assertions. For example, suppose that the Eastbound trains in figure 1 are characterized as:

> When the train has 3 cars, the load of the first two cars is twice the total load of Westbound cars, and when the train is longer, the load of the first two cars is equal the total load of Westbound cars!

How would one design an efficient algorithm which could discover such an assertion?

Let us now consider a problem of describing, say, the Eastbound trains not in the context of Westbound trains, but in the context of every possible train which is not Eastbound. This is a problem of determining a *characteristic description* of Eastbound trains (type Ia).

A trivial solution to this problem is a 'zero degree generalization' description, which is the disjunction of descriptions of individual trains. A more interesting solution (although still of 'zero degree generalization') would be some equivalence preserving transformation of such a disjunction, which would produce a computationally simpler description. Allowing a 'non-zero degree generalization' leads us to a great variety of possibilities, called the *version space* (Mitchell [1978]). As we mentioned before (Sec. A.1), the most studied solution is to determine the most specific conjunctive generalization (i.e., the longest list of common properties). Another solution is to determine the description of minimal cost whose degree of generality is under certain threshold (Stepp [1978]). INDUCE 1.1 gives a solution of the first type, namely, it produces a set of the most specific (longest) c-formulas (quantified logical products of VL_{21} selectors). Here are examples of such formulas:

For Eastbound trains (some of these formulas may also cover Westbound trains):

∃car[length(car) =short] [car–shape(car) =closed top] [nr–wheels=2]

(In every train there is a short car with closed top and two wheels)

∃car[position(car) =1] [car–shape(car) =engine]

(The first car in each train is engine)

∃car[position(car) =2] [car–shape(car) =open–top]

(The second car in each train has an open-top)

∃car[position(car) =2 ∨ 3] [load–shape(load) =triangle] [contains(car,load)]

(The second or third car in each train contains triangle)

[nr–cars=4 ∨ 5]

(number of cars is 4 or 5)

∀car[nr–wheels=2 ∨ 3]

(number of wheels in each car in every train is 2 or 3)

The logical product of these formulas is a characteristic description of Eastbound trains.

To keep this paper within reasonable limits, we will skip the discussion of problems of type Ic (i.e., the sequence prediction), referring the reader to paper by Diettrich [1980].

E. Learning From Observation

The major difference between problems of learning a characteristic description from examples (type IA), and problems of conceptual clustering in learning from observation (type II) is that in the latter problem the input is usually an arbitrary collection of entities, rather than a collection of examples representing a single predetermined conceptual class; and that the goal is to determine a partition of the collection into categories (in general, to determine a structure within the collection), such that each category represents a certain concept.

Problems of this type have been intensively studied in the area of cluster analysis and pattern recognition (as 'learning without teacher', or unsupervised learning). The methods which have been developed in these areas partition the entities into clusters, such that the entities within each cluster have a high 'degree of similarity', and entities of different clusters have a low 'degree of similarity'. The degree of similarity between two entities is typically a function (usually a reciprocal of a distance function), which takes into consideration only properties of these entities and not their relation to other entities, or to some predefined concepts. Consequently, clusters obtained this way rarely have any simple conceptual interpretation.

In this section we will briefly describe an approach to clustering which we call *conceptual clustering.* In this approach, entities are assembled into a single cluster, if together they represent some concept from a predefined set of concepts. For example, consider the set of points shown in Figure 2.

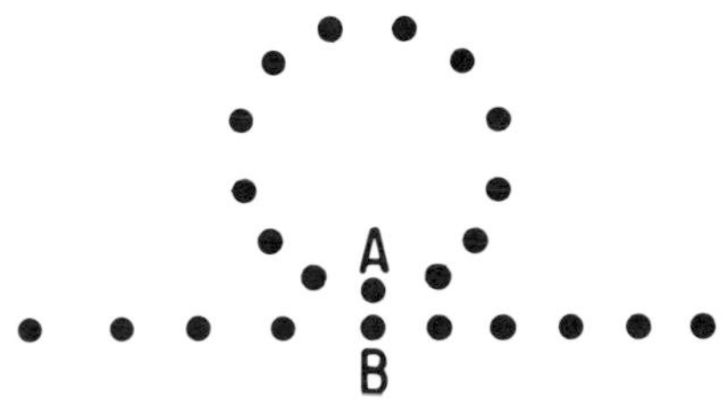

Figure 2.

A typical description of this set by a human is something like 'a circle on a straight line'. Thus, the points A and B, although closer to each other than to any other points, will be put into different clusters, because they are parts of different concepts.

Since the points in Figure 2 do not constitute a complete circle and straight line, the obtained conceptual clusters represent generalizations of these data points. Consequently, conceptual clustering can be viewed as a form of generalization of symbolic descriptions, similarly as problems of learning from examples. The input rules are symbolic descriptions of the entities in the collection. To interpret this problem as a special case of the paradigm in Sec. A.1, the collection is considered as a single generalization class.

If the concepts into which the collection is to be partitioned are defined as C-formulas, then the generalization rules discussed before would apply. The restriction imposed by the problem is that the C-formulas logically intersect, as each cluster should be disjoint from other clusters.

We will describe here briefly an algorithm for determining such a clustering, assuming that the concepts are simpler constructs than C-formulas, namely, non-quantified C-formulas with *unary selectors,* i.e., logical products of such selectors. Unary selectors are relational statements:

$$[x_i \# R_i]$$

where:

x_i is one of n predefined variables $(i=1,2,...,n)$
$\#$ is one of the relational operators $= \neq$
R_i is a subset of the value set of x_i.

A selector $[x_i = R_i]([x_i \neq R_i])$ is *satisfied* by a value of x_i, if this value is in relation $= (\neq)$ with some (all) values from R_i. Such restricted c-formulas are called VL_1 *complexes* or, briefly, *complexes* (Michalski [1980]).

Individual entities are assumed to be described by *events,* which are sequences of values of variables x_i:

$$(a_1,a_2,..., a_n)$$

where $a_i \in Dom(x_i)$, and $Dom(x_i)$ is the value set of $x_i, i=1,2,..., n$. An event e is said to *satisfy* a complex, if values of x_i in e satisfy all selectors. Suppose E is a set of observed events, each of which satisfies a complex C. If there exist events satisfying C which are not in E, then they are called *unobserved events.* The number of unobserved events in a complex is called the *absolute sparseness* of the complex. We will consider the following problem. Given is an event set E and an integer k. Determine k pairwise disjoint complexes such that:

1. they represent a partition of E into k subsets (a k-partition)
2. the total sparseness of the complexes is minimum.

The theoretical basis and an algorithm for a solution of this problem (in somewhat more general formulation, where the clustering criterion is not limited to sparseness) is described in Michalski [1980]. The algorithm is interactive, and its general structure is based on dynamic clustering method (Diday and Simon [1976]). Each step starts with k specially selected data events, called *seeds.* The seeds are treated as representatives of k classes, and this way the problem is reduced to essentially a classification problem (type 1b). The step ends with a determination of a set of k complexes defining a partition of E. From such complex a new seed is selected, and the obtained set of k seeds is the input to the next iteration. The algorithm terminates with a k partition of E, defined by k complexes, which have the minimum or sub-minimum total sparseness (or, generally, the assumed cost criterion).

Figure 3 (on the next page) presents an example illustrating this process. The space of all events is defined by variables x_1, x_2, x_3 and x_4, with sizes of their value sets 2, 5, 4 and 2, respectively. The space is represented as a diagram, where each cell represents an event. For example, cell marked e represents event(0,0,2,0).

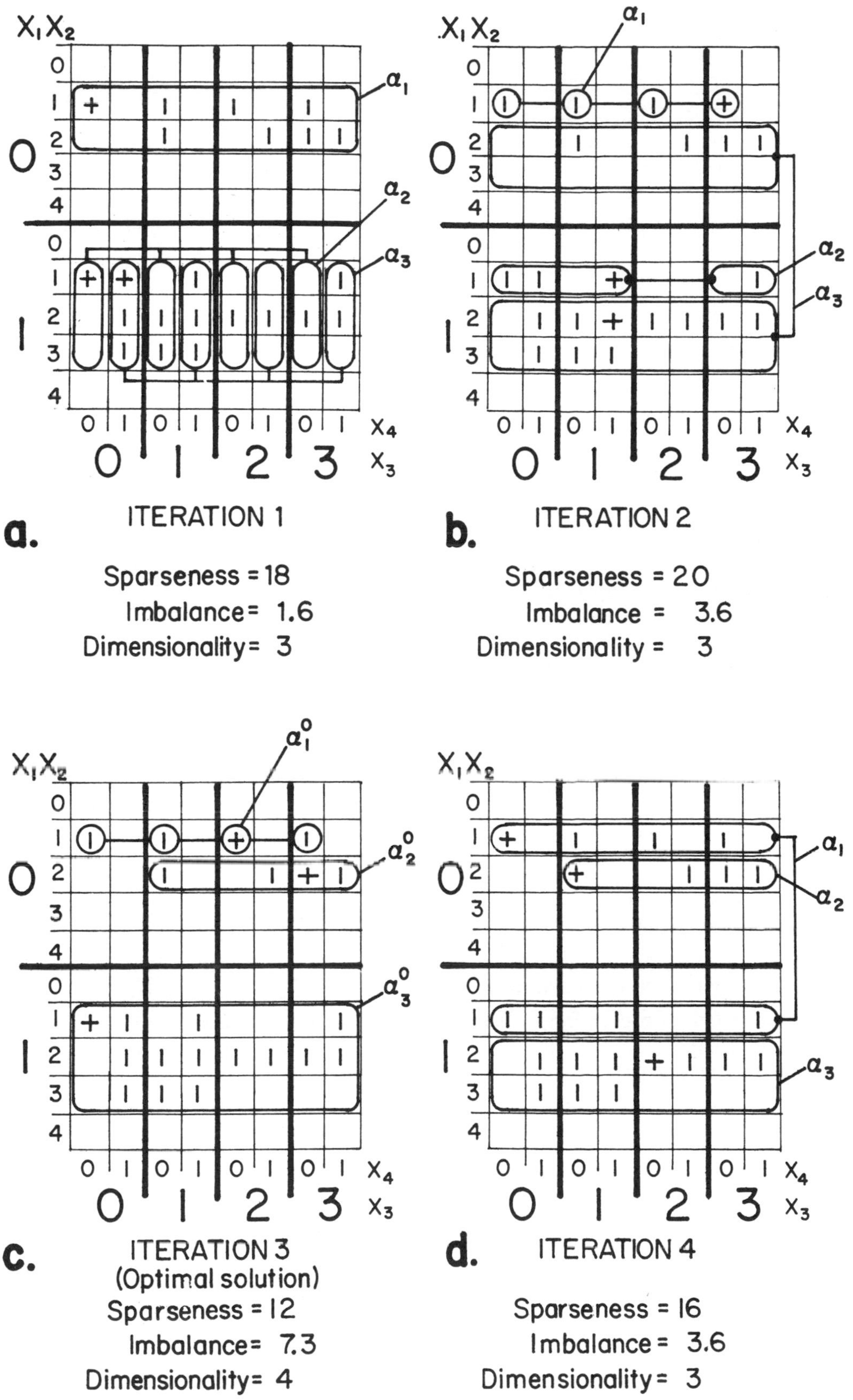

Figure 3. Iterative generation of a conjunctive clustering.

Cells marked by a vertical bar represent data events, while remaining cells represent unobserved events. Figure 3a also shows complexes obtained in the first iteration. Cells representing seed events in each iteration are marked by +. So in the first iteration, assuming k=3, three seeds were chosen: (0,1,0,0), (1,1,0,0) and (1,1,0,1). The complexes determined in this iteration are $\alpha, \alpha_2, \alpha_3$ (Figure 3a), with the total sparseness 18 (the total number of unmarked cells in these complexes). Figures 3b, c, and d show the results of the three consecutive iterations. The solution with the minimum sparseness is shown in Figure 3c. It consists of complexes:

$$\alpha_1^o = [x_1 = 0][x_2 = 1][x_4 = 0]$$

$$\alpha_2^o = [x_1 = 0][x_2 = 2][x_3 = 1..3]$$

$$\alpha_3^o = [x_1 = 1][x_2 = 1..3]$$

This result was obtained by program CLUSTER/PAF* implementing the algorithm in PASCAL language on Cyber 175 (Michalski and Stepp [1982]).

Another experiment with the program involved clustering 47 cases of soybean diseases. These cases represented four different diseases, as determined by plant pathologists (the program was not, of course, given this information). Each case was represented by an event of 35 many-valued variables. With k=4, the program partitioned all cases into four categories. These four categories turned out to be precisely the categories corresponding to individual diseases. The complexes defining the categories contained known characteristic symptoms of the corresponding diseases.

Program CLUSTER/PAF is very general and could be useful for a variety of tasks that require a determination of intrinsically disjunctive descriptions. For example, such tasks are splitting a goal into subgoals, discovering useful subcases in a collection of computational processes, partitioning specific facts into conceptual categories, formulating cases in program specification.

F. Summary

We have presented a view of inductive inference as a process of generalization of symbolic descriptions. The process is conducted by applying *generalization rules* and the *background knowledge rules* (representing problem specific knowledge) to the initial and intermediate descriptions. It is shown that both learning from examples and learning from observation can be viewed this way.

A form of learning from observation, called 'conceptual clustering' was described, which partitions a collection of entities into clusters, such that each cluster represents a certain concept. Presented methods for learning from examples (INDUCE) and automated conceptual clustering (CLUSTER/PAF) generate logic-style descriptions that are easy to comprehend and interpret by humans. Such descriptions can be viewed as formal specifications of programs solving tasks in the area of computer-based decision making and analysis of complex data.

G. Acknowledgement

A partial support of this research was provided by the National Science Foundation under grants MCS79−06614 and MCS82−05116. The author is grateful to Robert Stepp for useful discussions and for proofreading the paper.

---

* PAF stands for "Polish-American-French"

APPENDIX 1

Definition of variable-valued logic calculus V_{21}

Data rules, hypotheses, problem environment descriptions, and generalization rules are all expressed using the same formalism, that of variable-valued logic calculus VL_{21}*.
VL_{21} is an extension of predicate calculus designed to facilitate a compact and uniform expression of descriptions of different degrees and different types of generalization. The formalism also provides a simple linguistic interpretation of descriptions without losing the precision of the conventional predicate calculus.

There are three major differences between VL_{21} and the first order predicate calculus (FOPC):

1. In place of predicates, it uses *selectors* (or *relational statements)* as basic operands. A selector, in the most general form, specifies a relationship between one or more atomic functions and other atomic functions or constants. A common form of a selector is a test to ascertain whether the value of an atomic function is a specific constant or is a member of a set of constants.

   The selectors represent compactly certain types of logical relationships which can not be directly represented in FOPC but which are common in human descriptions. They are particularly useful for representing changes in the degree of generality of descriptions and for syntactically uniform treatment of descriptors of different types.
2. Each atomic function (a variable, a predicate, a function) is assigned a value set (domain), from which it draws values, together with a characterization of the structure of the value set.

   This feature facilitates a representation of the semantics of the problem and the application of generalization rules appropriate to the type of descriptors.
3. An expression in VL_{21} can have a truth status: TRUE, FALSE or ? (UNKNOWN).

The truth-status '?' provides an interpretation of a VL_{21} description in the situation, when e.g., outcomes of some measurements are not known.

An *atomic function* is a variable, or a function symbol followed by a pair of parentheses which enclose a sequence of atomic functions and/or constants. Atomic functions which have a defined interpretation in the problem under consideration are called *descriptors.*

A *constant* differs from a variable or a function symbol in that its value set is empty. If confusion is possible, a constant is typed in quotes.

---

* VL_{21} is a subset of a more complete system VL_2, which is a many valued-logic extension of predicate calculus.

Examples

Constants 2 * red
Atomic forms: x_1 color(box) on−top(pl,p2) $((x_1,g(x_2))$
Exemplary value sets:

$$D(x_1) = \{0,1,..., 10\}$$
$$D(\text{color}) = \{\text{red, blue}, \cdots\}$$
$$D(\text{on-top}) = \{\text{true, false}\}$$
$$D(f) = \{0,1,..., 20\}$$

A *selector* is a form

$$[L \ \# \ R]$$

where
L - called *referee,* is an atomic function, or a sequence of atomic functions separated by '.' . (The operator '.' is called the *internal conjunction.)*
- is one of the following relational operators:

$$= \neq \ \geqslant \ < \ \geqslant \ <$$

R - called *reference,* is a constant or atomic function, or a sequence of constants or atomic functions separated by operator 'V' or '..' . (The operators 'V' and '..' are called the *internal disjunction,* and the *range operator,* respectively.)

A selector in which the referee L is a simple atomic function and the reference R is a single constant is called an *elementary selector.* The selector has truth-status TRUE {or FALSE} with regard to a situation if the situation *satisfies* {*does not satisfy*} the selector, i.e., if the referee L is {is not} related by relatonal operator # to the reference R. The selector has the truth-status UNKNOWN (and is interpreted as being a *question),* if there is not sufficient information about the values of descriptors in L for the given situation. To simplify the exposition, instead of giving a definition of what it means that 'L is related by relational operator # to R', we will simply explain this by examples.

		Linguistic interpretation
(i)	[color(box1) = white]	color of box1 is white
(ii)	[length(box1) $\geqslant$ 2]	length of box1 is greater than or equal to 2
(iii)	[weight(box1) = 2..5]	weight of box1 is between 2 and 5,
(iv)	[blood-type(P1) = 0 V A V B]	blood-type of P1 is 0 or A or B
(v)	[on-top(box1,box2) = T] or simply [on-top(box1,box2)]	box1 is on top of box2
(vi)	[above(box1,box2) = 3'']	box1 is 3'' above box2
(vii)	[weight(box1) > weight(box3)]	the weight of box1 is greater than the weight of box3
(viii)	[length(box1) • length(box2) = 3]*	the length of box1 and box2 is 3
(ix)	[type(P_1) • type(P_2) = A V B]	the type of P_1 and the type of P_2 is either A or B.

Note the direct *correspondence of the selectors to linguistic interpretations.* Note also that some selectors can not be expressed in FOPC in a (pragmatically) equivalent form (e.g., (iv), (ix)).

A VL_{21} expression (or, here, simply VL expression) is defined by the following rules:

(i) A constant TRUE, FALSE, or 'UNKNOWN' is a VL expression

(ii) A selector is a VL expression

(iii) If V, V_1 and V_2 are VL expressions then so are:

(V)	formula in parentheses
$\neg V$	inverse
V_1 & V_2 or V_1V_2	conjunction
$V_1 \vee V_2$	disjunction
$V_1 \veebar V_2$	exception exclusive disjunction
$V_1 \rightarrow V_2$	metaimplication

where $\rightarrow \in \{\rightarrow, \leftrightarrow, ::>, =>, |<, |=, |>\}$

(implication, equivalence, decision assignment, inference, generalization, semantical equivalence, specialization)

$\exists x_1, x_2, \ldots, x_k(V)$	existentially quantified expression
$\forall x_1, x_2, \ldots, x_k(V)$	universally quantified expression

A VL formula can have truth-status TRUE(T), FALSE(F) or UNKNOWN(?). The interpretation given to connectives ˜ ('not'), &,('and'),V('or'),→, is defined in Fig. A1. (This interpretation is consistent with Kleen-Korner 3-valued logic.) An expression with the operator =>, |< or |= is assumed to always have the truth-status TRUE and with operator ::>, TRUE or ?. Operators $\veebar$ and $\leftrightarrow$ are interpreted:

$$V_1 \veebar V_2 \text{ is equivalent to } V_1 \& \neg V_2 \vee \neg V_1 \& V_2$$

$$V_1 \leftrightarrow V_2 \text{ is equivalent to } (V_1 \rightarrow V_2)(V_2 \rightarrow V_1)$$

* This expression is equivalent to [length(box1) =3] [length(box2) =3].

The truth-status of

$$\exists x(V) \text{ is } \begin{cases} \text{TRUE\{FALSE\}} & \text{if, there exist} \\ & \text{\{does not exist\} a value of x which makes} \\ & \text{the truth-status of V equal TRUE} \\ ? & \text{if it is not known whether there exist } \cdots \end{cases}$$

	~
?	?
F	T
T	F

&	?	F	T
?	?	F	?
F	F	F	F
T	?	F	T

V	?	F	T
?	?	?	T
F	?	F	T
T	T	T	T

→	?	F	T
?	?	?	T
F	T	T	T
T	?	F	T

DEFINITION OF CONNECTIVES
~, &, V, AND →
IN VL_{21}

Figure A1.

$$\forall x(V) \text{ is } \begin{cases} \text{TRUE \{FALSE\} if for every value of x} \\ \qquad\qquad \text{the truth–status of V is \{is not\} TRUE} \\ ? \qquad\qquad \text{if it is not known whether for every } \cdots \end{cases}$$

A VL expression in the form

$$QF_1, QF_2, \cdots \ (C_1 \vee C_2 \vee, \ldots, \vee C_l)$$

where QF_i is a quantifier form $\exists\ x_1, x_2, \ldots$, or $\forall\ x_1, x_2, \cdots$ and C_i is a conjunction of selectors (called a *complex)* is called a *disjunctive simple* VL expression (a *DVL* expression).

To make possible a name substitution operation, the following notation is adopted:

- If FORMULA is an arbitrary VL_{21} expression then V: FORMULA assigns name V to the FORMULA.
- If FORMULA is a VL_{21} expression containing quantified variables $P_1, P_2, \ldots, P_k$, and V is the name of the expression, then

$$P_i - V$$

denotes the quantified variable P_i in the FORMULA.

The latter construct enables one to refer in one expression to quantified variables inside of other expressions.

APPENDIX 2

Outline of the Top Level Algorithm of INDUCE 1.1.

1. At the first step, the data rules whose condition parts are in the disjunctive simple forms are transformed to a new set of rules, whose condition parts are in the form of *c-expressions. A c-expression (a conjunctive expression)* is a product of selectors accompanied by zero or more quantifier forms, i.e., forms $QFx_1,x_2,...,$ where QF denotes a quantifier. (Note, that due to the use of the internal disjunction and quantifiers, a c-expression represents a more general concept than a conjunction of predicates.)

2. A generalization class is selected, say K_i, and all c-expressions associated with this class are put into a set F1, and all remaining c-expressions are put into a set FO (the set F1 represents events to be *covered,* and set FO represents constraints, i.e., events not to be *covered).*

3. By application of inference rules representing background knowledge and constructive generalization rules, new selectors are generated. The most promising selectors (according to the preference criterion) are added to the c-expressions in F1 and F0.

4. A c-expression is selected from F1, and a set of consistent generalizations (a *restricted star)* of this expression is generated (Michalski and Stepp [1982]). This is done by starting with single selectors (called 'seeds'), selected from this c-expression as the most promising ones (according to the preference criterion). In each subsequent next step, a new selector is added to the c-expression obtained in the previous step (initially the seeds), until a specified number (parameter NCONSIST) of consistent generalizations is determined. Consistency is achieved when a c-expression has NULL intersection with the set FO. This 'rule growing' process is illustrated in Fig. A2.

5. The obtained c-expressions, and c-expressions in FO, are transformed to two sets El and E0, respectively, of VL_1 events (i.e., sequences of values of certain discrete variables).

   A procedure for generalizing VL_1 descriptions is then applied to obtain the 'best cover' (according to a user defined criterion) of set El against E0 (the procedure is a version of AQVAL/1 program Michalski and Larson [1978]).

   During this process, the *extension against,* the *closing the interval* and the *climbing generalization tree* rules are applied.

   The result is transformed to a new set of c-expressions (a restricted star) in which selectors have now appropriately generalized references.

6. The 'best' c-expression is selected from the restricted star.

7. If the c-expression completely covers F1, then the process repeats for another decision class. Otherwise, the set F1 is reduced to contain only the uncovered c-expressions, and steps 4 to 7 are repeated for the same generalization class.

   The implementation of the inductive process in INDUCE-1.1 consists of a large collection of specialized algorithms, each accomplishing certain tasks. Among the most important tasks are:

1. "Growing" rules.

2. Testing whether one c-expression is a generalization of ('covers') another c-expression. (This is done by testing for subgraph isomorphism).

3. Generalizating a c-expression by extending the selector references and forming irredundant c-expressions (includes application of AQVAL/1 procedure).

4. Generating new descriptors and new selectors.

Program INDUCE 1.1 has been implemented in PASCAL (for Cyber 175) its description is given in (Larson [1977] and Dietterich [1978]).

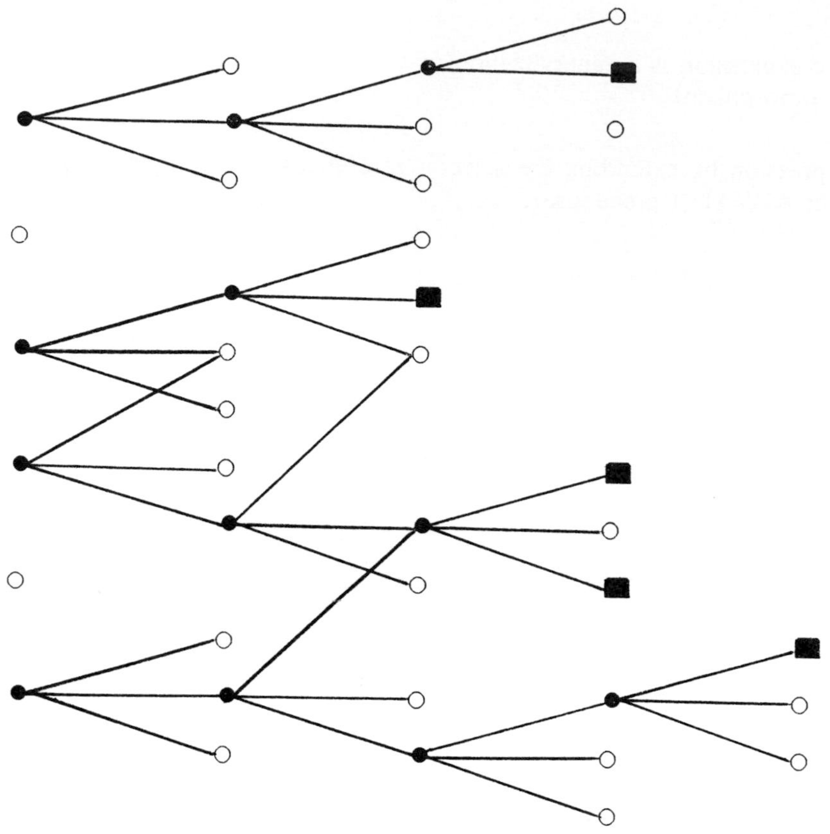

○ - a disgarded c-rule

● - an active c-rule

■ - a terminal node denoting a consistent c-rule

Each arc represents an operation of adding a new selector to a c-rule.

The branching factor is determined by parameter ALTER. The number of active rules (which are maintained for the next step of the rule growing process) is specified by parameter MAXSTAR. The number of terminal nodes (consistent generalizations) which program attempts to generate is specified by parameter NCONSIST.

Illustration of the rule growing process
(an application of the dropping selector rule in the reverse order)

Figure A2.

References

Banerji [1977]
R.B. Banerji, "Learning in structural description languages," Temple University Report to NSF Grant MCS 76—0—200 (1977).

Biermann [1978]
A.W. Biermann, "The inference of regular LISP programs from examples," *IEEE Trans. on Systems, Man, and Cybernetics,* Vol. SMC—8(8) (Aug. 1978) pp. 585—600.

Biermann and Feldman [1972]
A.W. Biermann and J. Feldman, "Survey of Results in Grammatical Inference," in *Frontiers of Pattern Recognition,* Academic Press, Inc., New York (1972), pp. 31—54.

Brachman [1978]
R.T. Brachman, "On the epistomological status of semantic networks," Report No. 3807, Bolt, Beranek and Newman (April 1978).

Burstall and Darlington [1977]
R.M. Burstall and J. Darlington, "A transformation system for developing recursive programs," *JACM, Vol. 24, No. 1* (1977) pp. 44—67.

Carnap [1962]
R. Carnap, "The aim of inductive logic," in *Logic, Methodology and Philosophy of Science,* E. Nagel, P. Suppes, and A. Tarski, eds., Stanford, California: Stanford University Press (1962) pp. 303—318.

Cohen [1977]
B.L. Cohen, "A powerful and efficient structural pattern recognition system," Artificial Intelligence, Vol. 9, No. 3 (December 1977).

Coulon and Kayser [1978]
D. Coulon and D. Kayser, "Learning criterion and inductive behavior," *Pattern Recognition,* Vol. 10, No. 1, pp. 19—25 (1978).

Davis [1976]
R. Davis, "Applications of Meta-level knowledge to the construction, maintenance, and use of large knowledge bases," Report No. 552, Computer Science Department, Stanford University (July 1976).

Diday and Simon [1976]
E. Diday and J.C. Simon, "Clustering Analysis," in *Communication and Cybernetics* 10, Ed. K.S. Fu, Springer-Verlag, Berlin, Heidelberg, New York (1976).

Dietterich [1980]
T.G. Dietterich, "A methodology of knolege layers for inducing descriptions of sequentially ordered events," Report No. 80—1024, Department of Computer Science, University of Illinois (May 1980).

Dietterich [1978]
T. Dietterich, "Description of Inductive program INDUCE 1.1," Internal Report, Department of Computer Science, University of Illinois at Urbana-Champaign (October 1978).

Dietterich and Michalski [1979]
T. Dietterich and R.S. Michalski, "Learning and generalization of characteristic descriptions: Evaluation criteria and comparative review of selected methods," Proceedings of the Sixth International Joint Conference on Artificial Intelligence, pp. 223–231, Tokyo (August 20–23, 1979).

Fikes, Hart and Nilsson [1972]
R.E. Fikes, R.E. Hart, and N.J. Nilsson, "Learning and executing generalized robot plans," Artificial Intelligence 3, (1972).

Hayes-Roth [1976]
F. Hayes-Roth, "Patterns of induction and associated knowledge acquisition algorithms," Pattern Recognition and Artificial Intelligence, ed. C. Chen, Academic Press, New York (1976).

Hayes-Roth and McDermott [1978]
F. Hayes-Roth and J. McDermott, "An interference matching technique for inducing abstractions," Communications of the ACM, No. 5, Vol. 21, pp. 401–411 (May 1978).

Hedrick [1974]
C.L. Hedrick, "A computer program to learn production systems using a semantic net," Ph.D. Thesis, Department of Computer Science, Carnegie-Mellon University, Pittsburg (July 1974).

Jouannaud and Kodratoff [1979]
J.P. Jouannaud and Y. Kodratoff, "Characterization of a class of functions synthesized from examples by a Summers-like method using a B.M.W. matching technique," *Sixth International Joint Conference on Artificial Intelligence* Tokyo (1979) pp. 440–447.

Larson [1977]
J. Larson, "INDUCE-1: An interactive inference program in VL_{21} logic system," Report No. UIUCDCS–R–77–876, Department of Computer Science, University of Illinois, Urbana, Illinois (May 1977).

Larson and Michalski [1977]
J. Larson and R.S. Michalski, "Inductive inference of VL decision rules," *Proceedings of the Workshop on Pattern-Directed Inference Systems,* Honolulu, Hawaii, (May 23–27, 1977) *SIGART Newsletter,* No. 63 (June 1977).

Lenat [1976]
D. Lenat, "AM: An artificial intelligence approach to discovery in mathematics as heuristic search," Computer Science Department, Report STAN–CS–76–570, Stanford University (July 1976).

Michalski [1980]
R.S Michalski, "Knowledge acquisition through conceptual clustering: A theoretical framework and an algorithm for partitioning data into conjunctive concepts, special issue on knowledge acquisition and induction," Inter. Journal on Policy Analysis and Information Systems, No. 3, 1980. (Also, Report No. 80–1026, Department of Computer Science, University of Illinois, May 1980.)

Michalski [1980]
R.S. Michalski, "Pattern recognition as rule-guided inductive inference," IEEE Trans. on Pattern Analysis and Machine Intelligence (July 1980).

Michalski [1978]
R.S. Michalski, "Pattern recognition as knowledge-guided computer induction," Report No. 78−927, Department of Computer Science, University of Illinois, Urbana, Illinois (June 1978).

Michalski [1973]
R.S. Michalski, "AQVAL/1—Computer implementation of a variable-valued logic system and the application to pattern recognition," *Proceedings of the First International Joint Conference on Pattern Recognition,* Washington, D.C., (October 30−November 1, 1973).

Michalski and Chilausky [1980]
R.S. Michalski and R.L. Chilausky, "Learning by being told and learning from examples," *Policy Analysis and Information Systems,* Special Issue on Knowledge Acquisition and Induction, No.2 (1980)

Michalski and Larson [1978]
R.S. Michalski and J. Larson, "Selection of most representative training examples and incremental generation of VL_1 hypotheses: the underlying methodology and the description of programs ESEL and AQ11," Report No. UIUCDCS−R−78−867, Department of Computer Science, University of Illinois, Urbana, Illinois (May 1978).

Michalski and Stepp [1982]
R.S. Michalski and R. Stepp, "Revealing conceptual structure in data by inductive inference." In: Machine Intelligence 10, D. Michie, J.E. Hayes, Y.H. Pao (Eds.), Ellis Horwood, Ltd., New York, 1982, pp. 173−196.

Michie [1977]
D. Michie, "New face of artificial intelligence," *Information 3* (1977) pp. 5−11.

Mitchell [1978]
T.M. Mitchell, "Vernion spaces: An approach to concept learning," Doctor of Philosophy Thesis, Stanford University (1978).

Morgan [1975]
C.G. Morgan, "Automated hypothesis generation using extended inductive resolution," Advance Papers of the 4th International Joint Conference on Artificial Intelligence, Vol. I, Tbilisi, Georgia (September 1975) pp. 351−356.

Pettorossi [1980]
A. Pettorossi, "An algorithm for reducing memory requirements in recursive programs using annotations," IBID.

Shaw, Swartout, and Green [1975]
D.E. Shaw, W.R. Swartout, and C.C. Green, "Inferring Lisp programs from examples," *Proceedings of the 4th International Conference on Artificial Intelligence,* Vol. I, pp. 351−356, Tbilisi (Sept. 1975).

Shortliffe [1974]
E.G. Shortliffe, "A rule based computer program for advising physicians antimicrobial therapy selection," Ph.D. Thesis, Computer Science Department, Stanford University (Oct. 1974).

Smith [1980]
D.R. Smith, "A survey of the synthesis of LISP programs from examples," International Workshop on Program Construction, Bonas (Sept. 1980).

Simon and Lea [1973]
H.A. Simon and G. Lea, "Problem solving and rule induction: A unified way," Carnegie-Mellon Complex Information Processing Working Paper No. 277, Revised June 14, 1973.

Stepp [1978]
R. Stepp, "The investigation of the UNICLASS inductive program AQ7UNI and user's guide," Report No. 949, Department of Computer Science, University of Illinois, Urbana, Illinois (November 1978).

Vere [1975]
S.A. Vere, "Induction of concepts in the predicate calculus," Advance Papers of the 4th International Joint Conference on Artificial Intelligence, Vol. I, pp. 351–356, Tbilisi, Georgia (September 1975).

Winston [1970]
P.H. Winston, "Learning structural descriptions from examples," Technical Report AI TR–231, MIT AI Lab, Cambridge, Massachusetts (1970).

Yau and Fu [1978]
K.C. Yau and K.S. Fu, "Syntactic shape of recognition using attributed grammars," *Proceedings of the 8th Annual EIA Symposium on Automatic Imagery Pattern Recognition* (1978).

Appendix

Some Examples of Program Synthesis

Alan W. Biermann
Duke University
Durham, NC 27706

A. Introduction

The details of some of the examples from Chapter 1 will be completed here.

B. The Manna-Waldinger Method

The technique begins by placing a theorem to be proved into sequent form.

assertions	*goals*	*outputs*
P(a)		
	R(a,z)	z

Thus, if P(a) is true, we seek z such that R(a,z) and that z is the desired output.

The deductive approach provides techniques for adding assertions and goals with their appropriate output entries to the initial sequent. The aim is to deduce a goal of "true" with a corresponding output entry in terms of primitive machine instructions. For the example problem, a sequent entry will be deduced giving the target program which removes the negative numbers from a list.

	goal	*output*
(0)	true	f(a) = if a = NIL then NIL else if neg(car(a)) then f(cdr(a)) else cons(car(a),f(cdr(a)))

The synthesis begins by stating the constraints of the problem in the form of transformations:

(1) R(a,NIL) => true if a = NIL
(2) R(a,u) => true if not(a=NIL) ∧ neg(car(a)) ∧ R(cdr(a),u)
(3) R(a,cons(car(a),u)) => true if not(a=NIL) ∧ not (neg(car(a))) ∧ R(cdr(a),u)

Rule (1) specifies the required output if the input is NIL. Rules (2) and (3) give properties about relation R necessary for the synthesis. Rule (2) asserts that if a is not NIL with a first element that is negative, that first element may be ignored in the calculaton. Rule (3) asserts that if a is not NIL, the first element is not negative, and the answer u is known for f(cdr(a)), then the first element should be added to the front of list u.

The transformation (1) can be applied to the original goal.

goal	*output*
R(a,z)	z

The substitution z=NIL is necessary yielding a new goal and output.

goal	*output*
a=NIL ∧ true	NIL

This can be rewritten as

	goal	*output*
(4)	a=NIL	NIL

indicating that if the goal a=NIL is achieved, the output NIL should be returned.

Similarly, transformation rules (2) and (3) can be applied to obtain additional entries in the sequent.

	goal	*output*
(5)	not(a=NIL)∧neg(car(a)) ∧R(cdr(a),u)	u
(6)	not(a=NIL)∧not(neg(car(a))) ∧R(cdr(a),u)	cons(car(a),u)

Next, we use the method for introducing recursion into the program synthesis. We noticed in (5) that a special case of the original goal R(a,z) has occurred. This leads one to suspect that an inductive argument might succeed so a new assertion is created, an inductive hypothesis.

assertion

```
(7)    if v<a then
                 if P(v) then
                       R(v,f(v))
```

Thus, by the usual inductive argument, we assume the correctness of f for all v smaller than a by some measure < and try to prove it for a. The recursion results from a GA-resolution between (5) and (7) with the substitution v ← cdr(a) and u ← f(v).

goal	*output*
not(a=NIL)∧neg(car(a)) ∧true∧ not(if cdr(a) < a then if P(cdr(a)) then false)	f(cdr(a))

This reduces to

	goal	*output*
(8)	not(a=NIL)∧neg(car(a))	f(cdr(a))

Recall that we are proceeding to create a program f(a), and note that a recursive call to that program was entered in the ouput column by this step. Thus we have seen how an inductive argument leads to a looping structure using this formalism.

A similar resolution of (6) and (7) yields

	goal	*output*
(9)	not(a=nil) ∧ not (neg(car(a)))	cons(car(a),f(cdr(a)))

GG-resolution between (8) and (9) with $P_1\theta$=neg(car(a)) yields

goal	*output*

not(a=NIL)∧ true∧
not(a=NIL)∧ not∧ (false)
	if neg(car(a)) then
	f(cdr(a))
	else
	cons(car(a),f(cdr(a)))

which reduces to

	goal	*output*

(10)	not(a=NIL)	if neg(car(a)) then
		f(cdr(a))
		else
		cons(car(a),f(cdr(a)))

The final program can be constructed using GG resolution on (4) and (10). The above steps can, in fact, be assembled to become a complete derivation of the target program as follows:

Step	*assertion*	*goal*	*output*
Problem Statement A	P(a)		
Problem Statement B		R(a,z)	z
Transform (1) on B		(4)	NIL
Transform (2) on B		(5)	u
Transform (3) on B		(6)	cons(-)
Inductive Hypothesis	(7)		
GA on (5) and (7)		(8)	f(cdr(a))
GA on (6) and (7)		(9)	cons(-)
GG on (8) and (9)		(10)	if
GG on (4) and (10)		(0)	program

C. The Bibel-Hörnig Method

The Bibel-Hörnig method would begin with the following dialog with the user.

```
INITIALIZE PROBLEM
f
INPUT VARIABLE
x
INPUT CONDITION
list(x)
OUTPUT CONDITION
if x=NIL then f(x)=NIL
otherwise f(x)=y where
    ∀u [member(u,y) <=> (member(u,x) ∧ not(neg(u)))]
```

We would expect the system to begin by generating code to handle the trivial case and then seek a recursive solution to the general case. Following this strategy would yield the code

f(x) = if x = NIL then NIL else g(x)

where g(x) is a program yet to be created.

Bibel and Hörnig argue that there are relatively few practical recursion schemes and that a program synthesizer need only try those few. Their method would pose the problem, find g(x) such that

$$g(x) = y \text{ where } x \neq NIL \wedge list(y) \wedge \forall u\,[member(u,y) <=> (member(u,x) \wedge nonneg(u))].$$

The strategy dictates that an element of the input is to be "guessed" and then used in computing the output. This "guessed" element can then be removed from the input and a recursive call can be made on the function. The most easily accessed member of input x is its first element car(x), so g(x) is rewritten with the added assertion that car(x) is either not on output y or on input y.

$$\begin{aligned} g(x) = y \text{ where } & x \neq NIL \wedge list(y) \wedge \\ & \forall u\,[member(u,y) <=> (member(u,x) \wedge nonneg(u))] \\ & \wedge [not(member(car(x),y)) \dot{\vee} (member(car(x),y))] \end{aligned}$$

Here $\dot{\vee}$ stands for an exclusive "or" operation. This is rewritten to consider the two cases separately, not(member(car(x),y)) and (member(car(x),y)).

$$\begin{aligned} g(x) = y \text{ where } & x \neq NIL \wedge list(y) \wedge \\ & [(\forall u\,[(member(u,y) <=> (member(u,x) \wedge nonneg(u))] \\ & \wedge (not(member(car(x),y)))\,] \\ \dot{\vee} & \\ \forall u[member(u,y) & <=> (member(u,x) \wedge nonneg(u))] \\ & \wedge (member(car(x),y))\,] \end{aligned}$$

Next, the system uses domain knowledge of the types (2) and (3) from the previous section to obtain a form where the recursion can be found.

$$\begin{aligned} g(x) = y \text{ where } & x \neq NIL \wedge list(y) \wedge \\ & \{[(\forall u[member(u,y) <=> (member(u,cdr(x)) \wedge not(neg(u)))] \\ & \wedge not(member(car(x),y))\,] \\ \dot{\vee} & \\ \exists\, y'[\forall u[member(u,y') & <=> (member(u,cdr(x)) \wedge not(neg(u)))] \\ & \wedge y = cons(car(x),y') \\ & \wedge member(car(x),y))\,]\} \end{aligned}$$

But in this form, the definition of f has recurred twice:

$$\begin{aligned} g(x) = y \text{ where } & x \neq NIL \wedge list(y) \wedge \\ & [(y = f(cdr(x)) \wedge not(member(car(x),y)) \\ & \dot{\vee} \\ & y' = f(cdr(x)) \wedge y = cons(car(x),y') \\ & \quad \wedge member(car(x),y))\,] \end{aligned}$$

(For simplicity, we have omitted some of the details concerning the case x=NIL. We leave it to the reader to fill them in.) This yields

$$
\begin{aligned}
g(x)=y \text{ where } & x\neq NIL \wedge list(y) \wedge \\
& [(y=f(cdr(x)) \wedge not(member(car(x),y)) \\
& \dot{\vee} \\
& y=cons(car(x),f(cdr(x))) \\
& \qquad \wedge member(car(x),y))\ ]
\end{aligned}
$$

Finally, the Bibel-Hörnig method attempts to discover the condition under which not(member(car(x),y)) is true. It generates a typical model and uses a theorem proving technique to show that the desired condition is (neg(car(x))). Thus the function g is synthesized as

$$
\begin{aligned}
g(x) = & \text{ if } neg(car(x)) \text{ then } f(cdr(x)) \\
& \text{ else } cons(car(x),f(cdr(x))).
\end{aligned}
$$

The the synthesis of f is completed with

$$f(x) = \text{if } x=NIL \text{ then } NIL \text{ else } g(x)$$

and the function g(x) has been constructed.

D. Synthesis Through Merge of Primitive Functions

The example output z=(2 9 4) can be written in terms of x=(−7 2 9 −3 4) using standard LISP functions.

$$
\begin{aligned}
z=&cons(car(cdr(x)), \\
&\quad cons(car(cdr(cdr(x))), \\
&\qquad cons(car(cdr(cdr(cdr(cdr(x))))), \\
&\qquad\quad NIL)))
\end{aligned}
$$

One can create the desired program by first breaking this expression into a set of *primitive forms* and then performing a merge operation on these primitives.

$$
\begin{aligned}
z &= f_1(x) \\
f_1(x) &= cons(f_2(x), f_5(x)) \\
f_2(x) &= f_3(cdr(x)) \\
f_3(x) &= f_4(car(x)) \\
f_4(x) &= x \\
f_5(x) &= cons(f_6(x), f_{10}(x)) \\
f_6(x) &= f_7(cdr(x)) \\
f_7(x) &= f_8(cdr(x)) \\
f_8(x) &= f_9(car(x)) \\
f_9(x) &= x \\
f_{10}(x) &= cons(f_{11}(x), f_{17}(x)) \\
f_{11}(x) &= f_{12}(cdr(x)) \\
f_{12}(x) &= f_{13}(cdr(x)) \\
f_{13}(x) &= f_{14}(cdr(x)) \\
f_{14}(x) &= f_{15}(cdr(x)) \\
f_{15}(x) &= f_{16}(car(x)) \\
f_{16}(x) &= x \\
f_{17}(x) &= NIL
\end{aligned}
$$

It turns out that this *trace* represents a rather inefficient calculation. Various car and cdr operations can be saved as explained in Chapter 17 by giving these operations precedence. Following the method of Chapter 17, the trace is revised to this.

$$\begin{aligned}
f_1(x) &= f_2(cdr(x)) \\
f_2(x) &= cons(f_3(x), f_5(x)) \\
f_3(x) &= f_4(car(x)) \\
f_4(x) &= x \\
f_5(x) &= f_6(cdr(x)) \\
f_6(x) &= cons(f_7(x), f_9(x)) \\
f_7(x) &= f_8(car(x)) \\
f_8(x) &= x \\
f_9(x) &= f_{10}(cdr(x)) \\
f_{10}(x) &= f_{11}(cdr(x)) \\
f_{11}(x) &= cons(f_{12}(x), f_{14}(x)) \\
f_{12}(x) &= f_{13}(car(x)) \\
f_{13}(x) &= x \\
f_{14}(x) &= NIL
\end{aligned}$$

Proceeding with the synthesis using the above fourteen functions, every possible merger is attempted. If a function becomes ambiguously defined due to a merger, a conditional is introduced to remove the problem. That is, if g becomes defined both as $g = f_1$ and $g = f_2$, then an attempt is made to define g as

$$\begin{aligned} g = cond(&(p_1,f_1), \\ &(p_2,f_2)) \end{aligned}$$

If predicates p_1 and p_2 can be defined so that the definition is successful, the new definition of g is maintained. However, if they cannot be found, then the merger is a failure and is discarded. Mergers may also be disallowed if they introduce infinite loops or contradictions as will be illustrated. The final program is the code remaining after all possible mergers have been completed.

The example synthesis thus begins with an attempt to merge f_1 and f_2.

$$\begin{aligned} f_1(x) = cond(&(p_1, f_1(cdr(x))) \\ &(p_2,cons(f_3(x), f_5(x)))) \end{aligned}$$

But from the example, we see that branch $f_1(cdr(x))$ is to be taken when x = (−7 2 9 −3 4) and the other is taken when x = (2 9 −3 4). So the predicate generator produces p_i's and the code becomes

$$\begin{aligned} f_1(x) = cond(&(neg(car(x)), f_1(cdr(x))), \\ &(T, cons(f_3(x), f_5(x)))) \end{aligned}$$

The merger of f_1 and f_2 appears to be successful. (It is possible a later contradiction would result in back up and a return to separate f_1 and f_2.)

Next we attempt to merge f_1 and f_3, but this leads to an infinite cons loop if car(x) is not negative. So this merger fails. Function f_3 will be distinct from f_1. Similarly f_5 must be distinct from f_1.

We could attempt to merge f_3 and f_5 to obtain

$$\begin{aligned} f_3(x) = f_5(x) = cond(&(p_1,f_4(car(x))) \\ &(p_2, f_6(cdr(x)))) \end{aligned}$$

But both branches are taken for $x = (2\ 9\ -3\ 4)$ so this merger fails also. Thus, the code

$$\begin{aligned} f_3(x) &= f_4(car(x)) \\ f_5(x) &= f_6(cdr(x)) \end{aligned}$$

is temporarily maintained as part of the final program.

Next, f_4 can be merged into f_1 with the addition of one predicate, and f_6 can be merged with f_1, yielding

$$\begin{aligned} f_1(x) &= cond((atom(x),x) \\ &\qquad (neg(car(x)),\ f_1(cdr(x))) \\ &\qquad (T,\ cons(f_3(x),\ f_5(x)))) \\ f_3(x) &= f_1(car(x)) \\ f_5(x) &= f_1(cdr(x)) \end{aligned}$$

In fact, subsequent mergers follow easily and the above program is the final program. The final partition on the fourteen functions becomes $\{f_1,f_2,f_4,f_6,f_8,f_{10},f_{11},f_{13}\}$, $\{f_3,f_7,f_{12}\}$, and $\{f_5,f_9,f_{14}\}$. (For simplicity, special considerations related to the merger of the NIL function f_{14} have been omitted here.

E. Synthesis Through Application of Production Rules

In Chapter 17, it was shown how the input-output graph may be drawn for this example. As explained there, the first production rule selected is routine P^o.

$$\begin{aligned} &[P^o_w,\ (X_o\ XL),\ next] ==> \\ &P^o_w\ (X_o,\ XL) = cons(car(X_o),\ next) \end{aligned}$$

Next, the nonlinearity of the input-output graph suggests the introduction of the branching rule from Chapter 17.

$$\begin{aligned} &[P^1_w,\ (X_1\ XL),\ next] ==> \\ &\quad P^1_w(X_1,\ XL) = \\ &\quad cond\ ((not(neg(car(X_1))),\ P^o_{w1}\ (cdr(X_1),\ X_1,\ XL)) \\ &\qquad (T,\ next)) \\ &\quad [P^o_{w1},\ (X_o\ X_1\ XL),\ next] \end{aligned}$$

Finally the looping schema from Chapter 1 is introduced and instantiated to obtain a third production rule.

$$\begin{aligned} &[P^2_2,\ (X_2\ XL),\ next] ==> \\ &P^2_w\ (X_2,\ XL) = \\ &\quad cond((atom(X_2),\ next) \\ &\qquad (T,\ P^1_{w1}\ (X_2,\ X_2,\ XL))) \\ &[P^1_{w1},\ (X_k\ X_2\ XL),\ P^2_w(cdr,(X_2),\ XL)] \end{aligned}$$

The target program is then generated by expanding the nonterminal $[P_2,\ (X_2),\ NIL]$ as follows.

$$\begin{aligned} &[P^2,\ (X_2,\ NIL] ==> \\ &P^2\ (X_2) = cond\ ((atom(X_2),\ NIL) \\ &\qquad\qquad (T,\ P^1_1\ (X_2,X_2))) \\ &[P^1_1,\ (X_1\ X_2),\ P^2(cdr(X_2))] \end{aligned}$$

This has generated a call for the P^1 rule with $w=1$, $XL=X_2$, and next=$P^2(cdr(X_2))$.

$$[P_1^1,(X_1\ X_2),\ P^2(cdr(X_2))] ==>$$
$$P_1^1\ (X_1,\ X_2) =$$
$$cond((not(neg(car(X_1))),\ P_{11}^o(cdr(X_1),X_1,\ X_2))$$
$$(T,\ P^2(cdr(X_2))))$$
$$[P_{11}^o,\ (X_o\ X_1\ X_2),\ P^2(cdr(X_2))]$$

This has produced a call for the P^o rule with $w=11$, $XL=X_1\ X_2$, and next=$P^2(cdr(X_2))$.

$$[P_{11}^o,\ (X_o\ XL),\ P^2(cdr(X_2))]==>$$
$$P_{11}^o(X_o,\ X_1,\ X_2)=cons(car(X_o),P^2(cdr(X_2)))$$

The union of the code generated by the above three expansions is the target program.

$$P^2(X_2)=cond((atom(X_2),NIL)$$
$$(T,\ P_1^1\ (X_2,X_2)))$$
$$P_1^1(X_1,X_2)=cond((not(neg(car(X_1))),\ P_{11}^o(cdr(X_1),X_1,X_2))$$
$$(T,\ P^2\ (cdr(X_2))))$$
$$P_{11}^o\ (X_o,X_1,X_2)=cons(car(X_o),\ P^2(cdr(X_2)))$$

AUTHOR INDEX

Abelson, R.P. 443, 459
Adam, A. 123, 124, 133
Aho, A. 88, 218, 221
Allen, F.E. 133
Amirchahy, M. 302
Anderson, E.D. 184, 198
Anderson, R.H. 436, 438, 458
Angluin, D. 25, 503, 505, 506, 507, 508, 509, 510, 511, 512
Aronson, A.R. 513
Arsac, J. 23, 28
Arvind, 277, 286
Ashcroft, E.A. 277, 286
Austin, G.A. 482
Back, R.J.R. 13, 223, 230, 234, 241
Backus, J. 161, 179, 277
Ballantine, A.M. 79, 88
Ballard, B.W. 12, 28
Balzer, R.M. 12, 28, 394, 419
Banerji, R. 25, 466, 467, 470, 482, 483, 484, 485, 498, 500, 501, 502, 521, 549
Barstow, D.R. 12, 13, 29, 98, 107, 201, 221, 372, 394, 419
Bartussek, W. 160, 166, 179
Barzdin, J.M. 308, 322, 511, 512
Bauer, F.L. 160, 179, 181, 290, 302
Bauer, M.A. 309, 322
Baum, R.I. 322, 512
Beick, H.R. 511, 514
Belz, F.C. 198
Bendix, P.B. 16, 161, 180, 373

Berger, J. 509, 512
Bibel, W. 4, 7, 8, 10, 69, 70, 72, 73, 75, 76, 80, 82, 84, 85, 87, 88, 221, 484, 485, 496, 501, 556, 557, 558
Bidoit, M. 10, 28, 133, 162, 163, 175, 179
Biermann, A.W. 3, 12, 28, 87, 88, 308, 309, 313, 316, 317, 320, 321, 322, 323, 372, 375, 379, 380, 383, 389, 392, 394, 399, 419, 420, 435, 439, 458, 484, 485, 501, 502, 505, 507, 512, 513, 518, 549, 553
Biggerstaff, T.J. 393, 394, 420
Bjorner, D. 180
Bledsoe, W.W. 42, 67, 72, 79, 88
Blikle, A. 227, 231, 241
Blum, E.K. 198
Blum, K.E. 241
Blum, L. 308, 322
Blum, M. 308, 322
Booth, T.L. 505, 507, 508, 514
Boullier, P. 184, 198
Boyer, R.S. 34, 66, 67, 133, 427, 430
Brachman, R.T. 518, 549
Brand, D. 224, 241
Broy, M. 158, 160, 181, 302
Bruner, J.S. 466, 470, 482
Buchanan, J.R. 437, 458
Burstall, R.M. 34, 63, 66, 67, 110, 118, 120, 133, 134, 140, 144, 147, 158, 160, 163, 179, 290, 293, 302, 423, 430, 518, 549
Carnap, R. 519, 549
Cartwright, R. 116, 118, 120
Case, J. 505, 506, 513
Castaing, J. 421, 422, 430
Chatelin, P. 290, 302
Cheatham, Jr., T.E. 134
Chen, C.H. 458, 460, 501, 550
Cheriton, D. 214, 221
Chilausky, R.L. 551
Choppy, C. 12, 159, 166, 179
Clarke, Jr., E.M. 110, 120
Cocke, J. 133
Cohen, B.L. 22, 23, 25, 463, 465, 466, 468, 482, 484, 485, 497, 498, 500, 501, 502, 521, 549
Colmerauer, A. 80, 88
Cook, C.M. 507, 508, 513
Costa, E. 23, 28
Coulon, D. 525, 549
Cousot, P. 13, 243, 244, 251, 254, 257, 258, 266, 268, 269, 270
Cousot, R. 13, 243, 244, 249, 254, 257, 258, 266, 269, 270
Crespi-Reghizzi, S. 509, 510, 513
Curry, H.B. 161, 179
Dahl, O.J. 10, 13, 28, 290, 302
Daley, R. 506, 513
Darlington, J.A. 12, 34, 53, 63, 66, 67, 98, 107, 133, 134, 139, 140, 141, 144, 147, 158, 160, 163, 176, 179, 290, 302, 423, 430, 549
Davis, R. 437, 444, 458, 518, 549
Degano, P.P. 421, 422, 430
DeMillo, R.A. 110, 120

Depper, P. 158
Derksen, J.A. 482
Dershowitz, N. 161, 179
Deschamp, Ph. 183, 185, 188, 198
Dewar, R. 80, 88
Diday, E. 538, 549
Dietterich, T.G. 521, 522, 530, 534, 536, 547, 549, 550
Dijkstra, E.W. 28, 220, 221, 224, 227, 228, 229, 241, 302
Donzeau-Gouge, V. 133, 134
Dosch, W. 158
Eder, E. 88
Eigemeier, H. 80, 88
Elcock, E.W. 107, 458
Elschlager, Q. 372
Elschlager, R. 29
Elspas, B. 133
Englemore, R.S. 445, 458
Erman, L.D. 442, 458, 459
Fargues, J. 323, 373
Faught, W.S. 433, 439, 458
Feather, M.S. 160, 163, 176, 179, 290, 302
Feigenbaum, E.A. 444, 459
Feldman, J.A. 485, 501, 505, 506, 508, 509, 510, 513, 518, 549
Feys, R. 161, 179
Fikes, R.E. 521, 550
Floyd, R.W. 13, 14, 28, 110, 118, 119, 120, 139, 158, 227, 241, 244, 255, 257, 270
Follett, R. 4, 10, 91, 99, 101, 102, 107
Fosdick, L.O. 134
Freivald, R.V. 506, 511, 512, 513
Fronhofer, B. 88
Fu, K.S. 484, 500, 505, 514, 518, 549, 552
Furbach, U. 501
Gaines, B.R. 507, 508, 514
Gaudel, M.C. 10, 11, 28, 160, 167, 176, 180, 183, 185, 188, 198
Gerhart, S.L. 13, 29, 134, 224, 236, 242, 394, 420
Gilchrist, B. 322, 372
Gillogly, J.J. 438, 458
Ginzberg, M.J. 29
Gloess, P. 123
Goguen, J.A. 10, 29, 160, 168, 179, 180, 184, 185, 198
Gold, E.M. 504, 505, 506, 507, 508, 511, 514, 308, 322
Goldman, N. 419
Gonzalez, R.C. 505, 514
Goodenough, J.B. 224, 242
Goodnow, J.J. 482
Gordon, M. 111, 120
Gostelow 277, 286
Green, C.C. 12, 29, 33, 36, 67, 80, 87, 88, 98, 107, 110, 120, 202, 221, 323, 372, 394, 420, 435, 458, 551
Gresse, C. 28, 29, 87, 88, 133
Greussay 373
Gries, D. 30, 221, 242, 244, 258, 259, 261, 271

Guida, G. 513
Guiho, G. 3, 10, 28, 29, 87, 88, 133, 318, 319, 320, 321, 323, 485, 497, 501
Guttag, J.V. 10, 29, 121, 140, 148, 156, 160, 164, 170, 180, 184, 185, 198, 400, 420
Halbwachs, H. 244, 251, 270
Hantler, S.L. 236, 242, 411, 420
Hardy, J. 372
Hardy, S. 309, 323, 399, 420
Harriman, D.C. 134
Harris, G. 437, 459
Hart, R.E. 550
Hayes, J.E. 201, 551
Hayes-Roth, B. 436, 444, 458
Hayes-Roth, F. 23, 29, 436, 437, 444, 458, 459, 460, 466, 482, 521, 550
Hecht, M.S. 134
Hedrick, C.L. 523, 527, 550
Hehner, E. 231, 242
Heidorn, G.E. 394, 420
Hendrix, G. 439, 459
Hewitt, C. 42, 67
Hoare, C.A.R. 13, 28, 29, 110, 111, 112, 113, 114, 115, 116, 118, 119, 120, 121, 140, 158, 227, 228, 242, 255, 271, 302, 411
Hoffman, C.M. 286
Holloway, G.H. 134
Hopcroft, J.E. 88, 218, 221
Hörnig, K.M. 4, 7, 8, 10, 69, 85, 89, 556, 557, 558
Horning, J.J. 10, 29, 121, 160, 180, 184, 198, 507, 508, 514
Horowitz, E. 180, 198, 420
Huet, G. 134, 160, 162, 164, 180, 290, 302, 336, 372
Hunt, E.B. 436, 459
Jantke, K.P. 511, 514
Johnson, D.L. 420
Jones, N. 266, 270, 271
Jouannaud, J.P. 15, 16, 87, 89, 161, 180, 318, 319, 320, 321, 323, 325, 326, 332, 347, 352, 358, 373, 485, 497, 501, 511, 514, 518, 550
Kahn, G. 134
Kamin, S. 161, 180
Kanoui, H. 88
Kant, E. 13, 29
Kaplan, R.M. 133, 135
Katz, S.M. 224, 242
Kayser, D. 525, 549
Keller, R.M. 244, 253, 271
Kerschenbaum, A. 220, 222
Kibler, D.F. 134
King, J.C. 134, 236, 242, 420, 444, 458
Klahr, P. 433
Knabe, Ch. 88
Knuth, D.E. 16, 110, 121, 161, 180, 184, 199, 329, 373
Kodratoff, Y. 3, 15, 16, 23, 28, 29, 87, 89, 312, 317, 318, 320, 321, 323, 325, 326, 332, 336, 342, 347, 350, 352, 358, 373, 421, 422, 428, 430, 431, 497, 502, 511, 514, 550
Kotovsky, K. 436, 459

Kott, L. 290, 302
Kowalski, R. 89, 484, 502
Kowaltowski, T. 118, 121
Krishnaswamy, R. 308, 322, 420, 435, 458, 513
Krumland, R. 29
Kruskal, J.B. 214, 215, 218, 219, 222
Kugel, P. 506, 514
Lamport, L. 14, 29, 244, 258, 259, 261, 263, 271
Lampson, B.W. 121
Lang, B. 134, 290, 302
Larson, J. 522, 530, 534, 546, 547, 550, 551
Laubsch 373
Laurent, J.P. 123, 124, 133
Lea, G. 521, 552
Lee, R.C.T. 33, 67, 202, 222
Leech, J. 180, 373
Lenat, D.B. 29, 372, 437, 459, 527
Lescanne, P. 159, 160, 179, 180, 181
Lesser, V.R. 442, 458, 459
Levi, G. 422, 431
Levitt, K. 133
Levy, J.J. 164, 180
Lipton, R.J. 120
Liskov, B.H. 29, 140, 158
London, R.L. 110, 121
Lorho, B. 194, 199
Loveman, D. 134
MacQueen, D.B. 302
Majster, M.E. 160, 181
Mandrioli, D. 513
Manna, Z. 4, 5, 6, 7, 10, 33, 34, 66, 67, 87, 89, 92, 106, 107, 109, 110, 111, 121, 202, 222, 224, 242, 327, 335, 366, 367, 373, 399, 420, 422, 431, 484, 501, 553
Mark, B. 29
Martin, W.A. 12, 29
Maryanski, P.J. 507, 508, 514
Mazaud, M. 183, 198
McCarthy, J. 110, 113, 116, 121, 308, 309
McCune, B.P. 29, 372
McDermott, J. 29, 437, 459, 482, 550
Meltzer, B. 120, 374
Michalski, R.S. 25, 482, 517, 518, 519, 520, 521, 525, 530, 534, 538, 540, 546, 550, 551
Michalsky, P.S. 323, 373
Michie, D. 107, 120, 201, 323, 374, 458, 519, 551
Milne, R. 184, 199
Milner, R. 120
Mistra, J. 221
Mitchell, J.G. 121
Mitchell, T.M. 507, 514, 535, 551
Moore, J.S. 34, 66, 67, 365, 374, 422, 427, 431
Morgan, C.G. 521, 551
Morgenstern, M. 29

Morris, F.L. 184, 199
Mosses, P.D. 184, 199
Moto-oka, T. 88
Muchnick, S.S. 266, 270, 271
Murray, N. 44, 47, 48, 67
Musser, D.R. 160, 180, 181, 195, 198, 199, 420
Mycroft, A. 301
Nagel, E. 549
Naur, P. 227, 242, 255, 271
Neel, D. 302
Neighbors, J.M. 134
Nelson, G. 42, 67
Ness, S. 373, 431
Niamir, B. 29
Nii, H.P. 444, 445, 458, 459
Nilsson, N.J. 37, 44, 67, 550
Oppen, D.C. 42, 67, 120
Osterweil, L.J. 134
Owicki, J. 14, 30, 244, 258, 259, 261, 271
Pair, C. 509, 512
Pao, Y.H. 201, 551
Papon, E. 318, 323, 336, 342, 373, 374
Parnas, D. 160, 166, 179
Partsch, H. 160, 181, 290, 302, 303
Partsch, W. 158
Paul, M. 241
Pepper, P. 290, 302, 303
Pequeno, T.H.C. 160, 181
Perlis, A.J. 120
Petry, F.E. 322, 512
Pettorossi, A. 14, 289, 290, 291, 292, 293, 294, 295, 296, 298, 301, 303, 518, 551
Plaisted, D.A. 161, 181
Plotkin, G.D. 336, 374
Pnueli, A. 14, 273, 286, 287
Poitiers 430
Popek, G.J. 121
Popplewell, C.M. 121
Poupon, J. 121
Prim, R.C. 214, 218, 222
Prywes, N.S. 14, 273, 275, 286, 287
Raulefs, P. 88
Reinig, F. 180
Rémy, J.L. 159, 160, 169, 176, 179, 181
Reynolds, J.C. 227, 231, 232, 242, 336, 374
Rich, C. 134
Robinet 179
Robinson, J.A. 7, 30, 40, 42, 67, 326, 336, 374
Rosen, B.K. 134
Rosenchein, S.J. 433
Rosenfeld, A. 513
Roussel, P. 465, 482

Rulifson, J.F. 481
Ruth, G.R. 134
Sammut, C.A. 22, 23, 25, 463, 466, 482, 484, 485, 497, 498, 501, 502
Sannella, D.T. 302
Schank, R.C. 443, 459
Schreiber, J.F. 501
Schwartz, J.T. 120
Schwarz, J. 289, 290, 303
Scott, D. 366, 374
Shapiro, E.Y. 23, 30, 507, 511, 515
Shastry, S. 287
Shaw, D.E. 29, 309, 323, 372, 518, 551
Shields, P. 508, 513
Shortliffe, E.H. 437, 459, 518, 551
Shrobe, H. 134
Siekmann, J. 88, 89
Siklossy, L. 309, 323, 374, 435, 459
Simon, H.A. 222, 436, 459, 521, 552
Simon, J.C. 538, 549
Sirovich, F. 422, 430, 431
Sites, R.L. 236, 242
Sloane, N.J.A. 504, 515
Smith, C. 505, 506, 512, 513
Smith, C.H. 505, 506, 515
Smith, D.R. 15, 30, 307, 316, 317, 320, 321, 322, 324, 372, 389, 392, 505, 515, 518, 551
Smith, J.P. 352, 374
Solomonoff, R.J. 508, 515
Standish, T.A. 134
Steinberg, L.I. 29, 372
Stepp, R. 521, 535, 540, 546, 551, 552
Summers, P.D. 15, 16, 30, 309, 310, 311, 312, 313, 314, 317, 319, 320, 321, 322, 324, 326, 327, 329, 374, 399, 420, 485, 497, 501
Sunguroff, A. 29
Suppes, P. 549
Sussman, G. 94, 107
Swain, P. 484, 500
Swartout, W.R. 323, 551
Sykes, D.A. 309, 323, 374, 435, 459
Takosu, S. 241
Tarjan, R.E. 134, Tarjan, R.E. 214, 221
Tarski, A. 549
Tate, A. 94, 107
Teitelman, W. 133, 135
Terrine, G. 147, 158, 167, 176, 180
Thatcher, J.W. 29, 160, 180, 181
Thomason, M.G. 505, 514
Tobias, J.M. 482
Townley, J.A. 134
Tramer, K. 88
Treuil, J.P. 485, 497, 501
Ullman, J.D. 134, 218, 221

Ullmann, J. 88
Van Caneghem, M. 88
Van der Mude, A. 507, 508, 515
Van Emden, M.H. 227, 231, 232, 241
Van Slyke, R. 220, 222
Veloso, P.A.S. 160, 169, 181
Vere, S.A. 23, 30, 436, 459, 521, 523, 552
Vuillemin, J. 139, 158, 164, 181, 373, 431
Wadge, W. 286, 287
Wadsworth, C. 120
Wagner, E.G. 29, 180, 181
Waldinger, R.J. 4, 5, 6, 7, 10, 29, 33, 34, 66, 67, 87, 89, 94, 107, 109, 110, 111, 121, 202, 222, 372, 420, 482, 484, 501, 553
Walker, A. 507, 508, 515
Wand 156
Warren, D. 484, 485, 501
Waterman, D.A. 433, 436, 437, 438, 444, 459, 460
Waters, R. 134, 135
Wegbreit, B. 87, 89, 118, 121, 290, 303
Wertz, H. 135
Wesson, R. 433
Wharton, R.M. 507, 515
Wiehagen, R. 506, 513
Wile, D. 419
Wilkins, D. 44, 67
Winston, P.H. 436, 460, 476, 482, 521, 527, 552
Wirsing, M. 156, 157, 158
Wirth, N. 227, 228, 242, 290, 303
Wossner, H. 160, 179, 302
Wright, J.B. 181
Yau, K.C. 518, 552
Yeh, R.T. 29, 180
Yelowitz, L. 420
Zarhi, R. 14, 273, 286, 287
Ziller, S.N. 158